A-Z LIVERPOOL

CONTENTS

Key to Map Pages	2-3
Large Scale City Centre	4-5
Map Pages	6-1
Postcode Map	126-127
Index to Hospitals & Hospices	222-224

REFERENCE

Motorway	**M57**
A Road	**A59**
Proposed	
Tunnel	
B Road	**B5188**
Dual Carriageway	
One-way Street	
Traffic flow on A Roads is also indicated by a heavy line on the driver's left.	
Restricted Access	
Pedestrianized Road	
Track / Footpath	
Residential Walkway	
Railway	Station / Level Crossing / Tunnel
Built-up Area	MANOR ST
Local Authority Boundary	
Posttown Boundary	
Postcode Boundary (within Posttown)	
Map Continuation	**60** / Large Scale City Centre **4**

Airport	✈
Car Park (selected)	P
Church or Chapel	†
Cycleway (selected)	🚲
Fire Station	■
Hospital	H
House Numbers (A & B Roads only)	13 / 8
Information Centre	i
National Grid Reference	445
Park & Ride	Marshalls Cross P+R
Police Station	▲
Post Office	★
Safety Camera with Speed Limit	(30)
Fixed cameras and long term road works cameras. Symbols do not indicate camera direction.	
Toilet: without facilities for the Disabled	▽
with facilities for the Disabled	▽
Disabled facilities only	▽
Viewpoint	☀
Educational Establishment	
Hospital or Healthcare Building	
Industrial Building	
Leisure or Recreational Facility	
Place of Interest	
Public Building	
Shopping Centre or Market	
Other Selected Buildings	

SCALE

Map Pages 6-125   1:18,103

0	¼	½ Mile
0	250	500	750 Metres

3½ inches (8

Map Pages 4-5   1:9,051

0	⅛	¼ Mile
0	100	200	300 Metres

11.05 cm to 1 km

C... **Limited**

Fairfield Road, Bor...
Telephone: 01732...
01732...
www.a-zmaps.co....
...napping data licensed
... with the permission of
...ajesty's Stationery Office.
...d. Licence number 100017302

Copyright © Geo...
Edition 5 2010
...PocketGPSWorld.com
...ht 2009 © PocketGPSWorld.com

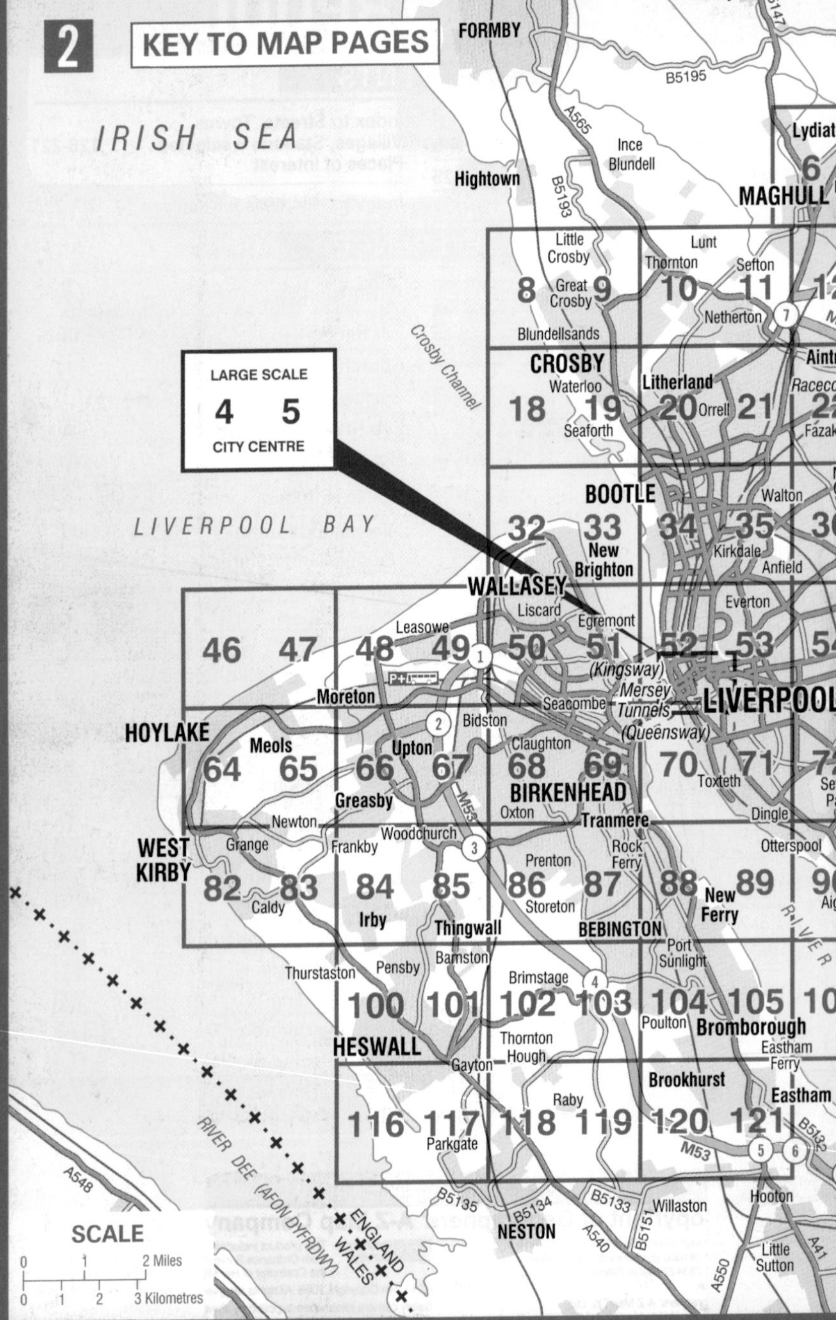

2 KEY TO MAP PAGES

FORMBY

Haskayne · A5147

B5195

IRISH SEA

Lydiate

6 MAGHULL

Hightown

Ince Blundell

A565

B5193

Little Crosby · Lunt · Sefton
8 Great **9** Thornton **10** **11** **12**
Crosby · Netherton · 7 · M5

Blundellsands

CROSBY

Waterloo · Litherland · **Aintree**
18 **19** **20** Orrell **21** **22** Racecourse
Seaforth · Fazaker

LARGE SCALE
4 5
CITY CENTRE

BOOTLE

Walton · No Gr

32 **33** **34** **35** **36**
New Brighton · Kirkdale · Anfield

LIVERPOOL BAY

WALLASEY

Liscard · Egremont · Everton

Leasowe
46 **47** **48 49 50 51 52 53 54**
· 1 · (Kingsway)

Moreton · P+L · Seacombe · Mersey **LIVERPOOL**
· 2 · Bidston · Tunnels
HOYLAKE · (Queensway)

Meols · Claughton
64 65 66 67 68 69 70 71 72
Upton · **BIRKENHEAD** · Toxteth · Sefton Park

Greasby · Oxton · **Tranmere**
Newton · Woodchurch · Dingle · Otterspool
WEST Grange · Frankby · Rock Ferry
KIRBY · 3 · Prenton · **88 89 90**
82 83 84 85 86 87 New Ferry · Aigb
Caldy · Irby · Storeton · **BEBINGTON**
Thingwall · Port Sunlight

Thurstaston · Pensby · Barnston
100 101 102 103 104 105 106
Brimstage · 4 · Poulton · **Bromborough**
HESWALL · Thornton Hough · Eastham Ferry
Gayton · **Brookhurst** · **Eastham**
Raby
116 117 118 119 120 121
Parkgate · M53 · 5 · 6
Willaston · Hooton · 7

B5135 · B5134 · B5133 · B5151 · A41
NESTON · A540 · A550 · Little Sutton

RIVER DEE (AFON DYFRDWY)
ENGLAND / WALES

A548

SCALE
0 · 1 · 2 Miles
0 · 1 · 2 · 3 Kilometres

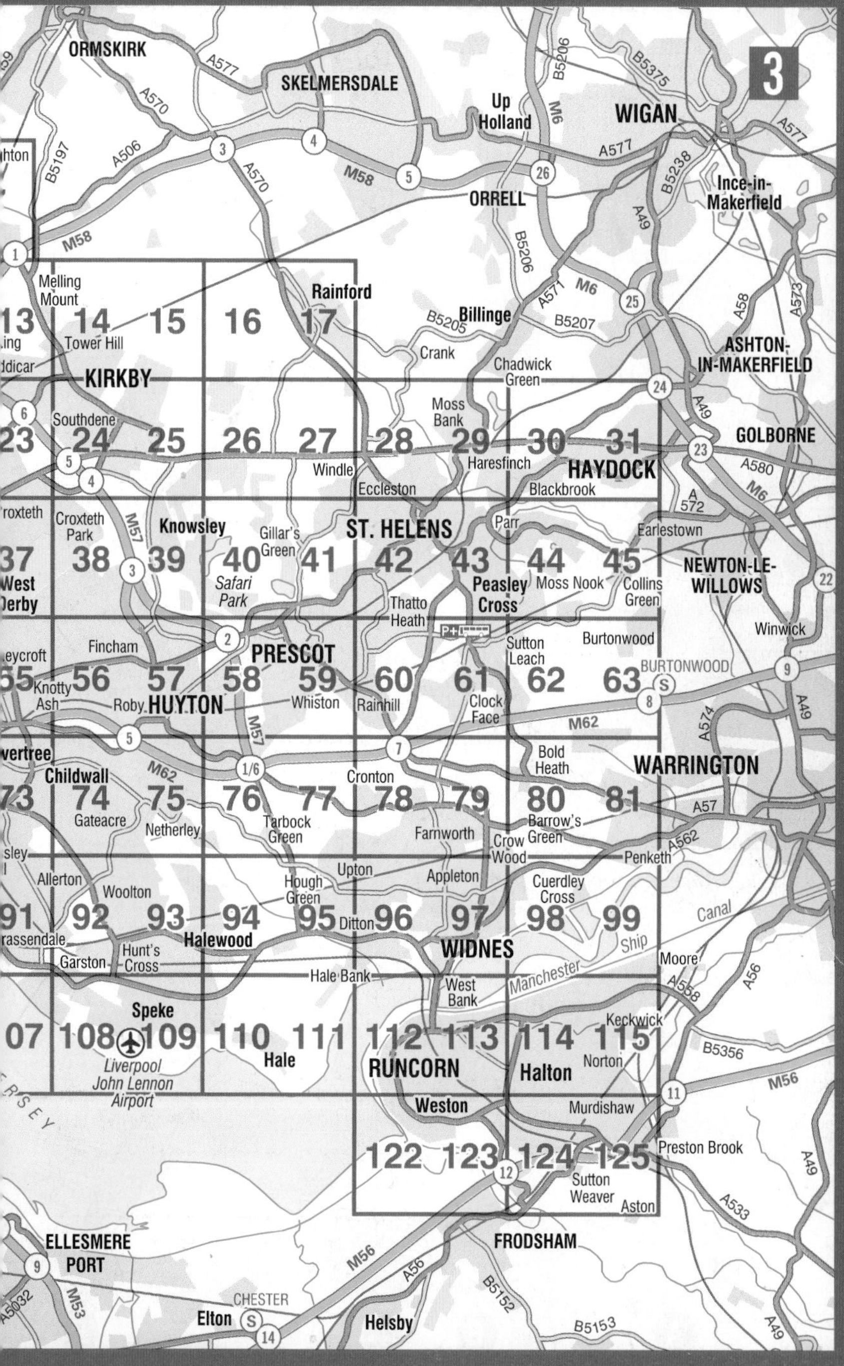

3
ORMSKIRK
SKELMERSDALE
Up Holland
WIGAN
ORRELL
Ince-in-Makerfield
Melling Mount
Rainford
Billinge
Tower Hill
KIRKBY
Crank
Chadwick Green
ASHTON-IN-MAKERFIELD
Southdene
Moss Bank
GOLBORNE
Windle
Eccleston
Haresfinch
HAYDOCK
Blackbrook
Croxteth
Croxteth Park
Knowsley
Gillar's Green
ST. HELENS
Parr
Earlestown
West Derby
Safari Park
Thatto Heath
Peasley Cross
Moss Nook
Collins Green
NEWTON-LE-WILLOWS
Winwick
Fincham
PRESCOT
Sutton Leach
Burtonwood
Knotty Ash
Roby
HUYTON
Whiston
Rainhill
Clock Face
Childwall
Cronton
Bold Heath
WARRINGTON
Gateacre
Netherley
Tarbock Green
Farnworth
Barrow's Green
Crow Wood
Penketh
Allerton
Woolton
Hough Green
Upton
Appleton
Cuerdley Cross
Ditton
Halewood
WIDNES
Garston
Hunt's Cross
Hale Bank
West Bank
Moore
Manchester Ship Canal
Speke
Keckwick
Liverpool John Lennon Airport
Hale
RUNCORN
Halton
Norton
Weston
Murdishaw
Preston Brook
Sutton Weaver
Aston
ELLESMERE PORT
FRODSHAM
Elton
Helsby
CHESTER

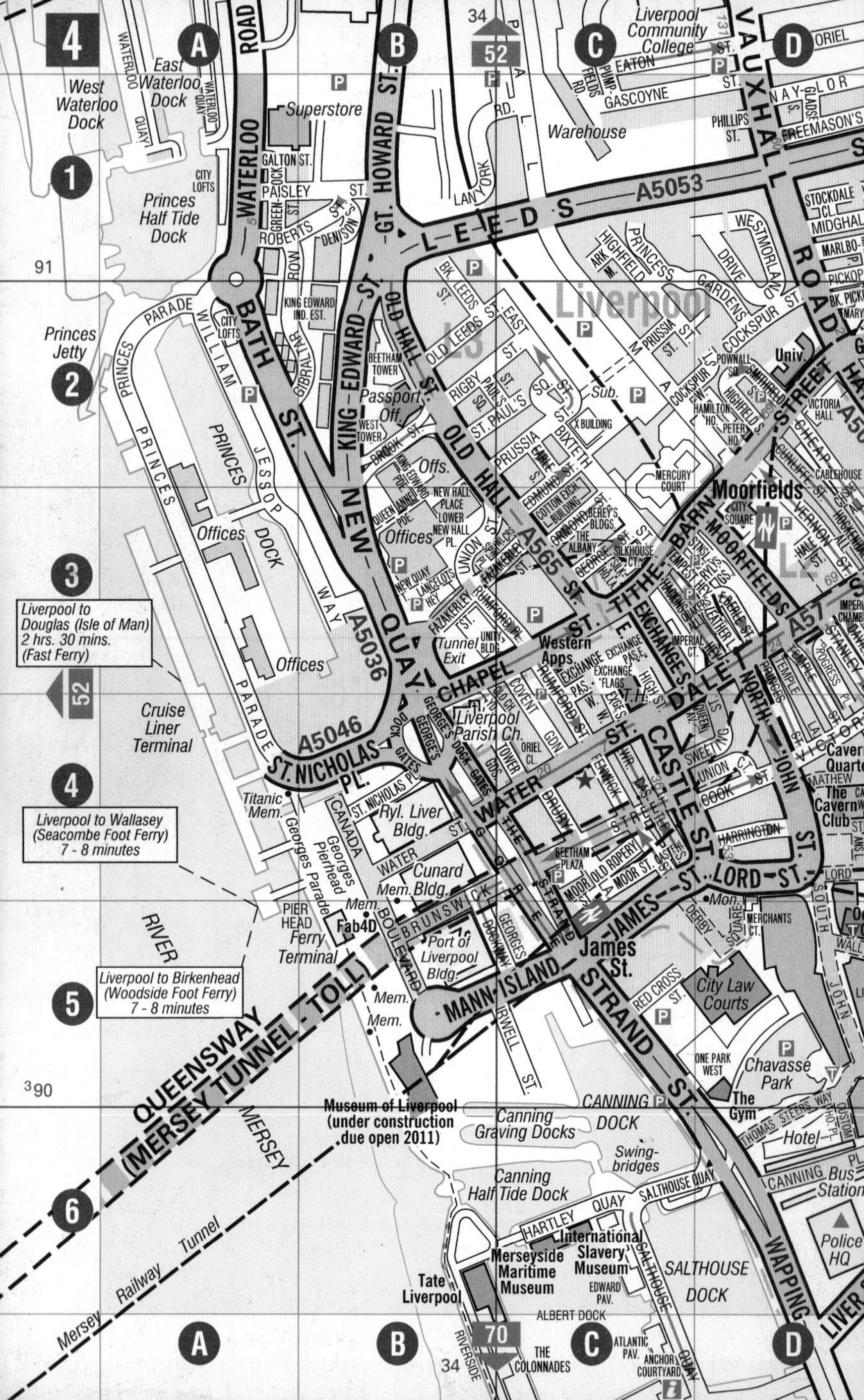
West Waterloo Dock
East Waterloo Dock
Princes Half Tide Dock
Princes Jetty
Liverpool to Douglas (Isle of Man) 2 hrs. 30 mins. (Fast Ferry)
Cruise Liner Terminal
Liverpool to Wallasey (Seacombe Foot Ferry) 7 - 8 minutes
Liverpool to Birkenhead (Woodside Foot Ferry) 7 - 8 minutes
RIVER MERSEY
QUEENSWAY (MERSEY TUNNEL - TOLL)
Mersey Railway Tunnel
Titanic Mem.
Georges Parade
Georges Pierhead
PIER HEAD Ferry Terminal
Fab4D
Ryl. Liver Bldg.
Cunard Mem. Bldg.
Port of Liverpool Bldg.
Museum of Liverpool (under construction due open 2011)
Canning Graving Docks
Canning Half Tide Dock
CANNING DOCK
Swing-bridges
Merseyside Maritime Museum
Tate Liverpool
International Slavery Museum
SALTHOUSE DOCK
ALBERT DOCK
THE COLONNADES
Liverpool Community College
Warehouse
Superstore
Liverpool
Moorfields
Western Apps.
Liverpool Parish Ch.
Tunnel Exit
James St.
City Law Courts
Chavasse Park
The Gym
Hotel
Bus Station
Police HQ
Cavern Quarter
The Cavern Club
WATERLOO ROAD
BATH ST.
NEW QUAY
GT. HOWARD ST.
LEEDS ST. A5053
OLD HALL ST.
TITHE BARN ST.
CHAPEL ST.
WATER ST.
DALE ST.
CASTLE ST.
LORD ST.
JAMES ST.
STRAND ST.
MANN ISLAND
WAPPING
VAUXHALL ROAD
MOORFIELDS
A5036
A5046
A565
A57
ST. NICHOLAS PL.
PRINCES PARADE
WILLIAM JESSOP WAY
KING EDWARD ST.
52
70
34
91
90

5
E
F
G
H
53
1
2
3
4
5
6
71
ATLANTIC POINT
THE REACH
EDGAR ST.
PEOVER ST.
COMUS ST.
CHRISTIAN ST.
RICHMOND ROW
BIRKETT ST.
PRIT ST.
WILLIAM HENRY ST.
SOHO ST.
SOHO PL.
BIDDER ST.
SIM ST.
CANTERBURY ST.
JOHN ST.
SALISBURY ST.
LANGSDALE ST.
STRADA WY.
CANTY WY.
CARVER ST.
MANSFIELD ST.
Sub.
Thurston Billiard & Snooker Mus.
WAKEFIELD ST.
HARKER ST.
QUEEN ANNE ST.
Football Pitch
RODERICK ST.
MARITIME PL.
BIRCHFIELD ST.
SPRINGFIELD
WILTON ST.
ISLINGTON
Liverpool John Moores University
JOSEPHS ST.
CRESCENT
TOM MANN CL.
GERARD ST.
ELF CT.
HOLY CROSS CL.
ST. STEPHEN'S PL.
ADDISON WY.
ADDISON
Holy Cross Catholic Prim. Sch.
HENRY EDWARD ST.
ADLINGTON HO.
BISPHAM HO.
STANDISH ST.
FONTENOY ST.
SCOTLAND RD.
Scotland Pl.
BYROM ST.
Offs.
CROSSHALL A5046 ST.
CHURCHILL WAY NORTH
CHURCHILL WAY SOUTH
HUNTER ST.
NEW ISLINGTON
GILDART ST.
DEVON ST.
STAFFORD ST.
CRAVEN ST.
CLIFFORD ST.
LAMBERT WY.
KEMPSTON ST.
NORTON ST.
FRASER ST.
Coach Sta.
CAMDEN ST.
WILDE ST.
COMMUTATION ROW
AUDLEY ST.
CONSTANCE ST.
BAYHORSE LA.
LONDON RD.
ANSON ST.
NORTH ST.
PRIMROSE HILL
TRUEMAN ST.
Univ.
CUERDEN ST.
MILL LA.
WILLIAM BROWN ST.
Uni.
Mus.
Lib.
Gallery
Mon.
Tunnel Entrance & Exit
DALE ST.
St. John's Gdn.
St. George's Hall
LONDON RD.
PEMBROKE PL.
BK. BRIDPORT ST.
BRIDPORT ST.
WARD ST.
ST. VINCENT ST.
HOTHAM ST.
NELSON ST.
SEYMOUR ST.
SEYMOUR TERRACE
HART ST.
GREEK ST.
MARQUIS ST.
MOOR PL.
GT. NEWTON ST.
GILL ST.
Juv. Ct.
OLD HAYMARKET
Municipal Offs.
Health Club
QUEEN SQ.
ST. JOHN'S LANE
Conservation Cen.
Millennium Ho.
Bus Sta.
HOOD ST.
Royal Ct. Thtre.
ST. GEORGE'S PL.
LIME ST.
Thtre.
LORD ST.
COAL ST.
LIME ST. CHAMBERS
LIME STREET
ST. ANDREWS GDS.
BRONTE ST.
DANSIE ST.
RUSSELL ST.
Sorting Office
Comm. Cen.
TROWBRIDGE ST.
ST. ANDREW STREET
NEW TN WY.
METQUARTER
WHITECHAPEL
DAWSON ST.
WILLIAMSON SQ.
ST. JOHN'S CEN.
Liverpool Playhouse
HOUGHTON ST.
Sub.
SKELHORNE ST.
BOLTON ST.
HILBRE ST.
GRAND CENTRAL
COPPERAS
HAWKE ST.
WARREN ST.
RUSSELL ST.
ROYAL MAIL ST.
AINSWORTH ST.
NHS Cen.
BK. LIME ST.
GREAT CHARLOTTE ST.
MITCHELL PL.
RANELAGH PL.
RICHMOND ST.
LEIGH ST.
WILLIAMSON ST.
TARLETON ST.
BASNETT ST.
PARKER ST.
CLAYTON SQ. SHOP. CEN.
CHURCH ST.
HILL ST.
BROWNLOW
Univ.
Design Academy
CLARENCE ST.
PLEASANT ST.
Sch.
Coll.
St. Nicholas's Catholic Prim. Sch.
POMONA ST.
CATHL WK.
ORFORD ST.
PLEASANT
SCHOOL LA.
The Bluecoat
BLUECOAT CHAMBERS
PETERS ARCADE
COLLEGE LA.
ALL. Th.
RANELAGH ST.
CENTRAL SHOP. CEN.
LYCEUM PL.
CENTRAL
BOLD ST.
CROPPER ST.
RENSHAW A5038 ST.
MOUNT ST.
NEWINGTON
CENTRAL GDNS.
BENSON ST.
MAY ST.
YMCA
PARADISE ST.
MANESTY'S LA.
HANOVER B5339
Open Eye Gall.
CONCERT SQ.
CONCERT ST.
WOOD ST.
SEEL ST.
DAVID
LEWIS ST.
HEATHFIELD ST.
BK. RENSHAW
OLDHAM PL.
OLDHAM ST.
John Moores University
GRADWELL ST.
WOLSTENHOLME SQUARE
LEVER CT.
TUNNAGE SQ.
PARR ST.
SLATER PL.
L1
DUKE ST.
FACT
ROPEWALKS SQ.
ST. PETER'S SQ.
ART HO. SQ.
COLQUITT ST.
MARYLAND ST.
HUNTER ST.
LEECE S. HARDMAN ST.
ST. LUKES PL.
CAMPBELL ST.
HENRY ST.
ARGYLE CT.
CLEVELAND SQ.
LIVERPOOL ARTS VILLAGE
THE CINNAMON BLDG.
THE FOUNDRY
BK. SEEL ST.
BK. COLQUITT ST.
BERRY ST.
BOLD PL.
ROSCOE LA.
RODNEY ST.
LIT. HARDMAN ST.
Phil. Hall
BK. HOPE PL.
Univ.
Unity Thtre.
HOPE PL.
CALEDONIA ST.
UP. HOPE PL.
LYDIA ANN ST.
LAKELAND CL.
MARL TIME WY.
YORK ST.
GILBERT ST.
SURREY ST.
FREDERICK ST.
GREETHAM ST.
PARK LA.
BECKWITH ST.
Comm. Cen.
DUKES TER.
SLATER ST.
SUFFOLK ST.
CIRCLE 109
MADISON SQ.
EAST VILLAGE
KENT ST.
CORNWALLIS ST.
Prim. Sch.
VINCENT CT.
KNIGHT ST.
BK. KNIGHT ST.
PILGRIM ST.
RICE ST.
FALKNER ST.
MOUNT ST.
Univ.

6
A
B
C
D
37
38
Nursery
Jackson's Bridge Farm
Canal Cottages
Canal Bank
Pygon's Hill
Sudell Bri.
Lane
Pye's Cotts.
Back
Hill Top Poultry Farm
Sudell
Pygon's Hill Farm
Spencers Hey
Swan
Riding School
Lydiate Hill Bri.
Leeds & Liverpool Canal
1
Station Rd.
Hall
Ryecrofts Farm
Home Farm
Southport Road
Sandy
Rose Hill Farm
Rose Hill
Nursery
Cherry Tree Farm
Rose Mount Nurseries
Pygon's Farm
Sudell Brook
Lollies Bri.
Sandhurst Wy.
Birchfield Wy.
Charlesworth Cl.
Lydiate
Silver Birch Wy.
Pye's Farm
2
Manion Av.
Manion Cl.
A5147
Moss
Sandy
Northway Nurseries
Pilling
Berry's Farm
Lydiate Bri.
Rec. Grd.
Pav.
Liverpool
Oakfield House
Road
Lane
Highway Farm
Lydiate House
Lambshear
Schs.
Mill Villas
L31
3
Kingfisher Ct.
Herons Ct.
Mallard Ho.
The Moorings
The Fieldings
Lydiate Prim. Sch.
Marshall's Cl.
Haigh
Oakhill
Knutsford Wk.
B5407
St. Thomas C of E Prim. Sch.
Coppull
Seafore Cl.
Sumners Turn Bri.
Fir Grove
Bells
Lane
Road
Liverpool
Kenyons
Bowl. Grns.
Ridgeway Park
Football Grd.
Maghull Brook
4
Virginia
Coronation
Ridgeway
Tunbridge
Greenbank
Rigby
Crawford Av.
Liverpool
Northway
Northway Prim. Sch.
03
Green
St. John Bosco Catholic Prim. Sch.
Prim. Sch.
The Round
Dodd's
Dodd's Park
Moss
5
West Meade
Towers Avenue
Roedean Cl.
Westway
Road
A5147 North
A59
Moss Side
Peel Farm
Lane
Westway
Mayhall Ct.
Windermere
Deyes
30
Empress Cl.
Milton Wy.
South Meade
Green
Westover Cl.
Swim. Pool
Deyes High Sch.
Buttermere Cl.
Glenn Park
Maghull
6
Meade
Lib.
Red Lion Shop. Cen.
Henry Cox Home
Bartlett Home
Cricket Grd.
Pav.
Lane
Liverpool Rd. Sth.
Prim. Sch.
Deyes
02
Manor House
Harrison Home
Damfield
Kennesse Green
Playing Field
11
12
B5422 Lane
Maghull Canal Bri.
Maricourt Catholic Upper & Lower High School

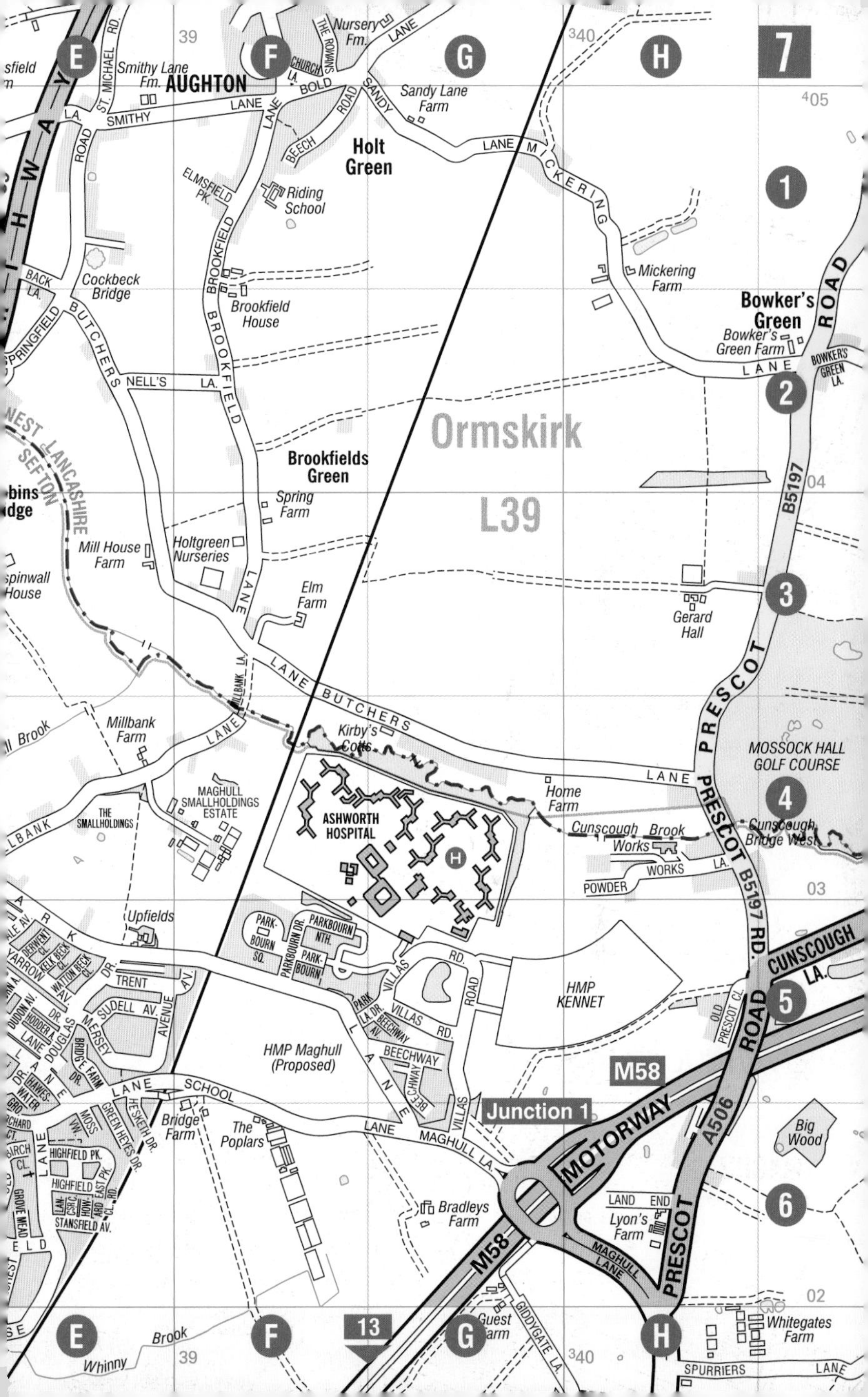

7
AUGHTON
Holt Green
Brookfields Green
Bowker's Green
Ormskirk
L39
Smithy Lane Fm.
Nursery Fm.
Sandy Lane Farm
Riding School
Cockbeck Bridge
Brookfield House
Mickering Farm
Bowker's Green Farm
Spring Farm
Holtgreen Nurseries
Mill House Farm
Elm Farm
Gerard Hall
Millbank Farm
Kirby's Cotts.
MOSSOCK HALL GOLF COURSE
Home Farm
Cunscough Brook
Cunscough Bridge West
Works
MAGHULL SMALLHOLDINGS ESTATE
THE SMALLHOLDINGS
ASHWORTH HOSPITAL
HMP KENNET
HMP Maghull (Proposed)
Upfields
Bridge Farm
The Poplars
Bradleys Farm
Lyon's Farm
Big Wood
Guest Farm
Whitegates Farm
Junction 1
M58
MOTORWAY
A506
B5197
PRESCOT ROAD
BUTCHERS LANE
BROOKFIELD LANE
MICKERING LANE
SMITHY LANE
BOLD LANE
SANDY LANE
NELL'S LA.
MILLBANK LANE
SCHOOL LANE
MAGHULL LA.
VILLAS RD.
PARK LANE
BEECHWAY
WORKS LA.
POWDER
CUNSCOUGH LA.
OLD PRESCOT CL.
LAND END
MAGHULL LANE
SPURRIERS LANE
GIDDYGATE LA.
Whinny Brook
WEST LANCASHIRE
SEFTON
13

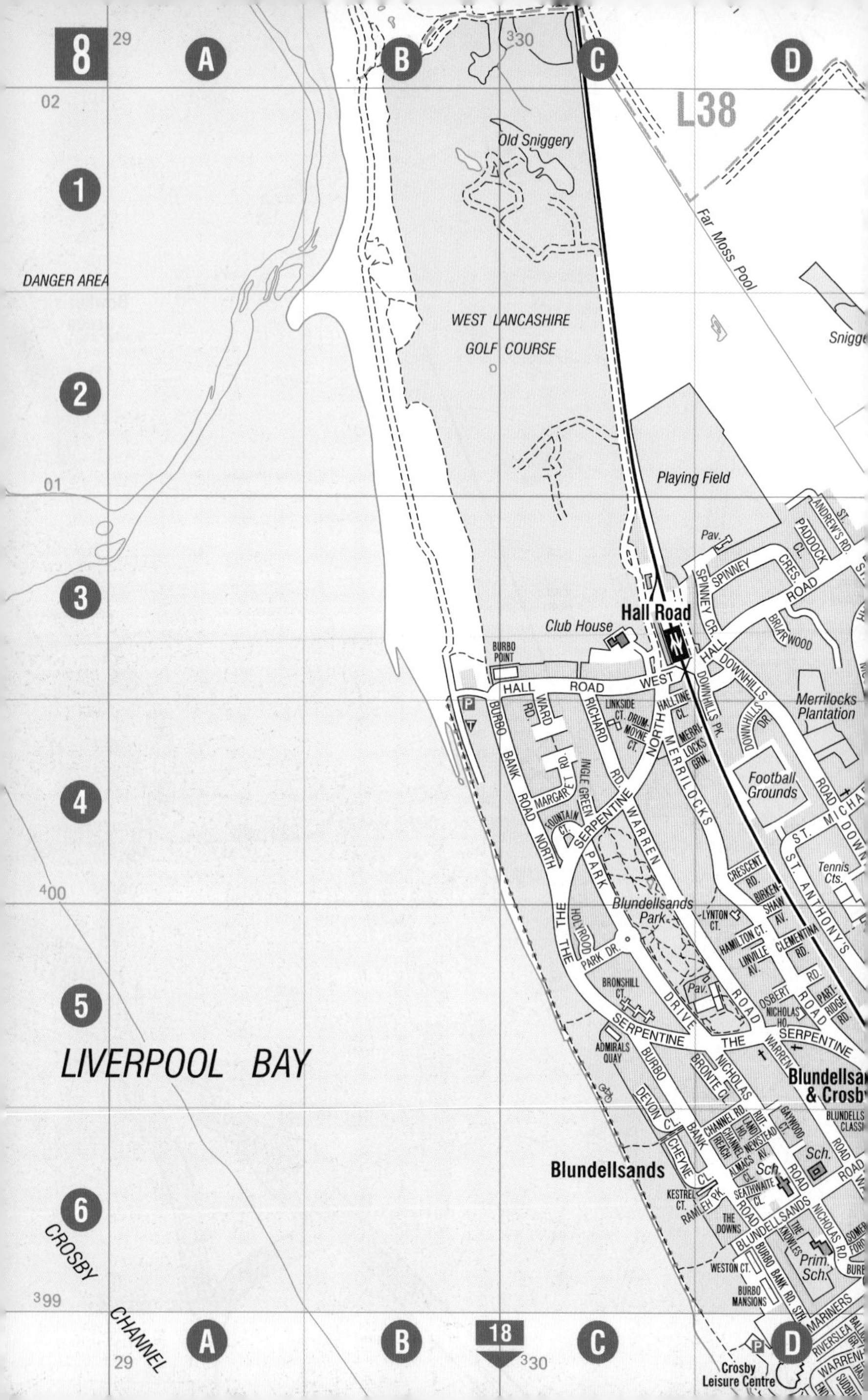

A
B
C
D
1
2
3
4
5
6
29
330
02
01
400
399
L38
Old Sniggery
Far Moss Pool
DANGER AREA
WEST LANCASHIRE
GOLF COURSE
Playing Field
Pav.
Hall Road
Club House
BURBO POINT
HALL ROAD WEST
Merrilocks Plantation
Football Grounds
Tennis Cts.
Blundellsands Park
LIVERPOOL BAY
CROSBY CHANNEL
Blundellsands
Blundellsands & Crosby
Sch.
Prim. Sch.
Crosby Leisure Centre
SPINNEY CR.
SPINNEY
PADDOCK CL.
CRES. ROAD
BRIARWOOD
DOWNHILLS
DOWNHILLS PK.
DOWNHILLS DR.
WARD RD.
RICHARD RD.
BURBO BANK ROAD NORTH
MARGARET RD.
INGLE GREEN
FOUNTAIN CT.
LINKSIDE CT.
DRUMMOYNE CT.
HALLTINE CL.
NORTH WARREN
MERRILOCKS
MERRILOCKS GRN.
SERPENTINE
PARK
THE
HOLYROOD
PARK DR.
CRESCENT RD.
BIRKENSHAW AV.
LYNTON CT.
HAMILTON CT.
LINVILLE AV.
CLEMENTINA RD.
ST. ANTHONY'S
ST. MICHAEL
BRONSHILL CT.
DRIVE
ROAD
OSBERT RD.
NICHOLAS HO.
PARTRIDGE RD.
THE SERPENTINE
ADMIRALS QUAY
BURBO
BRONTE CL.
NICHOLAS
DEVON CL.
BANK
CHANNEL RD.
CHANNEL REACH
RUTLAND HO.
NEWSTEAD AV.
GAYWOOD CT.
ALMACS CL.
CHEYNE CL.
KESTREL CT.
RAMLEH PK.
SEATHWAITE CL.
THE DOWNS
BLUNDELLSANDS
THE KNOWLES
NICHOLAS RD.
WESTON CT.
BURBO BANK RD. STH
BURBO MANSIONS
MARINERS
RIVERSLEA
BLUNDELLS CLASSIC
ROAD
18

9
E
F
G
H
1
2
3
4
5
6
10
19
Sunnyfield Farm
Trap Plantation
Border Plantation
MOSS LANE
B5193
INCE LANE
A565
High Farm
DELPH RD.
Delph Farm
St. Mary's Catholic Prim. Sch.
Sunnyfields
Bens Gorse
St. Joseph's Hospice
Thornton Wood
BACK LANE
Little Crosby
Kennel Plantation
Church Wood
Crosby Hall
Bens Gorse Belt
Well Farm
White House Farm
The Vista
Moor Hey Plantation
Model Farm
LITTLE CROSBY ROAD
ACKERS LANE
BACK LA.
VIRGIN'S LANE
Cottage Farm
Liverpool
Burying Ground Plantation
Playing Fields
Holy Family Catholic High School
St. Michael's C of E High School
Sports Ground
Cricket Grounds
Running Track
Moor Park
Crosby High Sch.
Tennis Cts.
MANOR ROAD
ST. MICHAEL'S ROAD
PRESTWICK DR.
ROEHAMPTON DR.
BOUNDARY DR.
OAKLANDS AV.
LONGFIELD AVENUE
DE VILLIERS AV.
CHESTNUT AV.
SYCAMORE AV.
ELM AVENUE
Tithebarn
MOOR LANE
L23
GREAT CROSBY
CAMBRIDGE ROAD
COLLEGE ROAD
Prim. Sch.
Health Club
THE BY-PASS
Crossroads Cen.
MOOR DR.
THE BYWAY
OLD FARM RD.
ASCOT PK.
MOORSIDE RD.
FOREFIELD LANE
ELMWOOD AV.
HILLCREST
LUPTON
NEWBOROUGH
LYNDHURST
Forefield Jun. Sch.
Moorside Park
Bowl. Grn.
NORTHERN AV.
ORCHARD DALE
THE PRECINCTS
LIVERPOOL ROAD
VICTORIA ROAD
ALEXANDRA RD.
Coronation Park
CORONATION ROAD
ENDBUTT LANE
BLAIR INDUSTRIAL ESTATE
SOUTH PARADE
MORNINGSIDE
Sacred Heart Catholic Coll.
KIMBERLEY DR.
KINGSWOOD DRIVE
Marine AFC (The Arriva Stadium)
BLUNDELLSANDS RD.
MERSEY RD.
HARLECH RD.
CAVENDISH RD.
A565 ROAD
MYERS RD.
Nazareth Ho.
Merchant Taylors' Boys' Sch.
BROWNMOOR LANE
BROWNMOOR PARK
Ten. Cts.
Alexandra Pk.
Lib.
Sch.
Coll.
Bowl. Grns.
VIEW ROAD
MORNINGTON AV.
PINEHURST AV.

10
A
B
C
D
1
2
3
4
5
6
Thornton
Liverpool
Lunt
Sefton Town
Windles Green
INCE LANE A565
SOUTHPORT RD.
GREEN LA.
LYDIATE LANE A5207
THORNTON TO SWIFTS
MOOR LANE A565
BUCKLEY HILL LANE
GORSEY LANE B5422
LONG LANE
HOLGATE
BACK LANE
RAKES LA.
LUNT ROAD
Holly Farm
Wrake's Farm
Hunt's Brook
St. Joseph's Hospice
Thornton Wood
Cottage Farm
Orchard House
Houghton Cotts.
Rothwell Cotts.
Lunt Farm
Thornton Garden of Rest Cemetery
Thornton Crematorium
Holy Family Catholic High School
Sports Ground
Comm. Cen.
Thornton Hall
The Hollies
Playing Field
Tan House Farm
Newfield Sch.
Chesterfield High Sch.
Orchard Farm
New Cotts.
Edge Farm
RIMROSE VALLEY COUNTRY PARK
Rimrose Brook
Moorside Park
Leeds & Liverpool Canal
Killen Green Park
IMPACT
Ford
L23
L21
20
9

E
F
G
H
36
37
6
Cricket Grd.
Manor House
Harrison Home
Harrison's Brook
St. Helen's Gutter
Dover's Brook
River Alt
SEFTON LANE
B5422
L31
MAGHULL
CLAREMONT AV.
ROSSLYN AVENUE
GAINSBOROUGH
OLD RACECOURSE RD.
LINCOLN GR.
SEFTON LANE IND. EST.
CROWN PL.
MEADWAY
HATHAWAY
Tennis Cts.
Maghull High School
Playing Field
Whinny Brook
LIVERPOOL AVENUE
ORMONDE AVENUE
FOURACRES
THE CRES.
Sefton Meadows
Dover's Bri.
Football Field
Bowl. Grn.
ROAD
SEFTON MILLS
SEFTON MILL LA.
MILL STREAM CL.
BRIDGES LA.
Sefton
GLEBE END
BRICKWALL LA.
OLD RECTORY GRN.
BRIDGES LANE
BRICKWALL GN.
COACH HO. CT.
L29
Old Alt Bri.
Netherton Brook
Mill Dam Bri.
Melling Brook
River Alt
Dunnings Bri. South
12
Brook House Farm
Moor Hey Brook
ISLAND LINK (Proposed)
NETHERTON
Pinfold Cottage Woodland Park
LANE
Manor House
CHAPEL LANE
Junction 7 (M57)
A59
SWITCH ISLAND
NORTHERN PERIMETER ROAD
A5207
STONYFIELD
The Grange Prim. Sch.
WATERSIDE
PARKWAY
YORK CL.
WINDSOR CL.
St. Ambrose Barlow Catholic College
COPY LANE
Prim. Sch.
APOLLO WAY
WITHAM CL.
SHROPSHIRE DR.
Copy Farm Pk.
Total Fitness
DUNNINGS BRIDGE ROAD
Superstore
ORMSKIRK RD.
Netherton Activity Cen.
Lib.
VALE Bri.
Netherton
WESTMINSTER AV.
PETERBOROUGH
BUCKFAST CL.
CANTERBURY
TRURO
FINLAY CT.
L30
GLOVER'S LANE
SHERBORNE AV.
MAGDALEN SQ.
ST. OSWALD'S
HOWARD FLOREY AV.
NIGHTINGALE
FREDERICK BANTING CL.
NAVIGATION CL.
CHARLOCK CL.
BARBERRY
Bootle High School
Swing Bri.
ALEXANDER FLEMING AV.
SCHWEITZER AV.
LOUIS BRAILLE CL.
JOSEPH LISTER CL.
CURIE AV.
ALBERT
BROWN'S LANE
MARIAN WAY
ALL SAINTS CL.
ST. BENET'S WY.
APRIL RISE
HEATHERS CFT.
Prim. Sch.
Netherton
Factory
Play. Fld.
Dunnings Canal Bri.
Odeon Cinema
Tenpin
SWITCH ISLAND LEISURE PARK
Warehouses
A5036
DUNNINGS BRIDGE
COPY LANE
CUMBERLAND GATE
EMERALD CL.
WHEATFIELD CL.
WATERWAY AV.
MANOR DR.
PROSPECT WY.
HOMESTEAD AV.
ORCHARD HEY
DOOLEY DRIVE
DEERBARN DRIVE
B5194
NETHERTON GRANGE
BECHERS CT.
Old Roan
Leeds & Liverpool Canal
Works
Warehouses
GRANGE RD.
WAKEFIELD
BECHERS BUSINESS
Works
ORMSKIRK RD.
AINTREE
RADLE
KEBLE
OUNDLE DR.
BRADFIELD
MUNICIPAL COURSE
ASHBOURNE
ELTON AV.
LINDEN
BARNFIELD CL.
STAND PARK
REGENT
LYMINGTON GRO.
LEONARD CHESHIRE DR.
21
2
3
4
5
1
400
399
01
02
81
42

MAGHULL
Maghull
Kennesse Green
Maricourt Catholic Upper & Lower High School
Old Hall Playing Fields
Maghull High School
Town Hall Play. Fld.
Hudson Prim. Sch.
Summerhill Prim. Sch.
Leeds & Liverpool Canal
M58 MOTORWAY
M58
M57 MOTORWAY
M57
Junction 7 (M57)
Superstore
Old Roan
AINTREE
Aintree Hall Farm
Aintree Davenhill Prim. Sch.
Wood Hall Farm
Bradshaw's Farm
Holy Fold
Brooklea
Town Meadow Cottages
Carr Cottage
Brooklands Farm
Melling Stone Bri.
Dunnings Bri. South
River Alt
Dover's Brook
Melling Brook
L29
L30
L31
L10
SEFTON LA.
B5422
LIVERPOOL RD.
A59
B5194
ORMSKIRK RD.
BREWERY LANE
ROCK LANE
SPENCER'S LANE
DUNNINGS BRIDGE RD.
MOORHEY RD.
Bull Bridge
Works
6
11
22

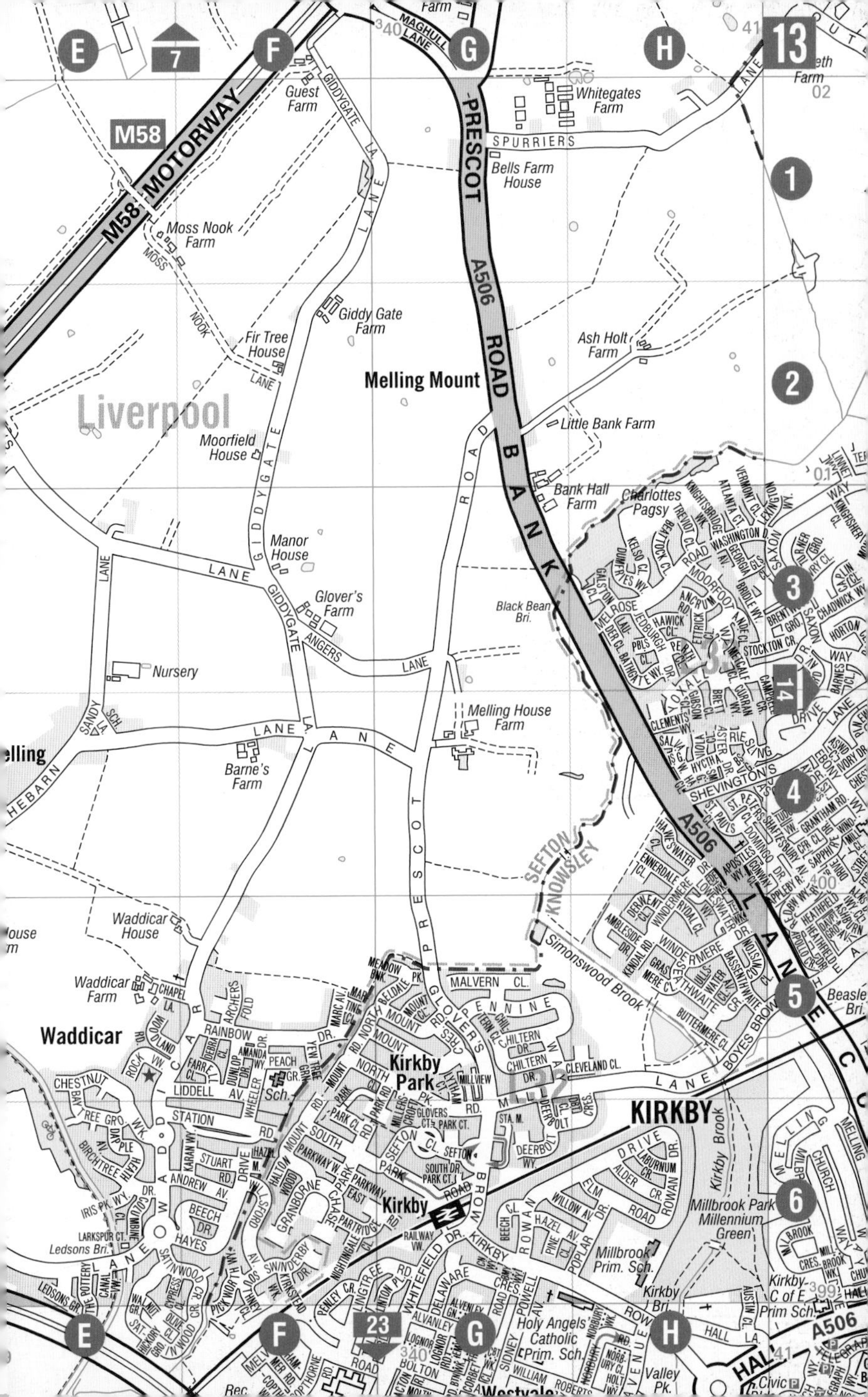

13
7
23
M58 MOTORWAY
M58
A506
PRESCOT ROAD
BANK LANE
Liverpool
Melling Mount
Waddicar
Kirkby Park
KIRKBY
Kirkby
Westvale
Whitegates Farm
Guest Farm
Bells Farm House
Moss Nook Farm
Giddy Gate Farm
Fir Tree House
Ash Holt Farm
Little Bank Farm
Moorfield House
Bank Hall Farm
Charlottes Pagsy
Manor House
Glover's Farm
Black Bean Bri.
Nursery
Melling House Farm
Barne's Farm
Waddicar House
Waddicar Farm
SEFTON
KNOWSLEY
Simonswood Brook
Kirkby Brook
Millbrook Park Millennium Green
Millbrook Prim. Sch.
Holy Angels' Catholic Prim. Sch.
Kirkby C of E Prim. Sch.
Kirkby Bri.
Ledsons Bri.
Valley Pk.

Hesketh Farm
Simonswood Brook
Depot (disused)
Basford Farm
Moss Cottage
Chickru Lodge
Grayson's Farm
The Bungalow
Brookfield Farm
Hesketh Shroggs
L31
SEFTON
Shacklady's Plantation
Liverpool
Simonswood
Wood House Farm
Heavy Testing
Gate House Bridge
Timber Yard
SIMONSWOOD INDUSTRIAL PARK
L33
Tower Hill
Woods Farm
Bridge Farm
Comm. Cen.
Prim. Sch.
Eastcroft Pk. Prim. Sch.
Primary Support Cen.
Overdale Prim. Sch.
Beasley's Bri.
KIRKBY
Northwood
Ruffwood School
St. Marie's Catholic Prim. Sch.
Playing Field
Playing Field
Kirkby Brook
Millennium Green
L32
Kirkby C of E Prim Sch.
Gala Bingo
Training Grd.
COUNTY ROAD
A506
HALL LANE
TOPGATE
SIMONSWOOD LANE
MOSS LANE
HEADBOLT LANE
BROOK HEY DRIVE
QUARRYSIDE DRIVE
ROUGH LANE
BOYES BROW
24
13

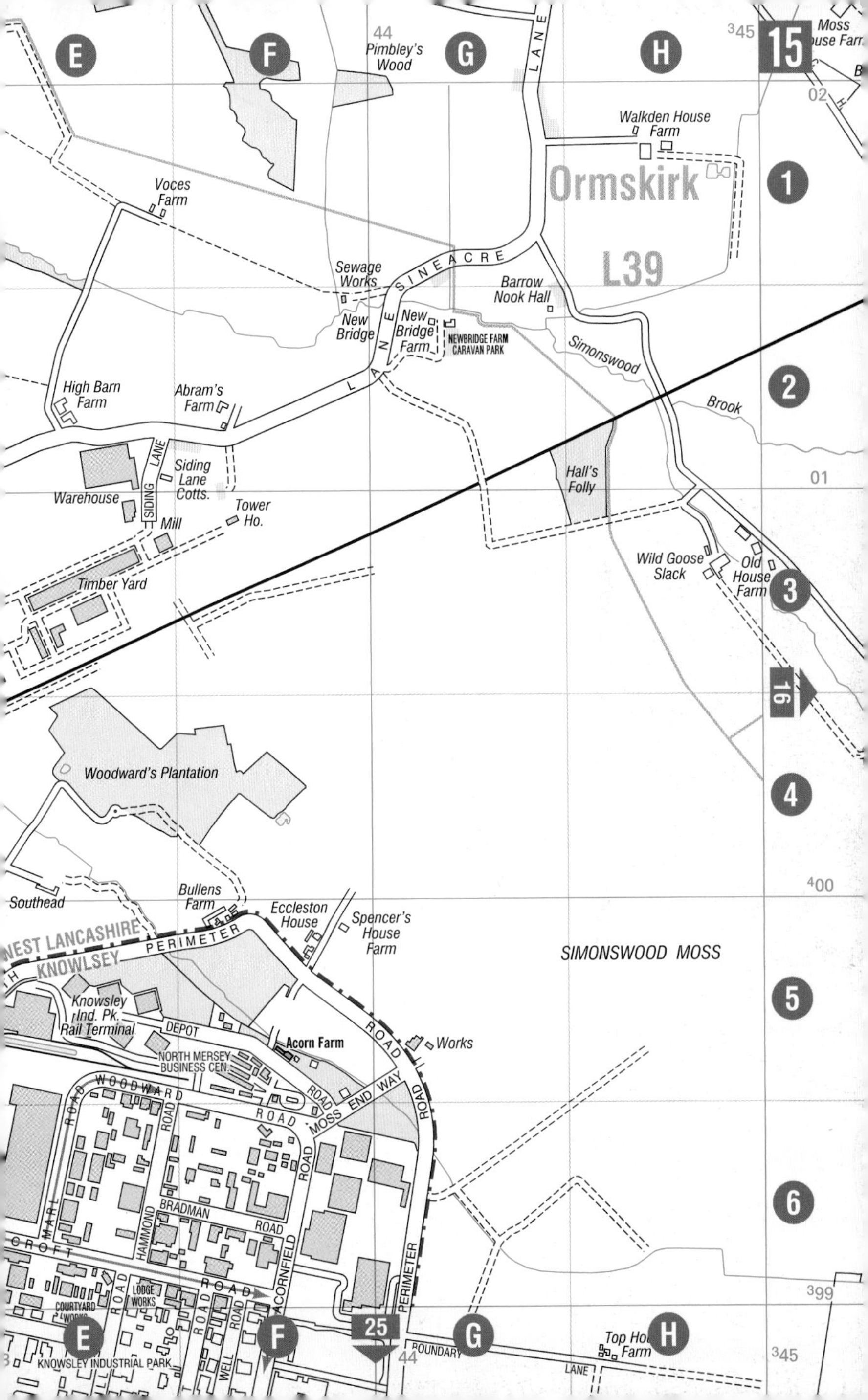

Walkden House
Farm

1

Ormskirk

Voces
Farm

L39

Sewage
Works

Barrow
Nook Hall

S I N E A C R E

New   New
Bridge   Bridge   Simonswood
               Farm   NEWBRIDGE FARM
                         CARAVAN PARK   **2**

High Barn   Brook
Farm   Abram's
              Farm   01

SIDING LANE

Siding   Hall's
Lane   Folly
Cotts.

Warehouse   Tower
             Ho.

Mill   Wild Goose   Old
                                    Slack   House
                                                    Farm
Timber Yard   **3**

                                                    16

                                                    4

Woodward's Plantation

                                                    400

Southead   Bullens
              Farm   Eccleston
                        House   Spencer's
NEST LANCASHIRE   House   SIMONSWOOD MOSS
                       PERIMETER   Farm
KNOWSLEY

              Knowsley
              Ind. Pk.   **5**
              Rail Terminal
                      DEPOT
          NORTH MERSEY   **Acorn Farm**   Works
          BUSINESS CEN

WOODWARD   ROAD

              ROAD

          ROAD   MOSS END WAY

                                                    6
CROFT   BRADMAN   ROAD

          ROAD

          ROAD   ACORNFIELD   ROAD

LODGE   PERIMETER
COURTYARD WORKS
WORKS
                         25   **G**   Top Hol   **H**
E   F   44   BOUNDARY   Farm
KNOWSLEY INDUSTRIAL PARK   LANE   345

16
Moss Ho. Fm.
Birchall's Wood
Rigby's Wood
SIDING LANE
A570
Rainford Brook
Nursery Plantation
Dairy Farm
Ormskirk
L39
Moss Farm
Simonswood Brook
Camholes Wood
Coach Road Farm
COACH ROAD
DAIRY FARM
Goose
Old House Farm
15
Moss Cottage
Simonswood Brook
WEST LANCASHIRE
ST. HELENS
Freddy's Wood
Blackburn's Plantation
SIMONSWOOD MOSS
Liverpool
L33
Clare's Moss Plantation
Brown Birch Farm
Aspinwall' Wood
Mossborough Hall
Mossborough Wood
MOSSBOROUGH HALL LANE
26
Bunker Hill Wood
Brown Birches
A B C D
1 2 3 4 5 6

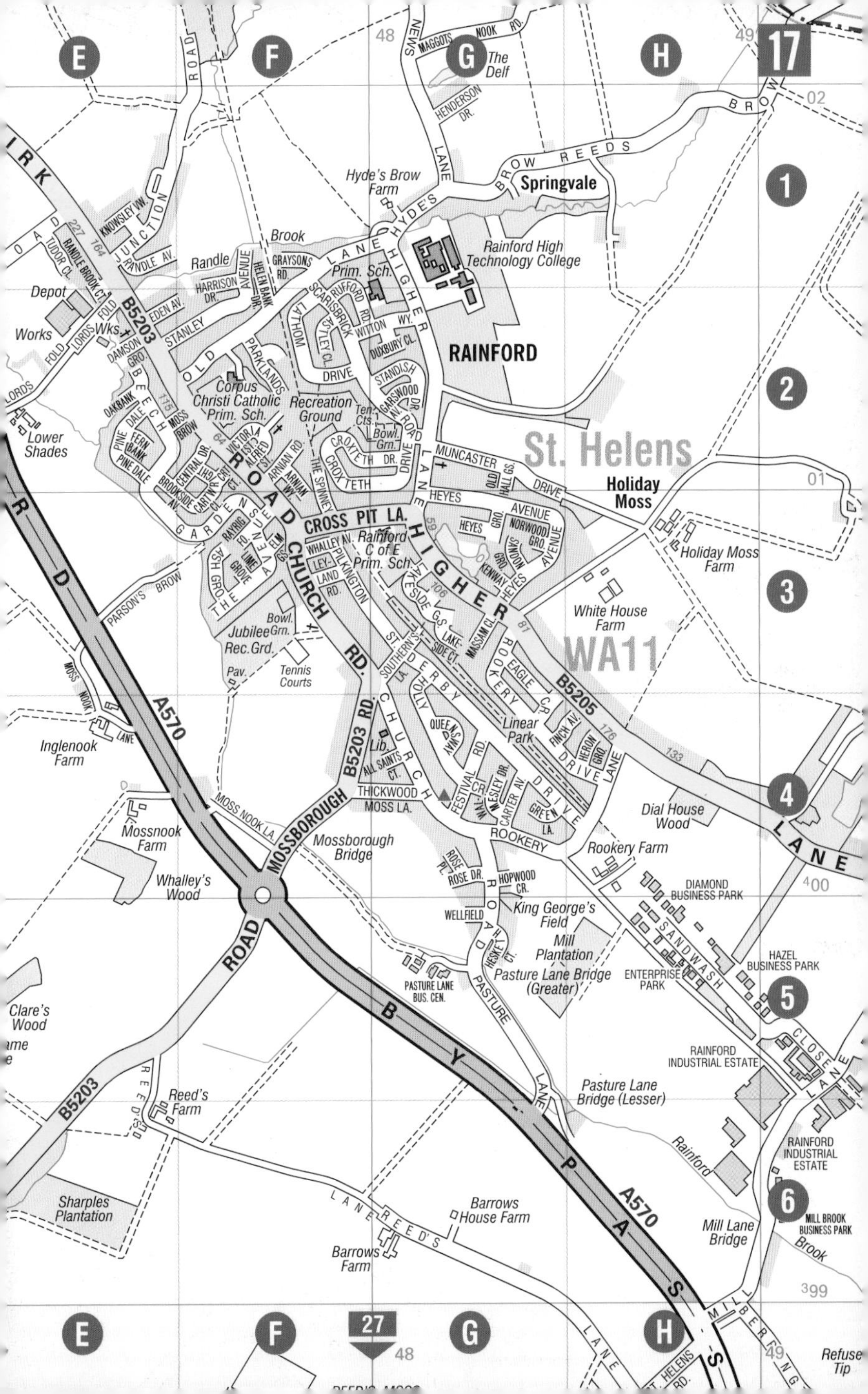

RAINFORD
St. Helens
WA11
Springvale
Holiday Moss
Rainford High Technology College
Hyde's Brow Farm
The Delf
Corpus Christi Catholic Prim. Sch.
Recreation Ground
Rainford C of E Prim. Sch.
Jubilee Rec.Grd.
Tennis Courts
Linear Park
White House Farm
Holiday Moss Farm
Dial House Wood
Rookery Farm
DIAMOND BUSINESS PARK
HAZEL BUSINESS PARK
ENTERPRISE PARK
RAINFORD INDUSTRIAL ESTATE
MILL BROOK BUSINESS PARK
King George's Field
Mill Plantation
Pasture Lane Bridge (Greater)
Pasture Lane Bridge (Lesser)
PASTURE LANE BUS. CEN.
Mossborough Bridge
Mossnook Farm
Whalley's Wood
Inglenook Farm
Lower Shades
Clare's Wood
Reed's Farm
Sharples Plantation
Barrows House Farm
Barrows Farm
Mill Lane Bridge
Refuse Tip
Depot
Works
Wks.
Lib.
Pav.
Bowl. Grn.
Ten. Cts.
A570
B5203
B5205
BY-PASS
CROSS PIT LA.
CHURCH ROAD
HIGHER LANE
MOSSBOROUGH RD.
REED'S LANE
SANDWASH CLOSE
MILL LANE
PASTURE LANE
ROOKERY DRIVE
MUNCASTER DRIVE
HEYES AVENUE
REEDS BROW
MAGGOTS NOOK RD.
27

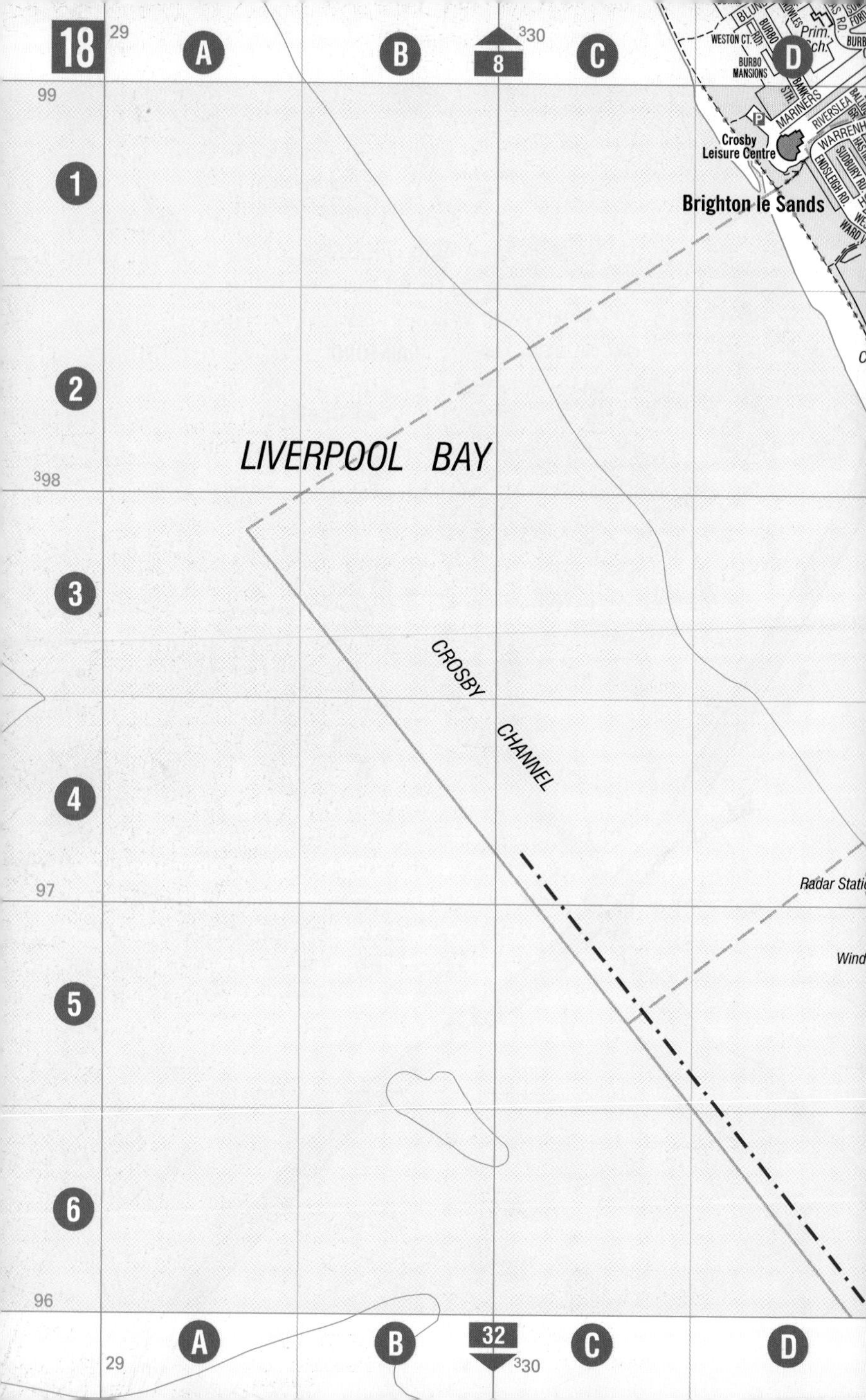

LIVERPOOL BAY

CROSBY CHANNEL

Brighton le Sands

Crosby
Leisure Centre

Radar Station

Wind

WESTON CT. RD.
BURBO
BURBO
MANSIONS
RIVERSLEA
WARREN
SUDBURY RD.
MARINERS
STR.
Prim.
Sch.

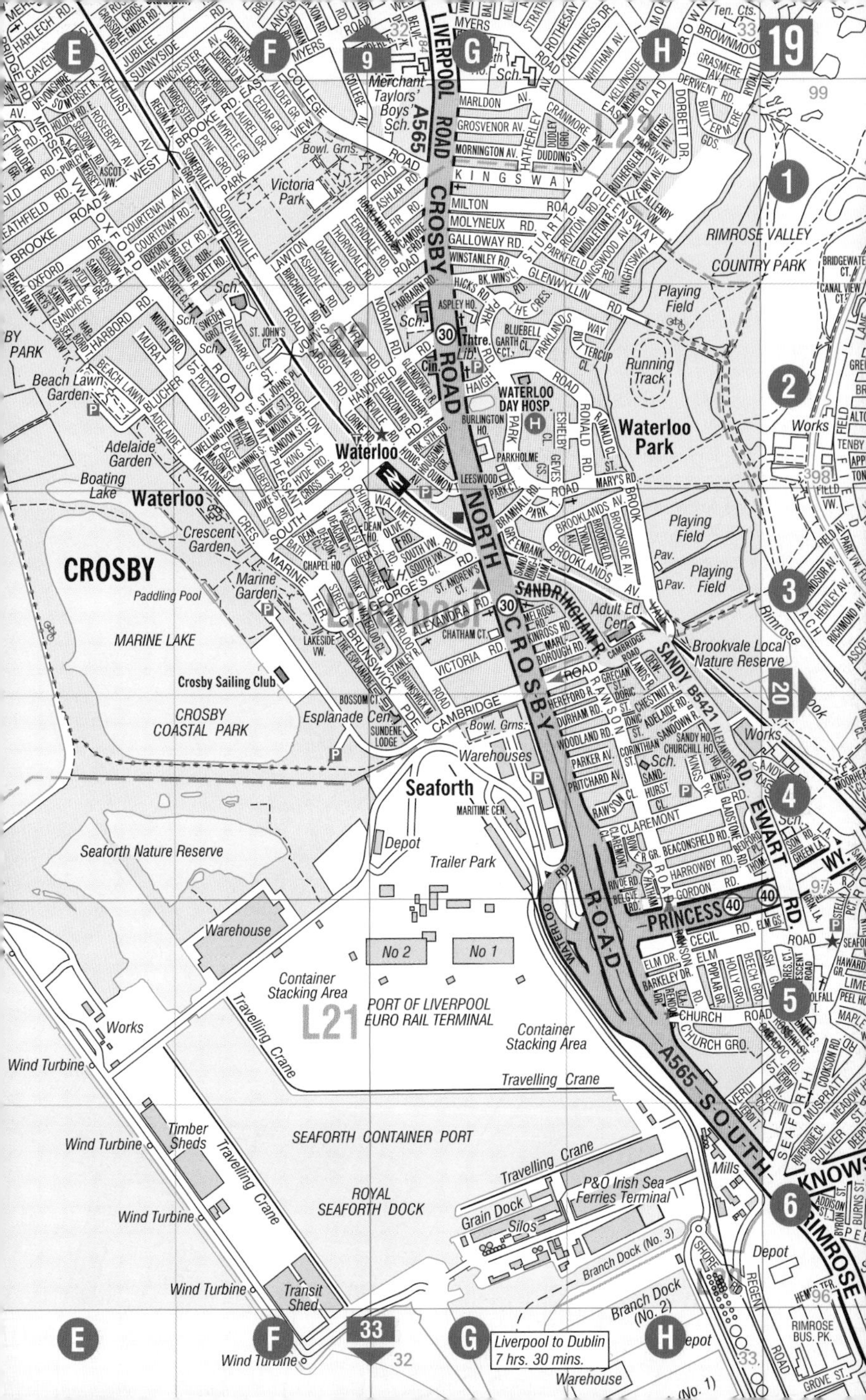

19
CROSBY
Waterloo
Seaforth
Waterloo Park
Victoria Park
RIMROSE VALLEY COUNTRY PARK
MARINE LAKE
Crosby Sailing Club
CROSBY COASTAL PARK
Seaforth Nature Reserve
SEAFORTH CONTAINER PORT
ROYAL SEAFORTH DOCK
PORT OF LIVERPOOL EURO RAIL TERMINAL
Container Stacking Area
P&O Irish Sea Ferries Terminal
Liverpool to Dublin 7 hrs. 30 mins.
Brookvale Local Nature Reserve
Merchant Taylors' Boys' Sch.
WATERLOO DAY HOSP.
Running Track
Playing Field
Grain Dock
Branch Dock (No. 3)
Branch Dock (No. 2)
Timber Sheds
Transit Shed
Wind Turbine
Trailer Park
Warehouse
LIVERPOOL ROAD
CROSBY ROAD NORTH
CROSBY ROAD
A565 SOUTH
A565
B5421
L21
L22
9
20
33

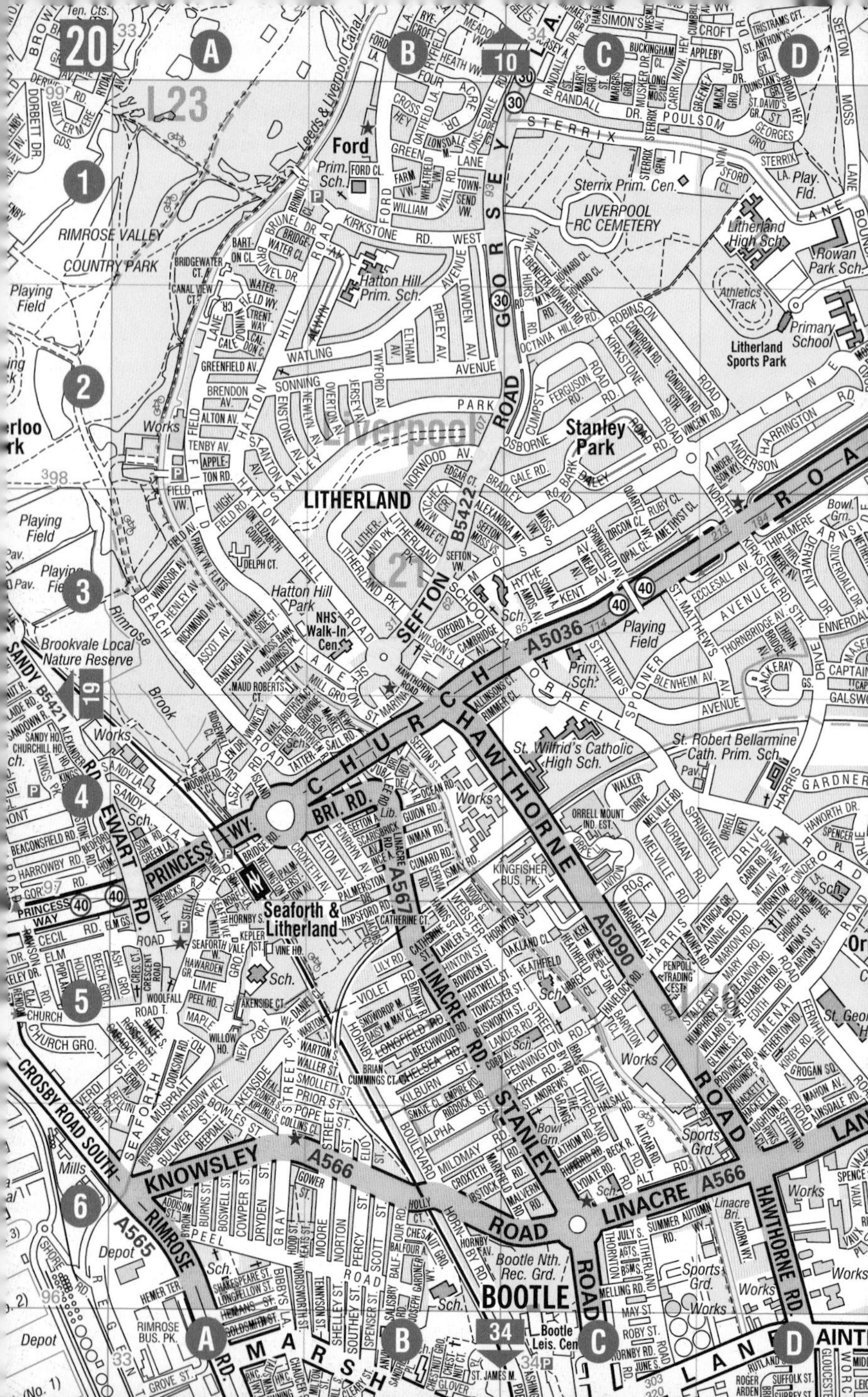
20
A
B
C
D
10
34
19
1
2
3
4
5
6
L23
L21
Ford
Ford Prim. Sch.
RIMROSE VALLEY COUNTRY PARK
Playing Field
Leeds & Liverpool Canal
Sterrix Prim. Cen.
LIVERPOOL RC CEMETERY
Litherland High Sch.
Rowan Park Sch.
Athletics Track
Primary School
Litherland Sports Park
Hatton Hill Prim. Sch.
Stanley Park
LITHERLAND
Hatton Hill Park
NHS Walk-In Cen.
Brookvale Local Nature Reserve
Rimrose Brook
Works
Seaforth & Litherland
St. Wilfrid's Catholic High Sch.
St. Robert Bellarmine Cath. Prim. Sch.
ORRELL MOUNT IND. EST.
KINGFISHER BUS. PK.
PENPOLL TRADING EST.
Bootle Nth. Rec. Grd.
BOOTLE
Bootle Leis. Cen.
RIMROSE BUS. PK.
Depot
Mills
Linacre Bri.
Sports Grd.
STERRIX LANE
GORSEY ROAD
B5422
SEFTON ROAD
HATTON HILL ROAD
PARK AVENUE
WATLING AVENUE
KIRKSTONE RD. WEST
CHURCH ROAD
A5036
HAWTHORNE ROAD
A5090
LINACRE ROAD
A566
LINACRE LANE
STANLEY ROAD
A567
KNOWSLEY ROAD
RIMROSE ROAD
A565
CROSBY ROAD SOUTH
PRINCESS WAY
EWART RD.
B5421
ORRELL ROAD
MOSS LANE
SEFTON LANE
HARRIS DRIVE
BRIDGE RD.
MARSH LANE

AINTREE
AINTREE RACECOURSE
Aintree
Warbreck Park
Bootle
Victoria Park
Orrell Park
Walton
Hartley's Village
HMP LIVERPOOL
Rice Lane Recreation Ground
Archbishops Beck Tennis Centre
Inland Container Depot
NETHERTON IND. ESTATE
BRIDLE ROAD IND. ESTATE
SEFTON BUSINESS PARK
VESTY BUSINESS PARK
Fire Service HQ
Savio High Sch.
Orrell Public Pleasure Grd.
Our Lady of Walsingham Catholic Primary School
St. Monica's Cath. Prim. Sch.
Carlton Bingo Club
Aintree Visitor Cen.
Fitness First
GRAYLAW INDUSTRIAL ESTATE
Kirkdale Cemet
DUNNINGS BRIDGE RD.
A5036
NETHERTON WAY
A5038
BAILEY DR.
ORMSKIRK ROAD
A59
MOOR LA.
WARBRECK MOOR
WALTON VALE
RICE LA.
HORNBY RD.
A5098
MOSS LA.
A566
LONGMOOR LANE
A506
LONG LA.
B5187
SOUTHPORT RD.
Leeds & Liverpool Canal
Rimrose Brook
Aintree Curve
E
F
G
H
1
2
3
4
5
6
11
22
35
36
37
96
97
98
99

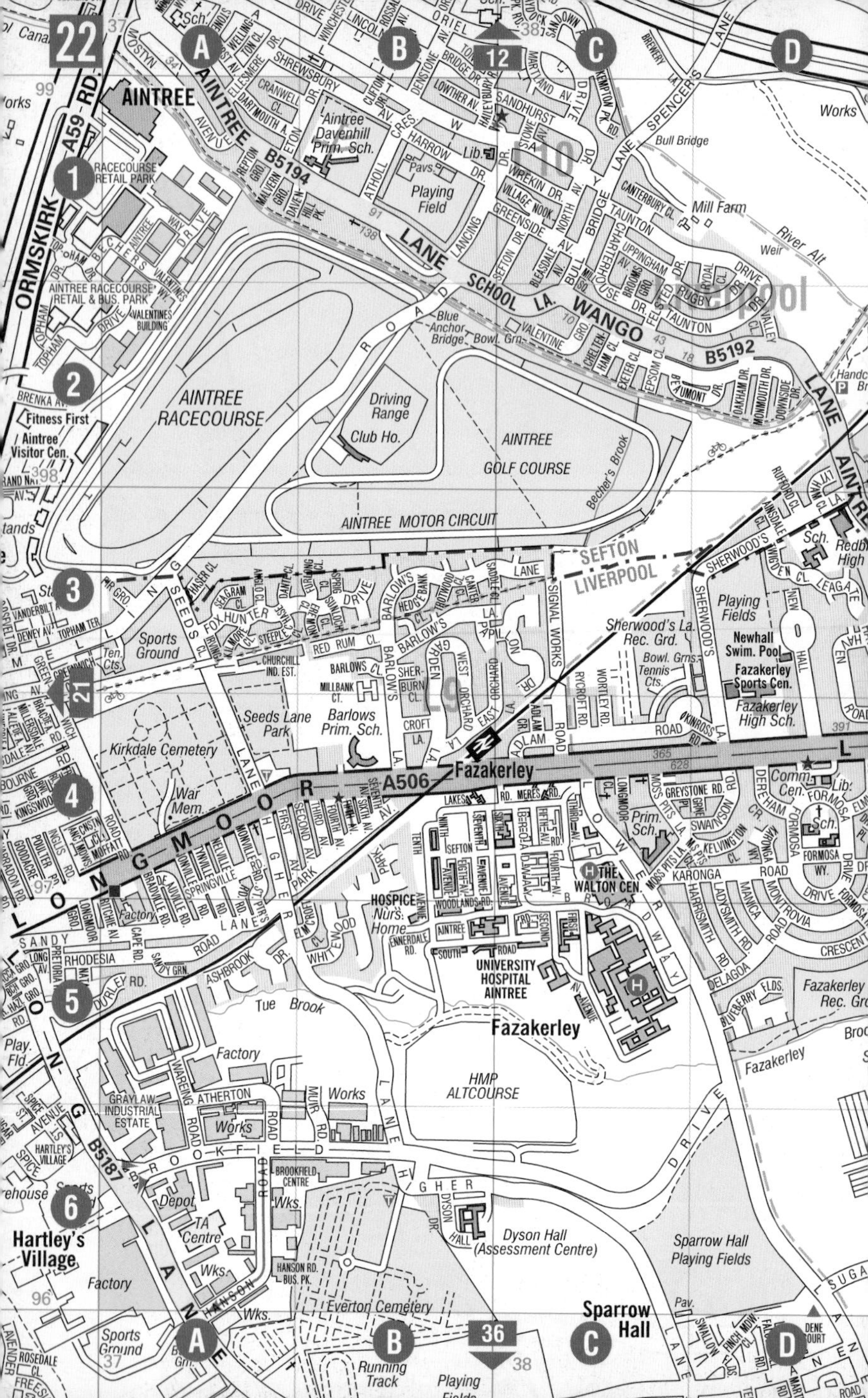
AINTREE
RACECOURSE RETAIL PARK
AINTREE RACECOURSE RETAIL & BUS. PARK
VALENTINES BUILDING
Fitness First
Aintree Visitor Cen.
AINTREE RACECOURSE
ORMSKIRK RD.
A59
AINTREE LANE
B5194
Aintree Davenhill Prim. Sch.
Playing Field
Pavs.
Lib.
SCHOOL LA.
WANGO LANE
B5192
Liverpool
Bull Bridge
Mill Farm
River Alt
Weir
Works
Blue Anchor Bridge
Bowl. Grn.
Driving Range
Club Ho.
AINTREE GOLF COURSE
Becher's Brook
AINTREE MOTOR CIRCUIT
SEFTON
LIVERPOOL
Sports Ground
Ten. Cts.
CHURCHILL IND. EST.
Seeds Lane Park
Barlows Prim. Sch.
Kirkdale Cemetery
War Mem.
Sherwood's La. Rec. Grd.
Bowl. Grns.
Tennis Cts.
Playing Fields
Newhall Swim. Pool
Fazakerley Sports Cen.
Fazakerley High Sch.
Fazakerley
A506
LONGMOOR
HOSPICE
Nurs. Home
THE WALTON CEN.
UNIVERSITY HOSPITAL AINTREE
Prim. Sch.
Comm. Cen.
Lib.
Sch.
Factory
Tue Brook
Fazakerley
HMP ALTCOURSE
Fazakerley Rec. Grd.
GRAYLAW INDUSTRIAL ESTATE
Works
BROOKFIELD CENTRE
Wks.
Depot
TA Centre
HANSON RD. BUS. PK.
Dyson Hall (Assessment Centre)
Sparrow Hall Playing Fields
Sparrow Hall
Everton Cemetery
Running Track
Playing Fields
Hartley's Village
Factory
Sports Ground
B5187
LOWER LANE
12
21
36
A
B
C
D
1
2
3
4
5
6

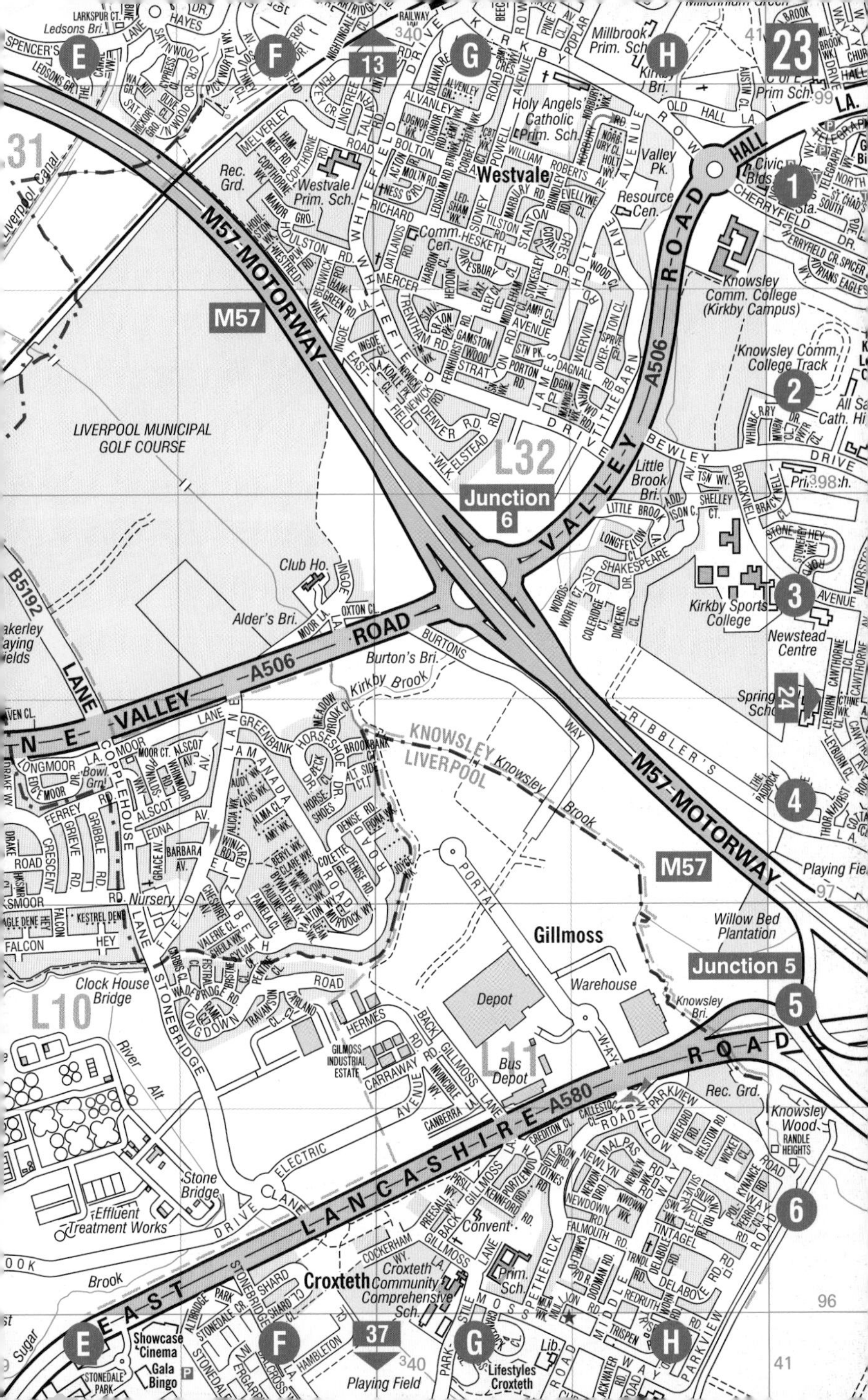

23
13
37
24
31
E
F
G
H
1
2
3
4
5
6
Westvale
Gillmoss
Croxteth
L32
L10
L11
M57
M57-MOTORWAY
Junction 6
Junction 5
VALLEY ROAD A506
EAST LANCASHIRE ROAD A580
LIVERPOOL MUNICIPAL GOLF COURSE
KNOWSLEY
LIVERPOOL
Westvale Prim. Sch.
Holy Angels' Catholic Prim. Sch.
Millbrook Prim. Sch.
Knowsley Comm. College (Kirkby Campus)
Knowsley Comm. College Track
Kirkby Sports College
Newstead Centre
Valley Pk.
Resource Cen.
Comm. Cen.
Rec. Grd.
Club Ho.
Alder's Bri.
Burton's Bri.
Kirkby Brook
Knowsley Brook
Knowsley Bri.
Willow Bed Plantation
Depot
Bus Depot
Warehouse
GILLMOSS INDUSTRIAL ESTATE
Clock House Bridge
Stone Bridge
Effluent Treatment Works
River Alt
Croxteth Community Comprehensive Sch.
Convent
Prim. Sch.
Showcase Cinema
Gala Bingo
Lifestyles Croxteth
Lib.
Playing Field
Knowsley Wood
Little Brook Bri.
Civic Bldgs.
Ledsons Bri.
B5192

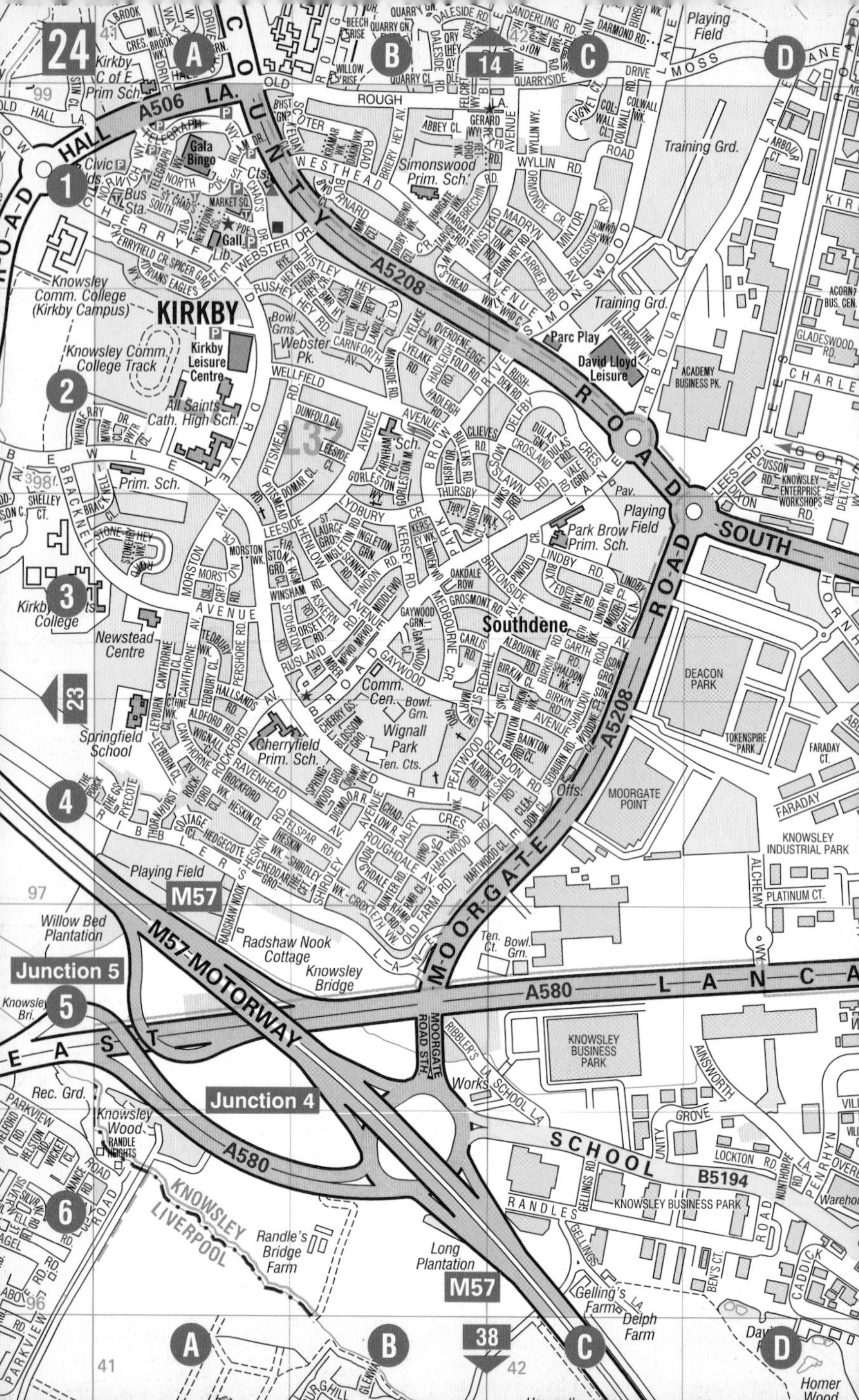

KIRKBY
Southdene
Kirkby C of E Prim Sch.
Civic Bldgs.
Bus Sta.
Gala Bingo
Knowsley Comm. College (Kirkby Campus)
Knowsley Comm. College Track
Kirkby Leisure Centre
All Saints Cath. High Sch.
Simonswood Prim. Sch.
Webster Pk.
Bowl. Grns.
Training Grd.
Parc Play
David Lloyd Leisure
ACADEMY BUSINESS PK.
ACORN BUS. CEN.
KNOWSLEY ENTERPRISE WORKSHOPS
Playing Field
Park Brow Prim. Sch.
Prim. Sch.
Kirkby College
Newstead Centre
Springfield School
Cherryfield Prim. Sch.
Comm. Cen.
Wignall Park
Ten. Cts.
DEACON PARK
TOKENSPIRE PARK
MOORGATE POINT
KNOWSLEY INDUSTRIAL PARK
PLATINUM CT.
FARADAY CT.
Willow Bed Plantation
Radshaw Nook Cottage
Knowsley Bridge
Junction 5
Junction 4
M57 MOTORWAY
A580
A5208
A506
B5194
KNOWSLEY BUSINESS PARK
Rec. Grd.
Knowsley Wood
Randle's Bridge Farm
Long Plantation
Gelling's Farm
Delph Farm
Homer Wood
KNOWSLEY
LIVERPOOL
MOORGATE ROAD
SCHOOL LA.
L32
14
23
38

Top House Farm
WEST LANCASHIRE
KNOWSLEY
BOUNDARY LANE
KNOWSLEY INDUSTRIAL PARK
COURTYARD WORKS
LODGE WORKS
BIRCHILL ROAD
STOCKPIT ROAD
DRAW WELL ROAD
BANK ROAD
CRANSTON RD.
CAPITOL TRADING PARK
YARDLEY CENTRE
YARDLEY ROAD
ACORNFIELD ROAD
Liverpool
Charnley Wood
Kirkby Moss
L33
Sandy Brow
RED CUT
Acornfield Plantation Local Nature Reserve
BECKETT CL.
THE WEB COMPLEX
CENTRO PARK
GALE RD.
BUSINESS RESOURCE CEN.
ACORNFIELD CL.
SPINNEY CL.
SPINNEY VW.
A5208 ROAD
PERIMETER RD.
MOLLY'S LANE
CUT LANE
SANDY BROW LANE
Sandy Lane Farm
Cooper's Moss Farm
Electricity Sub Station
OWEN RD.
COOPER'S LANE
Works
Moss Side
HEWITT'S
New Road Farm
A580 ROAD
Prescot
L34
Tincle Peg Farm
ORMSKIRK
B5202 LANE
KNOWSLEY BUSINESS PARK
Canrow Farm
CANROW LANE
Canrow Cotts.
Moss Plantation
Keeper's House
Scamper Plantation
WALK
OVERBROOK HOUSE
MILLBROOK CT.
KNOWSLEY
Dumbreeze Lodge
PATTEN'S LANE
Knowsley Park
Mill Cotts.
MAYPOLE CT.
MILL LANE
KNOWSLEY LANE
War Mem.
Village Hall
OLD MEADOW
TEYNHAM AVENUE
DUMBREEZE GRO.
WHITEGATE CL.
Corn Ground Plantation

15
26
39

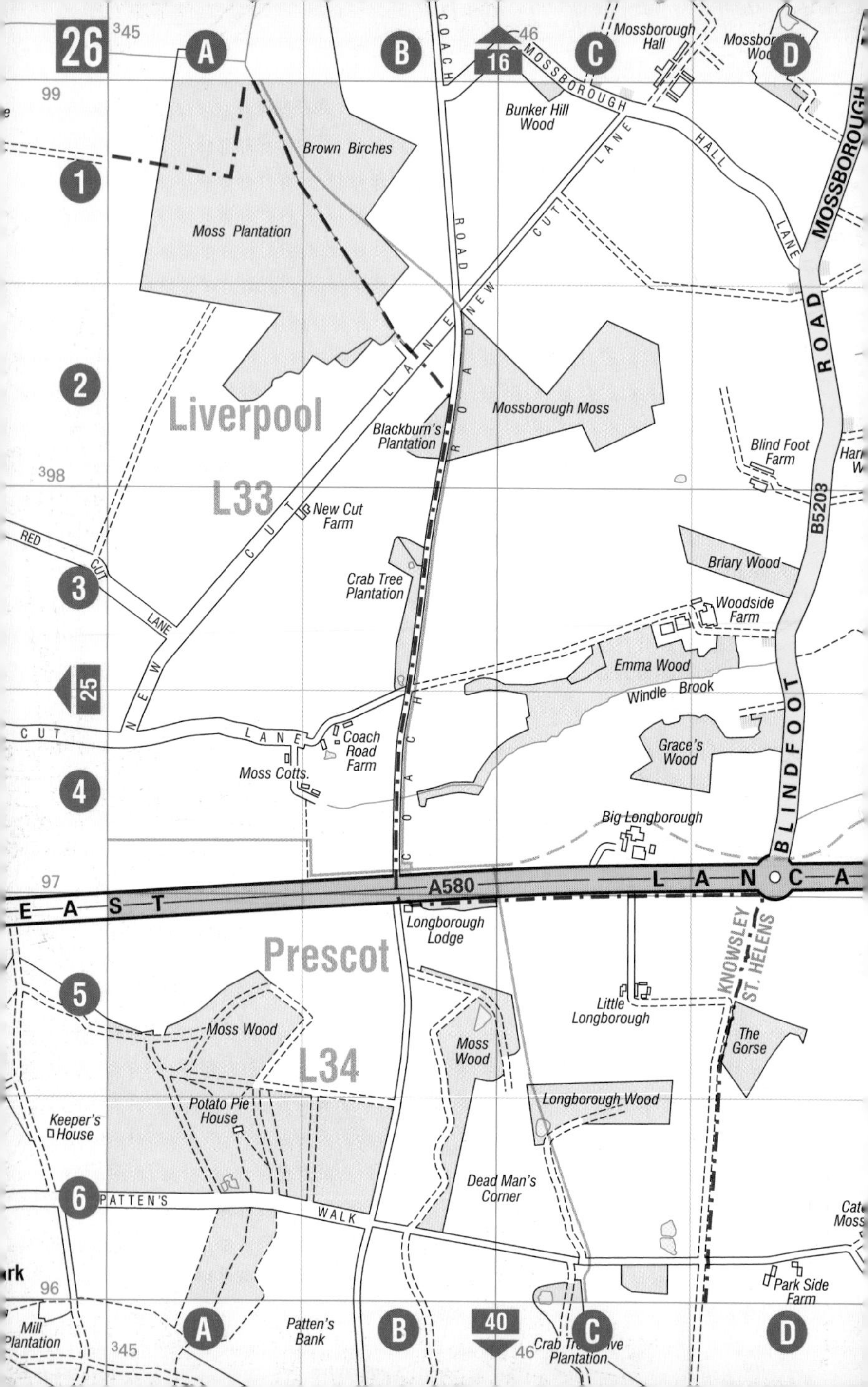

Brown Birches
Moss Plantation
Mossborough Hall
Mossborough Wood
Bunker Hill Wood
MOSSBOROUGH
HALL
LANE
COACH ROAD
NEW CUT LANE
MOSSBOROUGH ROAD
Liverpool
L33
Mossborough Moss
Blackburn's Plantation
Blind Foot Farm
B5203
New Cut Farm
RED CUT LANE
Crab Tree Plantation
Briary Wood
Woodside Farm
Emma Wood
Windle Brook
Grace's Wood
CUT LANE
Coach Road Farm
Moss Cotts.
BLINDFOOT
Big Longborough
EAST LANCA
A580
Longborough Lodge
Prescot
KNOWSLEY
ST. HELENS
Little Longborough
Moss Wood
L34
The Gorse
Longborough Wood
Potato Pie House
Keeper's House
Dead Man's Corner
PATTEN'S WALK
Park Side Farm
Mill Plantation
Patten's Bank
Crab Tree Plantation
345
46
99
98
97
96
A
B
C
D
1
2
3
4
5
6

16
25
40

27
17
28
41
WA11
WA10
St. Helens
Reed's Moss
Windle Moss
Moss Plantation
Inglewood Farm
Long Wood
Square Wood
Refuse Tip
Hill Top Ho.
Moss Farm
Watery Lane Farm
Liverpool St Helens Rugby Football Club
Pav.
Windle Brook Bridge
Windle Farm
Windle
Windle Brook
Catchdale Moss Farm
Orith Farm
Hilton's Farm
Higher Barrowfield Farm
Carmelite Convent
Recreation Ground
Library
Bleak Hill Prim. Sch.
Smithy Heritage Cen.
Eccleston
Howard Farm
Barrows Farm
Mill Lane Bridge
A570
A580
B5201
B5203
Rainford By-Pass
Reed's Lane
Moss Lane
Watery Lane
Sadler's Lane
Catchdale Moss Lane
Houghton's Lane
Green Lane
Lynton Way
Bleak Hill
Millbrook Lane
Broad Oak Road
Walmesley Road
Springfield Lane
Kiln Lane

28
A
B
C
D
1
2
3
4
5
6
27
42
WA11
WA10
St. Helens
Rainford Brook
Refuse Tip
FAIRFIELD INDEPENDENT HOSPITAL
RAINFORD HALL
STABLEYARD COTTS.
Lion House Wood
Nursery Wood
Fenny Bank Rough
Fenny Bank Farm
Square Wood
Berrington's Lane Cotts.
Grey House Farm
Dagnals Bridge Farm
Dagnals Bridge
Poverty Plantation
Long Wood
Pottery Farm
Hill Top Ho.
Potter's House Farm
Brook Wood
Windle Park Wood
Potter's Wood
Windle Hall Farm
Windle Hall
Windle Hall Bridge
RAINFORD BY-PASS
A570
B5201
RANK ROAD
SANDY LANE
BERRINGTONS LANE
EAST LANCASHIRE ROAD
A580
Windlehurst
St. Helens Crematorium
St. Helens Cemetery
Playing Fields
Windle
St. Thomas of Canterbury Catholic Prim. Sch.
Windlehurst Prim. Sch.
Cowley Language College
Victoria Park
The Mansion House
Bleak Hill Prim. Sch.
Youth Cen.
Prim. Sch.
Bishop Rd. Play. Flds.
Denton's Green
Cricket Ground
Bowling Greens
Cowley Hill
Recreation Ground
All Weather Pitch
Cricket Grd.
Ruskin Leisure
Eccleston
Smithy Heritage Cen.
Millbrook Rec. Grd.
The Rivington Cen. Prim. Sch.
Queens Park
De La Salle
RAINFORD ROAD
DENTONS GREEN LANE
BLEAK HILL

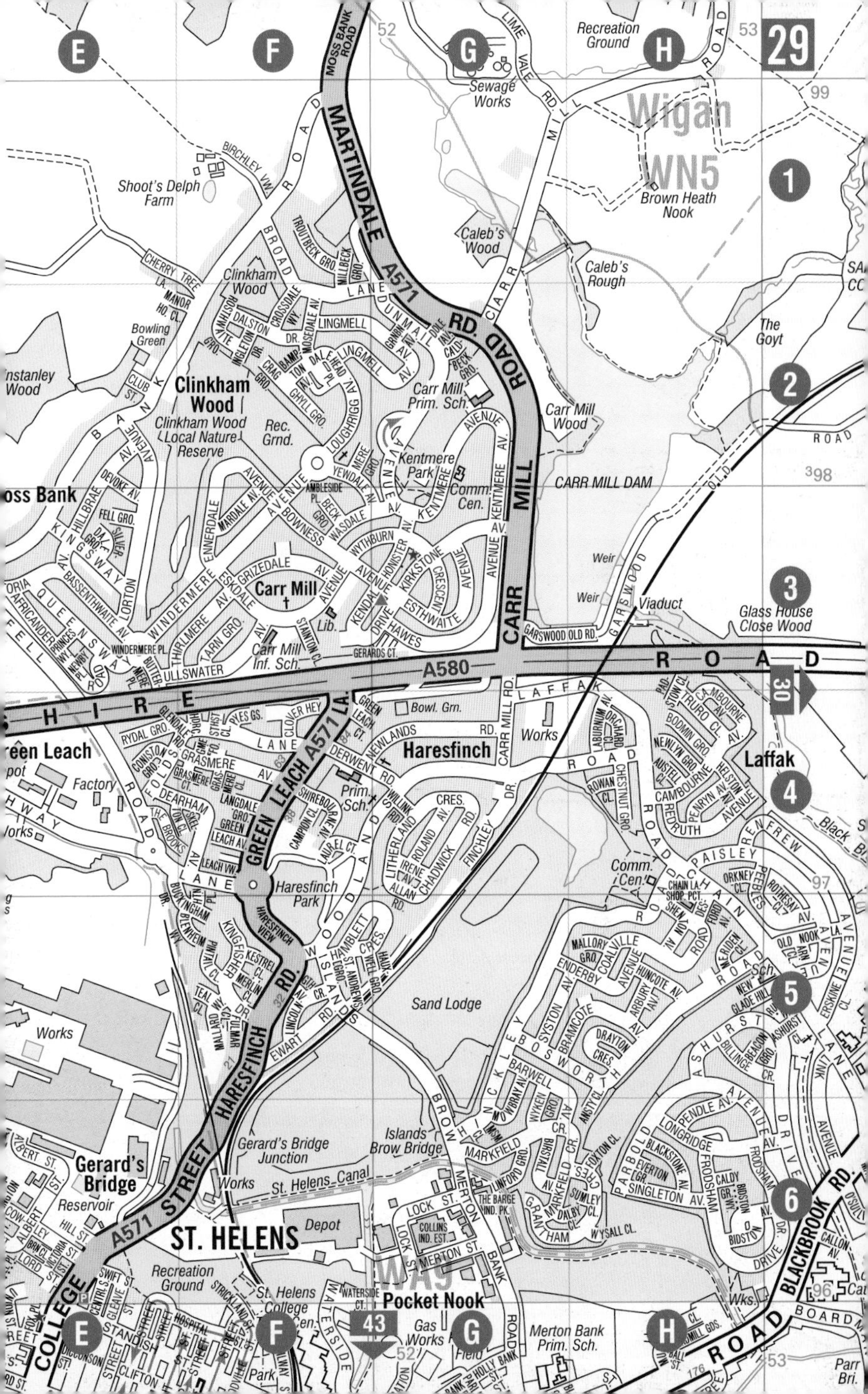

E
F
G
H
Recreation Ground
Sewage Works
Wigan
WN5
Brown Heath Nook
Shoot's Delph Farm
Caleb's Wood
Caleb's Rough
The Goyt
Clinkham Wood
Bowling Green
Clinkham Wood
Clinkham Wood Local Nature Reserve
Rec. Grnd.
Carr Mill Prim. Sch.
Carr Mill Wood
Kentmere Park
Comm. Cen.
CARR MILL DAM
Moss Bank
Carr Mill
Lib.
Carr Mill Inf. Sch.
Weir
Viaduct
Glass House Close Wood
MARTINDALE RD.
A571
CARR MILL ROAD
A580
ROAD
Haresfinch
Works
Laffak
Green Leach
Factory
Prim. Sch.
GREEN LEACH
Haresfinch Park
Comm. Cen.
Sand Lodge
HARESFINCH RD.
HARESFINCH STREET
Gerard's Bridge
Reservoir
Gerard's Bridge Junction
Islands Brow Bridge
St. Helens Canal
Works
Depot
ST. HELENS
Recreation Ground
St. Helens College
Pocket Nook
Gas Works
Merton Bank Prim. Sch.
COLLEGE STREET
BLACKBROOK RD.
ROAD
WA9
1
2
3
4
5
6
30
43

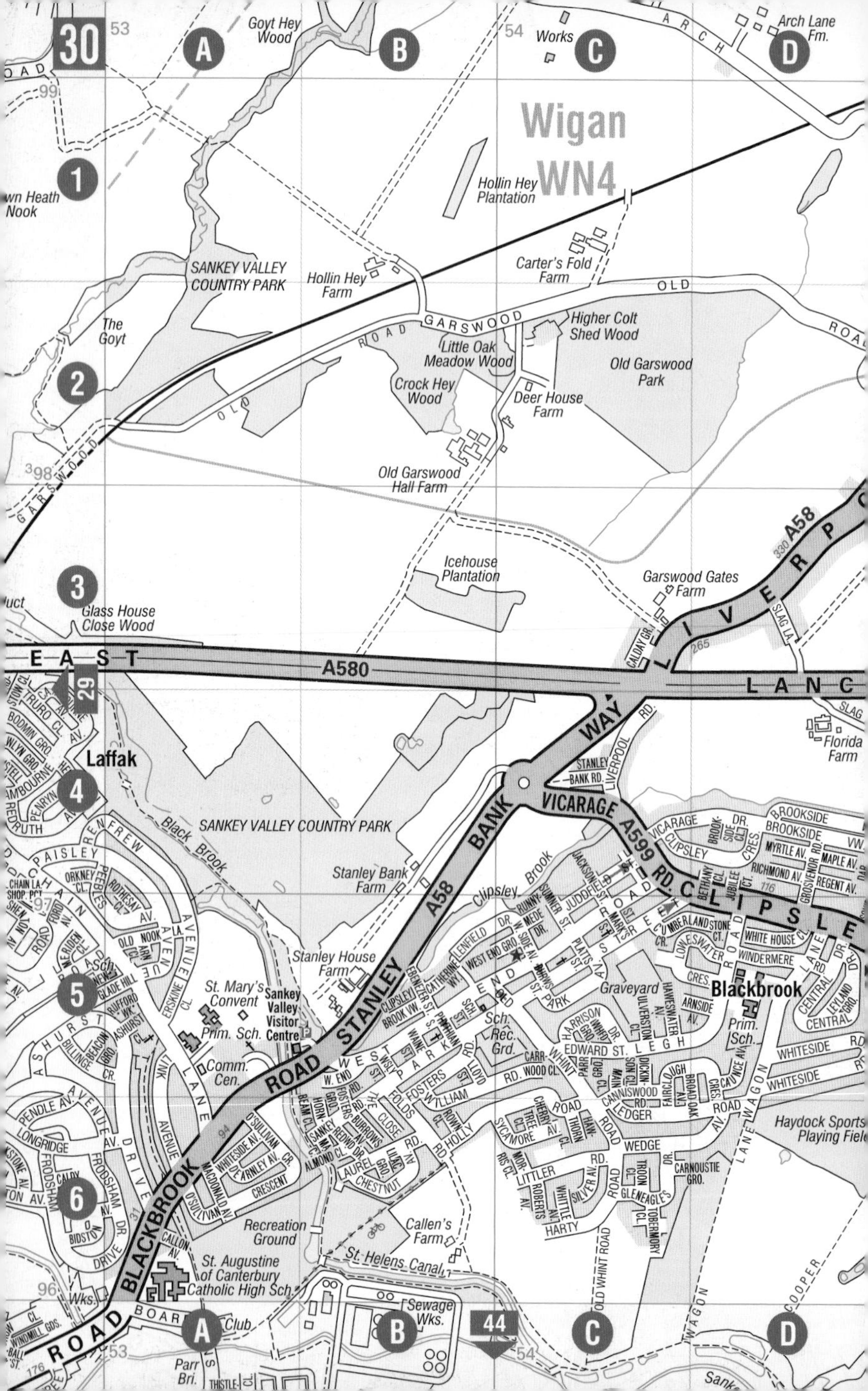
Wigan
WN4
Goyt Hey Wood
Works
Arch Lane Fm.
Hollin Hey Plantation
Carter's Fold Farm
SANKEY VALLEY COUNTRY PARK
Hollin Hey Farm
The Goyt
OLD GARSWOOD ROAD
Higher Colt Shed Wood
Little Oak Meadow Wood
Old Garswood Park
Crock Hey Wood
Deer House Farm
Old Garswood Hall Farm
Icehouse Plantation
Garswood Gates Farm
Glass House Close Wood
EAST LANCS ROAD
A580
A58
LIVERPOOL RD.
Laffak
SANKEY VALLEY COUNTRY PARK
Black Brook
Florida Farm
Stanley Bank Farm
Clipsley Brook
STANLEY BANK WAY
VICARAGE RD.
A599
CLIPSLEY LANE
Stanley House Farm
St. Mary's Convent
Sankey Valley Visitor Centre
Prim. Sch.
Comm. Cen.
BLACKBROOK ROAD
Graveyard
Blackbrook
Prim. Sch.
Sch. Rec. Grd.
Haydock Sports Playing Field
Recreation Ground
Callen's Farm
St. Helens Canal
St. Augustine of Canterbury Catholic High Sch.
Sewage Wks.
Wks.
Club
Parr Bri.
OLD WHINT ROAD
WAGON LANE
COOPER

29
44

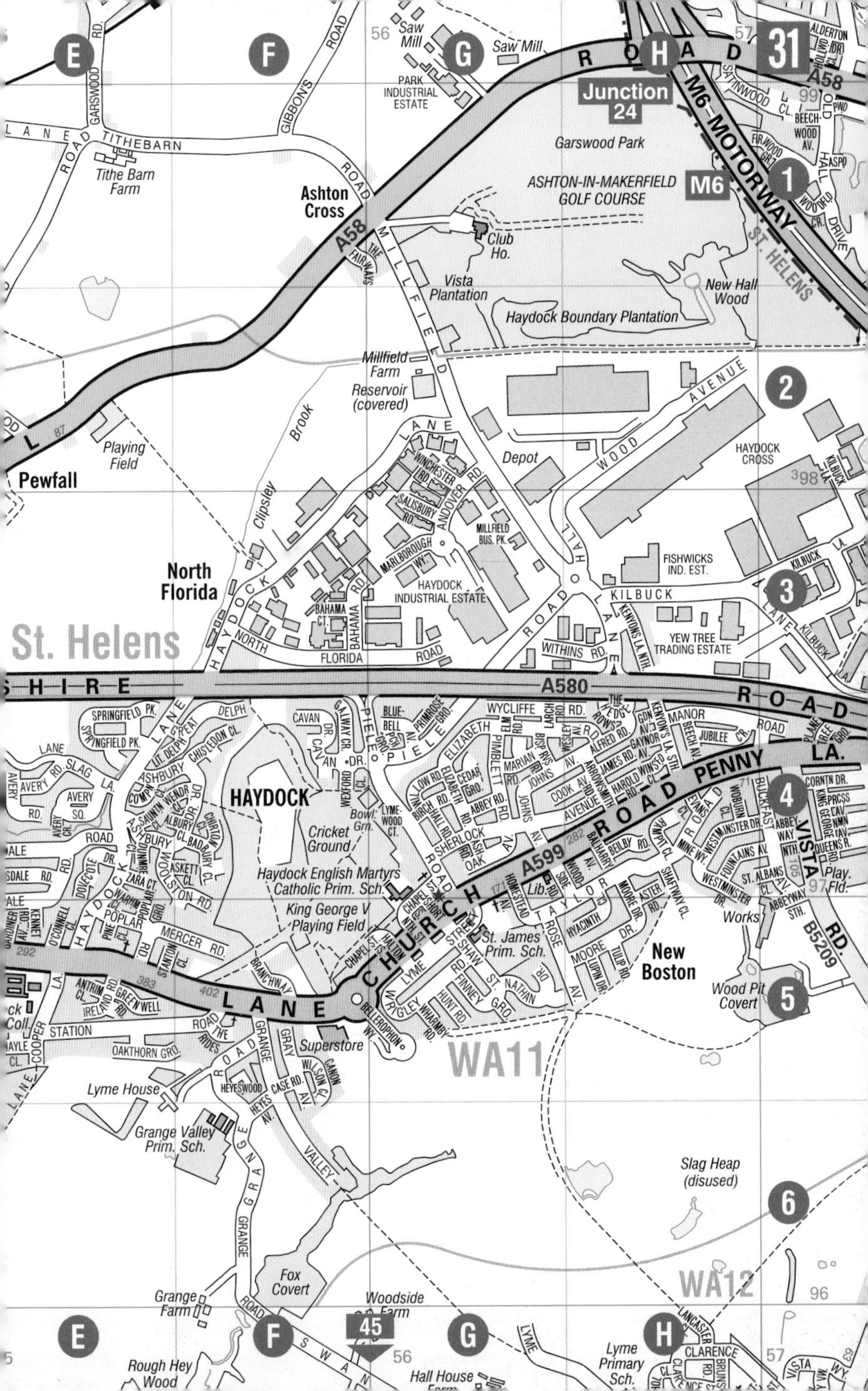

E
F
G
H
Saw Mill
Saw Mill
PARK INDUSTRIAL ESTATE
ROAD
Junction 24
M6 MOTORWAY
M6
A58
GARSWOOD RD.
GIBBON'S ROAD
TITHEBARN
LANE
ROAD
Tithe Barn Farm
Ashton Cross
Garswood Park
ASHTON-IN-MAKERFIELD GOLF COURSE
Club Ho.
Vista Plantation
Haydock Boundary Plantation
New Hall Wood
ST. HELENS
MILLFIELD
THE FAIRWAYS
SATINWOOD CL.
BEECH-WOOD AV.
FIRWOOD GR.
WOODFOLD CR.
DRIVE
HALL
OLD
ALDERTON
Millfield Farm
Reservoir (covered)
Brook
Playing Field
Pewfall
Clipsley
North Florida
St. Helens
LANE
WINCHESTER RD.
SALISBURY RD.
ANDOVER RD.
MARLBOROUGH WY.
MILLFIELD BUS. PK.
HAYDOCK INDUSTRIAL ESTATE
BAHAMA CT.
BAHAMA RD.
NORTH FLORIDA ROAD
HAYDOCK LANE
Depot
WOOD AVENUE
HAYDOCK CROSS
KILBUCK LA.
FISHWICKS IND. EST.
KILBUCK
HALL LANE
ROAD
KENYONS LA. NTH.
WITHINS RD.
YEW TREE TRADING ESTATE
KILBUCK LANE
SHIRE
A580
ROAD
SPRINGFIELD PK.
DELPH
CAVAN DR.
GALWAY CR.
BLUE-BELL AV.
PRIMROSE GRO.
PIELE RD.
WYCLIFFE RD.
MANOR
JUBILEE CR.
ROAD
PENNY LA.
SLAG LA.
AVERY RD.
AVERY SQ.
ASHBURY
HAYDOCK
Cricket Ground
Bowl. Grn.
WEXFORD
ELIZABETH
PIMBLETT
MARIAN RD.
JOHNS AV.
COOK AV.
AVENUE
JAMES RD.
HAROLD RD.
ALFRED RD.
ROAD
A599
VISTA
ABBEY WAY
WESTMINSTER DR.
FOUNTAINS AV.
ST. ALBANS CL.
Play. Fld.
Works
B5209
RD.
Haydock English Martyrs Catholic Prim. Sch.
King George V Playing Field
CHURCH
St. James Prim. Sch.
Lib.
TAYLOR
New Boston
Wood Pit Covert
MERCER RD.
POPLAR
STATION
OAKTHORN GRO.
LANE
Superstore
WA11
Lyme House
Grange Valley Prim. Sch.
GRANGE
VALLEY
HEYES AV.
Slag Heap (disused)
Fox Covert
WA12
Grange Farm
Woodside Farm
45
Rough Hey Wood
Hall House
Lyme Primary Sch.
CLARENCE
VISTA WY.

LIVERPOOL BAY
CROSBY CHANNEL
GREAT BURBO BANK
ROCK CHANNEL
WHARF
Fort Perch Rock
Marine Lake
Breakwater
MOCKBEGGAR
KING'S PARADE
A554
MARINE PROMENADE
New Brighton
Warren Golf Course
HARRISON PARK
HARRISON DRIVE
Wallasey Grove Rd.
Club House
Elleray Pk. Sch.
Mount Prim. Sch.
Captain's Pit
Earlston Gardens
ROWSON ST.
VICTORIA ROAD
WELLINGTON RD.
ALEXANDRA RD.
SEA ROAD
WARREN DRIVE
SANDCLIFFE ROAD
ROLLESTON DR.
MOUNT PLEASANT ROAD
GORSEHILL ROAD
ST. GEORGE'S MT.
ST. GEORGE'S RD.
SEABANK RD.
RAKE LA.

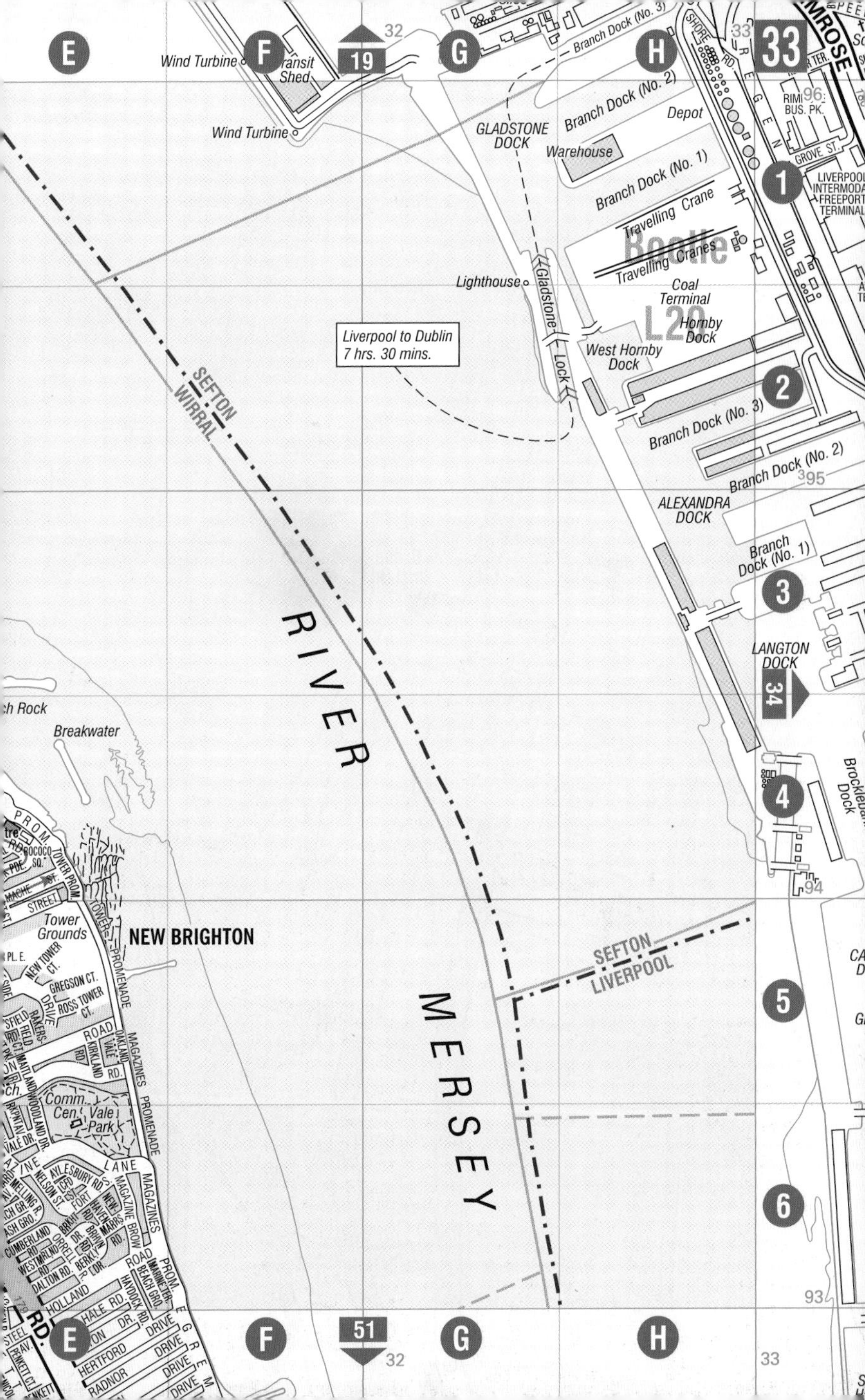

Wind Turbine

Transit Shed

Wind Turbine

GLADSTONE DOCK

Branch Dock (No. 3)

Branch Dock (No. 2)

Depot

Warehouse

RIMI BUS. PK.

96

GROVE ST

Branch Dock (No. 1)

Travelling Crane

LIVERPOOL INTERMODAL FREEPORT TERMINAL

1

Bootle

Travelling Cranes

L20

Lighthouse

Gladstone Lock

Liverpool to Dublin 7 hrs. 30 mins.

Coal Terminal

Hornby Dock

West Hornby Dock

2

Branch Dock (No. 3)

Branch Dock (No. 2)

395

ALEXANDRA DOCK

Branch Dock (No. 1)

SEFTON
WIRRAL

3

LANGTON DOCK

34

Brocklebank Dock

4

94

RIVER

Rock

Breakwater

SEFTON
LIVERPOOL

Tower Grounds

NEW BRIGHTON

CA D

Gr

5

PROMENADE

MAGAZINES PROMENADE

Comm. Cen. Vale Park

MAGAZINES

LANE

MAGAZINES BROW

M E R S E Y

6

93

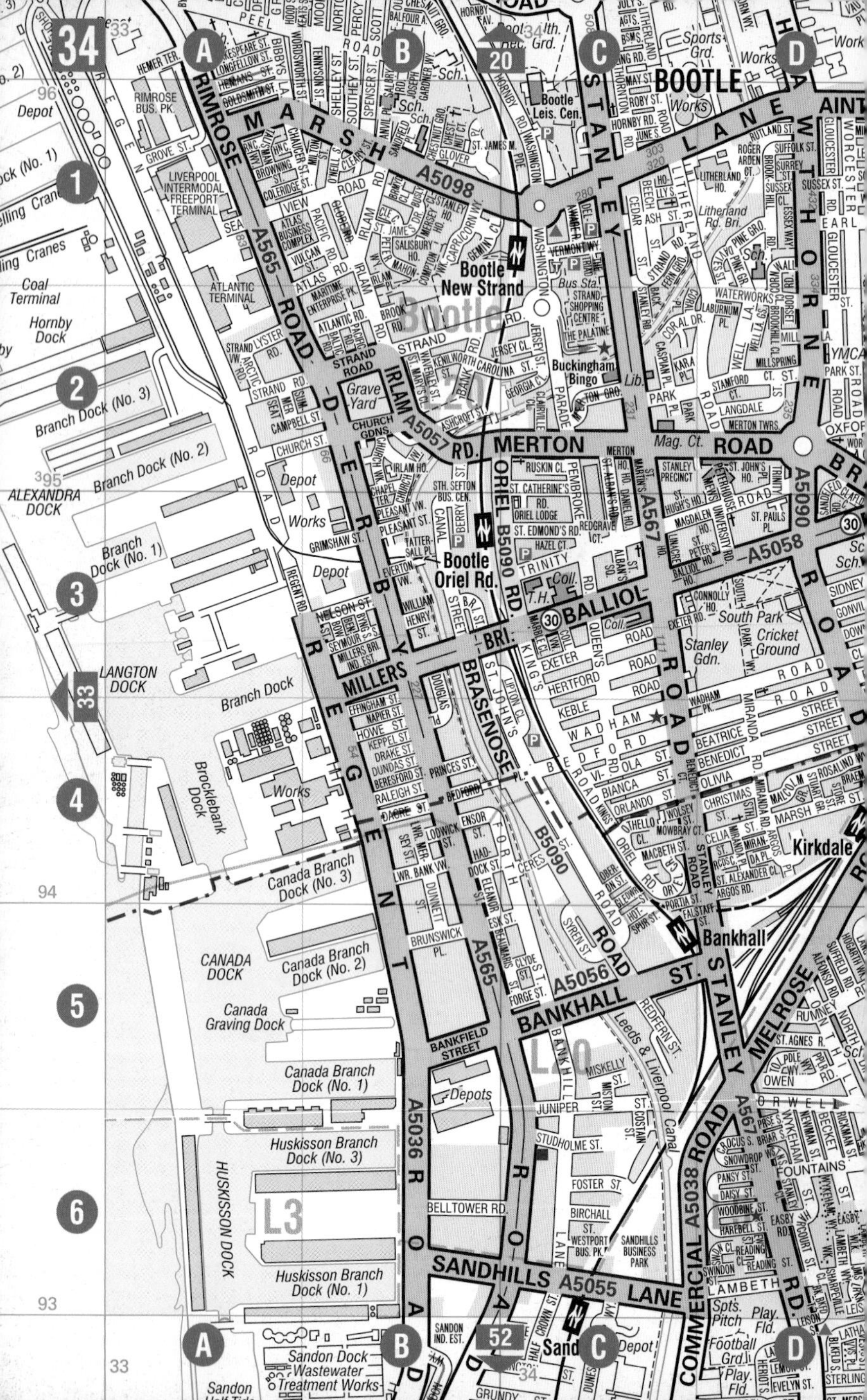

34
A
B
C
D
1
2
3
4
5
6
20
52
33
BOOTLE
Bootle New Strand
Bootle Oriel Rd.
Bankhall
Kirkdale
Sandhills
MARSH LANE
A5098
STANLEY ROAD
A567
RIMROSE ROAD
A565
DERBY ROAD
REGENT ROAD
A5036
MERTON ROAD
A5057
ORIEL RD.
B5090
BALLIOL ROAD
A5058
HAWTHORNE ROAD
A5090
MILLERS BRI.
BRASENOSE RD.
BANKHALL ST.
A5056
SANDHILLS LANE
A5055
COMMERCIAL ROAD
A5038
MELROSE RD.
IRLAM RD.
STRAND ROAD
Leeds & Liverpool Canal
L20
L3
Hornby Dock
Coal Terminal
Branch Dock (No. 3)
Branch Dock (No. 2)
Branch Dock (No. 1)
ALEXANDRA DOCK
LANGTON DOCK
Branch Dock
Brocklebank Dock
Canada Branch Dock (No. 3)
CANADA DOCK
Canada Branch Dock (No. 2)
Canada Graving Dock
Canada Branch Dock (No. 1)
Huskisson Branch Dock (No. 3)
HUSKISSON DOCK
Huskisson Branch Dock (No. 1)
Sandon Dock Wastewater Treatment Works
LIVERPOOL INTERMODAL FREEPORT TERMINAL
ATLANTIC TERMINAL
RIMROSE BUS. PK.
ATLAS BUSINESS COMPLEX
MARITIME ENTERPRISE PK.
Bootle Leis. Cen.
Buckingham Bingo
Bus Sta.
STRAND SHOPPING CENTRE
Grave Yard
CHURCH GDNS.
STH. SEFTON BUS. CEN.
South Park
Cricket Ground
Stanley Gdn.
SANDON IND. EST.
SANDHILLS BUSINESS PARK
WESTPORT BUS. PK.
BANKFIELD STREET
Depots
Works
Depot
Sports Grd.
Football Grd.
Play. Fld.
94
93
95
96
33
34

E
F
G
H
21
53
36
1
2
3
4
5
6
HMP LIVERPOOL
Rice Lane Recreation Ground
Hartley's Village
Sports Ground
Walton
Rice La.
HORNBY RD.
A5098
A5038
A5058
A580
A59
SEFTON NORTH
LIVERPOOL
Rice Lane City Farm
Walton Park Cemy.
Playing Field
WALTON HOSP.
CAVENDISH RETAIL PK.
Boating Lake
Recreation Ground
WALTON HALL PARK
Hillside High Sch.
Lifestyles Alsop
Lifestyles Walton
Playing Fields
All Weather Spts. Grd.
WALTON
QUEENS DRIVE
WALTON HALL AV.
HALE RD.
COUNTY ROAD
SOUTHPORT RD.
WALTON LANE
ANFIELD CEMETERY
Everton FC (Goodison Pk.)
Registrar's Office
Anfield Crematorium
North Liverpool Academy
STANLEY PARK
Abbey Lawns Nursing Home
Anfield
Liverpool FC Stadium (Proposed)
Liverpool FC (Anfield)
WALTON BRECK RD.
EVERTON VALLEY
ST. DOMINGO RD.
College
Swim. Pool
Bingo
Factories
Train. Cen.
Super-store
STANLEY PARK AVENUE
PRIORY RD.
ARKLES LANE
UTTING AVENUE

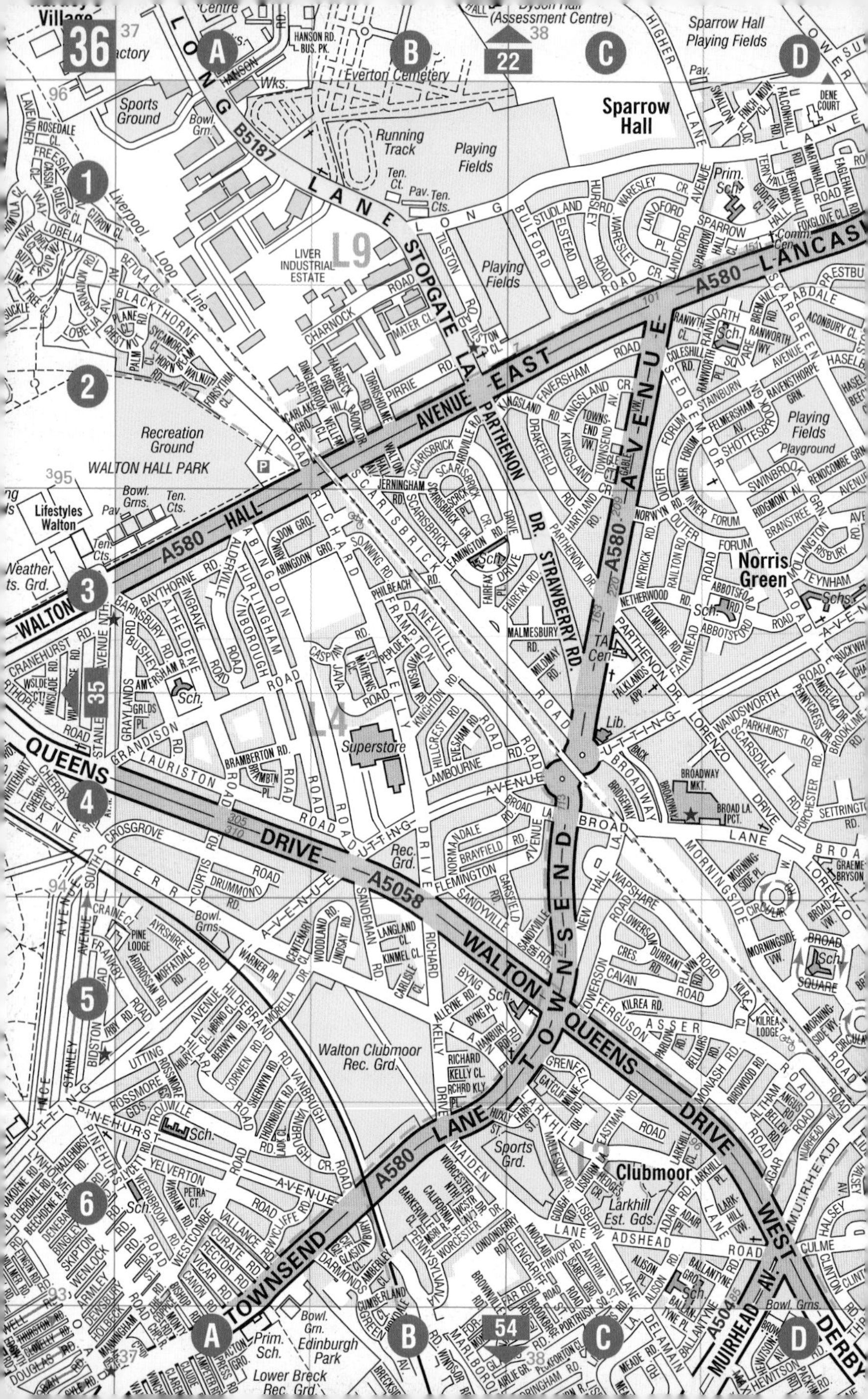
36
A
B
C
D
1
2
3
4
5
6
22
54
35
37
38
96
95
94
93
Dyson Hall
(Assessment Centre)
Sparrow Hall
Playing Fields
Sparrow Hall
Everton Cemetery
Sports Ground
Running Track
Playing Fields
LONG LANE
B5187
STOPGATE LA.
LIVER INDUSTRIAL ESTATE
L9
Liverpool Loop Line
Recreation Ground
WALTON HALL PARK
Lifestyles Walton
A580 HALL AVENUE EAST
A580 LANCASHIRE
PARTHENON DR.
STRAWBERRY RD.
A580 AVENUE
Norris Green
Playing Fields
Playground
QUEENS DRIVE
A5058
WALTON
L4
Superstore
Rec. Grd.
BROADWAY MKT.
BROAD LA. PCT.
BROAD LANE
TOWNSEND AVENUE
Walton Clubmoor Rec. Grd.
A580 LANE
TOWNSEND
Sports Grd.
Clubmoor
Larkhill Est. Gds.
QUEENS DRIVE
WEST DERBY
MUIRHEAD AV.
A5049
Bowl. Grn.
Edinburgh Park
Lower Breck Rec. Grd.
Prim. Sch.

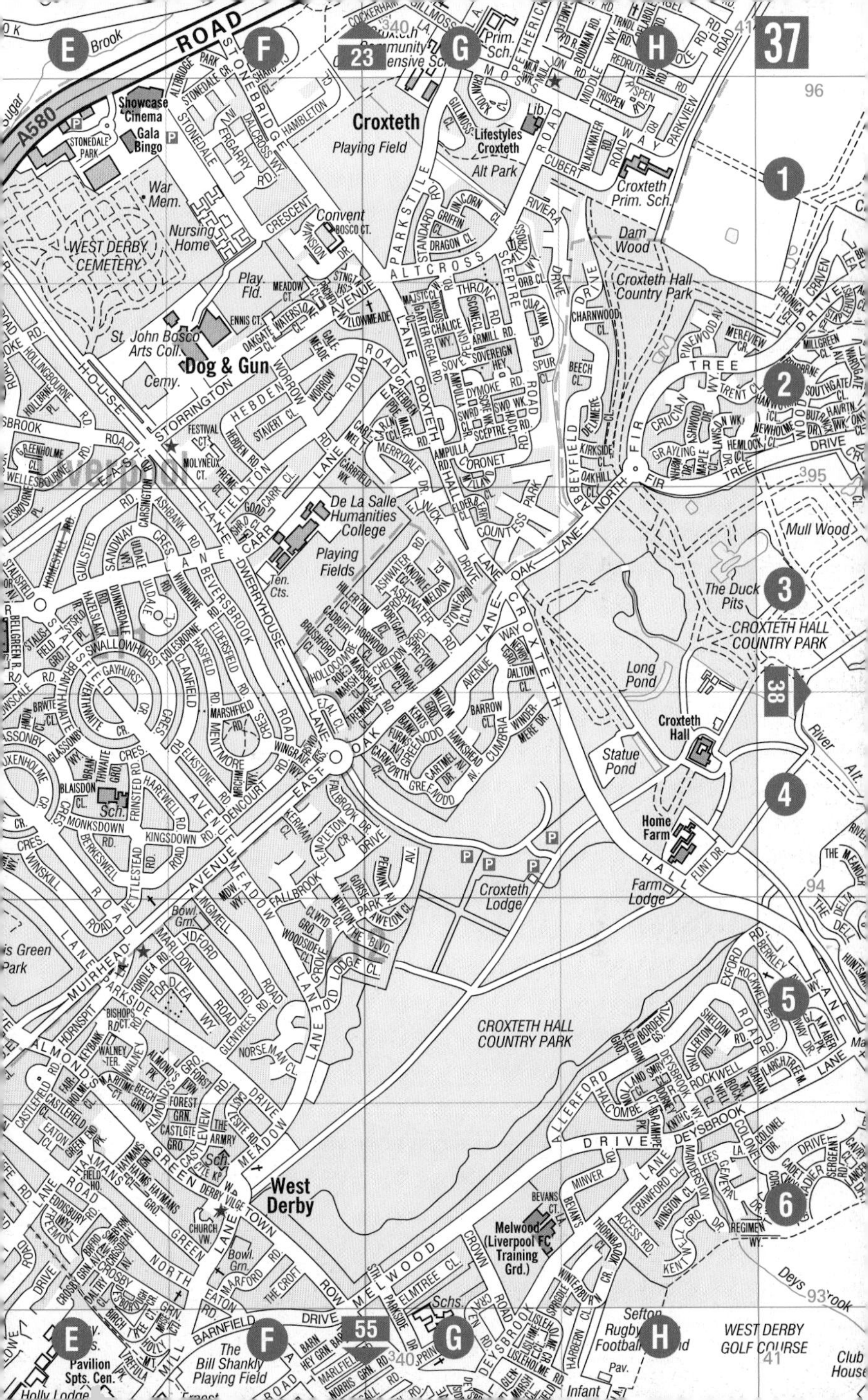

23
55
38
E
F
G
H
1
2
3
4
5
6
96
95
94
93
340
41
A580
ROAD
Brook
Showcase Cinema
Gala Bingo
STONEDALE PARK
War Mem.
WEST DERBY CEMETERY
Nursing Home
Play. Fld.
St. John Bosco Arts Coll.
Dog & Gun
Cemy.
Liverpool
Croxteth
Playing Field
Croxteth Community Comprehensive Sch.
Prim. Sch.
Lib.
Lifestyles Croxteth
Alt Park
Croxteth Prim. Sch.
Convent
Dam Wood
Croxteth Hall Country Park
Mull Wood
The Duck Pits
CROXTETH HALL COUNTRY PARK
Long Pond
Croxteth Hall
Statue Pond
Home Farm
Farm Lodge
Croxteth Lodge
River Alt
De La Salle Humanities College
Playing Fields
Ten. Cts.
Sch.
Bowl. Grn.
is Green Park
West Derby
Melwood (Liverpool FC Training Grd.)
Schs.
Sefton Rugby Football Ground
Pav.
Infant
WEST DERBY GOLF COURSE
Club House
Deys Brook
The Bill Shankly Playing Field
Pavilion Spts. Cen.
Holly Lodge
STONEBRIDGE LANE
STORRINGTON AVENUE
EAST LANE
CROXTETH LANE
ALTCROSS ROAD
MOSS WAY
PARKVIEW
PARKSTILE LANE
CARR LANE
EAST LANCASHIRE
OAK LANE
DWERRYHOUSE LANE
MUIRHEAD AVENUE
MUIRHEAD AVENUE EAST
CROXTETH HALL LANE
FIR TREE DRIVE NORTH
FIR TREE DRIVE SOUTH
DEYSBROOK LANE
DRIVE
ALMOND'S GREEN
WEST DERBY VILLAGE
TOWN ROW
MELWOOD DRIVE
BARNFIELD DRIVE
CROWN ROAD
CROXTETH HALL COUNTRY PARK

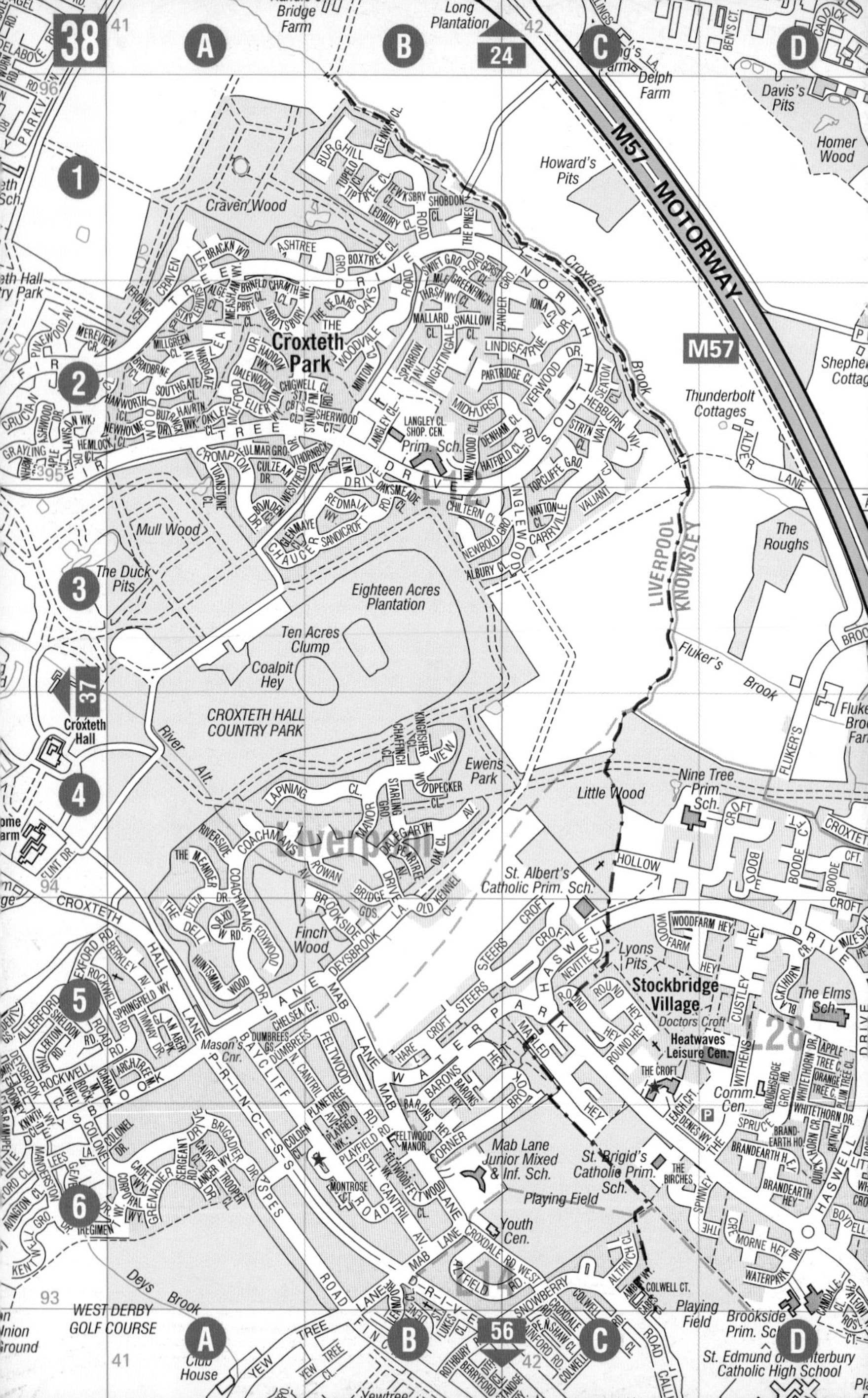
Croxteth Park
CROXTETH HALL COUNTRY PARK
Craven Wood
Mull Wood
The Duck Pits
Eighteen Acres Plantation
Ten Acres Clump
Coalpit Hey
Croxteth Hall
River Alt
Ewens Park
Little Wood
Finch Wood
Stockbridge Village
Lyons Pits
Howard's Pits
Thunderbolt Cottages
The Roughs
Fluker's Brook
Croxteth Brook
M57 MOTORWAY
Delph Farm
Davis's Pits
Homer Wood
Long Plantation
Bridge Farm
LIVERPOOL
KNOWSLEY
Nine Tree Prim. Sch.
St. Albert's Catholic Prim. Sch.
Heatwaves Leisure Cen.
Comm. Cen.
The Elms Sch.
Mab Lane Junior Mixed & Inf. Sch.
St. Brigid's Catholic Prim. Sch.
Playing Field
Youth Cen.
Brookside Prim. Sch.
WEST DERBY GOLF COURSE
Club House
Mason's Cnr.
Deys Brook
24
37
56

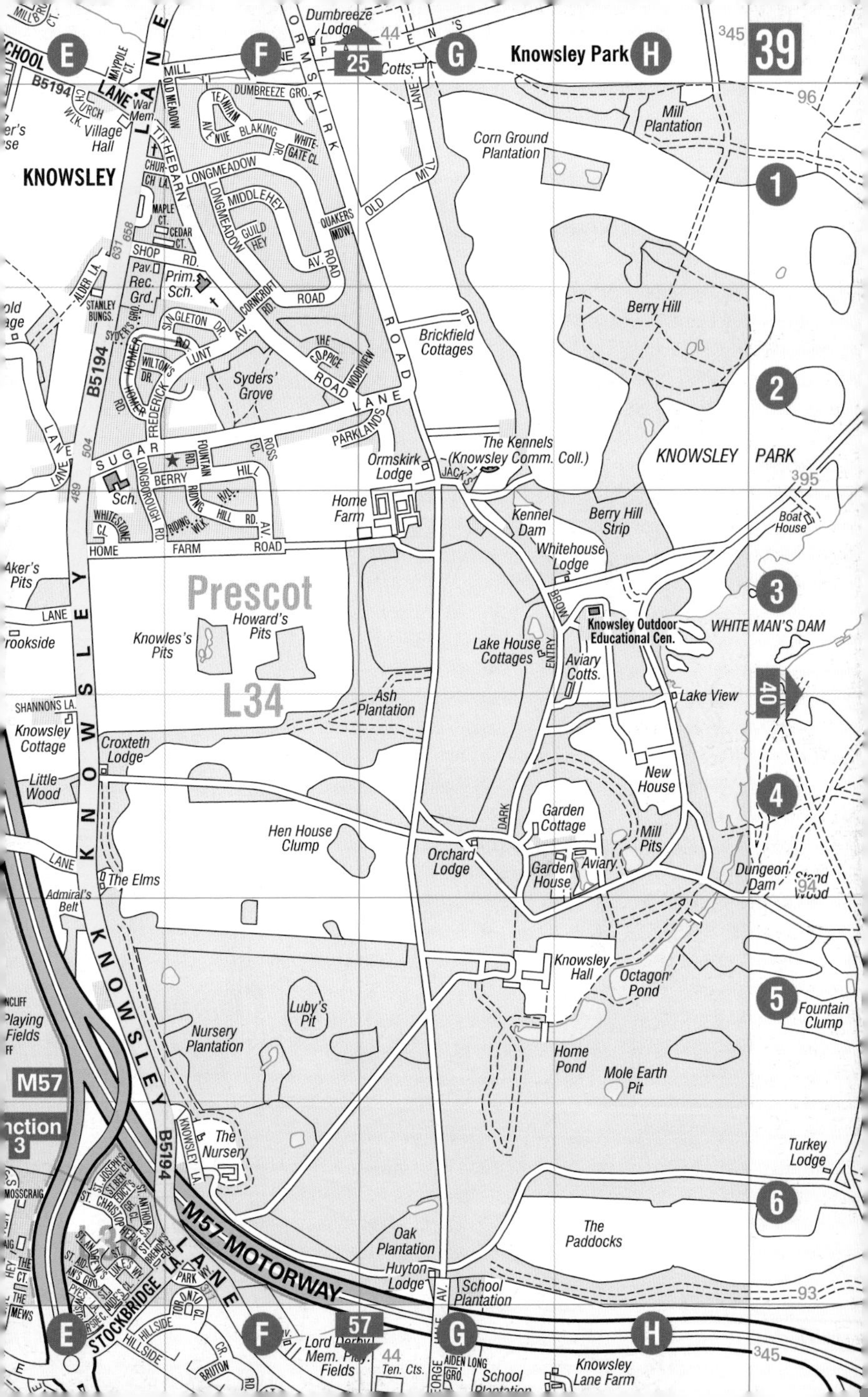

39
Knowsley Park
25
40
57
KNOWSLEY
Prescot
L34
KNOWSLEY PARK
Dumbreeze Lodge
Ormskirk Road
Mill Plantation
Corn Ground Plantation
Berry Hill
Brickfield Cottages
Syders' Grove
The Kennels (Knowsley Comm. Coll.)
Ormskirk Lodge
Home Farm
Kennel Dam
Berry Hill Strip
Boat House
Whitehouse Lodge
Knowsley Outdoor Educational Cen.
WHITE MAN'S DAM
Lake House Cottages
Aviary Cotts.
Lake View
Knowles's Pits
Howard's Pits
Ash Plantation
Croxteth Lodge
Knowsley Cottage
Little Wood
New House
Garden Cottage
Hen House Clump
Orchard Lodge
Garden House
Aviary
Mill Pits
Dungeon Dam
Stand Wood
The Elms
Admiral's Belt
Knowsley Hall
Octagon Pond
Fountain Clump
Luby's Pit
Nursery Plantation
Home Pond
Mole Earth Pit
The Nursery
Turkey Lodge
The Paddocks
Oak Plantation
Huyton Lodge
School Plantation
M57 MOTORWAY
Lord Derby Mem. Play. Fields
Knowsley Lane Farm
Knowsley Lane
Sugar Lane
Home Farm Road
Berry Hill Av.
B5194
M57
Junction 3

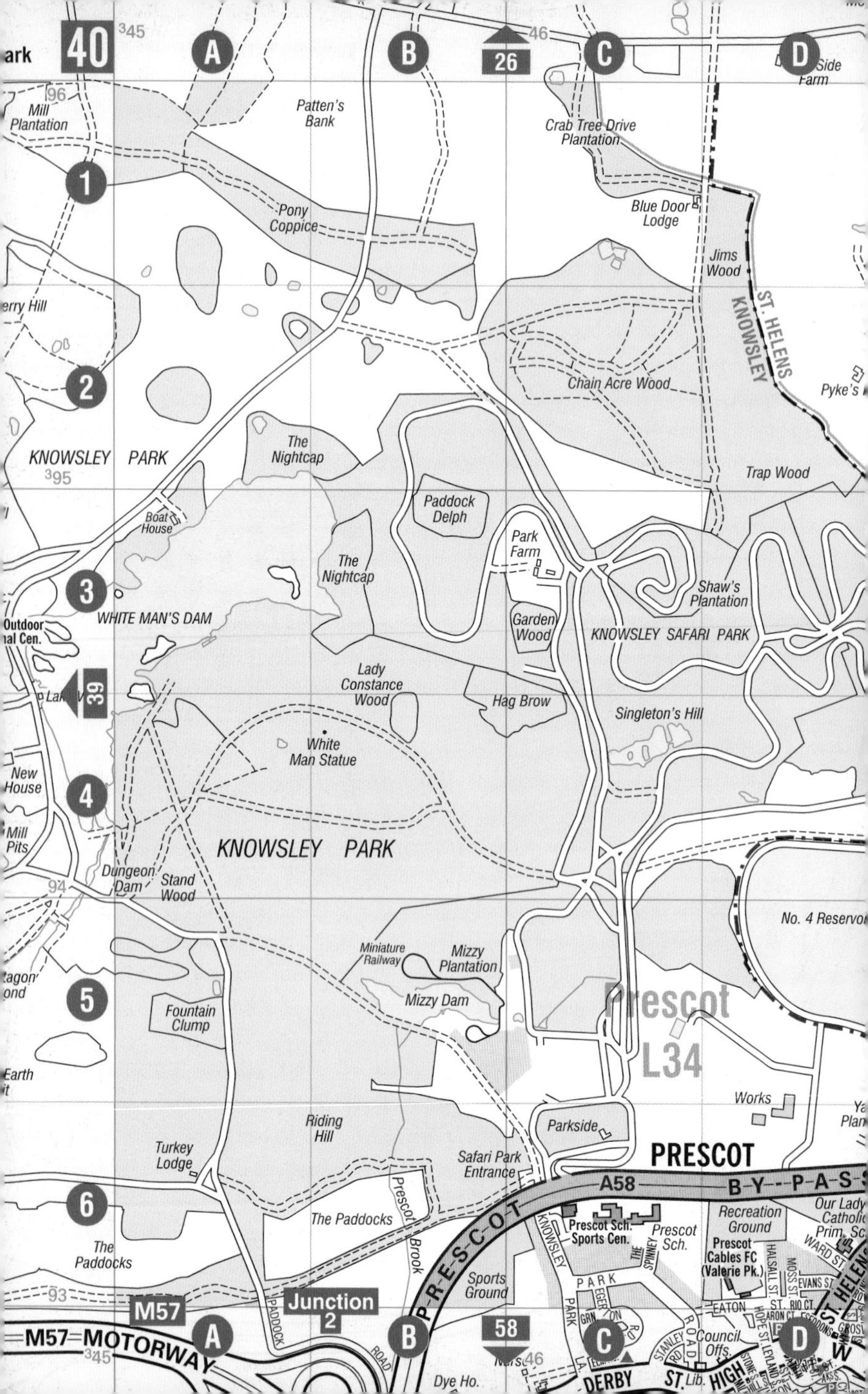
40
A
B
C
D
26
Mill Plantation
Patten's Bank
Crab Tree Drive Plantation
Side Farm
Pony Coppice
Blue Door Lodge
Jims Wood
ST. HELENS
KNOWSLEY
Chain Acre Wood
Pyke's
KNOWSLEY PARK
The Nightcap
Paddock Delph
Trap Wood
Boat House
Park Farm
The Nightcap
Shaw's Plantation
WHITE MAN'S DAM
Outdoor
Garden Wood
KNOWSLEY SAFARI PARK
39
Lady Constance Wood
Hag Brow
Singleton's Hill
White Man Statue
New House
Mill Pits
KNOWSLEY PARK
Dungeon Dam
Stand Wood
No. 4 Reservoir
Miniature Railway
Mizzy Plantation
Mizzy Dam
Fountain Clump
Prescot
L34
Earth
Works
Riding Hill
Parkside
Turkey Lodge
Safari Park Entrance
PRESCOT
A58
BY-PASS
PRESCOT
The Paddocks
Prescot Brook
Recreation Ground
Our Lady Catholic Prim. Sch.
Prescot Sch. Sports Cen.
Prescot Sch.
Prescot Cables FC (Valerie Pk.)
The Paddocks
Sports Ground
M57
Junction 2
M57 MOTORWAY
58
Council Offs.
DERBY
ST.
HIGH
Dye Ho.

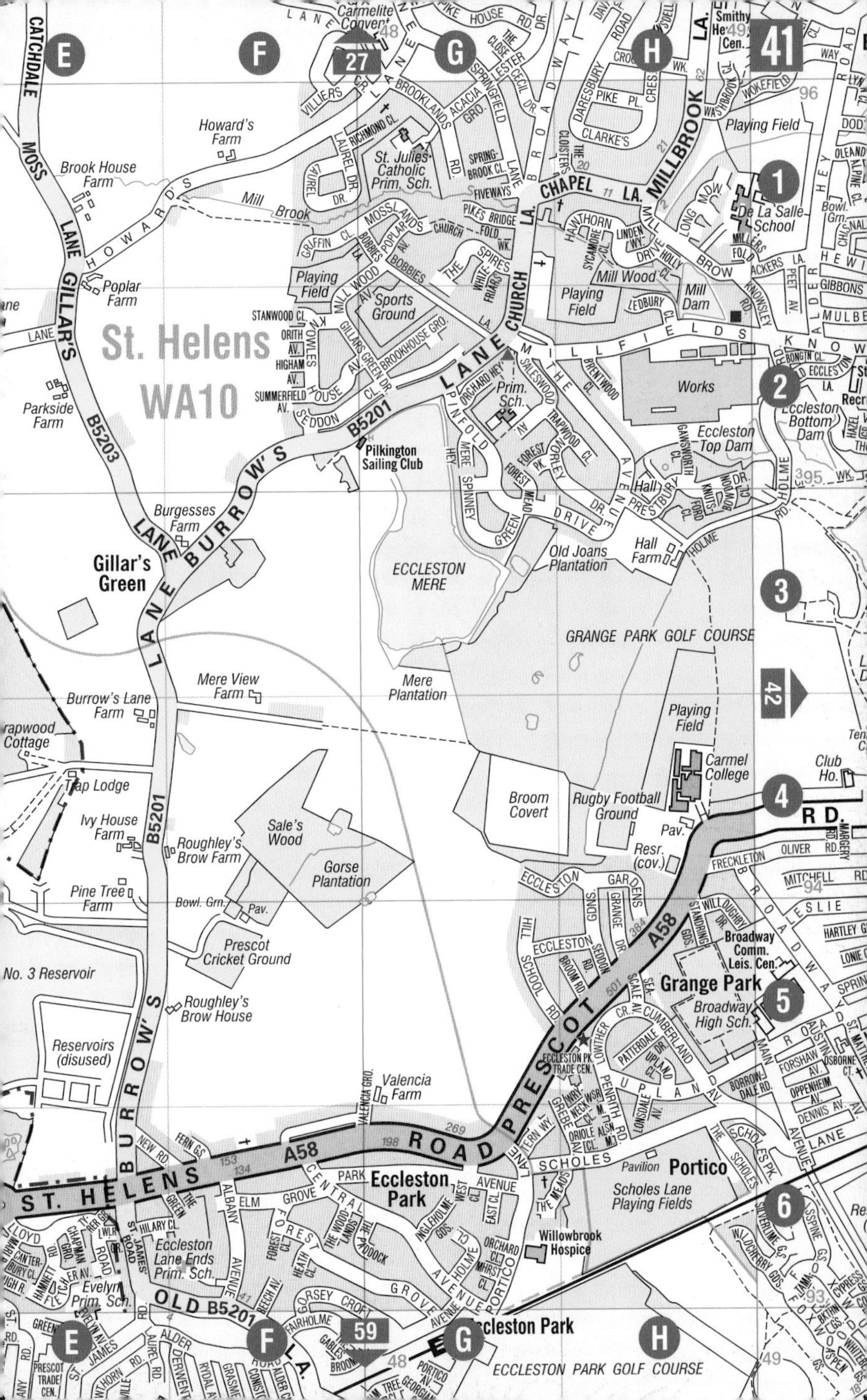

St. Helens
WA10
Gillar's Green
Eccleston Mere
Grange Park Golf Course
Grange Park
Eccleston Park
Portico
Eccleston Park Golf Course
Burrow's Lane
Gillar's Lane
Moss Lane
Catchdale
Church Lane
Chapel La.
Millbrook La.
Millfields
Prescot Road
St. Helens Road
Old B5201
B5201
B5203
A58
Howard's Farm
Brook House Farm
Poplar Farm
Parkside Farm
Burgesses Farm
Mere View Farm
Burrow's Lane Farm
Trap Lodge
Ivy House Farm
Roughley's Brow Farm
Pine Tree Farm
Roughley's Brow House
Valencia Farm
Hall Farm
St. Julies' Catholic Prim. Sch.
De La Salle School
Pilkington Sailing Club
Sports Ground
Playing Field
Works
Eccleston Bottom Dam
Eccleston Top Dam
Mill Dam
Mill Wood
Old Joans Plantation
Mere Plantation
Sale's Wood
Gorse Plantation
Prescot Cricket Ground
Broom Covert
Rugby Football Ground
Carmel College
Club Ho.
Broadway Comm. Leis. Cen.
Broadway High Sch.
No. 3 Reservoir
Reservoirs (disused)
Scholes Lane Playing Fields
Willowbrook Hospice
Eccleston Lane Ends Prim. Sch.
Evelyn Prim. Sch.
Eccleston Pk. Trade Cen.
Prescot Trade Cen.
Carmelite Convent
Smithy Heath Cen.

27
42
59

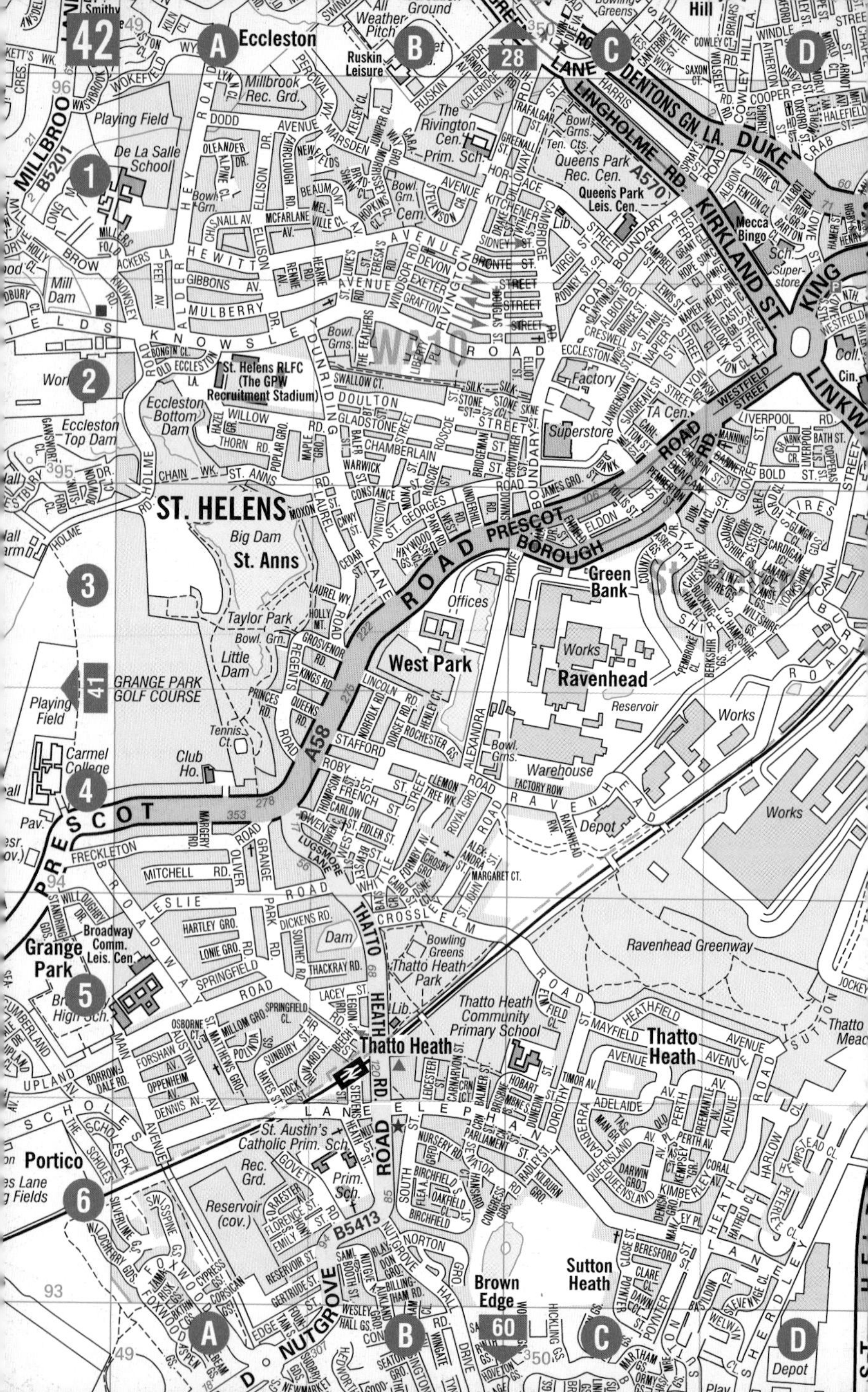

Eccleston
Ruskin Leisure
Millbrook Rec. Grd.
Playing Field
De La Salle School
The Rivington Cen.
Prim. Sch.
Queens Park Rec. Cen.
Queens Park Leis. Cen.
Mecca Bingo
Mill Dam
WA10
St. Helens RLFC (The GPW Recruitment Stadium)
Eccleston Bottom Dam
Eccleston Top Dam
Factory
Superstore
TA Cen.
ST. HELENS
Big Dam
St. Anns
Green Bank
Offices
Taylor Park
Little Dam
West Park
Works
Ravenhead
Reservoir
GRANGE PARK GOLF COURSE
Playing Field
Carmel College
Club Ho.
Warehouse
Depot
Broadway Comm. Leis. Cen.
Grange Park
Dam
Thatto Heath Park
Ravenhead Greenway
Thatto Heath Community Primary School
Thatto Heath
St. Austin's Catholic Prim. Sch.
Rec. Grd.
Reservoir (cov.)
Portico
Brown Edge
Sutton Heath
PRESCOT ROAD
A58
B5413
B5201
A570
DUKE ST.
KIRKLAND ST.
LINKWAY
NUTGROVE ROAD

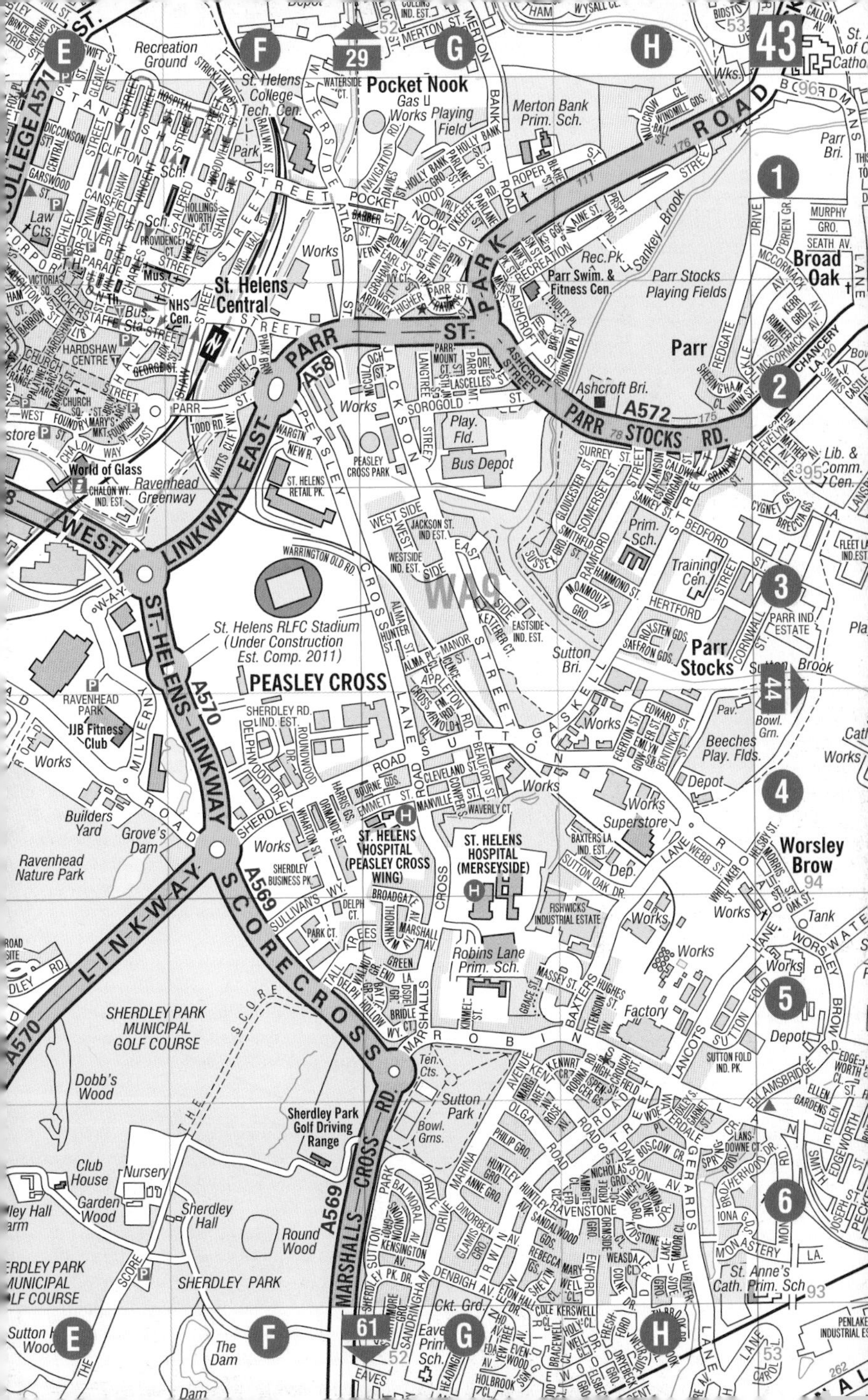

43
29
44
61
E
F
G
H
1
2
3
4
5
6
Pocket Nook
St. Helens Central
Parr
Broad Oak
Parr Stocks
Peasley Cross
Worsley Brow
WA9
Recreation Ground
St. Helens College Tech. Cen.
Merton Bank Prim. Sch.
Parr Swim. & Fitness Cen.
Parr Stocks Playing Fields
Ashcroft Bri.
Bus Depot
World of Glass
Ravenhead Greenway
St. Helens RLFC Stadium (Under Construction Est. Comp. 2011)
JJB Fitness Club
Ravenhead Nature Park
St. Helens Hospital (Peasley Cross Wing)
St. Helens Hospital (Merseyside)
Fishwicks Industrial Estate
Robins Lane Prim. Sch.
Sherdley Park Municipal Golf Course
Sherdley Park Golf Driving Range
Sutton Park
Sherdley Park
Sherdley Hall
Dobb's Wood
Round Wood
Club House
Nursery
Garden Wood
St. Anne's Cath. Prim. Sch
Penlake Industrial Est.
Sutton Fold Ind. Pk.
Parr Ind. Estate
Lib. & Comm. Cen.
A58
A570
A569
A571
A572
Parr Stocks Rd.
St. Helens Linkway
Linkway East
Linkway
Scorecross
Marshalls Cross Rd.
Park Road
Parr St.
Sutton Road
Robins Lane
Peasley Cross Lane
Jackson Street
Sherdley Road

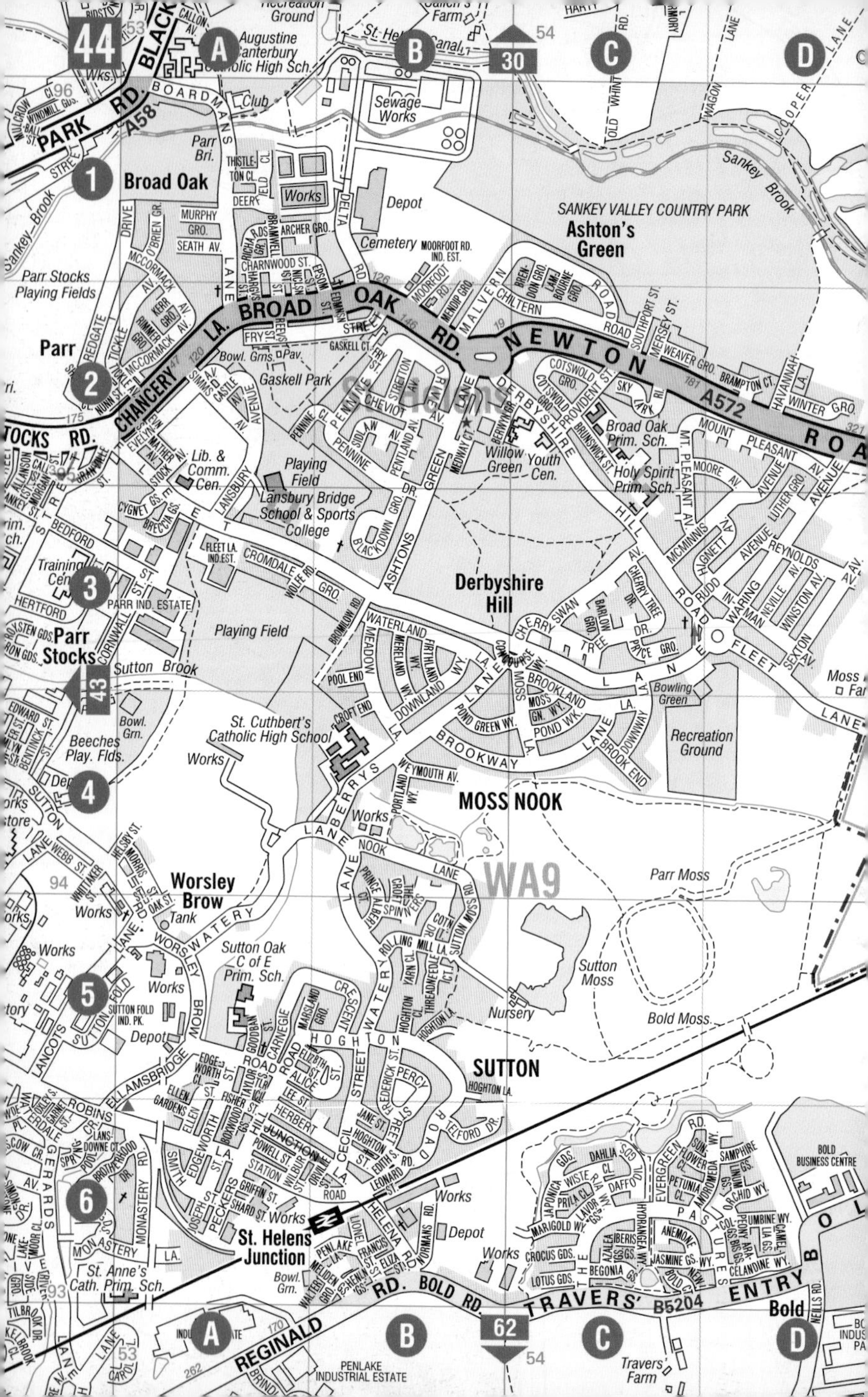
Broad Oak
Parr
Parr Stocks
Ashton's Green
SANKEY VALLEY COUNTRY PARK
Derbyshire Hill
MOSS NOOK
Worsley Brow
SUTTON
St. Helens Junction
Bold
WA9
BROAD OAK RD.
NEWTON ROAD
A572
A58
PARK RD.
CHANCERY LA.
FLEET LANE
B5204
TRAVERS' ENTRY
REGINALD RD.
BOLD RD.
Sewage Works
Depot
Cemetery
Gaskell Park
Playing Field
Lansbury Bridge School & Sports College
St. Cuthbert's Catholic High School
Sutton Oak C of E Prim. Sch.
St. Anne's Cath. Prim. Sch.
Broad Oak Prim. Sch.
Holy Spirit Prim. Sch.
Willow Green
Youth Cen.
Lib. & Comm. Cen.
Augustine Canterbury Catholic High Sch.
Recreation Ground
Parr Moss
Sutton Moss
Bold Moss
Sankey Brook
Sutton Brook
Parr Stocks Playing Fields
Beeches Play. Flds.
PENLAKE INDUSTRIAL ESTATE
BOLD BUSINESS CENTRE
Travers' Farm
PARR IND. ESTATE
SUTTON FOLD IND. PK.
FLEET LA. IND. EST.
MOORFOOT RD. IND. EST.
30
43
62
54
53

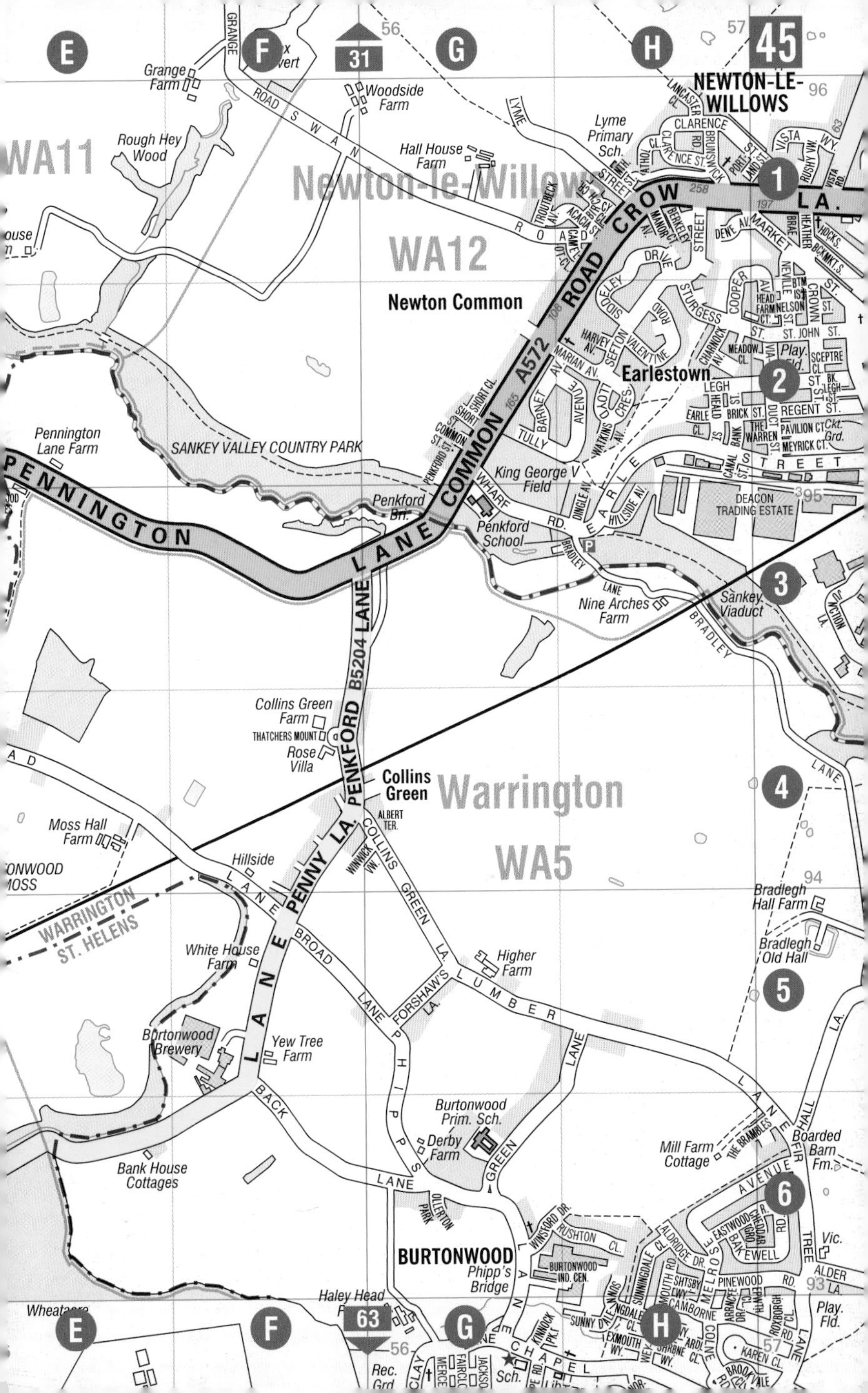

NEWTON-LE-WILLOWS
Newton-le-Willows
WA11
WA12
WA5
Newton Common
Earlestown
Warrington
Collins Green
BURTONWOOD
Grange Farm
Rough Hey Wood
Woodside Farm
Hall House Farm
Lyme Primary Sch.
Pennington Lane Farm
SANKEY VALLEY COUNTRY PARK
Penkford Bri.
King George V Field
Penkford School
DEACON TRADING ESTATE
Nine Arches Farm
Sankey Viaduct
Collins Green Farm
THATCHERS MOUNT
Rose Villa
Moss Hall Farm
Hillside
White House Farm
Burtonwood Brewery
Yew Tree Farm
Higher Farm
Bradlegh Hall Farm
Bradlegh Old Hall
Burtonwood Prim. Sch.
Derby Farm
Bank House Cottages
Mill Farm Cottage
Boarded Barn Fm.
Phipp's Bridge
BURTONWOOD IND. CEN.
Haley Head
Wheatacre
Rec. Grd.
Play. Fld.
Vic.
PENNINGTON LANE
COMMON LANE
CROW LA.
A572
ROAD
B5204
PENKFORD LANE
PENNY LA.
COLLINS GREEN LA.
BROAD LANE
LUMBER LANE
PHIPPS LANE
BACK LANE
GREEN LANE
SWAN ROAD
FIR TREE AVENUE
HALL LA.
BRADLEY LANE
WHARF RD.
EARLE ST.
CANAL ST.
REGENT ST.
MARKET ST.
STURGESS ST.
WARRINGTON
ST. HELENS
31
63

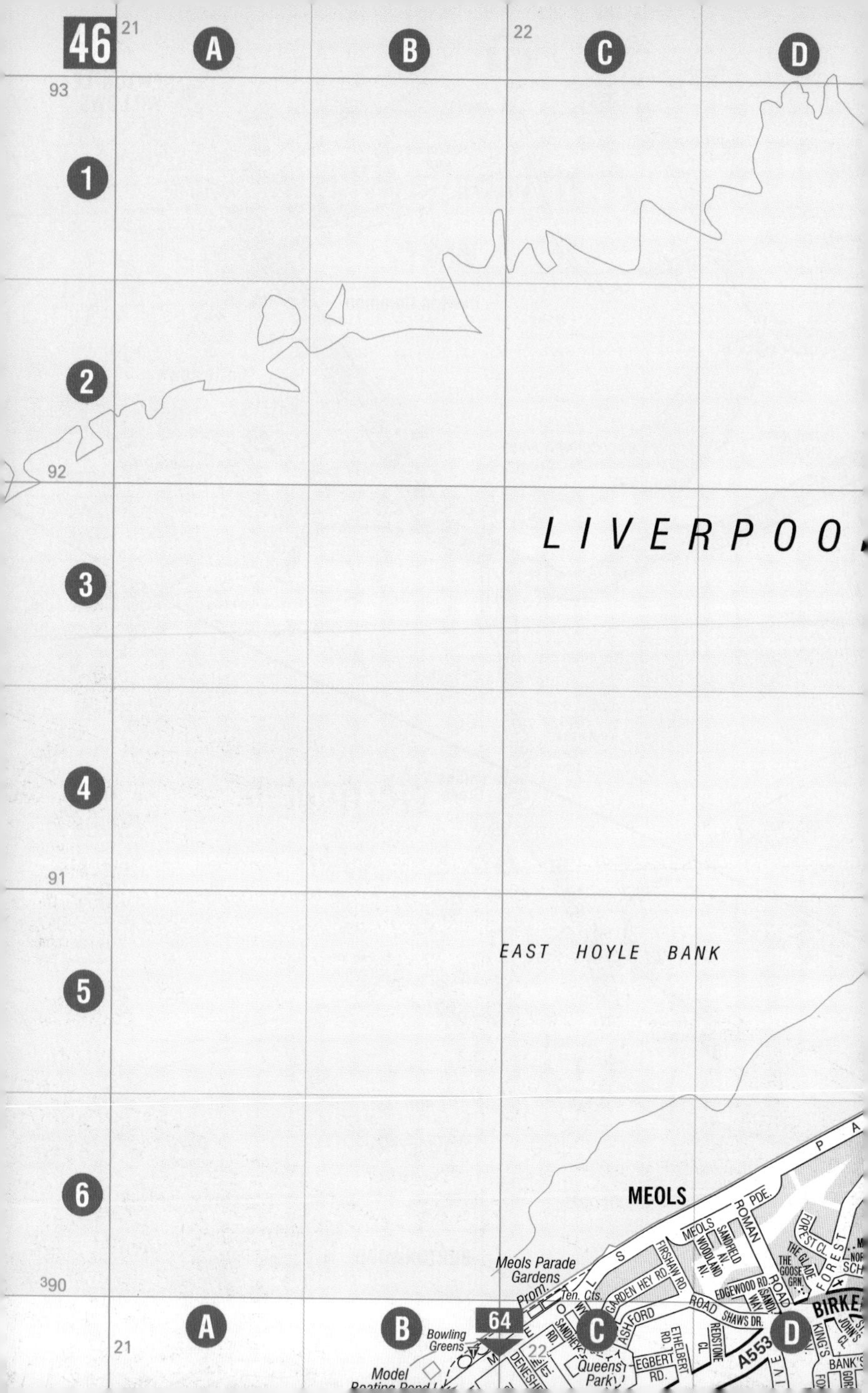

A B 22 C D

93

1

2

92

L I V E R P O O

3

4

91

EAST HOYLE BANK

5

6

390

21

A B *Bowling Greens* **64** C D

MEOLS

Meols Parade Gardens
Prom. Ten. Cts.

Model Boating Pond *Queens Park*

BIRKE

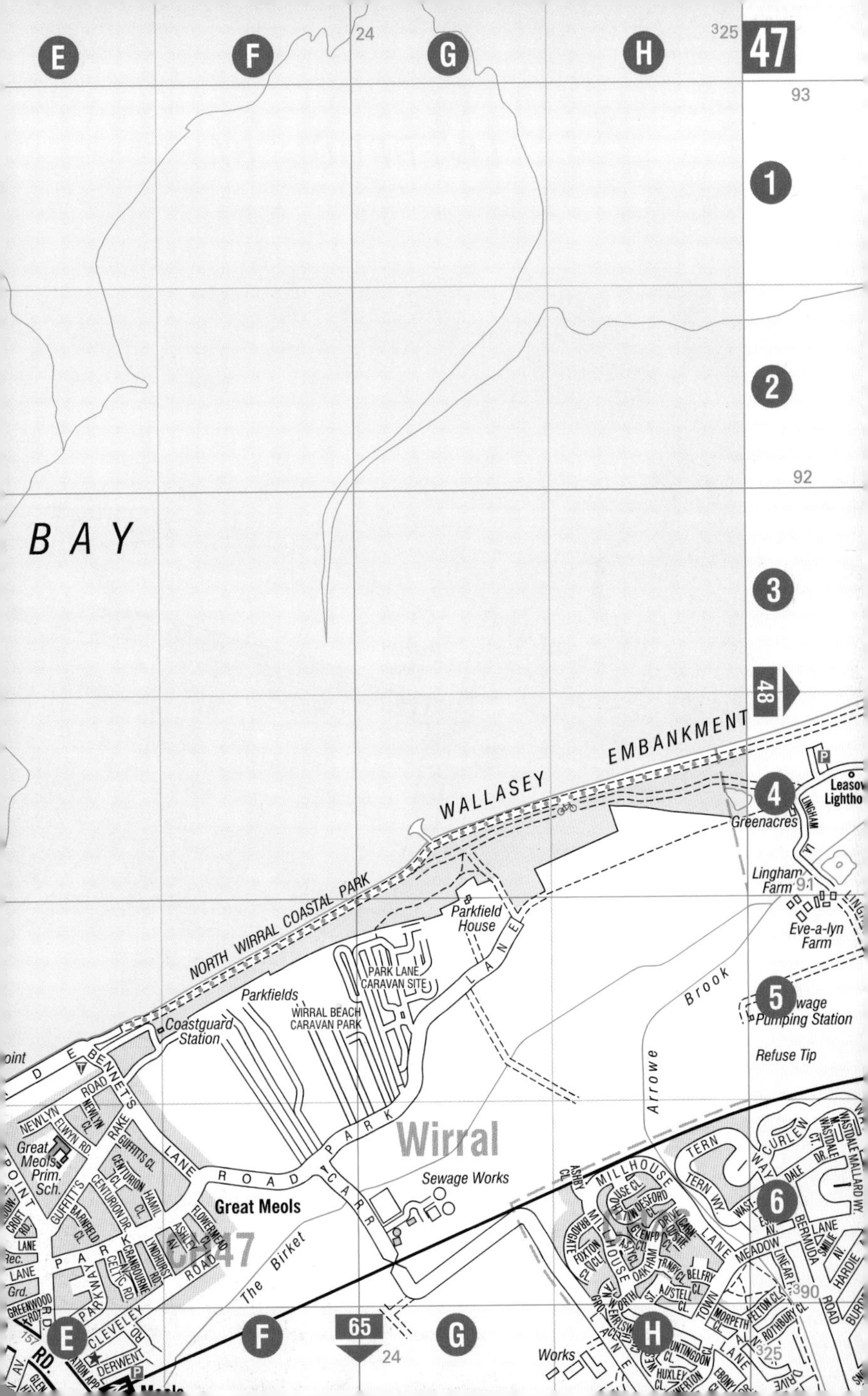

E F G H

325

1

2

92

3

48

B A Y

WALLASEY EMBANKMENT

4

Leaso
Lightho

Greenacres

*Lingham
Farm* 91

NORTH WIRRAL COASTAL PARK

*Eve-a-lyn
Farm*

*Parkfield
House*

PARK LANE
CARAVAN SITE

Parkfields

Brook

Arrowe

5 Sewage
Pumping Station

*Coastguard
Station*

WIRRAL BEACH
CARAVAN PARK

Refuse Tip

point

NEWLYN
RD

Great
Meols
Prim.
Sch.

ELWYN RD

MINN

RAKE

GRIFFITTS CL

CENTURION CL

HAMIL

CENTURION DR

BARNFIELD

FLOREANCE

CELTIC ST

CRANBOURNE

Wirral

CURLEW
WAY

TERN

MILLHOUSE LANE

WASTDALE

WASTDALE MALLARD WY

DALE

BERNADA
AV

6

390

Great Meols

LUNTS

Sewage Works

A 47

ASHBY
CL

SAGE CL

CLESFORD

MILLHOUSE

FOXTON

OAKHAM

TRAFFIC CL

BELFRY

AUSTELL

MEADOW
CL

BELFRY

The Birket

MORPETH

FELTON CL

EBONY
CL

HARDIE
AV

ROTHBURY
CL

GLOVE

DERWENT

CLEVELEY

CELANDINE

HUNTINGDON
CL

325

PARK

GREENWOOD
RD

CHRIST

LANE
Grd.

REC.
Grd.

RD.

Works

Meols

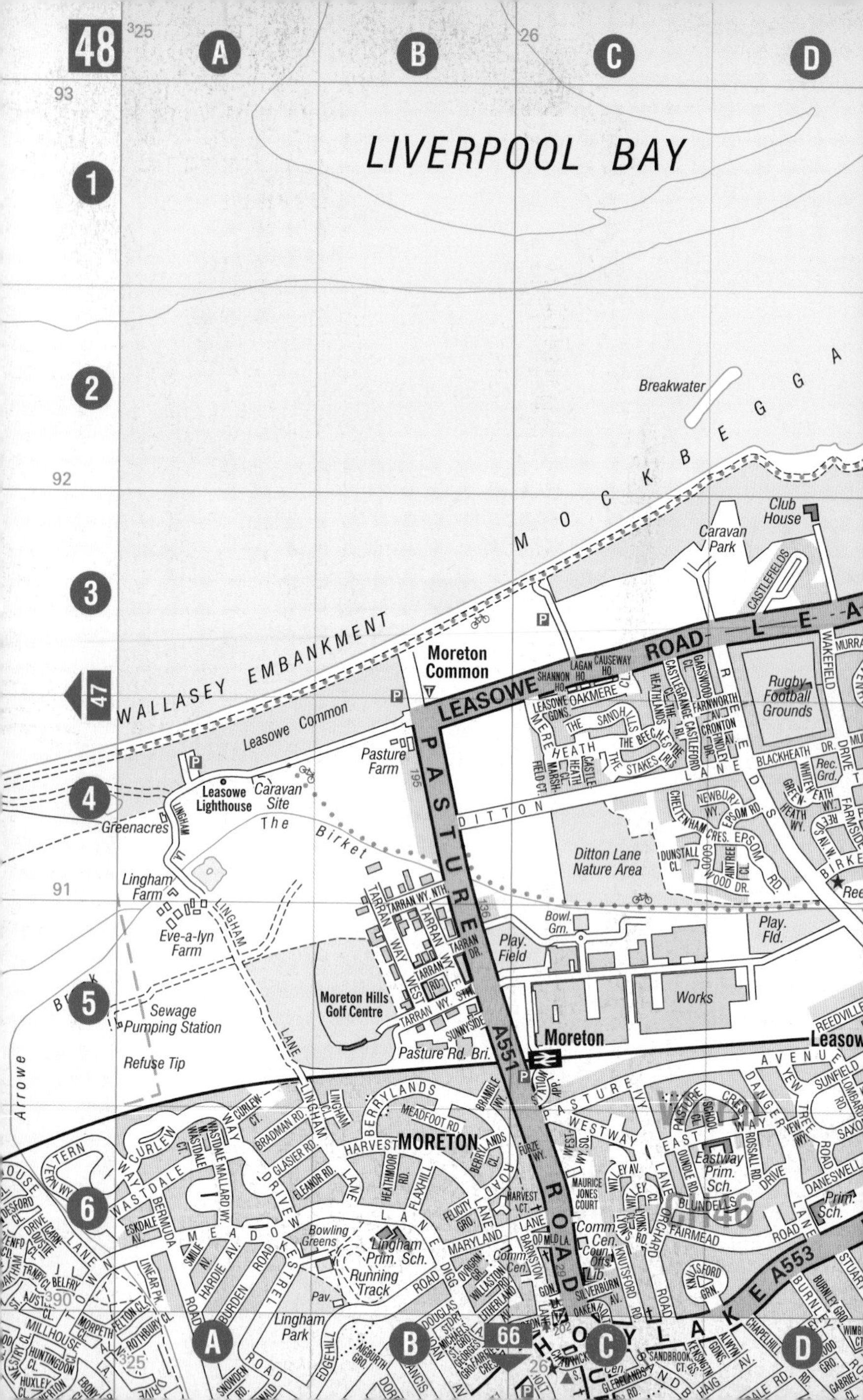
A
B
C
D
1
2
3
4
5
6
LIVERPOOL BAY
Breakwater
MOCKBEGGAR
WALLASEY EMBANKMENT
Leasowe Common
Moreton Common
Caravan Park
Club House
LEASOWE ROAD
Rugby Football Grounds
Pasture Farm
PASTURE ROAD
Leasowe Lighthouse
Caravan Site
Greenacres
The Birket
DITTON LANE
Ditton Lane Nature Area
Lingham Farm
Eve-a-lyn Farm
LINGHAM LANE
Play. Field
Bowl. Grn.
Play. Fld.
Works
Moreton Hills Golf Centre
Sewage Pumping Station
Refuse Tip
Arrowe
Pasture Rd. Bri.
Moreton
A551
MORETON
Bowling Greens
Lingham Prim. Sch.
Running Track
Pav.
Lingham Park
Eastway Prim. Sch.
Prim. Sch.
HOYLAKE ROAD
A553
Comm. Cen.
Coun. Offs.
Lib.
MEADOW LANE
FAIRMEAD ROAD
BLUNDELLS
KNUTSFORD ROAD
WESTWAY
EASTWAY
HARVEST LANE
BERRYLANDS
WASTDALE DRIVE
TERN WAY
CURLEW WAY
KESTREL ROAD
DIGG LANE
MARYLAND LANE
BURDEN ROAD
HARDIE AV.
BERMUDA
ESKDALE AV.
TARRAN WAY
SUNNYSIDE
DANGER AVENUE
YEW TREE ROAD
BLACKHEATH DR.
EPSOM RD.
CASTLEFORD
CASTLEFIELDS
WAKEFIELD

47
66

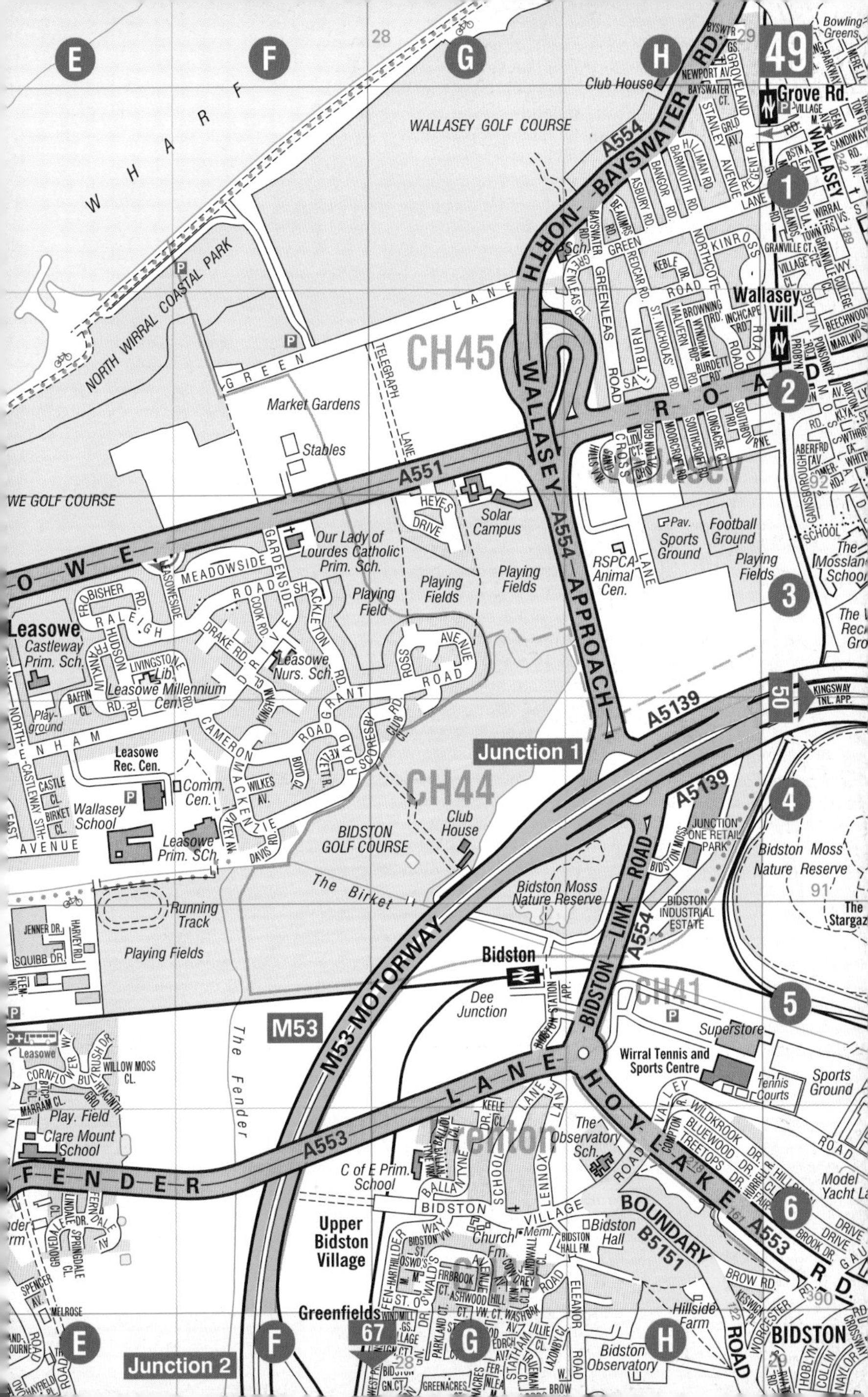
49
E
F
G
H
28
29
W H A R F
Club House
WALLASEY GOLF COURSE
NORTH WIRRAL COASTAL PARK
GREEN LANE
CH45
Market Gardens
Stables
TELEGRAPH LANE
A551
A554
NORTH BAYSWATER RD.
WALLASEY APPROACH
WE GOLF COURSE
LEASOWE
Our Lady of Lourdes Catholic Prim. Sch.
Solar Campus
HEYES DRIVE
Playing Field
Playing Fields
Sports Ground
Football Ground
RSPCA Animal Cen.
Leasowe
Castleway Prim. Sch.
Leasowe Nurs. Sch.
Leasowe Millennium Cen.
Leasowe Rec. Cen.
Comm. Cen.
Wallasey School
Leasowe Prim. SCh.
MEADOWSIDE
GARDENSIDE
SHACKLETON RD.
GRANT ROAD
CAMERON
MACKENZIE
ROSS AVENUE
Play-ground
Junction 1
CH44
A5139
50
KINGSWAY TNL. APP.
BIDSTON GOLF COURSE
Club House
Bidston Moss Nature Reserve
JUNCTION ONE RETAIL PARK
BIDSTON INDUSTRIAL ESTATE
The Birket
Running Track
Playing Fields
Bidston
Dee Junction
M53
M53 MOTORWAY
BIDSTON LINK ROAD
CH41
Superstore
Wirral Tennis and Sports Centre
Tennis Courts
Sports Ground
The Fender
A553
LANE
FENDER
HOYLAKE RD.
Clare Mount School
Play. Field
Leasowe
The Observatory Sch.
C of E Prim. School
BIDSTON VILLAGE
Upper Bidston Village
Church Fm.
Bidston Hall
BOUNDARY B5151
Greenfields
67
Junction 2
Hillside Farm
Bidston Observatory
BIDSTON
Grove Rd.
Wallasey Vill.
WALLASEY
Model Yacht La
1
2
3
4
5
6

50
Wallasey Gro. Rd.
Wallasey Vill.
32
49
68
A
B
C
D
1
2
3
4
5
6
WALLASEY
LEASOWE ROAD
SANDY LANE
St. Mary's Catholic College
B5427
Prim. Sch.
Cricket Grd.
CLAREMOUNT ROAD
Belvidere Rec. Ground
Liscard
The Oldershaw School
Tennis Courts
Superstore
CEMETERY
Earlston Gardens
Lib.
B5143
Cricket Grd.
The Delph Rec. Grd
WALLASEY A551 ROAD
ST. HILARY BROW
BRECK ROAD
VILLAGE
The Breck
The Mosslands School
Football Ground
Sports Ground
Playing Fields
The Wallacre Recreation Ground
KINGSWAY TUNNEL APP.
DOCKS LINK
A5139
B5145
Weatherhead High School
A5088
VICTORIA CENTRAL HOSPITAL
Bowling Greens
Park Prim. Sch.
Oxton Rd. Playing Fields
JUNCTION ONE RETAIL PARK
Bidston Moss Nature Reserve
The Stargazer
BIDSTON INDUSTRIAL ESTATE
Poulton Bridge
Warehouses
Refuse Incinerator
BRIDGE ROAD
A5058
Works
Lewis's Quay
Poulton Quay
Cheshire's Quay
Graving Dock No.3
Birkenhead CH41
DOCK ROAD
KINGSWAY
Victoria Park
Poulton
Gas Holders
GALLAGHER IND. EST.
WEST FLOAT IND. EST.
UVECO BUS. CEN.
WEST FLOAT
Sheds
Gillbrook Basin
Cavendish Wharf
Superstore
Tennis and Leisure Centre
Tennis Courts
Sports Ground
VALLEY ROAD BUSINESS PARK
Model Yacht Lake
Comm. Cen.
Birkenhead Nth.
BEAUFORT A5030 ROAD
WALLASEY
HOYLAKE A553 ROAD
Primary Sch.
Hillside Farm
BIDSTON
CORPORATION ROAD

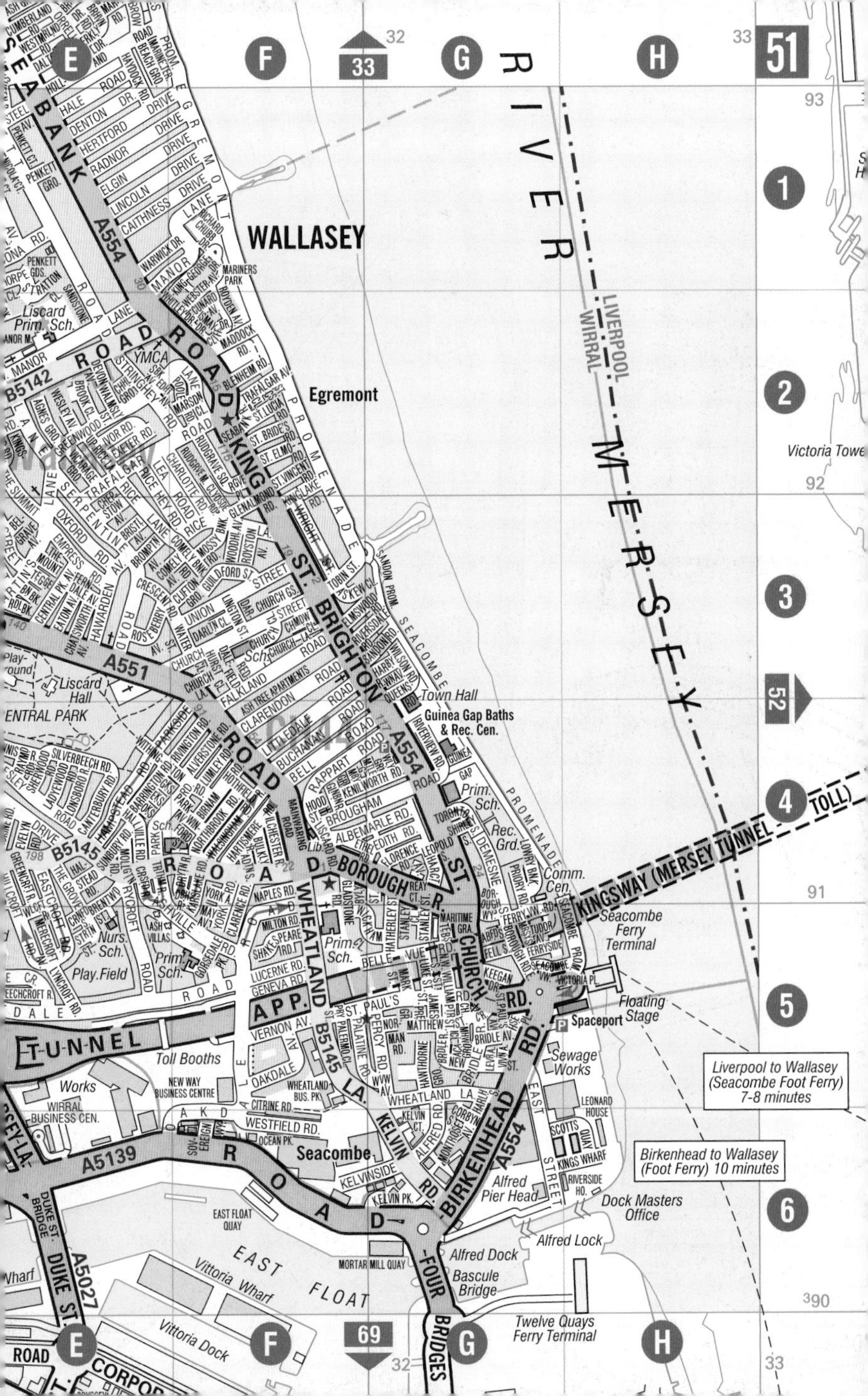
WALLASEY
Egremont
RIVER MERSEY
Seacombe
Town Hall
Guinea Gap Baths & Rec. Cen.
Seacombe Ferry Terminal
Floating Stage
Spaceport
Victoria Towe
Liverpool to Wallasey (Seacombe Foot Ferry) 7-8 minutes
Birkenhead to Wallasey (Foot Ferry) 10 minutes
Dock Masters Office
Alfred Lock
Alfred Dock
Bascule Bridge
Alfred Pier Head
Twelve Quays Ferry Terminal
EAST FLOAT
Vittoria Wharf
Vittoria Dock
EAST FLOAT QUAY
MORTAR MILL QUAY
KINGSWAY (MERSEY TUNNEL TOLL)
TUNNEL
Toll Booths
Works
WIRRAL BUSINESS CEN.
NEW WAY BUSINESS CENTRE
Liscard Hall
CENTRAL PARK
Liscard Prim. Sch.
MARINERS PARK
YMCA
Sewage Works
LEONARD HOUSE
KINGS WHARF
A554
A551
A5139
A5027
B5142
B5145
33
52
69

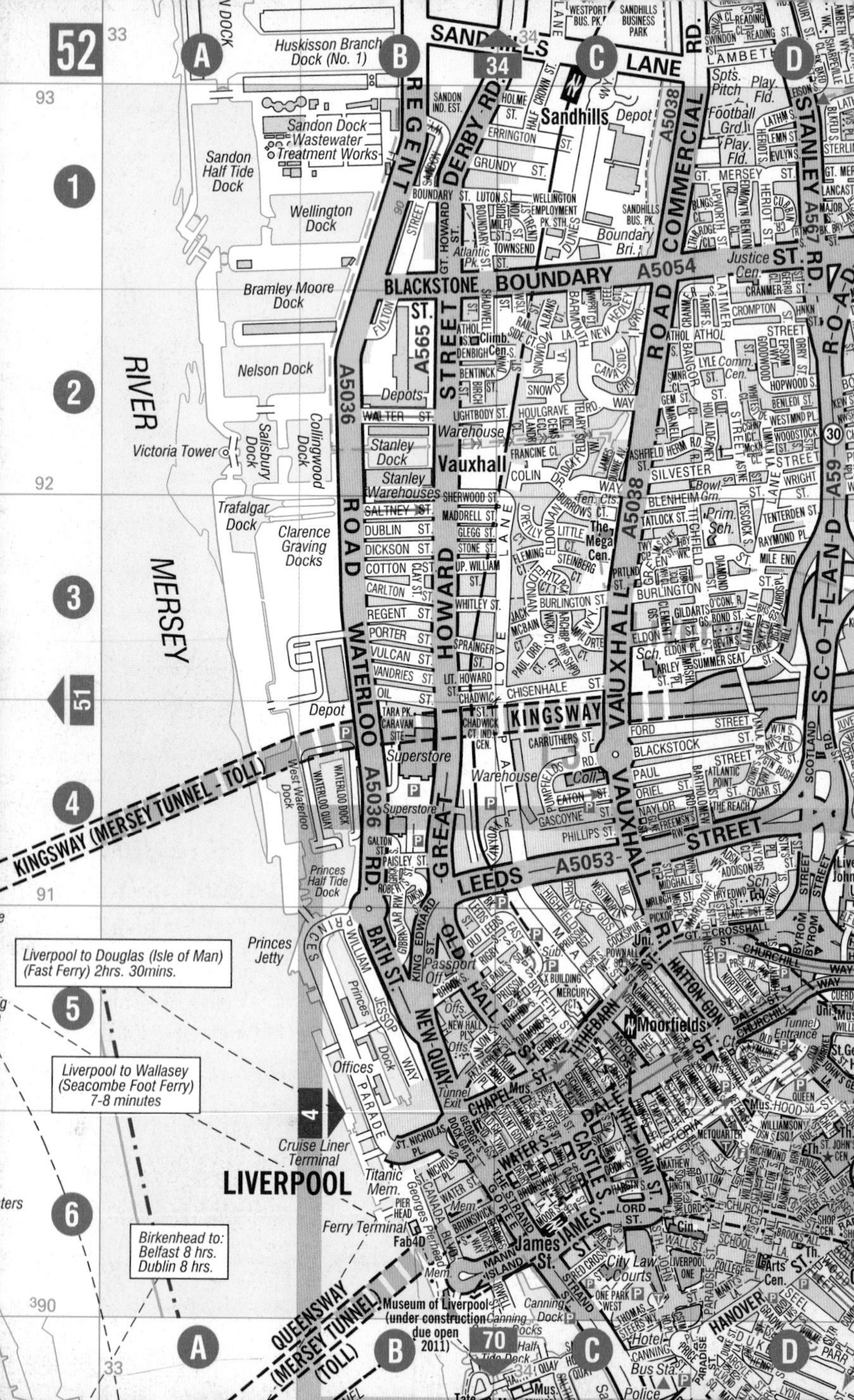

Huskisson Branch Dock (No. 1)
SANDHILLS LANE
34
Sandon Ind. Est.
Sandhills
Depot
Sandhills Business Park
Westport Bus. Pk.
Sandon Dock Wastewater Treatment Works
Sandon Half Tide Dock
Wellington Dock
Bramley Moore Dock
Nelson Dock
Salisbury Dock
Collingwood Dock
Victoria Tower
Stanley Dock
Stanley Warehouses
Trafalgar Dock
Clarence Graving Docks
RIVER MERSEY
51
REGENT ROAD
DERBY RD.
COMMERCIAL ROAD
A5038
STANLEY RD. A567
BLACKSTONE ST.
BOUNDARY A5054
Wellington Employment Pk. Sth.
Sandhills Bus. Pk.
Boundary Bri.
Atlantic Pk.
Justice Cen.
Play. Fld.
Football Grd.
Spts. Pitch
GREAT HOWARD STREET
A565
A5036
WATERLOO ROAD
Climb. Cen.
Depots
Warehouse
Vauxhall
The Mega Cen.
VAUXHALL ROAD
A5038
Comm. Cen.
Prim. Sch.
Sch.
SCOTLAND ROAD
A59
30
KINGSWAY
KINGSWAY (MERSEY TUNNEL - TOLL)
Depot
Tara Pk. Caravan Site
Superstore
Warehouse
Coll.
West Waterloo Dock
Waterloo Dock
Waterloo Quay
Princes Half Tide Dock
LEEDS STREET A5053
Princes Jetty
Liverpool to Douglas (Isle of Man) (Fast Ferry) 2hrs. 30mins.
Liverpool to Wallasey (Seacombe Foot Ferry) 7-8 minutes
Birkenhead to: Belfast 8 hrs. Dublin 8 hrs.
PRINCES PARADE
WILLIAM JESSOP WAY
Princes Dock
Offices
4
Cruise Liner Terminal
LIVERPOOL
Titanic Mem.
Ferry Terminal
Pier Head
Fab4D
Georges Pierhead Mem.
BATH ST.
NEW QUAY
OLD HALL ST.
Passport Off.
Moorfields
TITHEBARN ST.
DALE ST.
VICTORIA ST.
CHAPEL ST.
WATER ST.
CASTLE ST.
LORD ST.
JAMES ST.
James St.
THE STRAND
CHURCHILL WAY
Tunnel Exit
Tunnel Entrance
Mus.
Cin.
City Law Courts
Liverpool One
Canning Dock
Canning Half Tide Dock
Museum of Liverpool (under construction due open 2011)
QUEENSWAY (MERSEY TUNNEL) (TOLL)
70
HANOVER ST.
Hotel
Bus Sta.
Police
Arts Cen.
Uni.
A B C D
1 2 3 4 5 6
93 92 91 390
33 34

53
E
F
G
H
1
2
3
4
5
6
35
54
5
71
36
37
EVERTON VALLEY
ST. DOMINGO A5050 RD.
HEYWORTH ST.
EVERTON A580 RD.
BRECK A580
BRECK ROAD
OAKFIELD A5089 RD.
BELMONT ROAD
WEST DERBY A5049 ROAD
SHEIL ROAD
TOWNSEND LA.
KENSINGTON A5047
ISLINGTON
PRESCOT A57 ST.
LONDON RD.
PEMBROKE A5047 PL.
EDGE A5047
WAVERTREE B5178
ST. A5048
B5340
B5188
DURNING RD.
TUNNEL RD.
GROVE
OXFORD ST.
ST. DOMINGO VALE
ST. DOMINGO GROVE
ERSKINE ST.
BRUNSWICK RD.
LOW HILL
MOLYNEUX
BOALER
LIME ST.
Everton
Kensington
Edge Hill
Lifestyles Everton
North Liverpool Academy
Rupert Lane Rec. Grd.
Liverpool FC
Superstore
Govt. Offs.
Referral Unit
Grant Gds.
Kensington Gds.
LIVERPOOL UNI. DENTAL HOSP.
ROYAL LIVERPOOL UNIV. HOSP.
University of Liverpool
Liverpool Metropolitan Cath.
John Moores University
Sorting Office
Police Traffic HQ
Comm. Cen.
Sports Cen.
Gall.& Mus.
Coach Sta.
YMCA
Nursing Home
Football Pitch

54
36
72
A
B
C
D
1
2
3
4
5
6
TOWNSEND LA.
A580
Edinburgh Park
Lower Breck Rec. Grd.
Anfield Youth Club
Cabbage Hall
Nursing Home
Prim. Sch.
SUZANNE BOARDMAN HO.
ROCKY LANE W.
DERBY A5049 ROAD
WEST DERBY RD.
BELMONT RD.
SHEIL ROAD
B5188
Rec. Grd.
Tue Brook
MUIRHEAD AV.
QUEENS DRIVE
Lifestyles Peter Lloyd
Play. Fld.
Liverpool Community College
Cemy.
Schs.
PARK LODGE HOSP.
Adult Educ. Cen.
Newsham Ho.
NEWSHAM PARK
NEWSHAM DRIVE
GARDNER'S DRIVE
LISTER DRIVE
BOULEVARD
Playgrd.
Sub.
Depot
Bus Depot
Depots
Warehouse
Market
B5189
CARNEGIE ROAD
Fairfield
Bowl. Grns.
Bandstand
Elm Park
PRESCOT
KENSINGTON A57
Club Ho.
Athletic Grd.
Stanley
Market
Prim. Sch.
HOLT A5089 RD.
EDGE LANE
A5047
Botanic Gardens
WAVERTREE PARK
BOTANIC ESTATE
Works
DIGITAL WY.
WAVERTREE BOULEVARD
WAVERTREE TECHNOLOGY PARK
FARADAY TECHNOLOGY PARK
PIGHUE LANE
BINNS RD.
EDGE LANE RETAIL PARK
Hollywood Bowl
Total Fitness
Cineworld Liverpool
Wavertree Technology Park
B5179
Sandown Pk.
RATHBONE RD.
INNOVATION
B5178
ROAD
PICTON
Gala Bingo
WAVERTREE RETAIL PK.
Edge Hill
DURNING RD.
TUNNEL R.
WAVERTREE
LEC COMPLEX
Mersey Indoor Karting Cen.
L7

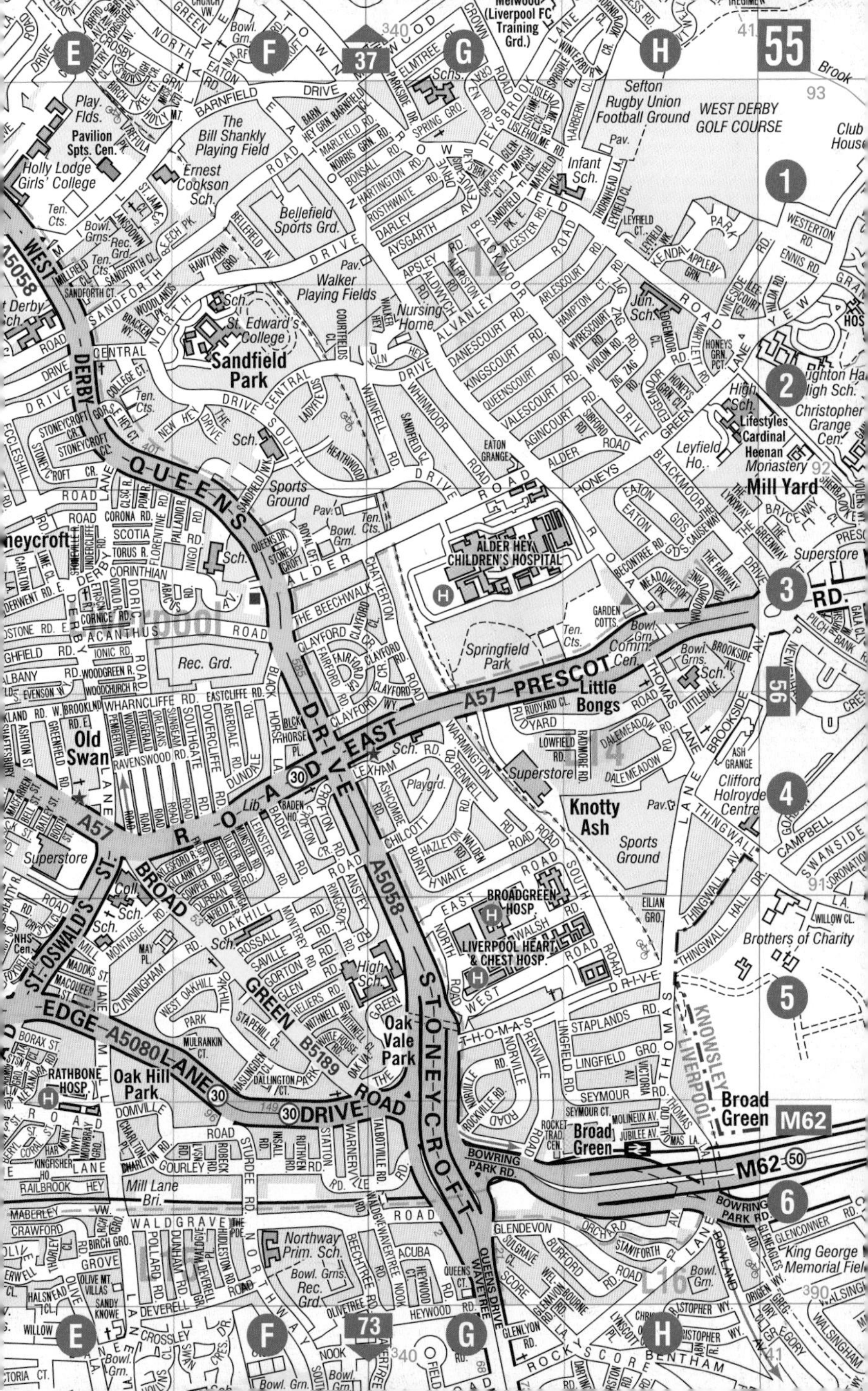

E
F
37
G
H
Melwood (Liverpool FC Training Grd.)
Sefton Rugby Union Football Ground
WEST DERBY GOLF COURSE
Club House
Brook
93
Play. Flds.
Pavilion Spts. Cen.
Holly Lodge Girls' College
The Bill Shankly Playing Field
Ernest Cookson Sch.
Bellefield Sports Grd.
Walker Playing Fields
Nursing Home
Infant Sch.
Jun. Sch.
1
2
3
4
5
6
St. Edward's College
Sandfield Park
Sports Ground
ALDER HEY CHILDREN'S HOSPITAL
Springfield Park
Leyfield Ho.
Lifestyles Cardinal Heenan High Sch.
Monastery
Mill Yard
Christopher Grange Cen.
Superstore
QUEENS DRIVE
A5058
WEST DERBY ROAD
A57 PRESCOT ROAD EAST
Little Bongs
Knotty Ash
Sports Ground
Clifford Holroyde Centre
Brothers of Charity
56
Liverpool
Rec. Grd.
Old Swan
Superstore
BROADGREEN HOSP.
LIVERPOOL HEART & CHEST HOSP.
Oak Vale Park
STONEYCROFT
EDGE LANE A5080
Oak Hill Park
RATHBONE HOSP.
BROAD GREEN
B5189
Broad Green
M62
Mill Lane Bri.
Northway Prim. Sch.
Bowl. Grns.
Rec. Grd.
King George V Memorial Field
L16
73
340
390
41
91
92

56
38
55
74
A
B
C
D
1
2
3
4
5
6
WEST DERBY GOLF COURSE
Deys Brook
Club House
Yewtree Cemetery
HOSPICE
Broughton Hall High Sch.
Christopher Grange Cen.
Lifestyles
Cardinal Heenan
Leyfield Ho.
Monastery
Mill Yard
Superstore
Mecca Bingo
A57
PRESCOT
ROAD
EAST
Dovecot Park
Dovecot
Dovecot Prim. Sch.
Roby Park Prim. Sch.
Bowring Sports Coll.
St. Margaret Mary's Catholic Jun. & Inf. Schs.
Playing Fields
Swanside
Brothers of Charity
Malvern Prim. Sch.
M62
Broad Green
BOWRING PARK RD.
ROBY A5080 ROAD
MOTORWAY
Junction 5
Club Ho.
Bowring Park Vis. Cen.
Bowring Park
King George V Memorial Field
Cricket Grd.
Court Hey
National Wildflower Centre
Court Hey Park
BOWRING PARK GOLF COURSE
Page Moss
Comm. Cen.
Playing Field
Brookside Prim. Sch.
St. Edmund of Canterbury Catholic High School
St. Dominic's Catholic Jun. & Inf. Schs.
Nursing Home
Finch
Govt. Offs.
Rec. Grd.
Playgrd.
Sch.
FINCH LANE
LIVERPOOL
KNOWSLEY
THINGWALL LANE
THOMAS LANE
CHILDWALL
PAGE MOSS
PILCH LANE
L12
L14
L16

M57 MOTORWAY
KNOWSLEY LANE
B5194
Prescot
L34
Longview
SETH POWELL WAY
A526
Woolfall Heath
A57
LIVERPOOL ROAD
King George V Sports Complex
Playing Fields
B5199
HUYTON LANE
Liverpool
HUYTON-WITH-ROBY
St. Aloysius Cath. Prim. Sch.
L36
HUYTON
Knowsley Hey School
Knowsley Comm. College
ROBY
Roby
Huyton
ROBY ROAD
TARBOCK ROAD
A5080
ARCHWAY
Huyton Leisure Cen.
McGoldrick Park
St. Joseph's Catholic Prim. Sch.
Superstore
Bus Sta.
Sawpit Park
Sports Ground
St. John's Millennium Grn.
M62
39
58
75

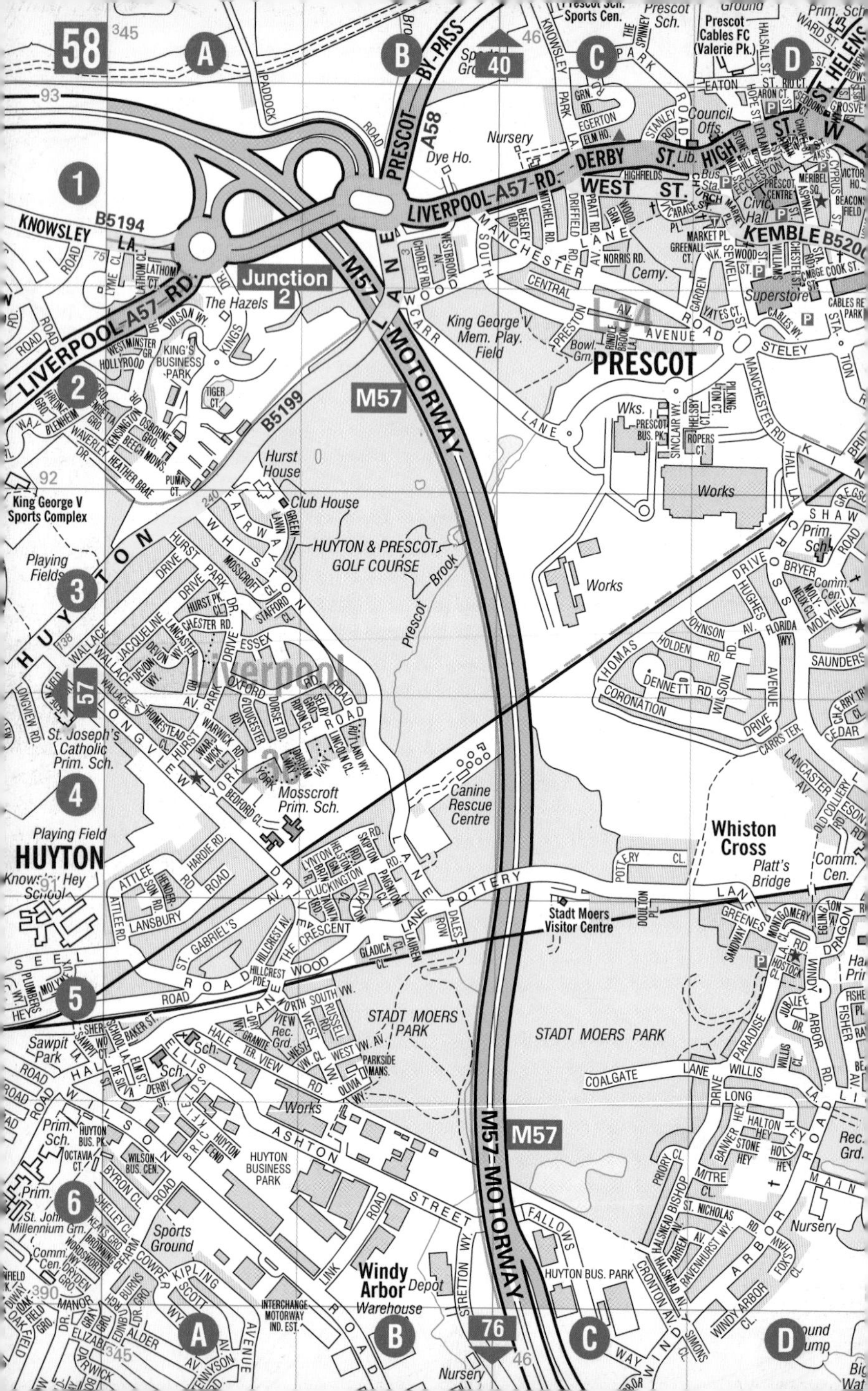

58
A
B
C
D
40
76
1
2
3
4
5
6
PRESCOT BY-PASS
A58
LIVERPOOL A57 RD.
DERBY ST.
HIGH ST.
WEST ST.
KEMBLE
B5200
KNOWSLEY LA.
B5194
Junction 2
M57
M57 MOTORWAY
B5199
HUYTON LANE
The Hazels
KING'S BUSINESS PARK
Hurst House
Club House
HUYTON & PRESCOT GOLF COURSE
Prescot Brook
King George V Mem. Play. Field
PRESCOT
Works
King George V Sports Complex
Playing Fields
St. Joseph's Catholic Prim. Sch.
Playing Field
HUYTON
Mosscroft Prim. Sch.
Canine Rescue Centre
Whiston Cross
Platt's Bridge
Comm. Cen.
POTTERY LANE
Stadt Moers Visitor Centre
STADT MOERS PARK
Sawpit Park
Works
HUYTON BUSINESS PARK
Sports Ground
Windy Arbor
Depot
Warehouse
INTERCHANGE MOTORWAY IND. EST.
HUYTON BUS. PARK
ASHTON STREET
WILSON ROAD
LINK ROAD
WINDY ARBOR RD.
Nursery
Prescot Sch. Sports Cen.
Prescot Sch.
Prescot Cables FC (Valerie Pk.)
Council Offs.
Lib.
Bus Sta.
Civic Hall
Superstore
Nursery
Dye Ho.
Cemy.
Bowl. Grn.
Sch.
Prim. Sch.
Rec. Grd.

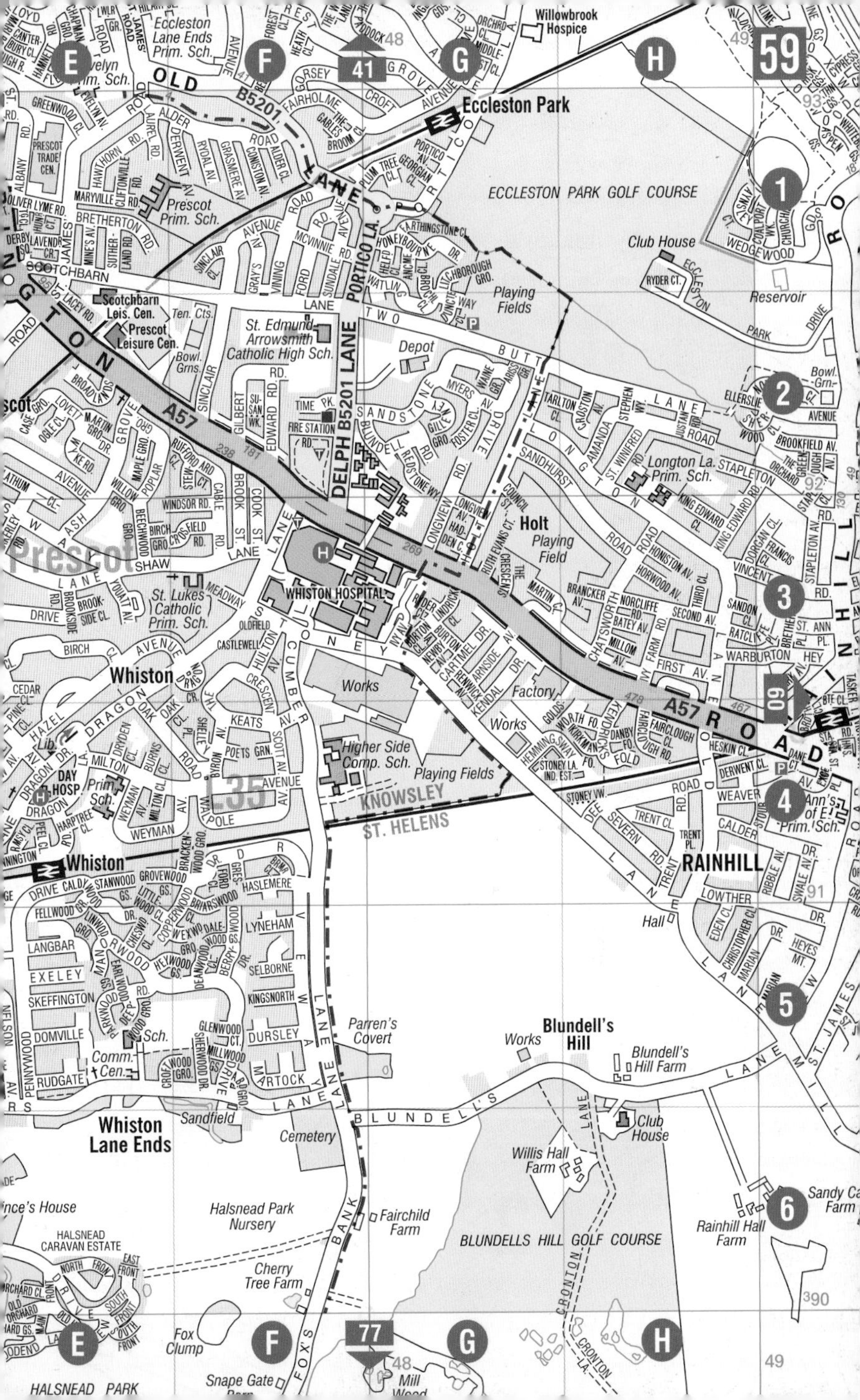

41
77
60
E
F
G
H
1
2
3
4
5
6
Willowbrook Hospice
Eccleston Lane Ends Prim. Sch.
Evelyn Prim. Sch.
Eccleston Park
ECCLESTON PARK GOLF COURSE
Club House
Reservoir
Prescot Trade Cen.
Prescot Prim. Sch.
Scotchbarn Leis. Cen.
Prescot Leisure Cen.
Ten. Cts.
Bowl. Grns.
St. Edmund Arrowsmith Catholic High Sch.
Depot
Playing Fields
Time Pk.
Fire Station
DELPH LANE
B5201
PORTICO LA.
OLD LANE
TWO BUTTS LANE
Holt
Playing Field
Longton La. Prim. Sch.
LONGTON LANE
WHISTON HOSPITAL
Prescot
Whiston
St. Lukes Catholic Prim. Sch.
Works
Factory
Higher Side Comp. Sch.
Playing Fields
KNOWSLEY
ST. HELENS
L35
A57
WARRINGTON ROAD
STONEY LANE
CUMBER LANE
RAINHILL
St. Ann's of E. Prim. Sch.
Day Hosp.
Prim. Sch.
Whiston
Sch.
Comm. Cen.
Hall
Blundell's Hill
Works
Blundell's Hill Farm
Club House
BLUNDELL'S LANE
Parren's Covert
Whiston Lane Ends
Sandfield
Cemetery
Willis Hall Farm
Halsnead Park Nursery
Fairchild Farm
BLUNDELLS HILL GOLF COURSE
Cherry Tree Farm
HALSNEAD CARAVAN ESTATE
Fox Clump
FOX'S BANK LANE
Snape Gate
Mill Wood
Rainhill Hall Farm
Sandy Ca Farm
HALSNEAD PARK
CRONTON LA.
MILL LANE
ST. JAMES
390
48
49

A
B
C
D
1
2
3
4
5
6
42
59
78
Sutton Heath
Brown Edge
NUTGROVE
Nut Grove
REEVE COURT VILLAGE
SCOTT CLINIC
Reservoir
Bowl. Grn.
HEATHER
B5204
ELTON HEAD
B5413
RAINHILL ROAD
St. John Vianney Catholic Prim. Sch.
Depot
Play. Fld.
Lea Green
Works
Elton Head Hall Farm
LOWFIELD INDUSTRIAL ESTATE
LEA GREEN BUSINESS PARK
EUROLINK BUS. PK.
Wks.
Training Centre
Micklehead Green Farm
Ansdell's Wood
Pendlebury Brook
St. Anne's Well
Rainhill
Rec. Grd.
Playing Field
Sports Grd.
WARRINGTON ROAD
A57
A570
ST. HELENS LINKWAY
Rainhill Nursery Sch.
Rainhill High Sch.
Loyola Hall
Prescot
St. Ann's C of E Prim. Sch.
Lib. Mus.
THE PRIORY
RAINHILL
Oakdene Prim. Sch.
Rainhill Hall Farm
Sandy Carr Farm
Briars Hey
Tower College
Chapel House Farm
Rainhill Stoops
Prim. Sch.
Brookhouse Bridge
Home Farm
Wood's House Farm
Junction 7
BLUNDELL'S LANE
MILL LANE
ASHTON
SCHOOL LANE
CHAPEL LANE
HALL LANE
MOOREWAY
LAVIEW
ST. JAMES
OWEN ROAD
KNOWSLEY RD.
ELLERSLIE AV.
STAPLETON
VINCENT
WARBURTON HEY
RITHERUP LANE
FIELD WY.
GARDENERS WY.
TEESDALE WY.
ELDERSWOOD
SHERDLEY CT.
ELLABY RD.
ANDSELL VS.
ROBY CL.
WEDGEWOOD
ECCLESTON PARK DRIVE
NOTTINGHAM CL.
BROOKFIELD AV.
KING EDWARD RD.
LOWTHER DR.
CALDER
WEAVER AV.
DERWENT CL.
HESKIN CL.
MOSSDALE
BISHOPDALE DR.
COVERDALE AV.
DEEPDALE
ALLENDALE
THE MEADOWS
OAKLANDS
ORCHARD DENE
CRAVEN RD.
LOWFIELD
SHERDLEY
LEASIDE
EUROLINK
MICKLEHEAD
CHEYNE WK.
MARYLEBONE AV.
FARRINGDON CL.
HARWORTH ROAD
ROSSINGTON GS.
3 49
3 50
3 90
93
92
91
49
739
597
650
635
816
307

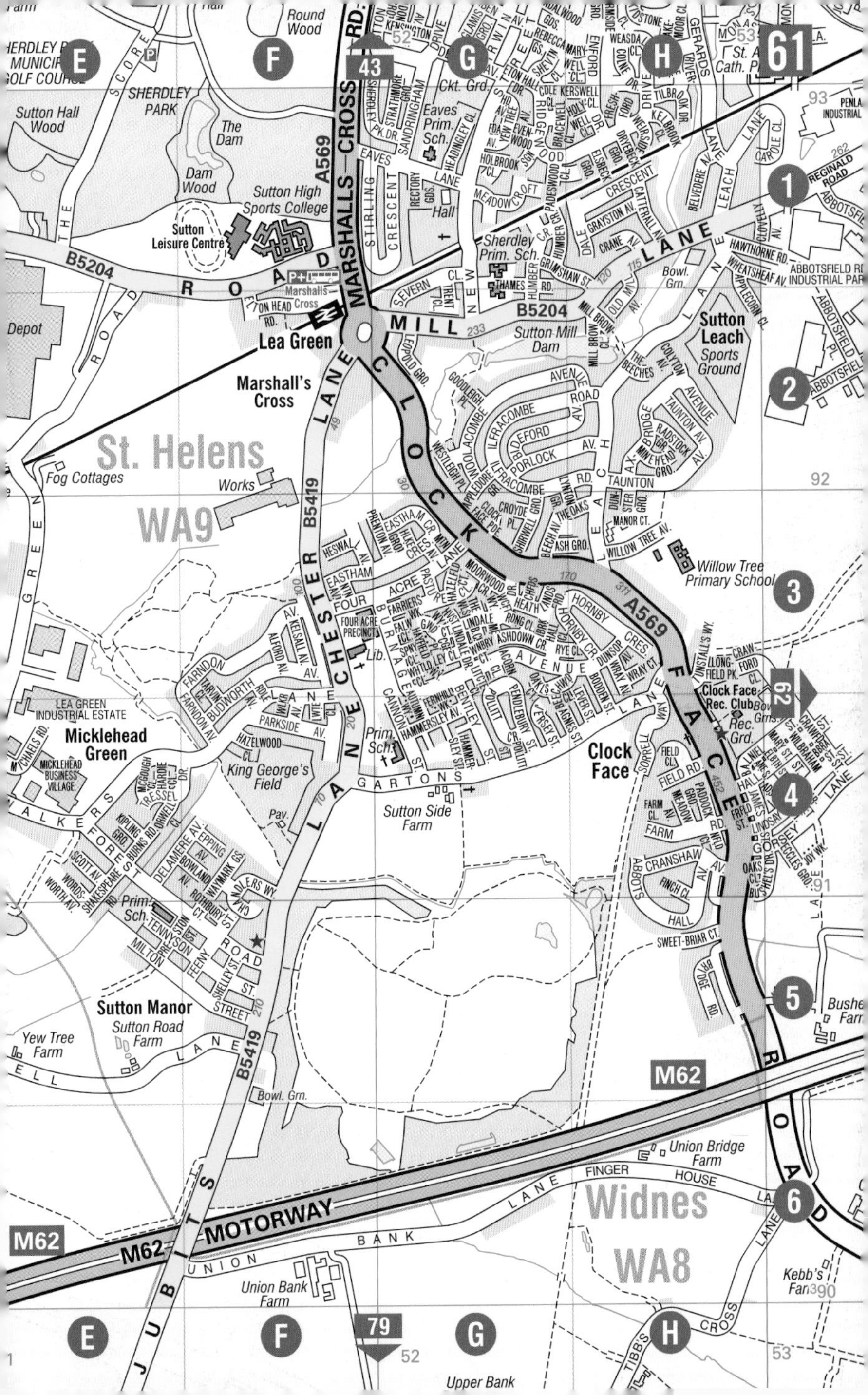
St. Helens
WA9
Widnes
WA8
Sutton Leisure Centre
Sutton High Sports College
Marshall's Cross
Lea Green
Sutton Leach Sports Ground
Willow Tree Primary School
Clock Face
Micklehead Green
Sutton Manor
King George's Field
Sutton Side Farm
Union Bank Farm
Union Bridge Farm
LEA GREEN INDUSTRIAL ESTATE
ABBOTSFIELD RD INDUSTRIAL PARK
Clock Face Rec. Club
Sherdley Prim. Sch.
Eaves Prim. Sch.
SHERDLEY PARK
Sutton Hall Wood
The Dam
Dam Wood
Round Wood
Sutton Mill Dam
Fog Cottages
Yew Tree Farm
Sutton Road Farm
Kebb's Farm
Upper Bank
MARSHALLS CROSS RD.
CLOCK FACE RD.
A569
B5204
B5419
M62 MOTORWAY
JUBITS LANE
MILL LANE
LEACH LANE
ROAD
43
62
79

62
St. Helens Junction
Penlake Industrial Estate
Reginald Road
B5204
Bold Rd.
Travers' Entry
Bold
44
Travers' Farm
Brindley Rd.
Lyon Ind. Est.
Abbotsfield Road
Abbotsfield Rd. Industrial Park
Northfield Riding Centre
Douglas Av.
Rosehill Av.
Neills Road
Gorsey Lane
Sutton Leach
Sports Ground
Bowl. Grn.
St. Helens
Abbotsfield Farm
WA9
Lodge Wood
Maypole Farm
Maypole Woods
Willow Tree Primary School
Clock Face Colliery Country Park
Nursery
Works
Clock Face
61
Home Farm
Middle Field Farm
Hall Lane
Ladies' Walk
Dog Kennel Plantation
Ladies' Walk Plantation
Currant Dam Plantation
Bushell's Farm
Joy Lane
Plain Plantation
M62
Widnes
Currant Dam Plantation
Old Hall Plantation
Booth's Wood
Union Bridge Farm
Finger House La.
Crow's Nest Farm
WA8
Coney Green Wood
Old Hall Farm
A569
Clock Face Road
Cross Lane
Kebb's Farm
Tibb's
Depot
80
Duck Wood

E
F
G
H
45
56
57
93
Wheatacre
Haley Head
Farm
Bridge
PHIPPS
RUSHTON CL.
BURTONWOOD
IND. CEN.
ALDRIDGE DR.
MELROSE
PINEWOOD
CAMBORNE
Vic.
ALDER
LA.
Play.
Fld.
KAREN CL.
FIR TREE LA.
ROXBORGH RD.
Primrose
Hill Fm.
FARMERS
LA.
Wheatacre
Farm
Wheatacre
Cottage
Rec.
Grd.
Pav.
CLAY
LANE
CHAPEL
LANE
SUNNY DALE
KINNOCK PK.
EXMOUTH WY.
WEYMOUTH RD.
Sch.
Lib.
Cem.
MERCER ST.
FAIRCLOUGH
JACKSON ST.
SHER-
WOOD
CR.
MILNTHORPE RD.
SEDGEWICK CR.
HAWKSHEAD
ROAD
HERBERT ST.
ACTON RD.
WEBB
KILSHAW RD.
ALMOND DR.
SPURLING
GLEAVE CL.
PERRINS RD.
KNIGHT RD.
GRN. JONES BROW
BROOKVALE
COLNE RD.
Comm.
Cen.
1
NORTH
RD.
HALEY RD.
MITCHELL AV.
STH.
Ashton's
Farm
BURTONWOOD
Lymedene
Moat
House
ST. HELENS
WARRINGTON
Clay Lane
Farm
Old Lodge
Farm
BARIN
2
Brook Head
Farm
LANE
92
HOUSE
Moat House
Farm
Warrington
3
Ivy
Cottage
Highfield
Joy Lane
Farm
JOY
LANE
JOY
LA.
BURTONWOOD
TAN
Finger
Post
WA5
LANE
WRIGHT'S
LANE
Warehouses
LIMEKILN
Limekiln
Farm
Warehouses
RD.
4
Airfield
(disused)
CHARON
WY.
91
Junction 8
M62
M62 MOTORWAY
BURTONWOOD RD.
5
Big Wood
Bell
BOULEVARD
ORION
OMEGA
Sorting
Office
6
AVENUE
WHITTLE
Lingley Mere
LINGLEY MERE
BUSINESS PARK
390
MATLOCK
MATLOCK
CL.
LEAMINGTON CL.
81
BOULEVARD
55

HOYLAKE
LIVERPOOL BAY
Meols Parade Gardens
Bowling Greens
Promenade
Model Boating Pond
Comm. Cen.
Lifeboat Sta.
Queens Park
Hoylake Cott.
Kingsmead School
Play. Flds.
MEOLS
Manor Road
Rec. Ground
Football Ground
The Bungalow
CH47
Hoylake
Play. Fld.
Sports Ground
Club House
New Hall Farm
HOYLAKE GOLF COURSE
ROYAL LIVERPOOL GOLF COURSE
The Birket
Playing Field
Red Rocks Marsh Nature Reserve
Hockey Pitch
Football Ground
Waste Site
Gilroy Nature Park
Newton Brook
West Kirby Grammar Sch.
WEST KIRBY
Grange Hill
War Meml.
Cemetery
Grange Hill Farm
Black Horse Hill Jun. & Inf. Schools
Hilbre High School
West Kirby
MARKET ST.
BIRKENHEAD RD.
A553
A540
MEOLS DRIVE
GREENBANK RD.
GILROY ROAD
SAUGHALL MASSIE RD.
FRANKBY RD. B5139
BLACK HORSE HILL
B5192
STANLEY RD.
NORTH PARADE
GRANGE RD.
46
82
LINGDALE COURT
Wirral

65
47
83
66
E
F
G
H
1
2
3
4
5
6
Great Meols
Meols
Fornalls Bridge
Playing Field
Wirral
CH48
CH49
A553 ROAD
HOYLAKE ROAD
Works
Refuse Tip
Clay Pit
Carr Hall Farm
Carr Farm
Green Gates Farm
Nursery
Saughall Massie
Barnacre
Prospect Farm
The Heyes
Oldfield Court
Oldfield Manor Farm
Three Lanes End Farm
Three Lanes End
Greasby Brook
MASSIE B5192
Rake House Farm
Long Rake Farm
Newton Hall Farm
China Plate Farm
Larton
Larton Hey Farm
Nursery
Greasby Bri.
War Memorial
Manor Ho. Farm
FRANKBY B5139
Football Ground
Royden Hall
Yew Tree Farm
The Birket

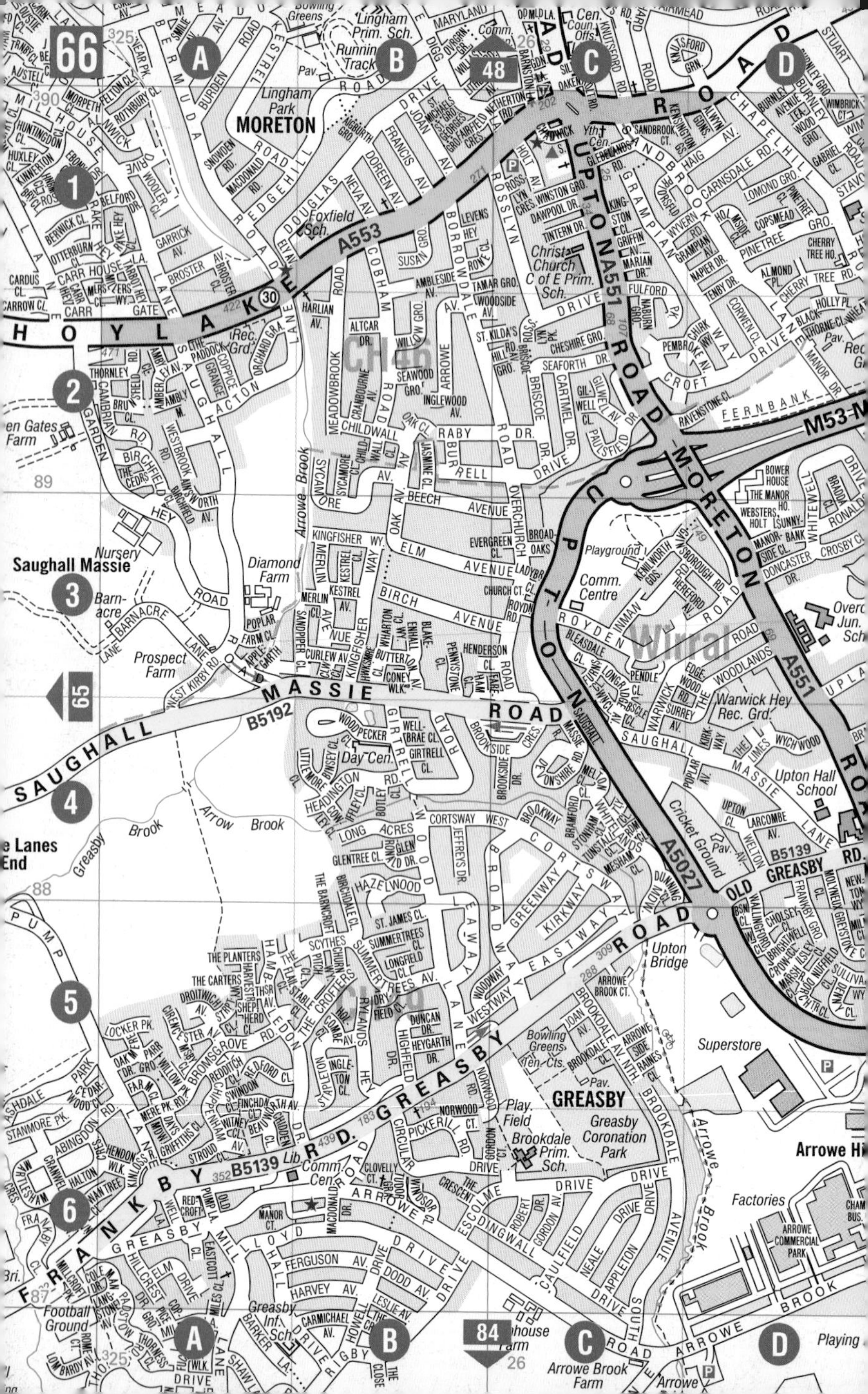

66
48
65
84
A
B
C
D
1
2
3
4
5
6
MORETON
Lingham Park
Lingham Prim. Sch.
Running Track
Bowling Greens
Foxfield Sch.
Christ Church C of E Prim. Sch.
HOYLAKE ROAD
A553
UPTON ROAD
A551
MORETON ROAD
M53
CH46
Wirral
Saughall Massie
SAUGHALL MASSIE ROAD
B5192
Diamond Farm
Prospect Farm
Nursery
Barnacre
Arrowe Brook
Greasby Brook
Playground
Comm. Centre
Day Cen.
Warwick Hey Rec. Grd.
Upton Hall School
Cricket Ground
A5027
Upton Bridge
Superstore
GREASBY
Greasby Coronation Park
Brookdale Prim. Sch.
Play. Field
FRANKBY ROAD
B5139
Lib.
Comm. Cen.
Football Ground
Greasby Inf. Sch.
ARROWE BROOK ROAD
Arrowe Brook Farm
ARROWE COMMERCIAL PARK
Factories
Playing
Arrowe Hi
OLD GREASBY RD.
BROADWAY
EASTWAY
CORTSWAY
GREENWAY
KIRKWAY

67
Bidston Village
49
Greenfields
BIDSTON
Bidston Observatory
BIDSTON HILL
Hillside Farm
Kennels
Recreation Ground
Beechwood
Silver Birch Wood
Bidston Windmill
Tam O'Shanter Urban Farm
Taylor's Wood
Park Wood
Manor Grn.
Cricket Ground
Junction 2
M53
MOTORWAY
The Fender
Nursery
Manor Prim. Sch.
Comm. Cen.
Rec. Cen.
Ford
Prenton
CH43
68
THE WIRRAL GOLF
Sports Gd.
UPTON
Upton
Hillside Prim. Sch.
St. Anselm's Coll. Sports Ground
Noctorum
Ridgeway High School
Playing Field
M53-MOTORWAY
A5027
UPTON BY-PASS
B5151
A551
Running Track
Woodchurch Leisure Cen.
Fender Prim. Sch.
Arrowe Hill Prim. Sch.
Woodchurch High Sch. Engineering College
St. Michael & All Angels
85

68
A
B
C
D
1
2
3
4
5
6
50
86
67
HOYLAKE RD.
A553
BEAUFORT RD.
CORPORATION ROAD
LAIRD STREET
PARK ROAD
A5027
B5151
BOUNDARY RD.
UPTON ROAD
BIDSTON ROAD
BIDSTON
Gillbrook Basin
FLOAT
Cavendish Wharf
Primary Sch.
Comm. Cen.
Bus Depot
Prim. Sch.
Flaybrick Hill Cemetery
Tam O'Shanter Urban Farm
Taylor's Wood
Rec. Ground
Cricket Ground
Rugby Grd.
Tennis Courts
Claughton
Birkenhead Sixth Form Coll.
BIRKENHEAD PARK
Birkenhead Pk.
Sports Grd.
Pavilion
Park High School
St. Anselm's College
Convent
Birkenhead High Sch.
Res. Cov.
Club House
THE WIRRAL LADIES GOLF COURSE
Play. Field
Tennis Courts
Prep Sch.
Play. Fld.
TA Centre
Ulverscroft Pav.
Hosp.
Noctorum
LC McAllester Memorial Field
Oxton
Mere Hall
Cricket Grd.
Recreation Ground
Townfield Prim. School
Oxton St. Saviour's C of E Prim. Sch.
Playing Field
The Arno
Shop. Cen.
TALBOT RD.
STORETON RD.
NOCTORUM ROAD
HOLMLANDS DRIVE
CLAUGHTON FIRS
CH43

BIRKENHEAD
TRANMERE
Rock Ferry
Birkenhead to:
Belfast 8 hrs.
Dublin 8 hrs.
Birkenhead to
Wallasey
(Foot Ferry)
10 minutes
QUEENSWAY
(MERSEY TUNNEL)
(TOLL)
Twelve Quays
Ferry Terminal
Alfred Dock
Alfred Lock
Vittoria Dock
Egerton Dock
Morpeth Dock
Sewage Works
Ferry Terminal
U-boat Story
Hamilton Sq.
Conway Pk.
Birkenhead Central
Green Lane
Birkenhead Priory
The Princess Dock
Outer Basin
Shipbuilding &
Engineering Works
Lairdside
Maritime
Cen.
Clifton Park
Mersey Park
Devonshire Park
Playing Fields
Victoria Park
51
70
87

Ⓐ   Ⓑ   Ⓒ   Ⓓ

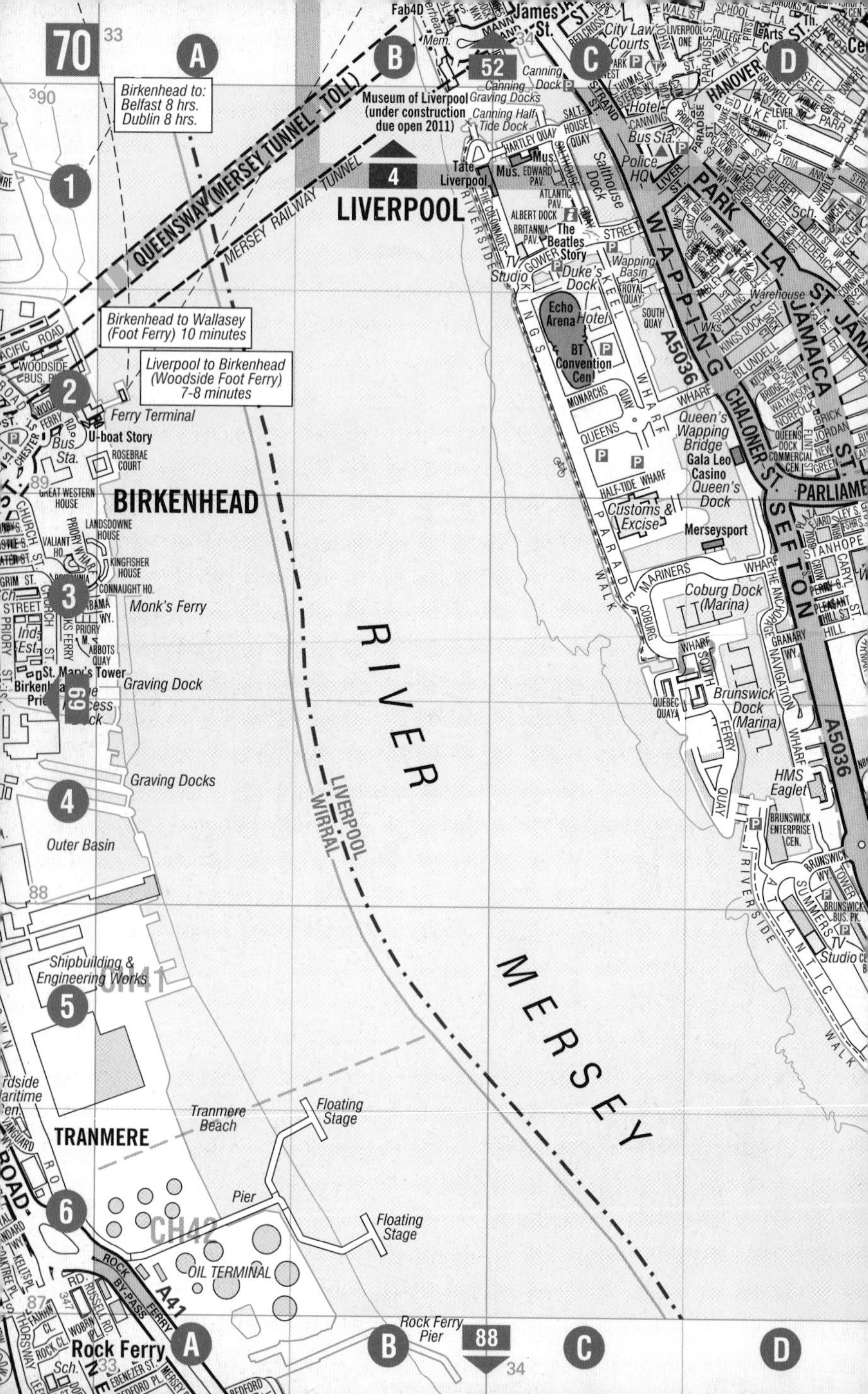

1

Birkenhead to:
Belfast 8 hrs.
Dublin 8 hrs.

QUEENSWAY (MERSEY TUNNEL - TOLL)

MERSEY RAILWAY TUNNEL

Fab4D

52 Canning
Graving Docks

Museum of Liverpool
(under construction
due open 2011)

Canning Half
Tide Dock

Tate
Liverpool

4

LIVERPOOL

James St.

Mann
St.

City Law
Courts

Mem.

HANOVER

Hotel

Mus.
EDWARD
PAV.

ATLANTIC
PAV.

BRITANNIA
PAV.

ALBERT DOCK

The Beatles
Story

TV
Studio

GOWER
STREET

Duke's
Dock

Wapping
Basin
ROYAL

South
Quay

Warehouse

KINGS DOCK

Police
HQ

PARK

Salthouse
Dock

Hartley Quay

SALT
HOUSE
QUAY

A5036

WAPPING

CHALONER ST.

2

Birkenhead to Wallasey
(Foot Ferry) 10 minutes

Liverpool to Birkenhead
(Woodside Foot Ferry)
7-8 minutes

Ferry Terminal

U-boat Story

ROSEBRAE
COURT

Bus.
Sta.

Echo
Arena

Hotel

BT
Convention
Cen

MONARCHS
QUAY

QUEENS
QUAY

Queen's
Wapping
Bridge
Gala Leo
Casino

Queen's
Dock

Half-Tide Wharf

BIRKENHEAD

GREAT WESTERN
HOUSE

LANDSDOWNE
HOUSE

VALIANT
HO.

KINGFISHER
HOUSE

CONNAUGHT HO.

Customs &
Excise

Merseysport

PARADE

WHARF

MARINERS

WHARF

JAMAICA ST.

PARLIAME

3

Monk's Ferry

St. Mary's Tower

Graving Dock

69

Ind
Est

PRIORY

ABBOTS
QUAY

MONKS FERRY

Birkenhead
Priory

Coburg Dock
(Marina)

CORBING

SEFTON

STANHOPE

4

Graving Docks

Outer Basin

Brunswick
Dock
(Marina)

QUEBEC
QUAYS

SOUTH
WHARF

NAVIGATION

GRANARY
WY

A5036

HMS
Eaglet

FERRY QUAY

88

5

Shipbuilding &
Engineering Works

BRUNSWICK
ENTERPRISE
CEN.

BRUNSWICK
BUS. STA.

TV
Studio

RIVERSIDE

ATLANTIC WALK

6

rdside
aritime
en

TRANMERE

CH42

Tranmere Beach

Floating
Stage

Pier

Floating
Stage

OIL TERMINAL

R I V E R

L I V E R P O O L   W I R R A L

M E R S E Y

87

ROAD

Rock Ferry

A41 BY-PASS

Sch

Ⓐ   Ⓑ

Rock Ferry
Pier

88

34

Ⓒ   Ⓓ

E
F
G
H
53
5
1
2
3
4
5
6
72
89
Edge Hill
Edge Hill
Granby
Liverpool Women's Hosp.
John Moores University
Sports Cen.
Senate Ho.
MYRTLE A5039 ST.
GROVE
GROVE ST.
PARLIAMENT
A562 STREET
UPPER A562
Lib.
Huskisson Mon.
Liverpool Cathedral
GT. GEORGE ST.
ST. JAMES PL.
PARK PL.
PARK RD.
A561 ROAD
PRINCES RD.
PRINCES AVENUE
B5175
WARWICK
UP. B5177
KINGSLEY ROAD
B5174
DEVONSHIRE RD.
BELVIDERE B5174 RD.
CROXTETH RD.
LODGE LANE A5089
SEFTON PK. RD.
AIGBURTH RD.
ULLET A5089
TUNNEL RD.
Princes Park
PRINCES PARK
Belvidere Academy
The Belvidere Sch.
Bellerive FCJ Catholic Coll.
The Lake
Lifestyles Park Rd.
All Weather Spts. Area
Spts. Cen.
Toxteth
Brunswick
Glacier Building
Brunswick Bus. Pk.
Greens Health & Fitness
Dingle
St. Michael's
St. Michael's Hamlet
Shorefields Sch.
Ckt. Grd.
The Turner Home
Rec. Grd.
Sefton Dr.
Alexandra Ho.
Sch.
Depot
Gala Bingo
HARRINGTON
SEFTON STREET
RIVERSIDE DRIVE
35
36
37
87
88
89
390

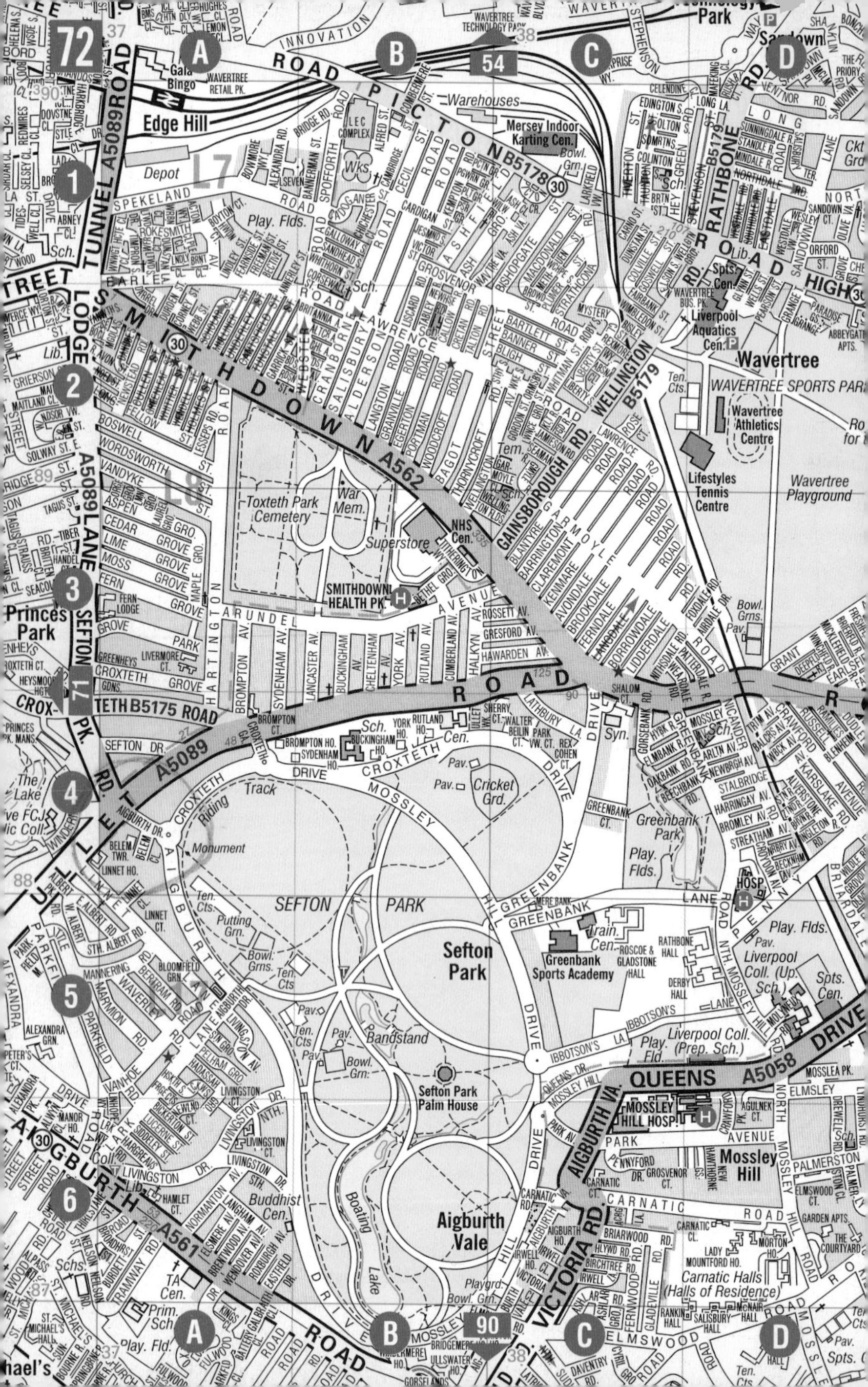
37
38
54
A
B
C
D
1
2
3
4
5
6
Edge Hill
Gala Bingo
Wavertree Retail Pk.
Wavertree Technology Park
Innovation Road
Picton Road B5178
Depot
L7
Warehouses
LEC Complex
Wks.
Mersey Indoor Karting Cen.
Sandown Pk.
Long Lane
Rathbone Road B5179
Wavertree
Wavertree Sports Park
Wavertree Athletics Centre
Lifestyles Tennis Centre
Wavertree Playground
Liverpool Aquatics Cen.
Wavertree Bus. Pk.
High St.
Tunnel Road A5089
Lodge Lane A5089
Sefton Pk. Rd.
Smithdown Road A562
Wellington Rd. B5179
Gainsborough Rd.
Garmoyle Road
L8
Toxteth Park Cemetery
War Mem.
Superstore
NHS Cen.
Smithdown Health Pk.
Arundel Avenue
Hartington Road
Princes Park
Croxteth Grove
Croxteth Road B5175
71
Ullet Road A5089
Play. Flds.
Sefton Park
Sefton Drive
Croxteth Drive
Mossley Drive
Riding Track
Monument
Cricket Grd.
Greenbank Park
Greenbank Drive
Greenbank Sports Academy
Train. Cen.
Roscoe & Gladstone Hall
Rathbone Hall
Derby Hall
Liverpool Coll. (Up. Sch.)
Liverpool Coll. (Prep. Sch.)
Spts. Cen.
Hosp.
Penny Lane
Bandstand
Sefton Park Palm House
Boating Lake
Aigburth Vale
Queens Drive A5058
Mossley Hill Hosp.
Mossley Hill
Aigburth Va.
Victoria Rd.
Carnatic Road
Carnatic Halls (Halls of Residence)
Aigburth Road A561
Buddhist Cen.
Livingston Dr.
Lark Lane
TA Cen.
Prim. Sch.
Play. Fld.
Elmswood Road
North Mossley Hill Road
88
89
87
90
30

73
E
F
G
H
55
91
74
1
2
3
4
5
6
Northway Prim. Sch.
CHILDWALL
Childwall School
Playing Fields
L15
L16
L18
Wavertree Green
Liverpool
Blue Coat Sch. Play. Flds.
The Blue Coat Sch.
Superstore
King David High Sch.
King David Prim. Sch.
Comm. Cen.
Clair Gdns.
Rec. Grd.
Liverpool Hope Uni. Coll.
HOPE PARK
Prim. Sch.
Spts. Grd.
Monastery
Jun. Sch.
Inf. Sch.
Calderstones Sch.
Liverpool Botanic Gardens
Open Air Theatre
Mansion House
CALDERSTONES PARK
Calderstones
Playground
Adventure Playground
Beechley Riding Cen. for Disabled People
All Weather Pitch
Geoffrey Hughes Memorial Ground
Running Track
Mossley Hill
LA Fitness
Odeon Cin.
TA Centre
Sports Ground
Rec. Grd.
QUEENS DRIVE
WAVERTREE
A5058
CHILDWALL ROAD
B5178
CHILDWALL VALLEY RD.
MENLOVE AVENUE
A562
MOSSLEY HILL
QUEENS DR. MOSSLEY HILL
ALLERTON RD.
MATHER AV.
B5180
WOOLTON ROAD
ROCKY LANE
THINGWALL ROAD
DUNBABIN ROAD
CHILDWALL ABBEY RD.
CHILDWALL PRIORY RD.
CHILDWALL PARK AV.
TAGGART AV.
GREEN LANE
DRUIDS CROSS RD.
YEW TREE ROAD
HEYWOOD RD.
CHURCH RD. NTH.
SMITHDOWN RD.
ALLERTON ROAD
CALDERSTONES ROAD
HARTHILL RD.
GREENHILL RD.
BEECH LANE
MEADWAY
WEST WAY
FIELD WAY
ABBEYSTEAD ROAD
PITVILLE AV.
ELM HALL DRIVE
DUDLOW LANE
HOPE PARK
HORNBY

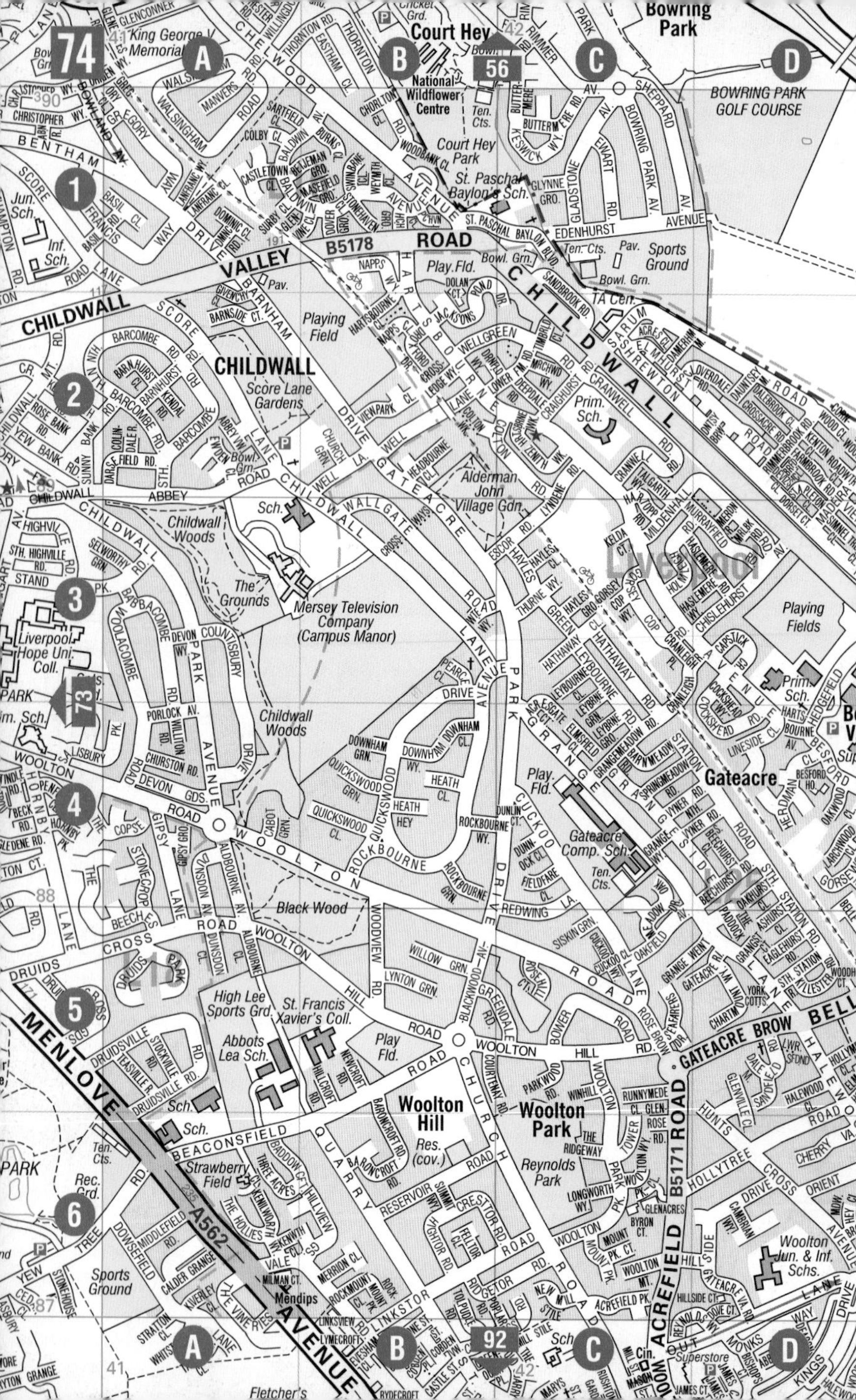
Court Hey
National Wildflower Centre
Court Hey Park
Bowring Park
BOWRING PARK GOLF COURSE
CHILDWALL
Childwall Woods
Mersey Television Company (Campus Manor)
Liverpool Hope Uni. Coll.
Gateacre
Gateacre Comp. Sch.
Woolton Hill
Woolton Park
Reynolds Park
Black Wood
High Lee Sports Grd.
St. Francis Xavier's Coll.
Abbots Lea Sch.
Strawberry Field
Woolton Jun. & Inf. Schs.
CHILDWALL VALLEY ROAD
B5178
WOOLTON ROAD
MENLOVE AVENUE
A562
ACREFIELD ROAD
B5171
GATEACRE BROW

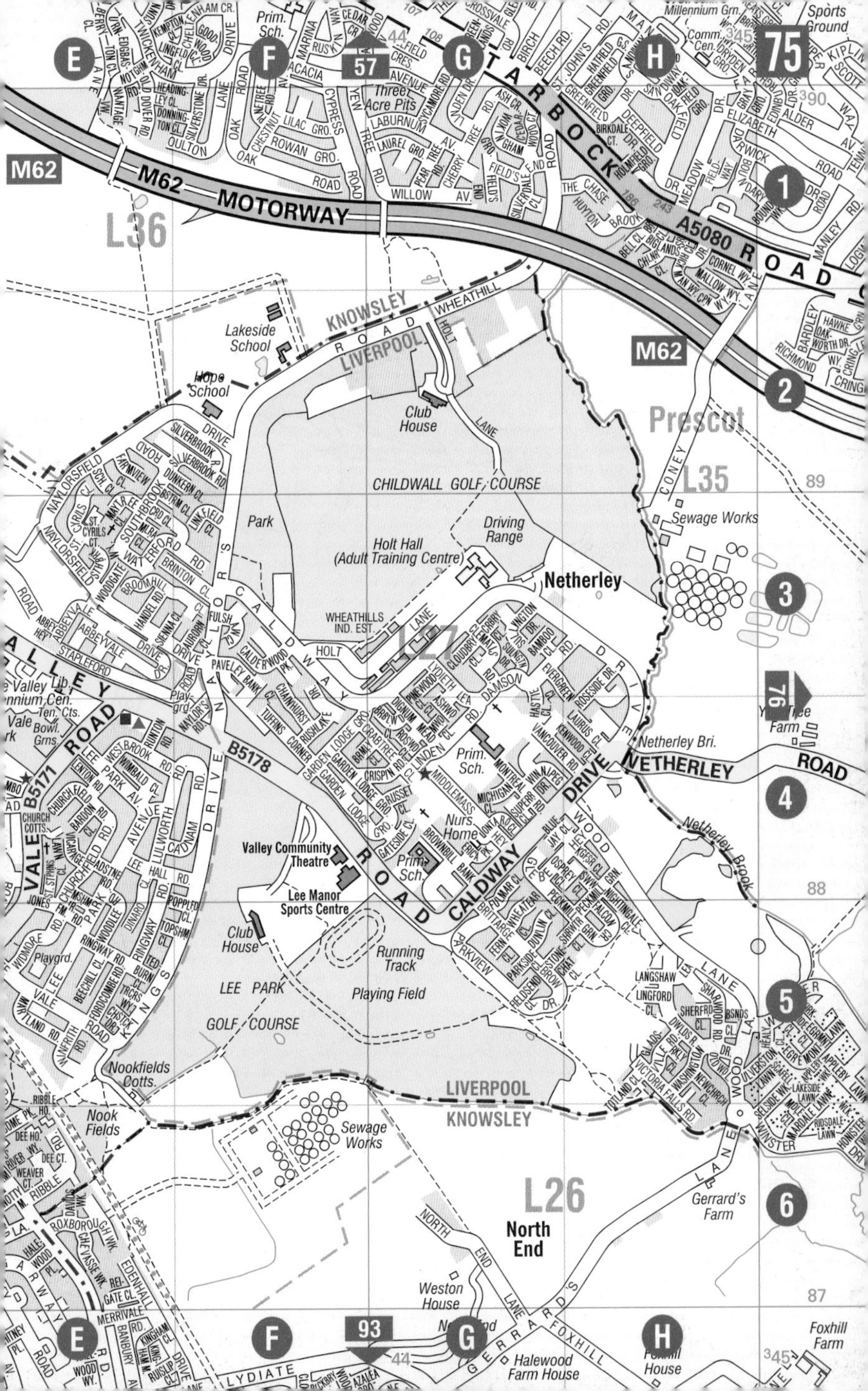
75
57
93
76
M62
M62 MOTORWAY
A5080 ROAD
TARBOCK ROAD
L36
L35
L27
L26
Prescot
Netherley
North End
KNOWSLEY
LIVERPOOL
LIVERPOOL ROAD
CHILDWALL GOLF COURSE
Driving Range
Holt Hall (Adult Training Centre)
Lakeside School
Hope School
Club House
Park
WHEATHILLS IND. EST.
CALDWAY DRIVE
NETHERLEY ROAD
Netherley Bri.
Netherley Brook
Sewage Works
Valley Community Theatre
Lee Manor Sports Centre
Running Track
Playing Field
LEE PARK GOLF COURSE
Nookfields Cotts.
Nook Fields
B5178
B5171
VALLEY ROAD
KINGS DRIVE
Prim. Sch.
Nurs. Home
Gerrard's Farm
Weston House
Halewood Farm House
Foxhill House
Foxhill Farm
Three Acre Pits
Sports Ground
Yew Tree Farm
GERRARDS LANE
FOXHILL LANE
NORTH END LANE
LYDIATE LANE
CONEY LANE
WOOD LANE
E
F
G
H
1
2
3
4
5
6
87
88
89

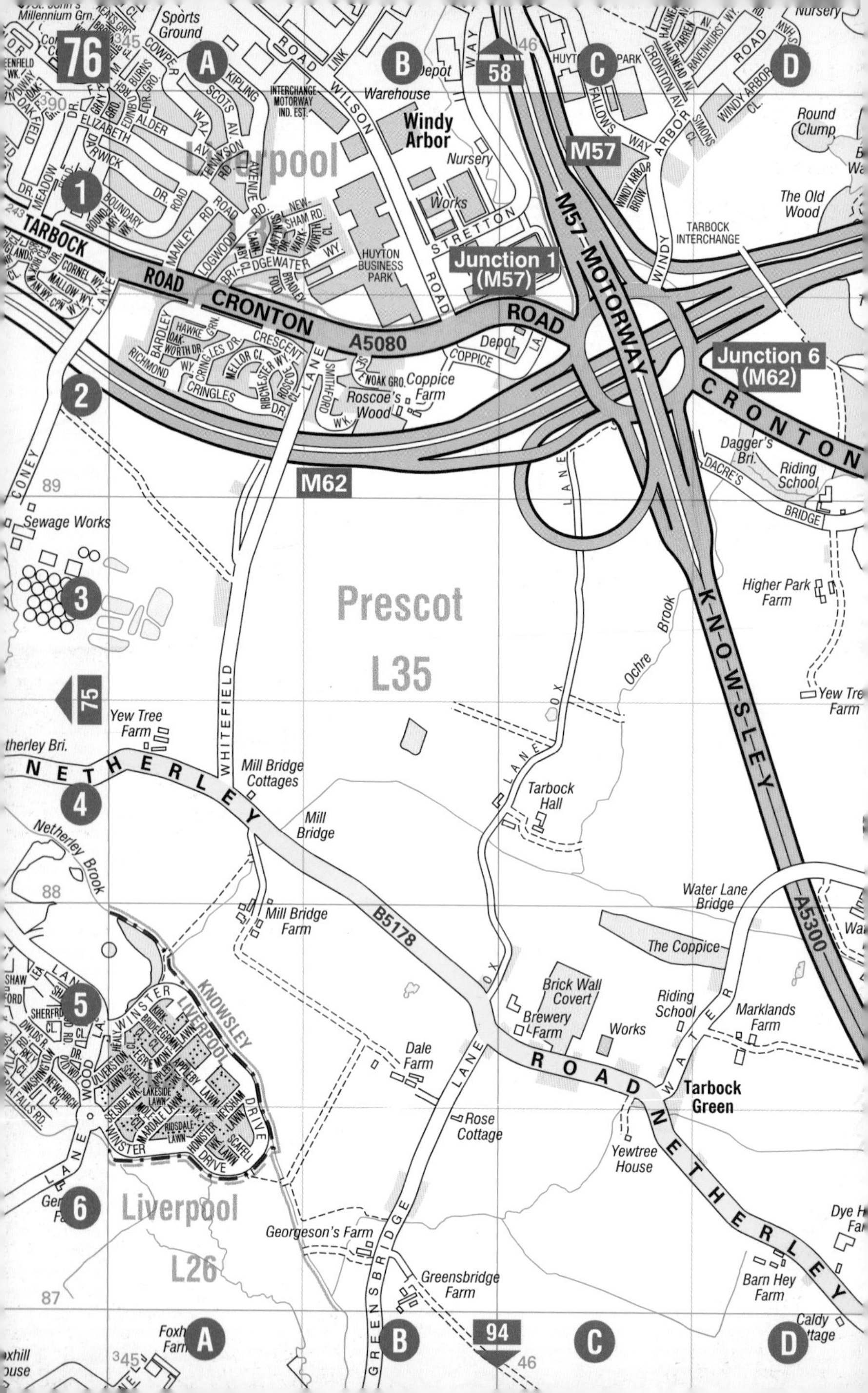
Liverpool
Prescot
L35
Liverpool
L26
Windy Arbor
Tarbock Green
CRONTON ROAD
A5080
M62
M57
M57 MOTORWAY
KNOWSLEY
A5300
Junction 1 (M57)
Junction 6 (M62)
TARBOCK INTERCHANGE
NETHERLEY ROAD
B5178
WHITEFIELD LANE
OX LANE
WATER LANE
GREENSBRIDGE LANE
WOOD LANE
DACRE'S BRIDGE
Sewage Works
Yew Tree Farm
Mill Bridge Cottages
Mill Bridge
Mill Bridge Farm
Netherley Brook
Tarbock Hall
Ochre Brook
Higher Park Farm
Riding School
Dagger's Bri.
Water Lane Bridge
The Coppice
Brick Wall Covert
Brewery Farm
Works
Marklands Farm
Dale Farm
Rose Cottage
Yewtree House
Georgeson's Farm
Greensbridge Farm
Barn Hey Farm
Round Clump
The Old Wood
Huyton Business Park
Interchange Motorway Ind. Est.
Warehouse
Depot
Nursery
Coppice Farm
Roscoe's Wood
Sports Ground
58
75
94

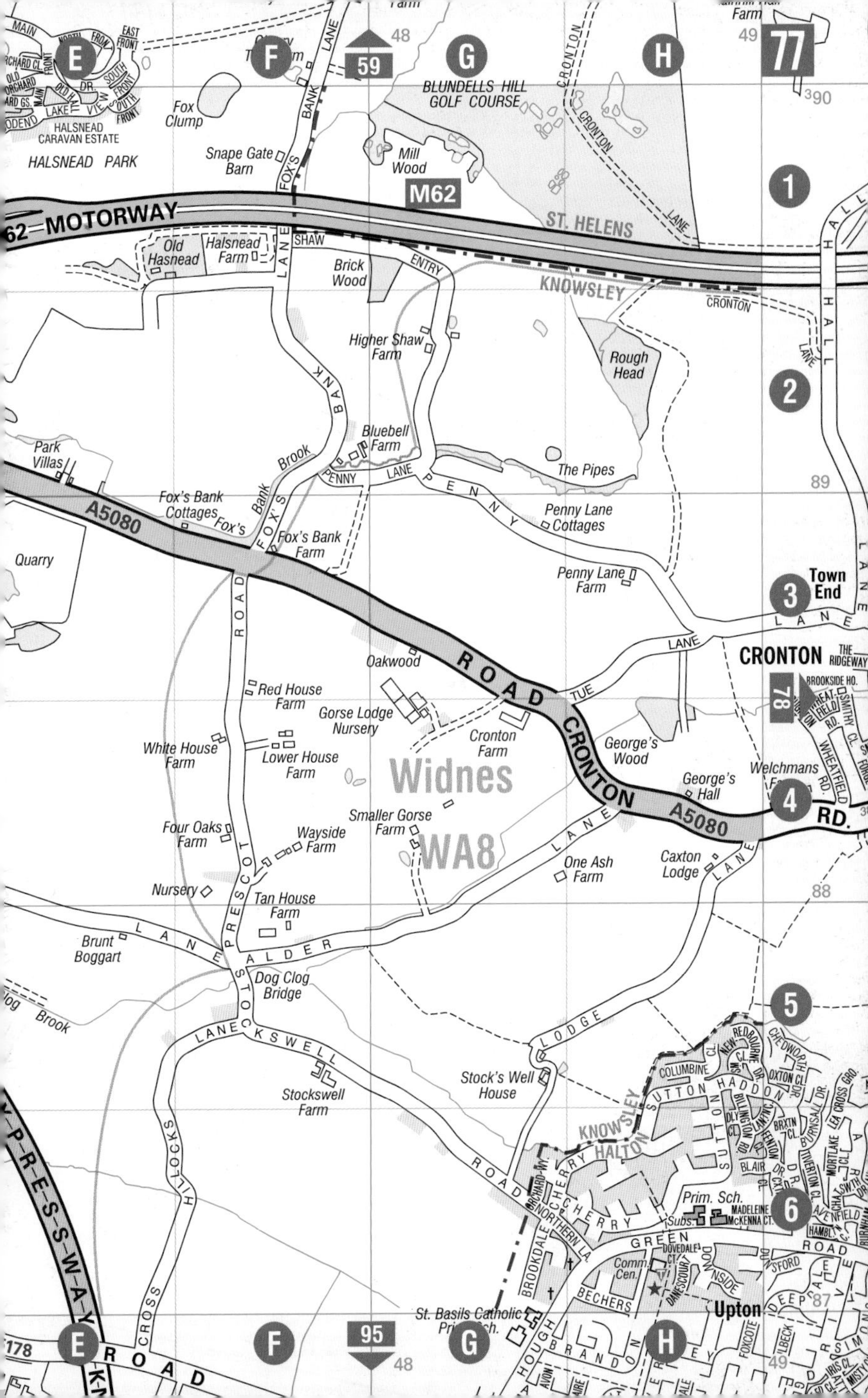
BLUNDELLS HILL GOLF COURSE
Fox Clump
HALSNEAD CARAVAN ESTATE
HALSNEAD PARK
Snape Gate Barn
Mill Wood
M62
M62 MOTORWAY
ST. HELENS
KNOWSLEY
Old Hasnead
Halsnead Farm
Brick Wood
Higher Shaw Farm
Rough Head
Bluebell Farm
The Pipes
Park Villas
Fox's Bank Cottages
A5080
Quarry
Fox's Bank Farm
Penny Lane Cottages
Penny Lane Farm
Town End
CRONTON
Oakwood
Red House Farm
Gorse Lodge Nursery
Cronton Farm
George's Wood
White House Farm
Lower House Farm
Widnes
WA8
George's Hall
Welchmans
Four Oaks Farm
Wayside Farm
Smaller Gorse Farm
One Ash Farm
Caxton Lodge
Nursery
Tan House Farm
Brunt Boggart
Dog Clog Bridge
Stock's Well House
Stockswell Farm
KNOWSLEY
HALTON
Prim. Sch.
Comm. Cen.
Upton
St. Basils Catholic Prim. Sch.
59
95
78

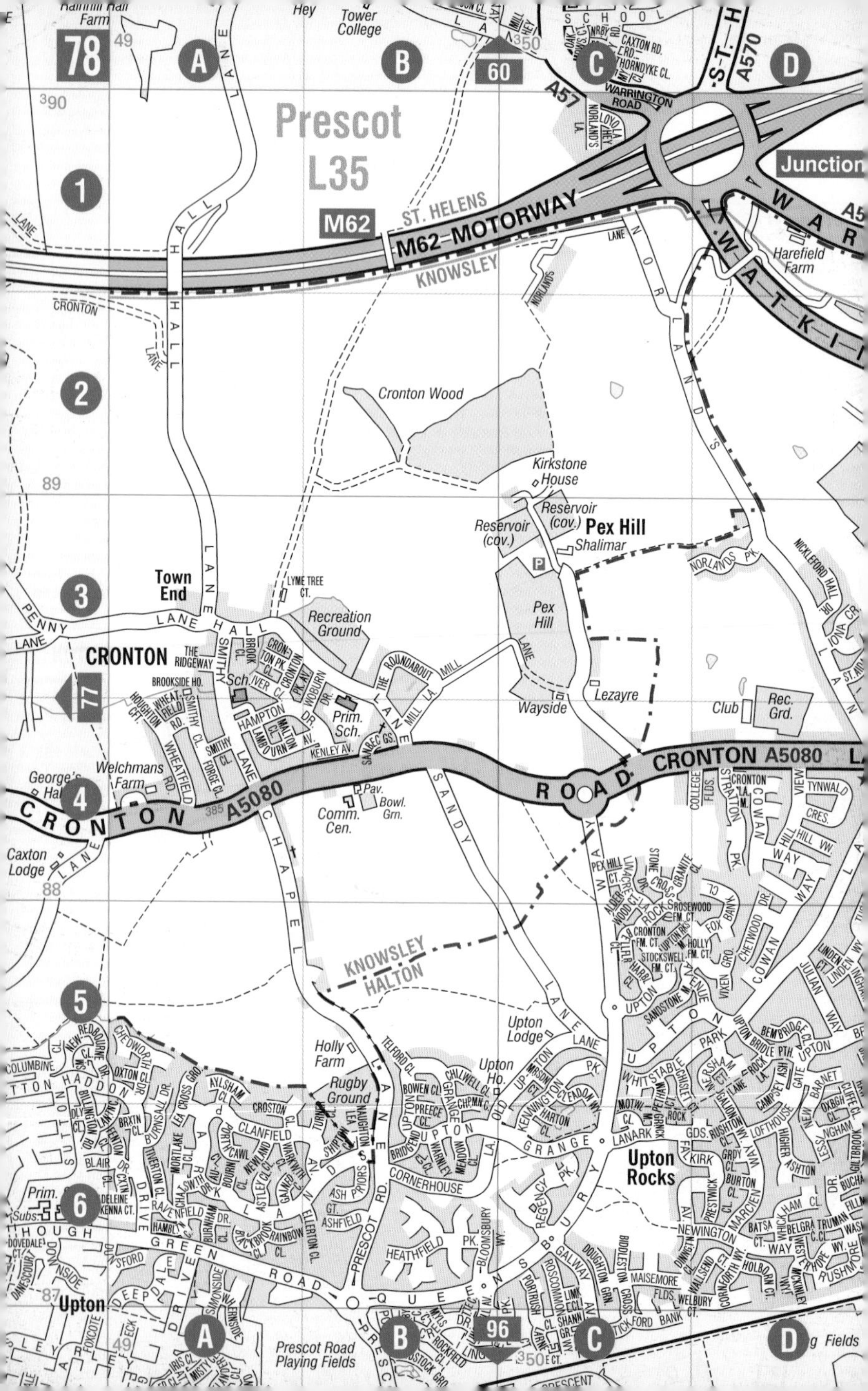

78
60
77
96
Prescot
L35
CRONTON
Town End
Pex Hill
Upton Rocks
Upton
Cronton Wood
Recreation Ground
Tower College
M62 MOTORWAY
CRONTON ROAD A5080
KNOWSLEY
HALTON
ST. HELENS
Prescot Road Playing Fields

79
61
80
97
E
F
G
H
1
2
3
4
5
6
M62
UNION BANK
JUBITS LANE
B5419
Union Bank Farm
Upper Bank Farm Cottage
TIBB'S CROSS LANE
Tibb's Cross Farm
Old Brook Hall Farm
ST. HELENS
HALTON
Bold Bridge Cottages
Wilmere House
Willowbank Farm
A57
ROAD
Nursery Farm
Bridge Farm
Model Farm
TWYFORD LANE
Bold Heath
FERNDALE CL.
A557
Widnes
WA8
Pavilion
Cranshaw Hall
CRANSHAW LA.
Glebe Farm
WILMERE LANE
Garden Centre
Rec. Ground
Bowling Greens
Lunt's Bridge Farm
Barnside
MILL GREEN
Mill Green Farm
Mill Green Cottage
LUNT'S HEATH ROAD
A5080
BOLD INDUSTRIAL ESTATE
WATKINSON WAY
DERBY ROAD
CORONER'S LANE
GLEBE LANE
Prim. Sch.
Grave Yd.
Farnworth C of E Prim. Sch.
Lunts Heath
Works
FARNWORTH
MOORFIELD
Moorfield Prim. Sch.
Youth Cen.
Club
Rec. Grd.
Cricket Grd.
Pav.
Widnes Crematorium
Cemetery
Widnes
LANCASTER ROAD
AVENUE
Fairfield High School
Playing Field
The Bongs
Brook
Bowyer's
BISHOPS WAY
Crow Wood Pk.
Tennis Cts.
Crow Wood
LOCKETT ROAD
Rose Gdn.
VICTORIA

Coney Green Wood
Old Hall Farm
Kebb's Farm
CLOCK FACE ROAD A569
Depot
Cross Farm
Duck Wood
Eccles Plantation
South Park Plantation
Club Ho.
MERSEY VALLEY GOLF COURSE
Nursery Farm
SCHOOL LA.
Bold Heath Plantation
WARRINGTON ROAD A57
Garden Centre
Bold Heath
FERNDALE CL.
Heathfield Farm
Bold Heath House Farm
Works
Widnes
WA8
ENTRY LANE
SANDY
Hayfield Farm
Greenside
MILL LANE
Barnside
MILL GREEN
Mill Green Cottage
South Lane Farm
SOUTH LA.
ST. HELENS
HALTON
SOUTH LANE A5080
DERBY RD.
Boundary Farm
Pendlebury Farm
Sunny Bank Cottages
Abbey Farm
Peel Farm
Barrow's Green
FARNWORTH
Sunnybank Woodland Park
Moorfield Prim. Sch.
Youth Cen.
Rec. Grd.
WEATES CL.
Whitfields Cross
CLOCK LANE
Fowl Farm
MOWCROFT
BACK LA.
Clock Lane Farm
Cuerdley Cross
A562
DAN'S RD.
WIDNES ROAD
Rosetree Farm
MOORFIELD ROAD
BARROW'S GREEN LANE

62
79
98

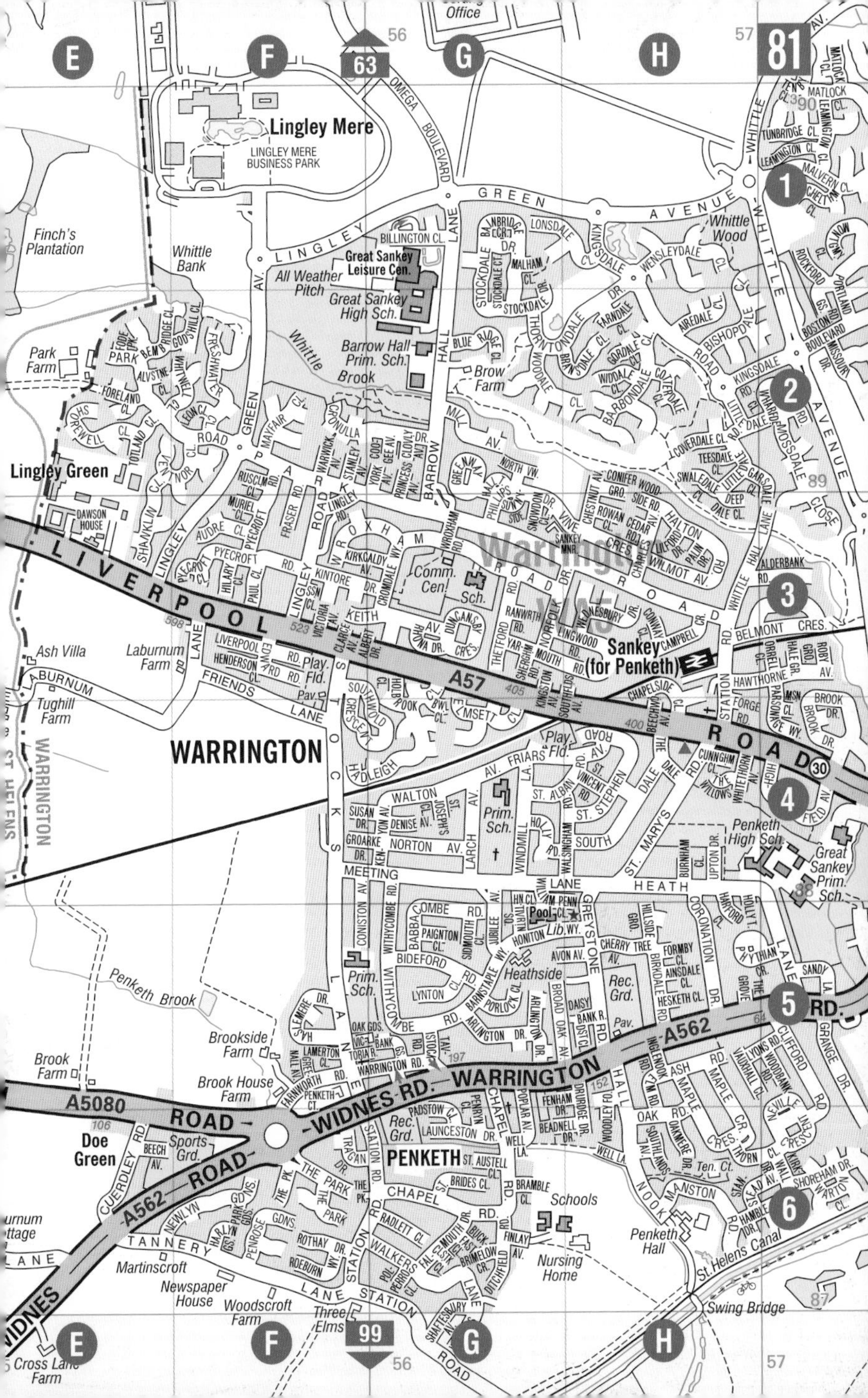

Lingley Mere
LINGLEY MERE BUSINESS PARK
Finch's Plantation
Whittle Bank
Great Sankey Leisure Cen.
All Weather Pitch
Great Sankey High Sch.
Barrow Hall Prim. Sch.
Whittle Brook
Brow Farm
Whittle Wood
Park Farm
Lingley Green
DAWSON HOUSE
LIVERPOOL ROAD
A57
Comm. Cen.
Sch.
Sankey (for Penketh)
Ash Villa
Laburnum Farm
Tughill Farm
WARRINGTON
Play. Fld.
Pav.
Prim. Sch.
Penketh High Sch.
Great Sankey Prim. Sch.
Pool
Lib.
Heathside
Rec. Grd.
Penketh Brook
Brookside Farm
Brook Farm
Brook House Farm
A5080
A562
WIDNES RD.
WARRINGTON ROAD
Doe Green
Sports Grd.
PENKETH
Schools
Nursing Home
Penketh Hall
St Helens Canal
Swing Bridge
Martinscroft
Newspaper House
Woodscroft Farm
Three Elms
Cross Lane Farm
63
99

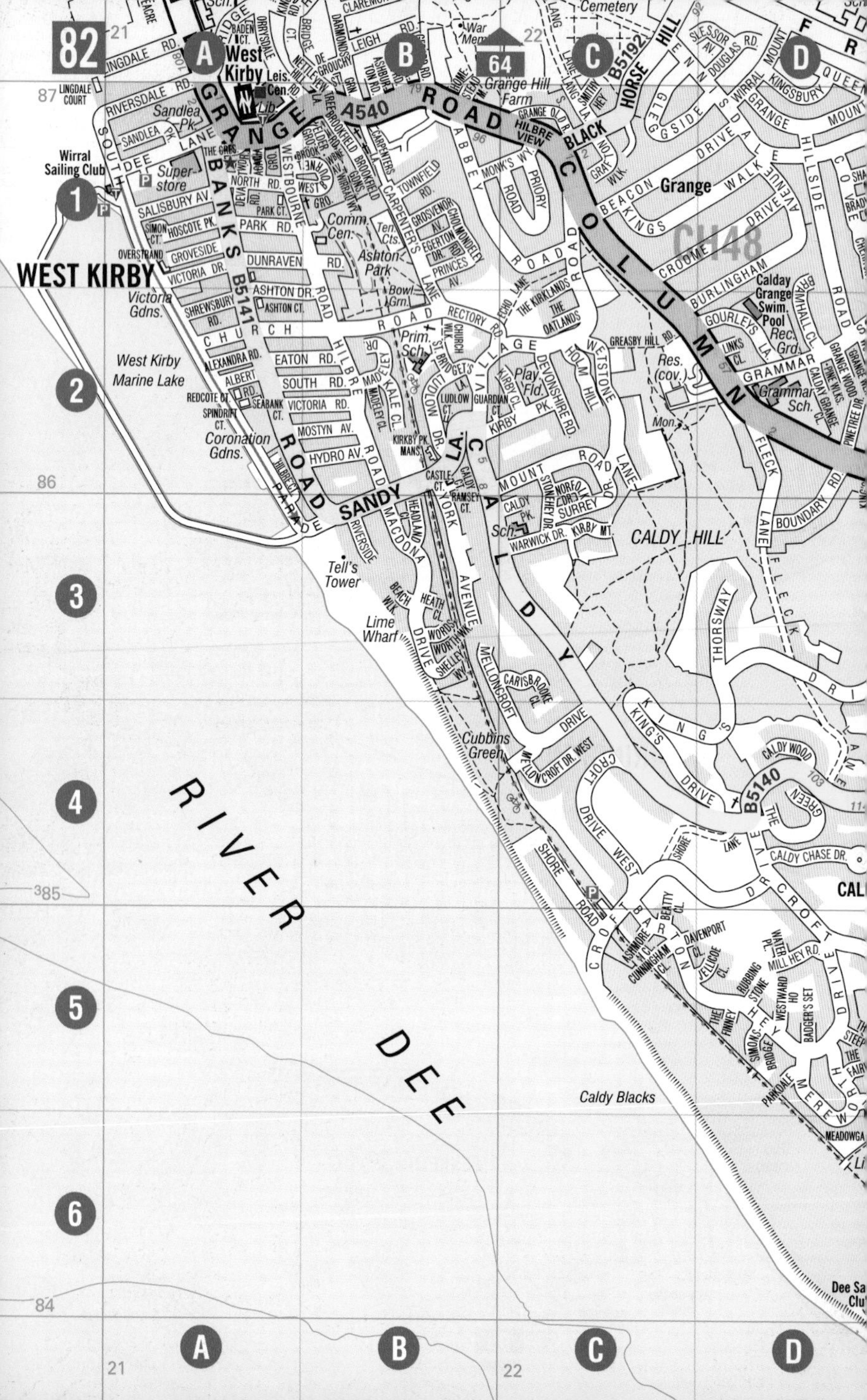

WEST KIRBY
West Kirby
Wirral Sailing Club
West Kirby Marine Lake
Victoria Gdns.
Coronation Gdns.
Sandlea Pk.
Super-store
Comm. Cen.
Ashton Park
Ten. Cts.
Bowl. Grn.
Prim. Sch.
Play Fld.
Grange Hill Farm
Grange
CH48
Calday Grange Swim. Pool
Rec. Grd.
Grammar Sch.
Res. (cov.)
Mon.
CALDY HILL
Tell's Tower
Lime Wharf
Cubbins Green
RIVER DEE
Caldy Blacks
Dee Sa Clu
GRANGE ROAD
A540
BANKS ROAD
B5141
COLUMN ROAD
B5192
B5140
BLACK HORSE HILL
SANDY LA.
CALDY ROAD
HILBRE ROAD
CHURCH ROAD
VILLAGE ROAD
MOUNT ROAD
KING'S DRIVE
CALDY CHASE DR.
SHORE ROAD
MELLONCROFT DR. WEST
CROFT DRIVE WEST
Cemetery
War Mem.

64

83
65
84
24
325
Larton
Larton Hey Farm
Nursery
Greasby
War Memorial
Manor Ho. Farm
Yew Tree Farm
Bay Tree Farm
Royden Hall
Bowling Green
Frankby
Hillcroft Poultry Farm
Newton
B5139
B5140
A540
Cemetery
Royden Manor
Birch House
Torpenhow
Nurseries
Football Ground
HILL BARK RD.
HILL BARK ROAD
ROYDEN PARK
Frankby Mere
Model Railway Centre
Quarry Farm
Hill Bark Farm House
Hill Bark
Roodee Mere
Irby Hi
Bowl. Grn.
Tennis Court
Playing Fields
Poultry Houses
Wirral
MONTGOMERY HILL
EAST FARM MEWS
Thurstaston Common Local Nature Reserve
PIKES HEY RD.
Paton Field (Sports Ground)
Pavilion
Hockey Pitch
Playing Field
Thurstaston Hill
Thur's Stone
Benty Farm
Strowan
Greasby Brook
Thurstaston Common Recreation Ground
Hillside Farm
SCHOOL LANE
Dawpool C of E Prim. School
DAWPOOL COTTAGES
TELEGRAPH ROAD
Club House
GOLF COURSE
Thurstaston
CH61
Dawpool
DAWPOOL FARM
Hill Farm
Rectory
CHURCH LA.
Thurstaston Hall
Church Farm Organics
Camping Site
Hall Farm
Copperfields
STATION ROAD
Nature Reserve
Caravan Park
GRANGE CROSS LANE
NEWTON PARK ROAD
LONG HEY ROAD
LINKS HEY ROAD
SANDY LANE
THURSTASTON ROAD
E
F
G
H
1
2
3
4
5
6

84
A
B
C
D
66
1
2
3
4
5
6
83
100
26
325
87
86
385
84
CH61
Football Ground
Greasby Inf. Sch.
Greenhouse Farm
Arrowe Brook Farm
Arrowe Bridge
Gorse Covert
Greasby Copse
Our Lady of Pity Catholic Prim. Sch.
Greasby Junior School
Arrowe Brook Farm
Fish Pond
Nicholson's Plantation
Green Gates
Redstones Farm
Quarry Farm
Hill Bark Farm House
Cricket Ground
Irby Hill
Irby Hill Farm
Arrowe Brook
Neilson's Plantation
Limbo Lane Plantation
Irby Prim. Sch.
Play. Field
Playing Fields
Irby Heath
Hall
Harrock Wood
Lib.
Manor Court
Irby Farm
IRBY
Irby Hall
Rectory
Church Farm
Camping Site
Hall Farm
Hill Farm
Cricket Ground
Greasby Brook
Arrowe Commercial Park
GREASBY RD.
LLOYD DR.
FERGUSON AV.
HARVEY AV.
ARROWE PARK RD.
ARROWE BROOK RD.
ARROWE BROOK LANE
MILL LANE
BARK RD.
HILL BARK RD.
ARROWE PARK RD.
LIMBO LANE
SANDY LANE
SANDY LA. NORTH
THORNS DRIVE
HEATHBANK AV.
HILLVIEW RD.
GLENWOOD DR.
THINGWALL RD.
IRBY RD.
THURSTASTON RD.
TELEGRAPH RD.
A540
CHURCH LA.
WOODLANDS RD.
RIDGEWOOD DR.
CORNELIUS DR.
KING'S DR.
WHALEY LA.
PARKWAY

85
67
101
98
E
F
G
H
1
2
3
4
5
6
CH49
Wirral
Woodchurch
Landican
Thingwall
Junction 3
M53
M53 MOTORWAY
A551
A552
B5138
ARROWE PARK ROAD
WOODCHURCH ROAD
BARNSTON ROAD
LANDICAN ROAD
LANDICAN LANE
WOODCHURCH LA.
HOME FARM ROAD
COMMONFIELD ROAD
SANDFIELD RD.
SCHOOLFIELD RD.
CHURCH LANE
CHILDWALL GREEN
POOL LA.
SHERRY LA.
MEADOW CRESCENT
NEW HEY ROAD
CARR BRIDGE RD.
GANNEY'S MEADOW
HOOLE ROAD
HOUGHTON RD.
PEMBERTON RD.
ARROWE PARK HOSPITAL
High Sch. Engineering College
St. Michael & All Angels Catholic Prim. Sch.
Playing Field
Subway
Playground
Superstore
Lib.
Hall
School
Sports Ground
PRENTON WAY BUS. UNITS
Total Fitness
Landican Cemetery and Crematorium
Bowling Greens
Tennis Courts
Pavilion
Day Care Centre
COUNTRY PARK
Miniature Golf Course
Club Ho.
Robinson's Plantation
Card Plantation
Home Farm
Old Hall Farm
E PARK GOLF COURSE
Nursery
HINGWALL ROAD
RD. EAST
MILL ROAD
The Farm
Caravan Park
GALLOPERS LA.
THINGWALL GRANGE
LWR. THINGWALL LANE
Thingwall Prim. Sch.
Stanley Sch.
PARKS LANE
SEVEN ACRES LANE
THE LEAS
AVENUE
BARNSDALE AV.
REGENTS CL.
Thingwall Rec. Cen.
Bowl. Grn.
Ten. Cts.
Res. (cov.)
Crosshill Reservoir (cov.)
MURRAYFIELD SPIRE HOSPITAL
Lower Heath Wood
Sewage Works
Football Ground
Cross Hill
HOLMWOOD DRIVE
HOLMWOOD AV.
STATION ROAD
STORETON LA.
PRIVATE DR.
OVERDALE AV.
Youth Centre
Prenton Brook
Riding Centre
Gills Lane Farm
GILLS LANE
THORNCROFT DR.
PENSBY RD.
WOODLANDS
Storet Brickfie

Junction 3
Townfield Prim. School
Oxton St. Saviour's C of E Prim. Sch.
Recreation Ground
Playing Field
Shop. Cen.
A552
B5151
Spts. Grd.
WOODCHURCH ROAD
STORETON ROAD
Prenton
CH43
Prenton Prim. Sch.
Lib.
Playing Field
Pav.
Walker Park
Prenton Dell
Old Rockferrians Rugby Ground
PRENTON
Club House
PRENTON GOLF COURSE
PRENTON WAY BUS. UNITS
Total Fitness
NORTH CHESHIRE TRADING ESTATE
M53 MOTORWAY
M53
CH49
CH61
Cow Hey Covert
Marsh Hey Covert
Ethel's Covert
Prenton Brook
Stanley Wood
Grange Farm
Wirral
Little Storeton
Storeton
Storeton Hall Farm
Storeton House Farm
Home Farm
Storeton Lodge
Storeton Brickfields
STATION ROAD
LANDICAN LANE
ROMAN ROAD
New Hey Covert
New Hey Triangle
Rake Hey

68
85
102

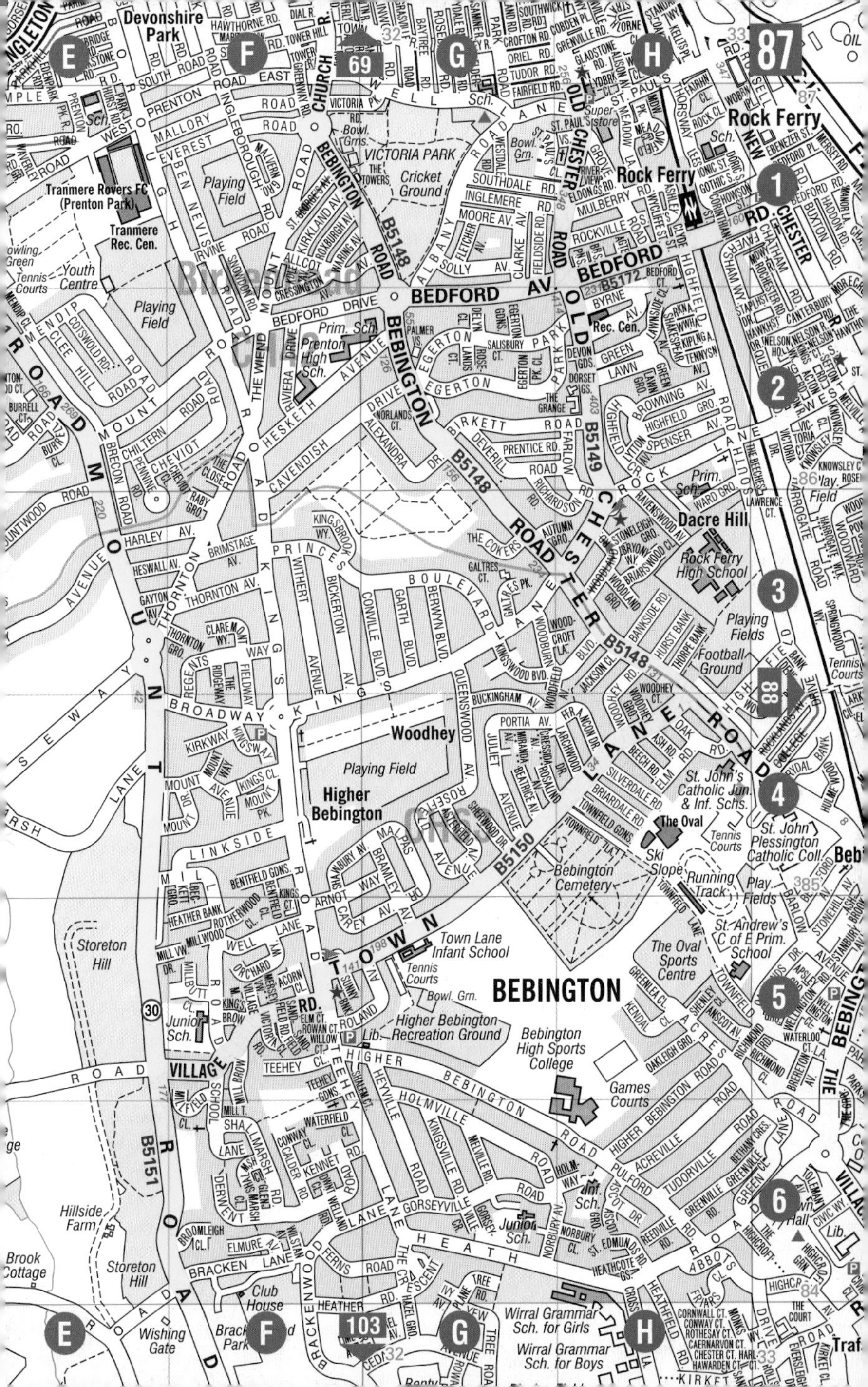

87
E
F
G
H
69
103
Devonshire Park
Rock Ferry
Tranmere Rovers FC (Prenton Park)
Tranmere Rec. Cen.
Youth Centre
Tennis Courts
Playing Field
VICTORIA PARK
Cricket Ground
Bowl. Grns.
Prim. Sch.
Prenton High Sch.
Rec. Cen.
Dacre Hill
Rock Ferry High School
Playing Fields
Football Ground
Woodhey
Higher Bebington
St. John's Catholic Jun. & Inf. Schs.
The Oval
Ski Slope
Running Track
Bebington Cemetery
St. John Plessington Catholic Coll.
St. Andrew's C of E Prim. School
The Oval Sports Centre
BEBINGTON
Town Lane Infant School
Higher Bebington Recreation Ground
Bebington High Sports College
Games Courts
Storeton Hill
Hillside Farm
Brook Cottage
Wishing Gate
Club House
Junior Sch.
Inf. Sch.
Wirral Grammar Sch. for Girls
Wirral Grammar Sch. for Boys
Town Hall
BEDFORD AV.
BEDFORD DRIVE
BEBINGTON ROAD
OLD CHESTER ROAD
MOUNT ROAD
KINGS LANE
TOWN LANE
HIGHER BEBINGTON ROAD
HEATH ROAD
PRINCES BOULEVARD
ROCK LANE
B5148
B5149
B5150
B5151
B5172
1
2
3
4
5
6

A
B
C
D
70
34
33
TERMINAL
Rock Ferry Pier
Rock Ferry
1
2
3
4
5
6
ROCK FERRY BY-PASS
A41
NEW CHESTER ROAD
B5136
ESPLANADE
RIVER
Rock Park
Football Grd.
Bus Depot
Play. Field
Dacre Hill
Rock Ferry High School
Playing Fields
Football Ground
Tennis Courts
New Ferry Park
87
CHESTER RD.
B5148
St. John's Cath. Jun. & Inf. Sch.
The Oval
St. John Plessington Catholic Coll.
Ski Slope
Running Track
385
Bebington
BEBINGTON
The Oval Sports Cen.
NEW FERRY
Playing Field
Sewage Works
Refuse Tip
Warehouse
DOCK RD. NORTH
Depot
Lady Lever Art Gall.
Mus
Prim. Sch.
War Meml.
Mayer Park
Council Offices
Lower Bebington
Ormerod Gdns.
Town Hall
Lib.
Port Sunlight Driving Range
Golf Course
Works
Bromborough Pool
Refuse Tip
Bromborough Pool Bridge
PORT SUNLIGHT
Port Sunlight
Sports Club
Sports Ground
Bowl. Grn.
OLD COURT HOUSE RD.
Pavilion
104
84
Trafalgar

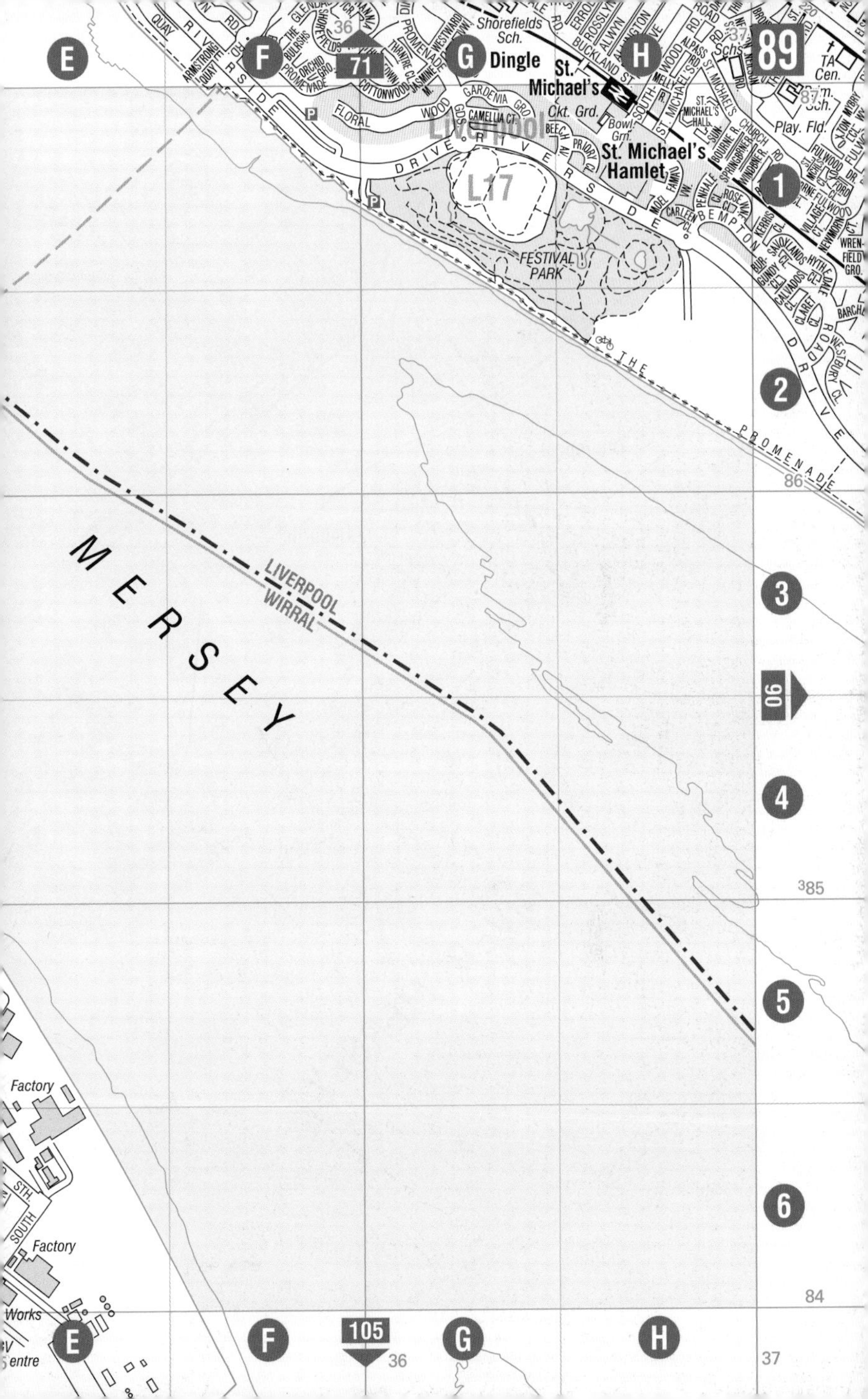

89
E
F
G
H
71
36
Dingle
Shorefields Sch.
St. Michael's
Ckt. Grd.
Bowl. Grn.
St. Michael's Hamlet
Liverpool
L17
FESTIVAL PARK
RIVERSIDE DRIVE
FLORAL WOOD
CAMELLIA CT.
GARDENIA GRO.
BUCKLAND ST.
ALWYN
ROSSLYN
ERROL
BEMPTON
ROAD
DRIVE
THE PROMENADE
TA Cen.
Prim. Sch.
Play. Fld.
86
MERSEY
LIVERPOOL
WIRRAL
90
1
2
3
4
5
6
385
84
Factory
Factory
Works
SOUTH
STH
105
36
37

90
A
B
C
D
1
2
3
4
5
6
72
89
106
37
38
86
85
84
Aigburth Vale
Carnatic Halls (Halls of Residence)
AIGBURTH RD.
ASHFIELD RD.
A5058
VICTORIA ROAD
ELMSWOOD
MOSSLEY HILL DR.
Prim. Sch.
Play. Fld.
RIVERSIDE
BEMPTON RD.
FULWOOD RD.
AMPTHILL RD.
ASHBOURNE RD.
LARKFIELD RD.
JERICHO LANE
OTTERSPOOL ROAD
Otterspool
Play. Flds.
Playing Fields
Otterspool Park
The Cottage
Aigburth
Sudley House
Sports Ground
Nurs. Home
Sch.
L17
High Sch.
Pav.
A561
Rec. Grd.
Sports Grd.
Alfred Holt Athletics Grd.
Play Area
Nursing Home
THE PROMENADE
OTTERSPOOL DRIVE
THE DRIVE
MERSEY ROAD
RIVERSDALE RD.
MOSSLEY HILL ROAD
ROSEMONT ROAD
BARKHILL ROAD
SUDLEY GRANGE
RIVER MERSEY
LIVERPOOL

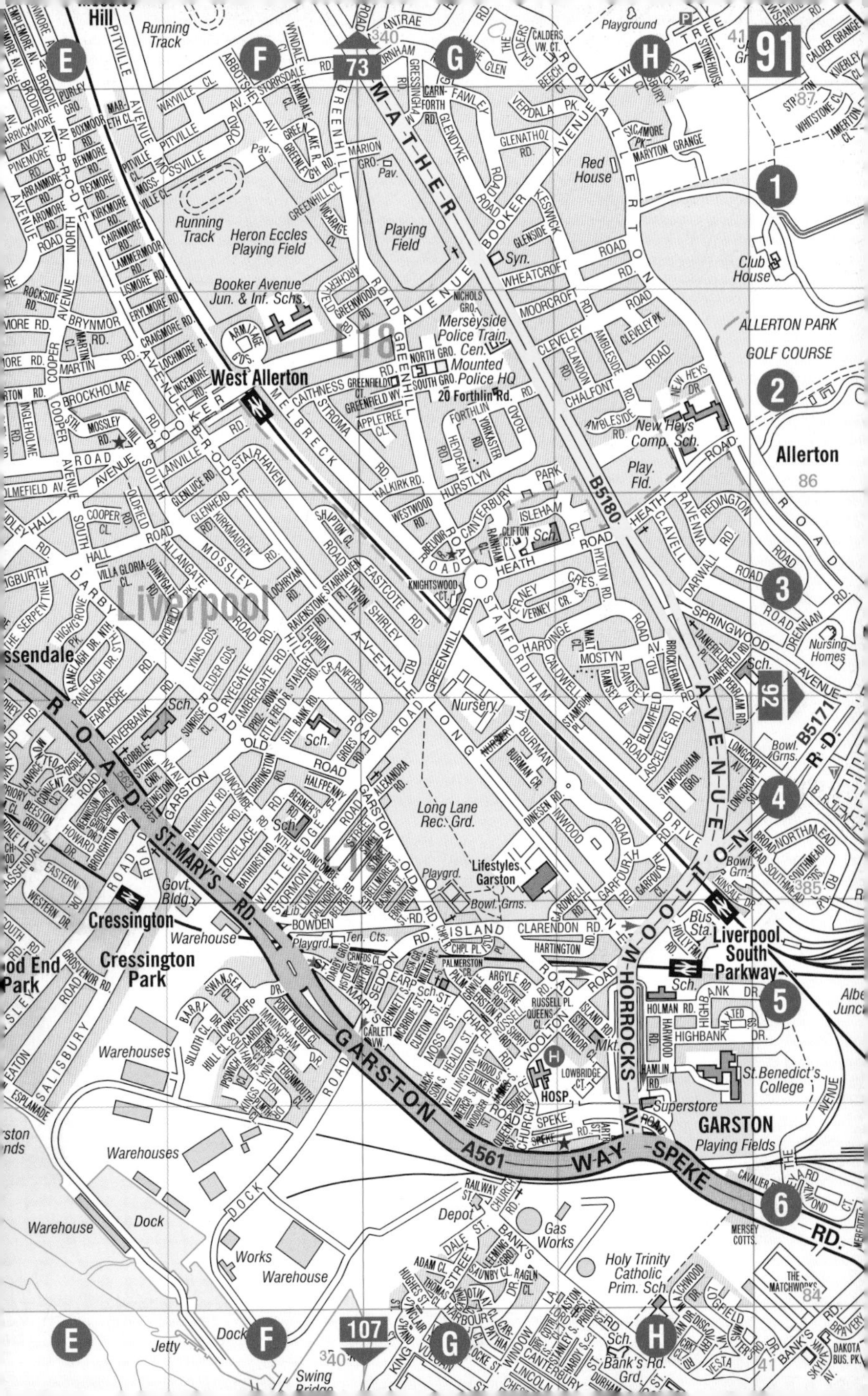
91
73
107
92
E
F
G
H
1
2
3
4
5
6
Liverpool
L18
L19
West Allerton
Allerton
Cressington
Cressington Park
Liverpool South Parkway
GARSTON
Allerton Park Golf Course
Heron Eccles Playing Field
Running Track
Playing Field
Red House
Club House
Booker Avenue Jun. & Inf. Schs.
Merseyside Police Train. Cen.
Mounted Police HQ
20 Forthlin Rd.
New Heys Comp. Sch.
Play. Fld.
Nursing Homes
Nursery
Long Lane Rec. Grd.
Lifestyles Garston
St. Benedict's College
GARSTON Playing Fields
Superstore
HOSP.
Gas Works
Holy Trinity Catholic Prim. Sch.
Warehouses
Warehouse
Dock
Works
Jetty
Depot
Govt. Bldg.
Swing Bridge
Bank's Rd. Grd.
Mkt.
Bus Sta.
A561
B5180
B5171
MATHER AVENUE
BOOKER AVENUE
ALLERTON ROAD
WOOLTON ROAD
GARSTON WAY
SPEKE RD.
ST. MARY'S RD.
AIGBURTH ROAD
MOSSLEY HILL
HORROCKS AV.
BRODIE AVENUE
MERSEY COTTS.
THE MATCHWORKS
DAKOTA BUS. PK.

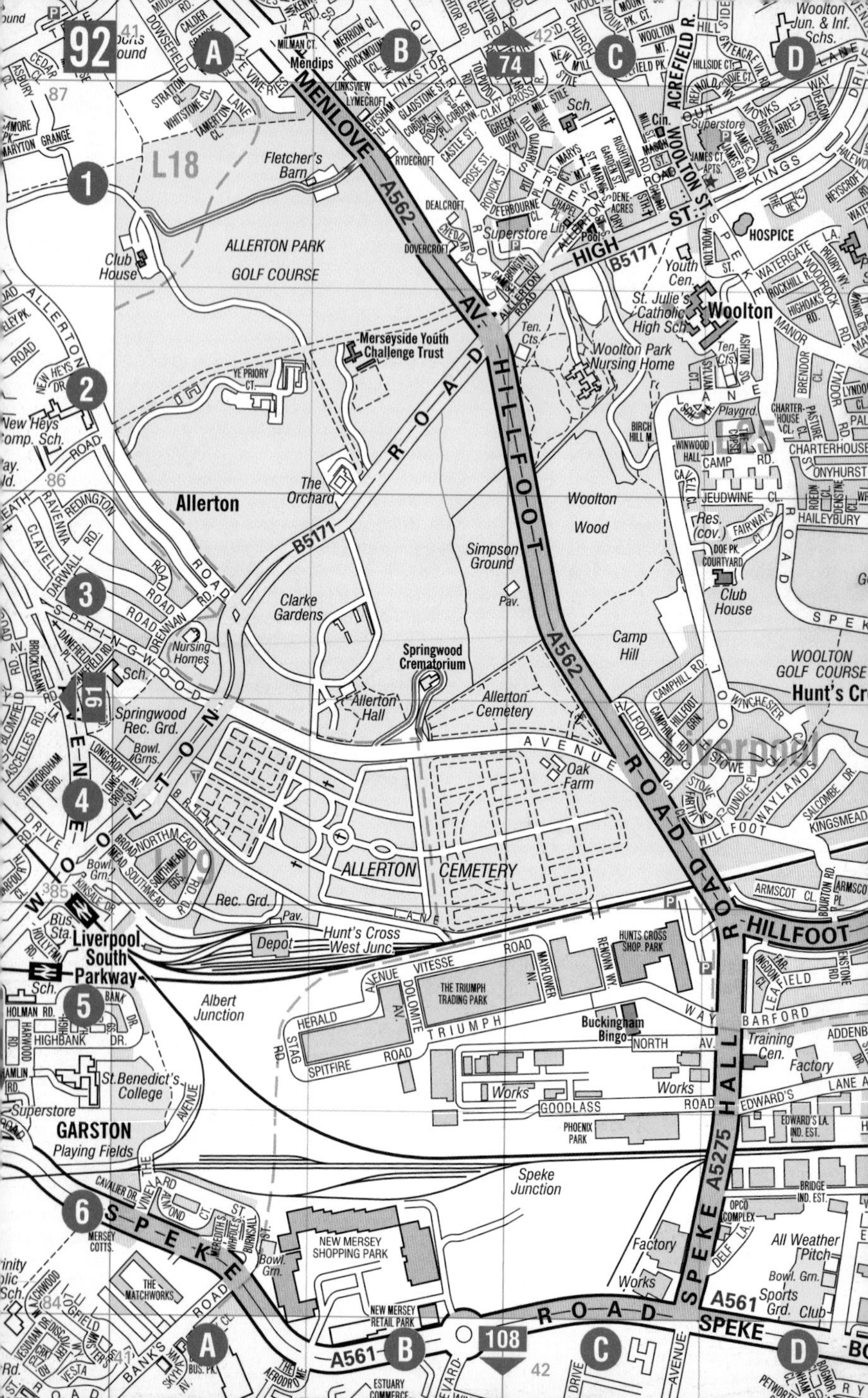

92
A
B
C
D
74
108
1
2
3
4
5
6
L18
MENLOVE
A562
AV.
HILLFOOT
ROAD
Mendips
Fletcher's Barn
ALLERTON PARK
GOLF COURSE
Club House
Merseyside Youth
Challenge Trust
The Orchard
Allerton
B5171
Clarke Gardens
Springwood
Crematorium
Allerton Hall
Allerton Cemetery
ALLERTON
CEMETERY
Simpson Ground
Woolton Wood
Camp Hill
Woolton Park
Nursing Home
St. Julie's
Catholic
High Sch.
Woolton
HIGH
ST.
HOSPICE
Superstore
WOOLTON
GOLF COURSE
Hunt's Cross West Junc.
Depot
Liverpool
South
Parkway
Albert
Junction
THE TRIUMPH
TRADING PARK
HUNTS CROSS
SHOP. PARK
Buckingham
Bingo
Works
Factory
Training Cen.
Speke
Junction
SPEKE
A5275
HALL
St.Benedict's
College
GARSTON
Playing Fields
NEW MERSEY
SHOPPING PARK
NEW MERSEY
RETAIL PARK
THE MATCHWORKS
A561
All Weather
Pitch
Sports
Grd.
Club
Springwood
Rec. Grd.
Nursing
Homes
New Heys
Comp. Sch.
Rec. Grd.
Oak Farm

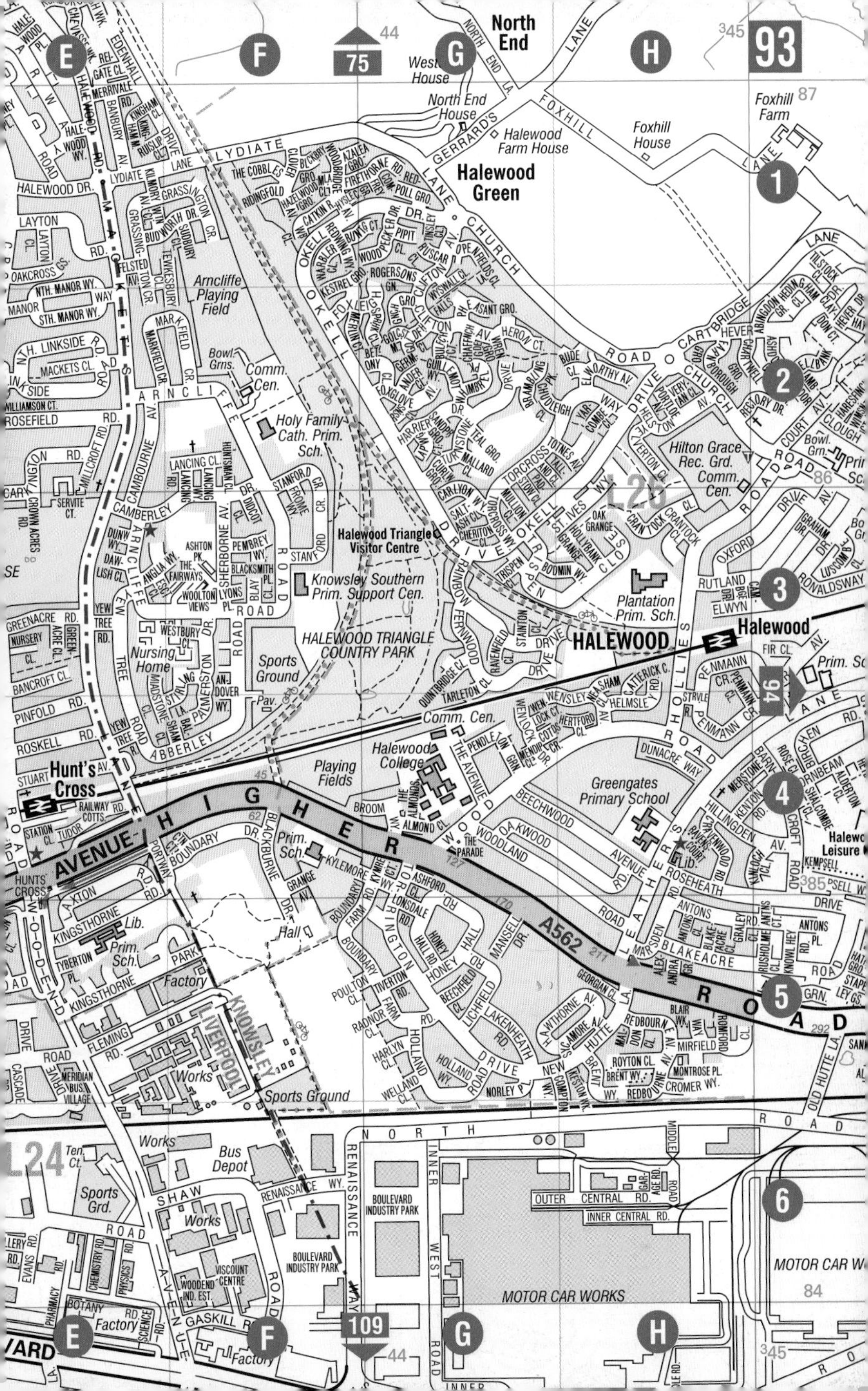

93
North End
Halewood Green
Foxhill Farm
Foxhill House
Halewood Farm House
North End House
West House
Arncliffe Playing Field
Holy Family Cath. Prim. Sch.
Halewood Triangle Visitor Centre
Knowsley Southern Prim. Support Cen.
HALEWOOD TRIANGLE COUNTRY PARK
Sports Ground
Nursing Home
Hilton Grace Rec. Grd. Comm. Cen.
Plantation Prim. Sch.
HALEWOOD
Halewood
L25
Halewood College
Playing Fields
Greengates Primary School
Hunt's Cross
HIGHER AVENUE
HIGHER ROAD
A562
Sports Ground
Works
Bus Depot
Sports Grd.
L24
BOULEVARD INDUSTRY PARK
VISCOUNT CENTRE
WOODEND IND. EST.
MOTOR CAR WORKS
NORTH ROAD
LYDIATE LANE
CHURCH ROAD
FOXHILL LANE
OKELL DRIVE
ARNCLIFFE ROAD
HOLLIES ROAD
WOODEND AVENUE
SHAW ROAD
LIVERPOOL
KNOWSLEY
109
75
94

Georgeson's Farm
Foxhill Farm
Foxhill House
Greensbridge Farm
Caldy Cottage
Prescot
L35
Cart Bridge
Green's Bridge Plantation
Green's Bridge
Ditton Brook
Hilton Grace Rec. Grd.
Prim. Sch.
The Hayes
Yew Tree Farm
Halewood
HALEWOOD
L26
Prim. Sch.
Halewood Caravan Park
Ireland's Farm
Highfield School
Halewood Leisure Cen.
Ditton Fold Farm
Liverpool
Brook Cottage
Finch Farm
Wellbrook Farm
RSPCA Centre
HIGHER A562 ROAD
SPEKE A562
Manor Farm
BOULEVARD A561
Ramsbrook Farm
Millfield
Burnt Mill Cottages
Crab Tree Rough
L24
MOTOR CAR WORKS
Hop Yard Wood
Sewage Works
Ramsbrook

76
93
110

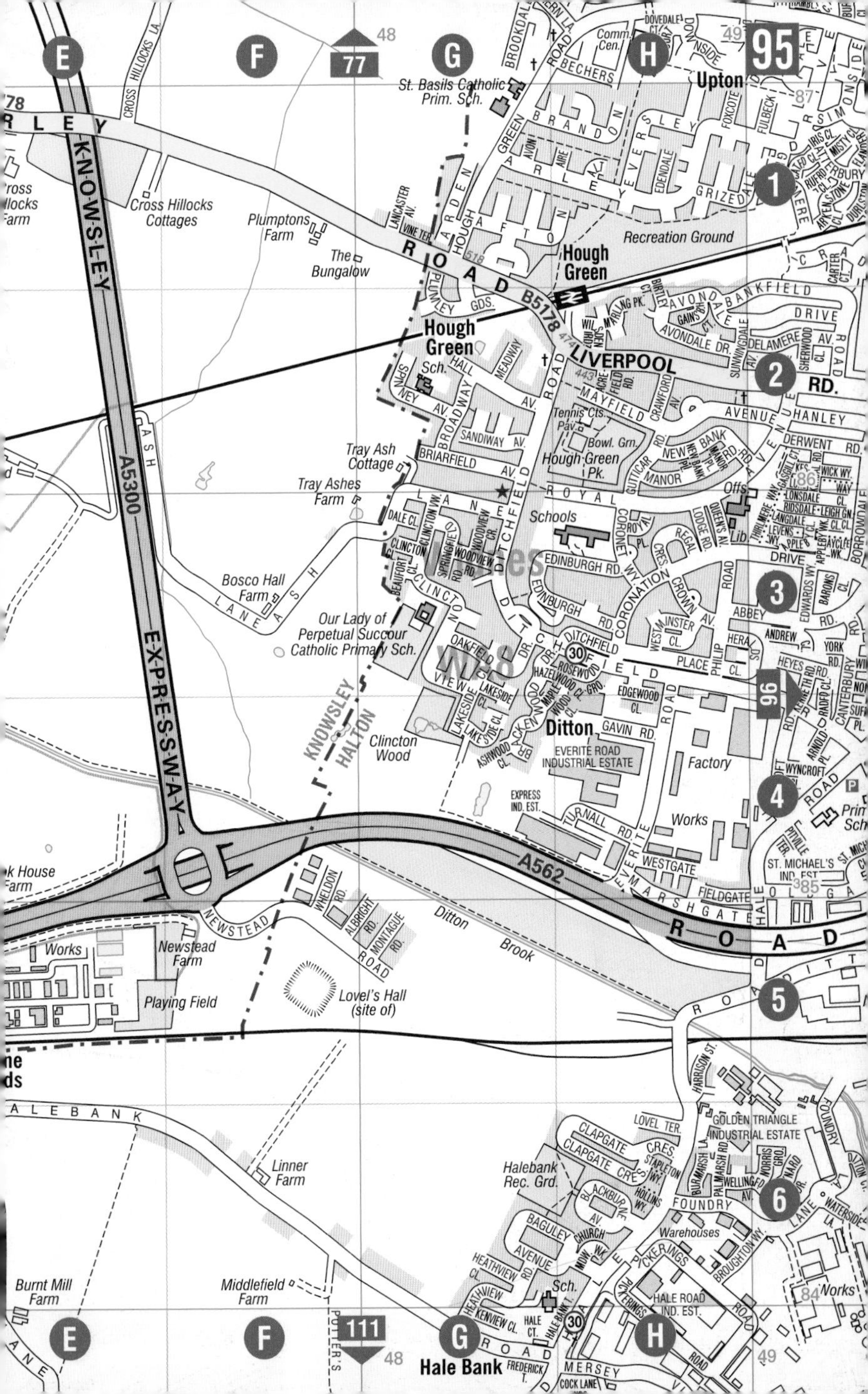
95
77
48
49
87
86
385
84
96
111
E
F
G
H
1
2
3
4
5
6
Upton
St. Basils Catholic Prim. Sch.
Comm. Cen.
BECHERS
BRANDON
EVERSLEY
FOXCOTE
FULBECK
SIMONSIDE
GRIZEDALE
EDENDALE
AVON
AIRE
ARLEY
AFTON
HOUGH GREEN
ARDEN
LANCASTER AV.
VINE TER.
Recreation Ground
Hough Green
B5178
ROAD
PLUMLEY GDS.
Hough Green Sch.
SPINNEY AV.
HALL
MEADWAY
BROADWAY
SANDIWAY AV.
BRIARFIELD AV.
LIVERPOOL RD.
AVONDALE DR.
BANKFIELD DRIVE
DELAMERE AV.
SUNNINGDALE AV.
SHERWOOD CL.
MAYFIELD
CRAWFORD AV.
HANLEY
AVENUE
DERWENT RD.
Tennis Cts. Pav.
Bowl. Grn.
Hough Green Pk.
NEW BANK PL.
MANOR
GUTTICAR RD.
ROYAL
Offs.
Lib.
THIRLMERE WAY
LONSDALE
RIDSDALE
LANGDALE
LEVENS
APPLEBY
AYCLIFFE
BORROWDALE
DRIVE
Schools
CORONET WY.
REGAL CRES.
LODGE RD.
QUEEN'S AV.
DITCHFIELD ROAD
EDINBURGH RD.
CORONATION
CROWN AV.
WESTMINSTER CL.
ABBEY RD.
EDWARDS WY.
BARONS CL.
ANDREW
YORK
HERALD
PHILIP
PLACE
HEYES RD.
CANTERBURY
Tray Ash Cottage
Tray Ashes Farm
LANE
DALE CL.
CLINCTON VW.
CLINCTON CL.
SPRINGFIELD RD.
WOODVIEW CR.
WOODVIEW RD.
BEAUFORT CL.
CLINCTON
Our Lady of Perpetual Succour Catholic Primary Sch.
OAKFIELD DR.
VIEW
LAKESIDE
LAKESIDE CL.
DITCHFIELD
ROSEWOOD
HAZELWOOD GRO.
MAPLE
BRACKENWOOD
ASHWOOD CL.
EDGEWOOD CL.
GAVIN RD.
Ditton
EVERITE ROAD INDUSTRIAL ESTATE
Factory
Works
KNOWSLEY
HALTON
Clincton Wood
EXPRESS IND. EST.
TURNALL RD.
EVERITE
WESTGATE
FIELDGATE
MARSHGATE
HALE
ST. MICHAEL'S IND. EST.
WYNCROFT
ARNOLD PL.
A562
Ditton Brook
ROAD
DITTON ROAD
Cross Hillocks Cottages
CROSS HILLOCKS LA.
Plumptons Farm
The Bungalow
KNOWSLEY EXPRESSWAY
A5300
ASH LANE
Bosco Hall Farm
NEWSTEAD
WHELDON RD.
ALBRIGHT RD.
MONTAGUE RD.
ROAD
Newstead Farm
Works
Playing Field
Lovel's Hall (site of)
HALEBANK
Linner Farm
Burnt Mill Farm
Middlefield Farm
POTTER'S
HARRISON ST.
LOVEL TER.
GOLDEN TRIANGLE INDUSTRIAL ESTATE
CLAPGATE CRES.
STAPLETON WY.
HOLLINS WY.
Halebank Rec. Grd.
BLACKBURNE AV.
BURMARSH LA.
PALMARSH RD.
NORRIS GRO.
WELLINGFORD AV.
FOUNDRY
FOUNDRY LANE
WATERSIDE LA.
Warehouses
BAGULEY AVENUE
CHURCH
MDW. WK.
BROUGHTON WY.
PICKERINGS ROAD
HEATHVIEW CL.
HEATHVIEW RD.
KENVIEW CL.
Sch.
HALE CT.
HALE BANK T.
HALE ROAD IND. EST.
Hale Bank
FREDERICK T.
MERSEY
COCK LANE
ROAD
Works
Prim. Sch.

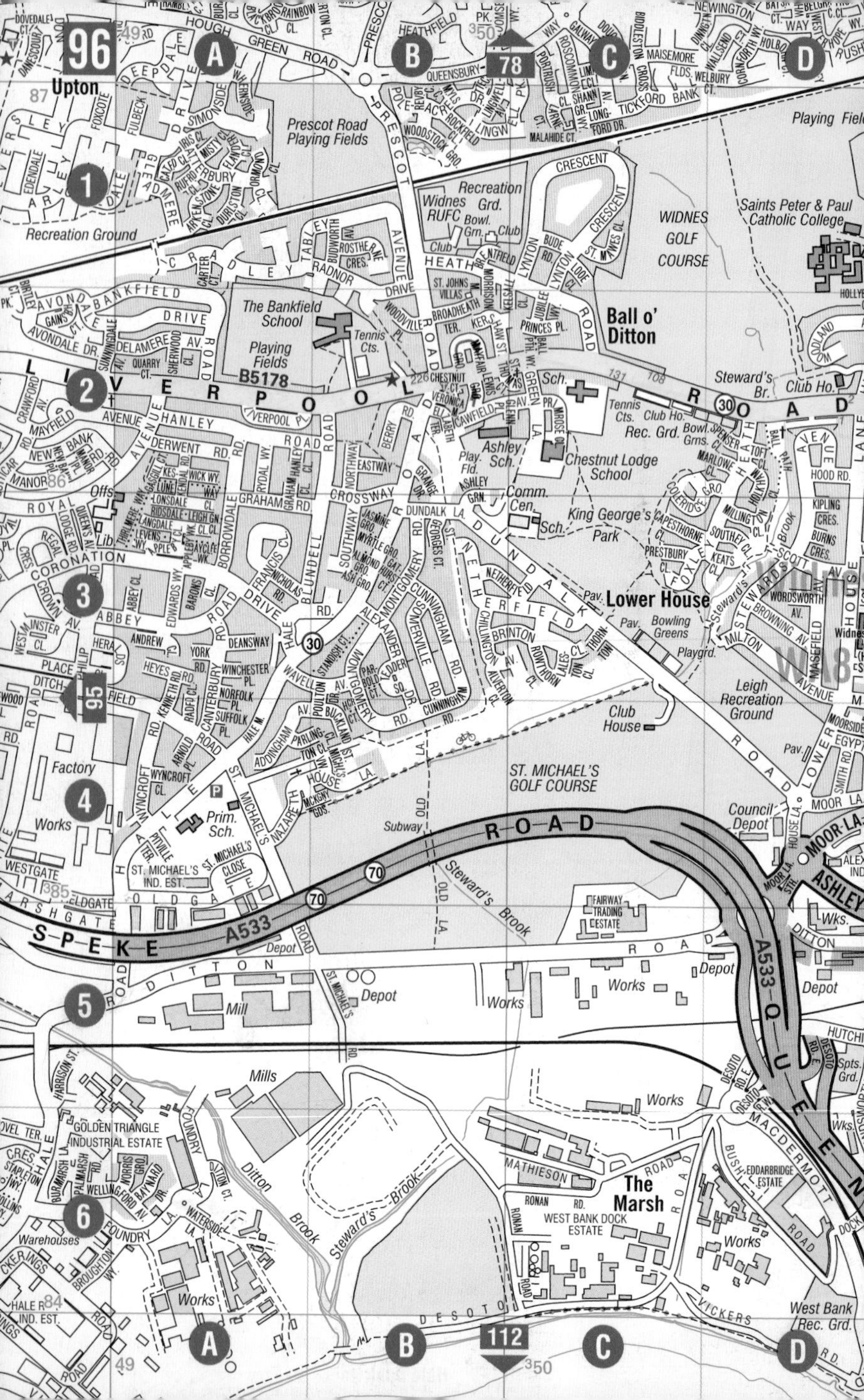

A
B
C
D
1
2
3
4
5
6
78
95
112
Upton
Hough Green Road
Prescot Road
Prescot Road Playing Fields
Queensbury
Heathfield
Newington
Maisemore
Biddleston Cross
Tickford Bank
Welbury Ct.
Longford Dr.
Malahide Ct.
Woodstock Gro.
Rockfield
Deepdale Drive
Simonside
Fulbeck
Foxcote
Edendale
Canterbury
Gleadmere
Arkenstone
Durliston
Ormond Cl.
Recreation Ground
Recreation Grd.
Widnes RUFC
Bowl. Grn.
Club
Crescent
Bude Rd.
Lynton Road
Lynton Crescent
St. Mawes Cl.
Looe Cl.
Widnes Golf Course
Saints Peter & Paul Catholic College
Playing Fields
Cradley
Tabley
Budworth Av.
Rostherne Av.
Radnor
Avenue
Heath
Brentfield
Drive
Morrison
Kelsall Cl.
Jubilee Wy.
Ball o' Ditton
St. Johns Villas
Broadheath Ter.
Woodville Pl.
Kershaw St.
Princes Pl.
The Bankfield School
Playing Fields
Tennis Cts.
B5178
Bankfield
Avondale Drive
Avondale Dr.
Sunningdale Av.
Delamere Av.
Sherwood Cl.
Quarry Ct.
Gains Ct.
Britley
Liverpool Road
Liverpool Pl.
Chestnut Ct.
Veronica M.
Elizabeth Ter.
Cawfield Av.
Glenn
Green La.
Primrose Cl.
Sch.
Tennis Cts.
Club Ho.
Rec. Grd.
Bowl. Grns.
Spenser Cl.
Steward's Br.
Club Ho.
Hanley Road
Hanley Cl.
Avenue
Crawford Av.
Mayfield Rd.
New Bank Pl.
Manor Rd.
Derwent Rd.
Rydal Wy.
Graham Rd.
Berry Rd.
Eastway
Northway
Ashley Sch.
Play. Fld.
Chestnut Lodge School
Marlowe Cl.
Heath
Toft Cl.
Hood Rd.
Kipling Cres.
Burns Cres.
Ball Path
Offs.
Royal
Lodge Rd.
Queen's Av.
Regal Cres.
Thirlmere Wy.
Lonsdale Cl.
Ridsdale
Langdale
Levens Wy.
Borrowdale
Crossway
Dundalk La.
Dundalk Road
Grange Dr.
Ashley Grn.
Comm. Cen.
Sch.
King George's Park
Coleridge Gro.
Capesthorne
Prestbury Cl.
Foxley
Southey Cl.
Keats Cl.
Millington Cl.
Holkham Cl.
Scott
Brook
Coronation
Crown Av.
Abbey Cl.
Abbey
Edwards Wy.
Barons Cl.
Francis Cl.
Nicholas Rd.
Blundell Rd.
Drive
Southway
Jasmine Gro.
Myrtle Gro.
Almond Gro.
Ash Gro.
Gathurst Ct.
Montgomery Rd.
Georges Ct.
Netherfield
Pav.
Lower House
Steward's
Browning Av.
Wordsworth Av.
Milton
Masefield
Avenue
WA8
Westminster Cl.
Herald's Cl.
Andrew
York Rd.
Deansway
Winchester Pl.
Norfolk Pl.
Suffolk Pl.
Heyes Rd.
Kenneth Rd.
Radfo Cl.
Canterbury Rd.
Hale Road
Hale M.
Standish Ct.
Alexander Dr.
Wavell Av.
Poulton Dr.
Parbold Ct.
Ledder Sq.
Cunningham Rd.
Somerville Rd.
Chillington Av.
Brinton Cl.
Rowthorn Cl.
Alverton Cl.
Thornton
Bowling Greens
Playgrd.
Leigh Recreation Ground
Philip
Place
Ditch Field
Wood
Road
Arnold Pl.
Wyncroft Cl.
Buckland St.
Addingham
Parlington Cl.
St. Michael's
House La.
Mckenny Gds.
Nazareth
Club House
St. Michael's Golf Course
Pav.
Moorside
Egypt
Smith Rd.
Lower House La.
Factory
Works
Prim. Sch.
St. Michael's Close
St. Michael's Ind. Est.
Pitville Ter.
Old La.
Subway
Road
Council Depot
Moor La.
Moor La. Sth.
Ashley
Westgate
Oldgate
Marshgate
Speke
A533
Steward's Brook
Fairway Trading Estate
Wks.
Ditton
Depot
Ditton Road
Mill
Depot
Works
A533 Queensway
Hutchi
Desoto
Spts. Grd.
Harrison St.
Mills
Works
Macdermott
Foundry
Golden Triangle Industrial Estate
Hale
Burmarsh La.
Palmarsh
Morris Gro.
Baynard
Wellingford Av.
Stapleton Wy.
Ditton Ct.
Ditton Brook
Steward's Brook
Mathieson Road
The Marsh
Ronan Rd.
Ronan
West Bank Dock Estate
Eddarbridge Estate
Bush
Dock Road
Foundry La.
Waterside La.
Warehouses
Broughton Wy.
Works
Hale Rd. Ind. Est.
Desoto
Vickers Rd.
West Bank Rec. Grd.
30
70
86
87
84
49
350
385

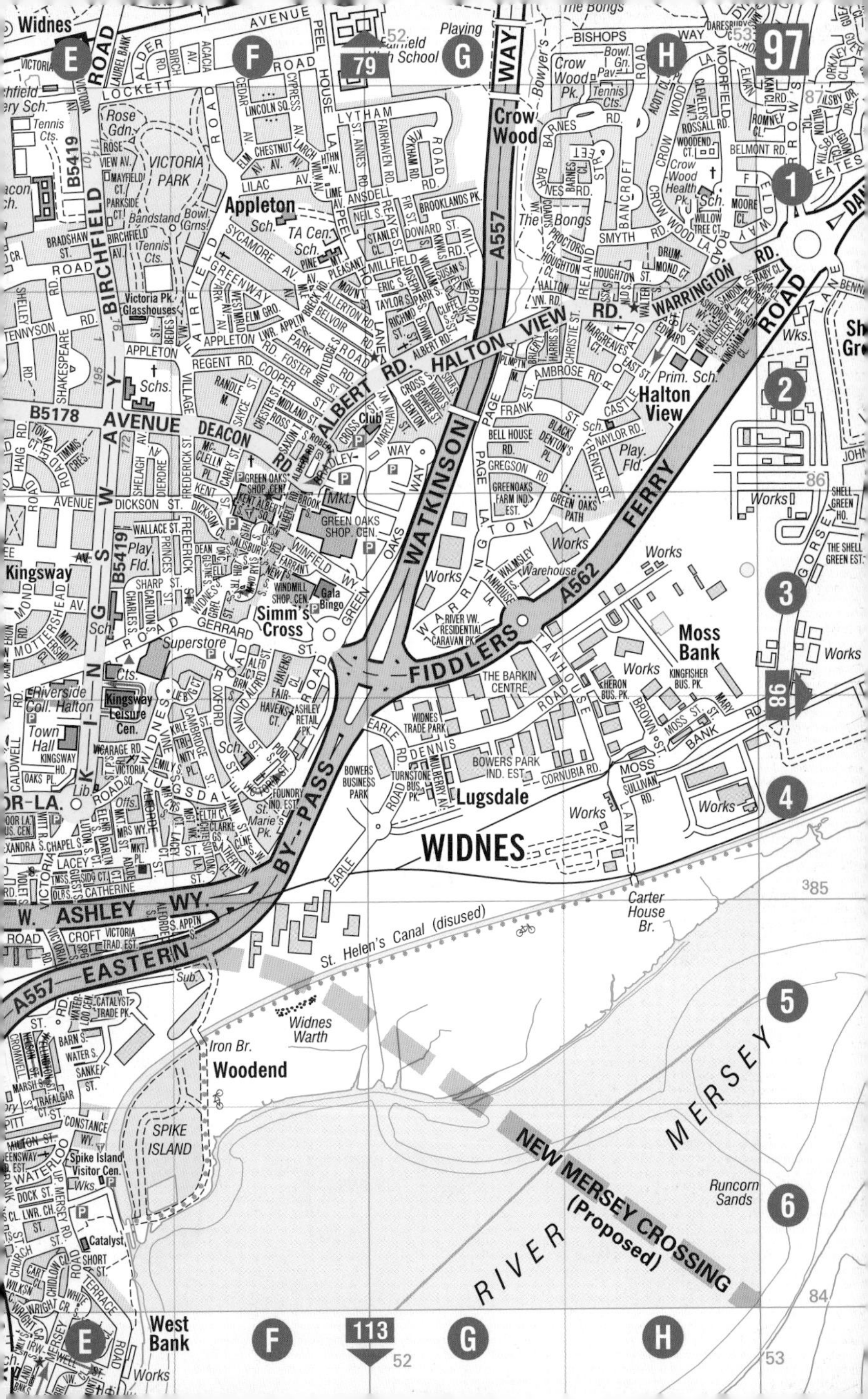

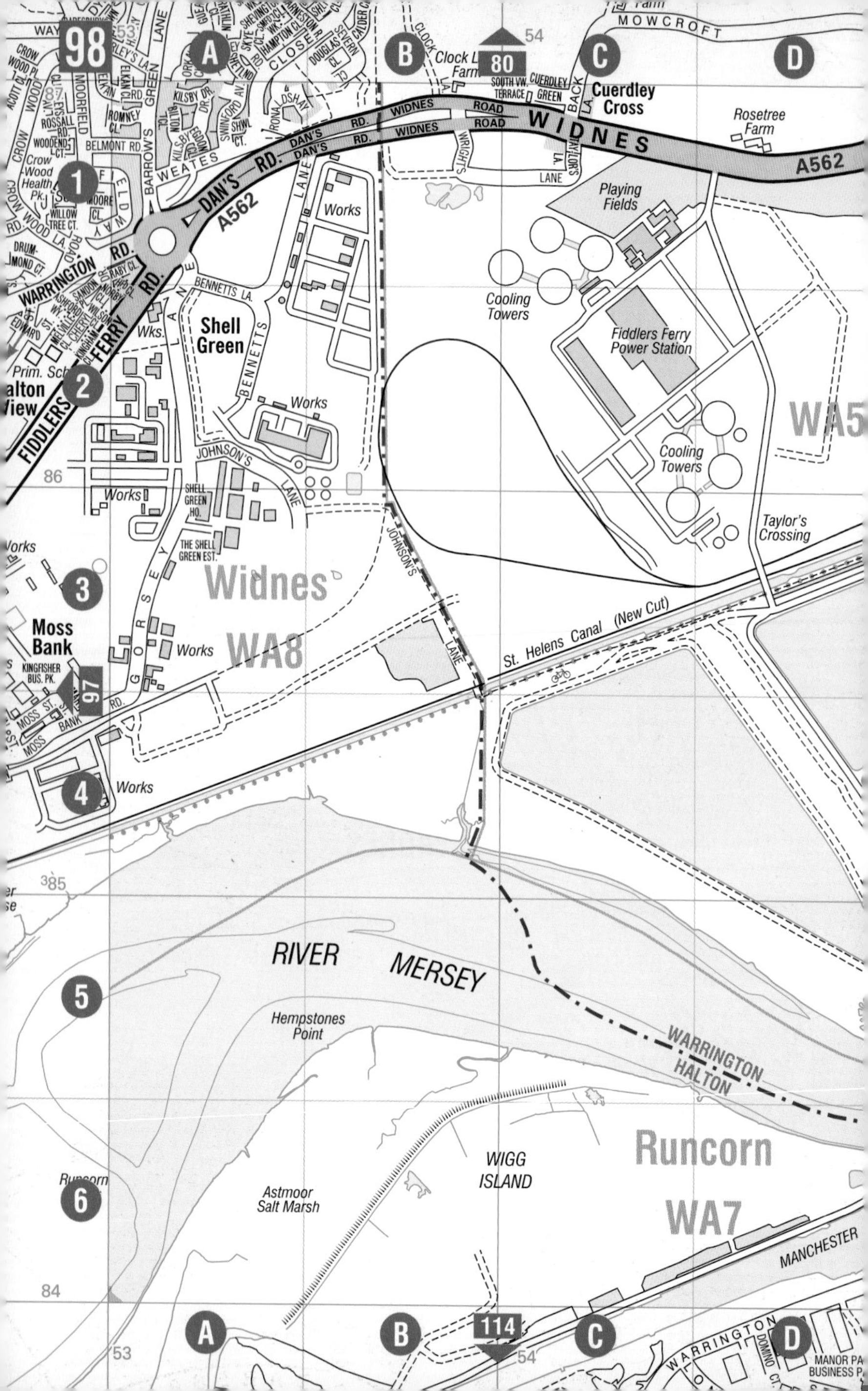

A
B
C
D
80
Clock Lane Farm
MOWCROFT
Cuerdley Cross
Rosetree Farm
WIDNES ROAD
DAN'S RD.
A562
Playing Fields
Works
Cooling Towers
Fiddlers Ferry Power Station
Shell Green
BENNETTS LANE
JOHNSON'S LANE
WA5
Taylor's Crossing
Widnes
WA8
St. Helens Canal (New Cut)
GORSEY LANE
WARRINGTON RD.
FIDDLERS FERRY RD.
Moss Bank
KINGFISHER BUS. PK.
97
Works
RIVER MERSEY
Hempstones Point
WARRINGTON
HALTON
Runcorn
WA7
WIGG ISLAND
Astmoor Salt Marsh
MANCHESTER
114
MANOR PARK BUSINESS PARK
1
2
3
4
5
6
53
54
86
85
84

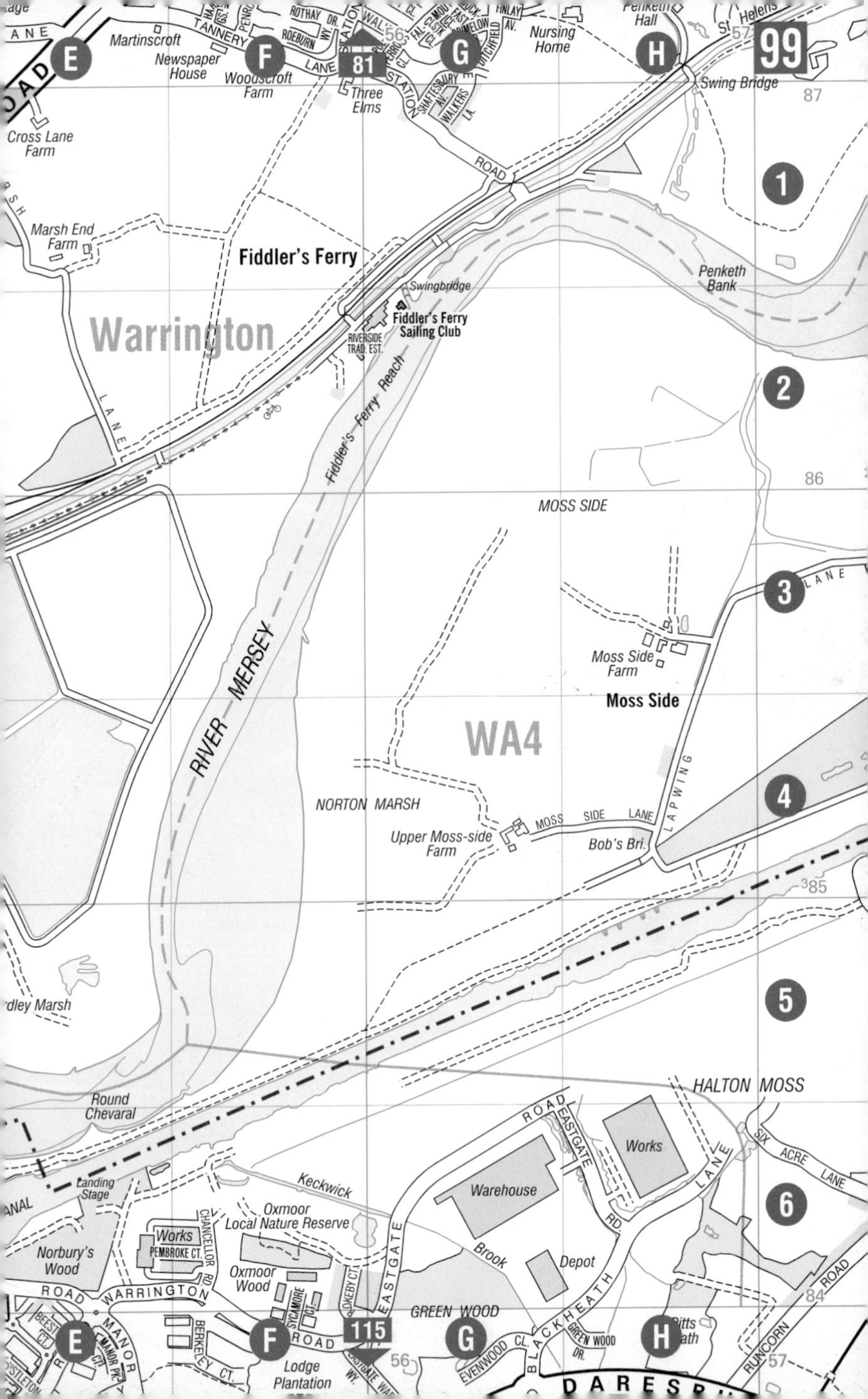

Martinscroft
Newspaper House
Woodscroft Farm
Cross Lane Farm
Three Elms
Nursing Home
Penketh Hall
Swing Bridge
Marsh End Farm
Fiddler's Ferry
Swingbridge
Fiddler's Ferry Sailing Club
RIVERSIDE TRAD. EST.
Warrington
Penketh Bank
Fiddler's Ferry Reach
RIVER MERSEY
MOSS SIDE
Moss Side Farm
Moss Side
WA4
NORTON MARSH
Upper Moss-side Farm
MOSS SIDE LANE
Bob's Bri.
LAPWING
rdley Marsh
HALTON MOSS
Round Chevaral
Landing Stage
Keckwick
Oxmoor Local Nature Reserve
Works
PEMBROKE CT.
Norbury's Wood
Oxmoor Wood
Warehouse
Brook
Depot
Works
EASTGATE
ROAD
SIX ACRE LANE
GREEN WOOD
WARRINGTON ROAD
MANOR
BLACKHEATH
GREEN WOOD DR.
EVENWOOD CL.
Lodge Plantation
BERKELEY CT.
SYCAMORE CT.
ROKEBY CT.
RUNCORN ROAD
DARESBU
81
115
E F G H
1 2 3 4 5 6

A
B
C
D
1
2
3
4
5
6
84
116
TELEGRAPH RD.
A540
Pensby High School for Boys
Pensby High School for Girls
Pensby Pk. Prim. Sch.
Catholic Prim. Sch.
Pensby Jun. & Inf. Schs.
Pensby Wood
Pensby Hall
Comm. Cen.
Day Cen.
Sports Ground
Cemetery
The Dungeon
Oldfield Farm
Cleaver Heath Nature Reserve
Dale Farm
Heswall Dales Local Nature Reserve
The Dales
The Cave
Poll Hill
Reservoir (covered)
Adult Train. Cen.
Puddy Dale
Superstore
Prim. Sch.
Playing Field
Holiday Camp
Sewage Works
Caravan Park
Slipway
White House
Dee Farm
Camping Site
Hall Farm
Rectory
RIVER DEE
Gayton Hole
CH60

85
E
F
G
H
Football Ground
Riding Centre
Gills Lane Farm
Youth Centre
1
2
3
4
5
6
Pensby
CH61
Prenton Brook
Beech Farm
Bank Farm
Barnston
Manor Farm
Carnsdale Farm
Wirral
Pensby House Farm
Greenheys Cottages
102
White House
Whitehouse Farm
Heswall Primary School
Whitfield Common
Tennis Courts
Dunster House
Cloverley
Heswall
Lane End Farm
Willow Bank House
CH63
Football Ground
Barnston Prim. Sch.
Gayton
Play Field
HESWALL
The Beacons
117
A551
A5137
A540
B5138
BARNSTON ROAD
BRIMSTAGE ROAD
CHESTER ROAD
WHITEHOUSE LANE
WHITFIELD LANE
GILLS LANE
STORETON LANE
DAWSTONE ROAD
MILL LANE

84
29

A   **B**   330 86   **C**   **D**

Farm
KEEPERS LANE
RED
Storeton
Lodge

1

CH61

New Hey
Covert

New Hey
Triangle

Rake Hey
Covert

Brimstage
Plantation

Ley Farm

2

383

Wirral

Iveston
Farm

Home
Farm

Lady
Farm

GREEN BANK

BRIMSTAGE

3

101

Brimstage
Hall

Brimstage

Melite
Cottage

A5137

Brimstage
Hall Courtyard

White
House

Whitehouse
Farm

Fairfield

The
Brooklet

WHITEHOUSE

LANE

Fairfield
Lodge

TALBOT   AVENUE

Dunster
House

Westwood
Hall

Cloverley

B 82 R   I   M   S   T   A   G   E

Lake
Lodge

4

all

5

Lane End
Farm

Willow Bank
House

Thornton
Manor

Manor Wood

Westmead

Drinkwater
Cottage

Crofts Bank
Cottages

6

Hesketh
Grange

GRANGE RD

Hill Top
Farm

THORNTON

81

A

B   118 330   **C**   **D**

29

Thornton
Hough

SMITHY HILL

GRANGE ROAD

Sch
ST GEORGE'S WY

Pav.

CHURCH RD

Graveyard

M53
M53-MOTORWAY
Junction 4
CH63
BRACKENWOOD GOLF COURSE
Brackenwood Park
Wirral Grammar Sch. for Girls
Wirral Grammar Sch. for Boys
Playing Field
Benty Hey
Recreation Ground
Stanton Rd. Prim. Sch.
Umberstone Covert
Lower Umberstone Covert
Claremont House
Poulton Royd
ST. JOHN'S HOSPICE
CLATTERBRIDGE HOSPITAL
CLAIRE HO. CHILDREN'S HOSPICE
CLATTERBRIDGE CENTRE FOR ONCOLOGY
Clatter Bridge
Clatter Brook
Wirral Manor House
New Rocklands
Rocklands Farm
Thornton Grange
Rocklands Lodge
Rugby Football Grd.
Thornton Common
Rugby Football Ground
Club Ho.
Willows Farm
Oakwood Farm
The Foxes
Brook Farm
Rose Bank
Bank Farm
Strawberry Farm
Grove Cotts.
Lancelyn Farm
Brook Cottage
Storeton Hill
Wishing Gate
Hillside Cottage
MOUNT ROAD
B5151
BRIMSTAGE ROAD
B5137
A5137
CLATTERBRIDGE ROAD
WILLASTON RD.
COMMON ROAD
B5136
THORNTON COMMON ROAD
STANTON ROAD
HEATH ROAD
CROSS LANE
POULTON ROYD DRIVE
PETER PRICE'S LA.
LANGDALE ROAD
BORROWDALE ROAD
RABY MERE RD.

87
104
119

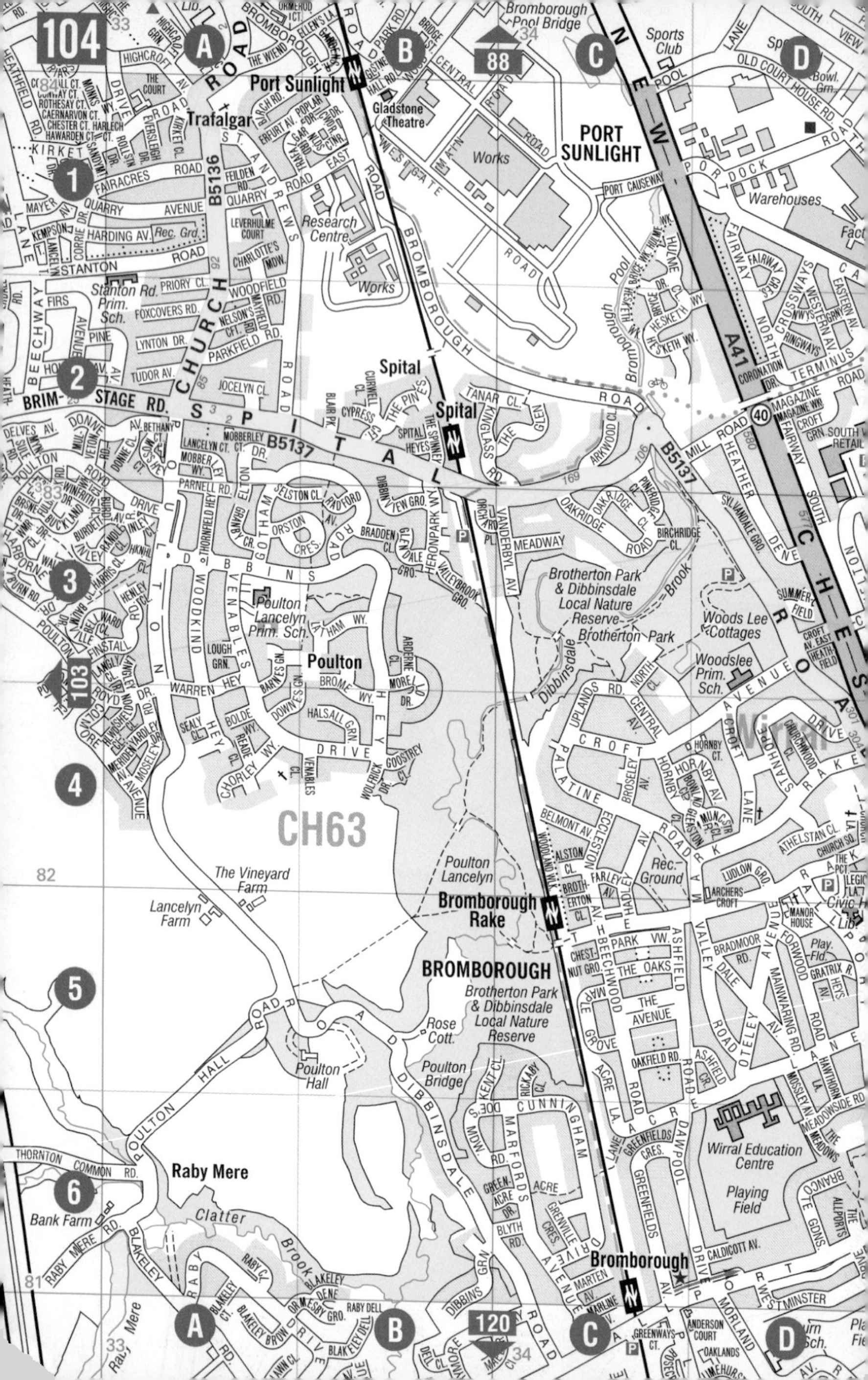
104
A
B
C
D
1
2
3
4
5
6
88
120
103
Bromborough Pool Bridge
Port Sunlight
Trafalgar
Gladstone Theatre
PORT SUNLIGHT
Works
Research Centre
Sports Club
Warehouses
OLD COURT HOUSE RD.
PORT CAUSEWAY
A41
B5136
B5137
CHURCH ROAD
BROMBOROUGH ROAD
SPITAL ROAD
BRIMSTAGE RD.
Spital
Stanton Rd. Prim. Sch.
Poulton Lancelyn Prim. Sch.
Poulton
DIBBINS HEY
POULTON ROAD
CH63
The Vineyard Farm
Lancelyn Farm
Poulton Lancelyn
Brotherton Park & Dibbinsdale Local Nature Reserve
Brotherton Park
Dibbinsdale
Woods Lee Cottages
Woodslee Prim. Sch.
Bromborough Rake
BROMBOROUGH
Rec. Ground
Rose Cott.
Poulton Hall
Poulton Bridge
POULTON HALL ROAD
DIBBINSDALE ROAD
Raby Mere
Clatter Brook
Bank Farm
THORNTON COMMON RD.
RABY MERE RD.
BLAKELEY
Wirral Education Centre
Playing Field
Bromborough
CUNNINGHAM
MARFORDS AVENUE
FAIRACRES ROAD
QUARRY AVENUE
STANTON ROAD
HARDING AV.
MEADWAY
CROFT AVENUE
PALATINE ROAD
THE OAKS
THE AVENUE
PARK VW.
ACRE LANE
DAWPOOL
GREENFIELDS
OTELEY AV.
MAINWARING RD.
VALLEY ROAD
PORT WESTMINSTER
MILL ROAD
MAGAZINE
CORONATION DR.
TERMINUS
82
81
33
34

E
F
G
H
89
121
106
36
37
84
383
82
81
1
2
3
4
5
6
Bromborough Port
RIVER MERSEY
Works
Factory
Odeon Cinema
Gala Bingo
Fitness First
Slack Wood
Oak Wood
Offices
Job's Ferry
Playing Field
Eastham Ferry
EASTHAM COUNTRY PARK
Eastham Woods
Oil Storage Depots
Long Plantation
Tennis Courts
The Warrens Farm
Leverhulme Sports Ground
Pavilion
Mayfields Remembrance Park
Custom House
Eastham Locks
Wirral Metropolitan College
Playing Field
Plymyard Cemetery
Tank Farm
Club House
Queen Elizabeth II Dock
CH62
WIRRAL INTERNATIONAL BUSINESS PARK
PLANTATION BUSINESS PARK
PLANTATION COURT
STADIUM CT.
APEX COURT
Cowpasture Wood
CROFT BUS. PARK
CROFT BUSINESS CEN.
CROFT TRADE PK.
CROFT TECH. PK.
LAKE ENT. PK.
GATEWAY PARK
RIVERBANK ROAD
STADIUM ROAD
COMMERCIAL ROAD
RIVERVIEW ROAD
PLANTATION ROAD
POWER ROAD
OLD HALL ROAD
RIVERWOOD ROAD
SOUTHWOOD RD.
BASSENDALE ROAD
GEORGIA AV.
BANKFIELD CT.
SKIDDAW RD.
HAWKSHEAD RD.
MARTINDALE RD.
BRUNEL RD.
WOODWAY CT.
LUMINA
HARDKNOTT RD.
GRISEDALE ROAD
WRYNOSE RD.
TEBAY ROAD
GREEN LANE
FERRY ROAD
LOCK RD.
WOOD HEATH WY.
DRIVE
TORR
PARK
A41
ROAD
WOODYEAR ROAD
GORDON AV.
GLYN AV.
Prim. Sch.
Mendell Prim. Sch.
MENDELL CL.
CARLETT
AVENUE

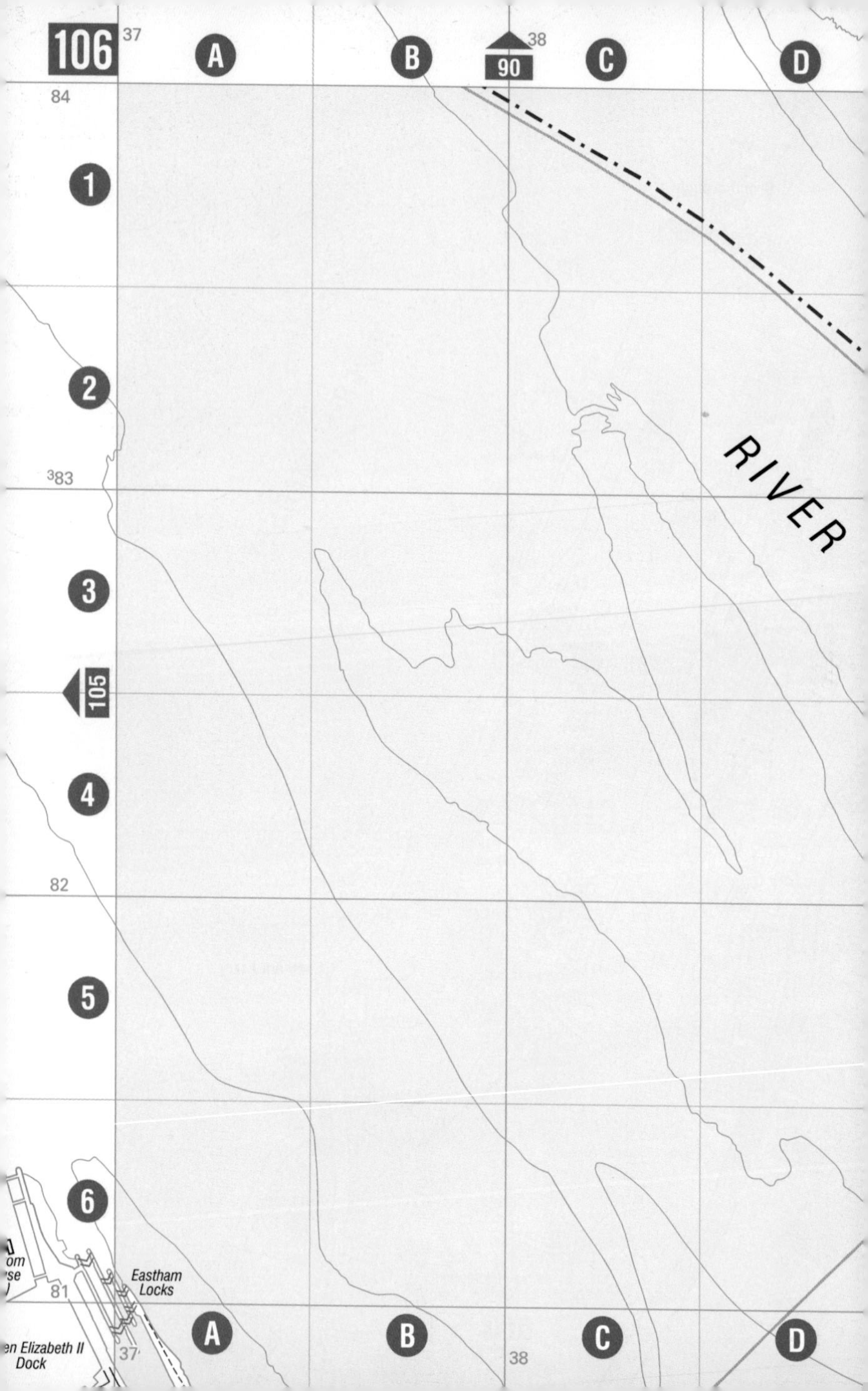

River

Queen Elizabeth II Dock

Eastham Locks

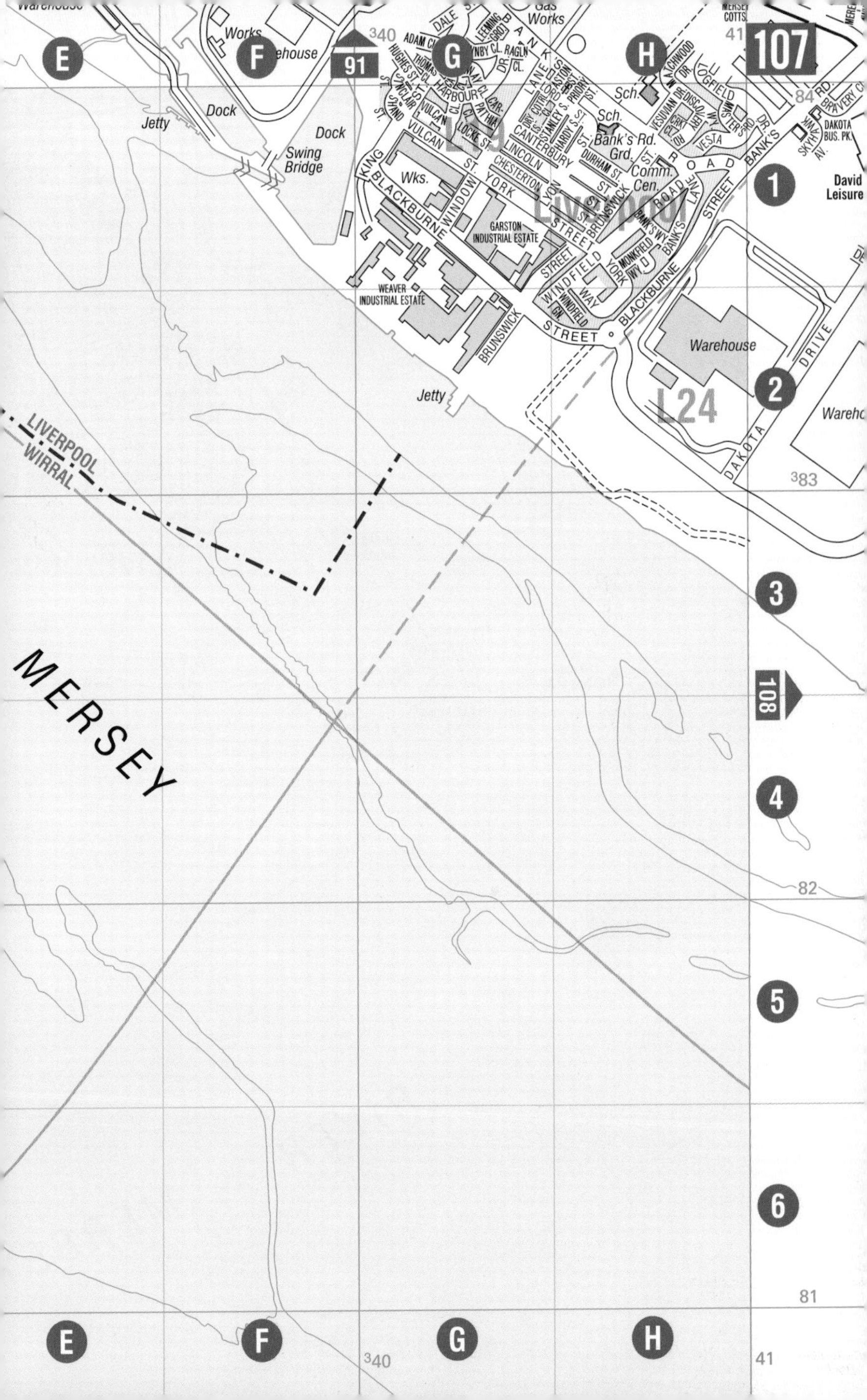

Warehouse
Works
Warehouse
Gas Works
Dock
Jetty
Dock
Swing Bridge
91
108
Wks.
GARSTON INDUSTRIAL ESTATE
WEAVER INDUSTRIAL ESTATE
Warehouse
Jetty
L19
L24
Liverpool
Sch.
Sch.
Bank's Rd. Grd.
Comm. Cen.
KING ST.
BLACKBURNE ST.
WINDOW LANE
YORK ST.
LYON ST.
VULCAN ST.
LINCOLN ST.
CANTERBURY ST.
CHESTERTON ST.
BRUNSWICK ST.
HARBOUR CL.
BANK'S ROAD
BANK'S LANE
STREET
WINDFIELD
YORK WAY
BLACKBURNE STREET
BANK'S WY.
MONKFIELD WY.
DAKOTA DRIVE
DAKOTA BUS. PK.
SKYHAWK AV.
BRAVERY CT.
VESTA
LOGFIELD
DISCOVERY RD.
WATCHWOOD DR.
VESUVIAN DR.
DAVID Leisure
LIVERPOOL
WIRRAL
MERSEY
E F G H
1 2 3 4 5 6
340 41 383 82 81

A
B
C
D
1
2
3
4
5
6
41
42
383
82
81
92
107
NEW MERSEY SHOPPING PARK
NEW MERSEY RETAIL PARK
THE MATCHWORKS
Bowl. Grn.
Factory
Works
A5275
All Weather Pitch
Sports Grd. Club
SPEKE ROAD
A561
Trinity Catholic Sch.
LOGFIELD
VESTA
Comm. Cen.
BANK'S ROAD
BLACKBURNE
BRAVERY CL.
DAKOTA BUS. PK.
SKYHAWK AV.
THE AERODROME
David Lloyd Leisure Centre
Hotel
ESTUARY COMMERCE PARK
BOULEVARD
WINDWOOD DR.
THE OFFICE QUARTER
LEEWARD DRIVE
SPEKE HALL AVENUE
ESTUARY
BANKS
CARTWRIGHTS FM. RD.
Works
PETWORTH CL.
BARNHAM CL.
BOGNOR RD.
MELBRNE
TONBRIDGE CL.
LENHAM WY.
BEXHILL CL.
SANDGATE CL.
DYMCHURCH
APPLEDORE CT.
COLWORTH
Speke Hall Rec. Grd.
DE HAVILLAND DRIVE
HURRICANE DR.
ESTUARY COMMERCE PARK
HERCULES DR.
LIVERPOOL INTERNATIONAL BUSINESS PARK
HURRICANE COR.
Warehouse
Warehouse
DAKOTA
SPINDUS ROAD
SPEKE HALL IND. EST.
STIRLING RD.
BLENHEIM WY.
SKY PARK INDUSTRIAL ESTATE
OWEN
BAILEY'S LA.
SPEKE HALL
WALK
Speke Dams
BANK'S LANE
Stockton's Wood
Liverpool
Speke Hall
The Clough
Speke Home Farm
Liverpool Sailing Club
P
RIVER MERSEY

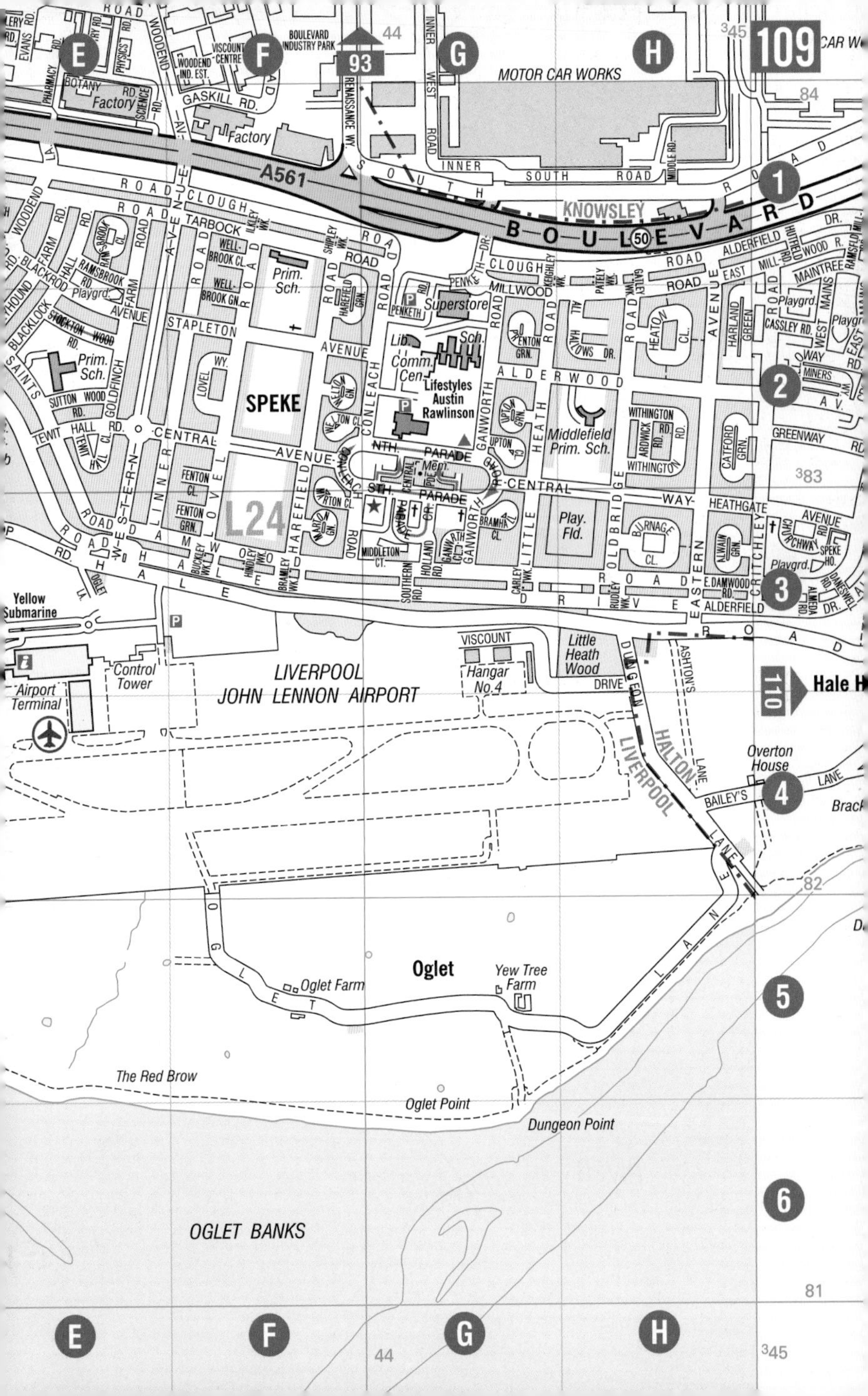

SPEKE
L24
A561
KNOWSLEY BOULEVARD
MOTOR CAR WORKS
BOULEVARD INDUSTRY PARK
WOODEND IND. EST.
VISCOUNT CENTRE
GASKILL RD.
Factory
Prim. Sch.
Superstore
Lib.
Comm. Cen.
Sch.
Lifestyles Austin Rawlinson
Middlefield Prim. Sch.
Play. Fld.
Playgrd.
Yellow Submarine
Control Tower
Airport Terminal
LIVERPOOL JOHN LENNON AIRPORT
Hangar No.4
Little Heath Wood
DUNGEON DRIVE
HALTON
LIVERPOOL
Overton House
BAILEY'S LANE
Oglet
Oglet Farm
Yew Tree Farm
The Red Brow
Oglet Point
Dungeon Point
OGLET BANKS
Hale H
93
110

MOTOR CAR WORKS
SOUTH ROAD
KNOWSLEY
BOULEVARD
SPEKE
A561
EAST ROAD
Hop Yard Wood
Mill Wood
LIVERPOOL
HALTON
Ramsbrook Farm
Millfield
Burnt Mill Cottages
BURNT
Sewage Works
Ramsbrook Bridge
RAMSBROOK
Ram's Brook
Weir
Ramsbrook Plantation
Clamley Park Plantation
Carr L
Bridg
ALDERFIELD DRIVE
ALDERFIELD ROAD
EAST ROAD
MIDDLE RD.
HUTFIELD RD.
MILLWOOD
MAINTREE
RAMSFLD RD.
MILLWOOD CT.
MILLWAY RD.
SANDHAM RD.
Playgrd.
WEST MAINS
EAST MAINS
OAK CRES.
CLAMLEY CT.
VIEW
CASSLEY RD.
ELLOWAY RD.
MINERS WY.
CROYDE RD.
MILLWOOD RD.
LEVRT RD.
HARLAND GREEN
HEATON CL.
AVENUE
ALDERWOOD
AVENUE
EAST ROAD
GREENWAY RD.
CATFORD GRN.
Alder Plantation
RINGSFIELD RD.
St. Ambrose Catholic Prim. Sch.
HEATHGATE
WAY
CRITCHLEY ROAD
CHURCHWAY RD.
AVENUE
SPEKE HO.
DAMWOOD
DANESWELL RD.
ALMEDA RD.
EASTERN AVENUE
ALDERFIELD DR.
ALDERFIELD
EAST
Playgrd.
HALE
ASHTON'S LANE
Hale Heath
LANE
Brook Farm
Liverpool
L24
Shetland Rescue Horse & Pony Sanctuary
Hoghton Tower Farm
MORCOTT LANE
CARLOW CL.
ARKLOW DRIVE
BANDON CL.
GREENORE DR.
ENNIS CL.
WEXFORD AV.
MALIN CL.
KILDARE CL.
HEAD CL.
LANE
HOLLY CL.
COCKLADE
PEPPER ST.
Comm. Cen.
STREET
TOWER
HIGH
ARAN CL.
LANGFORD
PHEASANT FLD.
LADYPOOL
ROAD
Overton House
BAILEY'S
Brackenholme
Dungeon Marsh
Old Plantation
Home Farm
HALE PARK
Rec. Grd.
Bowling Grn.
CARRIAGE CL.
Hale Hall
Ice House Plantation
Lady Pool
Rabbit Hey
LANE
Dungeon Banks
RIVER MERSEY
94
109
A B C D
1 2 3 4 5 6
345 46 84 83 82 81

E
Burnt Mill Farm

LANE

F
Mide Farm

95
HALEBANK

G
Heathview
HEATHVIEW
KENVIEW CL.
HALE CT.

AVENUE
Sch.
FREDERICK

H
Warehouses
PICKERINGS
PICKERINGS
BROAD
HALE ROAD IND. EST.
HALE ROAD
MERSEY

84

Works

Hale Bank

Hope Farm

POTTER'S LANE

POTTER'S LA.

Widnes

WA8

Little Boar's Wood

Keepers Cottage

Big Boar's Wood

ROAD

GARNETT'S

GARNETT'S LA.

COCK LANE ENDS

Depots

Shore House

Pickerings Pasture Visitor Centre

Pickerings Pasture Local Nature Reserve

1
er ard

2

³83

Ram's

Brook

HALE

GATE

LANE

Marsh Bri.

Hale Gate Farm

Hale Duck Decoy

Sewage Works

Green

OWN

Decoy Marsh

Hale Gate Marsh

3

112 ▶

BROOK GDS.

HALE

Parsonage Grn.

Manor Farm

WITHIN

CHURCH

Church Willow Bed

WAY WITHIN

Willow Bed

ROAD

Old Pits

RIVER

MERSEY

4

82

5

6

81

LIGHTHOUSE

house

Hale Head

A
B
C
D
96
111
122
1
2
3
4
5
6
49
350
84
383
82
81
RIVER
Runcorn Gap
RUNCORN
Higher Runcorn
Weston Point
Runcorn
Halton College (Runcorn Campus)
Bridgewater Lock (Disused)
The Pier
Pier
Alfred Pier
MANCHESTER SHIP CANAL
WESTON POINT EXPRESSWAY
A557
A533
Weston Point Light Railway
Beaconsfield Wood
Beacon Hill
Runcorn Hill Visitor Cen.
Runcorn Hill Local Nature Reserve
Westfield Prim. Sch.
Weston Point Prim. Sch.
Weston Point Docks
Old Basin
Timber Yard
Works
Warehouses
Warehouse
Depots
Depot
Football Grds.
Rec. Grd.
West Bank Rec. Grd.
HALE ROAD IND. EST.
DESOTO ROAD
VICKERS ROAD
PERCIVAL LANE
PICOW FARM ROAD
SANDY LANE
WESTFIELD ROAD
CROFTON
WESTON ROAD
HIGHLANDS ROAD
LYDIATE LA.
CHESHYRES LA.

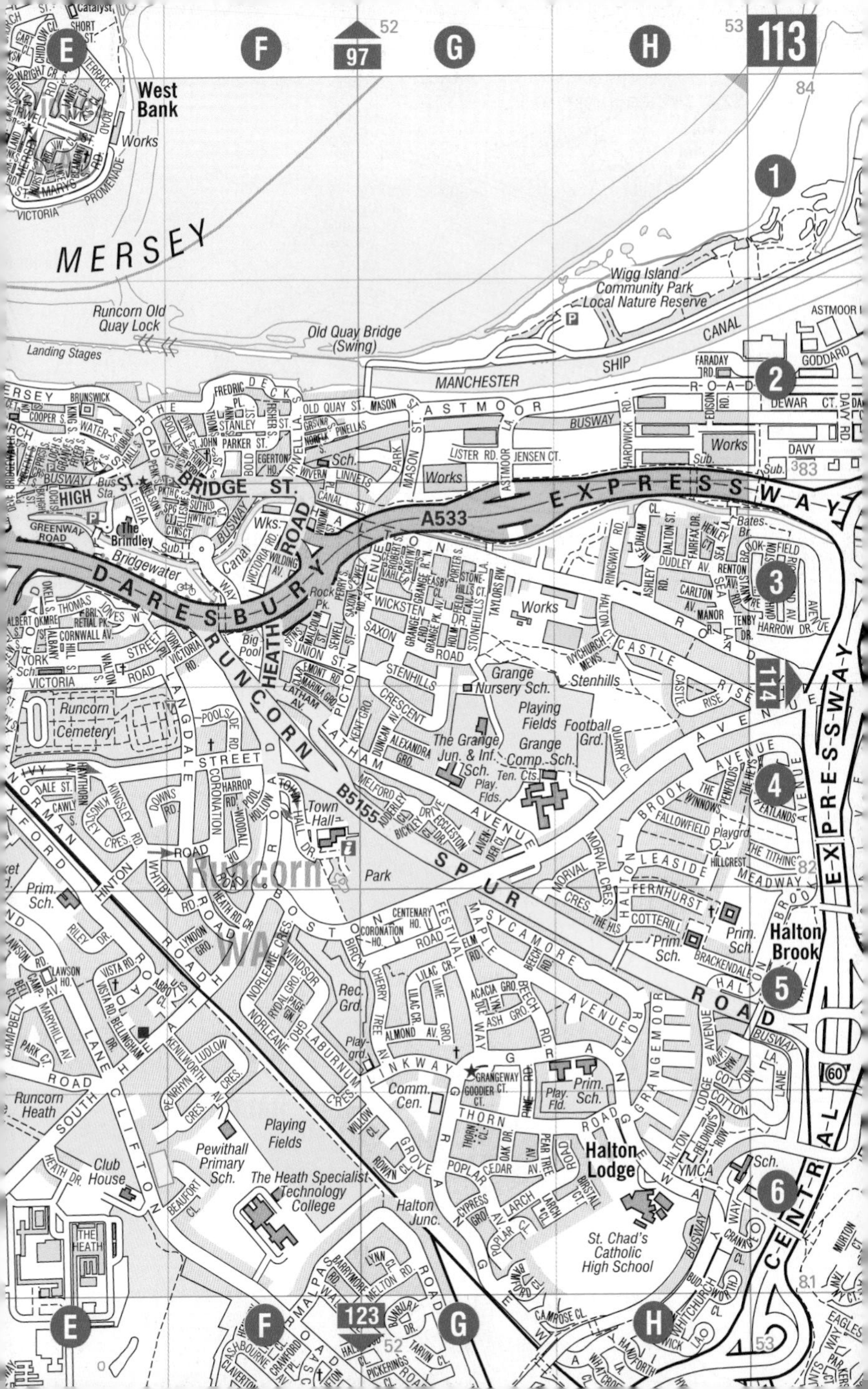

E
F
G
H
97
52
53
84
1
2
3
4
5
6
83
82
81
114
123
West Bank
Works
MERSEY
Wigg Island Community Park Local Nature Reserve
Runcorn Old Quay Lock
Landing Stages
Old Quay Bridge (Swing)
MANCHESTER
SHIP
CANAL
ASTMOOR ROAD
BUSWAY
FARADAY RD.
GODDARD
DEWAR CT.
DAVY
HARDWICK RD.
EDISON RD.
Works
LISTER RD.
JENSEN CT.
ASTMOOR LA.
HIGH ST.
BRIDGE ST.
The Brindley
GREENWAY ROAD
Bridgewater Canal
EXPRESSWAY
A533
DARESBURY
HEATH ROAD
Rock Pk.
Big Pool
Wks.
Sch.
PICTON AVENUE
WICKSTEN DR.
SAXON
STENHILLS CRESCENT
UNION ST.
VICTORIA
YORK
Runcorn Cemetery
LANGDALE
CORONATION RD.
RUNCORN SPUR
B5155
LATHAM AVENUE
Town Hall
Park
Runcorn
Works
Grange Nursery Sch.
Playing Fields
Football Grd.
Grange Comp. Sch.
The Grange Jun. & Inf. Sch.
Stenhills
CASTLE RISE
HALTON ROAD
HALTON BROOK AVENUE
MANOR
HARROW DR.
Bates Br.
Playgrd.
Prim. Sch.
Halton Brook
LEASIDE
FERNHURST
COTTERILL
MEADWAY
BOSTON AVENUE
SYCAMORE AVENUE
FESTIVAL
Rec. Grd.
LINKWAY
GRANGEWAY
Comm. Cen.
Play. Fld.
Prim. Sch.
Halton Lodge
YMCA
St. Chad's Catholic High School
Halton Junc.
Runcorn Heath
Club House
Pewithall Primary Sch.
Playing Fields
The Heath Specialist Technology College
THE HEATH
HEATH ROAD
CLIFTON
SOUTH
NORMAN
OXFORD
HINTON
GRANGEMOOR
GROVE
CENTRAL EXPRESSWAY
60
MALPAS
BUSWAY

Astmoor
ASTMOOR INDUSTRIAL ESTATE
MANCHESTER SHIP CANAL
Wigg Island Community Park Local Nature Reserve
Sewage Works
Castlefields
The Brow
Halton Castle
Halton Village
Halton Brook
Halton Lea
HALTON
Runcorn WA7
Haddocks Wood Playing Fields
Playing Fields
The Keeper's Cottage
Priory Cotts.
Pickerings Rough
St. Bertelines Wood
TOWN PARK
Sports Arena
Superstore
HALTON LEA SHOP. CEN.
Cineworld
Fitness First
TRIDENT PARK
HALTON GENERAL HOSPITAL
Halton Cemetery
Stockham Lodge Racquet & Health Club
A558
A533
B5155
DARESBURY
CENTRAL EXPRESSWAY

98
113
124

Sandymoor
Keckwick
Windmill Hill
Norton
Runcorn East
Warrington
WA4
EXPRESSWAY
A558
Junction 11
M56
MOTORWAY
CHESTER ROAD
A56
Bridgewater Canal
Lodge Plantation
GREEN WOOD
Pitts Heath
Dorchester Park Local Nature Reserve
Sandymoor Wood
Sandymoor Hall
BIG WOOD
Bog Wood
Village Farm
Poplar Farm
Keckwick Hill Bridge
George Gleave's Bridge
Crow's Nest
Red Brow
Aqueduct
DARESBURY PARK
Norton Water Tower
Railway Plantation
Marina House
Preston Brook Marina
Dukes Wharf
Windmill Farm
Hilltop Farm
Preston Brook
Catholic Prim. Sch.

99
125

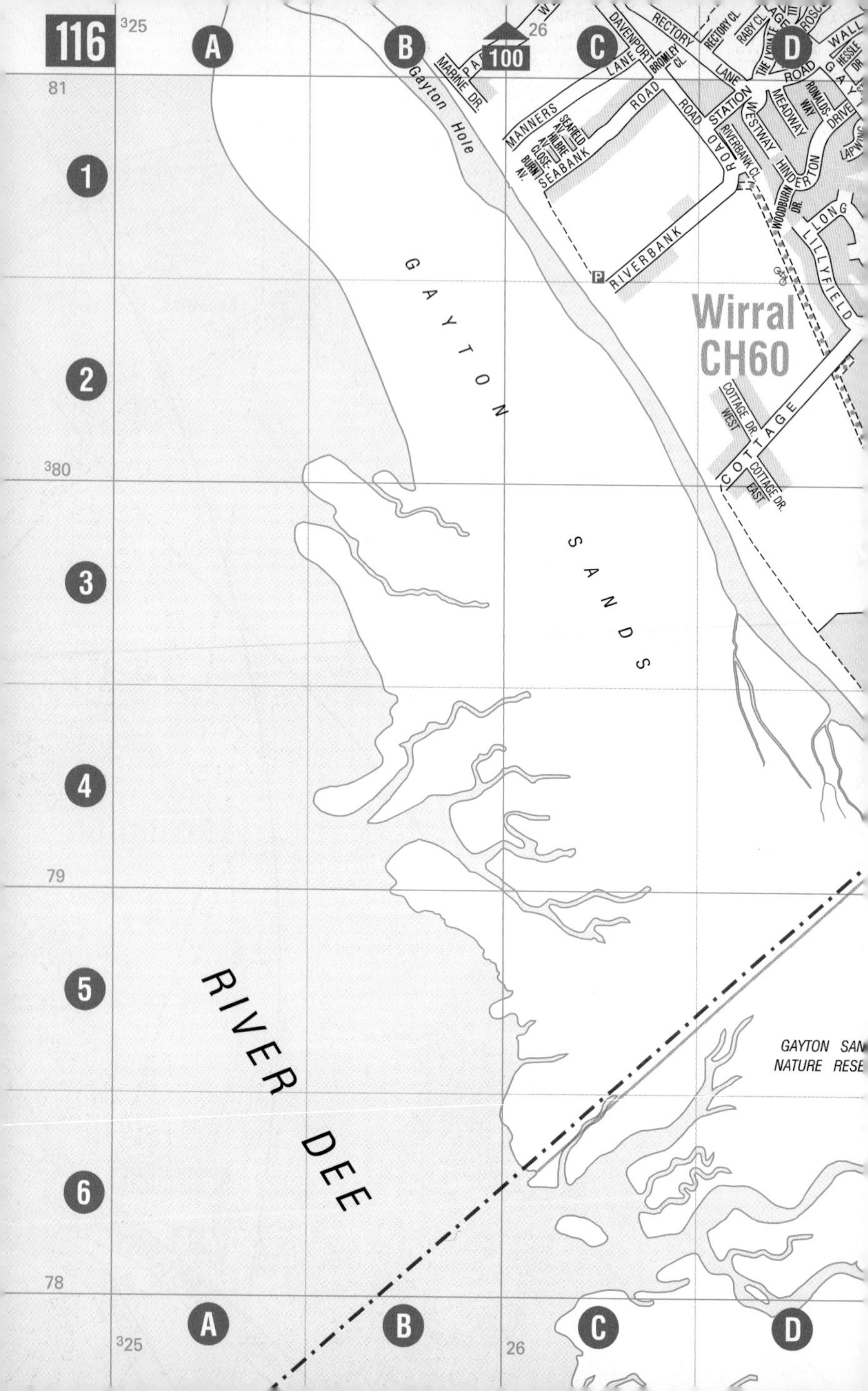

A **B** **C** **D**

81

1

2

³80

3

79

4

5

6

78

³25 26

A **B** **C** **D**

GAYTON

SANDS

Gayton Hole

MARINE DR

PA

26

100

DAVENPORT

RECTORY

CL

RECTORY CL

RABY CL

THE UPLANDS

AGE

VOSEL

WALL

HESKE

DRIVE

WAY

ROAD

LANE

PRIORY CL

LANE

ROAD

STATION

MEADOW

RONALDS WAY

HINDERTON DR

LONG

WESTWAY

DRIVE

MANNERS

SEAFIELD

AV

ROSS

ROAD

SEABANK

RIVERBANK CL

WOODBURN DR

LILLYFIELD

RIVERBANK

P

Wirral
CH60

COTTAGE

WEST DR

COTTAGE

EAST DR

GAYTON

COTTAGE

RIVER DEE

GAYTON SAN
NATURE RESE

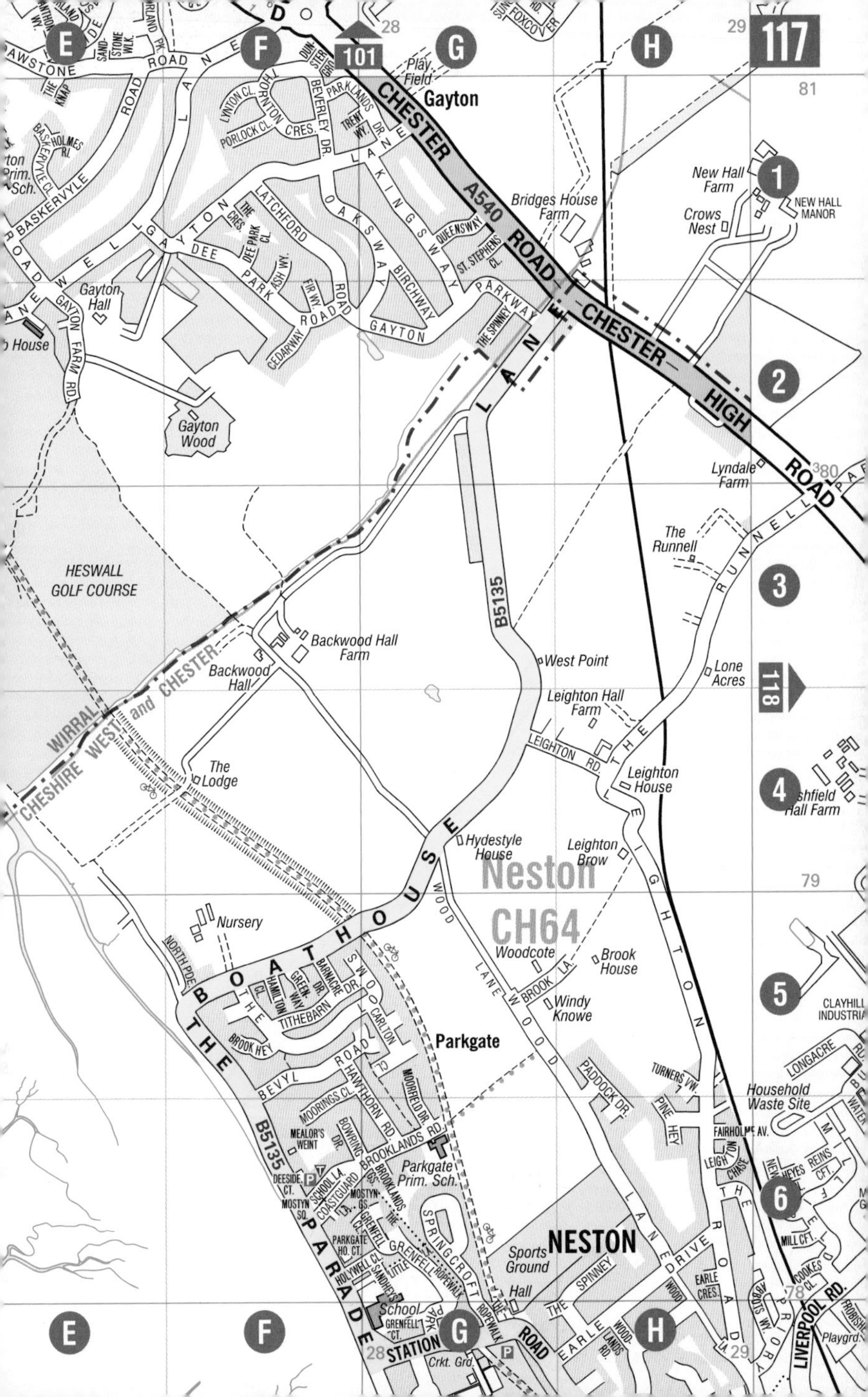

101
Gayton
Play Field
CHESTER ROAD
A540
CHESTER HIGH ROAD
New Hall Farm
NEW HALL MANOR
Crows Nest
Bridges House Farm
Lyndale Farm
The Runnell
RUNNELL
Gayton Hall
Gayton Wood
GAYTON FARM RD.
HESWALL GOLF COURSE
Backwood Hall Farm
Backwood Hall
West Point
Leighton Hall Farm
Lone Acres
118
LEIGHTON RD.
Leighton House
The Lodge
WIRRAL
CHESHIRE WEST and CHESTER
Hydestyle House
Leighton Brow
Neston
CH64
B5135
BOATHOUSE LANE
WOOD LANE
Nursery
NORTH PDE.
Woodcote
Brook House
BROOK LA.
Windy Knowe
Parkgate
THE PARADE
BEVYL ROAD
TITHEBARN DR.
BROOK HEY
HAWTHORN RD.
MOORINGS CL.
BROOKLANDS RD.
Parkgate Prim. Sch.
SPRINGCROFT
NESTON
Sports Ground
Hall
THE SPINNEY
School
STATION ROAD
Crkt. Grd.
PADDOCK DR.
TURNERS VW.
PINE HEY
FAIRHOLME AV.
LEIGHTON CHASE
THE PRIORY
EARLE CRES.
EARLE DRIVE
LIVERPOOL RD.
Household Waste Site
LONGACRE
CLAYHILL INDUSTRIAL
MILL CFT.
COOKES CL.
Playgrd.

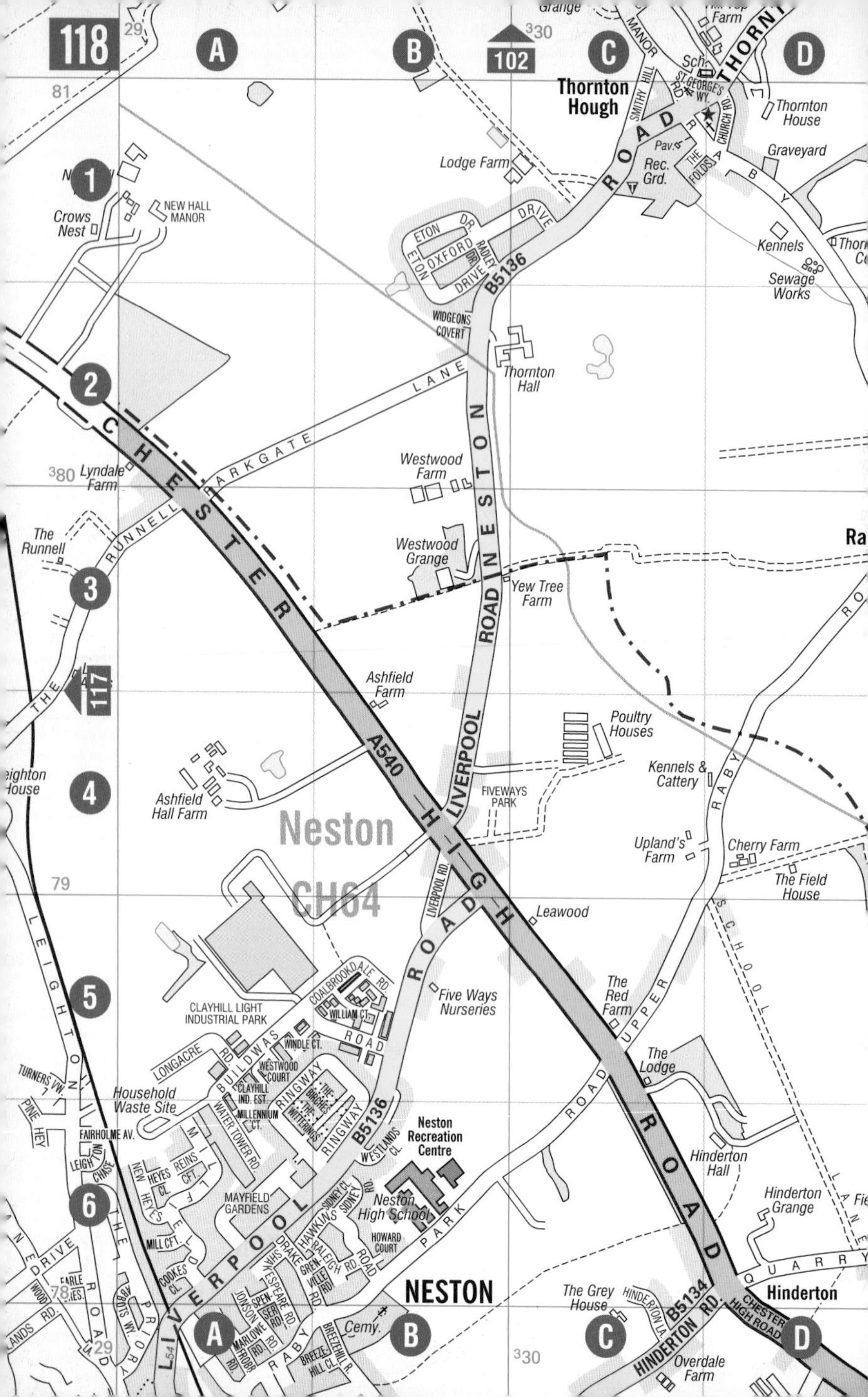
Thornton Hough
Thornton House
Graveyard
Lodge Farm
Rec. Grd.
Kennels
Sewage Works
Crows Nest
NEW HALL MANOR
Thornton Hall
Westwood Farm
Westwood Grange
Yew Tree Farm
Lyndale Farm
The Runnell
Ashfield Farm
Poultry Houses
Kennels & Cattery
FIVEWAYS PARK
Ashfield Hall Farm
Neston
CH64
Upland's Farm
Cherry Farm
The Field House
Leawood
Five Ways Nurseries
The Red Farm
CLAYHILL LIGHT INDUSTRIAL PARK
The Lodge
Household Waste Site
Neston Recreation Centre
Hinderton Hall
Hinderton Grange
MAYFIELD GARDENS
Neston High School
NESTON
The Grey House
Hinderton
Overdale Farm
Cemy.
CHESTER HIGH ROAD
LIVERPOOL ROAD
NESTON ROAD
PARKGATE LANE
A540
B5136
B5134
RABY ROAD
UPPER ROAD
SCHOOL LANE
QUARRY
PARK ROAD
LEIGHTON ROAD
THE PRIORY
HINDERTON RD.
RINGWAY
BUILDWAS RD.

102
117

Strawberry Farm
Groveside Cottages
Pear Tree Farm
103
32
Bank
RABY MERE RD.
33
Playing Field
Pavilion
Raby Vale
Raby Vale Cottage
Thornton Farm Coach House
Four Lanes End Farm
Four Lanes End
RABY MERE ROAD
Three Stacks
M53 MOTORWAY
M53
Raby Mere
81
Raby Hall
Raby Hall Farm Blws.
Raby Hall Farm
RABY HALL ROAD
MERE ROAD
Wirral
CH63
WILLASTON
B5151
Keeper's Cottage
HARGRAVE
380
Corner Farm
Grange Farm
THE GREEN
LOWBROW
Willowbrow Farm
WILLOW LANE
Hargrave Hall Farm
Hargrave Lane Cotts.
LANE
120
Hargrave Cottages
BENTY HEATH LANE
Raby House Farm
Raby House
79
ROAD
BIRKENHEAD
WIRRAL
CHESHIRE WEST and CHESTER
BLUEBELL LANE
Greenwood Nurseries
MILL LANE
Mill Cottages
Mill Lane Farm
Poultry Houses
The Lydiate
Tower Cott.
Theakston
Two Oaks Farm
LYDIATE LA.
B5151
ROAD
HANNS
B5133
HALL ROAD
Windle Hill
WEATHERSTONES COTTAGES
32
WHITEGATES CL.
WHITEGATES
CRES.
MEADOW
MEADOW CFT.
MEADOW CL.
LANE
Recreation Ground
Sch.
WILLASTON
MILL GRN.
ELM GRN.
ELM RD.
THE CHESTNUTS
33
BRIARDALE
DELAMORE'S ACRE
KNOWE CL.
78
E
F
G
H
1
2
3
4
5
6

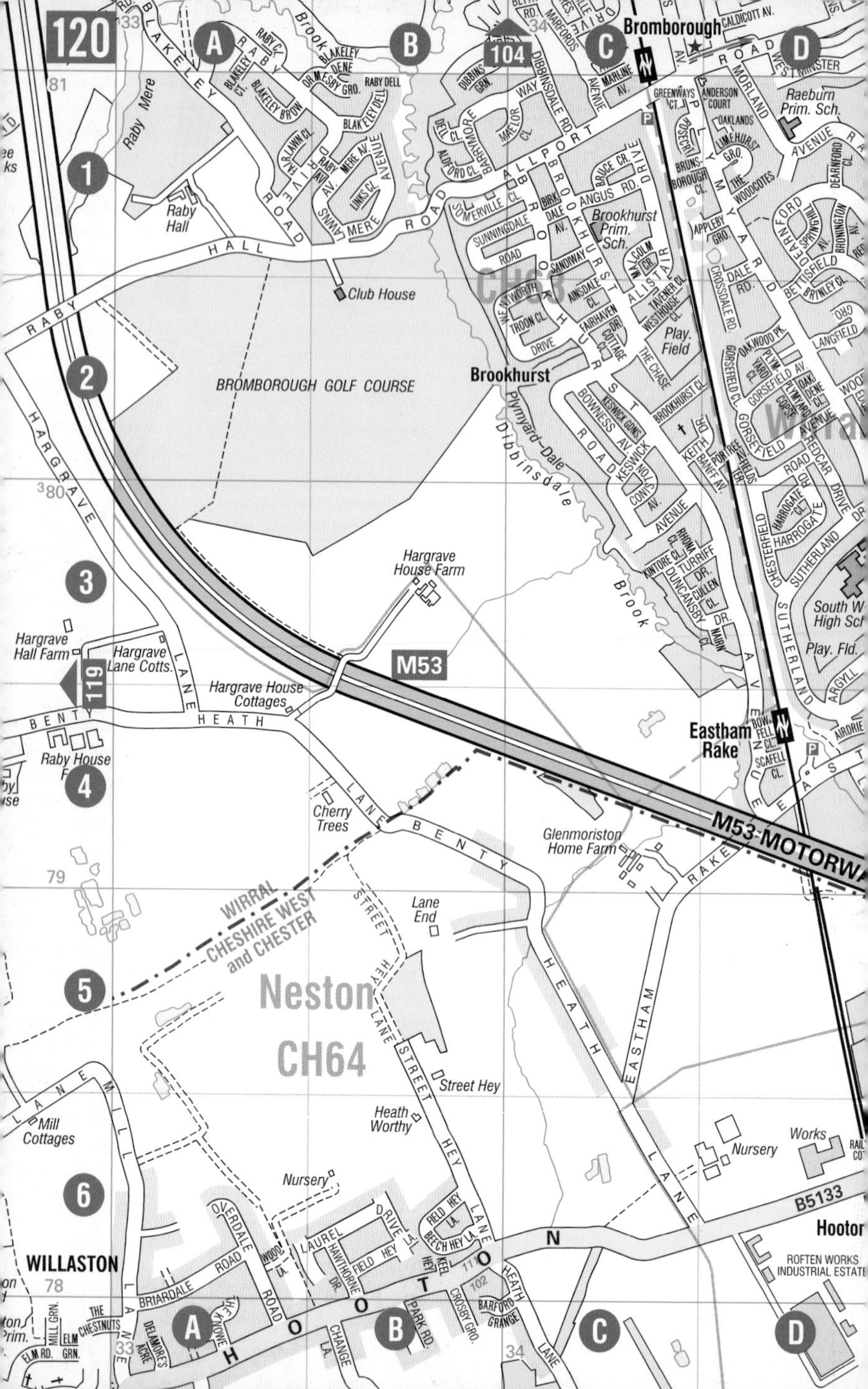

104
119
Bromborough
Raby Mere
Raby Hall
Club House
BROMBOROUGH GOLF COURSE
Brookhurst
Brookhurst Prim. Sch.
Raeburn Prim. Sch.
CH63
Play. Field
Plymyard Dale
Dibbinsdale Brook
Hargrave House Farm
M53
M53 MOTORWAY
Hargrave Hall Farm
Hargrave Lane Cotts.
Hargrave House Cottages
Raby House F
Cherry Trees
Glenmoriston Home Farm
Lane End
WIRRAL
CHESHIRE WEST and CHESTER
Neston
CH64
Street Hey
Heath Worthy
Mill Cottages
Nursery
WILLASTON
Eastham Rake
South W High Sch
Play. Fld.
Works
Nursery
B5133
Hootor
ROFTEN WORKS INDUSTRIAL ESTATE
HARGRAVE LANE
RABY HALL ROAD
BENTY HEATH LANE
STREET HEY LANE
HEATH LANE
EASTHAM RAKE
MILL LANE
HOOTON ROAD
ALLPORT ROAD
BROOKHURST ROAD
PLYMYARD AVENUE
BLAKELEY ROAD
RABY DRIVE
BRIARDALE ROAD
OVERDALE ROAD
LAUREL DRIVE
FIELD HEY LA.
BEECH HEY LA.
CROSBY GRO.
BARFORD GRANGE
PARK RD.
CHANGE LA.
THE KNOWE
DELAMORE'S ACRE
THE CHESTNUTS
MILL GRN.
ELM GRN.
ELM RD.
HAWTHORNE DR.
WOOD LA.
KESWICK AVENUE
BOWNESS AV.
SUTHERLAND DRIVE
CHESTERFIELD ROAD
HARROGATE RD.
REDCAR DRIVE
GORSEFIELD AVENUE
CROSSDALE RD.
APPLEBY GRO.
DIBBINSDALE RD.
MAELOR CL.
BARNMORE
DIBBINS GRN.
MARLINE AV.
GREENWAYS CT.
ANDERSON COURT
OAKLANDS
LIMEHURST GRO.
THE WOODCOTES
MORLAND AVENUE
WESTMINSTER
CALDICOTT AV.
ALISTAIR DRIVE
ANGUS RD.
BRUCE CR.
MALCOLM CR.
SUNNINGDALE ROAD
WENTWORTH DRIVE
TROON CL.
FAIRHAVEN DR.
THE CHASE
BROOKHURST CL.
KINTORE CL.
DUNCANSBY DR.
NAIRN CL.
CULLEN CL.
TURRIFF DR.
BOWFELL CL.
SCAFELL CL.
ARGYLL
AIRDRIE
LANGFIELD
BETTISFIELD
DEARNFORD
BRONINGTON AV.
ELM RD.

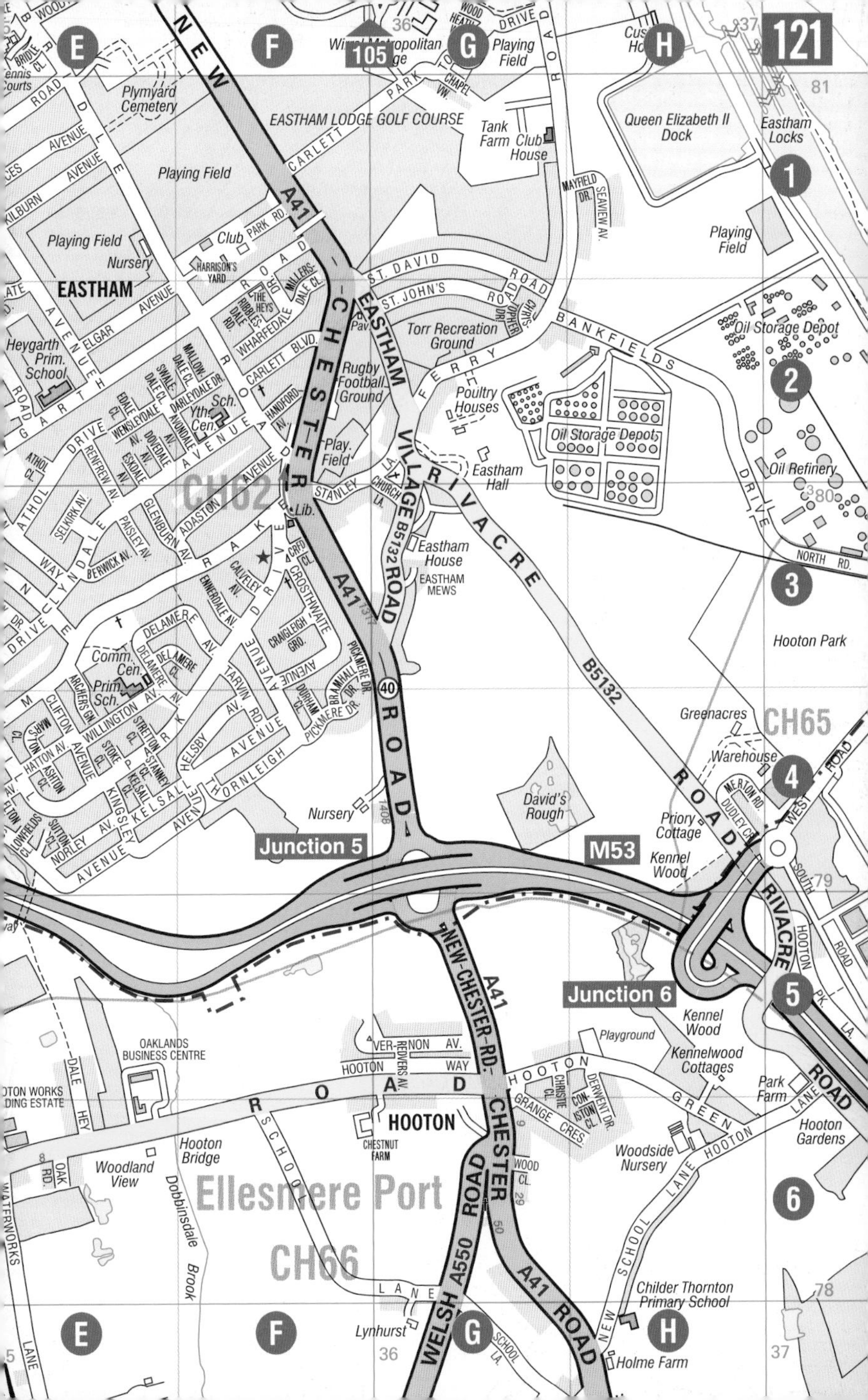
105
Playing Field
Plymyard Cemetery
EASTHAM LODGE GOLF COURSE
Tank Farm
Club House
Queen Elizabeth II Dock
Eastham Locks
Playing Field
Playing Field
Club
Nursery
EASTHAM
Heygarth Prim. School
Oil Storage Depot
Torr Recreation Ground
Rugby Football Ground
Poultry Houses
Oil Storage Depot
Play. Field
Eastham Hall
Oil Refinery
CH62
Eastham House
EASTHAM MEWS
Hooton Park
Comm. Cen.
Prim. Sch.
Greenacres
CH65
Warehouse
David's Rough
Priory Cottage
Nursery
Junction 5
M53
Kennel Wood
Junction 6
Kennel Wood
Playground
OAKLANDS BUSINESS CENTRE
Kennelwood Cottages
Park Farm
HOOTON
CHESTNUT FARM
Hooton Gardens
Hooton Bridge
Woodland View
Woodside Nursery
Ellesmere Port
CH66
Childer Thornton Primary School
Lynhurst
Holme Farm
NEW CHESTER ROAD
A41
B5132
RIVACRE ROAD
EASTHAM VILLAGE ROAD
HOOTON ROAD
WELSH ROAD A550
E
F
G
H
1
2
3
4
5
6
36
37
81
80
79
78

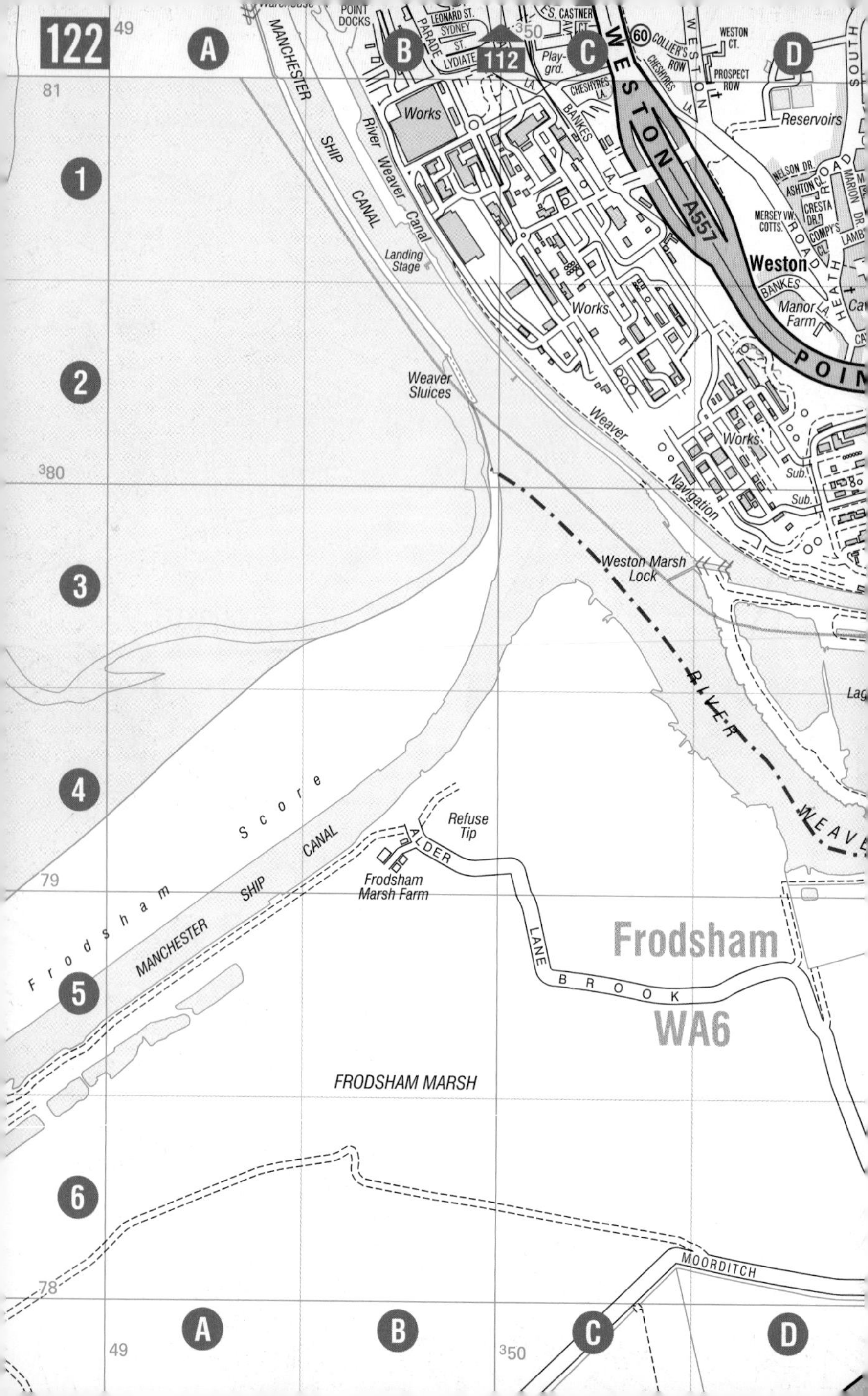
49
A
B
C
D
1
2
3
4
5
6
81
380
79
78
350
112
POINT DOCKS
MANCHESTER SHIP CANAL
River Weaver Canal
LEONARD ST.
SYDNEY ST.
PARADE
LYDIATE
Play-grd.
CASTNER CT.
WESTON
60
COLLIER'S ROW
CHESHYRES
WESTON CT.
PROSPECT ROW
CHESHYRES LA.
BANKES LA.
Works
Reservoirs
A557
NELSON DR.
ASHTON CL.
CRESTA DR.
MARION DR.
MERSEY VW. COTTS.
COMPY'S CL.
ROAD
HEATH
Weston
BANKES LA.
Manor Farm
POINT
Landing Stage
Weaver Sluices
Weaver Navigation
Sub.
Weston Marsh Lock
RIVER WEAVER
Frodsham Score
Refuse Tip
ALDER LANE
Frodsham Marsh Farm
BROOK
Frodsham
WA6
FRODSHAM MARSH
MOORDITCH

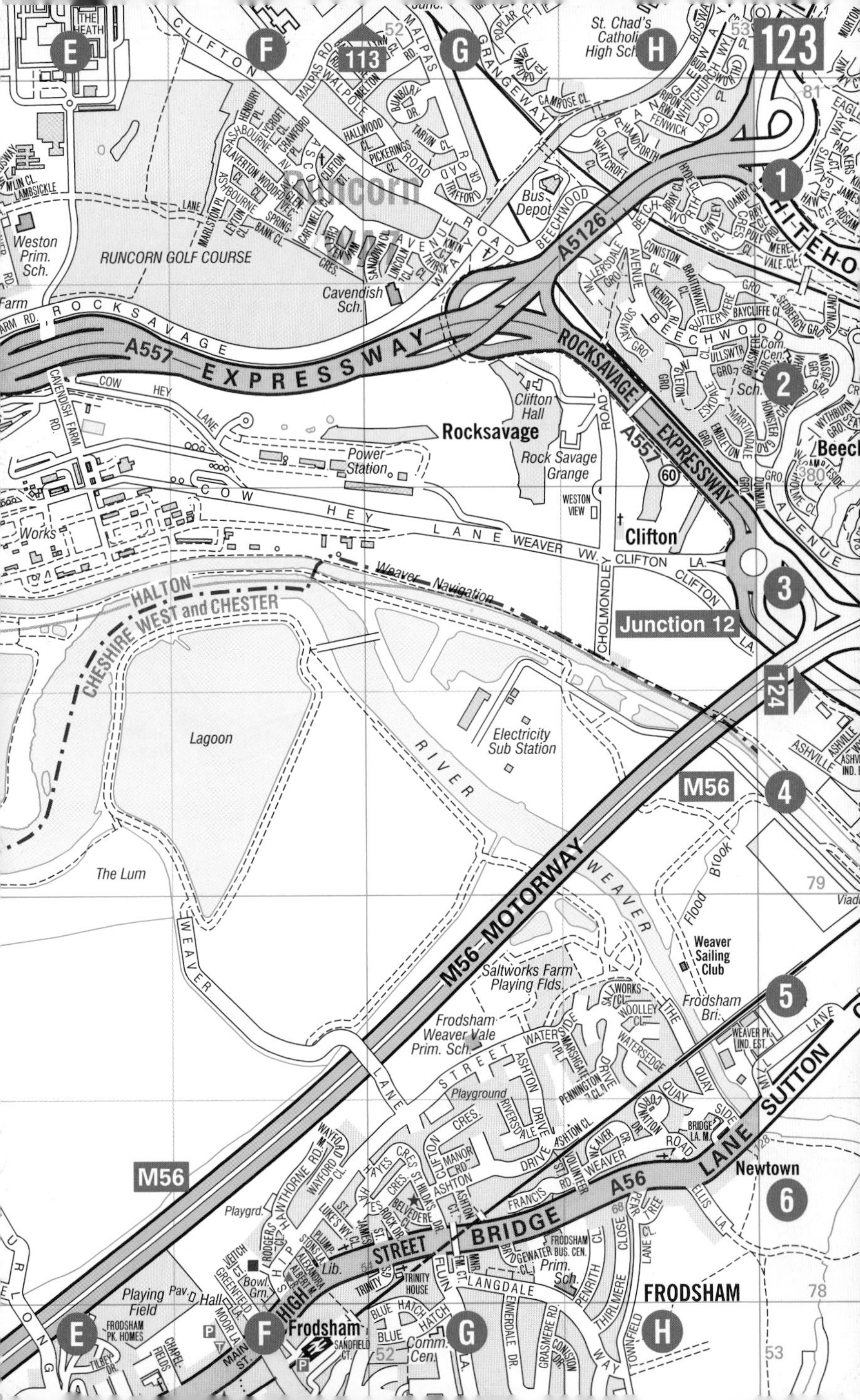

E
F
G
H
113
52
53
St. Chad's Catholic High Sch.
1
2
3
4
5
6
Runcorn
RUNCORN GOLF COURSE
Weston Prim. Sch.
Cavendish Sch.
A557 EXPRESSWAY
ROCKSAVAGE
A5126
Bus Depot
Rocksavage
Clifton Hall
Power Station
Rock Savage Grange
Clifton
Works
Junction 12
HALTON
CHESHIRE WEST and CHESTER
Weaver Navigation
Lagoon
Electricity Sub Station
RIVER WEAVER
M56 MOTORWAY
M56
The Lum
124
Weaver Sailing Club
Frodsham Bri.
Saltworks Farm Playing Flds.
Frodsham Weaver Vale Prim. Sch.
Playground
Newtown
A56
BRIDGE
HIGH STREET
SUTTON LANE
FRODSHAM
Frodsham
Playing Field
Pav.
Hall
Bowl. Grn.
Lib.
TRINITY HOUSE
FRODSHAM BUS. CEN.
Prim. Sch.
Comm. Cen.
FRODSHAM PK. HOMES
79
78
80
81

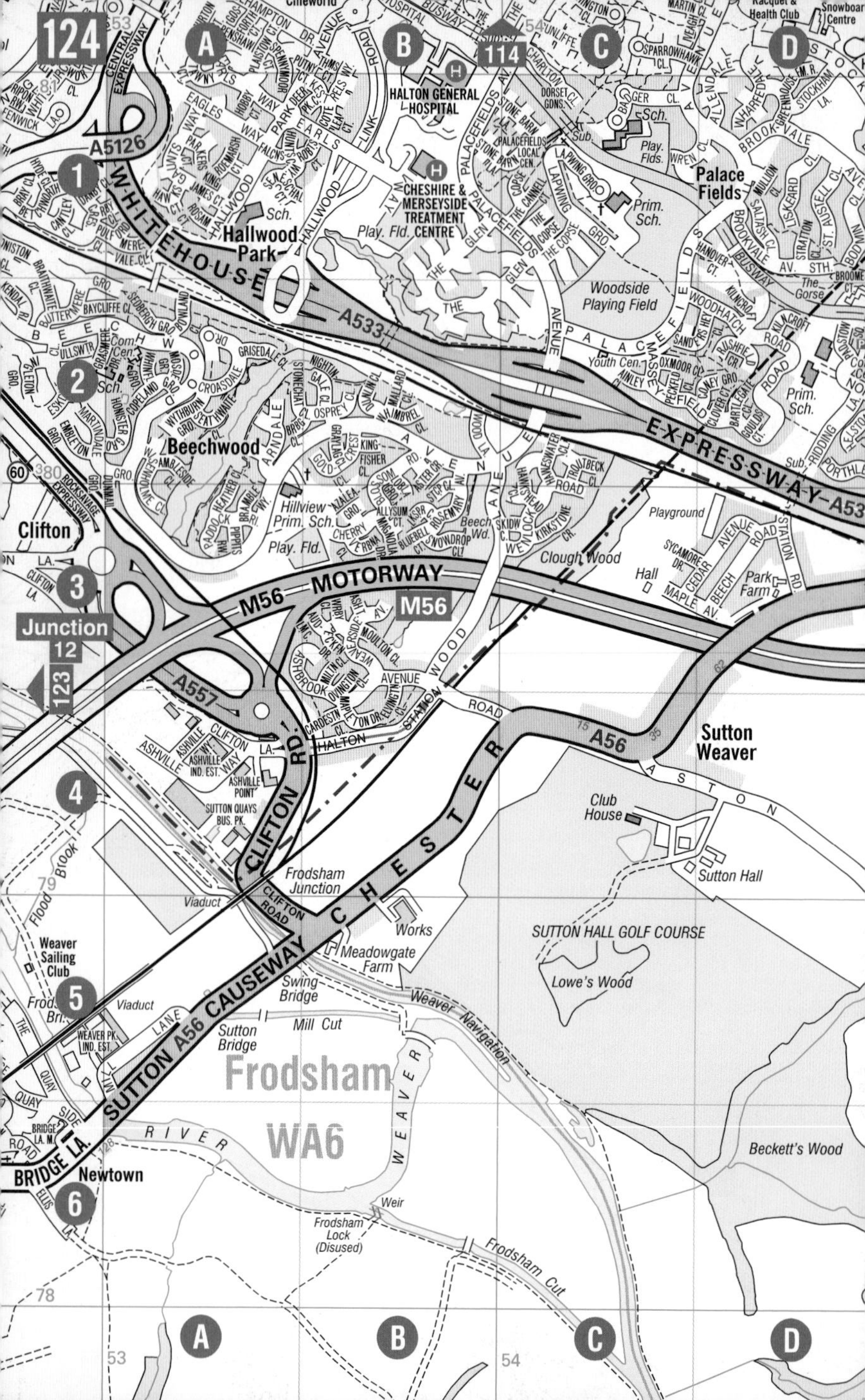

A
B
C
D
114
1
2
3
4
5
6
A5126
WHITEHOUSE
EXPRESSWAY
A533
CENTRAL EXPRESSWAY
HALTON GENERAL HOSPITAL
CHESHIRE & MERSEYSIDE TREATMENT CENTRE
Hallwood Park
Sch.
Play. Fld.
PALACEFIELDS AV.
Palace Fields
Prim. Sch.
Play. Flds.
Woodside Playing Field
Youth Cen.
Beechwood
Hillview Prim. Sch.
Play. Fld.
Beech Wd.
Clough Wood
Playground
Hall
Park Farm
Clifton
ROCKSAVAGE EXPRESSWAY
60
M56 MOTORWAY
M56
Junction 12
123
A557
CLIFTON RD.
ASHVILLE IND. EST.
ASHVILLE POINT
SUTTON QUAYS BUS. PK.
HALTON STATION ROAD
WOOD LANE
Frodsham Junction
Viaduct
CHESTER
A56
Sutton Weaver
ASTON
Club House
Sutton Hall
SUTTON HALL GOLF COURSE
Lowe's Wood
Works
Meadowgate Farm
Swing Bridge
Weaver Navigation
Mill Cut
Sutton Bridge
SUTTON A56 CAUSEWAY
Weaver Sailing Club
Flood Brook
WEAVER PK. IND. EST.
Frodsham
WA6
RIVER WEAVER
Weir
Frodsham Lock (Disused)
Frodsham Cut
Beckett's Wood
BRIDGE LA.
Newtown
53
54
78
79

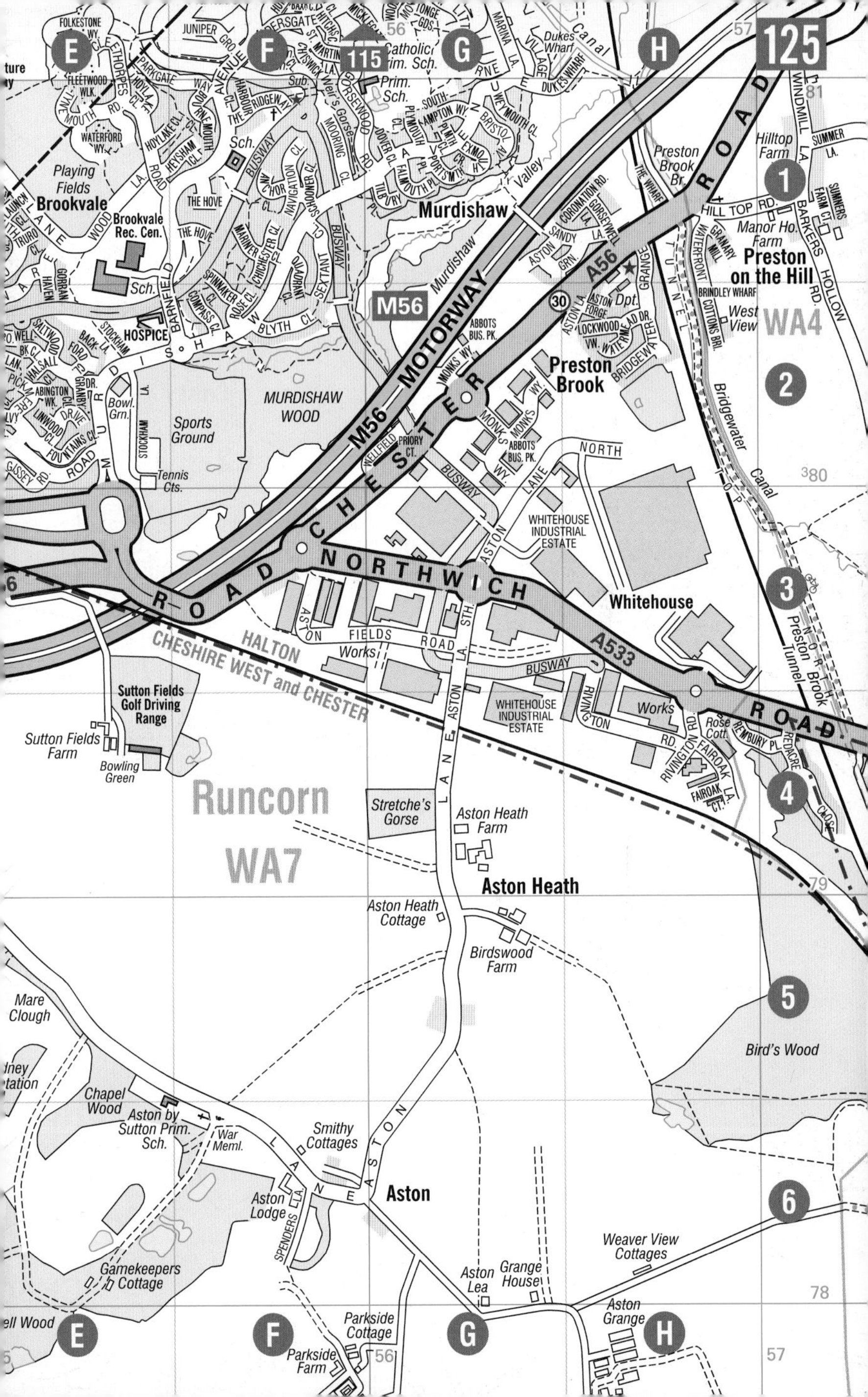

115
E
F
G
H
1
2
3
4
5
6
56
57
81
80
79
78
Brookvale
Playing Fields
Brookvale Rec. Cen.
Sch.
HOSPICE
Murdishaw
MURDISHAW WOOD
Sports Ground
Tennis Cts.
Bowl. Grn.
M56 MOTORWAY
M56
CHESTER ROAD
NORTHWICH ROAD
A56
A533
30
Preston Brook
Preston on the Hill
WA4
Hilltop Farm
Manor Ho. Farm
Preston Brook Br.
West View
Bridgewater Canal
Preston Brook Tunnel
Whitehouse
WHITEHOUSE INDUSTRIAL ESTATE
Works
ABBOTS BUS. PK.
ASTON FIELDS ROAD
HALTON
CHESHIRE WEST and CHESTER
Sutton Fields Golf Driving Range
Sutton Fields Farm
Bowling Green
Runcorn
WA7
Stretche's Gorse
Aston Heath Farm
Aston Heath
Aston Heath Cottage
Birdswood Farm
Bird's Wood
Mare Clough
Chapel Wood
Aston by Sutton Prim. Sch.
War Meml.
Smithy Cottages
Aston
Aston Lodge
SPENDERS LA.
Gamekeepers Cottage
Weaver View Cottages
Aston Lea
Grange House
Aston Grange
Parkside Cottage
Parkside Farm
ASTON LANE
Dukes Wharf
Catholic Prim. Sch.
Prim. Sch.
Murdishaw Valley

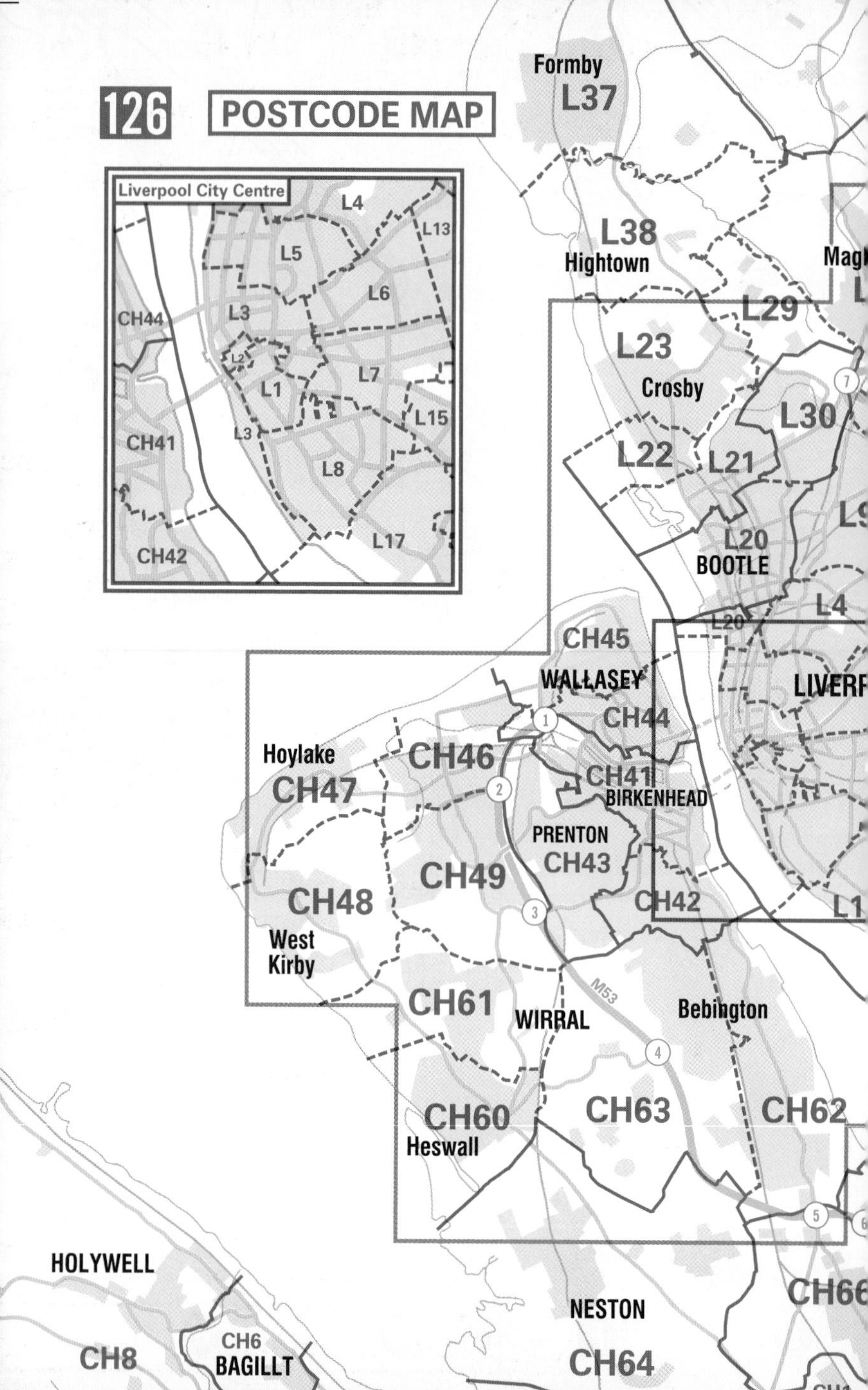

Liverpool City Centre

L4
L13
L5
L6
CH44
L3
L2
L1
L7
L15
CH41
L3
L8
CH42
L17

Formby
L37

L38
Hightown

Mag

L29
L

L23
Crosby

L30

7

L22
L21

L20
BOOTLE

L9

L20
L4

CH45

WALLASEY
1
CH44

LIVERF

Hoylake
CH47

CH46

2
CH41
BIRKENHEAD

PRENTON
CH43

LIVER

CH48
West
Kirby

CH49

3

CH42

L1

CH61
WIRRAL

M53

Bebington

4

CH60
Heswall

CH63

CH62

HOLYWELL

CH6
BAGILLT

NESTON

5

6

CH66

CH8

CH64

CH1

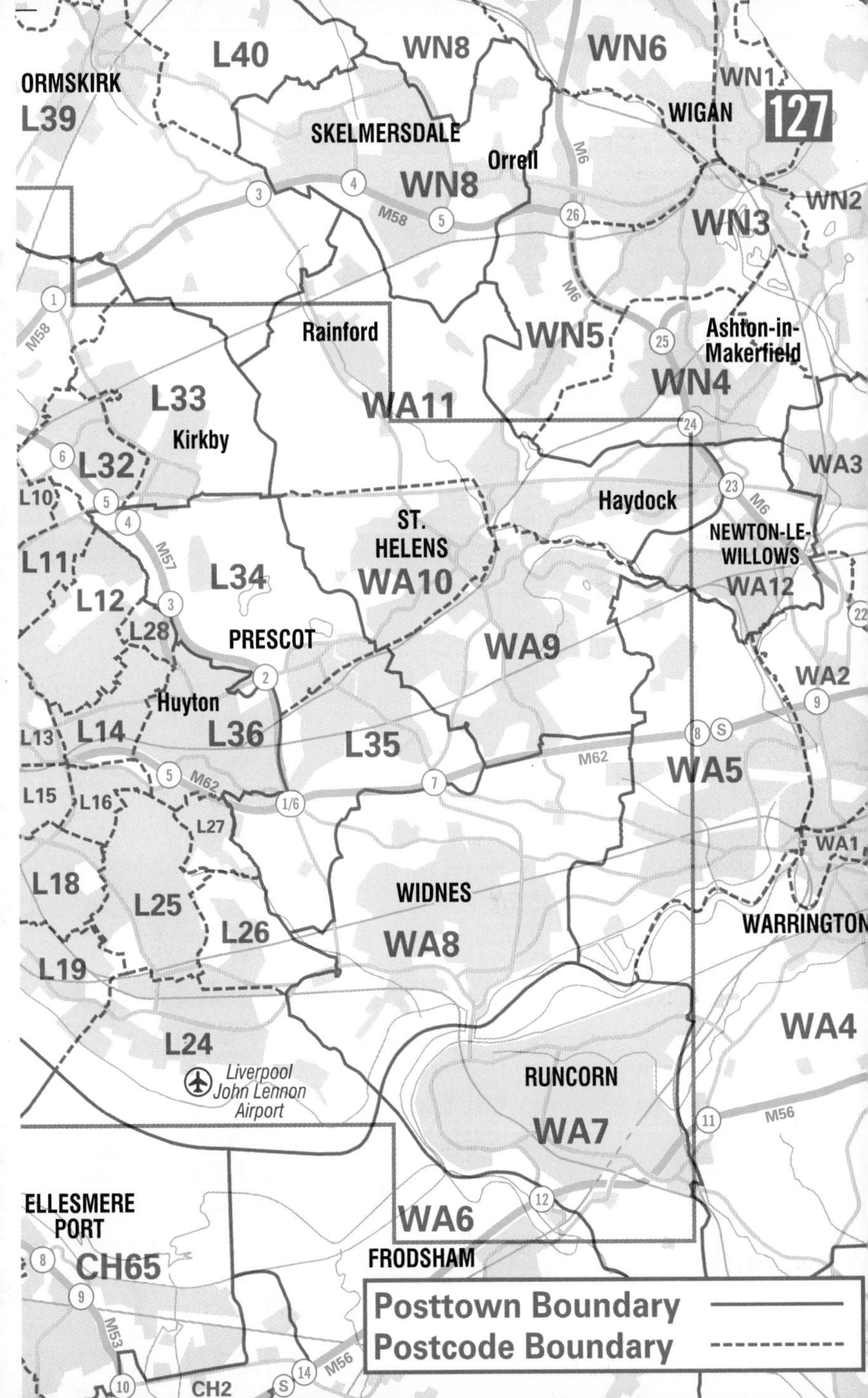

L40
WN8
WN6
WN1
ORMSKIRK
L39
WIGAN
SKELMERSDALE
Orrell
WN8
WN2
WN3
Rainford
WN5
Ashton-in-Makerfield
WN4
L33
WA11
Kirkby
WA3
L32
L10
Haydock
ST. HELENS
NEWTON-LE-WILLOWS
L11
L34
WA10
WA12
L12
L28
PRESCOT
WA9
WA2
Huyton
L13
L14
L36
L35
WA5
L15
L16
L27
WA1
L18
WIDNES
L25
L26
WARRINGTON
WA8
L19
WA4
L24
Liverpool John Lennon Airport
RUNCORN
WA7
ELLESMERE PORT
WA6
CH65
FRODSHAM
CH2
M58
M6
M57
M62
M56
M53
Posttown Boundary
Postcode Boundary

INDEX

Including Streets, Places & Areas, Industrial Estates,
Selected Flats & Walkways, Junction Names, Stations and Selected Places of Interest.

HOW TO USE THIS INDEX

1. Each street name is followed by its Postcode District, then by its Locality abbreviation(s) and then by its map reference;
e.g. **Abberley Rd.** L25: Hunts X . . . .4E **93** is in the L25 Postcode District and the Hunts Cross Locality and is to be found in square 4E on page **93**. The page number is shown in bold type.

2. A strict alphabetical order is followed in which Av., Rd., St., etc. (though abbreviated) are read in full and as part of the street name; e.g. **Ashcombe Rd.** appears after **Ash Cl.** but before **Ash Cres.**

3. Streets and a selection of flats and walkways that cannot be shown on the mapping, appear in the index with the thoroughfare to which they are connected shown in brackets; e.g. **Acresfield** L13: Liv . . . .5F **55** (off Broad Grn. Rd.)

4. Addresses that are in more than one part are referred to as not continuous.

5. Places and areas are shown in the index in BLUE TYPE and the map reference is to the actual map square in which the town centre or area is located and not to the place name shown on the map; e.g. **AINTREE** 1B **22**

6. An example of a selected place of interest is **Halton Castle** 4B **114**

7. An example of a station is **Aigburth Station (Rail)** . . . .3C **90**, also included is Park & Ride. e.g. **Leasowe (Park & Ride)** 5E **49**

8. Junction Names are shown in the index in BOLD CAPITAL TYPE; e.g. **HUNTS CROSS** 4E **93**

9. Map references for entries that appear on large scale pages **4** & **5** are shown first, with small scale map references shown in brackets; e.g. **Addison St.** L3: Liv 1E **5** (4D **52**)

GENERAL ABBREVIATIONS

All. : Alley	**Est.** : Estate	**Pde.** : Parade
App. : Approach	**Fld.** : Field	**Pk.** : Park
Arc. : Arcade	**Flds.** : Fields	**Pas.** : Passage
Av. : Avenue	**Gdn.** : Garden	**Pav.** : Pavilion
Bk. : Back	**Gdns.** : Gardens	**Pl.** : Place
Blvd. : Boulevard	**Ga.** : Gate	**Pct.** : Precinct
Bri. : Bridge	**Gt.** : Great	**Prom.** : Promenade
B'way. : Broadway	**Grn.** : Green	**Res.** : Residential
Bldg. : Building	**Gro.** : Grove	**Ri.** : Rise
Bldgs. : Buildings	**Hgts.** : Heights	**Rd.** : Road
Bus. : Business	**Ho.** : House	**Shop.** : Shopping
Cvn. : Caravan	**Ind.** : Industrial	**Sth.** : South
C'way. : Causeway	**Info.** : Information	**Sq.** : Square
Cen. : Centre	**Intl.** : International	**Sta.** : Station
Chu. : Church	**La.** : Lane	**St.** : Street
Cl. : Close	**Lit.** : Little	**Ter.** : Terrace
Comn. : Common	**Lwr.** : Lower	**Twr.** : Tower
Cnr. : Corner	**Mnr.** : Manor	**Trad.** : Trading
Cott. : Cottage	**Mans.** : Mansions	**Up.** : Upper
Cotts. : Cottages	**Mkt.** : Market	**Va.** : Vale
Ct. : Court	**Mdw.** : Meadow	**Vw.** : View
Cres. : Crescent	**Mdws.** : Meadows	**Vs.** : Villas
Cft. : Croft	**M.** : Mews	**Vis.** : Visitors
Dr. : Drive	**Mt.** : Mount	**Wlk.** : Walk
E. : East	**Mus.** : Museum	**W.** : West
Ent. : Enterprise	**Nth.** : North	**Yd.** : Yard

LOCALITY ABBREVIATIONS

Aig : **Aigburth**	Brom : **Bromborough**	Eccl : **Eccleston**
Ain : **Aintree**	Brook : **Brookvale**	Eccl P : **Eccleston Park**
Aller : **Allerton**	Burt : **Burton**	Ell P : **Ellesmere Port**
Ash M : **Ashton-in-Makerfield**	Burtw : **Burtonwood**	Faz : **Fazakerley**
Ast : **Astmoor**	Caldy : **Caldy**	Ford : **Ford**
Aston : **Aston**	Cas : **Castlefields**	Frank : **Frankby**
Augh : **Aughton**	Chil T : **Childer Thornton**	Frod : **Frodsham**
Barn : **Barnston**	Child : **Childwall**	Garst : **Garston**
Beb : **Bebington**	Clau : **Claughton**	Garsw : **Garswood**
Beech : **Beechwood**	Clftn : **Clifton**	Gate : **Gateacre**
Bic : **Bickerstaffe**	Clock F : **Clock Face**	Gras : **Grassendale**
Bid : **Bidston**	Coll G : **Collins Green**	Grea : **Greasby**
Bil : **Billinge**	Crank : **Crank**	Gt San : **Great Sankey**
Birke : **Birkenhead**	Cron : **Cronton**	Gt Sut : **Great Sutton**
Blun : **Blundellsands**	Crosb : **Crosby**	Hale : **Hale**
Bold : **Bold**	Crox : **Croxteth**	Hale B : **Hale Bank**
Bold H : **Bold Heath**	Cuerd : **Cuerdley**	Halew : **Halewood**
Boot : **Bootle**	Dares : **Daresbury**	Halt : **Halton**
Brim : **Brimstage**	Dutt : **Dutton**	Hatt : **Hatton**
Broad G : **Broad Green**	East : **Eastham**	Hay : **Haydock**

Hesw : **Heswall**
Hghr B : **Higher Bebington**
Hghr Wal : **Higher Walton**
Hoot : **Hooton**
Hoy : **Hoylake**
Hunts X : **Hunts Cross**
Huy : **Huyton**
Ince B : **Ince Blundell**
Irby : **Irby**
Kirkb : **Kirkby**
Kirkd : **Kirkdale**
Knott A : **Knotty Ash**
Know : **Knowsley**
Know I : **Knowsley Industrial Park**
Know P : **Knowsley Park**
Leas : **Leasowe**
Led : **Ledsham**
Lith : **Litherland**
Lit C : **Little Crosby**
Lit Sut : **Little Sutton**
Liv : **Liverpool**
Lwr W : **Lower Whitley**
Lyd : **Lydiate**
Mag : **Maghull**
Manor P : **Manor Park**
Mell : **Melling**
Meols : **Meols**
Moore : **Moore**
More : **Moreton**
Moss H : **Mossley Hill**
Murd : **Murdishaw**
Nest : **Neston**
N'ley : **Netherley**
N'ton : **Netherton**
New B : **New Brighton**
New F : **New Ferry**
Newt W : **Newton-le-Willows**
Noct : **Noctorum**
Norr G : **Norris Green**
Nort : **Norton**
Orm : **Ormskirk**
O'ton : **Oxton**
Pal F : **Palace Fields**
Park : **Parkgate**
Penk : **Penketh**
Pens : **Pensby**
Port S : **Port Sunlight**
Pren : **Prenton**
Presc : **Prescot**
Pres B : **Preston Brook**
Pres H : **Preston on the Hill**
Raby : **Raby**
Raby M : **Raby Mere**
Rainf : **Rainford**
Rainh : **Rainhill**
Roby : **Roby**
Rock F : **Rock Ferry**
Run : **Runcorn**
St H : **St Helens**
Sea : **Seaforth**
Seft : **Sefton**
Sim : **Simonswood**
Speke : **Speke**
Spit : **Spital**
Stockb V : **Stockbridge Village**
Store : **Storeton**
Sut L : **Sutton Leach**
Sut M : **Sutton Manor**
Sut W : **Sutton Weaver**
Tar G : **Tarbock Green**
Thing : **Thingwall**
Thorn : **Thornton**
Thorn H : **Thornton Hough**
Thurs : **Thurstaston**
Tran : **Tranmere**
Upton : **Upton**
Wall : **Wallasey**
Walt : **Walton**
Water : **Waterloo**
Wav : **Wavertree**
W Der : **West Derby**
W Kir : **West Kirby**
Westb : **Westbrook**
West : **Weston**
West P : **Weston Point**
Whis : **Whiston**
Wid : **Widnes**
Will : **Willaston**
Windle : **Windle**
Wind H : **Windmill Hill**
Woodc : **Woodchurch**
Woolt : **Woolton**

5athegallery *2E 43*
(off Bickerstaffe St.)
20 Forthlin Road (Childhood Home of Paul McCartney) **2G 91**

A

A41 Expressway CH42: Tran 6H **69**
Abacus Rd. L13: Liv 3E **55**
Abberley Cl. WA10: St H 2D **42**
Abberley Rd. L25: Hunts X 4E **93**
Abberton Pk. L30: N'ton 4G **11**
Abbey Cl. CH41: Birke 4H **69**
L33: Kirkb 1B **24**
WA8: Wid 3A **96**
Abbey Ct. L25: Woolt 1D **92**
Abbeyfield Dr. L12: Crox 3H **37**
Abbeygate Apartments L15: Wav 2D **72**
Abbey Hey WA7: Nort 5E **115**
Abbey M. L8: Liv 4H **71**
Abbey Rd. CH48: W Kir 1B **82**
L6: Liv .1A **54**
WA8: Wid 3H **95**
WA10: St H 4B **28**
WA11: Hay 4G **31**
Abbeystead Av. L30: N'ton 2G **21**
Abbeystead Rd. L15: Wav 1F **73**
Abbey St. CH41: Birke 4H **69**
Abbeyvale Dr. L25: Gate 3E **75**
Abbey Vw. L16: Child 2A **74**
Abbeyway Nth. WA11: Hay 4H **31**
Abbeyway Sth. WA11: Hay 5H **31**
Abbeywood Gro. L35: Whis 5F **59**
Abbot Cl. CH43: Bid 3G **67**
Abbotsbury Way L12: Crox 2A **38**
Abbots Bus. Pk. WA7: Pres B 2G **125**
(not continuous)
Abbots Dr. CH63: Beb 6H **87**
Abbotsfield Rd. WA9: Bold, St H 1A **62**
(not continuous)
Abbotsfield Rd. Ind. Est. WA9: St H . . .1A **62**
Abbotsford Ct. L23: Blun 6E **9**
Abbotsford Gdns. L23: Crosb 6E **9**
Abbotsford Rd. L11: Norr G 3D **36**
L23: Blun 6E **9**
Abbotsford St. CH44: Wall 5G **51**
Abbots Hall Av. WA9: Clock F 4H **61**
Abbots Quay CH41: Birke 3A **70**
Abbots Way CH48: W Kir 6C **64**
CH64: Nest 6A **118**
Abbott Dr. L20: Boot 6E **21**
Abbotts Cl. L18: Moss H 6F **73**
WA7: Run 5E **113**
Abbottshey Av. L18: Moss H 6F **73**
Abdale Rd. L11: Norr G 2D **36**
Abercrombie Rd. L33: Know I 4D **24**
Abercromby Sq. L7: Liv 1F **71**
Aberdale Rd. L13: Liv 4F **55**
Aberdeen St. CH41: Birke 2E **69**
Aberford Av. CH45: Wall 2A **50**
Abergele Rd. L13: Liv 5D **54**
Aber St. L6: Liv 4G **53**
Abingdon Gro. L4: Walt 3A **36**
L26: Halew 2A **94**
Abingdon Rd. CH49: Grea 6H **65**
L4: Walt 3A **36**
Abington Wlk. WA7: Brook 2E **125**
Abney Cl. L7: Liv 1H **71**
Aboyne Cl. L9: Walt 1G **35**
Abram St. L5: Liv 2E **53**
Abyssinia Cl. L15: Wav 2C **72**
Acacia Av. L36: Huy 6F **57**
WA8: Wid 6F **79**
Acacia Cl. CH49: Grea 1A **84**
Acacia Gro. CH44: Wall 5G **51**
CH48: W Kir 1A **82**
L9: Ain 5H **21**
WA7: Run 5G **113**
WA10: Eccl 1G **41**
Acacia St. WA12: Newt W 1H **45**
Academy Bus. Pk. L33: Know I 2D **24**
Acanthus Rd. L13: Liv 3E **55**
Access Rd. L12: W Der 6H **37**
Acer Leigh L17: Aig 1B **90**
Acheson Rd. L13: Liv 1C **54**
Achilles Ct. WA7: Cas 3C **114**
Ackers Hall Av. L14: Knott A 3B **56**
Ackers La. L23: Lit C 2E **9**
WA10: St H 1A **42**
Ackers Rd. CH49: Woodc 1G **85**
Ackers St. L34: Presc 1D **58**
Acland Rd. CH44: Wall 3D **50**
Aconbury Cl. L11: Norr G 2D **36**
Aconbury Pl. L11: Norr G 2D **36**
Acorn Bus. Cen. L33: Know I 1D **24**
Acorn Cl. CH63: Hghr B 5F **87**
WA9: Clock F 3G **61**
Acorn Ct. L8: Liv 3F **71**
Acorn Farm **5F 15**
Acornfield Cl. L33: Know I 3E **25**
Acornfield Plantation Local Nature Reserve **3F 25**
Acornfield Rd. L33: Know I 2F **25**
Acorn Way L20: Boot 6D **20**
Acrefield Ct. CH42: Tran 2D **86**
Acrefield Pk. L25: Woolt 6C **74**
Acrefield Rd. CH42: Tran 2D **86**
L25: Woolt 6C **74**
WA8: Wid 2H **95**
Acre Grn. L26: Halew 5A **94**
Acre La. CH60: Hesw 4G **101**
CH62: Brom 6C **104**
CH63: Brom 6C **104**
Acres Cl. L25: Gate 2C **74**
Acresfield *L13: Liv* *5F 55*
(off Broad Grn. Rd.)
Acresgate Ct. L25: Gate 4C **74**
Acres Rd. CH47: Meols 2F **65**
CH63: Beb 5H **87**
Acreville Rd. CH63: Beb 6H **87**
Acton Cl. WA11: Hay 5E **31**
Acton Gro. L6: Liv 1A **54**
Acton La. CH46: More 2A **66**
Acton Rake *L30: N'ton* *4D 10*
(off Higher End Pk.)
Acton Rd. CH42: Rock F 2A **88**
L32: Kirkb 1G **23**
WA5: Burtw 1G **63**
Acton Way L7: Liv 1A **72**
Acuba Gro. CH42: Tran 5G **69**
Acuba Rd. L15: Wav 6G **55**
Adair Pl. L13: Liv 6C **36**
Adair Rd. L13: Liv 6C **36**
Adam Cl. L19: Garst 6G **91**
Adamson Ho. WA7: Run 2C **112**
Adamson St. L7: Liv 5B **54**
Adam St. L5: Liv 1F **53**
Adaston Av. CH62: East 3F **121**
Adcote Cl. L14: Knott A 4B **56**
Adcote Rd. L14: Knott A 4B **56**
Addenbrook Cl. CH43: Bid 3G **67**
Addenbrooke Dr. L24: Speke 5D **92**
Adderley Cl. WA7: Run 4G **113**
Adderley St. L7: Liv 5H **53**
Addingham Av. WA8: Wid 4A **96**

Addingham Rd. L18: Moss H 4F **73**
Addington St. CH44: Wall 4F **51**
Addison Cl. L32: Kirkb 3H **23**
Addison Sq. WA8: Wid 2E **97**
Addison St. L3: Liv 1E **5** (4D **52**)
L20: Boot .6A **20**
Addison Way L3: Liv 1E **5** (4D **52**)
Adelaide Av. WA9: St H 6C **42**
Adelaide Ct. WA8: Wid 4E **97**
Adelaide Pl. L5: Liv 3E **53**
Adelaide Rd. CH42: Tran 5E **69**
L7: Liv 5H **53**
(not continuous)
L21: Sea .4H **19**
Adelaide St. CH44: Wall 4D **50**
Adelaide Ter. L22: Water 2E **19**
Adela Rd. WA7: Run 3D **112**
Adele Thompson Dr. L8: Liv 2G **71**
Adelphi St. CH41: Birke 3G **69**
Adkins St. L5: Liv 1G **53**
Adlam Cres. L9: Faz 4C **22**
Adlam Rd. L9: Faz 4C **22**
L10: Faz .4C **22**
Adler Way L3: Liv 6F **71**
Adlington Ho. L3: Liv 1E **5**
Adlington Rd. WA7: Wind H 3F **115**
Adlington St. L3: Liv 1E **5**
Admin Rd. L33: Know I 3E **25**
Admiral Gro. *L8: Liv* *4G 71*
(off High Pk. St.)
Admirals Quay L23: Blun 5C **8**
Admiral St. L8: Liv 4G **71**
Adrian's Way L32: Kirkb 1A **24**
Adshead Rd. L13: Liv 6C **36**
Adstone Rd. L25: Gate 4E **75**
Adswood Rd. L36: Huy 4G **57**
Aerodrome, The L24: Speke 1A **108**
Africander Rd. WA11: St H 3E **29**
Afton WA8: Wid 1G **95**
Agar Rd. L11: Norr G 6D **36**
Agate St. L5: Liv 2G **53**
Agincourt Rd. L12: W Der 2G **55**
Agnes Gro. CH44: Wall 2E **51**
Agnes Jones Ho. L8: Liv 1F **71**
Agnes Rd. CH42: Tran 6G **69**
L23: Blun .6E **9**
Agnes St. WA9: Clock F 4G **61**
Agnes Way L7: Liv 6H **53**
Agulnek Ct. L18: Moss H 6D **72**
Aiden Long Gro. L34: Know P 1G **57**
AIGBURTH 3C 90
Aigburth Dr. L17: Aig 4A **72**
Aigburth Gro. CH46: More 1B **66**
Aigburth Hall Av. L19: Aig 3D **90**
Aigburth Hall Rd. L19: Aig 3E **91**
Aigburth Ho. L17: Aig 6C **72**
Aigburth Rd. L17: Aig 5H **71**
L19: Aig, Gras 2C **90**
Aigburth Station (Rail) 3C 90
Aigburth St. L7: Liv 1H **71**
AIGBURTH VALE 6C 72
Aigburth Va. L17: Aig 1B **90**
(not continuous)
L18: Moss H 6C **72**
Ailsa Rd. CH45: Wall 2C **50**
Ainley Cl. WA7: Brook 2C **124**
Ainsdale Cl. CH61: Thing 6E **85**
CH63: Brom 2C **120**
L10: Faz 3D **22**
WA5: Penk 5H **81**
Ainsdale Rd. L20: Boot 6D **20**
Ainsworth Av. CH46: More 2A **66**
Ainsworth La. L34: Know 5D **24**
Ainsworth Rd. WA10: St H 6B **28**
Ainsworth St. L3: Liv 4H **5** (6E **53**)
AINTREE 1B 22
Aintree Cl. CH46: Leas 4D **48**
Aintree Ct. *L10: Ain* *6A 12*
(off Aintree La.)
Aintree La. L10: Ain 6A **12**
L10: Faz 2D **22**
Aintree Motor Circuit 3B **22**
Aintree Racecourse 2A **22**
Aintree Racecourse Retail & Bus. Pk.
L9: Ain 2H **21**
Aintree Rd. L9: Ain 5B **22**
L20: Boot .1D **34**
Aintree Station (Rail) 3H 21
Aintree Vis. Cen. &
Grand National Experience 2H **21**
Aintree Way L9: Ain 1A **22**
Airdale Cl. CH43: Bid 3G **67**
Airdale Rd. L15: Wav 3D **72**
Airdrie Cl. CH62: East 4D **120**
Aire WA8: Wid 1H **95**
Airedale Cl. WA5: Gt San 2H **81**
Airegate L31: Mag 5A **6**
Airlie Gro. L13: Liv 1B **54**
Airlie Rd. CH47: Hoy 3B **64**
Aisthorpe Gro. L31: Mag 2B **12**
Akbar, The CH60: Hesw 3A **100**
Akenside Ct. L20: Boot 5A **20**
Akenside St. L20: Boot 5A **20**
Alabama Way CH41: Birke 3H **69**
Alamein Rd. L36: Huy 3F **57**
Alan's Way L33: Kirkb 4A **14**
Alastair Cres. CH43: Pren 2B **86**
Alban Rd. L16: Child 1H **73**
Albany, The L3: Liv 3C **4**
Albany Av. L34: Eccl P 6F **41**
Albany Rd. CH42: Rock F 1G **87**
L7: Liv 5G **53**
L9: Ain 4H **21**
L13: Liv 3E **55**
L34: Presc 1E **59**
Albany Ter. WA7: Run 3E **113**
Albemarle Rd. CH44: Wall 4F **51**
Alberta Gro. L34: Presc 2H **57**
Albert Dock L3: Liv 6C **4** (1C **70**)
Albert Dr. WA5: Gt San 3F **81**
Albert Edward Rd. L7: Liv 5G **53**
(not continuous)
Albert Gro. L15: Wav 1E **73**
L23: Crosb .5F **9**
Albert Pk. L17: Aig 4H **71**
Albert Rd. CH42: Tran 5E **69**
CH47: Hoy 3B **64**
CH48: W Kir 2A **82**
L13: Liv 1B **54**
L22: Water 2F **19**
WA8: Wid .3F **97**
Albert Row WA6: Frod 6F **123**
Albert Schweitzer Av.
L30: N'ton 6F **11**
Albert Sq. WA8: Wid 3F **97**
Albert St. CH45: New B 4E **33**
L7: Liv 6G **53**
WA7: Run 3E **113**
WA10: St H 6E **29**
Albert Ter. WA5: Coll G 4G **45**
Albion Pl. CH45: New B 5D **32**
Albion St. CH41: Birke 3H **69**
(not continuous)
CH45: New B 5C **32**
L5: Liv 1E **53**
WA10: St H 2C **42**
(not continuous)
Albourne Rd. L32: Kirkb 3C **24**
Albright Rd. WA8: Wid 5F **95**
Albury Cl. L12: Crox 3B **38**
WA11: Hay 4E **31**
Albury Rd. L32: Kirkb 4B **24**
Alcester Rd. L12: W Der 1G **55**
Alchemy Way L33: Know I 4D **24**
Alcock St. WA7: Run 2E **113**
Aldams Gro. L4: Kirkd 4E **35**
Aldbourne Av. L25: Woolt 4A **74**
Aldbourne Cl. L25: Woolt 5A **74**
Alder Av. L36: Huy 1A **76**
WA8: Wid .6E **79**
Alderbank Rd. WA5: Gt San 3H **81**
Alder Cl. L34: Presc 1F **59**
Alder Cres. L32: Kirkb 6H **13**
Alderfield Dr. L24: Speke 1H **109**
Alder Gro. L22: Water 1F **19**
Alder Hey Rd. WA10: St H 2A **42**
Alder La. L34: Know 2D **38**
(not continuous)
WA5: Burtw 6H **45**
WA6: Frod 4B **122**
WA8: Cron 5F **77**
Alderley Av. CH41: Birke 2B **68**
Alderley Rd. CH44: Wall 4D **50**
CH47: Hoy 2B **64**
Alderman Rd. L24: Speke 5D **92**
Alderney Rd. L5: Liv 2D **52**
Alder Rd. CH63: Hghr B 1F **103**
L12: W Der 3F **55**
L34: Presc 1F **59**
Aldersey Cl. WA7: Wind H 4F **115**
Aldersey St. L3: Liv 4D **52**
Aldersgate CH42: Rock F 1H **87**
Aldersgate Av. WA7: Murd 6F **115**
Aldersgate Dr. L26: Halew 5A **94**
Alderson Rd. L15: Wav 2B **72**
Alderton Cl. L26: Halew 4A **94**
Alderton Dr. WN4: Ash M 1H **31**
Alderville Rd. L4: Walt 3A **36**
Alderwood Av. L24: Speke 2G **109**
Alderwood Ct. WA8: Wid 5C **78**
Alderwood Lodge *L24: Speke* *2A 110*
(off East Mains)
Aldford Cl. CH43: O'ton 1A **86**
CH63: Brom 1B **120**
Aldford Rd. L32: Kirkb 4A **24**
Aldridge Cl. L12: Crox 2A **38**
Aldridge Dr. WA5: Burtw 6H **45**
Aldrins La. L30: N'ton 5F **11**
Aldwark Rd. L14: Knott A 3C **56**
Aldwych Rd. L12: W Der 1G **55**
Aldykes L31: Mag 1C **12**
Alexander Dr. CH61: Pens 2C **100**
L31: Lyd 4C **6**
WA8: Wid .3B **96**
Alexander Fleming Av. L30: N'ton 5F **11**
Alexander Grn. L36: Huy 3G **57**
Alexander Ho. L21: Sea 4H **19**
L34: Presc 6D **40**
Alexander Wlk. *L4: Walt* *5F 35*
(off Florence St.)
Alexander Way *L8: Liv* *5F 71*
(off Park Hill Rd.)
Alexander Wharf *L31: Mag* *6B 6*
(off Damfield La.)
Alexandra Ct. *CH45: New B* *5C 32*
(off Alexandra Rd.)
L6: Liv 4H **53**
L23: Crosb .5F **9**
WA9: St H *5B 42*
(off Carnarvon St.)
Alexandra Dr. CH42: Rock F 2G **87**
L17: Aig 5H **71**
L20: Boot .5E **21**
WA10: St H 4B **42**
(not continuous)
Alexandra Grn. L17: Aig 5H **71**
Alexandra Gro. L26: Halew 5H **93**
WA7: Run 4G **113**
Alexandra Ho. L17: Aig 5H **71**
Alexandra Ind. Est. WA8: Wid 4D **96**
Alexandra M. WA6: Frod 6F **123**
Alexandra Mt. L21: Lith 3B **20**
Alexandra Pk. L17: Aig 6H **71**
Alexandra Rd. CH43: O'ton 4E **69**
CH45: New B 5C **32**
CH48: W Kir 2A **82**
L7: Liv 1A **72**
L13: Liv 5E **55**
L19: Garst 4G **91**
L22: Water 3G **19**
L23: Crosb .5F **9**
Alexandra St. WA8: Wid 4E **97**
WA10: St H 4B **42**
Alexandra Ter. *L8: Liv* *2F 71*
(off Princes Rd.)
Alexandra Vs. *L21: Lith* *3B 20*
(off Alexandra Mt.)
Alex Cl. L8: Liv 3F **71**
Alfonso Rd. L4: Kirkd 5D **34**

Alford Av. WA9: Sut M 3F **61**
Alforde St. WA8: Wid 4E **97**
(not continuous)
Alford St. L7: Liv 5C **54**
Alfred Cl. WA8: Wid 3F **97**
Alfred M. L1: Liv 2E **71**
Alfred Rd. CH43: O'ton 4E **69**
CH44: Wall 6G **51**
WA11: Hay 4H **31**
Alfred Stocks Ct. *L8: Liv* *6G 71*
(off Turner Cl.)
Alfred St. L15: Wav 1B **72**
WA8: Wid 3F **97**
WA10: St H 1F **43**
WA11: Rainf 2F **17**
Alfriston Rd. L12: W Der 1G **55**
Algernon St. WA7: Run 2D **112**
Alice Ct. WA8: Wid 1E **113**
Alice St. WA9: St H 5A **44**
Alicia Wlk. L10: Faz 4F **23**
Alison Av. CH42: Rock F 6H **69**
Alison Pl. L13: Liv 6C **36**
Alison Rd. L13: Liv 6C **36**
Alistair Dr. CH63: Brom 2C **120**
Allangate Cl. CH49: Grea 1A **84**
Allangate Rd. L19: Gras 3F **91**
Allan Rd. WA11: St H 4G **29**
Allanson St. WA9: St H 2H **43**
Allcot Av. CH42: Tran 1F **87**
Allenby Av. L23: Crosb 1H **19**
Allenby Sq. L13: Liv 5E **55**
Allendale WA7: Pal F 1D **124**
Allendale Av. L9: Ain 4H **21**
L35: Rainh 4B **60**
Allengate L23: Crosb 4G **9**
Allen Rd. WA7: West P 6B **112**
Allerford Rd. L12: W Der 6G **37**
ALLERTON 3H 91
Allerton Beeches
L18: Moss H 6G **73**
Allerton Dr. L18: Moss H 5F **73**
Allerton Gro. CH42: Tran 6G **69**
Allerton Rd. CH42: Tran 6F **69**
CH45: Wall 1C **50**
L18: Aller, Moss H 4E **73**
L25: Woolt 2B **92**
WA8: Wid 2F **97**
Allerton Station (Rail) 5H **91**
Allesley Rd. L14: Knott A 2B **56**
Alleyne Rd. L4: Walt 5B **36**
All Hallows Dr. L24: Speke 2H **109**
Allington St. L17: Aig 6H **71**
Allinsons Ct. L21: Lith 4B **20**
Allonby Cl. CH43: Noct 5A **68**
Allport La. CH62: Brom 5D **104**
(not continuous)
Allport Rd. CH62: Brom 1C **120**
CH63: Brom 1C **120**
Allports, The CH62: Brom 6D **104**
All Saints Cl. L30: N'ton 6E **11**
All Saints Ct. WA11: Rainf 4G **17**
All Saints Rd. L24: Speke 2E **109**
Allysum Ct. WA7: Beech 3B **124**
Alma Cl. L10: Faz 4F **23**
Almacs Cl. L23: Blun 6D **8**
Alman Ct. *L17: Aig* *6H 71*
(off Bryanston Rd.)
Alma Pl. WA9: St H 3G **43**
Alma Rd. L17: Aig 3C **90**
Alma St. CH41: Birke 3G **69**
CH62: New F 4A **88**
WA9: St H 3G **43**
Alma Ter. *L15: Wav* *1D 72*
(off Sandown La.)
Almeda Rd. L24: Speke 3A **110**
Almond Av. L30: N'ton 6C **10**
WA7: Run 5G **113**
Almond Cl. L26: Halew 4G **93**
WA11: Hay 6B **30**
Almond Ct. L19: Garst 6A **92**
Almond Dr. WA5: Burtw 1H **63**
Almond Gro. WA8: Wid 3B **96**
Almond Pl. CH46: More 1D **66**
Almonds, The L26: Halew 4G **93**
Almond's Grn. L12: W Der 5E **37**
Almond's Gro. L12: W Der 6E **37**
Almond's Pk. L12: W Der 5E **37**
Almonds Turn L30: N'ton 5D **10**
Almond Tree Cl. L24: Hale 4E **111**
Almond Way CH49: Grea 1A **84**
Alness Dr. L35: Rainh 5B **60**
Alnwick Dr. CH46: More 1H **65**
Aloeswood Cl. L6: Liv 2H **53**
Alpass Rd. L17: Aig 6H **71**
Alpha Dr. CH42: Rock F 2A **88**
Alpha St. L21: Lith 6B **20**
Alpine Cl. WA10: St H 1A **42**
Alresford Rd. L19: Aig 3D **90**
Alroy Rd. L4: Walt 6G **35**
Alscot Av. L10: Faz 4E **23**
Alscot Cl. L31: Mag 1B **12**
Alston Cl. CH62: Brom 4C **104**
Alstonfield Rd. L14: Knott A 3C **56**
Alston M. WA10: St H 6H **41**
Alston Rd. L17: Aig 3C **90**
Alt WA8: Wid 1H **95**
Alt Av. L31: Mag 2A **12**
Altbridge Pk. L11: Crox 1F **37**
(not continuous)
Altbridge Rd. L36: Huy 2F **57**
Altcar Av. L15: Wav 2B **72**
Altcar Dr. CH46: More 2B **66**
Altcar Rd. L20: Boot 6C **20**
Altcross Rd. L11: Crox 1G **37**
Altcross Way L11: Crox 1G **37**
Altfield Rd. L14: Knott A 6B **38**
Altfinch Cl. L14: Knott A 6C **38**
Altham Rd. L11: Norr G 6D **36**
Althorp St. L8: Liv 6F **71**
Altmoor Rd. L36: Huy 1F **57**
Alton Av. L21: Lith 2A **20**
Alton Rd. CH43: O'ton 4C **68**
L6: Liv 2B **54**
Alt Rd. L20: Boot 6C **20**
L36: Huy 4G **57**
Alt Side Ct. L10: Faz 4F **23**
Alt St. L8: Liv 2H **71**
Altway L10: Ain 6A **12**
Altway Ct. *L10: Ain* *6A 12*
(off Altway)
Alundale Ct. *L20: Boot* *2C 34*
(off Clairville Cl.)
Alundale Rd. L12: W Der 2A **56**
Alvanley Grn. L32: Kirkb 1G **23**
Alvanley Pl. CH43: O'ton 3E **69**
Alvanley Rd. L12: W Der 2G **55**
L32: Kirkb 1G **23**
Alva Rd. L35: Rainh 5B **60**
Alvega Cl. CH62: New F 4C **88**
Alverstone Av. CH41: Birke 2B **68**
Alverstone Cl. WA5: Gt San 2E **81**
Alverstone Rd. CH44: Wall 4F **51**
L18: Moss H 4D **72**
Alverton Cl. WA8: Wid 3B **96**
Alvina La. L4: Walt 6E **35**
L33: Kirkb 4C **14**
Alwain Grn. L24: Speke 3H **109**
Alwen St. CH41: Birke 6B **50**
Alwyn Av. L21: Lith 2B **20**
Alwyn Cl. L17: Aig 6H **71**
Alwyn Gdns. CH46: More 1D **66**
Alwyn St. L17: Aig 6H **71**
Amanda Rd. L10: Faz 4F **23**
L35: Rainh 2H **59**
Amanda Way L31: Mell 5F **13**
Amaury Cl. L23: Thorn 4B **10**
Amaury Rd. L23: Thorn 4B **10**
Ambassador Dr. L26: Halew 2A **94**
Ambergate Cl. WA9: St H 6H **43**
Ambergate Rd. L19: Gras 4F **91**
Amberley Av. CH46: More 2A **66**
Amberley Cl. CH46: More 2A **66**
L6: Liv 6B **36**
Amberley St. L8: Liv 2G **71**
Amber Way L14: Knott A 6C **38**
Ambleside Av. CH46: More 1B **66**
Ambleside Cl. CH61: Thing 5E **85**
CH62: Brom 6E **105**
WA7: Beech 2A **124**
Ambleside Dr. L33: Kirkb 5H **13**
Ambleside Pl. WA11: St H 2F **29**
Ambleside Rd. L18: Aller 2H **91**
L31: Mag 5C **6**
Amelia Cl. L6: Liv 4F **53**
WA8: Wid 5F **79**
Amersham Rd. L4: Walt 3A **36**
(not continuous)
Amery Gro. CH42: Tran 1E **87**
Amethyst Cl. L6: Liv 3H **53**
L21: Lith 3C **20**
Amherst Rd. L17: Aig 1A **90**
Amidian Ct. *CH44: Wall* *4D 50*
(off Poulton Rd.)
Amity St. L8: Liv 4F **71**
Amos Av. L21: Lith 3C **20**
Ampleforth Cl. L32: Kirkb 2G **23**
Ampthill Rd. L17: Aig 1A **90**
Ampulla Rd. L11: Crox 2G **37**
Amy Wlk. L10: Faz 4F **23**
Ancaster Rd. L17: Aig 1A **90**
Ancholme Cl. L35: Whis 1G **59**
Anchorage, The L3: Liv 3D **70**
Anchorage La. L18: Moss H 6C **72**
Anchor Cl. WA7: Murd 1F **125**
Anchor Courtyard L3: Liv 6C **4**
Ancient Mdws. L9: Ain 4H **21**
Ancroft Rd. L14: Knott A 4C **56**
Ancrum Rd. L33: Kirkb 3H **13**
Anders Dr. L33: Kirkb 4C **14**
Anderson Cl. CH61: Irby 5E **85**
L35: Rainh 6B **60**
Anderson Ct. CH62: Brom 1D **120**
Anderson Rd. L21: Lith 2D **20**
Anderson St. L5: Liv 1E **53**
(not continuous)
Anderson Trad. Est. *WA8: Wid* *5E 97*
(off Croft St.)
Anderson Way L21: Lith 2D **20**
Anderton Ter. L36: Roby 5E **57**
Andover Rd. WA11: Hay 3G **31**
Andover Way L25: Hunts X 3F **93**
Andrew Av. L31: Mell 6E **13**
Andrew Cl. WA8: Wid 3A **96**
Andrew Ho. *L8: Liv* *2F 71*
(off Birley Ct.)
Andrew St. L4: Walt 4F **35**
Andrew's Wlk. CH60: Hesw 5F **101**
Andromeda Way WA9: Bold 6D **44**
Anemone Way WA9: Bold 6C **44**
ANFIELD 6G **35**
Anfield 6G **35**
Anfield Ct. L4: Walt 6G **35**
Anfield Crematorium L4: Walt 5H **35**
Anfield Rd. L4: Walt 6F **35**
Angela St. L7: Liv 1H **71**
Angelica Dr. L11: Norr G 3D **36**
Angelica Rd. L33: Kirkb 5B **14**
Angers La. L31: Mell 3F **13**
Anglesea Rd. L9: Walt 2G **35**
Anglesea Way L8: Liv 5F **71**
Anglesey Rd. CH44: Wall 2D **50**
CH48: W Kir 5A **64**
Anglezark Cl. L7: Liv 5H **53**
Anglian Ct. *L8: Liv* *2E 71*
(off Blair St.)
Anglia Way L25: Hunts X 3E **93**
Anglo Cl. L9: Ain 3A **22**
Angus Rd. CH63: Brom 1C **120**
L11: Norr G 5D **36**
Annandale Cl. L33: Kirkb 3H **13**
Ann Conway Ho. *L15: Wav* *2C 72*
(off Garmoyle Cl.)
Anne Gro. WA9: St H 6G **43**
Annerley St. L7: Liv 1A **72**
Annesley Rd. CH44: Wall 4E **51**
L17: Aig 1A **90**
Anne St. WA9: Clock F 4H **61**
Annie Rd. L20: Boot 5D **20**
Ann St. WA7: Run 2F **113**

Ann St. W. WA8: Wid 4F 97
Anscot Av. CH63: Beb 5H 87
Ansdell Dr. WA10: Eccl 6H 27
Ansdell Rd. WA8: Wid 1F 97
Ansdell Vs. Rd. L35: Rainh 3A 60
Anson St. L3: Liv 3H 5 (5F 53)
Anstey Cl. CH46: More 6H 47
Anstey Rd. L13: Liv 4F 55
Ansty Cl. WA11: St H 6H 29
Anthony's Way CH60: Hesw 6E 101
Anthorn Cl. CH43: Noct 5H 67
Antonio St. L20: Boot 4D 34
Antons Cl. L26: Halew 5H 93
Antons Ct. L26: Halew 5A 94
Antons Rd. CH61: Pens 6E 85
L26: Halew 5H 93
Antrim Cl. WA11: Hay 5E 31
Antrim St. L13: Liv 6C 36
Anvil Cl. L20: Boot 1B 34
Anzacs, The CH62: Port S 5C 88
Anzio Rd. L36: Huy 3F 57
Apex Ct. CH62: Brom 4E 105
Apollo Ct. *CH44: Wall* *2F 51*
(off Rudgrave Sq.)
Apollo Cres. L33: Kirkb 5A 14
Apollo Way L6: Liv 2H 53
L30: N'ton 5F 11
Apostles Way L33: Kirkb 4H 13
Appin Rd. CH41: Birke 4G 69
Appleby Cl. WA8: Wid 3A 96
Appleby Dr. L30: N'ton 6C 10
Appleby Grn. L12: W Der 1H 55
Appleby Gro. CH62: Brom 1D 120
Appleby Lawn L27: N'ley 5A 76
Appleby Rd. L33: Kirkb 5A 14
Appleby Wlk. L27: N'ley 5A 76
WA8: Wid 3A 96
Applecorn Cl. WA9: Sut L 1H 61
Apple Ct. *L6: Liv* *4H 53*
(off Coleridge St.)
Appledore Ct. L24: Speke 1D 108
Appledore Gro. WA9: Sut L 3G 61
Applegarth CH46: More 3A 66
APPLETON 1F 97
Appleton Dr. CH49: Grea 6C 66
Appleton Rd. L4: Walt 4H 35
L21: Lith 2A 20
L32: Kirkb 5A 14
WA8: Wid 2F 97
WA9: St H 3G 43
Appleton St. WA8: Wid 5F 97
Appleton Village WA8: Wid 2E 97
Apple Tree Cl. L24: Hale 4E 111
L28: Stockb V 5D 38
Appletree Cl. L18: Aller 2G 91
Applewood Cl. L26: Halew 2A 94
April Gro. L6: Liv 2B 54
April Ri. L30: N'ton 6E 11
Apsley Av. CH45: Wall 1D 50
Apsley Brow L31: Mag 6A 6
Apsley Gro. CH63: Beb 5A 88
Apsley Rd. CH62: New F 3B 88
L12: W Der 1G 55
Aqua Complex, The 6E 35
Aquarius Cl. L14: Knott A 3C 56
Arabis Gdns. WA9: Bold 6D 44
Aragon Cl. L31: Mag 4D 6
Aragon Ct. WA7: Manor P 2E 115
Aran Cl. L24: Hale 3D 110
Arborn Dr. CH49: Upton 3E 67
Arbour Ct. L33: Know I 1D 24
Arbour La. L33: Know I 2C 24
Arbury Av. WA11: St H 5H 29
Arcadia Av. L31: Lyd 4C 6
Archbishops Beck Tennis Cen. 6G 21
Archbishop Warlock Ct. L3: Liv 3C 52
Archbrook M. *L13: Liv* *2C 54*
(off Sutton St.)
Archer Cl. L4: Kirkd 6E 35
Archerfield Rd. L18: Aller 1F 91
Archer Gro. WA9: St H 1A 44
Archers Ct. *CH49: Woodc* *1E 85*
(off Childwall Grn.)
Archers Cft. CH62: Brom 4D 104
Archers Fold L31: Mell 5F 13
Archers Grn. CH62: East 3E 121
Archer St. L4: Kirkd 6E 35
Archers Way CH49: Woodc 1E 85
Arch La. WN4: Garsw 1D 30
Arch Vw. Cres. L1: Liv 1E 71
Archway Rd. L36: Huy 5F 57
Arctic Rd. L20: Boot 2A 34
Arden WA8: Wid 1G 95
Ardennes Rd. L36: Huy 4G 57
Arderne Cl. CH63: Spit 3B 104
Ardleigh Cl. L13: Liv 5D 54
Ardleigh Gro. L13: Liv 5D 54
Ardleigh Pl. L13: Liv 5D 54
Ardleigh Rd. L13: Liv 5C 54
Ardmore Rd. L18: Moss H 1E 91
Ardrossan Rd. L4: Walt 5A 36
Ardville Rd. L11: Norr G 2B 36
Ardwick Rd. L24: Speke 2H 109
Ardwick St. WA9: St H 2G 43
Argo Rd. L22: Water 2F 19
Argos Pl. L20: Kirkd 4D 34
Argos Rd. L20: Kirkd 4D 34
Argyle Ct. L1: Liv 6E 5
Argyle Rd. L4: Walt 1H 53
L19: Garst 5G 91
Argyle St. CH41: Birke 3G 69
L1: Liv 6E 5 (1D 70)
WA10: St H 6D 28
Argyle St. Sth. CH41: Birke 4G 69
Argyll Av. CH62: East 3D 120
Aries Cl. L14: Knott A 2C 56
Ariss Gro. L35: Whis 2G 59
Arkenstone Cl. WA8: Wid 1A 96
Arkle Rd. CH43: Bid 1B 68
Arkles La. L4: Walt 6G 35
Arkles Rd. L4: Walt 1G 53
Arklow Dr. L24: Hale 3D 110
Ark Royal Way CH41: Tran 5H 69
Arkwood Cl. CH62: Spit 2C 104
Arkwright Ct. WA7: Ast 2B 114
Arkwright Rd. WA7: Ast 2B 114
Arkwright St. L5: Liv 2E 53
Arlescourt Rd. L12: W Der 2G 55
Arley Cl. CH43: Bid 3G 67
Arley Dr. WA8: Wid 1G 95
Arley St. L3: Liv 3C 52
Arlington Av. L18: Moss H 4D 72
Arlington Ct. CH43: O'ton 4B 68
Arlington Dr. WA5: Penk 5G 81
Arlington Rd. CH45: Wall 1A 50
Armill Rd. L11: Crox 2G 37
Armitage Gdns.
L18: Aller 2F 91
Armley Rd. L4: Walt 6H 35
Armour Gro. L13: Liv 5E 55
Armoury, The L12: W Der 6F 37
Armscot Cl. L25: Hunts X 4D 92
Armscot Pl. L25: Hunts X 4D 92
Armstrong Quay L3: Liv 6F 71
Arncliffe Dr. WA5: Burtw 1H 63
Arncliffe Rd. L25: Hunts X, Woolt 3E 93
Arndale WA7: Beech 2A 124
Arnhem Rd. L36: Huy 3G 57
Arnian Rd. WA11: Rainf 2F 17
Arnian Way WA11: Rainf 2F 17
Arno Ct. CH43: O'ton 6D 68
Arnold Av. WA10: St H 6B 28
Arnold Cl. WA9: St H 4G 43
Arnold Cres. L8: Liv 3G 71
Arnold Gro. L15: Wav 1E 73
Arnold Pl. WA8: Wid 4A 96
Arnold St. CH45: Wall 2D 50
Arno Rd. CH43: O'ton 6D 68
Arnot Cl. WA10: St H 6D 28
Arnot St. L4: Walt 4F 35
Arnot Way CH63: Hghr B 5F 87
Arnside L21: Lith 3D 20
Arnside Av. L35: Rainh 3G 59
WA11: Hay 5D 30
Arnside Rd. CH43: O'ton 5C 68
CH45: Wall 2D 50
Arnside Rd. L7: Liv 6A 54
L36: Huy 5D 56
Aron Ct. L34: Presc 1D 58
Arrad St. L7: Liv 1F 71
Arran Cl. WA11: St H 5A 30
Arranmore Rd. L18: Moss H 1E 91
Arriva Stadium, The 6E 9
Arrivato Plaza *WA10: St H* *2F 43*
(off Hall St.)
Arrowe Av. CH46: More 2B 66
Arrowe Brook La. CH49: Grea 2B 84
Arrowe Brook Rd. CH49: Woodc 1D 84
Arrowe Commercial Pk.
CH49: Upton 6D 66
Arrowe Country Pk. 2D 84
Arrowe Ct. *CH49: Woodc* *1E 85*
(off Childwall Grn.)
ARROWE HILL .6D 66
Arrowe Pk. Rd.
CH49: Upton, Woodc 5E 67
Arrowe Rd. CH49: Grea 6B 66
Arrowe Side CH49: Grea 5C 66
Arrowsmith Rd. WA11: Hay 4H 31
Art Ho. Sq. L1: Liv 6G 5
Arthur St. CH41: Birke 2E 69
(not continuous)
L9: Walt .2F 35
L19: Garst 6H 91
WA7: Run 3E 113
Arundel Av. CH45: Wall 1B 50
L8: Liv 3A 72
L17: Liv .3A 72
Arundel Cl. CH61: Pens 6C 84
L8: Liv 3G 71
Arundell Cl. WA5: Burtw 1H 63
Arundel St. L4: Walt 4E 35
Arvon St. L20: Boot 5D 20
Asbridge St. L8: Liv 3H 71
Asbury Cl. L18: Aller 6H 73
Asbury Rd. CH45: Wall 1H 49
Ascot Av. L21: Lith 3A 20
WA7: Run 1F 123
Ascot Dr. CH63: Beb 6H 87
L33: Kirkb 4A 14
Ascot Gro. CH63: Beb 6H 87
Ascot Pk. L23: Crosb 5H 9
Ascot Vw. L22: Water 1E 19
Ascroft Rd. L9: Ain 3H 21
Ashbank Rd. L11: Norr G 3E 37
Ashbourne Av. L23: Blun 5E 9
L30: N'ton 1E 21
WA7: Run 1F 123
Ashbourne Cres. L36: Huy 5D 56
Ashbourne Rd. L17: Aig 1A 90
Ashbrook Av. WA7: Sut W 3A 124
Ashbrook Dr. L9: Ain 5A 22
Ashbrook Ter. CH63: Beb 5A 88
Ashburn Av. L33: Kirkb 5A 14
Ashburnham Way L3: Liv 4E 53
Ashburton Av. CH43: Clau 3B 68
Ashburton Rd. CH43: Clau 3A 68
CH44: Wall 3D 50
CH48: W Kir 6B 64
Ashbury Cl. L14: Knott A 1D 56
WA7: Wind H 3F 115
Ashbury Dr. WA11: Hay 4E 31
Ashbury Rd. L14: Knott A 1D 56
Ashby Cl. CH46: More 6H 47
Ash Cl. L15: Wav 1C 72
Ashcombe Rd. L14: Knott A 4G 55
Ash Cres. L36: Huy 1G 75
Ashcroft Dr. CH61: Hesw 2D 100
Ashcroft Rd. L33: Know I 6D 14
Ashcroft St. L20: Boot 2B 34
WA9: St H 2G 43
(not continuous)
Ashdale L36: Huy 5F 57
Ashdale Pk. CH49: Grea 6H 65
Ashdale Rd. L9: Walt 1G 35
L18: Moss H 4E 73
L22: Water 1F 19
Ashdown Cres. WA9: Clock F 3G 61
Ashdown Dr. CH49: Grea 1A 84

Ashdown Gro. L26: Halew 2A 94
Ashfarm Ct. L14: Knott A 4B 56
Ashfield L15: Wav 1B 72
L35: Rainh 4B 60
Ashfield Ct. WA10: St H 2D 42
(off Glover St.)
Ashfield Cres. CH62: Brom 5D 104
Ashfield Rd. CH62: Brom 5C 104
L17: Aig 1B 90
L35: Presc 2C 52
Ashfield St. L5: Liv 4G 93
Ashford Cl. L26: Halew 4G 93
Ashford Rd. CH41: Birke 1C 68
CH47: Meols 1C 64
Ashford Way WA8: Wid 2H 97
Ash Grange L14: Knott A 4H 55
Ash Gro. CH45: New B 6E 33
L15: Wav 1B 72
L21: Sea .5A 20
L35: Presc 3E 59
WA7: Run 5G 113
WA8: Wid 3B 96
WA9: Clock F 3G 61
WA11: Rainf 3F 17
Ash La. WA8: Wid 2E 95
Ashlar Gro. L17: Aig 1C 90
Ashlar Rd. L17: Aig 1C 90
L22: Water 1G 19
Ashlea Rd. CH61: Pens 2D 100
Ashleigh Rd. L31: Mag 2D 12
Ashley Av. CH47: Meols 6F 47
Ashley Bus. Cen. L34: Presc 1E 59
(off Pottery Flds.)
Ashley Cl. L33: Kirkb 4A 14
L35: Rainh 5B 60
Ashley Grn. WA8: Wid 3B 96
Ashley Retail Pk. WA8: Wid 4F 97
Ashley Rd. WA7: Run 3H 113
Ashley St. CH42: Rock F 1H 87
Ashley Way WA8: Wid 5E 97
Ashley Way W. WA8: Wid 4D 96
Ashmore Cl. CH48: Caldy 5C 82
Ashmuir Hey L32: Kirkb 2B 24
Ashover Av. L14: Knott A 3C 56
Ash Priors WA8: Wid 6B 78
Ashridge St. WA7: Run 2D 112
Ash Rd. CH42: Tran 5F 69
CH63: Hghr B 4H 87
L21: Lith 4A 20
WA5: Penk 5H 81
WA11: Hay 4G 31
Ash St. L20: Boot 1C 34
Ashton Av. L35: Rainh 6A 60
Ashton Cl. CH62: East 4E 121
WA6: Frod 6H 123
WA7: West 1D 122
Ashton Ct. CH48: W Kir 2A 82
WA6: Frod 6G 123
ASHTON CROSS 1F 31
Ashton Dr. CH48: W Kir 2A 82
L25: Hunts X 4D 92
WA6: Frod 5G 123
Ashton Pk. L25: Hunts X 3F 93
ASHTON'S GREEN 2B 44
Ashtons Grn. Dr. WA9: St H 3B 44
Ashton's La. L24: Hale 3H 109
Ashton Sq. L25: Woolt 2D 92
Ashton St. L3: Liv 5F 53
L13: Liv .4E 55
Ash Tree Apartments CH44: Wall 4F 51
Ashtree Gro. L12: Crox 1A 38
Ashurst Cl. L25: Gate 5D 74
WA11: St H 5A 30
Ashurst Dr. WA11: St H 5H 29
Ash Va. L15: Wav 1C 72
Ash Vs. CH44: Wall 5E 51
Ashville Ind. Est. WA7: Sut W 4A 124
Ashville Point WA7: Sut W 4A 124
Ashville Rd. CH41: Birke 3C 68
CH43: Clau 3C 68
CH44: Wall 5F 51
Ashville Way WA7: Sut W 4A 124
Ashwater Rd. L12: W Der 3G 37
Ash Way CH60: Hesw 1F 117

Ashwell St. L8: Liv 2E 71
Ashwood Cl. L27: N'ley 4G 75
L33: Kirkb 4A 14
WA8: Wid 4G 95
Ashwood Ct. CH43: Bid 6G 49
Ashwood Dr. L12: Crox 2H 37
Askern Rd. L32: Kirkb 3B 24
Askett Cl. WA11: Hay 4F 31
Askew Cl. CH44: Wall 3F 51
Askew St. L4: Walt 4F 35
Askham Cl. L8: Liv 2H 71
Aspen Cl. CH60: Hesw 5H 101
L33: Kirkb 3B 14
Aspendale Rd. CH42: Tran 5F 69
Aspen Gdns. WA9: St H 1A 60
Aspen Gro. L8: Liv 3A 72
Aspenwood WN4: Ash M 1H 31
Aspes Rd. L12: W Der 6A 38
Aspinall St. CH41: Birke 2E 69
L34: Presc 1D 58
Aspley Ho. L22: Water 2G 19
Asquith Av. CH41: Birke 2D 68
Asser Rd. L11: Norr G 5C 36
Assheton Wlk. L24: Hale 3E 111
Assissian Cres. L30: N'ton 5E 11
Aster Cres. WA7: Beech 2B 124
Aster Dr. L33: Kirkb 4H 13
Asterfield Av. CH63: Hghr B 4G 87
Aster Rd. WA11: Hay 4H 31
Astley Cl. WA8: Wid 6A 78
WA11: Rainf 2F 17
Astley Rd. L36: Huy 1G 57
ASTMOOR 2B 114
Astmoor Bri. La. WA7: Cas 3B 114
Astmoor Ind. Est. WA7: Ast 2A 114
(not continuous)
Astmoor La. WA7: Ast 2G 113
WA7: Cas 3B 114
Astmoor Rd. WA7: Ast 2G 113
Astmoor Spine Rd.
WA7: Ast 2C 114
ASTON 6F 125
Aston Cl. CH43: O'ton 6B 68
Aston Flds. Rd. WA7: Pres B 3F 125
Aston Forge WA7: Pres B 2H 125
Aston Grn. WA7: Pres B 1G 125
ASTON HEATH 4G 125
Aston La. WA7: Aston, Sut W 4D 124
WA7: Pres B 2H 125
Aston La. Nth. WA7: Pres B 3G 125
Aston La. Sth. WA7: Pres B 4G 125
Aston St. L19: Garst 6H 91
Astonwood Rd. CH42: Tran 6F 69
Astor St. L4: Walt 3F 35
Atheldene Rd. L4: Walt 3A 36
Athelstan Cl. CH62: Brom 4D 104
Atherton Cl. L5: Liv 2E 53
Atherton Ct. CH45: New B 5C 32
(off Alexandra Rd.)
Atherton Dr. CH49: Woodc 6E 67
Atherton Ho. CH45: New B 5D 32
Atherton Rake L30: N'ton 5D 10
Atherton Rd. L9: Ain 5A 22
Atherton St. CH45: New B 4C 32
L34: Presc 1D 58
WA10: St H 6D 28
Athol Cl. CH62: East 2E 121
WA12: Newt W 1H 45
Athol Dr. CH62: East 3E 121
Atholl Cres. L10: Ain 1B 22
Athol St. CH41: Birke 2G 69
L5: Liv 2C 52
(Bangor St., not continuous)
L5: Liv 2B 52
(Denbigh St.)
Atkinson Gro. L36: Huy 3H 57
Atlanta Ct. L33: Kirkb 3H 13
Atlantic Av. L8: Liv 6C 4 (10 70)
Atlantic Point L3: Liv 1E 5 (4D 52)
Atlantic Rd. L20: Boot 2B 34
Atlantic Terminal L20: Boot 2A 34
Atlantic Way L3: Liv 4D 70
L30: Boot 3E 21

Atlas Bus. Complex L20: Boot 1A 34
Atlas Rd. L20: Boot 1B 34
Atlas St. WA9: St H 1F 43
Atterbury Cl. WA8: Wid 1A 96
Atterbury St. L8: Liv 4E 71
Attlee Rd. L36: Huy 4A 58
Attwood St. L4: Walt 6F 35
Atwell St. L6: Liv 3G 53
Aubourn Cl. WA8: Wid 6A 78
Aubrey Ct. L6: Liv 3G 53
Auburn Rd. CH45: Wall 6C 32
L13: Liv .1C 54
Aubynes, The CH45: Wall 6A 32
Auckland Rd. L18: Moss H 4E 73
Audlem Av. CH43: O'ton 6B 68
Audlem Cl. WA7: Sut W 3B 124
Audley Dr. L3: Liv 2H 5 (5E 53)
Audre Cl. WA5: Gt San 3F 81
Audrey Wlk. L10: Faz 4F 23
AUGHTON 1F 7
Aughton Cl. CH49: Upton 4E 67
Aughton Rd. L20: Boot 6D 20
Augusta Cl. L13: Liv 5E 55
August Rd. L6: Liv 2B 54
August St. L20: Boot 6C 20
Aukland Gro. WA9: St H 1B 60
Aurorean Cl. L27: N'ley 3F 75
Austell Cl. WA11: St H 4H 29
Austin Av. WA10: St H 5A 42
Austin Cl. L32: Kirkb 6H 13
Austin St. CH44: Wall 5C 50
Autumn Gro. CH42: Rock F 3G 87
Autumn Way L20: Boot 6C 20
WA9: Clock F 4G 61
Avalon Ter. L20: Boot 1B 34
(off Tennyson St.)
Avebury Cl. WA8: Wid 6A 80
Avelon Cl. CH43: Noct 4H 67
L31: Lyd 2A 6
Avenue, The CH62: Brom 5C 104
L19: Garst 6A 92
L26: Halew 4G 93
L36: Huy .4G 57
WA10: Eccl 2H 41
WA11: Rainf 3F 17
Avery Cres. WA11: Hay 4E 31
Avery Rd. WA11: Hay 4E 31
Avery Sq. WA11: Hay 4E 31
Aviary Ct. L9: Walt 5F 21
(off Dove Rd.)
Aviemore Rd. L13: Liv 4D 54
Avington Cl. L12: W Der 6H 37
Avis Wlk. L10: Faz 4F 23
Avolon Rd. L12: W Der 2H 55
Avon WA8: Wid 1G 95
Avon Av. WA5: Penk 5G 81
Avon Cl. L4: Kirkd 5E 35
L33: Kirkb 3B 14
Avon Ct. L23: Crosb 4G 9
Avondale Av. CH46: More 6D 48
CH62: East 2F 121
L31: Mag .1A 12
Avondale Dr. WA8: Wid 2H 95
Avondale Rd. CH47: Hoy 2B 64
L15: Wav .3C 72
WA11: Hay 4E 31
Avonmore Av. L18: Moss H 6E 73
Avon St. CH41: Birke 6B 50
L6: Liv 2H 53
Awelon Cl. L12: W Der 5G 37
Awesome Walls Climbing Cen. 2B 52
Axbridge Av. WA9: Sut L 2H 61
Axholme Cl. CH61: Thing 6F 85
Axholme Rd. CH61: Thing 6F 85
Ayala Cl. L9: Walt 4F 21
Aycliffe Rd. WA9: St H 1B 60
Aycliffe Wlk. WA8: Wid 3A 96
Aylesbury Av. CH43: O'ton 1A 86
Aylesbury Rd. CH45: New B 6E 33
Aylesford Rd. L13: Liv 4E 55
Aylsham Cl. WA8: Wid 5A 78
Aylsham Dr. CH49: Upton 2E 67
Aylton Rd. L36: Huy 3D 56

Aylward Pl. *L20: Boot* *1B* ***34***
(off Glover Pl.)
Aynsley Ct. WA9: St H 1H **59**
Ayres Ct. WA9: St H 6C **42**
Ayr Rd. L4: Walt 3G **35**
Ayrshire Gdns. WA10: St H 3C **42**
Ayrshire Rd. L4: Walt 5A **36**
Aysgarth Av. L12: W Der 1G **55**
Aysgarth Rd. CH45: Wall 1B **50**
Ayton La. L16: Child 2G **73**
Azalea Gdns. WA9: Bold 6C **44**
Azalea Gro. L26: Halew 1F **93**
WA7: Beech 3B **124**

B

Babbacombe Rd. L16: Child 3A **74**
WA5: Penk 5G **81**
Bk. Barlow La. L4: Kirkd 5E **35**
Bk. Beau St. L5: Liv 3E **53**
Bk. Bedford St. *L7: Liv* *1F* ***71***
(off Cambridge St.)
Bk. Belmont Rd. L6: Liv 2H **53**
Bk. Berry St. L1: Liv 6G **5**
Bk. Blackfield Ter. L4: Kirkd 6D **34**
Bk. Bold St. L1: Liv 5G **5**
Bk. Boundary Cl. L5: Kirkd 1D **52**
Bk. Bridge Rd. *L23: Blun* *6E* ***9***
(off Riverslea Rd.)
Bk. Bridport St. L3: Liv 3G **5**
Back B'way. L11: Norr G 4C **36**
Bk. Canning St. L8: Liv 1F **71**
Bk. Catharine St. *L8: Liv* *1F* ***71***
(off Little St Bride St.)
Bk. Chadwick Mt. L5: Liv 6E **35**
Bk. Chatham Pl. *L7: Liv* *6H* ***53***
(off Queensland St.)
Bk. Colquitt St. L1: Liv 6G **5** (1E **71**)
Bk. Commutation Row L3: Liv 2G **5**
Bk. Dovecot Pl. L14: Knott A 3B **56**
Bk. Egerton St. Nth. *L8: Liv* *2F* ***71***
(off Egerton St.)
Bk. Egerton St. Sth. *L8: Liv* *2F* ***71***
(off Egerton St.)
Bk. Falkner St. Sth. L8: Liv 1G **71**
Backford Cl. CH43: O'ton 6A **68**
WA7: Brook 2E **125**
Backford Rd. CH61: Irby 6B **84**
Bk. Gillmoss La. L11: Crox 5G **23**
Bk. Granton Rd. *L5: Liv* *1G* ***53***
(off Salisbury Rd.)
Bk. Guilford St. L6: Liv 4F **53**
Bk. Hadfield Pl. *L25: Woolt* *1C* ***92***
(off Church Rd.)
Bk. High St. *L25: Woolt* *1C* ***92***
(off High St.)
WA7: Run 3E **113**
Bk. Holland Pl. *L7: Liv* *6H* ***53***
(off Wavertree Rd.)
Bk. Hope Pl. L1: Liv 6H **5**
Bk. Huskisson St. L8: Liv 2F **71**
Bk. Irvine St. *L7: Liv* *6G* ***53***
(off Up. Mason St.)
Bk. Kelvin Gro. *L8: Liv* *3G* ***71***
(off Kelvin Gro.)
Bk. Knight St. L1: Liv 6G **5**
Back La. L23: Lit C 1G **9**
L29: Seft, Thorn 2C **10**
L39: Augh 1D **6**
WA5: Coll G 6F **45**
WA5: Cuerd 1C **98**
Bk. Langham St. L4: Walt 5F **35**
Bk. Leeds St. L3: Liv 1B **4** (4B **52**)
Bk. Legh St. WA12: Newt W 2H **45**
Bk. Lime St. L1: Liv 4F **5**
Bk. Little Canning St. *L8: Liv* *2F* ***71***
(off Lit. Canning St.)
Bk. Luton Gro. L4: Walt 5F **35**
Bk. Market St. WA12: Newt W 1H **45**
Bk. Maryland St. L1: Liv 6H **5**
Bk. Menai St. CH41: Birke 3E **69**
Bk. Mersey Vw. L22: Water 1E **19**
Bk. Mount St. L22: Water 2F **19**
Bk. Mulberry St. L7: Liv 1F **71**
Bk. Oliver St. *CH41: Birke* *3G* ***69***
(off Argyle St.)
Bk. Orford St. *L15: Wav* *1D* ***72***
(off Sandown La.)
Bk. Percy St. *L8: Liv* *2F* ***71***
(off Percy St.)
Bk. Pickop St. L3: Liv 2D **4**
Bk. Price St. CH41: Birke 2F **69**
Bk. Renshaw St. L1: Liv 5G **5** (6E **53**)
Bk. Rockfield Rd. *L4: Walt* *6F* ***35***
(off Blessington Rd.)
Back St Bride St. *L8: Liv* *1F* ***71***
(off Little St Bride St.)
Bk. Sandon St. L8: Liv 2F **71**
Bk. Sandown La. *L15: Wav* *1D* ***72***
(off Sandown La.)
Bk. Seaman Rd. *L15: Wav* *2C* ***72***
(off Seaman Rd.)
Back Seaview CH47: Hoy 2B **64**
Bk. Seel St. L1: Liv 6F **5**
Bk. Sir Howard St. *L8: Liv* *1F* ***71***
(off Sir Howard St.)
Bk. South Rd. L22: Water 2G **19**
Bk. Stanley Rd. L20: Boot 2C **34**
Bk. Towerlands St. *L7: Liv* *6H* ***53***
(off Church Mt.)
Bk. Wellesley Rd. *L8: Liv* *5G* ***71***
(off The Elms)
Bk. Westminster Rd. L4: Kirkd 5E **35**
Bk. Windsor Vw. *L8: Liv* *2H* ***71***
(off Lodge La.)
Bk. Winstanley Rd. L22: Water 1G **19**
Bk. York Ter. L5: Liv 1E **53**
Badbury Cl. WA11: Hay 4F **31**
Badby Wood L33: Kirkb 5B **14**
Baddow Cft. L25: Woolt 6A **74**
Baden Ct. CH48: W Kir 6A **64**
Baden Ho. L13: Liv 4F **55**
Baden Rd. L13: Liv 4F **55**
Bader Cl. CH61: Pens 2C **100**
Badger Cl. WA7: Pal F 1C **124**
Badger's Set CH48: Caldy 5D **82**
Badger Way CH43: Pren 3A **86**
Badminton St. L8: Liv 6F **71**
Baffin Cl. CH46: Leas 3E **49**
Bagnall St. L4: Walt 6G **35**
Bagot St. L15: Wav 2B **72**
Baguley Av. WA8: Hale B 6G **95**
Bahama Cl. WA11: Hay 3F **31**
Bahama Rd. WA11: Hay 3F **31**
Bailey Ct. L20: Boot 4E **21**
Bailey Dr. L20: Boot 5E **21**
Baileys Cl. WA8: Wid 4E **79**
Bailey's La. L24: Hale 4H **109**
L24: Speke 2C **108**
L26: Halew 3A **94**
Bailey St. L1: Liv 1E **71**
Bailey Way L31: Mag 2A **12**
Bainbridge Cres.
WA5: Gt San 1G **81**
Bainton Cl. L32: Kirkb 4C **24**
Bainton Rd. L32: Kirkb 4C **24**
Baker Rd. WA7: West P 6B **112**
Bakers Grn. Rd. L36: Huy 3G **57**
Baker St. L6: Liv 4G **53**
L36: Huy 5A **58**
WA9: St H 2G **43**
Baker Way L6: Liv 4G **53**
Bakewell Gro. L9: Ain 4H **21**
Bakewell Rd. WA5: Burtw 6H **45**
Bala Gro. CH44: Wall 4C **50**
Bala St. L4: Walt 1H **53**
Balcarres Av. L18: Moss H 4D **72**
Baldwin Av. L16: Child 1A **74**
Baldwin St. WA10: St H 1E **43**
Bales, The L30: N'ton 5G **11**
Balfe St. L21: Sea 5A **20**
Balfour Av. L20: Boot 6B **20**
Balfour Rd. CH43: O'ton 4D **68**
CH44: Wall 5C **50**
L20: Boot 6B **20**
Balfour St. L4: Walt 6F **35**
WA7: Run 4D **112**
WA10: St H 2B **42**
Balham Cl. WA8: Wid 5E **79**
Balharry Av. WA11: Hay 4H **31**
Balker Dr. WA10: St H 6D **28**
Ballantrae Rd. L18: Moss H 6G **73**
Ballantyne Dr. CH43: Bid 6G **49**
Ballantyne Gro. L13: Liv 6C **36**
L20: Boot 5E **21**
Ballantyne Pl. L13: Liv 6C **36**
Ballantyne Rd. L13: Liv 1C **54**
Ballantyne Wlk. CH43: Bid 6G **49**
Ballard Rd. CH48: W Kir 6E **65**
Ball Av. CH45: New B 5C **32**
Balliol Cl. CH43: Bid 6G **49**
Balliol Gro. L23: Blun 1D **18**
Balliol Ho. L20: Boot 3C **34**
Balliol Rd. L20: Boot 3C **34**
BALL O' DITTON 2C **96**
Ball Path WA8: Wid 2D **96**
Ball Path Way WA8: Wid 2C **96**
Ball's Rd. CH43: O'ton 5D **68**
Balls Rd. E. CH41: Birke 4E **69**
Ball St. WA9: St H 1H **43**
Balmer St. WA9: St H 5B **42**
Balmoral Av. L23: Crosb 6G **9**
WA9: St H 6G **43**
Balmoral Cl. L33: Kirkb 4A **14**
Balmoral Ct. L13: Liv 2C **54**
Balmoral Gdns. CH43: Pren 2B **86**
Balmoral Gro. CH43: Noct 6H **67**
Balmoral Rd. CH45: New B 4E **33**
L6: Liv 3A **54**
L9: Walt 5G **21**
L31: Mag 6B **6**
WA8: Wid 5D **78**
Balmoral Way L34: Presc 2H **57**
Balm St. L7: Liv 5H **53**
Balniel St. WA9: Clock F 4H **61**
Balsham Cl. L25: Hunts X 4F **93**
Baltic Rd. L20: Boot 2B **34**
Baltic St. L4: Walt 6G **35**
Baltimore St. L1: Liv 6H **5** (1E **71**)
Bamboo Cl. L27: N'ley 3G **75**
Bamford Cl. WA7: Run 6G **113**
Bampton Av. WA11: St H 2F **29**
Bampton Rd. L16: Child 1H **73**
Banbury Av. L25: Woolt 1E **93**
Banbury Ct. *L20: Boot* *1D* ***34***
(off Worcester Rd.)
Banbury Way CH43: O'ton 1A **86**
Bancroft Cl. L25: Hunts X 3E **93**
Bancroft Rd. WA8: Wid 1H **97**
Bandon Cl. L24: Hale 3D **110**
Banff Av. CH63: East 2D **120**
Bangor Rd. CH45: Wall 1H **49**
Bangor St. L5: Liv 2C **52**
Bankburn Rd. L13: Liv 1C **54**
Bank Dene CH42: Rock F 3A **88**
Bankes La. WA7: West P 1C **122**
(not continuous)
Bankfield Ct. CH62: Brom 2F **105**
L13: Liv 2D **54**
Bankfield Rd. L13: Liv 1D **54**
WA8: Wid 2H **95**
Bankfields Dr. CH62: East 2H **121**
Bankfield St. L20: Kirkd 5B **34**
Bank Gdns. WA5: Penk 5G **81**
Bankhall La. L20: Kirkd 5C **34**
Bankhall Station (Rail) 5C **34**
Bankhall St. L20: Kirkd 5C **34**
Bankland Rd. L13: Liv 2D **54**
Bank La. L31: Mell 2G **13**
L33: Kirkb 2G **13**
Bank Rd. L20: Boot 2B **34**
Banks, The CH45: Wall 6A **32**
Bank's Av. CH47: Meols 1D **64**
Bankside WA7: Pres B 6G **115**
Bankside Ct. L21: Lith 3A **20**
Bankside Rd. CH42: Rock F 3H **87**
Bank's La. L19: Garst 1H **107**
L24: Speke 3B **108**

Banks Rd. CH48: W Kir 1A 82
    CH60: Hesw 6A 100
    L19: Garst 6G 91
Bank St. CH41: Birke 3G 69
    WA8: Wid 1E 113
    WA10: St H 2C 42
    WA12: Newt W 2H 45
Bank's Way L19: Garst 1H 107
Bankville Rd. CH42: Tran 6G 69
Banner Hey L35: Whis 6D 58
Bannerman St. L7: Liv 1B 72
Banner St. L15: Wav 2C 72
    WA10: St H 2D 42
Banner Wlk. WA10: St H 2D 42
                                (off Banner St.)
Banning Cl. CH41: Birke 2F 69
Banstead Gro. L15: Wav 2F 73
Barbara Av. L10: Faz 4E 23
Barbara St. WA9: Clock F 4A 62
Barberry Cl. CH46: More 1H 65
Barberry Cres. L30: N'ton 5G 11
Barber St. WA9: St H 1G 43
Barbondale Cl. WA5: Gt San 2H 81
Barbour Dr. L20: Boot 5E 21
Barbrook Way L9: Walt 2H 35
Barchester Dr. L17: Aig 2A 90
Barclay St. L8: Liv 5F 71
Barcombe Rd. CH60: Hesw 4H 101
Bardley Cres. L35: Tar G 2A 76
Bardon Cl. L25: Gate 4E 75
Bardsay Rd. L4: Walt 4F 35
Barford Cl. CH43: Bid 3F 67
Barford Grange CH64: Will 6B 120
Barford Rd. L25: Hunts X 5D 92
    L36: Huy 1H 57
Bargate Water WA9: St H 1B 60
Barge Ind. Pk., The
    WA9: St H 6G 29
Barington Dr. WA7: Murd 6G 115
Barkbeth Rd. L36: Huy 2E 57
Barkbeth Wlk. L36: Huy 2E 57
Barkeley Dr. L21: Sea 5H 19
Barker Cl. L36: Huy 1H 75
Barker La. CH49: Grea 1A 84
                                (not continuous)
Barker Rd. CH61: Irby 5D 84
Barkers Hollow Rd.
    WA4: Dutt, Pres H 1H 125
Barkerville Cl. L13: Liv 6B 36
Barker Way L6: Liv 2H 53
Barkhill Rd. L17: Aig 2D 90
Barkin Cen., The WA8: Wid 3G 97
Barkis Cl. L8: Liv 4F 71
Bark Rd. L21: Lith 2C 20
Barleyfield CH61: Pens 1C 100
Barlow Av. CH63: Beb 5A 88
Barlow Gro. WA9: St H 3C 44
Barlow La. L4: Kirkd 5E 35
Barlows Cl. L9: Ain 3B 22
Barlow's La. L9: Ain 3B 22
Barlow St. L4: Kirkd 5E 35
Barmouth Rd. CH45: Wall 1H 49
Barmouth Way L5: Liv 2C 52
Barnacre Dr. CH64: Park 5F 117
Barnacre La. CH46: More 3H 65
Barnard Rd. CH43: O'ton 4D 68
Barn Cl. L30: N'ton 5G 11
Barncroft CH61: Pens 2D 100
    WA7: Nort 6F 115
Barncroft, The CH49: Grea 5B 66
Barncroft Pl. L23: Crosb 3G 9
Barncroft Rd. L26: Halew 4A 94
Barndale Rd. L18: Moss H 5D 72
Barnes Cl. L33: Kirkb 3A 14
    WA8: Wid 1H 97
Barnes Dr. L31: Lyd 3B 6
Barnes Rd. CH63: Spit 3A 104
Barnes Rd. WA8: Wid 1G 97
Barnes St. L6: Liv 2G 53
Barneston Rd. WA8: Wid 6A 80
Barnet Cl. L7: Liv 1A 72
Barnett Av. WA12: Newt W 2G 45
Barnfield Av. WA7: Murd 2F 125

Barfield Cl. CH47: Meols 6E 47
    L12: W Der 1F 55
    L30: N'ton 1E 21
Barnfield Dr. L12: W Der 1F 55
Barnham Cl. L24: Speke 1D 108
Barnham Dr. L16: Child 2A 74
Barn Hey CH47: Hoy 4A 64
Barn Hey Cres. CH47: Meols 1F 65
Barn Hey Grn. L12: W Der 1F 55
Barn Hey Rd. L33: Kirkb 1C 24
Barnhill Rd. L15: Wav 3E 73
Barnhurst Cl. L16: Child 2A 74
Barnhurst Rd. L16: Child 2A 74
Barn La. WA5: Burtw 2H 63
Barnmeadow Rd. L25: Gate 4C 74
Barnsbury Rd. L4: Walt 3A 36
Barnsdale Av. CH61: Thing 6F 85
Barnside Ct. L16: Child 2A 74
Barnstaple Way WA5: Penk 5G 81
BARNSTON 2G 101
Barnston La. CH46: More 6C 48
Barnston Rd. CH60: Hesw 6F 101
    CH61: Barn, Thing 4F 85
    L9: Ain .4H 21
Barnston Towers Cl. CH60: Hesw . . .5G 101
Barnstream Cl. L27: N'ley 3E 75
Barn St. WA8: Wid 5E 97
Barnton Cl. L20: Boot 5C 20
Barnwell Av. CH44: Wall 2D 50
Barnwood Rd. L36: Huy 3D 56
Baroncroft Rd. L25: Woolt 5B 74
Barons Cl. WA7: Cas 4B 114
    WA8: Wid 3A 96
Barons Hey L28: Stockb V 5B 38
Barren Gro. CH43: O'ton 5D 68
Barrington Rd. CH44: Wall 4E 51
    L15: Wav 3C 72
Barrow Cl. L12: W Der 4G 37
Barrowfield Rd. WA10: Eccl 6G 27
Barrow Hall La. WA5: Gt San 2G 81
Barrows Cotts. L35: Whis 4E 59
                                (off Cross La.)
BARROW'S GREEN 5H 79
Barrows Grn. La. WA8: Wid 1A 98
Barrow's Row WA8: Wid 5F 79
Barrow St. WA10: St H 2E 43
Barrymore Rd. L13: Liv 4D 54
    WA7: Run 6F 113
Barrymore Way CH63: Brom 1B 120
Bartholomew Cl. L35: Rainh 6C 60
Bartlegate Cl. WA7: Brook 2D 124
Bartlett St. L15: Wav 2C 72
Barton Cl. CH47: Hoy 3A 64
    L21: Lith 1A 20
    WA7: Murd 6F 115
    WA10: St H 1D 42
Barton Hey Dr. CH48: Caldy 5C 82
Barton Rd. CH47: Hoy 3A 64
    L9: Walt 1F 35
Barton St. CH41: Birke 3E 69
                                (not continuous)
Barwell Av. WA11: St H 5G 29
Bary Dr. L19: Garst 5F 91
Basil Cl. L16: Child 1A 74
Basildon Cl. WA9: St H 6D 42
Basil Rd. L16: Child 1H 73
Basing St. L19: Garst 4G 91
Baskervyle Cl. CH60: Hesw 1E 117
Baskervyle Rd. CH60: Hesw 1E 117
Basnett St. L1: Liv 4E 5 (6D 52)
Bassendale Rd. CH62: Brom 3E 105
Bassenthwaite Av. CH43: Noct 4H 67
    L33: Kirkb 5H 13
    WA11: St H 3E 29
Bates Cres. WA10: St H 5B 42
Batey Av. L35: Rainh 3H 59
Batherton Cl. WA8: Wid 4F 97
Bathgate Way L33: Kirkb 3H 13
Bath St. CH62: Port S 6B 88
    L3: Liv 2A 4 (5B 52)
    L22: Water 3F 19
    WA10: St H 2D 42
Bathurst Rd. L19: Gras 4F 91

Batley St. L13: Liv 4E 55
Battenberg St. L7: Liv 5G 53
Battersea Ct. WA8: Wid 6D 78
Battery Cl. L17: Aig 1A 90
Baucher Dr. L20: Boot 4E 21
Baumville Dr. CH63: Spit 3H 103
Baxter Cl. WA7: Murd 6F 115
                                (not continuous)
Baxters La. WA9: St H 5H 43
Baxters La. Ind. Est. WA9: St H 4H 43
Baycliffe Cl. WA7: Beech 2H 123
Baycliff Rd. L12: W Der 5A 38
Bayfield Rd. L19: Gras 4E 91
Bayhorse La. L3: Liv 2H 5 (5F 53)
Baynard Dr. WA8: Hale B 6A 96
Baysdale Cl. L8: Liv 5G 71
Bayswater Cl. WA7: Nort 1H 115
Bayswater Ct. CH45: Wall 1H 49
Bayswater Gdns. CH45: Wall 6A 32
Bayswater Rd. CH45: Wall 1H 49
Baythorne Rd. L4: Walt 3A 36
Bay Tree Gro. WA9: St H 5G 43
Baytree Gro. L31: Mell 6E 13
Baytree Rd. CH42: Tran 6G 69
    CH48: Frank 1F 83
Bay Vw. Dr. CH45: Wall 6A 32
Bayvil Cl. WA7: Murd 6G 115
Beach Bank L22: Water 1E 19
Beachcroft Rd. CH47: Meols 6E 47
Beach Gro. CH45: Wall 6E 33
Beach Lawn L22: Water 2E 19
Beach Rd. CH47: Hoy 3A 64
    L21: Lith 4B 20
                                (off Bridge Rd.)
    L21: Lith 3A 20
                                (Windsor Av.)
Beach Wlk. CH48: W Kir 3B 82
Beacon Ct. CH60: Hesw 5E 101
Beacon Dr. CH48: W Kir 1C 82
Beacon Gro. WA11: St H 5H 29
Beacon Hill Vw. WA7: West P 6B 112
Beacon Ho. L5: Liv 3E 53
                                (off Portland Pl.)
Beacon La. CH60: Hesw 5E 101
    L5: Liv .1F 53
Beacon Pde. CH60: Hesw 5E 101
Beacons, The CH60: Hesw 6E 101
Beaconsfield L34: Presc 1D 58
Beaconsfield Cl. CH42: Tran 6H 69
Beaconsfield Cres. WA8: Wid 5E 79
Beaconsfield Gro. WA8: Wid 5F 79
Beaconsfield Rd. CH62: New F 4B 88
    L21: Sea 4H 19
    L25: Woolt 6A 74
    WA7: Run 5C 112
    WA8: Wid 6F 79
    WA10: St H 6A 28
Beaconsfield St. L8: Liv 3G 71
Beaconsfield Ter. L19: Garst 5F 91
                                (off St Mary's Rd.)
Beadnell Dr. WA5: Penk 6G 81
Beames Cl. L7: Liv 6A 54
Beamont St. WA8: Wid 1E 113
Beatles Story, The 1C 70
Beatrice Av. CH63: Hghr B 4G 87
Beatrice St. L20: Boot 4D 34
Beattock Cl. L33: Kirkb 3H 13
Beatty Cl. CH48: Caldy 5C 82
    L35: Whis 5D 58
Beatty Rd. L13: Liv 4E 55
Beauclair Dr. L15: Wav 2F 73
Beaufort Cl. WA7: Run 6F 113
    WA8: Wid 3G 95
Beaufort Dr. CH44: Wall 2A 50
Beaufort Rd. CH41: Birke 6B 50
Beaufort St. L8: Liv 3E 71
                                (Hill St.)
    L8: Liv .3E 71
                                (Mann St.)
    L8: Liv .4E 71
                                (Northumberland St.)
    WA9: St H 4G 43
Beaumaris Ct. CH43: O'ton 4D 68

Beaumaris Dr. CH61: Thing 5F 85
Beaumaris Rd. CH45: Wall 1H 49
Beaumaris St. L20: Kirkd 5C 34
(not continuous)
Beaumaris Way WA7: Cas 3B 114
Beaumont Av. WA10: St H 1B 42
Beaumont Dr. L10: Ain 2C 22
Beaumont St. L8: Liv 2H 71
Beau St. L3: Liv 3E 53
Beauworth Av. CH49: Grea 6A 66
Beaver Gro. L9: Ain 5G 21
BEBINGTON 1H 103
Bebington Rd. CH42: Rock F, Tran 1F 87
CH62: New F 5A 88
CH63: Beb 5A 88
Bebington Station (Rail) 4A 88
Bechers WA8: Wid 6H 77
Bechers Bus. Cen. L30: N'ton 1G 21
Bechers Ct. L30: N'ton 6H 11
Bechers Dr. L9: Ain 1A 22
Bechers Row L9: Walt 5F 21
Beck Cl. L10: Faz 4F 23
Beckenham Av. L18: Moss H 4D 72
Beckenham Cl. WA8: Wid 5H 79
Beckenham Rd. CH45: New B 4D 32
Becket St. L4: Kirkd 6D 34
(not continuous)
Beckett Cl. L33: Know I 3E 25
Beckett Gro. CH63: Hghr B 4F 87
Beck Gro. WA11: St H 3F 29
Beckinsale Cl. L26: Halew 2A 94
Beck Rd. L20: Boot 6C 20
Beckwith Ct. *CH41: Birke 1E 69*
(off Beckwith St.)
Beckwith St. CH41: Birke 1D 68
L1: Liv 6E 5 (1D 70)
Beckwith St. E. CH41: Birke 2F 69
Becky St. L6: Liv 2H 53
Becontree Rd. L12: W Der 3H 55
Bective St. L7: Liv 1A 72
Bedale Wlk. L33: Kirkb 6B 14
Bedburn Dr. L36: Huy 4D 56
Bede Cl. L33: Kirkb 3A 14
Bedford Av. CH42: Rock F 2G 87
L31: Mell 3D 12
Bedford Cl. L7: Liv 1F 71
L36: Huy 4A 58
Bedford Ct. CH42: Rock F 1H 87
L7: Liv 2F 71
(off Bedford St. Sth.)
Bedford Dr. CH42: Rock F 2F 87
Bedford Pl. CH42: Rock F 1A 88
L20: Boot 4B 34
L21: Sea 4H 19
Bedford Rd. CH42: Rock F 1H 87
CH45: Wall 1D 50
L4: Walt 4C 34
L20: Boot 4C 34
Bedford Rd. E. CH42: Rock F 1A 88
Bedford St. WA9: St H 3H 43
Bedford St. Nth. L7: Liv 6F 53
Bedford St. Sth. L7: Liv 1F 71
(not continuous)
Bedford Wlk. *L7: Liv 1F 71*
(off Bedford Cl.)
Beecham Cl. L36: Huy 6F 57
Beech Av. CH49: Upton 3B 66
CH61: Pens 1E 101
L17: Aig 1H 89
L23: Crosb 3A 10
L31: Mell 6F 13
L34: Eccl P 6F 41
WA5: Penk 6E 81
WA9: Clock F 3G 61
WA11: Hay 4H 31
Beechbank Rd. L18: Moss H 4C 72
Beechburn Cres. L36: Huy 4D 56
Beechburn Rd. L36: Huy 4C 56
Beech Cl. L12: Crox 2H 37
L32: Kirkb 6G 13
Beech Ct. CH42: Tran 5F 69
L18: Moss H 6G 73
Beechcroft L31: Mag 6C 6
Beechcroft Rd. CH44: Wall 5E 51
Beechdale Rd. L18: Moss H 5E 73
Beechdene Rd. L4: Walt 6H 35
Beeches, The CH42: Rock F 2A 88
CH46: Leas 4C 48
L18: Moss H 4H 73
WA8: Wid 5H 79
(off Hampton Ct. Way)
WA9: Sut L 2H 61
Beechfield L31: Mag 6D 6
L36: Roby 5E 57
(off Church Rd.)
Beechfield Cl. CH60: Hesw 6E 101
L26: Halew 5G 93
Beechfield Rd. L18: Moss H 5H 73
Beech Gdns. *WA7: Run 5G 113*
(off Beech Rd.)
WA11: Rainf 2E 17
Beech Grn. L12: W Der 5E 37
Beech Gro. L9: Ain 5H 21
L21: Sea 5H 19
L30: N'ton 1G 21
Beech Hey La. CH64: Will 6B 120
Beechill Cl. L25: Gate 5E 75
Beech La. L18: Moss H 4G 73
Beech Lawn L19: Gras 4D 90
Beech Mdws. L34: Presc 2A 58
Beech Mt. L7: Liv 5A 54
Beech Pk. L12: W Der 1E 55
L23: Crosb 3H 9
Beech Ri. L33: Kirkb 6B 14
Beech Rd. CH42: Tran 5E 69
CH60: Hesw 5G 101
CH63: Hghr B 4H 87
L4: Walt 3G 35
L36: Huy 6G 57
L39: Augh 1F 7
WA7: Run 5G 113
WA7: Sut W 3D 124
Beech St. L7: Liv 5A 54
L20: Boot 1C 34
WA10: St H 5B 42
Beech Ter. L7: Liv 5A 54
Beech Tree Ct. *L19: Gras 4D 90*
(off Beechwood Rd.)
Beechtree Rd. L15: Wav 6F 55
Beechurst Cl. L25: Gate 4D 74
Beechurst Rd. L25: Gate 4D 74
Beechwalk, The L14: Knott A 3F 55
Beechway CH63: Beb 2H 103
L31: Mag 5G 7
Beechway Av. L31: Mag 5G 7
BEECHWOOD
CH43 1G 67
WA7 2A 124
Beechwood Av. CH45: Wall 2A 50
L26: Halew 4G 93
WA5: Gt San 4H 81
WA7: Beech 1G 123
WN4: Ash M 1H 31
Beechwood Cl. L19: Gras 4E 91
WA9: Clock F 4G 61
Beechwood Ct. *CH49: Woodc 2F 85*
(off Childwall Grn.)
L31: Mag 6E 7
(off Deyes La.)
Beechwood Dr. CH43: Bid 2G 67
Beechwood Gdns. L19: Gras 4D 90
Beechwood Grn. L19: Gras 4E 91
Beechwood Gro. L35: Presc 3E 59
Beechwood Recreation Cen. 2G 67
Beechwood Rd. CH62: Brom 5C 104
L19: Gras 4D 90
L21: Lith 5B 20
Beechwood Rd. Sth.
L19: Gras 5D 90
Beesands Cl. L27: N'ley 5H 75
Beesley Rd. L34: Presc 1C 58
Beeston Cl. CH43: Bid 3G 67
Beeston Ct. WA7: Manor P 1E 115
Beeston Dr. CH61: Pens 1D 100
L30: N'ton 4H 11
Beeston Gro. L19: Gras 4E 91
Beeston St. L4: Kirkd 5E 35
Beetham Plaza L2: Liv 4C 4
Beetham Twr. L3: Liv 2B 4
Beetham Way L33: Kirkb 6B 14
Begonia Gdns. WA9: Bold 6C 44
Beilby Rd. WA11: Hay 4H 31
Beldale Pk. L32: Kirkb 5G 13
Beldon Cres. L36: Huy 4D 56
Belem Cl. L17: Aig 4A 72
Belem Twr. L17: Aig 4A 72
Belfast Rd. L13: Liv 4F 55
Belfield Cres. L36: Huy 6G 57
Belfield Dr. CH43: O'ton 6D 68
Belford Dr. CH46: More 1A 66
Belfort Rd. L25: Gate 5D 74
Belfry Cl. CH46: More 6H 47
L12: W Der 1A 56
Belgrave Av. CH44: Wall 3E 51
Belgrave Cl. WA8: Wid 6A 80
Belgrave Rd. L17: Aig 6H 71
L21: Sea 4H 19
Belgrave St. CH44: Wall 2D 50
Belgravia Ct. WA8: Wid 6D 78
Belhaven Rd. L18: Moss H 4D 72
Bellair Av. L23: Crosb 5A 10
Bellairs Rd. L11: Norr G 5C 36
Bellamy Rd. L4: Walt 3E 35
Bell Cl. L36: Huy 1H 75
Belldene Gro. CH61: Hesw 3D 100
Bellefield Av. L12: W Der 1F 55
Bellerophon Way WA11: Hay 5G 31
BELLE VALE 4E 75
Belle Va. Rd. L25: Gate 5D 74
Belle Va. Shop. Cen.
L25: Gate 3D 74
Belle Vue Rd. CH44: Wall 5G 51
L25: Gate 5D 74
Bellew Rd. L11: Norr G 6D 36
Bellfield Cres. CH45: New B 5C 32
Bellflower Cl. WA8: Wid 5C 78
Bellgreen Rd. L11: Norr G 3E 37
Bell Ho. Rd. WA8: Wid 2G 97
Bellingham Dr. WA7: Run 5E 113
Bellini Cl. L21: Sea 5A 20
Bellis Gro. L33: Kirkb 4H 13
Bell La. L35: Rainh 5E 61
WA9: Sut M 5E 61
Bellmore St. L19: Garst 4G 91
Bell Rd. CH44: Wall 4F 51
Bell's Cl. L31: Lyd 3B 6
Bells La. L31: Lyd 4A 6
Bell St. L13: Liv 4E 55
Belltower Rd. L20: Kirkd 6B 34
Bellward Cl. CH63: Spit 3H 103
Belmont CH41: Birke 4E 69
Belmont Av. CH62: Brom 4C 104
Belmont Cres. WA5: Gt San 3H 81
Belmont Dr. CH61: Pens 1E 101
L6: Liv 2A 54
Belmont Gro. CH43: O'ton 4E 69
L6: Liv 2A 54
Belmont Pl. *L19: Garst 5G 91*
(off Shrewsbury Rd.)
Belmont Rd. CH45: New B 4D 32
CH48: W Kir 6B 64
L6: Liv 2H 53
WA8: Wid 1H 97
Belmont St. WA10: St H 2B 42
Belmont Vw. *L6: Liv 2A 54*
(off W. Derby Rd.)
Beloe St. L8: Liv 5F 71
Belper St. L19: Garst 5F 91
Belsford Way L24: Speke 1D 108
Belston Rd. L16: Child 1H 73
Belton Rd. L36: Huy 1F 57
(not continuous)
Belvedere *WA7: Run 2E 113*
(off Cooper St.)
Belvedere Av. WA9: Sut L 1H 61
Belvedere Cl. *L34: Presc 6E 41*
(off Marlborough Rd.)
WA6: Frod 6G 123
Belvidere Pk. L23: Crosb 6G 9

Belvidere Rd. CH45: Wall 1B **50**
  L8: Liv 4G **71**
  L23: Crosb 6F **9**
Belvoir Rd. L18: Aller 3G **91**
  WA8: Wid 2F **97**
Bembridge Cl. WA5: Gt San 2E **81**
  WA8: Wid 5D **78**
Bempton Rd. L17: Aig 1H **89**
Benbow Cl. L8: Liv 1B **68**
Benbow St. L20: Boot 3B **34**
Benedict Cl. CH49: Woodc 5F **67**
Benedict Ct. L20: Boot 4C **34**
Benedict St. L20: Boot 4D **34**
Benfleet Ho. L19: Aig 4D **90**
  (off The Spinnakers)
Benledi St. L5: Liv 2D **52**
Benmore Rd. L18: Moss H 1E **91**
Bennet's La. CH47: Meols 5E **47**
Bennetts Hill CH43: O'ton 5D **68**
Bennetts La. WA8: Wid 2A **98**
Bennett St. L19: Garst 5G **91**
Bennett Wlk. CH61: Pens 2D **100**
Ben Nevis Rd. CH42: Tran 1F **87**
Bennison Dr. L19: Gras 4E **91**
Ben's Ct. L34: Know 6D **24**
Benson Cl. CH49: Upton 5D **66**
Benson St. L1: Liv 5G **5** (6E **53**)
Bentfield L17: Aig 3D **90**
Bentfield Cl. CH63: Hghr B 4F **87**
Bentfield Gdns. CH63: Hghr B 4F **87**
Bentham Cl. CH43: Noct 6A **68**
Bentham Dr. L16: Child 1H **73**
Bentinck Cl. CH41: Birke 3E **69**
Bentinck Pl. CH41: Birke 3E **69**
Bentinck St. CH41: Birke 3E **69**
  (not continuous)
  L5: Liv 2B **52**
  WA7: Run 2D **112**
  WA9: St H 4H **43**
Bentley Rd. CH43: O'ton 5D **68**
  CH61: Pens 6D **84**
  L8: Liv 3H **71**
Bentley St. WA9: Clock F 4G **61**
Benton Cl. L5: Liv 1D **52**
Bent Way CH60: Hesw 4E **101**
Benty Cl. CH63: Hghr B 1G **103**
Benty Farm Gro. CH61: Pens 6E **85**
Benty Heath La. CH64: Will 4G **119**
  CH66: Hoot 4B **120**
Benwick Rd. L32: Kirkb 1F **23**
Berbice Rd. L18: Moss H 4E **73**
Beresford Av. CH63: Beb 4A **88**
Beresford Cl. CH43: O'ton 4C **68**
Beresford Ct. CH43: O'ton 4C **68**
Beresford Rd. CH43: O'ton 4B **68**
  CH45: Wall 6B **32**
  L8: Liv 5F **71**
Beresford St. L5: Liv 3E **53**
  L20: Boot 4B **34**
  WA9: St H 6C **42**
Berey's Bldgs. L3: Liv 3C **4**
Bergen Cl. L20: Boot 3E **35**
Berkeley Av. CH43: Pren 2B **86**
Berkeley Dr. CH49: Woodc 1E **85**
  (off Childwall Grn.)
  WA7: Manor P 1F **115**
  WA12: Newt W 1H **45**
Berkeley Rd. CH45: New B 6E **33**
Berkeley Rd. L23: Crosb 4E **9**
Berkeswell Rd. L11: Norr G 4E **37**
Berkley Av. L12: W Der 5A **38**
Berkley Cl. L8: Liv 3F **71**
Berkley St. L8: Liv 2F **71**
Berkshire Gdns. WA10: St H 3D **42**
Bermondsey Gro. WA8: Wid 5H **79**
Bermuda Rd. CH46: More 6A **48**
Bernard Av. CH45: New B 6E **33**
Berner's Rd. L19: Gras 4F **91**
Berner St. CH41: Birke 1F **69**
Berrington Av. L25: Woolt 1C **92**
Berringtons La. L11: Rainf 1H **27**
Berryford Rd. L14: Knott A 1B **56**
Berry Hill Av. L34: Know 2F **39**

Berrylands Cl. CH46: More 6B **48**
Berrylands Rd. CH46: More 6B **48**
Berry Rd. WA8: Wid 2B **96**
Berrys La. WA9: St H 4B **44**
Berry St. L1: Liv 6G **5** (1E **71**)
  L20: Boot 3B **34**
Berry St. Ind. Est. L20: Boot 4D **34**
  (off Berry St.)
Berrywood Dr. L35: Whis 5F **59**
Bertha Gdns. CH41: Birke 1B **68**
Bertha St. CH41: Birke 1B **68**
Bertram Cl. CH47: Meols 1D **64**
Bertram Dr. CH47: Meols 1C **64**
Bertram Dr. Nth. CH47: Meols 1D **64**
Bertram Rd. L17: Aig 5A **72**
Berwick Av. CH62: East 3E **121**
Berwick Cl. CH46: More 1H **65**
  L6: Liv 3A **54**
Berwick Dr. L23: Crosb 4E **9**
Berwick St. L6: Liv 3H **53**
Berwyn Av. CH47: Hoy 2C **64**
  CH61: Thing 5E **85**
Berwyn Blvd. CH63: Hghr B 3D **100**
Berwyn Dr. CH61: Hesw 3G **87**
Berwyn Gro. WA9: St H 2B **44**
Berwyn Rd. CH44: Wall 2E **51**
  L4: Walt 5A **36**
Beryl Rd. CH43: Noct 4G **67**
Beryl St. L13: Liv 6E **55**
Beryl Wlk. L10: Faz 4F **23**
Besford Ho. L25: Gate 4D **74**
Besford Rd. L25: Gate 4D **74**
Bessborough Rd. CH43: O'ton 5D **68**
Bessbrook Rd. L17: Aig 1C **90**
Bessemer St. L8: Liv 5F **71**
Beta Cl. CH62: New F 4A **88**
Betchworth Cres. WA7: Beech 1H **123**
Bethany Cl. WA11: Hay 4D **30**
Bethany Ct. CH63: Spit 2A **104**
Bethany Cres. CH63: Beb 6H **87**
Bethel Gro. L17: Liv 3B **72**
Betjeman Gro. L16: Child 1B **74**
Betony Cl. L26: Halew 2G **93**
Bettisfield Av. CH62: Brom 2D **120**
Betula Cl. L9: Walt 1A **36**
Bevan Cl. WA8: Wid 1B **60**
Bevans Ct. L12: W Der 6G **37**
Bevan's La. L12: W Der 6H **37**
Bevan Way WA8: Wid 6F **79**
Beverley Dr. CH60: Hesw 1F **117**
Beverley Gdns. CH61: Thing 5F **85**
Beverley Rd. CH45: Wall 1B **50**
  CH62: New F 3B **88**
  L15: Wav 3E **73**
Beversbrook Rd. L11: Norr G 3F **37**
Bevington Bush L3: Liv 4D **52**
Bevington Hill L3: Liv 3D **52**
Bevington St. L3: Liv 3D **52**
Bevyl Rd. CH64: Park 5F **117**
Bewey Cl. L8: Liv 5E **71**
Bewley Dr. L32: Kirkb 2H **23**
Bewsey St. WA10: St H 4B **42**
Bexhill Cl. L24: Speke 1D **108**
Bexhill Gdns. WA9: St H 1A **60**
Bianca St. L20: Boot 4C **34**
Bibbys La. L20: Boot 6A **20**
Bibby St. L13: Liv 4D **54**
Bickerstaffe St. L3: Liv 4E **53**
  WA10: St H 2E **43**
Bickerton Av. CH63: Hghr B 3F **87**
Bickerton St. L17: Aig 6A **72**
Bickley Cl. WA7: Run 4D **96**
Bidder St. L3: Liv 1H **5** (4E **53**)
Biddleston Cross WA8: Wid 6C **78**
Bideford Av. WA9: Sut L 2G **61**
Bideford Rd. WA5: Penk 5G **81**
Bidson Link Rd. CH44: Wall 5H **49**
BIDSTON 1H **67**
Bidston Av. CH41: Birke 2A **68**
  CH45: Wall 1A **50**
  WA11: St H 6H **29**
Bidston Ct. CH43: Noct 2A **68**

Bidston Grn. Ct. CH43: Bid 1G **67**
Bidston Grn. Dr. CH43: Bid 1G **67**
Bidston Hall Farm CH43: Bid 6G **49**
Bidston Ind. Est. CH44: Wall 4H **49**
Bidston Link Rd. CH43: Bid 5H **49**
Bidston Moss CH44: Wall 4H **49**
Bidston Moss Nature Reserve 4A **50**
Bidston Rd. CH43: Clau, O'ton 3A **68**
  L4: Walt 5H **35**
Bidston Station (Rail) 5G **49**
Bidston Sta. App. CH43: Bid 5G **49**
Bidston Vw. CH43: Bid 6G **49**
Bidston Village Rd. CH43: Bid 6G **49**
Bidston Way WA11: St H 6H **29**
Bidston Windmill 2H **67**
Bigdale Dr. L33: Kirkb 6B **14**
Bigham Rd. L6: Liv 4A **54**
Biglands Dr. L36: Huy 1H **75**
Big Mdw. Rd. CH49: Woodc 5E **67**
Billinge Cres. WA11: St H 5H **29**
Billingham Rd. WA9: St H 6B **42**
Billings Cl. L5: Kirkd 1D **52**
Billington Cl. WA5: Gt San 1G **81**
Billington Rd. WA8: Wid 5H **77**
Bilston Rd. L17: Aig 3C **90**
Bilton Cl. WA8: Wid 1A **98**
Bingley Rd. L4: Walt 6H **35**
Binns Rd. L7: Liv 5C **54**
  L13: Liv 5C **54**
Binns Rd. Ind. Est. L13: Liv 6D **54**
Binns Way L13: Liv 6D **54**
Binsey Cl. CH49: Upton 4B **66**
Birbeck Rd. L33: Kirkb 6C **14**
Birbeck Wlk. L33: Kirkb 6C **14**
Birchall St. L20: Kirkd 6C **34**
Birch Av. CH49: Upton 3B **66**
  L9: Ain 5H **21**
  WA10: St H 5D **28**
Birch Cl. CH43: O'ton 6D **68**
  L31: Mag 6E **7**
  L35: Whis 3E **59**
Birch Ct. L8: Liv 5G **71**
  (off Weller Way)
Birch Cres. WA12: Newt W 1H **45**
Birchdale Cl. CH49: Grea 4B **66**
Birchdale Rd. L9: Walt 1G **35**
  L22: Water 1F **19**
Birchen Rd. L26: Halew 4A **94**
Birches, The CH44: Wall 5G **51**
  CH64: Nest 5B **118**
  L28: Stockb V 6C **38**
Birches Cl. CH60: Hesw 5E **101**
Birchfield CH46: More 2A **66**
Birchfield Av. WA8: Wid 1E **97**
Birchfield Cl. CH46: More 3A **66**
  L7: Liv 5C **54**
Birchfield Rd. L4: Walt 3G **35**
  L7: Liv 5C **54**
  WA8: Wid 4E **79**
Birchfield St. L3: Liv 1H **5** (4E **53**)
  WA9: St H 6B **42**
Birchfield Way L31: Lyd 2A **6**
Birch Gdns. WA10: St H 5D **28**
Birch Gro. CH45: New B 6E **33**
  L15: Wav 6E **55**
  L35: Presc 3E **59**
  L36: Huy 5F **57**
Birch Heys CH48: Frank 2G **83**
Birch Hill M. L25: Woolt 2C **92**
Birchill Rd. L33: Know I 1E **25**
Birchley St. WA10: St H 1E **43**
Birchley Vw. WA11: St H 1F **29**
Birchmere CH60: Hesw 3C **100**
Birchmuir Hey L32: Kirkb 2B **24**
Birchridge Cl. CH62: Spit 3C **104**
Birch Rd. CH43: O'ton 6D **68**
  CH47: Meols 1E **65**
  CH63: Beb 1A **104**
  L36: Huy 6G **57**
  WA7: Run 5F **113**
  WA8: Wid 6F **79**
  WA11: Hay 4G **31**
Birch St. L5: Liv 2B **52**

Birch Tree Av. WA11: St H 3D 28
Birch Tree Ct. L12: W Der 1E 55
Birchtree Dr. L31: Mell 6E 13
Birchtree Rd. L17: Aig 6C 72
Birchview Way CH43: Noct 4H 67
Birchway CH60: Hesw 1G 117
Birchwood Av. CH41: Birke 2G 69
Birchwood Cl. CH41: Birke 2F 69
Birchwood Way L33: Kirkb 4C 14
Bird St. L7: Liv 2A 72
Birdwood Rd. L11: Norr G 5D 36
Birkdale Av. CH63: Brom 1C 120
Birkdale Cl. L6: Liv 1B 54
   L36: Roby 6E 57
Birkdale Ct. L36: Huy 1H 75
Birkdale Rd. WA5: Penk 5H 81
   WA8: Wid 4F 79
BIRKENHEAD 3H 69
Birkenhead Central Station (Rail) 4G 69
Birkenhead North Station (Rail) 6B 50
Birkenhead Park Station (Rail) 1D 68
Birkenhead Priory 3H 69
Birkenhead Rd. CH44: Wall 6G 51
   CH47: Hoy, Meols 1C 64
   CH64: Will 5F 119
Birkenshaw Av. L23: Blun 4D 8
Birket Av. CH46: Leas 4D 48
Birket Cl. CH46: Leas 4E 49
Birket Ho. CH41: Birke 2F 69
Birket Sq. CH46: Leas 4D 48
Birkett Rd. CH42: Rock F 2G 87
   CH48: W Kir 5B 64
Birkett St. L3: Liv 1G 5 (4E 53)
Birkin Cl. L32: Kirkb 3C 24
Birkin Rd. L32: Kirkb 3C 24
Birkin Wlk. L32: Kirkb 3C 24
Birley Ct. L8: Liv 2F 71
Birnam Dr. L35: Rainh 5B 60
Birnam Rd. CH44: Wall 4F 51
Birstall Av. WA11: St H 6G 29
Birstall Rd. L7: Run 6H 113
Birstall Rd. L6: Liv 4H 53
Birt Cl. L8: Liv 2H 71
Birtley Ct. WA8: Wid 2H 95
Bisham Pk. WA7: Nort 2F 115
Bishopdale Cl. WA5: Gt San 2H 81
Bishopdale Dr. L35: Rainh 4B 60
Bishop Dr. L35: Whis 6C 58
Bishopgate St. L15: Wav 1C 72
Bishop Reeves Rd. WA11: Hay 4G 31
Bishop Rd. CH44: Wall 5D 50
   L6: Liv 6A 36
   WA10: St H 6C 28
Bishops Ct. CH43: O'ton 6D 68
   L12: W Der 5E 37
   L25: Woolt 1D 92
Bishop Sheppard Ct. L3: Liv 3C 52
Bishops Way WA8: Wid 6H 79
Bisley St. CH45: Wall 2D 50
   L15: Wav .2C 72
Bispham Dr. CH47: Meols 2E 65
Bispham Ho. L3: Liv 1E 5
Bittern Cl. WA7: Nort 5F 115
Bixteth St. L3: Liv 2C 4 (5C 52)
Blackberry Gro. L26: Halew 1F 93
BLACKBROOK 5C 30
Blackbrook Cl. L9: Walt 2G 35
   WA8: Wid 6A 78
Blackbrook Rd. WA11: St H 6A 30
Blackburne Av. WA8: Hale B 6H 95
Blackburne Dr. L25: Hunts X 4F 93
Blackburne Pl. L8: Liv 1F 71
Blackburne St. L19: Garst 1G 107
Blackburne Ter. L8: Liv 1F 71
   (off Blackburne Pl.)
Black Cat Ind. Est. WA8: Wid 5D 96
Black Denton's Pl. WA8: Wid 2G 97
Blackdown Gro. WA9: St H 3B 44
Blackfield St. L5: Kirkd 1D 52
Blackheath Dr. CH46: Leas 4D 48
Blackheath La. WA7: Manor P 1G 115
Black Horse Cl. CH48: W Kir 6C 64
Black Horse Hill CH48: W Kir 1C 82

Black Horse La. L13: Liv 3F 55
Black Horse Pl. L13: Liv 4F 55
Blackhorse St. WA9: St H 1H 43
Blackhurst Rd. L31: Lyd 2B 6
Blackley Gro. L33: Kirkb 3C 14
   (off Carl's Way)
Blacklock Hall Rd. L24: Speke 2E 109
Blacklow Brow L36: Huy 5F 57
Blackmoor Dr. L12: W Der 1G 55
Blackpool St. CH41: Birke 4G 69
Blackrod Av. L24: Speke 1E 109
Blacksmith Pl. L25: Hunts X 3F 93
Blackstock Ct. L30: N'ton 5D 10
   (off Granams Cft.)
Blackstock St. L3: Liv 4C 52
Blackstone Av. WA11: St H 6H 29
Blackstone St. L5: Liv 1B 52
Blackthorn Cres. L28: Stockb V 5D 38
Blackthorne Cl. CH46: More 2D 66
Blackthorne Rd. L9: Walt 2A 36
Blackwater Rd. L11: Crox 1H 37
Blackwood Av. L25: Woolt 5B 74
Blair Ct. CH43: Clau 3D 68
Blair Dr. WA8: Wid 6H 77
Blair Ind. Est. L21: Crosb 6H 9
Blair Pk. CH63: Spit 2B 104
Blair St. L8: Liv 2E 71
Blair Wlk. L26: Halew 5H 93
Blaisdon Cl. L11: Norr G 4E 37
Blakeacre Cl. L26: Halew 5H 93
Blakeacre Rd. L26: Halew 5H 93
Blakefield Rd. L23: Thorn 3C 10
Blakeley Brow CH63: Raby M 1A 120
Blakeley Cl. CH63: Raby M 1A 120
Blakeley Dell CH63: Raby M 1B 120
Blakeley Dene CH63: Raby M 6B 104
Blakeley Rd. CH63: Raby M 6A 104
Blakeney Cl. CH49: Upton 2E 67
Blakenhall Way CH49: Upton 3B 66
Blaking Dr. L34: Know 1F 39
Blantyre Rd. L15: Wav 3C 72
Blantyre St. WA7: Run 2D 112
Blay Cl. L25: Hunts X 3F 93
Blaydon Cl. L30: N'ton 2F 21
Blaydon Gro. WA9: St H 6B 42
Blaydon Wlk. CH43: Clau 3A 68
Bleak Hill Cl. WA10: Windle 4A 28
Bleak Hill Rd. WA10: Eccl, Windle 6H 27
Bleasdale Av. L10: Ain 1C 22
Bleasdale Cl. CH49: Upton 3C 66
Bleasdale Rd. L18: Moss H 5F 73
Bleasdale Way L21: Ford 5B 10
Blenheim Av. L21: Lith 3C 20
Blenheim Dr. L34: Presc 2H 57
Blenheim Rd. CH44: Wall 2F 51
   L18: Moss H 4D 72
Blenheim St. L5: Liv 3C 52
Blenheim Way L2: Speke 2D 108
   WA11: St H 5F 29
Blessington Rd. L4: Walt 6F 35
Bletchley Av. CH44: Wall 3B 50
Bligh St. L15: Wav 2C 72
Blindfoot Rd. WA11: Rainf 4D 26
Blisworth St. L21: Lith 5B 20
Blithedale Ct. CH42: Rock F 2A 88
   (off The Hawthornes)
Blomfield Rd. L19: Aller 4H 91
Bloomfield Grn. L17: Aig 5A 72
Bloomsbury Ct. CH47: Hoy 3A 64
Bloomsbury Way WA8: Wid 6B 78
Blossom Gro. L32: Kirkb 4B 24
Blossom St. L20: Boot 6C 20
Blucher St. L22: Water 2E 19
Bluebell Av. CH41: Birke 1B 68
   WA11: Hay 4G 31
Bluebell Cl. L22: Water 2E 19
   L32: Kirkb .5A 14
Bluebell Ct. WA7: Beech 3B 124
Blue Bell La. L36: Huy 3G 57
Bluebell Cl. CH64: Nest 6E 119
Blueberry Flds. L10: Faz 5D 22
Bluecoat, The 5E 5 (6D 52)
Bluecoat Chambers L1: Liv 5E 5

Bluefields St. L8: Liv 2F 71
Blue Hatch WA6: Frod 6G 123
Blue Jay Cl. L27: N'ley 4G 75
Blue Ridge Cl. WA5: Gt San 2G 81
Bluestone La. L31: Mag 6D 6
Bluewood Dr. CH41: Birke 6H 49
Blundell Rd. L35: Whis 2G 59
   WA8: Wid .3A 96
BLUNDELLSANDS 6D 8
Blundellsands Classic L23: Blun 6D 8
Blundellsands Ct. L23: Blun 6D 8
   (off Blundellsands Rd. W.)
Blundellsands & Crosby Station (Rail)
   . . . . .5E 9
Blundellsands Rd. E. L23: Blun 5E 9
Blundellsands Rd. W. L23: Blun 6D 8
Blundells Dr. CH46: More 6C 48
BLUNDELL'S HILL 5H 59
Blundell's La. L35: Rainh 6G 59
Blundell St. L1: Liv 2D 70
Blyth Cl. WA7: Murd 2F 125
Blythe Av. WA8: Wid 5F 79
Blyth Hey L30: N'ton 5D 10
Blyth Rd. CH63: Brom 6C 104
Blythswood St. L17: Aig 6H 71
Boaler St. L6: Liv 4G 53
Boaler St. Ind. Est. L6: Liv 4H 53
   (off Tulloch St.)
Boardmans La. WA9: St H 1A 44
   WA11: St H 1A 44
Boathouse La. CH64: Park 5F 117
Bobbies La. WA10: Eccl 1G 41
Bob Paisley Ct. L5: Liv 1G 53
   (off Adkins St.)
Bodden St. WA9: Clock F 3H 61
Bodley St. L4: Walt 6F 35
Bodmin Cl. WA7: Brook 1D 124
Bodmin Gro. WA11: St H 4H 29
Bodmin Rd. L4: Walt 4F 35
Bodmin Way L26: Halew 3G 93
Bognor Cl. L24: Speke 1D 108
Bolan St. L13: Liv 4E 55
BOLD 6D 44
Bold Bus. Cen. WA9: Bold 6D 44
Bolden Cl. L30: N'ton 2F 21
Bolde Way CH63: Spit 4A 104
BOLD HEATH .2A 80
Bold Ind. Est. WA8: Wid 4G 79
Bold Ind. Pk. WA9: Bold 1D 62
Bold La. L39: Augh 1F 7
   WA5: Coll G 6D 44
   WA9: Bold 6D 44
Bold Pl. L1: Liv 6H 5
Bold Rd. WA9: St H 6D 44
Bold St. L1: Liv 5F 5 (6D 52)
   WA7: Run .2F 113
   WA8: Wid .4E 97
   WA10: St H 2D 42
Boleyn, The L31: Mag 4D 6
Boleyn Ct. WA7: Manor P 2E 115
Bollington Cl. CH43: O'ton 6B 68
Bolton Av. L32: Kirkb 1G 23
Bolton Cl. WA9: St H 1G 43
Bolton Rd. CH62: Port S 6B 88
Bolton Rd. E. CH62: Port S 5B 88
Bolton St. L3: Liv 4G 5 (6E 53)
   WA9: St H .1G 43
   (not continuous)
Bolton Wlk. L32: Kirkb 1G 23
Bonchurch Dr. L15: Wav 6D 54
Bond St. L3: Liv 3D 52
   L34: Presc 1D 58
Bonnington Av. L23: Crosb 4E 9
Bonnington Cl. WA10: St H 2A 42
Bonsall Rd. L12: W Der 1F 55
Boode Cft. L28: Stockb V 4D 38
Booker Av. L18: Moss H, Aller 2E 91
Booth St. L13: Liv 4E 55
   WA9: St H .6B 42
Boothwood Cl. L7: Liv 6H 53
BOOTLE 2C 34
Bootle Leisure Cen. 1C 34
Bootle New Strand Station (Rail) 1C 34

Borax St. L13: Liv 5E 55
Bordehill Gdns. L12: W Der 5H 37
Border Rd. CH60: Hesw 5F 101
Border Way L5: Liv 1E 53
Borella Rd. L13: Liv 1D 54
Borough Pavement CH41: Birke . . .3G 69
Borough Pl. CH41: Birke 3G 69
(off Grange Rd. E.)
Borough Rd. CH41: Birke 6E 69
CH42: Rock F, Tran 6E 69
CH44: Wall 4F 51
WA10: St H 3C 42
Borough Rd. E. CH41: Birke 3G 69
CH44: Wall 5G 51
Borough Way CH44: Wall 5G 51
Borrowdale Rd. CH46: More 1B 66
CH63: Beb 1G 103
L15: Wav 3C 72
WA8: Wid 3A 96
WA10: St H 5H 41
Bosco Ct. L11: Crox 1F 37
Boscow Cres. WA9: St H 6H 43
Bosnia St. L8: Liv 6G 71
Bossom Ct. L22: Water 4F 19
Bostock St. L5: Liv 2D 52
Boston Av. WA7: Run 5F 113
Boston Blvd. WA5: Gt San 2H 81
Boswell Rd. CH43: Pren 2B 86
Boswell St. L8: Liv 2A 72
L20: Boot 6A 20
Bosworth Cl. CH63: Spit 3H 103
Bosworth Rd. WA11: St H 5G 29
Botanic Est. L7: Liv 6B 54
Botanic Gro. L7: Liv 6A 54
Botanic Pl. L7: Liv 5A 54
Botanic Rd. L7: Liv 6A 54
Botany Rd. L24: Speke 6E 93
Botley Cl. CH49: Upton 4B 66
Boulevard L6: Liv 3B 54
Boulevard, The L8: Liv 3G 71
L12: W Der 5F 37
Boulevard Industry Pk. L24: Halew 6F 93
(not continuous)
Boulton Av. CH48: W Kir 5B 64
CH62: New F 3B 88
Boundary Dr. L23: Crosb 3F 9
L25: Hunts X 4F 93
Boundary Farm Rd. L26: Halew 5F 93
Boundary La. CH60: Hesw 5E 101
L6: Liv .3H 53
L33: Kirkb 1G 25
Boundary Rd. CH43: Bid, Noct 6H 49
CH48: W Kir 3D 82
CH62: Port S 4B 88
L21: Lith 1D 20
(not continuous)
L36: Huy 1H 75
WA10: St H 2C 42
Boundary St. L5: Liv 1B 52
Boundary St. E. L5: Liv 1E 53
Boundary Wlk. L36: Huy 1A 76
Bourne Gdns. WA9: St H 4G 43
Bournemouth Cl. WA7: Murd 1F 125
Bourne St. L6: Liv 4H 53
Bourton Rd. L25: Hunts X 4D 92
Bousfield St. L4: Walt 6E 35
Bowden Cl. L12: Crox 3A 38
Bowden Rd. L19: Garst 5F 91
Bowden St. L21: Lith 5B 20
Bowdon Rd. CH45: Wall 1C 50
Bowen Cl. WA8: Wid 5B 78
Bower Gro. L21: Sea 4H 19
Bower Ho. CH49: Upton 2D 66
Bower Rd. CH60: Hesw 5G 101
L25: Woolt 5C 74
L36: Huy 3G 57
Bowers Bus. Pk. WA8: Wid 4F 97
Bowers Pk. Ind. Est. WA8: Wid 4G 97
Bower St. WA8: Wid 2G 97
Bowfell Cl. CH62: East 4D 120
Bowfield Rd. L19: Gras 4F 91

Bowgreen Cl. CH43: Bid 2G 67
BOWKER'S GREEN 2H 7
Bowker's Grn. La. L39: Augh, Bic 2H 7
Bowland Av. L16: Child 6H 55
WA9: Sut M 4F 61
Bowland Cl. CH62: Brom 4D 104
WA7: Beech 2A 124
Bowland Dr. L21: Ford 5C 10
Bowles St. L20: Boot 6A 20
Bowley Rd. L13: Liv 2D 54
Bowmore Way L7: Liv 1A 72
Bowness Av. CH43: Pren 1C 86
CH63: Brom 2C 120
WA11: St H 3F 29
Bowood Cl. L8: Liv 6F 71
Bowring Dr. CH64: Park 6F 117
BOWRING PARK 6C 56
Bowring Pk. Av. L16: Child 6C 56
Bowring Pk. Rd. L14: Broad G 6G 55
Bowring Pk. Vis. Cen. 6C 56
Bowring St. L8: Liv 5G 71
Bowscale Cl. CH49: Upton 4C 66
Bowscale Rd. L11: Norr G 4E 37
Boxdale Cl. L18: Moss H 5E 73
Boxdale Rd. L18: Moss H 5E 73
Boxgrove Rd. WA8: Wid 6F 79
Boxmoor Rd. L18: Moss H 1E 91
Boxtree Cl. L12: Crox 1B 38
Boxwood Cl. L36: Roby 5E 57
Boxwood Gdns. WA9: St H 6A 44
Boycott St. L5: Liv 1G 53
Boyd Cl. CH46: Leas 4F 49
Boydell Cl. L28: Stockb V 6D 38
Boyer Av. L31: Mag 2B 12
Boyes Brow L33: Kirkb 5H 13
Boyes Ct. L31: Mag 2B 12
Boyton Ct. L7: Liv 1A 72
Brabant Rd. L17: Aig 2C 90
Braby Rd. L21: Lith 5C 20
Bracewell Cl. WA9: Clock F 1G 61
Bracken Cl. WA9: Clock F 3G 61
Brackendale CH49: Woodc 6G 67
WA7: Run 5H 113
Brackendale Av. L9: Ain 4H 21
Bracken Dr. CH48: W Kir 1E 83
Brackenhurst Dr.
CH45: New B 6E 33
Brackenhurst Grn. L33: Kirkb 1A 24
Bracken La. CH63: Hghr B 6F 87
Brackenside CH60: Hesw 3D 100
Bracken Wlk. L32: Kirkb 2H 23
(off Wervin Rd.)
Bracken Way L12: W Der 2E 55
Bracken Wood L12: Crox 1A 38
Brackenwood Dr. WA8: Wid 4G 95
Brackenwood Gro. L35: Whis 4F 59
Brackenwood Rd. CH63: Hghr B 6F 87
Brackley Cl. CH44: Wall 4C 50
WA7: Run 2D 112
Brackley St. WA7: Run 2D 112
Bracknell Av. L32: Kirkb 2H 23
Bracknell Cl. L32: Kirkb 3H 23
Bradbourne Cl. L12: Crox 2A 38
Bradda Cl. CH49: Upton 2D 66
Braddan Av. L13: Liv 2C 54
Bradden Cl. CH63: Spit 3B 104
Bradewell Cl. L4: Kirkd 5E 35
Bradewell St. L4: Kirkd 5E 35
Bradfield Av. L10: Ain 6A 12
Bradfield St. L7: Liv 5A 54
Bradgate Cl. CH46: More 6H 47
Bradkirk Ct. L30: N'ton 4D 10
Bradley Fold L36: Huy 1A 76
Bradley La. WA5: Burtw 3H 45
WA12: Newt W 3H 45
Bradley Rd. L21: Lith 2B 20
Bradley Way WA8: Wid 2F 97
Bradman Cl. CH45: Wall 2D 50
Bradman Rd. CH46: More 6A 48
L33: Know I 1H 25
Bradmoor Rd. CH62: Brom 5D 104
Bradshaw Cl. WA10: St H 1B 42
Bradshaw St. WA8: Wid 1E 97

Bradshaw Wlk. L20: Boot 1B 34
(off St James Dr.)
Bradstone Cl. L10: Faz 5F 23
Bradville Rd. L9: Ain 4A 22
Bradwell Cl. CH48: W Kir 1D 82
Braehaven Rd. CH45: New B 6E 33
Braemar Cl. L35: Whis 4F 59
Braemar Ho. CH43: O'ton 4B 68
Braemar St. L20: Kirkd 4D 34
Braemore Rd. CH44: Wall 3B 50
Braeside Gdns. CH49: Upton 4D 66
Brae St. L7: Liv 5H 53
Brahms Cl. L8: Liv 3H 71
Braid St. CH41: Birke 1F 69
Braidwood Ct. CH41: Birke 4E 69
(off Mount Gro.)
Brainerd St. L13: Liv 2C 54
Braithwaite Cl. L35: Rainh 4A 60
WA7: Beech 1H 123
Bramberton Pl. L4: Walt 4A 36
Bramberton Rd. L4: Walt 4A 36
Bramble Av. CH41: Birke 1B 68
Bramble Cl. WA5: Penk 6G 81
Brambles, The WA5: Burtw 6H 45
Bramble Way CH46: More 5B 48
WA7: Beech 3A 124
Bramblewood Cl. CH43: Noct 5H 67
L27: N'ley 4G 75
Brambling Cl. WA7: Beech 2A 124
Brambling Pk. L26: Halew 2G 93
Bramcote Av. WA11: St H 5G 29
Bramcote Cl. L33: Kirkb 5C 14
Bramcote Rd. L33: Kirkb 5B 14
Bramcote Wlk. L33: Kirkb 5B 14
Bramerton Cl. CH48: W Kir 6A 64
Bramford Cl. CH49: Upton 4C 66
Bramhall Cl. CH48: W Kir 1D 82
L24: Speke 3G 109
Bramhall Dr. CH62: East 4F 121
Bramhall Rd. L22: Water 3G 19
Bramhope Pk. L12: W Der 6H 37
Bramley Av. CH63: Hghr B 4G 87
Bramley Cl. L27: N'ley 4F 75
Bramleys, The L31: Mag 2A 12
Bramley Wlk. L24: Speke 3F 109
Bramley Way L32: Kirkb 6G 13
Brampton Cl. L32: Kirkb 5A 14
Brampton Dr. WA9: St H 2D 44
Brampton Dr. L8: Liv 1G 71
Bramwell Av. CH43: Pren 2C 86
Bramwell St. WA9: St H 1A 44
Branchway WA11: Hay 5F 31
Brancker Av. L35: Rainh 3H 59
Brancote Cl. CH43: Clau 3B 68
Brancote Gdns. CH43: Clau 3B 68
CH62: Brom 6D 104
Brancote Mt. CH43: Clau 3B 68
Brancote Rd. CH43: Clau 3B 68
Brandearth Hey L28: Stockb V 6D 38
Brandearth Rd. L28: Stockb V 6D 38
Brandon WA8: Wid 1G 95
Brandon St. CH41: Birke 3H 69
Brandreth Cl. L35: Rainh 4A 60
Branfield Cl. L12: Crox 2A 38
Bransdale Rd. WA5: Gt San 2H 81
Branstree Av. L11: Norr G 3D 36
Branthwaite Cl. L11: Norr G 4E 37
Branthwaite Cres. L11: Norr G 3E 37
Branthwaite Gro. L11: Norr G 4E 37
Brasenose Rd. L20: Boot 3B 34
Brassey St. CH41: Birke 1D 68
L8: Liv .3E 71
Brattan Rd. CH41: Birke 5E 69
Braunton Rd. CH45: Wall 1C 50
L17: Aig .3C 90
Bravery Cl. L19: Speke 1A 108
Braybrooke Rd. L11: Norr G 2E 37
Bray Cl. WA7: Beech 1H 123
Braydon Cl. L25: Hunts X 5E 93
Brayfield Rd. L4: Walt 4B 36
Bray Rd. L24: Speke 1E 109
Bray St. CH41: Birke 1D 68
Breccia Gdns. WA9: St H 3A 44

Brechin Rd. L33: Kirkb 1B **24**
Breckfield Pl. L5: Liv 2F **53**
Breckfield Rd. Nth. L5: Liv 1F **53**
Breckfield Rd. Sth. L6: Liv 2G **53**
Breck Pl. CH44: Wall 4C **50**
Breck Rd. CH44: Wall 3B **50**
L4: Walt 3F **53**
L5: Liv 3F **53**
WA8: Wid 2F **97**
Breckside Av. CH44: Wall 3A **50**
Breckside Pk. L6: Liv 1A **54**
Brecon Av. L30: N'ton 2F **21**
Brecon Rd. CH42: Tran 2E **87**
Brecon St. L6: Liv 4H **53**
Brecon Wlk. *L30: N'ton* *2G **21***
(off Durham Av.)
Breeze Cl. L9: Walt 2F **35**
Breeze Hill L9: Walt 2D **34**
L20: Boot 2D **34**
Breezehill Cl. CH64: Nest 6B **118**
Breezehill Rd. CH64: Nest 6B **118**
Breeze La. L9: Walt 2F **35**
Brelade Rd. L13: Liv 3D **54**
Bremhill Rd. L11: Norr G 2D **36**
Bremner Cl. L7: Liv 6A **54**
Brenda Cres. L23: Thorn 2A **10**
Brendale Av. L31: Mag 1A **12**
Brendan's Way L30: N'ton 6E **11**
Brendon Av. L21: Lith 2A **20**
Brendon Gro. WA9: St H 1C **44**
Brendor Rd. L25: Woolt 2D **92**
Brenig St. CH41: Birke 6B **50**
Brenka Av. L9: Ain 2H **21**
Brentfield WA8: Wid 1B **96**
Brent Way L26: Halew 5H **93**
(not continuous)
Brentwood Av. L17: Aig 6A **72**
L23: Crosb 4H **9**
Brentwood Cl. WA10: Eccl 2H **41**
Brentwood Ct. *CH49: Woodc* *1E **85***
(off Childwall Grn.)
Brentwood Gro. L33: Kirkb 3A **14**
Brentwood St. CH44: Wall 4E **51**
Brereton Av. CH63: Beb 5A **88**
L15: Wav 3E **73**
Brereton Cl. WA7: Cas 5C **114**
(not continuous)
Bretherton Pl. L35: Rainh 3A **60**
Bretherton Rd. L34: Presc 1E **59**
Bretlands Rd. L23: Thorn 3B **10**
Brett Cl. L33: Kirkb 4H **13**
Brett St. CH41: Birke 1D **68**
Brewery La. L31: Mell 5C **12**
(not continuous)
Brewster St. L4: Kirkd 4E **35**
L20: Boot 4E **35**
Breydon Gdns. WA9: St H 1C **60**
Brian Av. CH61: Irby 5D **84**
Brian Cummings Ct. L21: Lith 5B **20**
Briardale Rd. CH42: Tran 5E **69**
CH44: Wall 5G **51**
CH63: Hghr B 4H **87**
CH64: Will 6A **120**
L18: Moss H 4D **72**
Briar Dr. CH60: Hesw 5E **101**
L36: Huy 5F **57**
Briarfield Av. WA8: Wid 2G **95**
Briarfield Rd. CH60: Hesw 5E **101**
Briars Cl. L35: Rainh 6B **60**
Briars Grn. WA10: St H 6D **28**
Briars La. L31: Mag 6D **6**
Briar St. L4: Kirkd 6D **34**
Briarswood Cl. CH42: Rock F 3H **87**
L35: Whis 4F **59**
Briarwood L23: Blun 3D **8**
WA7: Nort 5D **114**
Briarwood Rd. L17: Aig 6C **72**
Briary Cl. CH60: Hesw 4F **101**
Brickfields L36: Huy 6A **58**
Brick St. L1: Liv 2D **70**
WA12: Newt W 2H **45**
Brickwall Grn. L29: Seft 2F **11**
Brickwall La. L29: Seft 4D **10**
Bride St. L4: Walt 3F **35**
Bridewell Ct. WA8: Wid 6F **79**
Bridge Ct. CH48: W Kir 6A **64**
L30: N'ton 5D **10**
Bridge Cft. L21: Ford 6C **10**
Bridgecroft Rd. CH45: Wall 1D **50**
Bridge Farm Cl. CH49: Woodc 5F **67**
Bridge Farm Dr. L31: Mag 5E **7**
Bridgefield Cl. L25: Gate 2D **74**
Bridgeford Av. L12: W Der 6E **37**
Bridge Gdns. L12: W Der 4B **38**
Bridge Ind. Est. L24: Speke 6D **92**
Bridge La. L30: N'ton 6E **11**
WA6: Frod 6G **123**
Bridge La. M. WA6: Frod 6H **123**
Bridgeman St. WA10: St H 2B **42**
(not continuous)
Bridgemere Cl. L7: Liv 4B **54**
Bridgemere Ho. L17: Aig 1B **90**
Bridgend Cl. WA8: Wid 6B **78**
Bridgenorth Rd. CH61: Pens 1C **100**
Bridge Retail Pk. WA7: Run 3E **113**
Bridge Rd. CH48: W Kir 6A **64**
L7: Liv 1B **72**
L18: Moss H 6E **73**
L21: Lith 4A **20**
(not continuous)
L23: Blun 6E **9**
L31: Mag 2B **12**
L34: Presc 2D **58**
L36: Roby 5E **57**
WA9: Clock F 5H **61**
Bridges La. L29: Seft 2F **11**
Bridge St. CH41: Birke 2G **69**
(not continuous)
CH62: Port S 6B **88**
(not continuous)
L20: Boot 3B **34**
WA7: Run 3F **113**
WA10: St H 2E **43**
Bridge Vw. Cl. WA8: Wid 1E **113**
Bridge Vw. Dr. L33: Kirkb 5B **14**
Bridge Wlk. *WA7: Pal F* *6B **114***
(off Halton Lea Shop. Cen.)
Bridgewater Cl. L21: Lith 1A **20**
WA6: Frod 6G **123**
Bridgewater Ct. L21: Lith 1A **20**
Bridgewater Grange
WA7: Pres B 2H **125**
Bridgewater Ho. WA7: Run 2C **112**
Bridgewater St. L1: Liv 2D **70**
WA7: Run 2E **113**
Bridgewater Way L36: Huy 1A **76**
Bridgeway L11: Norr G 4C **36**
Bridgeway E. WA7: Wind H 3E **115**
Bridgeway W. WA7: Wind H 3D **114**
Bridle Av. CH44: Wall 5G **51**
Bridle Cl. CH43: Bid 3F **67**
CH62: Brom 6E **105**
Bridle Ct. WA9: St H 5G **43**
Bridle Pk. CH62: Brom 6E **105**
Bridle Rd. CH44: Wall 5G **51**
CH62: Brom, East 6E **105**
L30: N'ton 3E **21**
Bridle Rd. Ind. Est. L30: N'ton 3F **21**
Bridle Way L30: N'ton 3F **21**
L33: Kirkb 3H **13**
Bridport St. L3: Liv 3G **5** (5E **53**)
Brierfield Rd. L15: Wav 3D **72**
Brierley Cl. *L30: N'ton* *5H **11***
(off Beeston Dr.)
Brierley Ter. WA8: Wid 2G **97**
Briery Hey Av. L33: Kirkb 1B **24**
Brigadier Dr. L12: W Der 6A **38**
Brightgate Cl. L7: Liv 1H **71**
BRIGHTON LE SANDS 1D **18**
Brighton Rd. L22: Water 2F **19**
L36: Huy 4B **58**
Brighton St. CH44: Wall 3F **51**
Brighton Va. L22: Water 1E **19**
Bright St. CH41: Birke 3E **69**
(not continuous)
L6: Liv 4G **53**
Brightwell Cl. CH49: Upton 5D **66**
WA5: Gt San 4G **81**
Brill St. CH41: Birke 1D **68**
Brimelow Cres. WA5: Penk 6G **81**
BRIMSTAGE 3D **102**
Brimstage Av. CH63: Hghr B 3F **87**
Brimstage Cl. CH60: Hesw 6G **101**
Brimstage Grn. CH60: Hesw 5H **101**
Brimstage Hall 3C **102**
Brimstage La. CH63: Brim, Store 3D **102**
Brimstage Rd. CH60: Hesw 6G **101**
CH63: Beb, Brim, Hghr B 6G **101**
L4: Walt 3E **35**
Brimstage St. CH41: Birke 4E **69**
Brindley, The 3E **113**
Brindley Cl. L21: Lith 1A **20**
Brindley Rd. L32: Kirkb 1G **23**
WA7: Ast 2B **114**
WA9: St H 1A **62**
Brindley St. L8: Liv 3D **70**
WA7: Run 2D **112**
Brindley Wharf WA4: Pres H 2H **125**
Brinley Cl. CH62: Brom 2D **120**
Brinton Cl. L27: N'ley 3E **75**
WA8: Wid 3B **96**
Brisbane Av. CH45: New B 5C **32**
Brisbane St. WA9: St H 6B **42**
Briscoe Av. CH46: More 2C **66**
Briscoe Dr. CH46: More 2C **66**
Bristol Av. CH44: Wall 3E **51**
WA7: Murd 1G **125**
Bristol Rd. L15: Wav 3E **73**
Britannia Av. L15: Wav 2B **72**
Britannia Cres. L8: Liv 6F **71**
Britannia Ho. CH41: Birke 3H **69**
Britannia Pav. L3: Liv 1C **70**
Britannia Rd. CH45: Wall 3C **50**
Britonside Av. L32: Kirkb 3C **24**
Brittarge Brow L27: N'ley 5G **75**
Britten Cl. L8: Liv 3H **71**
Broadacre Cl. L18: Moss H 4H **73**
Broadbelt St. L4: Walt 3F **35**
Broadfield Av. CH43: Bid 1F **67**
Broadfield Cl. CH43: Bid 2F **67**
Broadfields WA7: Nort 5E **115**
Broadgate Av. WA9: St H 4G **43**
BROAD GREEN 5H **55**
Broad Grn. Rd. L13: Liv 4E **55**
Broad Green Station (Rail) 6H **55**
Broadheath Av. CH43: Bid 2G **67**
Broadheath Ter. WA8: Wid 2B **96**
Broad Hey L30: N'ton 6D **10**
Broad Hey Cl. L25: Woolt 6D **74**
Broadhurst St. L17: Aig 6A **72**
Broadlands L35: Presc 2E **59**
Broad La. CH60: Hesw 4A **100**
L4: Walt 4C **36**
L11: Norr G 4C **36**
L32: Kirkb 3B **24**
WA5: Coll G 4E **45**
WA11: St H 1F **29**
Broad La. Pct. L11: Norr G 4D **36**
Broadleaf Rd. L19: Gras 4D **90**
Broadmead CH60: Hesw 6G **101**
L19: Aller 4A **92**
BROAD OAK 1B **44**
Broad Oak Av. WA5: Penk 5G **81**
WA11: Hay 5C **30**
Broad Oak Rd. WA9: St H 2A **44**
Broadoak Rd. L14: Knott A 3B **56**
L31: Mag 6D **6**
Broadoaks CH49: Upton 3C **66**
Broad Pl. L11: Norr G 5D **36**
Broads, The WA9: St H 1C **60**
Broad Sq. L11: Norr G 5D **36**
Broadstone Dr. CH63: Spit 3H **103**
Broad Vw. L11: Norr G 5D **36**
Broadway CH45: Wall 2B **50**
CH49: Grea 4C **66**
CH63: Hghr B 4F **87**
L9: Ain 4C **22**
L11: Norr G 4C **36**
WA8: Wid 2G **95**

Broadway WA10: Eccl 1G 41
   WA10: St H 5A 42
Broadway Av. CH45: Wall 2B 50
Broadway Community Leisure Cen.
   . . . . .5H 41
Broadway Mkt. L11: Norr G 4C 36
Broadwood Av. L23: Mag 2A 12
Broadwood St. L15: Wav 2C 72
Brock Av. L31: Mag 5D 6
Brockenhurst Rd. L9: Walt 6G 21
Brock Gdns. L24: Hale 3E 111
Brock Hall Cl. WA9: Clock F 3G 61
Brockhall Cl. L35: Whis 1G 59
Brockholme Rd. L18: Moss H 2E 91
Brocklebank La. L19: Aller 3H 91
Brockley Av. CH45: New B 4D 32
Brock St. L4: Kirkd 5E 35
Brodie Av. L18: Moss H 6E 73
   L19: Aig, Aller 2F 91
BROMBOROUGH 5C 104
BROMBOROUGH POOL 6D 88
BROMBOROUGH PORT 2E 105
Bromborough Rake Station (Rail) . .5C 104
Bromborough Rd. CH63: Beb 6A 88
Bromborough Station (Rail) 6C 104
Bromborough Village Rd.
   CH62: Brom 4E 105
Brome Way CH63: Spit 3B 104
Bromilow Rd. WA9: St H 3B 44
Bromley Av. L18: Moss H 4D 72
Bromley Cl. CH60: Hesw 6C 100
   L26: Halew .2A 94
Bromley Rd. CH45: New B 6C 32
Brompton Av. CH44: Wall 3E 51
   L17: Liv 4A 72
   L23: Crosb .6E 9
   L33: Kirkb .4C 14
Brompton Ct. L17: Liv 4A 72
Brompton Ho. L17: Aig 4B 72
Bromsgrove Rd. CH49: Grea 5A 66
Bromyard Cl. L20: Boot 1B 34
Bronington Av. CH62: Brom 1D 120
Bronshill Ct. L23: Blun 5C 8
Bronte Cl. L23: Blun 5D 8
Bronte St. L3: Liv 3H 5
   WA10: St H 1B 42
Brook, The L31: Mag 1C 12
Brookbank Cl. L10: Faz 4F 23
Brookbridge Rd. L13: Liv 1C 54
Brook Cl. CH44: Wall 2E 51
   WA8: Cron .3A 78
Brookdale WA8: Wid 6G 77
Brookdale Av. Nth. CH49: Grea 5C 66
Brookdale Av. Sth. CH49: Grea 5C 66
Brookdale Cl. CH49: Grea 5C 66
Brookdale Rd. L15: Wav 3C 72
Brook Dr. WA5: Gt San 4H 81
Brook End WA9: St H 4C 44
Brooke Rd. E. L22: Water 1F 19
Brooke Rd. W. L22: Water 1E 19
Brookfield Av. L22: Water 3H 19
   L23: Crosb .6F 9
   L35: Rainh .2A 60
   WA7: Run .3H 113
Brookfield Cen. L9: Ain 6A 22
Brookfield Dr. L9: Ain, Faz 6A 22
Brookfield Gdns. CH48: W Kir 1B 82
Brookfield Ho. L36: Huy 4G 57
Brookfield La. L39: Augh 2F 7
Brookfield Rd. CH48: W Kir 1B 82
BROOKFIELDS GREEN 2F 7
Brook Furlong WA6: Frod 5C 122
Brook Hey CH64: Park 5F 117
Brook Hey Dr. L33: Kirkb 5B 14
Brook Hey Wlk. L33: Kirkb 6C 14
Brookhill Cl. L20: Boot 2D 34
Brookhill Rd. L20: Boot 1D 34
Brookhouse Gro. WA10: Eccl 2G 41
BROOKHURST 2C 120
Brookhurst Av. CH62: East 1C 120
   CH63: Brom, East 1C 120
Brookhurst Cl. CH63: Brom 2C 120
Brookhurst Rd. CH63: Brom 1C 120

Brookland La. WA9: St H 3C 44
Brookland Rd. CH41: Birke 4F 69
Brookland Rd. E. L13: Liv 4E 55
Brookland Rd. W. L13: Liv 4E 55
Brooklands CH41: Birke 2F 69
Brooklands, The L36: Huy 6G 57
Brooklands Av. L22: Water 3G 19
Brooklands Dr. L31: Mag 1B 12
Brooklands Gdns. CH64: Park 6G 117
Brooklands Pk. WA8: Wid 1G 97
Brooklands Rd. CH64: Park 6G 117
   WA10: Eccl 1G 41
Brook La. CH64: Park 5G 117
Brook Lea Ho. L21: Ford 6C 10
Brooklet Rd. CH60: Hesw 5G 101
Brooklime Rd. L11: Norr G 4D 36
Brook Mdw. CH61: Irby 4C 84
Brook Pk. L31: Mag 2A 12
Brook Rd. L9: Walt 1G 35
   L20: Boot .2B 34
   L23: Thorn .3A 10
   L31: Mag 1C 12
Brooks, The WA11: St H 4E 29
Brooks All. L1: Liv 5E 5 (6D 52)
Brookside L12: W Der 5B 38
   L31: Mag 6D 6
Brookside Av. L14: Knott A 4H 55
   L22: Water .3H 19
   WA10: Eccl 6H 27
   WA11: Rainf 2E 17
Brookside Cl. L35: Presc 3E 59
   WA11: Hay .4D 30
Brookside Ct. L23: Crosb 5G 9
Brookside Cres. CH49: Upton 4B 66
Brookside Dr. CH49: Upton 4C 66
Brookside Rd. L35: Presc 3E 59
Brookside Vw. WA11: Hay 4D 30
Brookside Way WA11: Hay 4D 30
Brook St. CH41: Birke 1E 69
   CH62: Port S 5A 88
   L3: Liv 2B 4 (5B 52)
   L35: Whis 2F 59
   WA7: Run 3E 113
     (not continuous)
   WA8: Wid .3F 97
   WA10: St H 2E 43
Brook St. E. CH41: Birke 2G 69
Brook Ter. CH48: W Kir 1A 82
   WA7: Run .4A 114
Brookthorpe Ct. CH45: Wall 1E 51
BROOKVALE 2E 125
Brook Va. L22: Water 3H 19
Brookvale Av. Nth. WA7: Brook 1D 124
Brookvale Av. Sth. WA7: Brook 1D 124
Brookvale Cl. WA5: Burtw 1H 63
Brookvale Local Nature Reserve . . .3H 119
Brookvale Recreation Cen. 1E 125
Brook Wlk. CH61: Irby 4B 84
Brookway CH43: Pren 2A 86
   CH45: Wall .2C 50
   CH49: Grea 4C 66
Brookway La. WA9: St H 4B 44
Brookwood Ct. L33: Kirkb 5B 14
Brookwood Rd. L36: Huy 3G 57
Broom Cl. L34: Eccl P 1F 59
Broome Ct. WA7: Brook 1D 124
Broomfield Cl. CH60: Hesw 4A 100
Broomfield Gdns. L9: Walt 6F 21
Broomfield Rd. L9: Walt 6F 21
     (not continuous)
Broom Hill CH43: Clau 2B 68
Broomhill Cl. L27: N'ley 3E 75
Broomlands CH60: Hesw 5D 100
Broomleigh Cl. CH63: Hghr B 6F 87
Broom Rd. WA10: St H 5H 41
Brooms Gro. L10: Ain 1C 22
Broom Way L26: Halew 4G 93
Broseley Av. CH62: Brom 4C 104
Broster Av. CH46: More 1A 66
Broster Cl. CH46: More 1A 66
Brosters La. CH47: Meols 1D 64
Brotherhood Dr. WA9: St H 6H 43
Brotherton Cl. CH62: Brom 4C 104

Brotherton Park &
   Dibbinsdale Local Nature Reserve
   . . . . .3C 104
Brougham Av. CH41: Tran 5H 69
Brougham Rd. CH44: Wall 4F 51
Brougham Ter. L6: Liv 4G 53
     (off W. Derby Rd.)
Broughton Av. CH48: W Kir 6A 64
Broughton Dr. L19: Gras 4E 91
Broughton Hall Rd. L12: W Der 2A 56
Broughton Rd. CH44: Wall 4D 50
Broughton Way WA8: Hale B 6H 95
BROW, THE .4B 114
Brow La. CH60: Hesw 6D 100
Brownbill Bank L27: N'ley 4G 75
BROWN EDGE 6B 42
Browning Av. CH42: Rock F 2H 87
   WA8: Wid .3D 96
Browning Cl. L36: Huy 6H 57
Browning Rd. CH45: Wall 2H 49
   L13: Liv 1D 54
   L22: Water .1F 19
Browning St. L20: Boot 1A 34
Brownlow Arc. WA10: St H 2E 43
Brownlow Hill L3: Liv 4G 5 (6E 53)
Brownlow Rd. CH62: New F 4B 88
Brownlow St. L3: Liv 6F 53
Brownmoor Cl. L23: Crosb 5A 10
Brownmoor La. L23: Crosb 6H 9
Brownmoor Pk. L23: Crosb 6H 9
Brown's La. L30: N'ton 6F 11
Brown St. WA8: Wid 4H 97
Brownville Rd. L13: Liv 6B 36
Brow Rd. CH43: Bid 6H 49
Brow Side L5: Liv 3F 53
Broxholme Way L31: Mag 2B 12
Broxton Av. CH43: Pren 1B 86
   CH48: W Kir 6B 64
Broxton Cl. WA8: Wid 6A 78
Broxton Rd. CH45: Wall 1B 50
Broxton St. L15: Wav 1C 72
Bruce Cres. CH63: Brom 1C 120
Bruce St. L8: Liv 5G 71
   WA10: St H 2C 42
Brunel Dr. L21: Lith 1A 20
Brunel M. L6: Liv 2G 53
Brunel Rd. CH62: Brom 4F 105
Brunner Rd. WA8: Wid 3E 97
Brunsborough Cl. CH62: Brom 1C 120
Brunsfield Cl. CH46: More 2A 66
Brunstath Cl. CH60: Hesw 4G 101
Brunswick WA7: Run 2E 113
Brunswick Bus. Pk. L3: Liv 4D 70
     (not continuous)
Brunswick Cl. L4: Kirkd 5E 35
Brunswick Ct. CH41: Birke 2G 69
     (off Brunswick M.)
Brunswick Ent. Cen. L3: Liv 4D 70
Brunswick M. CH41: Birke 2G 69
   L22: Water .3G 19
Brunswick Pde. L22: Water 3F 19
Brunswick Pl. L20: Kirkd 5B 34
Brunswick Rd. L6: Liv 4F 53
   WA12: Newt W 1H 45
Brunswick Station (Rail) 5E 71
Brunswick St. L2: Liv 5B 4 (6C 52)
   L3: Liv 5B 4 (6B 52)
   L19: Garst .2G 107
     (not continuous)
   WA9: St H .2C 44
Brunswick Way L3: Liv 4D 70
Brunt La. L19: Aller 4A 92
Brushford Cl. L12: W Der 3F 37
Bruton Rd. L36: Huy 1F 57
     (not continuous)
Bryanston Rd. CH42: Tran 1C 86
   L17: Aig 6H 71
Bryant Rd. L21: Lith 5B 20
Bryce Dr. CH62: Brom 2C 104
Bryce Wlk. CH62: Brom 1C 104
Bryceway, The L12: Knott A 3H 55
Brydges St. L7: Liv 6G 53
Bryer Rd. L35: Presc 3D 58

Bryn Bank CH44: Wall 3E **51**
Brynmor Rd. L18: Moss H 2E **91**
Brynmoss Av. CH44: Wall 3B **50**
Brynn St. WA8: Wid 3F **97**
WA10: St H 1E **43**
Bryony Way CH42: Rock F 3H **87**
Brythen St. L1: Liv 4F **5** (6D **52**)
BT Convention Cen. **2C 70**
Buccleuch St. CH41: Birke 6B **50**
Buchanan Cl. WA8: Wid 6D **78**
Buchanan Rd. CH44: Wall 4F **51**
L9: Walt 2F **35**
Buckfast Av. WA11: Hay 4H **31**
Buckfast Cl. L30: N'ton 5F **11**
WA5: Penk 6G **81**
Buckfast Ct. WA7: Nort 2G **115**
Buckingham Av. CH43: Clau 2B **68**
CH63: Hghr B 4G **87**
L17: Liv 3B **72**
WA8: Wid 5E **79**
Buckingham Bingo
Bootle 2C 34
Liverpool, Poplar Bank 5G 57
Liverpool, Triumph Way 5C 92
Buckingham Cl. L30: N'ton 6C **10**
WA10: St H 3C **42**
Buckingham Ct. L33: Kirkb 6B **14**
Buckingham Dr. WA11: St H 4E **29**
Buckingham Ho. L17: Aig 4B **72**
Buckingham Rd. CH44: Wall 3B **50**
L9: Walt 5G **21**
L13: Liv 1B **54**
L31: Mag 1A **12**
Buckingham St. L5: Liv 2E **53**
Buckland Cl. WA8: Wid 4B **96**
Buckland Dr. CH63: Spit 3H **103**
Buckland St. L17: Aig 6H **71**
Buckley Hill La. L29: Seft 5D **10**
Buckley Wlk. L24: Speke 3F **109**
Buckley Way L30: N'ton 4D **10**
Buckthorn Cl. L28: Stockb V 6D **38**
Buckthorn Gdns. WA9: St H 1A **60**
Buckwheat Dr. L11: Norr G 3D **36**
Bude Cl. CH43: Bid 3G **67**
Bude Ho. *CH43: Bid 3G **67***
(off Bude Cl.)
Bude Rd. WA8: Wid 1C **96**
Budworth Av. WA8: Wid 1B **96**
WA9: Sut M 4F **61**
Budworth Cl. CH43: O'ton 5A **68**
WA7: Run 6H **113**
Budworth Ct. CH43: O'ton 4B **68**
Budworth Dr. L25: Woolt 1E **93**
Budworth Rd. CH43: Noct, O'ton 5A **68**
Buerton Cl. CH43: Noct 5A **68**
Buffs La. CH60: Hesw 4F **101**
Buildwas Rd. CH64: Nest 5A **118**
Bulford Rd. L9: Faz 1C **36**
Bulkeley Rd. CH44: Wall 4F **51**
Bull Bri. La. L10: Ain 1C **22**
Bullens Rd. L4: Walt 5F **35**
L32: Kirkb 2B **24**
Bullfinch Ct. L26: Halew 2G **93**
Bull La. L9: Ain 4H **21**
L9: Walt 5F **21**
Bullrush Dr. CH46: More 5E **49**
Bulrushes, The L17: Aig 6F **71**
Bulwer St. CH42: Rock F 1H **87**
L5: Liv 2G **53**
L20: Boot 6A **20**
Bunbury Dr. WA7: Run 1G **123**
Bundoran Rd. L17: Aig 1C **90**
Bunter Rd. L32: Kirkb 4B **24**
Bunting Ct. L26: Halew 1F **93**
Burbo Bank Rd. L23: Blun 5C **8**
Burbo Bank Rd. Nth. L23: Blun 4B **8**
Burbo Bank Rd. Sth. L23: Blun 6D **8**
Burbo Cres. L23: Blun 6D **8**
Burbo Mans. L23: Blun 6D **8**
Burbo Point L23: Blun 3C **8**
Burbo Way CH45: Wall 5A **32**
Burden Rd. CH46: More 1A **66**
Burdett Av. CH63: Spit 3H **103**
Burdett Cl. CH63: Spit 3A **104**
Burdett Rd. CH45: Wall 2H **49**
L22: Water 1F **19**
Burdett St. L17: Aig 6A **72**
Burford Av. CH44: Wall 4B **50**
Burford Rd. L16: Child 6G **55**
Burgess Gdns. L31: Mag 5B **6**
Burgess St. L3: Liv 2H **5** (5E **53**)
Burghill Rd. L12: Crox 1B **38**
Burgundy Cl. L17: Aig 1A **90**
Burland Cl. WA7: Run 4D **112**
Burland Rd. L26: Halew 5A **94**
Burleigh M. *L5: Liv 1F **53***
(off Burleigh Rd. Sth.)
Burleigh Rd. Nth. L5: Liv 1F **53**
Burleigh Rd. Sth. L5: Liv 1F **53**
Burley Cl. L32: Kirkb 2B **24**
Burlingham Av. CH48: W Kir 2D **82**
Burlington Ho. L22: Water 2G **19**
Burlington Rd. CH45: New B 4D **32**
Burlington St. CH41: Birke 3G **69**
L3: Liv 3C **52**
Burman Cres. L19: Garst 4G **91**
Burman Rd. L19: Garst 4G **91**
Burmarsh La. WA8: Hale B 6H **95**
Burnage Av. WA9: Clock F 3G **61**
Burnage Cl. L24: Speke 3H **109**
Burnand St. L4: Walt 6F **35**
Burnard Cl. L33: Kirkb 1B **24**
Burnard Cres. L33: Kirkb 1B **24**
Burnard Wlk. L33: Kirkb 1B **24**
Burnell Cl. WA10: St H 2D **42**
Burnham Cl. WA5: Penk 4H **81**
WA8: Wid 6A **78**
Burnham Rd. L18: Moss H 6G **73**
Burnie Av. L20: Boot 6E **21**
Burnley Av. CH46: More 1D **66**
Burnley Cl. L6: Liv 3G **53**
Burnley Gro. CH46: More 6D **48**
Burnley Rd. CH46: More 6D **48**
Burnsall Dr. WA8: Wid 6A **78**
Burnsall St. L19: Garst 6A **92**
Burns Av. CH45: Wall 2C **50**
Burns Cl. L16: Child 1B **74**
L35: Whis 4E **59**
Burns Cres. WA8: Wid 3D **96**
Burns Gro. L36: Huy 6A **58**
Burnside Av. CH44: Wall 5D **50**
Burnside Rd. CH44: Wall 5D **50**
Burns Rd. WA9: Sut M 4E **61**
Burns St. L20: Boot 6A **20**
Burnt Ash Cl. L19: Gras 4D **90**
Burnthwaite Rd. L14: Knott A 4G **55**
Burnt Mill La. WA8: Hale B 6D **94**
Burrell Cl. CH42: Tran 2E **87**
Burrell Ct. CH42: Tran 2E **87**
Burrell Dr. CH46: More 2B **66**
Burrell Rd. CH42: Tran 2E **87**
Burrell St. L4: Walt 5F **35**
Burroughs Gdns. L3: Liv 3D **52**
Burrow's Av. WA11: Hay 6B **30**
Burrows Ct. L3: Liv 3C **52**
*WA9: St H 2A **44***
(off Chancery La.)
Burrow's La. L34: Eccl P 6E **41**
WA10: Eccl 3F **41**
Burrows St. WA11: Hay 5C **30**
Burton Av. CH45: Wall 2A **50**
L35: Rainh 3G **59**
Burton Cl. L1: Liv 1D **70**
L35: Rainh 3G **59**
WA8: Wid 6D **78**
Burtonhead Ct. *WA9: St H 4F **43***
(off Harris Gdns.)
Burtonhead Rd. WA9: St H 3D **42**
WA10: St H 3D **42**
Burton St. L5: Kirkd 1C **52**
Burtons Way L32: Kirkb 3G **23**
BURTONWOOD **1G 63**
Burtonwood Cotts. WA9: St H 3E **45**
Burtonwood Ind. Cen. WA5: Burtw 6H **45**
Burtonwood Rd.
WA5: Burtw, Gt San, Westb 3H **63**
Burtree Rd. L14: Knott A 1C **56**
Burwain Ho. L19: Aig 4D **90**
Burwell Cl. L33: Kirkb 6C **14**
Burwell Wlk. L33: Kirkb 6C **14**
Burwen Dr. L9: Walt 5F **21**
Busby's Cotts. CH45: New B 5D **32**
Bushell Ct. CH43: O'ton 5C **68**
Bushel's Dr. WA9: Clock F 4H **61**
Bushey Rd. L4: Walt 3A **36**
Bushley Cl. L20: Boot 1B **34**
Bush Rd. WA8: Wid 6D **96**
Bush Way CH60: Hesw 5B **100**
Business Resource Cen.
L33: Know I 3E **25**
Butchers La. L39: Augh 2E **7**
Bute St. L5: Liv 4E **53**
(not continuous)
Butleigh Rd. L36: Huy 2F **57**
Butler Cres. L6: Liv 4H **53**
Butler St. L6: Liv 3H **53**
Buttercup Cl. CH46: More 5E **49**
L22: Water 2H **19**
Buttercup Way L9: Walt 1H **35**
Butterfield St. L4: Walt 6F **35**
Buttermere Av. CH43: Noct 3G **67**
WA11: St H 3E **29**
Buttermere Cl. L31: Mag 6D **6**
L33: Kirkb 5H **13**
Buttermere Ct. *CH41: Birke 4E **69***
(off Penrith St.)
Buttermere Gdns. L23: Crosb 1H **19**
Buttermere Gro. WA7: Beech 2H **123**
Buttermere Rd. L16: Child 1C **74**
Buttermere St. L8: Liv 2H **71**
Butterton Av. CH49: Upton 3B **66**
Butterwick Dr. L12: Crox 2A **38**
Button St. L2: Liv 4E **5** (6D **52**)
Buxted Rd. L32: Kirkb 3C **24**
Buxted Wlk. L32: Kirkb 3C **24**
Buxton La. CH44: Wall 2A **50**
Buxton Rd. CH42: Rock F 1A **88**
Byerley St. CH44: Wall 4F **51**
Byland Cl. WA8: Wid 4G **79**
Byles St. L8: Liv 5G **71**
Byng Pl. L4: Walt 5B **36**
Byng Rd. L4: Walt 5B **36**
Byng St. L20: Boot 3B **34**
By-Pass, The L23: Crosb 5G **9**
Byrne Av. CH42: Rock F 2H **87**
Byrne Avenue Recreation Cen. **2H 87**
Byrom St. L3: Liv 2F **5** (5D **52**)
Byron Av. L12: W Der 6E **37**
L35: Whis 4F **59**
Byron Cl. CH43: Pren 3B **86**
L36: Huy 6A **58**
WA10: St H 6E **29**
Byron Ct. L25: Woolt 6C **74**
Byron Rd. L23: Blun 5E **9**
L31: Lyd 4C **6**
Byron St. L19: Garst 6G **91**
L20: Boot 6A **20**
WA7: Run 4E **113**
Byron Ter. L23: Blun 5D **8**
Byton Wlk. L33: Kirkb 5C **14**
Bywater Way L10: Faz 4F **23**
Byway, The L23: Crosb 4G **9**

C

CABBAGE HALL **1H 53**
Cabes Cl. L14: Knott A 6C **38**
Cablehouse L2: Liv 2D **4**
Cable Rd. CH47: Hoy 2A **64**
L35: Presc 2F **59**
Cables Retail Pk. L34: Presc 2D **58**
Cable Yd., The *L2: Liv 2D **4***
(off Cheapside)
Cabot Grn. L25: Woolt 4A **74**
Cadbury Cl. L12: W Der 3F **37**
Caddick Rd. L34: Know 6D **24**
Cadet Way L12: W Der 6A **38**
Cadnam Rd. L25: Gate 4F **75**

Cadogan St. L15: Wav 1B **72**
Cadwell Rd. L31: Lyd 2A **6**
Caernarvon Cl. CH49: Upton 3E **67**
WA7: Cas 3B **114**
Caernarvon Ct. CH63: Beb 1H **103**
Caerwys Gro. CH42: Tran 5G **69**
Caesars Cl. WA7: Cas 3A **114**
Cains Brewery 3E 71
Caird St. L6: Liv 4G **53**
Cairn Ct. WA9: St H 5B **42**
Cairnmore Rd. L18: Moss H 1E **91**
Cairns St. L8: Liv 3G **71**
Cairo St. L4: Kirkd 4E **35**
WA10: St H 4B **42**
Caithness Ct. WA7: Run 3F **113**
Caithness Dr. CH45: Wall 1E **51**
L23: Crosb 6H **9**
Caithness Gdns. CH43: Pren 2B **86**
Caithness Rd. L18: Aller 2F **91**
Calcott Rake L30: N'ton 5E **11**
(not continuous)
Calday Grange Cl. CH48: W Kir 2D **82**
Calday Grange Swimming Pool 1D 82
Calday Gro. WA11: Hay 3C **30**
Caldbeck Gro. WA11: St H 2G **29**
Caldbeck Rd. CH62: Brom 3D **104**
Calder Av. CH43: Pren 1C **86**
Calder Cl. L33: Kirkb 3C **14**
WA8: Wid 6B **80**
Calder Dr. L18: Moss H 4G **73**
L31: Mag 5E **7**
L35: Rainh 4H **59**
Calder Edge L18: Moss H 5G **73**
Calderfield Rd. L18: Moss H 4H **73**
Calder Grange L18: Aller 6A **74**
Calderhurst Dr. WA10: Windle 5H **27**
Calder Pk. Ct. L18: Moss H 5H **73**
Calder Rd. CH63: Hghr B 6F **87**
L5: Liv 1F **53**
Calders, The L18: Moss H 6G **73**
CALDERSTONES 6G 73
Calderstones Av. L18: Moss H 4G **73**
Calderstones Ct. L18: Moss H 5G **73**
Calderstones Pk. 6G 73
Calderstones Rd. L18: Moss H 5F **73**
Calders Vw. Ct. L18: Moss H 6G **73**
Calderwood Pk. L27: N'ley 3F **75**
Caldicott Av. CH62: Brom 6D **104**
Caldon Cl. L21: Lith 2A **20**
Caldway Dr. L27: N'ley 3F **75**
Caldwell Cl. L33: Kirkb 5B **14**
Caldwell Dr. CH49: Woodc 1F **85**
Caldwell Rd. L19: Aller 3G **91**
WA8: Wid 4E **97**
Caldwell St. WA9: St H 2H **43**
CALDY 4D 82
Caldy Chase Dr. CH48: Caldy 4D **82**
Caldy Ct. CH48: W Kir 2B **82**
Caldy Gro. WA11: St H 6H **29**
Caldy Pk. CH48: W Kir 3C **82**
Caldy Rd. CH45: Wall 2D **50**
CH48: Caldy, W Kir 2B **82**
L9: Ain 4G **21**
Caldy Wood CH48: Caldy 4D **82**
Caldywood Dr. L35: Whis 4E **59**
Caledonian Cres. L21: Lith 2A **20**
Caledonia St. L7: Liv 6H **5** (1F **71**)
Calgarth Rd. L36: Huy 2E **57**
Calgary Way L36: Huy 2E **57**
California Rd. L13: Liv 6B **36**
Callaghan Cl. L5: Liv 2D **52**
Callander Rd. L6: Liv 4B **54**
Callard Cl. L27: N'ley 3E **75**
Callestock Cl. L11: Crox 6H **23**
Callington Cl. L14: Knott A 1C **56**
Callon Av. WA11: St H 6A **30**
Callow Rd. L15: Wav 2B **72**
Calmet Cl. L5: Liv 1E **53**
Calmington La. WA7: Nort 1H **115**
Calne Cl. CH61: Irby 4B **84**
Calstock Cl. WA5: Penk 6G **81**
Calthorpe St. L19: Garst 5F **91**
Calthorpe Way CH43: Noct 3H **67**
Calton Av. L18: Moss H 4E **73**
Calvados Cl. L17: Aig 2A **90**
Calvary Cl. L12: W Der 6A **38**
Calveley Av. CH62: East 3F **121**
Calveley Cl. CH43: O'ton 6A **68**
Calveley Gro. L26: Halew 5A **94**
Calverley Cl. WA7: Brook 2E **125**
Calvers WA7: Halt 4A **114**
Camberley Dr. L25: Hunts X 3E **93**
Camberwell Pk. Rd. WA8: Wid 5H **79**
Camborne Av. L25: Woolt 2E **93**
Camborne Cl. WA7: Brook 1E **125**
Camborne Rd. WA5: Burtw 1H **63**
Cambourne Av. WA11: St H 4H **29**
Cambrian Cl. *CH46: More 2H 65*
(off Cambrian Rd.)
Cambrian Rd. CH46: More 2A **66**
Cambrian Way L25: Woolt 6D **74**
Cambria St. Nth. L6: Liv 4H **53**
Cambria St. Sth. L6: Liv 4H **53**
Cambridge Av. L21: Lith 3B **20**
L23: Crosb 5F **9**
Cambridge Ct. L7: Liv 1F **71**
Cambridge Dr. L23: Crosb 4E **9**
L26: Halew 3H **93**
Cambridge Rd. CH42: Tran 1D **86**
CH45: New B 6D **32**
CH62: Brom 5E **105**
L9: Ain 3H **21**
L20: Boot 3D **34**
L21: Sea 3H **19**
L22: Water 4G **19**
L23: Crosb 4E **9**
WA10: St H 1C **42**
Cambridge St. L7: Liv 1F **71**
(not continuous)
L15: Wav 1B **72**
(not continuous)
L34: Presc 1D **58**
WA7: Run 3G **113**
WA8: Wid 4F **97**
Camdale Cl. L28: Stockb V 6D **38**
Camden Cl. CH49: Woodc 5F **67**
Camden Ct. WA7: Nort 4F **115**
Camden Pl. CH41: Birke 3G **69**
Camden St. L3: Liv 2G **5** (5E **53**)
Camelford Rd. L11: Crox 6H **23**
Camellia Ct. L17: Aig 1G **89**
Camellia Gdns. WA9: Bold 6D **44**
Camelot Cl. WA12: Newt W 1H **45**
Camelot Ter. *L20: Boot 1B 34*
(off Tennyson St.)
Camelot Way WA7: Cas 5C **114**
Cameo Cl. L6: Liv 3H **53**
Cameron Av. WA7: Run 5C **112**
Cameron Rd. CH46: Leas 4F **49**
WA8: Wid 3E **97**
Cameron St. L7: Liv 5A **54**
Cammell Ct. CH43: Clau 3D **68**
Campbell Av. WA7: Run 5E **113**
Campbell Cl. WA7: Run 5E **113**
Campbell Cres. L33: Kirkb 3H **13**
WA5: Gt San 3H **81**
Campbell Dr. L14: Broad G 4A **56**
Campbell Sq. L1: Liv 6E **5**
Campbell St. L1: Liv 6E **5** (1D **70**)
L20: Boot 2A **34**
WA10: St H 1C **42**
Campbeltown Rd. CH41: Tran 5H **69**
Camperdown St. CH41: Birke 3H **69**
Camphill Rd. L25: Woolt 3C **92**
Campion Cl. WA11: St H 4F **29**
Campion Gro. L33: Kirkb 5B **14**
Campion Way L36: Huy 2H **75**
Camp Rd. L25: Woolt 2D **92**
Campsey Ash WA8: Wid 5D **78**
Campus Dr. WA7: Run 3C **112**
Camrose Cl. WA7: Run 1G **123**
Cam St. L25: Woolt 1B **92**
Canada Blvd. L3: Liv 4B **4** (6B **52**)
Canal Bank L31: Lyd 1B **6**
Canal Cotts. L31: Lyd 1B **6**
Canal Reach WA7: Wind H 3E **115**
Canal Side WA7: West P 6B **112**
Canalside Gro. L5: Liv 2C **52**
Canal St. L20: Boot 3B **34**
WA7: Run 3F **113**
WA10: St H 3D **42**
WA12: Newt W 2H **45**
Canal Vw. L31: Mell 6E **13**
Canal Vw. Ct. L21: Lith 2A **20**
Canberra Av. WA9: St H 6C **42**
Canberra La. L11: Crox 6G **23**
Candia Towers *L5: Liv 1E 53*
(off Jason St.)
Cannell Ct. WA7: Pal F 1C **124**
Canning Pl. L1: Liv 6D **4** (1C **70**)
Canning St. CH41: Birke 2G **69**
L8: Liv 1F **71**
L22: Water 2F **19**
Canniswood Rd. WA11: Hay 5C **30**
Cannock Grn. L31: Mag 6A **6**
Cannonbury Cl. WA7: Halt 5C **114**
Cannon Hill CH43: Clau 3D **68**
Cannon Mt. CH43: Clau 3D **68**
Cannon St. WA9: Clock F 4G **61**
Canon Rd. L6: Liv 6A **36**
Canon St. WA7: Run 2E **113**
Canon Wilson Cl. WA11: Hay 5F **31**
Canova Cl. *L27: N'ley 5H 75*
(off Victoria Falls Rd.)
Canrow La. L34: Know 6F **25**
Cansfield St. WA10: St H 1E **43**
Canterbury Av. L22: Water 6F **9**
Canterbury Cl. L10: Ain 1C **22**
L34: Presc 6E **41**
Canterbury Pk. L18: Aller 3G **91**
Canterbury Rd. CH42: Rock F 2A **88**
CH44: Wall 4E **51**
WA8: Wid 4A **96**
Canterbury St. L3: Liv 1H **5** (4E **53**)
L19: Garst 1G **107**
WA10: St H 6C **28**
Canterbury Way L3: Liv 1H **5** (4F **53**)
L30: N'ton 5F **11**
Canter Cl. L9: Ain 3B **22**
Cantley Cl. WA7: Beech 1H **123**
Cantsfield St. L7: Liv 2A **72**
Canvey Cl. L15: Wav 2F **73**
Capella Cl. L17: Aig 4C **90**
Cape Rd. L9: Ain 5A **22**
Capesthorne Cl. WA8: Wid 3C **96**
Capital Ga. L3: Liv 5F **53**
Capitol Trad. Pk. L33: Know I 1F **25**
Caplin Cl. L33: Kirkb 3A **14**
Capper Gro. L36: Huy 4G **57**
Capricorn Cres. L14: Knott A 2B **56**
Capricorn Way L20: Boot 1B **34**
Capstick Cres. L25: Gate 3D **74**
Captain Charles Jones Wlk.
CH44: Wall 2F 51
(off Webster Av.)
Captains Cl. L30: Boot 3D **20**
Captain's Grn. L30: Boot 3D **20**
Captain's La. L30: Boot 3E **21**
Caradoc Rd. L21: Sea 5A **20**
Caraway Cl. *L23: Thorn 4B 10*
(off Tanhouse Rd.)
Caraway Gro. WA10: St H 1B **42**
Carbis Cl. L10: Faz 5E **23**
Carden Cl. L4: Kirkd 6E **35**
Cardeston Cl. WA7: Sut W 4B **124**
Cardiff Way L19: Garst 5F **91**
Cardigan Av. CH41: Birke 3F **69**
Cardigan Cl. WA10: St H 3D **42**
Cardigan Rd. CH45: New B 6D **32**
Cardigan St. L15: Wav 1B **72**
Cardigan Way L6: Liv 3H **53**
L30: N'ton 5H **11**
Cardus Cl. CH46: More 1H **65**
Cardwell Rd. L19: Garst 5H **91**
Cardwell St. L7: Liv 1G **71**
Carey Av. CH63: Hghr B 5F **87**
Carey St. WA8: Wid 2F **97**
Carfax Rd. L33: Kirkb 5C **14**
Cargill Gro. CH42: Rock F 3B **88**

Carham Rd. CH47: Hoy .3C **64**
Carillion Cl. L11: Crox .2G **37**
Carina Ct. L17: Aig .4D **90**
Carisbrooke Cl. CH48: Caldy .3C **82**
Carisbrooke Pl. L4: Kirkd .4F **35**
Carisbrooke Rd. L4: Kirkd, Walt .3E **35**
L20: Boot .3E **35**
Carkington Rd. L25: Woolt .2E **93**
Carlake Gro. L9: Ain .2A **36**
Carland Cl. L10: Faz .5F **23**
Carlaw Rd. CH42: Tran .1C **86**
Carleen Cl. L17: Aig .1H **89**
Carlett Blvd. CH62: East .2F **121**
Carlett Pk. CH62: East .1F **121**
Carlett Vw. L19: Garst .5G **91**
Carley Wlk. L24: Speke .3G **109**
Carlile Way L33: Kirkb .3B **14**
Carlingford Cl. L8: Liv .2G **71**
Carlisle Av. L30: N'ton .2F **21**
Carlisle Cl. L4: Walt .5B **36**
Carlisle M. CH43: O'ton .4E **69**
Carlis Rd. L32: Kirkb .3B **24**
Carlow Cl. L24: Hale .3C **110**
Carlow St. WA10: St H .4B **42**
Carlsruhe Ct. L8: Liv .4G **71**
Carl's Way L33: Kirkb .3C **14**
Carlton Av. WA7: Run .3H **113**
Carlton Bingo Club .5F **21**
Carlton Cl. CH64: Park .5G **117**
Carlton La. CH47: Meols .1C **64**
L13: Liv .3E **55**
Carlton Mt. CH42: Tran .6G **69**
Carlton Rd. CH42: Tran .5E **69**
CH45: New B .5D **32**
CH63: Beb .1B **104**
Carlton St. L3: Liv .3B **52**
L34: Presc .1D **58**
WA8: Wid .3E **97**
WA10: St H .2C **42**
Carlton Ter. CH47: Meols .1C **64**
L23: Crosb .5F **9**
Carlyon Way L26: Halew .3G **93**
Carmarthen Cres. L8: Liv .3D **70**
Carmel Cl. CH45: New B .5D **32**
Carmel Ct. WA8: Wid .5F **79**
Carmelite Cres. WA10: Eccl .6G **27**
Carmichael Av. CH49: Grea .1B **84**
Carnaby Cl. L36: Huy .1A **76**
Carnarvon Ct. L9: Walt .2F **35**
Carnarvon Rd. L9: Walt .2F **35**
Carnarvon St. WA9: St H .5B **42**
Carnatic Cl. L18: Moss H .6D **72**
Carnatic Ct. L18: Moss H .6C **72**
Carnatic Rd. L18: Moss H .6C **72**
Carnation Rd. L9: Walt .2H **35**
Carnegie Av. L23: Crosb .6F **9**
Carnegie Cres. WA9: St H .5A **44**
Carnegie Rd. L13: Liv .3C **54**
Carnforth Av. L32: Kirkb .2B **24**
Carnforth Cl. CH41: Birke .4E **69**
L12: W Der .4G **37**
Carnforth Rd. L18: Moss H .1G **91**
Carno St. L15: Wav .1C **72**
Carnoustie Cl. CH46: More .6H **47**
L12: W Der .1B **56**
Carnoustie Gro. WA11: Hay .6C **30**
Carnsdale Rd. CH46: More .1D **66**
Carol Dr. CH60: Hesw .5G **101**
Carole Cl. WA9: Sut L .1A **62**
Carolina St. L20: Boot .2B **34**
Caroline Pl. CH43: O'ton .4D **68**
Caroline St. WA8: Wid .4F **97**
Caronia St. L19: Garst .6G **91**
Carpathia St. L19: Garst .1G **107**
Carpenter's La. CH48: W Kir .1B **82**
Carpenters Row L1: Liv .6E **5** (1D **70**)
Carraway Rd. L11: Crox .5G **23**
Carr Bri. Rd. CH49: Woodc .5F **67**
Carr Cl. L11: Norr G .3F **37**
Carr Cft. L21: Ford .6B **10**
Carrfield Av. L23: Crosb .6A **10**
Carrfield Wlk. L11: Norr G .2F **37**
Carr Ga. CH46: More .2H **65**
Carr Hey CH46: More .2H **65**
Carr Hey Cl. CH49: Woodc .1G **85**
Carr Ho. La. CH46: More .1H **65**
Carriage Cl. L24: Hale .4D **110**
Carrick Ct. L23: Crosb .6A **10**
Carrickmore Av. L18: Moss H .1E **91**
Carrington Rd. CH45: Wall .1E **51**
Carrington St. CH41: Birke .1C **68**
Carr La. CH46: More .6F **47**
CH47: Hoy .3B **64**
CH47: Meols .6F **47**
CH48: W Kir .4D **64**
L11: Norr G .3D **36**
L24: Hale .3D **110**
L34: Presc .2B **58**
L36: Roby .6E **57**
WA8: Hale B .6E **95**
Carr La. E. L11: Norr G .3F **37**
Carr La. Ind. Est. CH47: Hoy .3C **64**
Carr Mdw. Hey L30: N'ton .1C **20**
CARR MILL .3G **29**
Carr Mill Rd. WA11: St H .4G **29**
WN5: Bil .2G **29**
Carrock Rd. CH62: Brom .3E **105**
Carrow Cl. CH46: More .2H **65**
Carr Rd. L20: Boot .4D **20**
Carrs Ter. L35: Whis .4D **58**
Carr St. WA10: St H .6B **28**
Carruthers St. L3: Liv .4C **52**
Carrville Way L12: Crox .3C **38**
Carrwood Cl. WA11: Hay .5C **30**
Carsdale Rd. L18: Moss H .4E **73**
Carsgoe Rd. CH47: Hoy .3C **64**
Carsington Rd. L11: Norr G .3E **37**
Carstairs Rd. L6: Liv .3B **54**
Carsthorne Rd. CH47: Hoy .3C **64**
Cartbridge La. L26: Halew .2H **93**
Carter Av. WA11: Rainf .4G **17**
Carters, The CH49: Grea .5A **66**
L30: N'ton .5G **11**
Carter St. L8: Liv .2F **71**
Carterton Rd. CH47: Hoy .3C **64**
Cartmel Av. L31: Mag .5D **6**
WA10: St H .4C **28**
Cartmel Cl. CH41: Birke .4E **69**
L36: Huy .3F **57**
Cartmel Dr. CH46: More .2C **66**
L12: W Der .4G **37**
L35: Rainh .3G **59**
Cartmell Cl. WA7: Run .1F **123**
Cartmel Rd. L36: Huy .2E **57**
Cartmel Ter. L11: Norr G .2F **37**
Cartmel Way L36: Huy .3E **57**
Cartwright Cl. WA11: Rainf .3F **17**
Cartwright Ct. WA11: Rainf .2F **17**
Cartwrights Farm Rd. L24: Speke .1C **108**
Cartwright St. WA7: Run .3G **113**
Carver St. L3: Liv .1H **5** (4F **53**)
Caryl Gro. L8: Liv .5E **71**
Caryl St. L8: Liv .4E **71**
(Atterbury St.)
L8: Liv .4E **71**
(Park St.)
L8: Liv .3D **70**
(Stanhope St.)
Cascade Rd. L24: Speke .5E **93**
Case Gro. L35: Presc .2E **59**
Case Rd. WA11: Hay .5F **31**
Cases St. L1: Liv .4F **5** (6D **52**)
Cashel Rd. CH41: Birke .5D **50**
Caspian Pl. L20: Boot .2C **34**
Caspian Rd. L4: Walt .3B **36**
Cassia Cl. L9: Walt .1H **35**
Cassino Rd. L36: Huy .4G **57**
Cassio St. L20: Boot .3E **35**
Cassley Rd. L24: Speke .2A **110**
Cassville Rd. L18: Moss H .3E **73**
Castell Gro. WA10: St H .2D **42**
Castle Av. WA9: St H .2A **44**
Castlebridge Ct. *CH42: Rock F .2H **87***
(off Old Chester Rd.)
Castle Cl. CH46: Leas .4E **49**
Castle Ct. CH48: W Kir .2B **82**
Castle Dr. CH60: Hesw .5D **100**
Castlefield Cl. L12: W Der .6E **37**
Castlefield Rd. L12: W Der .6E **37**
CASTLEFIELDS .3C **114**
Castlefields CH46: Leas .3D **48**
Castlefields Av. E. WA7: Cas .4C **114**
Castlefields Av. Nth. WA7: Cas .3A **114**
Castlefields Av. Sth. WA7: Cas .4B **114**
Castlefields Local Cen. WA7: Cas .3C **114**
Castleford Ri. CH46: Leas .4C **48**
Castleford St. L15: Wav .2E **73**
Castlegate Gro. L12: W Der .6F **37**
Castlegrange Cl. CH46: Leas .3C **48**
Castleheath Cl. CH46: Leas .4C **48**
Castle Hill L2: Liv .4C **4**
Castle Keep L12: W Der .6F **37**
Castle Mt. *CH60: Hesw .5D **100***
(off The Mount)
Castle Ri. WA7: Run .3H **113**
Castle Rd. CH45: Wall .1C **50**
WA7: Halt .5B **114**
Castlesite Rd. L12: W Der .5F **37**
Castle St. CH41: Birke .3H **69**
L2: Liv .4C **4** (6C **52**)
L25: Woolt .1B **92**
WA8: Wid .2H **97**
Castleton Dr. L30: N'ton .5H **11**
Castletown Cl. L16: Child .1A **74**
Castleview Rd. L12: W Der .6F **37**
Castleway Nth. CH46: Leas .3E **49**
Castleway Sth. CH46: Leas .4E **49**
Castlewell L35: Whis .3F **59**
Castlewood Rd. L6: Liv .2H **53**
Castner Av. WA7: West P .6C **112**
Castor St. L6: Liv .2H **53**
Catalyst Science Discovery Cen. .6E **97**
Catalyst Trade Pk. WA8: Wid .5E **97**
Catchdale Moss La. WA10: Eccl .5E **27**
Catford Cl. WA8: Wid .1A **96**
Catford Grn. L24: Speke .2H **109**
Catharine St. L8: Liv .1F **71**
Cathcart St. CH41: Birke .2F **69**
Cathedral Cl. L1: Liv .2E **71**
Cathedral Ct. *L1: Liv .2F **71***
(off Gambier Ter.)
Cathedral Ga. L1: Liv .1E **71**
Cathedral Rd. L6: Liv .1A **54**
Cathedral Wlk. L3: Liv .5H **5** (6F **53**)
Catherine Ct. *L21: Lith .5B **20***
(off Linacre Rd.)
Catherine St. CH41: Birke .3F **69**
L21: Lith .5B **20**
WA8: Wid .4E **97**
Catherine Way WA11: Hay .5B **30**
Catkin Rd. L26: Halew .1F **93**
Catonfield Rd. L18: Moss H .4H **73**
Catterall Av. WA9: Sut L .1H **61**
Catterick Cl. L26: Halew .3H **93**
Caulfield Dr. CH49: Grea .6C **66**
Caunce Av. WA11: Hay .5D **30**
Causeway, The CH62: Port S .6B **88**
L12: W Der .3H **55**
Causeway Cl. CH62: Port S .5B **88**
Causeway Ho. CH46: Leas .3C **48**
Cavalier Dr. L19: Garst .6H **91**
Cavan Dr. WA11: Hay .4F **31**
Cavan Rd. L11: Norr G .5C **36**
Cavell Cl. L25: Woolt .2C **92**
Cavendish Dr. CH42: Rock F .2F **87**
L9: Walt .2G **35**
Cavendish Farm Rd. WA7: West .2D **122**
Cavendish Gdns. L8: Liv .4G **71**
Cavendish Retail Pk. L9: Walt .2G **35**
Cavendish Rd. CH41: Birke .2D **68**
CH45: New B .4D **32**
L23: Blun .6E **9**
Cavendish St. CH41: Birke .1D **68**
WA7: Run .3D **112**
(not continuous)
Cavern Club, The .4D **4**
Cavern Ct. *L6: Liv .4H **53***
(off Coleridge St.)
Cavern Quarter .4D **4**

Cavern Walks L2: Liv ... 4D 4
Cawdor St. L8: Liv ... 3G 71
WA7: Run ... 2D 112
Cawfield Av. WA8: Wid ... 2B 96
Cawley St. WA7: Run ... 4E 113
Cawthorne Av. L32: Kirkb ... 4A 24
Cawthorne Cl. L32: Kirkb ... 3A 24
Cawthorne Wlk. L32: Kirkb ... 4A 24
Caxton Cl. CH43: Bid ... 3G 67
WA8: Wid ... 6A 78
Caxton Rd. L35: Rainh ... 6C 60
Cazneau St. L3: Liv ... 4D 52
Cearns Rd. CH43: O'ton ... 4C 68
Cecil Dr. WA10: Eccl ... 6G 27
Cecil Rd. CH42: Tran ... 1D 86
CH45: Wall ... 3C 50
CH62: New F ... 3B 88
L21: Sea ... 5H 19
Cecil St. L15: Wav ... 1B 72
WA9: St H ... 6B 44
Cedar Av. CH63: Hghr B ... 1G 103
WA7: Run ... 6G 113
WA7: Sut W ... 3C 124
WA8: Wid ... 1F 97
Cedar Cl. L18: Aller ... 6H 73
L35: Whis ... 3E 59
Cedar Ct. L34: Know ... 1F 39
Cedar Cres. L36: Huy ... 6F 57
Cedardale Pk. WA8: Wid ... 5A 80
Cedardale Rd. L9: Walt ... 1G 35
Cedar Gro. L8: Liv ... 3A 72
L22: Water ... 1F 19
L31: Mag ... 3B 12
WA11: Hay ... 4G 31
Cedar Rd. L9: Ain ... 5H 21
L35: Whis ... 4D 58
WA5: Gt San ... 3H 81
Cedars, The CH46: More ... 2A 66
L12: Crox ... 2B 38
Cedar St. CH41: Birke ... 4F 69
L20: Boot ... 1C 34
WA10: St H ... 3B 42
Cedar Ter. *L8: Liv ... 3A 72*
(off Cedar Gro.)
Cedarway CH60: Hesw ... 2F 117
Cedarwood Cl. CH49: Grea ... 5H 65
Cedarwood Ct. L36: Huy ... 1G 75
Celandine Way WA9: Bold ... 6D 44
Celebration Dr. L6: Liv ... 2A 54
Celendine Cl. L15: Wav ... 1C 72
Celia St. L20: Kirkd ... 4D 34
Celtic Rd. CH47: Meols ... 6E 47
Celtic St. L8: Liv ... 3G 71
Celt St. L6: Liv ... 3H 53
Cemeas Cl. L5: Liv ... 2C 52
Centenary Cl. L4: Walt ... 5A 36
Centenary Ho. WA7: Run ... 5G 113
Central Av. CH62: Brom ... 4C 104
L24: Speke ... 2F 109
L34: Eccl P ... 6F 41
L34: Presc ... 1C 58
Central Bldgs. *L23: Crosb ... 5G 9*
(off Church Rd.)
Central Dr. L12: W Der ... 2E 55
WA11: Hay ... 5D 30
WA11: Rainf ... 2F 17
Central Expressway WA7: Run ... 6A 114
Central Gdns. L1: Liv ... 5G 5
Central Library ... *2F 5*
(off Cuerden St.)
Central Pde. L24: Speke ... 2G 109
Central Pk. Av. CH44: Wall ... 3E 51
Central Rd. CH62: Port S ... 5B 88
(Osborne Ct.)
CH62: Port S ... 6B 88
(Wood St.)
Central Shop. Cen. L1: Liv ... 5F 5 (6D 52)
Central Sq. L31: Mag ... 5C 6
Central Station (Rail) ... 5F 5 (6D 52)
Central St. WA10: St H ... 1E 43
Central Way L24: Speke ... 2G 109
Centreville Rd. L18: Moss H ... 3E 73
Centre Way L36: Huy ... 5G 57
Centro Pk. L33: Know I ... 3E 25
Centurion Cl. CH47: Meols ... 6E 47
Centurion Dr. CH47: Meols ... 6E 47
Centurion Row WA7: Cas ... 3B 114
Century Bldgs. L3: Liv ... 5D 70
Century Rd. L23: Crosb ... 5F 9
Ceres Ct. CH43: Bid ... 2G 67
Ceres St. L20: Kirkd ... 4C 34
Cestrian Dr. CH61: Thing ... 6E 85
Chadlow Rd. L32: Kirkb ... 4B 24
Chadwell Rd. L33: Kirkb ... 5B 14
Chadwick Ct. Ind. Cen. L3: Liv ... 4B 52
Chadwick Rd. WA7: Ast ... 2A 114
WA11: St H ... 4G 29
Chadwick St. CH46: More ... 1C 66
L3: Liv ... 3B 52
Chadwick Way L33: Kirkb ... 3A 14
Chaffinch Cl. L12: W Der ... 4B 38
Chaffinch Glade L26: Halew ... 2G 93
Chainhurst Cl. L27: N'ley ... 3F 75
Chain La. WA11: St H ... 4H 29
Chain La. Shop. Pct. WA11: St H ... 4H 29
Chain Wlk. WA10: St H ... 2A 42
Chalfont Rd. L18: Aller ... 2H 91
Chalfont Way L28: Stockb V ... 6D 38
Chalgrave Cl. WA8: Wid ... 6B 80
Chalice Way L11: Crox ... 2G 37
Chalkwell Dr. CH60: Hesw ... 6G 101
Challis St. CH41: Birke ... 6A 50
Challoner Cl. L36: Huy ... 1H 75
Chaloner Gro. L19: Gras ... 5D 90
Chaloner St. L3: Liv ... 2D 70
Chalon Way E. WA10: St H ... 2E 43
Chalon Way Ind. Est. WA10: St H ... 3E 43
Chalon Way W. WA10: St H ... 2D 42
Chamberlain Dr. L33: Kirkb ... 4B 14
Chamberlain St. CH41: Tran ... 5G 69
CH44: Wall ... 5C 50
WA10: St H ... 2B 42
Chamomile Cl. L11: Norr G ... 3D 36
Champions Bus. Pk. CH49: Upton ... 6D 66
Chancellor Ct. L8: Liv ... 1G 71
Chancellor Rd. WA7: Manor P ... 6F 99
Chancel St. L4: Kirkd ... 6D 34
Chancery La. WA9: St H ... 2A 44
Chandlers Ct. WA7: Run ... 4C 112
Chandlers Way WA9: Sut M ... 4F 61
Chandos St. L7: Liv ... 6H 53
Change La. CH64: Will ... 6B 120
Changford Grn. L33: Kirkb ... 6C 14
Changford Rd. L33: Kirkb ... 5C 14
Channel, The CH45: Wall ... 5A 32
Channell Rd. L6: Liv ... 4A 54
Channel Reach L23: Blun ... 6D 8
Channel Rd. L23: Blun ... 6D 8
Chantrell Rd. CH48: W Kir ... 1E 83
Chantry, The WA10: St H ... 5B 28
Chantry Cl. CH43: Bid ... 3F 67
Chantry Wlk. CH60: Hesw ... 1E 117
Chapel Av. L9: Walt ... 5G 21
Chapelcroft Ct. L12: W Der ... 1G 55
Chapelfields WA6: Frod ... 6E 123
Chapel Gdns. L5: Liv ... 2D 52
Chapelhill Rd. CH46: More ... 1D 66
Chapel Ho. L22: Water ... 3F 19
L31: Mag ... 6C 6
Chapel La. L30: N'ton ... 4F 11
L31: Mell ... 5E 13
L35: Rainh ... 6C 60
WA5: Burtw ... 1G 63
WA8: Cron, Wid ... 4A 78
WA10: Eccl ... 1H 41
Chapel Pl. L19: Garst ... 5G 91
L25: Woolt ... 1C 92
Chapel Rd. CH47: Hoy ... 1C 64
L6: Liv ... 1A 54
L19: Garst ... 5G 91
(not continuous)
WA5: Penk ... 6G 81
Chapelside Cl. WA5: Gt San ... 3H 81
Chapel St. L3: Liv ... 3B 4 (5B 52)
L34: Presc ... 1D 58
WA8: Wid ... 4E 97
Chapel St. WA10: St H ... 6D 28
WA11: Hay ... 5F 31
(not continuous)
Chapel Ter. L20: Boot ... 2B 34
Chapel Vw. CH62: East ... 1G 121
Chapel Yd. *L15: Wav ... 2E 73*
(off Waterloo St.)
Chapman Cl. L8: Liv ... 4E 71
WA8: Wid ... 5B 78
Chapman Gro. L34: Presc ... 6E 41
Chardstock Dr. L25: Gate ... 5E 75
Charing Cross CH41: Birke ... 4F 69
Charlcombe St. CH42: Tran ... 5F 69
Charlecote St. L8: Liv ... 6F 71
Charles Av. WA5: Gt San ... 3H 81
Charles Berrington Rd. L15: Wav ... 3E 73
Charles Best Grn. *L30: N'ton ... 5F 11*
(off Albert Schweitzer Av.)
Charles Rd. CH47: Hoy ... 3B 64
Charles St. CH41: Birke ... 2F 69
WA8: Wid ... 3E 97
WA10: St H ... 1E 43
Charleston Rd. L8: Liv ... 5F 71
Charlesville CH43: O'ton ... 4D 68
Charlesville Ct. CH43: O'ton ... 4D 68
Charles Wlk. L14: Broad G ... 4B 56
Charlesworth Cl. L31: Lyd ... 2A 6
Charleywood Rd. L33: Know I ... 2D 24
Charlock Cl. L30: N'ton ... 5G 11
Charlotte Rd. CH44: Wall ... 2F 51
Charlotte's Mdw. CH63: Beb ... 1A 104
Charlotte Wlk. WA8: Wid ... 4F 97
Charlotte Way L1: Liv ... 4F 5
Charlton Cl. WA7: Pal F ... 6C 114
Charlton Ct. CH43: Clau ... 3B 68
L25: Hunts X ... 4F 93
Charlton Pl. L13: Liv ... 6E 55
Charlton Rd. L13: Liv ... 6E 55
Charlwood Av. L36: Huy ... 6G 57
Charlwood Cl. CH43: Bid ... 3G 67
Charmalue Av. L23: Crosb ... 5H 9
Charmouth Cl. L12: Crox ... 2A 38
Charnley Dr. L15: Wav ... 1G 73
Charnock Av. WA12: Newt W ... 2H 45
Charnock Rd. L9: Ain ... 2B 36
Charnwood Cl. L12: Crox ... 2H 37
Charnwood Rd. L36: Huy ... 4D 56
Charnwood St. WA9: St H ... 1A 44
Charon Way WA5: Westb ... 4H 63
Charter Ho. *CH44: Wall ... 3F 51*
(off Church St.)
Charterhouse Cl. L25: Woolt ... 2D 92
Charterhouse Dr. L10: Ain ... 1C 22
Charterhouse Rd. L25: Woolt ... 2D 92
Chartmount Way L25: Gate ... 5D 74
Chartwell Gro. L26: Halew ... 2H 93
Chase, The CH60: Hesw ... 5E 101
CH63: Brom ... 2C 120
L36: Huy ... 1H 75
Chaser Cl. L9: Ain ... 3A 22
Chasewater WA7: Nort ... 1H 115
Chase Way L5: Liv ... 3E 53
Chatbrook Cl. L17: Aig ... 4D 90
Chater Cl. *L35: Whis ... 1G 59*
(off Watling Way)
Chatham Cl. L21: Sea ... 4H 19
Chatham Ct. L22: Water ... 3G 19
Chatham Pl. L7: Liv ... 6H 53
Chatham Rd. CH42: Rock F ... 1A 88
Chatham St. L7: Liv ... 1F 71
L8: Liv ... 1F 71
Chatsworth Av. CH44: Wall ... 3E 51
L9: Walt ... 6F 21
Chatsworth Dr. L7: Liv ... 6H 53
WA8: Wid ... 6A 78
Chatsworth Rd. CH42: Rock F ... 1A 88
CH61: Pens ... 6D 84
L35: Rainh ... 3H 59
Chatteris Ct. *WA10: St H ... 4B 42*
(off Bewsey St.)
Chatteris Pk. WA7: Nort ... 3G 115
Chatterton Dr. WA7: Murd ... 5G 115
Chatterton Rd. L14: Knott A ... 3G 55

Chaucer Dr. L12: Crox 3A 38
Chaucer Rd. WA10: St H 5B 28
Chaucer St. L3: Liv 4D 52
  L20: Boot 1A 34
  WA7: Run 4E 113
Cheadle Av. L13: Liv 4D 54
Cheapside L2: Liv 2D 4 (5C 52)
Cheapside All. L2: Liv 3D 4
Cheddar Cl. L25: Woolt 1B 92
Cheddar Gro. L32: Kirkb 4A 24
  WA5: Burtw 6H 45
Cheddon Way CH61: Pens 1C 100
Chedworth Dr. WA8: Wid 5A 78
Chedworth Rd. L14: Knott A 3A 56
Cheldon Rd. L12: W Der 3G 37
Chelford Cl. CH43: Bid 2G 67
Chellow Dene L23: Thorn 3A 10
Chelmsford Cl. L4: Kirkd 6D 34
  (off Harcourt St.)
Chelsea, The CH45: New B 4E 33
  (off Tower Prom.)
Chelsea Ct. L12: W Der 5A 38
Chelsea Lea L9: Walt 5F 21
Chelsea Rd. L9: Walt 5G 21
  L21: Lith 5B 20
Cheltenham Av. L17: Liv 3B 72
Cheltenham Cl. L10: Ain 2C 22
  WA5: Gt San 1H 81
Cheltenham Cres. CH46: Leas 4C 48
  L36: Roby 6F 57
  WA7: Run 1F 123
Cheltenham Rd. CH45: Wall 1A 50
Chelwood Av. L16: Child 6A 56
Chemistry Rd. L24: Speke 6E 93
Chenotrie Gdns. CH43: Noct 4H 67
Chepstow Av. CH44: Wall 3E 51
Chepstow St. L4: Walt 4E 35
Chequers Gdns. L19: Aig 3D 90
Cheriton Av. CH48: W Kir 1D 82
Cheriton Cl. L26: Halew 3G 93
Chermside Rd. L17: Aig 2C 90
Cherry Av. L4: Walt 4H 35
Cherrybank CH44: Wall 5D 50
Cherry Blossom Rd. WA7: Beech . . .3B 124
Cherry Cl. L4: Walt 4H 35
  WA12: Newt W 1H 45
Cherrydale Rd. L18: Moss H 5E 73
Cherryfield Cres. L32: Kirkb 1A 24
Cherryfield Dr. L32: Kirkb 1H 23
Cherry Gdns. CH47: Hoy 2B 64
  L32: Kirkb 4B 24
Cherry La. L4: Walt 4H 35
Cherry Sq. CH44: Wall 3D 50
Cherry Sutton WA8: Wid 6G 77
Cherry Tree Av. WA5: Penk 5H 81
  WA7: Run 5G 113
Cherry Tree Cl. L24: Hale 4E 111
  L35: Whis 4D 58
  WA11: Hay 6C 30
Cherry Tree Dr. WA9: St H 3C 44
Cherry Tree Ho. CH46: More 1D 66
Cherry Tree La. WA11: St H 1E 29
Cherry Tree Rd. CH46: More 1D 66
  L36: Huy 1G 75
Cherry Vw. L25: Woolt 6D 74
Cherry Vw. L33: Kirkb 6D 74
Cherrywood Av. L26: Halew 2B 94
Cheryl Dr. WA8: Wid 2H 97
Cheshire Acre CH49: Woodc 6E 67
Cheshire Av. L10: Faz 4F 23
Cheshire Gdns. WA10: St H 3C 42
Cheshire Gro. CH46: More 2C 66
Cheshire Way CH61: Pens 2D 100
Cheshyre Dr. WA7: Halt 4B 114
Cheshyres La.
  WA7: West, West P 1C 122
  (not continuous)
Chesnell Gro. L33: Kirkb 4C 14
Chesney Cl. L8: Liv 3E 71
Chesnut Gro. CH42: Tran 5F 69
Chesnut Rd. L21: Sea 4H 19
Chester Av. L30: N'ton 2F 21

Chester Cl. L23: Crosb 5B 10
  WA7: Cas 3C 114
Chester Ct. CH63: Beb 1H 103
Chesterfield Dr. L33: Kirkb 4A 14
Chesterfield Rd. CH62: East 3D 120
  L23: Crosb 4A 10
Chesterfield St. L8: Liv 2E 71
Chester High Rd. CH64: Burt, Nest . .2H 117
Chester La. WA9: Sut M, St H 3F 61
Chester Rd. CH60: Hesw 6F 101
  CH66: Chil T, Gt Sut, Hoot, Lit Sut

    .6G 121
  L6: Liv 2B 54
  L36: Huy 3A 58
  WA4: Dares 3F 125
  WA7: Sut W, Pres B 5B 124
Chester St. CH41: Birke 3H 69
  CH44: Wall 4C 50
  L8: Liv 2E 71
  L34: Presc 1A 60
  WA8: Wid 2F 97
Chesterton St. L19: Garst 1G 107
Chester Wlk. L36: Huy 1B 58
  (off Chester Rd.)
Chestnut Av. L23: Crosb 3H 9
  L36: Huy 1F 75
  WA5: Gt San 3H 81
  WA8: Wid 1F 97
  WA11: Hay 6B 30
Chestnut Cl. CH49: Grea 2A 84
  L35: Whis 3E 59
Chestnut Ct. L20: Boot 1B 34
  WA8: Wid 2B 96
Chestnut Farm CH66: Hoot 6G 121
Chestnut Gro. CH62: Brom 5C 104
  L15: Wav 1D 72
  L20: Boot 6B 20
  (not continuous)
  WA11: St H 4H 29
Chestnut Ho. L20: Boot 4H 29
  (off St James Dr.)
Chestnut Rd. L9: Walt 2H 35
Chestnuts, The CH64: Will 6H 119
Chestnut Wlk. L31: Mell 5E 13
Cheswood Cl. L35: Whis 5E 59
Cheswood Ct. CH49: Woodc 1E 85
  (off Childwall Grn.)
Chetton Dr. WA7: Murd 6G 115
Chetwood Av. L23: Crosb 4H 9
Chetwood Dr. WA8: Wid 5D 78
Chetwynd Cl. CH43: O'ton 5B 68
Chetwynd Rd. CH43: O'ton 4C 68
Chetwynd St. L17: Aig 6H 71
Chevasse Wlk. L25: Woolt 6E 75
Cheverton Cl. CH49: Woodc 6F 67
Chevin Rd. L9: Walt 6G 21
Cheviot Av. WA9: St H 2B 44
Cheviot Cl. CH42: Tran 2F 87
Cheviot Rd. CH42: Tran 2E 87
  L7: Liv 1C 54
Cheviot Way L33: Kirkb 3B 14
Cheyne Cl. L23: Blun 6C 8
Cheyne Gdns. L19: Aig 3D 90
Cheyne Wlk. WA9: St H 1D 60
Chichester Cl. L15: Wav 1B 72
  WA7: Murd 1F 125
Chidden Cl. CH49: Grea 6A 66
Chidlow Cl. WA8: Wid 6E 97
Chigwell Cl. L12: Crox 2A 38
Chilcott Rd. L14: Knott A 4G 55
Childers St. L13: Liv 4E 55
CHILDWALL 2A 74
Childwall Abbey Rd. L16: Child 3H 73
Childwall Av. CH46: More 2B 66
  L15: Wav 2B 72
Childwall Bank Rd. L16: Child 2H 73
Childwall Cl. CH46: More 2B 66
Childwall Cres. L16: Child 2H 73
Childwall Fiveways L15: Wav 2G 73
Childwall Grn. CH49: Woodc 1E 85
Childwall La. L14: Broad G 5C 56
  L16: Child 3B 74
  L25: Child 3B 74

Childwall Mt. Rd. L16: Child 2H 73
Childwall Pk. Av. L16: Child 3H 73
Childwall Pas. L14: Broad G 5C 56
  (off Pilch La.)
Childwall Priory Rd. L16: Child 2H 73
Childwall Rd. L15: Wav 2E 73
Childwall Valley Rd. L16: Child 2H 73
  L25: Gate 2C 74
  L27: N'ley 2C 74
Chilhem Cl. L8: Liv 5F 71
Chilington Av. WA8: Wid 3B 96
Chillerton Rd. L12: W Der 5H 37
Chillingham St. L8: Liv 6G 71
Chiltern Cl. L12: Crox 3B 38
  L32: Kirkb 5G 13
Chiltern Dr. L32: Kirkb 5G 13
Chiltern Rd. CH42: Tran 2E 87
  WA9: St H 2B 44
Chilton Cl. L31: Mag 6C 6
Chilton Ct. L31: Mag 6C 6
Chilton M. L31: Mag 6C 6
Chilwell Cl. WA8: Wid 5B 78
China Farm La. CH48: W Kir 5E 65
Chippenham Av. CH49: Grea 5A 66
Chirkdale St. L4: Kirkd 4E 35
  (not continuous)
Chirk Way CH46: More 2D 66
Chirton Cl. WA11: Hay 4F 31
Chisenhale St. L3: Liv 3C 52
Chisledon Cl. WA11: Hay 4F 31
Chislehurst Av. L25: Gate 3D 74
Chislet Cl. WA8: Wid 5C 78
Chisnall Av. WA10: St H 1A 42
Chiswell St. L7: Liv 5A 54
Chiswick Cl. WA7: Murd 6F 115
Cholmondeley Rd.
  CH48: W Kir 1B 82
  WA7: Clftn 3H 123
Cholmondeley St. WA8: Wid 1E 113
Cholsey Cl. CH49: Upton 5D 66
Chorley Rd. L34: Presc 1B 58
Chorley's La. WA8: Wid 6H 79
Chorley St. WA10: St H 1D 42
Chorley Way CH63: Spit 4A 104
Chorlton Cl. L16: Child 1B 74
  WA7: Wind N 4F 115
Chorlton Gro. CH45: Wall 2H 49
Christchurch Rd. CH43: O'ton 5D 68
Christian St. L3: Liv 1F 5 (4E 53)
Christie Cl. CH66: Hoot 5G 121
Christie St. WA8: Wid 2H 97
Christleton Cl. CH43: O'ton 1H 85
Christleton Ct. WA7: Manor P 1E 115
Christmas St. L20: Kirkd 4D 34
Christopher Cl. L16: Child 1H 73
  L35: Rainh 5H 59
Christopher Dr. CH62: East 2G 121
Christophers Cl. CH61: Pens 1E 101
Christopher St. L4: Walt 5F 35
Christopher Taylor Ho.
  L31: Mag 1B 12
Christopher Way L16: Child 1H 73
Christowe Wlk. L11: Crox 6G 23
  (off Kennford Rd.)
Chris Ward Cl. L7: Liv 6A 54
Chudleigh Cl. L26: Halew 2G 93
Chudleigh Rd. L13: Liv 4D 54
Chung Hok Ho. L1: Liv 2E 71
  (off Pine M.)
Church All. L1: Liv 5E 5 (6D 52)
Church Av. L9: Ain 4H 21
Church Cl. CH44: Wall 3F 51
Church Cotts. L25: Gate 4E 75
Church Ct. CH49: Upton 3C 66
Church Cres. CH44: Wall 5G 51
Churchdown Cl. L14: Knott A 3B 56
Churchdown Gro. L14: Knott A 3A 56
Churchdown Rd. L14: Knott A 3A 56
Church Dr. CH62: Port S 5B 88
Church End L24: Hale 4D 110
Church End M. L24: Hale 4E 111
Church Farm CH63: Beb 6A 88
Church Farm Ct. CH60: Hesw 6D 100

Church Farm Organics 6H 83
Churchfield Ct. *L25: Gate* *5E 75*
　(off Jones Farm Rd.)
Churchfield Rd. L25: Gate 4E 75
Churchfields WA8: Wid 4F 79
　WA9: Clock F 3G 61
Church Flats L4: Walt 3F 35
Church Gdns. CH44: Wall 3F 51
　L20: Boot .2B 34
Church Grn. L16: Child 2B 74
　L32: Kirkb 6A 14
Church Gro. L21: Sea 5H 19
Church Hill CH45: Wall 2B 50
Churchill Av. CH41: Birke 2D 68
Churchill Gdns. WA9: St H 1A 60
Churchill Gro. CH44: Wall 2E 51
Churchill Ho. L21: Sea 4H 19
Churchill Ind. Est. L9: Ain 3A 22
Churchill Mans. *WA7: Run* *2E 113*
　(off Cooper St.)
Churchill Way Nth.
　L3: Liv 2E 5 (5D 52)
Churchill Way Sth.
　L3: Liv 3E 5 (5D 52)
Churchlands *CH44: Wall* *5G 51*
　(off Bridle Rd.)
Church La. CH44: Wall 3F 51
　(not continuous)
　CH49: Woodc 1F 85
　CH61: Thurs 6H 83
　CH62: Brom 4D 104
　CH62: East 3G 121
　L4: Walt .3F 35
　L17: Aig .2C 90
　L34: Know 1E 39
　L39: Augh 1F 7
　WA10: Eccl 2G 41
Churchmeadow Cl. CH44: Wall 3F 51
Church Mdw. La. CH60: Hesw 6C 100
Church Mdw. Wlk. WA8: Hale B 6H 95
Church Mt. CH42: Rock F 2A 88
Church Rd. CH42: Tran 6F 69
　CH44: Wall 5G 51
　CH48: W Kir 2A 82
　CH49: Upton 4E 67
　CH63: Beb 2A 104
　CH63: Thorn H 1D 118
　L4: Walt .3G 35
　L13: Liv .5D 54
　L15: Wav 3E 73
　L19: Garst 6G 91
　L20: Boot 5D 20
　L21: Lith .4B 20
　(not continuous)
　L21: Sea .5H 19
　L22: Water 3F 19
　L23: Crosb 5F 9
　L24: Hale 4E 111
　L25: Woolt 5B 74
　L26: Halew 1G 93
　L31: Mag 2B 12
　L36: Roby 5E 57
　WA11: Hay 5G 31
　WA11: Rainf 3F 17
Church Rd. Nth. L15: Wav 2E 73
Church Rd. Sth. L25: Woolt 1C 92
Church Rd. W. L4: Walt 3F 35
Church Sq. CH62: Brom 4D 104
　WA10: St H 2E 43
Church St. CH41: Birke 3H 69
　(not continuous)
　CH44: Wall 3F 51
　L1: Liv 4E 5 (6D 52)
　L20: Boot 2A 34
　L34: Presc 1D 58
　WA7: Run 2E 113
　WA8: Wid 6E 97
　WA10: St H 2E 43
Church Ter. CH42: Tran 6F 69
Church Vw. L12: W Der 6F 37
　L20: Boot 2B 34
Churchview Rd. CH41: Birke 1D 68

Church Wlk. CH48: W Kir 2B 82
　L20: Boot 2B 34
　L34: Know 1E 39
　WA10: Eccl 1G 41
Churchward Ct. *L25: Woolt* *1C 92*
　(off Garden St.)
Church Way L30: N'ton 5D 10
　L32: Kirkb 6A 14
Churchway Rd. L24: Speke 3A 110
Churchwood Cl. CH62: Brom 4D 104
Churchwood Ct.
　CH49: Woodc *2F 85*
　(off Childwall Grn.)
Churnet St. L4: Kirkd 5E 35
Churn Way CH49: Grea 5B 66
Churston Rd. L16: Child 4A 74
Churton Av. CH43: O'ton 6B 68
Churton Ct. L6: Liv 4G 53
Ciaran Cl. L12: W Der 5H 37
Cicely St. L7: Liv 6H 53
Cinder La. L18: Moss H 4G 73
　L20: Boot 4D 20
Cineworld Cinema
　Halton Lea 6A 114
　Liverpool 6D 54
　St Helens 2D 42
Cinnamon Bldg., The L1: Liv 6F 5
Circle 109 L1: Liv 6F 5
Circular Dr. CH49: Grea 6B 66
　CH60: Hesw 4D 100
　CH62: Port S 4B 88
Circular Rd. CH41: Birke 4F 69
Circular Rd. E. L11: Norr G 5D 36
Circular Rd. W. L11: Norr G 5D 36
Cirencester Av. CH49: Grea 5A 66
CISS GREEN 3D 110
Citadel, The *2E 43*
　(off Waterloo St.)
Citrine Rd. CH44: Wall 5F 51
Citron Cl. L9: Walt 1H 35
City Gdns. WA10: St H 4D 28
City Lofts L3: Liv 1A 4
　(Waterloo Rd.)
　L3: Liv 2A 4
　(William Jessop Way)
City Rd. L4: Walt 4F 35
　WA10: St H 4D 28
City Sq. L2: Liv 3D 4
Civic Cl. CH63: Beb 6A 88
Civic Way CH63: Beb 6A 88
　L36: Huy .5G 57
Clairville Cl. L20: Boot 2C 34
Clairville Ct. *L20: Boot* *2C 34*
　(off Clairville Cl.)
Clairville Way L13: Liv 2C 54
Clamley Ct. L24: Speke 2A 110
Clamley Gdns. L24: Hale 3E 111
Clandon Rd. L18: Aller 2H 91
Clanfield Av. WA8: Wid 6A 78
Clanfield Rd. L11: Norr G 3F 37
Clapgate Cres. WA8: Hale B 6H 95
Clapham Rd. L4: Walt 1H 53
Clare Cl. WA9: St H 6C 42
Clare Cres. CH44: Wall 3B 50
Claremont Av. L31: Mag 1H 11
　WA8: Wid 5G 79
Claremont Cl. L21: Sea 4H 19
Claremont Ct. CH45: Wall 1B 50
Claremont Dr. WA8: Wid 5F 79
Claremont Rd. CH48: W Kir 6B 64
　L15: Wav 3C 72
　L21: Sea .4H 19
　L23: Crosb 5G 9
　WA7: Run 3F 113
Claremont Way
　CH63: Hghr B 3F 87
Claremount Dr. CH63: Beb 1H 103
Claremount Rd. CH45: Wall 6B 32
Clarence Av. WA5: Gt San 3F 81
　WA8: Wid 5E 79
Clarence Cl. WA9: St H 3G 43
Clarence Rd. CH42: Tran 6E 69
　CH44: Wall 5F 51

Clarence St. L3: Liv 4H 5 (6E 53)
　WA7: Run 2D 112
　WA12: Newt W 1H 45
Clarence Ter. WA7: Run 2E 113
Clarendon Cl. CH43: O'ton 4E 69
　WA7: Murd 6F 115
Clarendon Gro. L31: Lyd 2B 6
Clarendon Rd. CH44: Wall 4F 51
　L6: Liv 1A 54
　L19: Garst 5G 91
　L21: Sea .5H 19
Clare Rd. L20: Boot 3D 34
Claret Cl. L17: Aig 2A 90
Clare Wlk. L10: Faz 4F 23
Clare Way CH45: Wall 2B 50
Claribel St. L8: Liv 3G 71
Clarke Av. CH42: Rock F 1G 87
Clarke Gdns. WA8: Wid 4F 97
Clarke's Cres. WA10: Eccl 1H 41
Clarks Ter. WA7: West P 5B 112
Classic Rd. L13: Liv 3E 55
Clatterbridge Rd. CH63: Spit 6F 103
Claude Rd. L6: Liv 1A 54
CLAUGHTON 2B 68
Claughton Cl. L7: Liv 6A 54
Claughton Dr. CH44: Wall 4D 50
Claughton Firs CH43: O'ton 5D 68
Claughton Grn. CH43: O'ton 4C 68
Claughton Pl. CH41: Birke 3E 69
Claughton Rd. CH41: Birke 3E 69
Claughton St. WA10: St H 1E 43
Clavell Rd. L19: Aller 3H 91
Claverton Cl. WA7: Run 1F 123
Clay Cross Rd. L25: Woolt 1B 92
Claydon Ct. L26: Halew 2A 94
Clayfield Cl. L20: Boot 3D 34
Clayford Cres. L14: Knott A 3F 55
Clayford Pl. L14: Knott A 3F 55
Clayford Rd. L14: Knott A 3G 55
Clayford Way L14: Knott A 3G 55
Clayhill Ind. Est. CH64: Nest 5A 118
Clayhill Light Ind. Pk. CH64: Nest . .5A 118
Clay La. WA5: Burtw 1G 63
　WA10: Eccl 2E 41
Claypole Cl. L7: Liv 1A 72
Clay St. L3: Liv 3B 52
Clayton Cl. WA10: St H 2C 42
Clayton Cres. WA7: Run 4D 112
　WA8: Wid 2D 96
Clayton La. CH44: Wall 5C 50
Clayton Pl. CH41: Birke 4E 69
Clayton Sq. L1: Liv 4F 5
Clayton Sq. Shop. Cen.
　L1: Liv 4F 5 (6D 52)
Clayton St. CH41: Birke 4E 69
Cleadon Cl. L32: Kirkb 4C 24
Cleadon Rd. L32: Kirkb 4C 24
Cleadon Way WA8: Wid 5C 78
Clearwater Cl. L7: Liv 5H 53
Cleary St. L20: Boot 1B 34
Cleaver Heath Nature Reserve . . .3B 100
Clee Hill Rd. CH42: Tran 2E 87
Cleethorpes Rd. WA7: Murd 6E 115
Clegg St. L5: Liv 3E 53
Clematis Rd. L27: N'ley 3G 75
Clement Gdns. L3: Liv 3C 52
Clementina Rd. L23: Blun 5D 8
Clements Way L33: Kirkb 4H 13
Clemmey Dr. L20: Boot 5E 21
Clent Av. L31: Lyd, Mag 4B 6
Clent Gdns. L31: Lyd 4B 6
Clent Rd. L31: Mag 4B 6
Cleopas St. L8: Liv 5F 71
Cleveland Cl. L32: Kirkb 5H 13
Cleveland Sq. L1: Liv 6E 5 (1D 70)
Cleveland St. CH41: Birke 1D 68
　WA9: St H 4G 43
Cleveley Pk. L18: Aller 2H 91
Cleveley Rd. CH47: Meols 1E 65
　L18: Aller .2G 91
Cleveleys Av. WA8: Wid 1H 97
Cleves, The L31: Mag 4D 6
Clieves Rd. L32: Kirkb 2B 24

Cliff, The CH45: New B 5B 32
Cliff Dr. CH44: Wall 2F 51
Cliffe St. WA8: Wid 2G 97
Clifford Rd. CH44: Wall 4E 51
WA5: Penk 5H 81
Clifford St. CH41: Birke 1C 68
L3: Liv 2H 5 (5E 53)
Cliff Rd. CH44: Wall 4B 50
Cliff St. L7: Liv 5A 54
CLIFTON 3H 123
Clifton Av. CH62: East 4E 121
L23: Crosb 4G 9
(off Liverpool Rd.)
L26: Halew 2G 93
Clifton Ct. CH41: Birke 4F 69
L19: Aller 3G 91
WA7: Run 1F 123
Clifton Cres. CH41: Birke 3G 69
WA6: Frod 6G 123
Clifton Dr. L10: Ain 1B 22
Clifton Ga. *CH41: Birke 4G 69*
(off Clifton Rd.)
Clifton Gro. CH44: Wall 3F 51
L5: Liv 3E 53
Clifton La. WA7: Clftn 3H 123
(not continuous)
CLIFTON PARK 4F 69
Clifton Rd. CH41: Birke 4F 69
L6: Liv 2B 54
WA7: Run 6E 113
WA7: Sut W 4A 124
Clifton Rd. E. L6: Liv 2B 54
Clifton St. L19: Garst 5G 91
WA10: St H 1E 43
Cliftonville Rd. L34: Presc 1E 59
Clincton Cl. WA8: Wid 3G 95
Clincton Vw. WA8: Wid 3G 95
CLINKHAM WOOD 2F 29
Clinkham Wood Local Nature Reserve 2E 29
Clinton Pl. L12: W Der 6D 36
Clinton Rd. L12: W Der 6D 36
Clint Rd. L7: Liv 6A 54
Clint Rd. W. L7: Liv 6A 54
Clint Way *L7: Liv 6A 54*
(off Clint Rd.)
Clipper Vw. CH62: New F 3C 88
Clipsley Brook Vw. WA11: Hay 5B 30
Clipsley Cres. WA11: Hay 4C 30
Clipsley La. WA11: Hay 5D 30
Clive Rd. CH43: O'ton 5E 69
CLOCK FACE 4H 61
Clock Face Colliery Country Pk. 3B 62
Clock Face Pde. WA9: Sut L 3G 61
Clock Face Recreation Club 3H 61
Clock Face Rd.
WA8: Bold H, Clock F 2G 61
WA9: Clock F 2G 61
Clock La. WA5: Cuerd 6B 80
Clocktower Dr. L9: Walt 2F 35
Clock Twr. St. WA10: St H 2D 42
Cloisters, The L23: Crosb 6F 9
WA10: Eccl 1H 41
Clorain Cl. L33: Kirkb 6C 14
Clorain Rd. L33: Kirkb 6C 14
Close, The CH49: Grea 1B 84
CH61: Irby 5B 84
CH63: Hghr B 2F 87
L9: Walt 1F 35
L23: Crosb 6F 9
L28: Stockb V 6E 39
WA10: Eccl 6G 27
WA11: Hay 6B 30
Closeburn Av. CH60: Hesw 1C 116
Close St. WA9: St H 6C 42
Cloudberry Cl. L27: N'ley 3G 75
Clough, The WA7: Halt 4B 114
Clough Rd. L24: Speke 1F 109
(not continuous)
L26: Halew 2A 94
Clovelly Av. WA5: Gt San 2G 81
WA9: St H 1A 62
Clovelly Ct. CH49: Grea 6B 66
Clovelly Gro. WA7: Brook 2D 124
Clovelly Rd. L4: Walt 1H 53
Clover Av. L26: Halew 1F 93
Clover Ct. WA7: Brook 2D 124
Cloverdale Rd. L25: Gate 2D 74
Clover Dr. CH41: Birke 6A 50
Cloverfield WA7: Nort 6E 115
Clover Hey WA11: St H 4F 29
CLUBMOOR 6C 36
Club St. WA11: St H 2E 29
Clwyd Gro. L12: W Der 5F 37
Clwyd St. CH41: Birke 3F 69
CH45: New B 6C 32
Clyde Rd. L7: Liv 5C 54
Clydesdale Rd. CH44: Wall 2F 51
CH47: Hoy 1B 64
Clyde St. CH42: Rock F 1H 87
L20: Kirkd 5C 34
Coach Ho. Ct. L29: Seft 3E 11
Coach Ho. M. L25: Woolt 6E 75
Coachmans Dr. L12: W Der 4A 38
Coach Rd. L39: Bic 1A 16
WA11: Kirkb 4B 26
WA11: Rainf, Bic 4B 16
Coadys Way WA8: Wid 1G 97
Coalbrookdale Rd. CH64: Nest 5B 118
Coalgate La. L35: Whis 5C 58
Coalport Wlk. WA9: St H 1A 60
Coal St. L3: Liv 3G 5 (5E 53)
Coalville Rd. WA11: St H 5H 29
Coastal Dr. CH45: Wall 5A 32
Coastal Point *CH46: Leas 3C 48*
(off Leasowe Rd.)
Coastguard La. CH64: Park 6F 117
Cobb Av. L21: Lith 5B 20
Cobbles, The L26: Halew 1F 93
Cobblestone Cnr. L19: Gras 4E 91
Cobden Av. CH42: Tran 6H 69
Cobden Ct. CH42: Tran 6H 69
Cobden Pl. CH42: Tran 6H 69
L25: Woolt 1B 92
Cobden St. L6: Liv 4F 53
L25: Woolt 1B 92
(not continuous)
Cobden Vw. L25: Woolt 1B 92
Cobham Av. L9: Walt 5F 21
Cobham Rd. CH46: More 1B 66
Cobham Wlk. L30: N'ton 5D 10
Coburg St. CH41: Birke 3F 69
Coburg Wharf L3: Liv 3C 70
Cochrane St. L5: Liv 2F 53
Cockburn St. L8: Liv 5F 71
Cockerell Cl. L4: Walt 6F 35
Cockerham Way L11: Crox 6F 23
Cock Glade L35: Whis 6D 58
Cocklade La. L24: Hale 4D 110
Cock La. Ends WA8: Hale B 1H 111
Cockshead Rd. L25: Gate 4D 74
Cockshead Way L25: Gate 3D 74
Cockspur St. L3: Liv 2D 4 (5C 52)
Cockspur St. W. L3: Liv 2C 4 (5C 52)
Coerton Rd. L9: Ain 4H 21
Cokers, The CH42: Rock F 3G 87
Colbern Cl. L31: Mag 1C 12
Colby Cl. L16: Child 1A 74
Colden Cl. L12: W Der 6A 38
Colebrooke Rd. L17: Aig 6H 71
Coleman Dr. CH49: Grea 6H 65
Colemere Dr. CH61: Thing 5F 85
Coleridge Av. WA10: St H 1B 42
Coleridge Ct. L32: Kirkb 3H 23
Coleridge Dr. CH62: New F 4A 88
Coleridge Gro. WA8: Wid 2C 96
Coleridge St. L6: Liv 4H 53
L20: Boot 1A 34
Colesborne Rd. L11: Norr G 3F 37
Coles Cres. L23: Thorn 3B 10
Coleshill Rd. L11: Norr G 2C 36
Cole St. CH43: O'ton 3E 69
Colette Rd. L10: Faz 4F 23
Coleus Cl. L9: Walt 1H 35
Colin Cl. L36: Roby 6E 57
Colindale Rd. L16: Child 2A 74
Colin Dr. L3: Liv 2C 52
Colinton St. L15: Wav 1C 72
College Av. L23: Crosb 6F 9
College Cl. CH43: Bid 3F 67
CH45: Wall 1A 50
College Ct. L12: W Der 2E 55
College Dr. CH63: Beb 4A 88
College Flds. L36: Huy 6G 57
WA8: Wid 4D 78
College Grn. Flats L23: Crosb 6F 9
College La. L1: Liv 5E 5 (6D 52)
College Rd. L23: Crosb 5E 9
College Rd. Nth. L23: Blun 4E 9
College St. WA10: St H 1E 43
(not continuous)
College St. Nth. L6: Liv 4F 53
College St. Sth. L6: Liv 4F 53
College Vw. L20: Boot 3C 34
L36: Huy 5G 57
Collier's Row WA7: West 6C 112
Collier St. WA7: Run 2D 112
Collingwood Cl. L4: Kirkd 5D 34
Collingwood Rd. CH63: Beb 1B 104
Collin Rd. CH43: Bid 1A 68
Collins Cl. L20: Boot 6A 20
COLLINS GREEN 4F 45
Collins Grn. La. WA5: Coll G 4G 45
Collins Ind. Est. WA9: St H 6G 29
Colmoor Cl. L33: Kirkb 3B 14
Colmore Av. CH63: Spit 4H 103
Colmore Rd. L11: Norr G 3C 36
Colne Dr. WA9: St H 6H 43
Colne Rd. WA5: Burtw 1H 63
Colonel Dr. L12: W Der 6H 37
Colonnades, The L3: Liv 6C 4 (1B 70)
Colquitt St. L1: Liv 6G 5 (1E 71)
Coltart Rd. L8: Liv 3H 71
Colton Rd. L25: Gate 2C 74
Colton Wlk. L25: Gate 2B 74
Columbia La. CH43: O'ton 5D 68
Columbian Cl. L30: N'ton 6E 11
Columbia Rd. CH43: O'ton 5D 68
L4: Walt 3G 35
L34: Presc 1E 59
Columbine Cl. L31: Mell 6E 13
WA8: Wid 5H 77
Columbine Way WA9: Bold 6D 44
Columbus Dr. CH61: Pens 2C 100
Columbus Quay L3: Liv 6E 71
Columbus Way *L21: Lith 4B 20*
(off Bridge Rd.)
Column Rd. CH48: Caldy, W Kir 1C 82
Colville Rd. CH44: Wall 3C 50
Colville St. L15: Wav 1C 72
Colwall Cl. L33: Kirkb 1C 24
Colwall Rd. L33: Kirkb 1C 24
Colwall Wlk. L33: Kirkb 1C 24
Colwell Cl. L14: Knott A 6C 38
Colwell Ct. L14: Knott A 6C 38
Colwell Rd. L14: Knott A 1C 56
Colworth Rd. L24: Speke 1D 108
Colwyn Rd. L13: Liv 5D 54
Colwyn St. CH41: Birke 1C 68
Colyton Av. WA9: Sut L 2H 61
Combermere St. L8: Liv 3F 71
L15: Wav 1B 72
Comely Av. CH44: Wall 3E 51
Comely Bank Rd. CH44: Wall 3F 51
Comer Gdns. L31: Lyd 4B 6
Comfrey Gro. L26: Halew 1G 93
Commerce Way L8: Liv 2H 71
Commercial Rd. CH62: Brom 2E 105
L5: Kirkd 1C 52
Common, The WA7: Halt 5C 114
Commonfield Rd. CH49: Woodc 2F 85
Common Rd. WA12: Newt W 2G 45
Common St. WA9: St H 6B 42
WA12: Newt W 2G 45
Commutation Row L3: Liv 2G 5 (5E 53)
Company's Cl. WA7: West 1D 122
Compass Cl. WA7: Murd 2F 125
Compass Ct. CH45: Wall 5B 32
Compton Cl. WA11: Hay 4E 31

Compton Rd. CH41: Birke 6H 49
  L6: Liv 3G 53
Compton Wlk. L20: Boot 1B 34
Compton Way L26: Halew 5G 93
Comus St. L3: Liv 1F 5 (4D 52)
Concert Sq. L1: Liv 5F 5
Concert St. L1: Liv 5F 5 (6D 52)
Concordia Av. CH49: Upton 4E 67
Concourse Way WA9: St H 3B 44
Condor Cl. L19: Garst 5H 91
Condron Rd. Nth. L21: Lith 2C 20
Condron Rd. Sth. L21: Lith 2C 20
Coney Cres. L23: Thorn 4B 10
Coney Gro. WA7: Brook 2D 124
Coney La. L35: Tar G 2H 75
  L36: Huy 2H 75
Coney Wlk. CH49: Upton 3B 66
Congress Gdns. WA9: St H 6B 42
Conifer Cl. L9: Walt 2H 35
  L33: Kirkb 4A 14
Conifer Gro. WA5: Gt San 2H 81
Conifers, The L31: Mag 4B 6
Coningsby Dr. CH45: Wall 3C 50
Coningsby Rd. L4: Walt 6G 35
Coniston Av. CH43: Noct 4G 67
  CH45: Wall .6A 32
  CH63: East 3C 120
  L34: Presc 1F 59
  WA5: Penk 5F 81
Coniston Cl. CH66: Hoot 6H 121
  L9: Ain 4H 21
  L33: Kirkb 5H 13
  WA7: Beech 1H 123
Coniston Dr. WA6: Frod 6G 123
Coniston Gro. WA11: St H 4E 29
Coniston Ho. L17: Aig 1C 90
Coniston Rd. CH61: Irby 5B 84
  L31: Mag 5D 6
Coniston St. L5: Liv 1G 53
Conleach Rd. L24: Speke 2G 109
Connaught Cl. CH41: Birke 1C 68
Connaught Ho. CH41: Birke 3A 70
Connaught Rd. L7: Liv 5G 53
  (not continuous)
Connaught Way CH41: Birke 1C 68
Connolly Av. L20: Boot 6E 21
Connolly Ho. L20: Boot 3D 34
Consett Rd. WA9: St H 1B 60
Constables Cl. WA7: Cas 4C 114
Constance St. L3: Liv 2H 5 (5F 53)
  WA10: St H .3B 42
Constance Way WA8: Wid 6E 97
Constantine Av. CH60: Hesw 4E 101
Convent Cl. CH42: Tran 5F 69
  L19: Gras 4E 91
Conville Blvd. CH63: Hghr B 3G 87
Conway Cl. CH63: Hghr B 6F 87
  L33: Kirkb 4H 13
  WA5: Gt San 3H 81
Conway Ct. CH63: Beb 1H 103
Conway Dr. CH41: Birke 3F 69
Conway Ho. L6: Liv 3A 54
Conway Park Station (Rail) 2G 69
Conway St. CH41: Birke 2F 69
  (not continuous)
  L5: Liv 2E 53
  WA10: St H .3B 42
Conwy Ct. WA7: Cas 3C 114
Conwy Dr. L6: Liv 2H 53
Coogee Av. WA5: Gt San 2G 81
Cook Av. WA11: Hay 4G 31
Cookes Cl. CH64: Nest 3F 49
Cooks Cl. L23: Crosb 4F 9
Cookson Rd. L21: Sea 5A 20
Cookson St. L1: Liv 2E 71
Cooks Rd. L23: Crosb 4F 9
Cook St. CH41: Birke 4F 69
  L2: Liv 4D 4 (6C 52)
  L34: Presc 1D 58
  L35: Whis 3F 59
Coombe Dr. WA7: Run 5D 112
Coombe Rd. CH61: Irby 4C 84

Cooperage Cl. L8: Liv 5E 71
Cooper Av. WA12: Newt W 2H 45
Cooper Av. Nth. L18: Moss H 2E 91
Cooper Av. Sth. L19: Aig 2E 91
Cooper Cl. L19: Aig 3E 91
Cooper La. WA11: Hay 1D 44
Cooper's La. L33: Know I 5F 25
Coopers Row L22: Water 3G 19
  (off Brunswick Pde.)
Cooper St. WA7: Run 2E 113
  WA8: Wid 2F 97
  WA10: St H .1D 42
Copeland Cl. CH61: Pens 1C 100
Copeland Gro. WA7: Beech 2A 124
Copperas Hill L3: Liv 4G 5 (6E 53)
Copperas St. WA10: St H 2D 42
Copperfield Cl. L8: Liv 4F 71
Copperwood WA7: Nort 4E 115
Copperwood Dr. L35: Whis 5E 59
Coppice, The CH45: Wall 6C 32
  L4: Walt 1A 54
  L34: Know 2F 39
Coppice Cl. CH43: Bid 3F 67
  WA7: Cas 4D 114
Coppice Cres. L36: Huy 3H 57
Coppice Grange CH46: More 2A 66
Coppice Gro. CH49: Grea 1A 84
Coppice La. L35: Tar G 2B 76
Copplehouse Ct. L10: Faz 4E 23
  (off Copplehouse La.)
Copplehouse La. L10: Faz 4E 23
Coppull Rd. L31: Lyd 3B 6
Copse, The L18: Moss H 4E 91
  L25: Woolt .2D 92
  WA7: Pal F 1C 124
  (not continuous)
Copse Gro. CH61: Irby 4C 84
Copsmead CH46: More 1D 66
Copthorne Rd. L32: Kirkb 1F 23
Copthorne Wlk. L32: Kirkb 1F 23
Copy Cl. L30: N'ton 4F 11
Copy La. L30: N'ton 4F 11
Copy Way L30: N'ton 4F 11
Coral Av. L36: Huy 4F 57
  WA9: St H 6D 42
Coral Cl. L32: Kirkb 1G 23
Coral Dr. L20: Boot 2C 34
Coral Ridge CH43: Bid 2H 67
Coral St. L13: Liv 6E 55
Corbet St. L32: Kirkb 1G 23
Corbet Wlk. L32: Kirkb 1G 23
Corbridge Rd. L16: Child 2G 73
Corbyn St. CH44: Wall 6G 51
Corfu St. CH41: Birke 3E 69
Corinthian Av. L13: Liv 3E 55
Corinthian St. CH42: Rock F 1H 87
  L21: Sea 4H 19
Corinth Twr. L5: Liv 1E 53
  (off Anderson St.)
Corinto St. L8: Liv 2F 71
Corkdale Rd. L9: Walt 6H 21
Cormorant Cen., The
  WA7: Run .3C 112
Cormorant Cl. CH45: Wall 5A 32
Cormorant Dr. WA7: Run 2C 112
Corncroft Rd. L34: Know 2F 39
Corndale Rd. L18: Moss H 5E 73
Cornelius Dr. CH61: Pens 6D 84
Cornel Way L36: Huy 1H 75
Corner Brook L28: Stockb V 6B 38
Cornerhouse La. WA8: Wid 6B 78
Cornett Rd. L9: Ain 4H 21
Corney St. L7: Liv 2A 72
Cornfields Cl. L19: Garst 5F 91
Cornflower Way CH46: More 5E 49
Cornforth Way WA8: Wid 6D 78
Cornhill L1: Liv 1D 70
Cornice Rd. L13: Liv 3E 55
Corniche Rd. CH62: Port S 5B 88
Cornmill Lodge L31: Mag 5B 6
Corn St. L8: Liv 4E 71
Cornubia Rd. WA8: Wid 4G 97
Cornwall Av. WA7: Run 3E 113

Cornwall Cl. CH62: New F 3B 88
  WA7: Cas 4B 114
Cornwall Cl. CH63: Beb 1H 103
Cornwall Dr. CH43: Pren 2C 86
Cornwallis St. L1: Liv 1D 70
  (not continuous)
Cornwall Rd. L20: Boot 1D 34
  WA8: Wid 6F 79
Cornwall St. WA9: St H 3H 43
Cornwood Cl. L25: Gate 2D 74
Corona Av. L31: Lyd 2B 6
Corona Rd. CH62: Port S 5C 88
  L13: Liv 3E 55
  L22: Water .2F 19
Coronation Av. CH45: New B 6D 32
  L14: Broad G 4A 56
Coronation Bldgs. CH45: Wall 2D 50
  (off Wallasey Rd.)
  CH48: W Kir 5C 64
Coronation Dr. CH62: Brom 2D 104
  L14: Broad G 4A 56
  L23: Crosb 6F 9
  L35: Presc .3C 58
  WA5: Penk .5H 81
  WA6: Frod .6H 123
  WA8: Wid 3H 95
  WA11: Hay .4H 31
Coronation Ho. WA7: Run 5G 113
Coronation Rd. CH47: Hoy 3A 64
  L23: Crosb 6F 9
  L31: Lyd 4B 6
  WA7: Pres B 1H 125
  WA7: Run .4F 113
  WA10: Windle 6A 28
Coroner's La. WA8: Wid 4E 79
Coronet Rd. L11: Crox 2G 37
Coronet Way WA8: Wid 3H 95
Corporal Way L12: W Der 6A 38
Corporation Rd. CH41: Birke 1B 68
Corporation St. WA9: St H 1E 43
  WA10: St H .1E 43
  (not continuous)
Corrie Dr. CH63: Beb 1H 103
Corsewall St. L7: Liv 1B 72
Corsican Gdns. WA9: St H 6A 42
Cortsway CH49: Grea 4C 66
Cortsway W. CH49: Grea 4B 66
Corwen Cl. CH43: Bid 3F 67
  CH46: More 2D 66
Corwen Cres. L14: Broad G 5B 56
Corwen Dr. L30: N'ton 5H 11
Corwen Rd. CH47: Hoy 2C 64
  L4: Walt 5A 36
Cosgrove Cl. L6: Liv 6B 36
Costain St. L20: Kirkd 6C 34
Cote Lea Ct. WA7: Pal F 1B 124
Cotham St. WA10: St H 2E 43
Coton Way L32: Kirkb 6G 13
Cotsford Cl. L36: Huy 3E 57
Cotsford Pl. L36: Huy 3E 57
Cotsford Rd. L36: Huy 3E 57
Cotsford Way L36: Huy 3E 57
Cotswold Gro. WA9: St H 2C 44
Cotswold Rd. CH42: Tran 2E 87
Cotswolds Cres. L26: Halew 4G 93
Cotswold St. L7: Liv 5H 53
Cottage Cl. CH63: Brom 2C 120
  L32: Kirkb 4A 24
Cottage Dr. E. CH60: Hesw 2D 116
Cottage Dr. W. CH60: Hesw 2D 116
Cottage La. CH60: Hesw 2D 116
Cottage Pl. WA9: Clock F 3G 61
Cottage St. CH41: Birke 2F 69
Cottenham St. L6: Liv 4H 53
Cotterdale Cl. WA5: Gt San 2H 81
  WA9: St H 1G 61
Cotterill WA7: Run 5H 113
Cottesbrook Cl. L11: Norr G 2E 37
Cottesbrook Pl. L11: Norr G 2E 37
Cottesbrook Rd. L11: Norr G 2E 37
Cottesmore Dr. CH60: Hesw 5H 101
Cotton Exchange Bldg. L3: Liv 3C 4
Cotton La. WA7: Run 5H 113

Cottons Bri. WA4: Pres H 2H 125
Cotton St. L3: Liv 3B 52
Cotton Ter. WA9: St H 5B 44
Cottonwood L17: Aig 1G 89
Cottrell Cl. L19: Garst 1G 107
Coulport Cl. L14: Knott A 3C 56
Coulsdon Pl. L8: Liv 5G 71
Coulthard Rd. CH42: Rock F 3A 88
Coulton Rd. WA8: Wid 6A 80
Council St. L35: Rainh 3G 59
Countess Pk. L11: Crox 3G 37
Countisbury Dr. L16: Child 3A 74
County Dr. WA10: St H 3C 42
County Rd. L4: Walt 4F 35
L32: Kirkb 5A 14
Court, The CH63: Beb 1A 104
L28: Stockb V 6E 39
Court Av. L26: Halew 2A 94
Courtenay Av. L22: Water 1E 19
Courtenay Rd. CH47: Hoy 3A 64
L22: Water 1E 19
L25: Woolt 5B 74
Courtfields Cl. L12: W Der 2F 55
COURT HEY 6B 56
Court Hey L31: Mag 6D 6
Court Hey Av. L36: Roby 5C 56
Court Hey Dr. L16: Child 6B 56
Court Hey Pk. 1B 74
Court Hey Rd. L16: Child 6B 56
Courthope Rd. L4: Walt 3H 35
Courtier Cl. L5: Liv 3E 53
Courtland Rd. L18: Moss H 4F 73
Courtney Av. CH44: Wall 4C 50
Courtney Rd. CH42: Rock F 3A 88
Courtyard, The L18: Moss H 6D 72
Courtyard Works L33: Know I 6E 15
Covent Gdn. L2: Liv 3C 4 (6C 52)
Coventry Av. L30: N'ton 2F 21
Coventry Rd. L15: Wav 3E 73
Coventry St. CH41: Birke 3F 69
Coverdale Av. L35: Rainh 4B 60
Coverdale Cl. WA5: Gt San 2H 81
Covertside CH48: W Kir 1D 82
Cowan Dr. L6: Liv 3G 53
Cowan Way WA8: Wid 5D 78
Cowdrey Av. CH43: Bid 6G 49
Cow Hey La. WA7: Clftn 2E 123
(not continuous)
Cowley Cl. CH49: Upton 4B 66
Cowley Ct. WA10: St H 6C 28
COWLEY HILL 6D 28
Cowley Hill La. WA10: St H 6C 28
Cowley Rd. L4: Walt 4F 35
Cowley St. WA10: St H 6E 29
Cowper Rd. L13: Liv 4F 55
Cowper St. L20: Boot 6A 20
WA9: St H 4G 43
Cowper Way L36: Huy 6A 58
Coylton Av. L35: Rainh 5B 60
Crab St. WA10: St H 1D 42
Crab Tree Cl. L24: Hale 3E 111
Crabtree Cl. L27: N'ley 4G 75
Crabtree Fold WA7: Nort 5E 115
Cradley WA8: Wid 1A 96
Crag Gro. WA11: St H 2F 29
Craigburn Rd. L13: Liv 1C 54
Craighurst Rd. L25: Gate 2C 74
Craigleigh Gro. CH62: East 3F 121
Craigmore Rd. L18: Moss H 2E 91
Craigside Av. L12: W Der 6E 37
Craigs Rd. L13: Liv 1C 54
Craigwood Way L36: Huy 4D 56
Craine Cl. L4: Walt 5H 35
Cramond Av. L18: Moss H 4D 72
Cranage Cl. WA7: Run 6H 113
Cranberry Cl. L27: N'ley 3G 75
WA10: St H 6D 28
Cranborne Rd. L15: Wav 2B 72
Cranbourne Av. CH41: Birke 2C 68
CH46: More 2B 66
CH47: Meols 6E 47
Crane Av. WA9: Sut L 1H 61
Cranehurst Rd. L4: Walt 3H 35
Cranfield Rd. L23: Crosb 4A 10
Cranford Cl. CH62: East 3F 121
Cranford Rd. L19: Gras 3F 91
Cranford St. CH44: Wall 5E 51
Crank Rd. WA11: Crank, St H 4A 28
Cranleigh Gdns. L23: Crosb 5F 9
Cranleigh Pl. L25: Gate 3C 74
Cranleigh Rd. L25: Gate 3C 74
Cranmer St. L5: Liv 2C 52
(not continuous)
Cranmore Av. L23: Crosb 1G 19
Cranshaw Av. WA9: Clock F 4H 61
Cranshaw La. WA8: Wid 4F 79
Cranston Cl. WA10: St H 6A 28
Cranston Rd. L33: Know I 1E 25
Crantock Cl. L11: Crox 1G 37
L26: Halew 3H 93
Crantock Gro. WA10: Windle 4A 28
Cranwell Cl. L10: Ain 1A 22
Cranwell Rd. CH49: Grea 6H 65
L25: Gate 2C 74
Cranwell Wlk. *L25: Gate* *2C 74*
(off Cranwell Rd.)
Crask Wlk. L33: Kirkb 5B 14
Craven Cl. CH41: Birke 3F 69
Craven Lea L12: Crox 2A 38
Craven Rd. L12: W Der 6G 37
L35: Rainh 4A 60
Craven St. CH41: Birke 3E 69
L3: Liv 2H 5 (5E 53)
Cravenwood Rd. L26: Halew 4H 93
Crawford Av. L18: Moss H 4D 72
L31: Mag 4A 6
WA8: Wid 2H 95
Crawford Cl. L12: W Der 6H 37
WA9: Clock F 3H 61
Crawford Dr. L15: Wav 6E 55
Crawford Pk. L18: Moss H 6D 72
Crawford Pl. WA7: Run 1F 123
Crawford St. WA9: Clock F 3A 62
Crawford Way L7: Liv 5D 54
Crawshaw Ct. L36: Huy 3D 56
Crediton Cl. L11: Crox 6G 23
Creek, The CH45: Wall 5A 32
Cremona Cnr. *L22: Water* *2G 19*
(off South Rd.)
Cremorne Hey L28: Stockb V 6D 38
Crescent, The CH48: W Kir 1A 82
CH49: Grea 6B 66
CH60: Hesw 1F 117
CH61: Pens 5D 84
CH63: Hghr B 6G 87
L20: Boot 5E 21
L22: Water 2G 19
L23: Thorn 3A 10
L24: Speke 1E 109
L31: Mag 2A 12
L35: Whis 3F 59
L36: Huy 5A 58
Crescent Ct. L21: Sea 5A 20
Crescent Rd. CH44: Wall 3E 51
L9: Walt 1H 35
L21: Sea 5A 20
L23: Blun 4D 8
Crescent Row *WA7: Run* *3D 112*
(off Hankey St.)
Crescents, The L35: Rainh 3G 59
Cressida Av. CH63: Hghr B 4G 87
Cressingham Rd. CH45: New B 5D 32
Cressington Av. CH42: Tran 2F 87
Cressington Esplanade L19: Gras 5E 91
CRESSINGTON PARK 4E 91
Cressington Station (Rail) 4E 91
Cresson Ct. CH43: O'ton 4B 68
Cresswell Cl. L26: Halew 2A 94
Cresswell St. L6: Liv 3F 53
(not continuous)
Cresta Dr. WA7: West 1D 122
Cresttor Rd. L25: Woolt 6B 74
Creswell St. WA10: St H 2C 42
Cretan Rd. L15: Wav 2B 72
Crete Towers L5: Kirkd 1E 53
Crewe Grn. CH49: Woodc 1E 85
Cricket Cl. L19: Garst 1H 107
Cricklade Cl. L20: Boot 1B 34
Cringles Dr. L35: Tar G 2A 76
Crispin Rd. L27: N'ley 4G 75
Crispin St. WA10: St H 2C 42
Critchley Rd. L24: Speke 3A 110
Critchley Way L33: Kirkb 5B 14
Croasdale Dr. WA7: Beech 2A 124
Crockett's Wlk. WA10: Eccl 6H 27
Crocus Av. CH41: Birke 2B 68
Crocus Gdns. WA9: Bold 6C 44
Crocus St. L5: Kirkd 6D 34
Croft, The CH49: Grea 1B 84
L12: W Der 6F 37
L28: Stockb V 5C 38
L31: Lyd 2A 6
L32: Kirkb 4B 24
WA7: Halt 4B 114
WA9: St H 4B 44
Croft Av. CH62: Brom 4C 104
Croft Av. E. CH62: Brom 3D 104
Croft Bus. Cen. CH62: Brom 3E 105
Croft Bus. Pk. CH62: Brom 3E 105
Croft Cl. CH43: Noct 5A 68
Croft Dr. CH46: More 2C 66
CH48: Caldy 5C 82
Croft Dr. E. CH48: Caldy 4D 82
Croft Dr. W. CH48: Caldy 4C 82
Croft Edge CH43: O'ton 6D 68
Croft End WA9: St H 4B 44
Crofters, The CH49: Grea 5B 66
Crofters La. L33: Kirkb 4C 14
Croftfield L31: Mag 6D 6
Croft Grn. CH62: Brom 2D 104
Croft La. CH62: Brom 4D 104
L9: Ain 4B 22
Crofton Cres. L13: Liv 4F 55
Crofton Rd. CH42: Tran 6G 69
L13: Liv 4F 55
WA7: Run 4C 112
Croft St. WA8: Wid 5E 97
Croftsway CH60: Hesw 5B 100
Croft Technology Pk. CH62: Brom 4F 105
Croft Trade Pk. CH62: Brom 3E 105
Croft Way L23: Thorn 4B 10
Croftwood Gro. L35: Whis 5E 59
Cromarty Rd. CH44: Wall 3B 50
L13: Liv 4D 54
Cromdale Gro. WA9: St H 3A 44
Cromdale Way WA5: Gt San 3G 81
Cromer Dr. CH45: Wall 2C 50
Cromer Rd. CH47: Hoy 2A 64
L17: Aig 2C 90
Cromer Way L26: Halew 5H 93
Cromford Rd. L36: Huy 2G 57
Crompton Ct. L18: Moss H 4H 73
Crompton Dr. L12: Crox 2A 38
Cromptons La. L18: Moss H 5H 73
Crompton St. L5: Liv 2D 52
Cromwell Rd. L4: Walt 3F 35
Cromwell St. WA8: Wid 5E 97
Crondall Gro. L15: Wav 2F 73
CRONTON 4A 78
Cronton Av. CH46: Leas 4D 48
L35: Whis 6C 58
Cronton Farm Ct. WA8: Wid 5C 78
Cronton La. L35: Rainh 1H 77
WA8: Cron 2H 77
WA8: Wid 4C 78
Cronton Pk. Av. WA8: Cron 3A 78
Cronton Pk. Cl. WA8: Cron 3A 78
Cronton Rd. L15: Wav 4E 73
L35: Tar G 2A 76
WA8: Cron 4H 77
Cronulla Dr. WA5: Gt San 2F 81
Croome Dr. CH48: W Kir 1C 82
Croppers Hill Ct. *WA10: St H* *3C 42*
(off Prescot Rd.)
Cropper St. L1: Liv 5G 5 (6E 53)
CROSBY 2E 19
Crosby Civic Hall (Theatre) 2G 19
Crosby Cl. CH49: Upton 3D 66
Crosby Grn. L12: W Der 6E 37

Crosby Gro. CH64: Will 6B 120
WA10: St H 4B 42
Crosby Leisure Cen. 1D 18
Crosby Rd. Nth. L22: Water 1G 19
Crosby Rd. Sth. L21: Sea 3G 19
L22: Water 3G 19
Crosby Sailing Club 3F 19
Crosender Rd. L23: Crosb 6E 9
Crosfield Cl. L7: Liv 6A 54
Crosfield Rd. CH44: Wall 4E 51
L7: Liv 6A 54
L35: Presc 3E 59
Crosfield Wlk. L7: Liv 6A 54
(off Crosfield Cl.)
Crosgrove Rd. L4: Walt 4A 36
Crosland Rd. L32: Kirkb 2C 24
Cross, The CH62: Brom 4E 105
Crossacre Rd. L25: Gate 2D 74
Crossdale Rd. CH62: Brom 1D 120
L23: Crosb 6E 9
Crossdale Way WA11: St H 2F 29
Cross Farm Rd. WA9: St H 4G 43
Crossfield St. WA9: St H 2F 43
Crossford Rd. L14: Knott A 1C 56
Cross Gates WA8: Wid 6B 80
Crosshall St. L1: Liv 3E 5 (5D 52)
Cross Hey L21: Ford 1B 20
L31: Mag 2C 12
Cross Hey Av. CH43: Noct 4H 67
Cross Hillocks La. WA8: Wid 1E 95
Cross La. CH45: Wall 2H 49
CH63: Beb 1H 103
L35: Presc, Whis 3D 58
Crossledge Way L25: Gate 2B 74
Crossley Dr. CH60: Hesw 5B 100
L15: Wav 1E 73
Crossley Rd. WA10: St H 5B 42
Cross Mdw. Ct. WA9: St H 3G 43
(off Appleton Rd.)
Cross Pit La. WA11: Rainf 3F 17
Cross St. CH41: Birke 3H 69
CH62: Port S 6B 88
L22: Water 2F 19
L34: Presc 6E 41
WA7: Run 2E 113
WA8: Wid 2F 97
(not continuous)
WA10: St H 2E 43
Crossvale Rd. L36: Huy 6G 57
Crossway CH43: Bid 1A 68
WA8: Wid 3B 96
Crossway, The CH63: Raby 3E 119
Crossways CH62: Brom 2D 104
L25: Gate 3B 74
Crosswood Cres. L36: Huy 4E 57
Crosthwaite Av. CH62: East 3F 121
Croston Av. L35: Rainh 2H 59
Croston Cl. WA8: Wid 6A 78
Crouch St. L5: Liv 1G 53
WA9: St H 5H 43
Crow La. W. WA12: Newt W 1H 45
Crowmarsh Cl. CH49: Upton 5D 66
Crown Acres Rd. L25: Woolt 3E 93
Crown Av. WA8: Wid 3H 95
Crown Ga. WA7: Pal F 6B 114
Crown Rd. L12: W Der 6G 37
Crown Sta. Pl. L7: Liv 1G 71
Crown St. L7: Liv 5F 53
(Elizabeth St.)
L7: Liv .1G 71
(Rosemary Cl.)
L8: Liv .1G 71
WA9: St H 6B 42
WA12: Newt W 2H 45
Crownway L36: Huy 3F 57
Crow St. L8: Liv 3D 70
Crowther St. WA10: St H 2C 42
CROW WOOD 1H 97
Crow Wood La. WA8: Wid 1H 97
Crow Wood Pl. WA8: Wid 6H 79
Croxdale Rd. L14: Knott A 6C 38
Croxdale Rd. W. L14: Knott A 6B 38
Croxeth Ga. L17: Aig 4A 72

CROXTETH 1G 37
Croxteth Av. CH44: Wall 3D 50
L21: Lith 4A 20
Croxteth Cl. L31: Mag 4D 6
Croxteth Ct. L8: Liv 3H 71
Croxteth Dr. L17: Aig 4A 72
WA11: Rainf 2F 17
Croxteth Gro. L8: Liv 3A 72
Croxteth Hall 4H 37
Croxteth Hall Country Pk. 4A 38
Croxteth Hall La. L11: Crox 2G 37
L12: Crox, W Der 3G 37
Croxteth La. L34: Know 4D 38
Croxteth Rd. L8: Liv 3H 71
L20: Boot 6B 20
Croxteth Vw. L32: Kirkb 4B 24
Croyde Pl. WA9: Sut L 3G 61
Croyde Rd. L24: Speke 2A 110
Croydon Av. L18: Moss H 4C 72
Croylands St. L4: Kirkd 5E 35
Crucian Way L12: Crox 2H 37
Crump St. L1: Liv 2E 71
Crutchley Av. CH41: Birke 1D 68
Crystal Cl. L13: Liv 5E 55
Cubbin Cres. L5: Kirkd 1D 52
Cubert Rd. L11: Crox 1G 37
Cuckoo Cl. L25: Gate 5C 74
Cuckoo La. L25: Gate 4C 74
Cuckoo Way L25: Gate 5C 74
Cuerden St. L13: Liv 2F 5 (5D 52)
CUERDLEY CROSS 1C 98
Cuerdley Grn. WA5: Cuerd 6C 80
Cuerdley Rd. WA5: Penk 6E 81
Culford Cl. WA7: Wind H 4F 115
Cullen Av. L20: Boot 6D 20
Cullen Cl. CH63: East 3D 120
Cullen Dr. L21: Lith 4A 20
Cullen Rd. WA7: West P 6B 112
Cullen St. L8: Liv 2A 72
Culme Rd. L12: W Der 6D 36
Culzean Cl. L12: Crox 2A 38
Cumberland Av. CH43: Pren 1C 86
L17: Liv 3B 72
L30: N'ton 6C 10
WA10: St H 5H 41
Cumberland Cl. L6: Liv 6B 36
Cumberland Cres. WA11: Hay 5C 30
Cumberland Ga. L30: N'ton 5G 11
Cumberland Rd. CH45: New B 6E 33
Cumberland St. L1: Liv 3D 4 (5C 52)
Cumber La. L35: Whis 3F 59
Cumbria Way L12: W Der 4G 37
Cummings St. L1: Liv 6G 5 (1E 71)
Cumpsty Rd. L21: Lith 2C 20
Cunard Av. CH44: Wall 4E 51
Cunard Cl. CH43: Bid 3G 67
Cunard Rd. L21: Lith 4B 20
Cunliffe Cl. WA7: Pal F 6C 114
Cunliffe St. L2: Liv 2D 4 (5C 52)
Cunningham Cl. CH48: Caldy 5C 82
WA5: Gt San 4H 81
Cunningham Dr. CH63: Brom 6C 104
WA7: Run 5C 112
(not continuous)
Cunningham Rd. L13: Liv 5E 55
WA8: Wid 3B 96
Cunscough La. L31: Mag 5H 7
Cuper Cres. L36: Huy 3F 57
Curate Rd. L6: Liv 6A 36
Curlender Cl. CH41: Birke 6A 50
Curlender Way L24: Hale 3E 111
Curlew Av. CH49: Upton 3B 66
Curlew Cl. CH49: Upton 3B 66
Curlew Ct. CH46: More 6A 48
Curlew Gro. L26: Halew 2G 93
Curlew Way CH46: More 6A 48
Curran Way L33: Kirkb 4H 13
Curtana Cres. L11: Crox 2G 37
Curtis Rd. L4: Walt 4A 36
Curwell Cl. CH63: Spit 2B 104
Curzon Av. CH41: Birke 2D 68
CH45: New B 5D 32

Curzon Rd. CH42: Tran 1D 86
CH47: Hoy 2A 64
L22: Water 2G 19
Curzon St. WA7: Run 4D 112
Cusson Rd. L33: Know I 2D 24
Custley Hey L28: Stockb V 5D 38
Custom Ho. Pl. L1: Liv 6D 4 (1C 70)
Cut La. L33: Kirkb 4G 25
Cygnet Cl. L33: Kirkb 1C 24
Cygnet Gdns. WA9: St H 3A 44
Cynthia Rd. WA7: Run 4D 112
Cypress Av. WA8: Wid 6F 79
Cypress Cl. L31: Mell 6E 13
Cypress Cft. CH63: Spit 2B 104
Cypress Gdns. WA9: St H 6A 42
Cypress Gro. WA7: Run 6G 113
Cypress Rd. L36: Huy 1F 75
Cyprian's Way L30: N'ton 6E 11
Cyprus Gro. L8: Liv 5G 71
Cyprus St. L34: Presc 1D 58
Cyprus Ter. CH45: New B 6D 32
Cyril Gro. L17: Aig 1C 90

D

Dacre Hill 3H 87
Dacre's Bri. La. L35: Tar G 2D 76
Dacre St. CH41: Birke 3G 69
L20: Boot 4B 34
Dacy Rd. L5: Liv 2G 53
Daffodil Cl. WA8: Wid 5A 80
Daffodil Gdns. WA9: Bold 6C 44
Daffodil Rd. CH41: Birke 2B 68
L15: Wav 3F 73
Dagnall Rd. L32: Kirkb 2G 23
Dahlia Cl. L9: Walt 1H 35
WA9: Bold 6C 44
Dairy Farm Rd. WA11: Rainf 3B 16
Dairylands Cl. L18: Moss H 3G 73
Daisy Bank Rd. WA5: Penk 5H 81
Daisy Gro. L7: Liv 6H 53
(off Dorothy St.)
Daisy M. L21: Lith 5B 20
Daisy Mt. L31: Mag 1C 12
Daisy St. L5: Kirkd 6D 34
Dakin Wlk. L33: Kirkb 1B 24
Dakota Bus. Pk. L19: Speke 1A 108
Dakota Dr. L24: Speke 2H 107
Dalby Cl. WA11: St H 6G 29
Dalcross Way L11: Crox 1F 37
Dale Av. CH60: Hesw 4D 100
CH62: Brom 5D 104
Dale Acre Dr. L30: N'ton 6C 10
Dale Av. CH60: Hesw 4D 100
CH62: Brom 5D 104
Dalebrook Cl. L25: Gate 2D 74
Dale Cl. L31: Mag 5B 6
WA8: Wid 3G 95
Dale Ct. CH60: Hesw 5D 100
Dale Cres. WA9: Sut L 1H 61
Dale End Rd. CH61: Barn 1G 101
Dale Gdns. CH60: Hesw 4B 100
Dalegarth Av. L12: W Der 4B 38
Dale Hall L18: Moss H 1D 90
Dalehead Pl. WA11: St H 2F 29
Dale Hey CH44: Wall 4D 50
CH66: Hoot 5E 121
Dalehurst Cl. CH44: Wall 3F 51
Dale La. L33: Kirkb 4C 14
Dalemeadow Rd. L14: Knott A 4H 55
Dale Rd. L25: Gate 5D 74
Dale Rd. CH62: Brom 1D 120
DALES, THE 5C 100
Daleside Cl. CH61: Irby 5D 84
Daleside Rd. L33: Kirkb 6B 14
Daleside Wlk. L33: Kirkb 6B 14
Dales Row L36: Huy 5B 58
Dale St. L2: Liv 3D 4 (5C 52)
L19: Garst 6G 91
WA7: Run 4E 113
Dalesway CH60: Hesw 5C 100
Dale Vw. Cl. CH61: Pens 6E 85
Dalewood L12: Crox 2A 38

Dalewood Gdns. L35: Whis 5F 59
Daley Pl. L20: Boot 4E 21
Daley Rd. L21: Lith 2C 20
Dallas Gro. L9: Ain 5G 21
Dallington Ct. L13: Liv 5F 55
Dalmeny St. L17: Aig 6H 71
Dalmorton Rd. CH45: New B 5D 32
Dalry Cres. L32: Kirkb 4B 24
Dalrymple St. L5: Liv 2D 52
Dalry Wlk. L32: Kirkb 4B 24
Dalston Dr. WA11: St H 2F 29
Dalton Cl. L12: W Der 3G 37
Dalton Ct. WA7: Ast 2A 114
Dalton Rd. CH45: New B 6E 33
Dalton St. WA7: Run 3H 113
Daltry Cl. L12: W Der 6E 37
Dalwood Cl. WA7: Murd 6G 115
Damerham M. L25: Gate 2C 74
Damfield La. L31: Mag 6B 6
Damson Gro. WA11: Rainf 2E 17
Damson Rd. L27: N'ley 3G 75
Damwood Rd. L24: Speke 3E 109
Danby Cl. L5: Liv 2F 53
WA7: Beech 1H 123
Danby Fold L35: Rainh 4H 59
Dane Cl. CH61: Irby 5D 84
Dane Ct. L35: Rainh 4A 60
Danefield Pl. L19: Aller 3H 91
Danefield Rd. CH49: Grea 1A 84
L19: Aller 3H 91
Danefield Ter. *L19: Aller* *4H 91*
(off Mather Av.)
Danehurst Rd. CH45: Wall 6B 32
L9: Ain 4H 21
Danescourt Rd. CH41: Birke 1C 68
L12: W Der 2G 55
Danescroft WA8: Wid 6H 77
Daneshill Cl. L17: Aig 4D 90
Dane St. L4: Walt 4F 35
Daneswell Dr. CH46: More 6D 48
Daneswell Rd. L24: Speke 3A 110
Daneville Rd. L4: Walt 3B 36
Danger La. CH46: More 5D 48
Daniel Cl. L20: Boot 5A 20
Daniel Davies Dr. L8: Liv 2G 71
Daniel Ho. L20: Boot 3C 34
Dannette Hey L28: Stockb V 1E 57
Dansie St. L3: Liv 4H 5 (6F 53)
Dan's Rd. WA8: Wid 1A 98
Dante Cl. L9: Ain 3A 22
Danube St. L8: Liv 2A 72
Dapple Heath Av. L31: Mell 6E 13
Darby Gro. L19: Garst 5F 91
Darby Rd. L19: Gras 3E 91
Darent Rd. WA11: Hay 4D 30
Daresbury Cl. L32: Kirkb 1G 23
Daresbury Ct. WA8: Wid 6H 79
Daresbury Expressway
WA4: Moore, Dares 3B 114
WA7: Run, Ast, Wind H, Nort 3E 113
Daresbury Pk. WA4: Dares 5H 115
(not continuous)
Daresbury Rd. CH44: Wall 3C 50
WA10: Eccl 1H 41
Dark Entry L34: Know P 4G 39
Dark La. L31: Mag 6C 6
Darley Cl. WA8: Wid 6H 77
Darleydale Dr. CH62: East 2F 121
Darley Dr. L12: W Der 1G 55
Darlington Cl. CH44: Wall 3F 51
Darlington Ct. WA8: Wid 4E 97
Darlington St. CH44: Wall 3F 51
Darmond Rd. L33: Kirkb 6C 14
Darmond's Grn. CH48: W Kir 6B 64
Darmonds Grn. Av. L6: Liv 6B 36
Darnley St. L8: Liv 4E 71
Darrel Dr. L7: Liv 2A 72
Darsefield Rd. L16: Child 2A 74
Dartford Cl. L14: Knott A 1B 56
Dartington Rd. L16: Child 1H 73
Dartmouth Av. L10: Ain 1A 22
Dartmouth Dr. L30: N'ton 5C 10
WA10: Windle 5A 28
Darwall Rd. L19: Aller 3H 91
Darwen St. L5: Liv 2C 52
Darwick Dr. L36: Huy 1H 75
Darwin Gro. WA9: St H 6C 42
Daryl Rd. CH60: Hesw 4E 101
Daulby St. L3: Liv 5F 53
Dauntsey Brow L25: Gate 2D 74
Dauntsey M. L25: Gate 2D 74
Davenham Av. CH43: O'ton 6B 68
Davenham Cl. CH43: O'ton 1B 86
Davenham Ct. L15: Wav 2F 73
Davenhill Pk. L10: Ain 1A 22
Davenport Cl. CH48: Caldy 5C 82
Davenport Gro. L33: Kirkb 5A 14
Davenport Rd. CH60: Hesw 6C 100
Davenport Row WA7: Run 5H 113
Daventree Rd. CH45: Wall 2D 50
Daventry Rd. L17: Aig 1C 90
David Lewis St. L1: Liv 5E 5 (6D 52)
David Lloyd Leisure
Liverpool **2C 24**
Speke **1A 108**
Davidson Rd. L13: Liv 4D 54
David St. L8: Liv 5F 71
Davids Wlk. L25: Woolt 6E 75
Davies Cl. WA8: Wid 1E 113
Davies St. L1: Liv 3D 4 (5C 52)
L20: Boot 1D 34
WA9: St H 1G 43
Davis Rd. CH46: Leas 4F 49
Davy Cl. WA10: Eccl 6H 27
Davy Rd. WA7: Ast 2A 114
Davy St. L5: Liv 1G 53
Dawber Cl. L6: Liv 3G 53
Dawlish Cl. L25: Hunts X 3E 93
Dawlish Rd. CH44: Wall 3B 50
CH61: Irby 6A 84
Dawn Cl. WA9: St H 6C 42
Dawn Wlk. *L10: Faz* *4F 23*
(off Panton Way)
Dawpool Cotts. CH48: Caldy 5G 83
Dawpool Dr. CH46: More 1C 66
CH62: Brom 6C 104
Dawpool Farm CH61: Thurs 6H 83
Dawson Av. CH41: Birke 1D 68
WA9: St H 6H 43
Dawson Gdns. L31: Mag 5B 6
Dawson Ho. WA5: Gt San 3E 81
Dawson St. L1: Liv 4E 5 (6D 52)
Dawson Way L1: Liv 4F 5
Dawstone Ri. CH60: Hesw 6D 100
Dawstone Rd. CH60: Hesw 6D 100
Days Mdw. CH49: Grea 6A 66
Day St. L13: Liv 4E 55
Deacon Cl. L22: Water 3F 19
Deacon Ct. L22: Water 3F 19
L25: Woolt 1D 92
Deacon Pk. L33: Know I 3D 24
Deacon Rd. WA8: Wid 2F 97
Deacon Trad. Est. WA12: Newt W 3H 45
Deakin St. CH41: Birke 1B 68
Dealcroft L25: Woolt 1B 92
Dean Av. CH45: Wall 1A 50
Dean Cl. WA8: Wid 3F 97
Dean Dillistone Ct. *L1: Liv* *2E 71*
(off Cathedral Ga.)
Deane Rd. L7: Liv 5A 54
Dean Ho. L22: Water 3G 19
Dean Patey Ct. L1: Liv 1E 71
Deansburn Rd. L13: Liv 1C 54
Deanscales Rd. L11: Norr G 3D 36
Dean St. L22: Water 3F 19
WA8: Wid 3F 97
Deans Way CH41: Birke 1B 68
Deansway WA8: Wid 3A 96
Deanwood Cl. L35: Whis 5F 59
Dearham Av. WA11: St H 4E 29
Dearne Cl. L12: W Der 2A 56
Dearnford Av. CH62: Brom 1D 120
Dearnford Cl. CH62: Brom 1D 120
Dearnley Av. WA11: St H 6A 30
Deauville Rd. L9: Ain 4A 22
Debra Cl. L31: Mell 5F 13
Dee Cl. L33: Kirkb 3B 14
Dee Ct. L25: Gate 6E 75
Dee Ho. L25: Gate 6E 75
Dee La. CH48: W Kir 1A 82
Deeley Cl. L7: Liv 6A 54
Dee Pk. Cl. CH60: Hesw 1F 117
Dee Pk. Rd. CH60: Hesw 1F 117
Deepdale WA8: Wid 6A 78
Deepdale Av. L20: Boot 6A 20
WA11: St H 2G 29
Deepdale Cl. CH43: Bid 3G 67
WA5: Gt San 3H 81
Deepdale Dr. L35: Rainh 4B 60
Deepdale Rd. L25: Gate 2C 74
Deepfield Dr. L36: Huy 1H 75
Deepfield Rd. L15: Wav 3D 72
Deepwood Gro. L35: Whis 5E 59
Deerbarn Dr. L30: N'ton 5H 11
Deerbolt Cl. L32: Kirkb 6G 13
Deerbolt Cres. L32: Kirkb 6G 13
Deerbolt Way L32: Kirkb 6G 13
Deerbourne Cl. L25: Woolt 1B 92
Deerfield Cl. WA9: St H 1A 44
Dee Rd. L35: Rainh 4H 59
Deer Pk. Ct. WA7: Pal F 1A 124
Dee Sailing Club **6D 82**
Deeside CH60: Hesw 5A 100
Deeside Cl. CH43: Bid 3F 67
Deeside Ct. CH64: Park 6F 117
Dee Vw. Rd. CH60: Hesw 5D 100
De Grouchy St. CH48: W Kir 6B 64
De Havilland Dr.
L24: Speke 1A 108
Deirdre Av. WA8: Wid 2E 97
Dekker Rd. L33: Kirkb 3A 14
Delabole Rd. L11: Crox 6H 23
De Lacy Row WA7: Cas 3C 114
Delagoa Rd. L10: Faz 5D 22
Delamain Rd. L13: Liv 1C 54
Delamere Av. CH62: East 3E 121
WA8: Wid 2A 96
WA9: Sut M 4E 61
Delamere Cl. CH43: Bid 3F 67
CH62: East 3E 121
L12: Crox 2H 37
Delamere Gro. *CH44: Wall* *5G 51*
(off Tudor Av.)
Delamere Pl. WA7: Run 4D 112
Delamore Pl. L4: Kirkd 4E 35
Delamore's Acre CH64: Will 6A 120
Delamore St. L4: Kirkd 4E 35
Delavor Cl. CH60: Hesw 5C 100
Delavor Rd. CH60: Hesw 5B 100
Delaware Cres. L32: Kirkb 6G 13
Delaware Rd. L20: Boot 1C 34
Delfby Cres. L32: Kirkb 2C 24
Delf La. L4: Walt 3G 35
L24: Speke 6D 92
Dell, The CH42: Rock F 2B 88
L12: W Der 5A 38
Della Robbia Ho. *CH41: Birke* *4F 69*
(off Clifton Rd.)
Dell Cl. CH63: Brom 1B 120
Dell Ct. CH43: Pren 2B 86
Dellfield La. L31: Mag 6D 6
Dell Gro. CH42: Rock F 3B 88
Dell La. CH60: Hesw 6F 101
Dellside Gro. WA9: St H 5G 43
Dell St. L7: Liv 5A 54
Delph Ct. L21: Lith 3A 20
WA9: St H 5F 43
Delphfield WA7: Nort 5F 115
Delph Hollow Way WA9: St H 5F 43
Delph La. L35: Whis 2F 59
WA4: Dares 2H 115
Delph Rd. L23: Lit C 1F 9
Delphwood Dr. WA9: St H 4F 43
Delta Dr. L12: W Der 5A 38
Delta Rd. L21: Lith 4B 20
WA9: St H 1B 44
Delta Rd. E. CH42: Rock F 2B 88
Delta Rd. W. CH42: Rock F 2B 88
Deltic Pl. L33: Know I 2D 24

Deltic Way L30: N'ton 3G **21**
L33: Know I 3D **24**
Delves Av. CH63: Spit 2H **103**
Delyn Cl. CH42: Rock F 2G **87**
Demesne St. CH44: Wall 4G **51**
Denbigh Av. WA9: St H 6G **43**
Denbigh Ct. WA7: Cas 3C **114**
Denbigh Rd. CH44: Wall 4F **51**
L9: Walt 2F **35**
Denbigh St. L5: Liv 2B **52**
Dencourt Rd. L11: Norr G 4F **37**
Deneacres L25: Woolt 1C **92**
Dene Av. WA12: Newt W 1H **45**
Denebank Rd. L4: Walt 6H **35**
Denecliff L28: Stockb V 5D **38**
Dene Ct. L9: Faz 1D **36**
Denehurst Cl. WA5: Penk 5H **81**
Deneshey Rd. CH47: Meols 1C **64**
Denes Way L28: Stockb V 6C **38**
Denford Rd. L14: Knott A 2B **56**
Denham Cl. CH43: Bid 2G **67**
L12: Crox .2B **38**
Denise Av. WA5: Penk 4G **81**
Denise Rd. L10: Faz 4F **23**
Denison Gro. WA9: St H 6C **42**
Denison St. L3: Liv 1B **4** (4B **52**)
Denman Dr. L6: Liv 3A **54**
Denman Gro. *CH44: Wall* *5G* ***51***
(off Tudor Av.)
Denman St. L6: Liv 4H **53**
Denman Way L6: Liv 3A **54**
Denmark St. L22: Water 2F **19**
Dennett Cl. L31: Mag 2B **12**
Dennett Rd. L35: Presc 3C **58**
Denning Dr. CH61: Irby 4B **84**
Dennis Av. WA10: St H 6A **42**
Dennis Rd. WA8: Wid 4G **97**
Denny Cl. CH49: Upton 5D **66**
Denston Cl. CH43: Bid 2F **67**
Denstone Av. L10: Ain 1B **22**
Denstone Cl. L25: Woolt 3D **92**
Dentdale Dr. L5: Liv 3E **53**
Denton Dr. CH45: Wall 1E **51**
Denton Gro. L6: Liv 2A **54**
DENTON'S GREEN 6C **28**
Dentons Grn. La. WA10: St H 6B **28**
Denton St. L8: Liv 5F **71**
WA8: Wid .2G **97**
Dentwood St. L8: Liv 5G **71**
Denver Rd. L32: Kirkb 2G **23**
Depot Rd. L33: Know I 5F **15**
Derby Bldgs. *L7: Liv* *6H* ***53***
(off Irvine St.)
Derby Dr. WA11: Rainf 3G **17**
Derby Gro. L31: Mag 3B **12**
Derby Hall L17: Aig 5C **72**
Derby La. L13: Liv 3E **55**
Derby Rd. CH42: Tran 6F **69**
CH45: Wall 1C **50**
L5: Kirkd .1B **52**
L20: Boot .2B **34**
L20: Kirkd 2B **34**
L36: Huy .5G **57**
(not continuous)
WA8: Wid .6E **79**
DERBYSHIRE HILL 3D **44**
Derbyshire Hill Rd.
WA9: St H .2C **44**
Derby Sq. L2: Liv 5D **4** (6C **52**)
L34: Presc 1E **59**
Derby St. L13: Liv 4D **54**
L19: Garst 1G **107**
L34: Presc 1C **58**
L36: Huy .5A **58**
Derby Ter. L36: Huy 4G **57**
Dereham Av. CH49: Upton 2E **67**
Dereham Cres. L10: Faz 4D **22**
Dereham Way WA7: Nort 2F **115**
Derna Rd. L36: Huy 3F **57**
Derringstone Cl. WA10: St H 4B **42**
Derwent Av. L34: Presc 1F **59**
Derwent Cl. CH63: Hghr B 6F **87**
L31: Mag 5E **7**
Derwent Cl. L33: Kirkb 5H **13**
L35: Rainh 4H **59**
Derwent Ct. L18: Moss H 4H **73**
Derwent Dr. CH45: Wall 1C **50**
CH61: Pens 1D **100**
CH66: Hoot 5H **121**
L21: Lith .3D **20**
Derwent Rd. CH43: O'ton 5D **68**
CH47: Meols 1E **65**
CH63: Hghr B 6F **87**
L23: Crosb 6H **9**
WA8: Wid .2A **96**
WA11: St H 4F **29**
Derwent Rd. E. L13: Liv 3E **55**
Derwent Rd. W. L13: Liv 3D **54**
Derwent Sq. L13: Liv 3E **55**
Desborough Cres. L12: W Der 6E **37**
Desford Av. WA11: St H 5H **29**
Desford Cl. CH46: More 6H **47**
Desford Rd. L19: Aig 3C **90**
De Silva St. L36: Huy 5A **58**
Desmond Cl. CH43: Bid 2G **67**
Desmond Gro. L23: Crosb 6H **9**
Desoto Rd. WA8: Wid 1B **112**
Desoto Rd. E. WA8: Wid 5D **96**
Desoto Rd. W. WA8: Wid 5D **96**
Deva Cl. L33: Kirkb 2A **14**
Deva Rd. CH48: W Kir 1A **82**
Deveraux Dr. CH44: Wall 4D **50**
Deverell Gro. L15: Wav 6F **55**
Deverell Rd. L15: Wav 1E **73**
Deverill Rd. CH42: Rock F 2G **87**
Devilla Cl. L14: Knott A 2C **56**
De Villiers Av. L23: Crosb 4G **9**
Devisdale Gro. CH43: Bid 2G **67**
Devizes Cl. L25: Gate 2D **74**
Devizes Dr. CH61: Irby 4B **84**
Devoke Av. WA11: St H 2E **29**
Devon Av. CH45: Wall 2E **51**
Devon Cl. L23: Blun 5C **8**
Devon Ct. *L5: Liv* *2G* ***53***
(off Tynemouth Cl.)
Devondale Rd. L18: Moss H 4E **73**
Devon Dr. CH61: Pens 1C **100**
Devonfield Rd. L9: Walt 6F **21**
Devon Gdns. CH42: Rock F 2H **87**
L16: Child 4A **74**
Devon Pl. WA8: Wid 6E **79**
Devonport St. L8: Liv 4F **71**
Devonshire Cl. CH43: O'ton 4D **68**
L33: Kirkb 5A **14**
DEVONSHIRE PARK 6E **69**
Devonshire Pl. CH43: O'ton 4C **68**
L5: Liv 1E **53**
(not continuous)
WA7: Run 3E **113**
Devonshire Rd. CH43: O'ton 4D **68**
CH44: Wall 3D **50**
(not continuous)
CH48: W Kir 2C **82**
CH49: Upton 4C **66**
CH61: Pens 1C **100**
L8: Liv 4G **71**
L22: Water 1E **19**
WA10: St H 6B **28**
Devonshire Rd. W. L8: Liv 4G **71**
Devon St. L3: Liv 2H **5** (5E **53**)
WA10: St H 1B **42**
Devonwall Gdns. L8: Liv 4H **71**
Devon Way L16: Child 3A **74**
L36: Huy .3A **58**
(not continuous)
Dewar Ct. WA7: Ast 2A **114**
Dewberry Cl. CH42: Tran 5F **69**
Dewey Av. L9: Ain 3H **21**
Dewlands Rd. L21: Sea 3H **19**
Dewsbury Rd. L4: Walt 1H **53**
Dexter St. L8: Liv 3E **71**
Deycroft Av. L33: Kirkb 5C **14**
Deycroft Wlk. L33: Kirkb 5C **14**
Deyes Ct. L31: Mag 6D **6**
Deyes End L31: Mag 6D **6**
Deyes La. L31: Mag 6C **6**
Deyes Lane Swimming Pool 6C **6**
Deysbrook La. L12: W Der 1G **55**
Deysbrook Side L12: W Der 1G **55**
Deysbrook Way L12: W Der 5H **37**
Dial Rd. CH42: Tran 6F **69**
Dial St. L7: Liv 5A **54**
Diamond Bus. Pk. WA11: Rainf 4H **17**
Diamond St. L5: Liv 3D **52**
Diana Rd. L20: Boot 4D **20**
Diana St. L4: Walt 5G **35**
Diane Ho. *L8: Liv* *2F* ***71***
(off Birley Ct.)
Dibbinsdale Rd. CH63: Brom 5B **104**
Dibbins Grn. CH63: Brom 1B **120**
Dibbins Hey CH63: Spit 3A **104**
Dibbinview Gro. CH63: Spit 3B **104**
Dibb La. L23: Lit C 2E **9**
Dicconson St. WA10: St H 1E **43**
Dickens Av. CH43: Pren 2B **86**
Dickens Cl. CH43: Pren 2B **86**
L32: Kirkb 3H **23**
Dickenson St. L1: Liv 1D **70**
Dickens Rd. WA10: St H 5A **42**
Dickens St. L8: Liv 3F **71**
Dickinson Cl. WA11: Hay 5C **30**
Dickson Cl. WA8: Wid 3F **97**
Dickson St. L3: Liv 3B **52**
WA8: Wid .3E **97**
(not continuous)
Didcot Cl. L25: Hunts X 3F **93**
Didsbury Cl. L33: Kirkb 1B **24**
Digg La. CH46: More 6B **48**
Digmoor Rd. L32: Kirkb 4B **24**
Digmoor Wlk. L32: Kirkb 4B **24**
Dignum Mead L27: N'ley 4G **75**
Dilloway St. WA10: St H 1C **42**
Dinaro Cl. L25: Gate 5E **75**
Dinas La. L36: Huy 3C **56**
Dinas La. Pde. L14: Huy 3C **56**
Dinesen Rd. L19: Garst 4G **91**
DINGLE 6F **71**
Dingle Av. WA12: Newt W 3H **45**
Dinglebrook Rd. L9: Ain 2A **36**
Dingle Brow L8: Liv 6G **71**
Dingle Grange *L8: Liv* *6G* ***71***
(off Dingle Brow)
Dingle Gro. L8: Liv 5G **71**
Dingle La. L8: Liv 6G **71**
Dingle Mt. L8: Liv 6G **71**
Dingle Rd. CH42: Tran 5E **69**
L8: Liv 6F **71**
Dingle Va. L8: Liv 6G **71**
Dingley Av. L9: Walt 5F **21**
Dingwall Dr. CH49: Grea 6B **66**
Dinmore Rd. CH44: Wall 3D **50**
Dinnington Ct. WA8: Wid 6C **78**
Dinorban Av. WA9: St H 6G **43**
Dinorwic Rd. L4: Walt 1G **53**
Dinsdale Rd. CH62: Brom 3E **105**
Discovery Cl. L19: Garst 1H **107**
Ditchfield Pl. WA8: Wid 3H **95**
Ditchfield Rd. WA5: Penk 6G **81**
WA8: Wid .3G **95**
DITTON 3A **96**
Ditton Ct. WA8: Hale B 6A **96**
Ditton La. CH46: Leas 4B **48**
Ditton Rd. WA8: Wid 5A **96**
Dixon M. L30: N'ton 5E **11**
Dixon Rd. L33: Know I 2D **24**
Dobson St. L6: Liv 3G **53**
Dock Rd. CH41: Birke 5C **50**
L19: Garst 6F **91**
WA8: Wid .6D **96**
(not continuous)
Dock Rd. Nth. CH62: Port S 5C **88**
Dock Rd. Sth. CH62: Brom 1D **104**
Docks Link CH44: Wall 4B **50**
Docks Rd. WA7: Run 3C **112**
Dock St. WA8: Wid 6E **97**
Dodd Av. CH49: Grea 6B **66**
WA10: St H 1A **42**
Doddridge Rd. L8: Liv 4E **71**
Dodd's La. L31: Mag 5B **6**

Dodleston Cl. CH43: Noct 5H **67**
Dodman Rd. L11: Crox 6H **23**
DOE GREEN 6F **81**
Doe Pk. Courtyard L25: Woolt 3D **92**
Doe's Mdw. Rd. CH63: Brom 6B **104**
DOG & GUN 2F **37**
Dolan Ct. L25: Gate 1B **74**
Dolomite Av. L24: Speke 5B **92**
Domar Cl. L32: Kirkb 2B **24**
Dombey Pl. *L8: Liv 3F **71***
(off Dombey St.)
Dombey St. L8: Liv 3F **71**
Domingo Dr. L33: Kirkb 4H **13**
Dominic Cl. L16: Child 1A **74**
Dominic Rd. L16: Child 1A **74**
Dominion St. L6: Liv 2A **54**
Domino Ct. WA7: Manor P 1D **114**
Domville L35: Whis 5E **59**
Domville Dr. CH49: Woodc 6E **67**
Domville Rd. L13: Liv 6E **55**
Donaldson Ct. L5: Liv 1G **53**
Donaldson St. L5: Liv 1G **53**
Donalds Way L17: Aig 2C **90**
Doncaster Dr. CH49: Upton 3D **66**
Donegal Rd. L13: Liv 4F **55**
Donne Av. CH63: Spit 2H **103**
Donne Cl. CH63: Spit 2A **104**
Donnington Cl. L36: Roby 1F **75**
Donsby Rd. L9: Ain 5H **21**
Dooley Dr. L30: N'ton 5H **11**
Doon Cl. L4: Kirkd 5E **35**
Dorans La. L2: Liv 4D **4** (6C **52**)
Dorbett Dr. L23: Crosb 1H **19**
Dorchester Cl. CH49: Upton 5D **66**
Dorchester Dr. L33: Kirkb 4C **14**
Dorchester Pk. CH43: Noct 6H **67**
WA7: Nort 2F **115**
Dorchester Pk. Local Nature Reserve 2F **115**
Dorchester Rd. L25: Gate 3D **74**
Dorchester Way CH43: Noct 6H **67**
WA5: Burtw 1H **63**
Doreen Av. CH46: More 1B **66**
Dorgan Cl. L35: Rainh 3H **59**
Doric Rd. L13: Liv 3E **55**
Doric St. CH42: Rock F 1H **87**
L21: Sea 4H **19**
Dorien Rd. L13: Liv 5D **54**
Dorincourt CH43: O'ton 5C **68**
Dorking Gro. L15: Wav 3F **73**
Dorney Ct. L12: W Der 6H **37**
Dorothy St. L7: Liv 6H **53**
WA9: St H 6C **42**
Dorrington Cl. WA7: Murd 5F **115**
Dorrington Wlk. *L5: Liv 3E **53***
(off Courtier Cl.)
Dorrit St. L8: Liv 3F **71**
Dorset Av. L15: Wav 2B **72**
Dorset Cl. L20: Boot 2D **34**
Dorset Ct. L25: Gate 3D **74**
Dorset Dr. CH61: Pens 1C **100**
Dorset Gdns. CH42: Rock F 2H **87**
WA7: Pal F 1C **124**
Dorset Rd. CH45: New B 6C **32**
CH48: W Kir 6C **64**
L6: Liv 1B **54**
L36: Huy 4A **58**
WA10: St H 4B **42**
Doughton Grn. WA8: Wid 6C **78**
Douglas Av. WA9: Bold 1D **62**
Douglas Cl. L13: Liv 3D **54**
WA8: Wid 6B **80**
Douglas Dr. CH46: More 1B **66**
L31: Mag 5E **7**
Douglas Pl. L20: Boot 3B **34**
Douglas Rd. CH48: W Kir 6D **64**
L4: Walt 1H **53**
Douglas St. CH41: Birke 3G **69**
WA10: St H 2B **42**
Douglas Way L33: Kirkb 3B **14**
Doulton Cl. CH43: Bid 2F **67**
Doulton Pl. L35: Whis 5C **58**
Doulton St. WA10: St H 2B **42**
Douro Pl. L13: Liv 5D **54**
Douro St. L5: Liv 3E **53**
DOVECOT 3B **56**
Dovecot Av. L14: Knott A 4B **56**
Dovecote Dr. WA11: Hay 4E **31**
Dovecot Pl. *L14: Knott A 3B **56***
(off Dovecot Av.)
Dove Ct. L25: Woolt 6D **74**
Dovedale Av. CH62: East 2E **121**
L31: Mag 5B **6**
Dovedale Cl. CH43: Pren 1B **86**
Dovedale Ct. WA8: Wid 6H **77**
Dovedale Rd. CH45: Wall 6C **32**
CH47: Hoy 1B **64**
L18: Moss H 4D **72**
Dovepoint Rd. CH47: Meols 6E **47**
Dovercliffe Rd. L13: Liv 4F **55**
Dover Cl. CH41: Birke 2F **69**
WA7: Murd 1G **125**
Dovercroft L25: Woolt 1B **92**
Dover Gro. L16: Child 1B **74**
Dove Rd. L9: Walt 5F **21**
Dover Rd. L31: Mag 3A **12**
Dover St. L3: Liv 6F **53**
WA7: Run 2F **113**
Dovesmead Rd. CH60: Hesw 6G **101**
Dovestone Cl. L7: Liv 1H **71**
Dove St. L8: Liv 2H **71**
Dovey St. L8: Liv 4G **71**
Doward St. WA8: Wid 1G **97**
Dowhills Dr. L23: Blun 4D **8**
Dowhills Pk. L23: Blun 3D **8**
Dowhills Rd. L23: Blun 3D **8**
Downes Grn. CH63: Spit 4A **104**
Downgreen Cl. L32: Kirkb 2G **23**
Downham Cl. L25: Woolt 4B **74**
Downham Dr. CH60: Hesw 5E **101**
Downham Grn. L25: Woolt 4B **74**
Downham Rd. CH42: Tran 6F **69**
Downham Rd. Nth. CH61: Hesw 3E **101**
Downham Rd. Sth. CH60: Hesw 5E **101**
Downham Way L25: Woolt 4B **74**
Downing Cl. CH43: O'ton 6D **68**
Downing Rd. L20: Boot 3D **34**
Downing St. L5: Liv 2G **53**
Downlands Rd. L27: N'ley 5H **75**
Downland Way WA9: St H 4B **44**
Downs, The L23: Blun 6D **8**
Downside WA8: Wid 6H **77**
Downside Cl. L30: N'ton 5E **11**
Downside Dr. L10: Ain 2D **22**
Downs Rd. WA7: Run 4E **113**
WA10: St H 3B **42**
Downway La. WA9: St H 4C **44**
Dowsefield La. L18: Aller 6A **74**
Dragon Cl. L11: Crox 1G **37**
Dragon Cres. L35: Whis 3F **59**
Dragon Dr. L35: Whis 4E **59**
Dragon La. L35: Whis 5D **58**
Dragon Wlk. *L11: Crox 1G **37***
(off Dragon Cl.)
Dragon Yd. WA8: Wid 5F **79**
Drake Cl. L10: Faz 4E **23**
L35: Whis 5E **59**
Drake Cres. L10: Faz 4D **22**
Drakefield Rd. L11: Norr G 2C **36**
Drake Gdns. WA9: St H 1C **60**
Drake Pl. L10: Faz 4D **22**
Drake Rd. CH46: Leas 3F **49**
CH64: Nest 6A **118**
L10: Faz 4D **22**
Drake St. L20: Boot 4B **34**
WA10: St H 1B **42**
Drake Way L10: Faz 4E **23**
Draw Well Rd. L33: Know I 1F **25**
Draycott St. L8: Liv 6F **71**
Drayton Cl. CH61: Irby 6B **84**
WA7: Run 4D **112**
Drayton Cres. WA11: St H 5H **29**
Drayton Rd. CH44: Wall 4F **51**
L4: Walt 3G **35**
Drennan Rd. L19: Aller 3A **92**
Drewell Rd. L18: Moss H 6D **72**
Driffield Rd. L34: Presc 1C **58**
Drinkwater Gdns. L3: Liv 4E **53**
Drive, The L12: W Der 2F **55**
Driveway L35: Whis 4F **59**
Droitwich Av. CH49: Grea 5A **66**
Dromore Av. L18: Moss H 6E **73**
Dronfield Way L25: Gate 2B **74**
(not continuous)
Droxford Dr. L25: Gate 2B **74**
Druids Cross Gdns. L18: Moss H 5H **73**
Druids Cross Rd. L18: Moss H 5H **73**
Druids Pk. L18: Moss H 5A **74**
Druidsville Rd. L18: Moss H 5A **74**
Druids Way CH49: Woodc 1E **85**
Drum Cl. L14: Knott A 2C **56**
Drummond Ct. WA8: Wid 1H **97**
Drummond Rd. CH47: Hoy 4A **64**
L4: Walt 4A **36**
L23: Thorn 5B **10**
Drummoyne Ct. L23: Blun 4C **8**
Druridge Dr. WA5: Penk 5H **81**
Drury La. L2: Liv 4C **4** (6C **52**)
Drybeck Gro. WA9: St H 1H **61**
Dryburgh Way *L4: Kirkd 5E **35***
(off Bradwell St.)
Dryden Cl. CH43: Bid 2G **67**
L35: Whis 4E **59**
Dryden Gro. L36: Huy 6H **57**
Dryden Rd. L7: Liv 6C **54**
Dryden St. L5: Liv 3D **52**
L20: Boot 6A **20**
Dryfield Cl. CH49: Grea 5B **66**
Dublin St. L3: Liv 3B **52**
Ducie St. L8: Liv 3H **71**
Duckinfield St. L3: Liv 6F **53**
Duck Pond La. CH42: Tran 1C **86**
Duddingston Av. L18: Moss H 4E **73**
L23: Crosb 1G **19**
Duddon Av. L31: Mag 5E **7**
Duddon Cl. CH43: O'ton 6B **68**
Dudley Av. WA7: Run 3H **113**
Dudley Cl. CH43: O'ton 5D **68**
Dudley Cres. CH65: Hoot 4H **121**
Dudley Gro. L23: Crosb 1G **19**
Dudley Pl. WA9: St H 2H **43**
Dudley Rd. CH45: New B 5C **32**
L18: Moss H 4D **72**
Dudlow Ct. L18: Moss H 4G **73**
Dudlow Dr. L18: Moss H 4G **73**
Dudlow Gdns. L18: Moss H 4G **73**
Dudlow La. L18: Moss H 3F **73**
Dudlow Nook Rd. L18: Moss H 3G **73**
Dugdale Cl. L19: Gras 4E **91**
Duke Cl. WA7: Run 3D **112**
Duke of York Cotts. CH62: Port S 5A **88**
Dukes Rd. L5: Liv 1E **53**
Dukes Ter. L1: Liv 6G **5** (1E **71**)
Duke St. CH41: Birke 6E **51**
CH45: New B 5D **32**
L1: Liv 6E **5** (1D **70**)
L19: Garst 5G **91**
L22: Water 3F **19**
L34: Presc 1D **58**
WA10: St H 1D **42**
Duke St. Bri. CH41: Birke 6E **51**
Duke St. La. L1: Liv 6E **5** (1D **70**)
Dukes Wharf WA7: Pres B 1G **125**
Dulas Grn. L32: Kirkb 2C **24**
Dulas Rd. L15: Wav 3F **73**
L32: Kirkb 2C **24**
Dulson Way L34: Presc 2A **58**
Dulverton Rd. L17: Aig 3C **90**
Dumbarton St. L4: Walt 4E **35**
Dumbrees Gdns. L12: W Der 5A **38**
Dumbrees Rd. L12: W Der 5A **38**
Dumbreeze Gro. L34: Know 1F **39**
Dumfries Way L33: Kirkb 3H **13**
Dunacre Way L26: Halew 4H **93**
Dunbabin Rd. L15: Wav 3F **73**
L16: Child 3G **73**
Dunbar St. L4: Walt 3F **35**
Dunbeath Av. L35: Rainh 6B **60**
Dunbeath Cl. L35: Rainh 6B **60**

Duncan Av. WA7: Run 4G 113
Duncan Cl. WA10: St H 3C 42
Duncan Dr. CH49: Grea 5B 66
Duncansby Cres. WA5: Gt San 3G 81
Duncansby Dr. CH63: East 3C 120
Duncan St. CH41: Birke 3H 69
   L1: Liv 2E 71
   WA10: St H 2C 42
Dunchurch Rd. L14: Knott A 2B 56
Duncombe Rd. Nth. L19: Gras 4F 91
Duncombe Rd. Sth. L19: Garst 4F 91
Duncote Cl. CH43: O'ton 5C 68
   L35: Whis .2G 59
Dundale Rd. L13: Liv 4F 55
Dundalk La. WA8: Wid 3B 96
Dundalk Rd. WA8: Wid 3B 96
Dundas St. L20: Boot 4B 34
Dundee Gro. CH44: Wall 4C 50
Dundonald Rd. L17: Aig 2C 90
Dundonald St. CH41: Birke 1C 68
Dunedin St. WA9: St H 6C 42
Dunes Way L5: Kirkd 1C 52
Dunfold Cl. L32: Kirkb 2B 24
Dungeon La. L24: Hale 3H 109
Dunham Cl. CH62: East 4F 121
Dunham Rd. L15: Wav 6F 55
Dunkeld Cl. L6: Liv 4G 53
Dunkerron Cl. L27: N'ley 2F 75
Dunlin Cl. L27: N'ley 5G 75
   WA7: Beech 2B 124
Dunlin Ct. L25: Gate 4C 74
Dunlins Ct. CH45: Wall 5A 32
Dunlop Dr. L31: Mell 5F 13
Dunlop Rd. L24: Speke 3E 109
Dunluce St. L4: Walt 4E 35
Dunmail Av. WA11: St H 2G 29
Dunmail Gro. WA7: Beech 3A 124
Dunmore Rd. L13: Liv 4C 54
Dunmow Way L25: Hunts X 3E 93
Dunnerdale Rd. L11: Norr G 3E 37
Dunnett St. L20: Kirkd 4B 34
Dunning Cl. CH49: Upton 4C 66
Dunnings Bri. Rd. L30: N'ton 2E 21
Dunnings Wlk. L30: N'ton 5G 11
Dunnock Cl. L25: Gate 4C 74
Dunraven Rd. CH48: W Kir 1A 82
Dunriding La. WA10: St H 2B 42
Dunscroft WA9: St H 6H 43
Dunsdon Cl. L25: Woolt 5A 74
Dunsdon Rd. L25: Woolt 4A 74
Dunsford WA8: Wid 6A 78
Dunsmore Cl. WA11: Hay 4E 31
Dunsop Av. WA9: Clock F 3H 61
Dunstall Cl. CH46: Leas 4C 48
Dunstan La. L7: Liv 1A 72
Dunstan St. L15: Wav 1C 72
Dunster Gro. CH60: Hesw 6F 101
   WA9: Sut L 3H 61
Durants Cotts. L31: Mag 2C 12
Durban Av. L23: Crosb 4G 9
Durban Rd. CH45: Wall 1D 50
   L13: Liv 5F 55
Durden St. L7: Liv 2A 72
Durham Av. L30: N'ton 2F 21
Durham M. E. L30: N'ton 2G 21
Durham M. W. L30: N'ton 2G 21
Durham Rd. L21: Sea 4G 19
   WA8: Wid .6F 79
Durham St. L19: Garst 1H 107
Durham Way L30: N'ton 2G 21
   L36: Huy 4A 58
Durley Dr. CH43: Pren 2A 86
Durley Pk. Cl. CH43: Pren 3A 86
Durley Rd. L9: Ain 5H 21
Durlston Cl. WA8: Wid 1A 96
Durning Rd. L7: Liv 6A 54
Durrant Rd. L11: Norr G 5C 36
Dursley L35: Whis 5F 59
Durston Rd. L16: Child 1H 73
Dutton Dr. CH63: Spit 3H 103
Duxbury Cl. L31: Mag 4D 6
   WA11: Rainf 2G 17
Dwerryhouse La. L11: Norr G 3F 37

Dyke St. L6: Liv 3G 53
Dykin Cl. WA8: Wid 6A 80
Dykin Rd. WA8: Wid 6H 79
Dylan Cl. L4: Walt 6F 35
Dymchurch Rd. L24: Speke 1D 108
Dymoke Rd. L11: Crox 2G 37
Dymoke Wlk. L11: Crox 2G 37
             (off Dymoke Rd.)
Dyson Hall Dr. L9: Faz 6B 22
Dyson St. L4: Walt 4F 35

E

Eagle Cres. WA11: Rainf 3G 17
Eagle Dene L10: Faz 5E 23
Eaglehall Rd. L9: Faz 1D 36
Eaglehurst Rd. L25: Gate 5D 74
Eagles Cl. L32: Kirkb 1A 24
Eaglesfield Cl. WA9: St H 6H 43
Eagles Way WA7: Pal F 1A 124
Ealing Cl. WA7: Nort 4F 115
Ealing Rd. L9: Ain 4H 21
Eanleywood Farm Cl. WA7: Nort 6E 115
Eanleywood La. WA7: Nort 6E 115
Eardisley Rd. L18: Moss H 3E 73
Earle Cl. WA12: Newt W 2H 45
Earle Cres. CH64: Nest 6H 117
Earle Rd. L7: Liv 1A 72
   WA8: Wid .4G 97
Earle St. L3: Liv 2C 4 (5C 52)
   WA12: Newt W 3H 45
Earl Rd. L20: Boot 1D 34
Earl's Cl. L23: Crosb 6F 9
Earlsfield Rd. L15: Wav 3D 72
Earlston Rd. CH45: Wall 1C 50
Earl St. CH62: New F 3B 88
   WA9: St H .1G 43
Earls Way WA7: Pal F 6A 114
Earlswood Cl. CH46: More 1H 65
Earlwood Gdns. L35: Whis 5E 59
Earp St. L19: Garst 5G 91
Easby Cl. WA7: Run 3G 113
Easby Rd. L4: Kirkd 6E 35
   L5: Kirkd 6D 34
Easby Wlk. L4: Kirkd 6D 34
Easedale Wlk. L33: Kirkb 4H 13
Easenhall Cl. WA8: Wid 5F 79
Easington Rd. WA9: St H 1B 60
E. Albert Rd. L17: Aig 5H 71
East Bank CH42: Tran 6E 69
Eastbourne M. L9: Ain 4H 21
          (off Eastbourne Rd.)
Eastbourne Rd. CH41: Birke 3E 69
   L9: Ain 4H 21
   L22: Water .1D 18
Eastbourne Wlk. L6: Liv 3F 53
Eastbury Cl. WA8: Wid 4G 79
Eastcliffe Rd. L13: Liv 4F 55
East Cl. L34: Eccl P 6G 41
Eastcote Rd. L19: Aller 3G 91
Eastcott Cl. CH49: Grea 6A 66
Eastcroft Rd. CH44: Wall 4E 51
Eastdale Rd. L15: Wav 1D 72
E. Dam Wood Rd. L24: Speke 3H 109
Eastern Av. CH62: Brom 1D 104
   L24: Speke 3H 109
Eastern Dr. L19: Gras 4E 91
E. Farm M. CH48: Caldy 3F 83
Eastfield Dr. L17: Aig 6A 72
Eastfield Wlk. L32: Kirkb 2C 24
E. Float Quay CH41: Birke 6F 51
East Front L35: Whis 6E 59
Eastgate Rd. WA7: Manor P 6H 99
Eastgate Way WA7: Manor P 6G 99
           (not continuous)
EASTHAM 2E 121
Eastham Cl. L16: Child 6B 56
Eastham Country Pk. 5G 105
Eastham Cres. WA9: Clock F 3F 61
EASTHAM FERRY 5G 105
Eastham M. CH62: East 3G 121

Eastham Rake CH62: East 5C 120
Eastham Rake Station (Rail) 4D 120
Eastham Village Rd. CH62: East . . .2G 121
Eastlake Av. L5: Liv 2F 53
E. Lancashire Rd.
   L11: Crox, Norr G 2C 36
   L33: Know I 2C 36
   L34: Know 2C 36
   WA10: Eccl, St H, Windle 2C 36
   WA11: St H 2C 36
East La. WA7: Pal F 6B 114
Eastleigh Dr. CH61: Irby 4B 84
East Mains L24: Speke 2A 110
Eastman Rd. L13: Liv 6C 36
East Meade L31: Mag 5B 6
E. Millwood Rd. L24: Speke 1H 109
East O'Hills Cl. CH60: Hesw 4E 101
Easton Rd. CH62: New F 3B 88
   L36: Huy 5C 56
East Orchard La. L9: Ain 4B 22
E. Prescot Rd. L14: Knott A 4G 55
East Rd. L14: Broad G 5G 55
   L24: Halew 6A 94
   L31: Mag 6E 7
East Side WA9: St H 3G 43
Eastside Ind. Est. WA9: St H 3G 43
East St. CH41: Birke 5G 51
   L3: Liv 2C 4 (5C 52)
   L22: Water .2F 19
   L34: Presc .1E 59
   WA8: Wid .2H 97
Eastview Cl. CH43: Noct 5H 67
East Village L1: Liv 6G 5
East Way CH46: More 6C 48
Eastway CH49: Grea 5C 66
   L31: Mag 5C 6
           (not continuous)
   WA7: Pal F 6B 114
   WA8: Wid .2B 96
Eastwood L17: Aig 6G 71
   WA7: Wind H 3E 115
Eastwood Rd. WA5: Burtw 6H 45
Eaton Av. CH44: Wall 3E 51
   L20: Boot 6D 20
          (off Aughton Rd.)
   L21: Lith 4B 20
Eaton Cl. L12: W Der 6E 37
   L36: Roby 5F 57
Eaton Gdns. L12: W Der 3H 55
Eaton Grange L12: W Der 2G 55
Eaton Rd. CH43: O'ton 4D 68
   CH48: W Kir 2A 82
   L12: W Der 6F 37
          (not continuous)
   L19: Gras 5E 91
   L31: Mag 3B 12
   WA10: St H 5B 28
Eaton Rd. Nth. L12: W Der 6E 37
Eaton St. L44: Wall 2D 50
   L3: Liv 1C 4 (4C 52)
   L34: Presc .6D 40
   WA7: Run .3E 113
Eaves La. WA9: St H 1G 61
Ebenezer Howard Rd. L21: Ford 1C 20
Ebenezer Rd. L7: Liv 5A 54
Ebenezer St. CH42: Rock F 1A 88
   WA11: Hay 5B 30
Eberle St. L2: Liv 3D 4 (5C 52)
Ebony Cl. CH46: More 1H 65
Ebony Way L33: Kirkb 4A 14
Ebor La. L5: Liv 3E 53
Ebrington St. L19: Garst 5G 91
Ecclesall Av. L21: Lith 3D 20
Eccles Gro. WA9: Clock F 4A 62
Ecclesfield Rd. WA10: Eccl 6G 27
Eccles Rd. L9: Walt 2D 74
Eccleshall Rd. CH62: Port S 5C 88
Eccleshill Rd. L13: Liv 2E 55
ECCLESTON .6A 28
Eccleston Av. CH62: Brom 4C 104
Eccleston Cl. CH43: O'ton 6B 68
Eccleston Dr. WA7: Run 4G 113
Eccleston Gdns. WA10: St H 4G 41

ECCLESTON PARK 6G 41
Eccleston Pk. Dr. L35: Rainh 1H 59
Eccleston Park Station (Rail) 1G 59
Eccleston Pk. Trade Cen.
WA10: St H 5G 41
Eccleston Rd. L9: Walt 5F 21
Eccleston St. L34: Presc 1D 58
WA10: St H 2C 42
Echo Arena 2C 70
Echo La. CH48: W Kir 2C 82
Edale Cl. CH62: East 2E 121
Edale Rd. L18: Moss H 5F 73
Eddarbridge Est. WA8: Wid 6D 96
Eddisbury Rd. CH44: Wall 2E 51
CH47: Hoy 5A 64
CH48: W Kir 5A 64
Eddisbury Way L12: W Der 6E 37
Eden Av. WA11: Rainf 2E 17
Eden Cl. L33: Kirkb 3B 14
L35: Rainh 5H 59
Edendale WA8: Wid 1H 95
Eden Dr. Nth. L23: Crosb 6A 10
Eden Dr. Sth. L23: Crosb 6A 10
Edenfield Cres. L36: Huy 4H 57
Edenfield Rd. L15: Wav 3D 72
Edenhall Dr. L25: Woolt 6E 75
Edenhurst Av. CH44: Wall 2E 51
L16: Child 1C 74
Edenhurst Ct. L36: Huy 3D 56
Edenpark Rd. CH42: Tran 6E 69
Eden Sq. L2: Liv 2D 4
Eden St. L8: Liv 2H 71
Eden Va. L30: N'ton 5E 11
Edgar Ct. CH41: Birke 2F 69
L21: Lith 2B 20
Edgar St. L3: Liv 1E 5 (4D 52)
Edgbaston Cl. L36: Roby 6E 57
Edgbaston Way CH43: Bid 1G 67
Edgefield Cl. CH43: Noct 5H 67
Edgefold Rd. L32: Kirkb 2B 24
Edge Gro. L7: Liv 5B 54
EDGE HILL 6H 53
Edgehill Rd. CH46: More 1A 66
Edge Hill Station (Rail) 1A 72
Edge La. L7: Liv 6H 53
L13: Liv 6H 53
L23: Thorn 3A 10
Edge La. Dr. L13: Liv 5E 55
Edge La. Retail Pk. L13: Liv 5D 54
Edgeley Gdns. L9: Walt 5F 21
Edgemoor Cl. CH43: Bid 2F 67
L12: W Der 2H 55
L23: Thorn 4B 10
Edgemoor Dr. CH61: Irby 4A 84
L10: Faz 4E 23
L23: Thorn 4A 10
Edgemoor Rd. L12: W Der 2H 55
Edge St. WA9: St H 1A 60
Edgewell Dr. L15: Wav 1F 73
Edgewood Cl. WA8: Wid 3H 95
Edgewood Dr. CH62: Brom 2D 120
Edgewood Rd. CH47: Meols 6D 46
CH49: Upton 3D 66
Edgeworth Cl. WA9: St H 5A 44
Edgeworth St. WA9: St H 6A 44
Edgworth Rd. L4: Walt 1H 53
Edinburgh Cl. L30: N'ton 3G 21
Edinburgh Dr. CH43: Pren 2C 86
L36: Huy 1A 76
Edinburgh Rd. CH45: Wall 2D 50
L7: Liv 5G 53
(not continuous)
WA8: Wid 3G 95
Edington St. L15: Wav 1C 72
Edison Rd. WA7: Ast 2H 113
Edith Rd. CH44: Wall 4G 51
L4: Walt 1G 53
L20: Boot 5D 20
Edith St. WA7: Run 2D 112
WA9: St H 6B 44
Edmondson St. WA9: St H 2B 44
Edmonton Cl. L5: Kirkd 1D 52
Edmund St. L3: Liv 3C 4 (5C 52)
Edna Av. L10: Faz 4E 23
Edrich Av. CH43: Bid 1G 67
Edward Jenner Av. L30: N'ton 6F 11
Edward Pav. L3: Liv 6C 4 (1C 70)
Edward Rd. CH47: Hoy 3C 64
L35: Whis 2F 59
WA5: Gt San 3F 81
Edward's La. L24: Speke 5D 92
Edward's La. Ind. Est. L24: Speke 6D 92
Edward St. WA8: Wid 2H 97
WA9: St H 4H 43
WA11: Hay 5C 30
Edwards Way WA8: Wid 3A 96
Edwin St. WA8: Wid 2G 97
Effingham St. L20: Boot 4B 34
Egan Ct. *CH41: Birke 2G 69*
(off Lord St.)
Egan Rd. CH43: Bid 1A 68
Egbert Rd. CH47: Meols 1C 64
Egdon Cl. WA8: Wid 1A 98
Egerton Ct. CH41: Birke 2G 69
Egerton Dr. CH48: W Kir 1B 82
Egerton Gdns. CH42: Rock F 2G 87
Egerton Gro. CH45: Wall 2D 50
Egerton Ho. WA7: Run 2F 113
Egerton Pk. CH42: Rock F 2G 87
Egerton Pk. Cl. CH42: Rock F 2G 87
Egerton Rd. CH43: Clau 3C 68
CH62: New F 4B 88
L15: Wav 2B 72
L34: Presc 1C 58
Egerton St. CH45: New B 5D 32
L8: Liv 2F 71
WA7: Run 2D 112
WA9: St H 4H 43
Egerton Wharf CH41: Birke 1G 69
Eglington Av. L35: Whis 5D 58
EGREMONT 2F 51
Egremont Cl. L27: N'ley 5A 76
Egremont Lawn L27: N'ley 5A 76
Egremont Prom. CH44: Wall 1F 51
CH45: Wall 1F 51
Egypt St. WA8: Wid 4D 96
Eighth Av. L9: Ain 4B 22
Eilian Gro. L14: Knott A 5H 55
Elaine Cl. WA8: Wid 1G 97
Elaine Price Ct. WA7: Run 4D 112
Elaine St. L8: Liv 3F 71
Elderberry Cl. L11: Crox 3G 37
Elderdale Rd. L4: Walt 6H 35
Elderflower Rd. WA10: St H 6C 28
Elder Gdns. L19: Gras 3F 91
Elder Gro. CH48: W Kir 1B 82
Eldersfield Rd. L11: Norr G 3F 37
Elderswood L35: Rainh 3A 60
Elderwood Rd. CH42: Tran 6G 69
Eldon Cl. *WA10: St H 3C 42*
(off Eldon St.)
Eldon Gro. *L3: Liv 3D 52*
(off Limekiln La.)
Eldonian Way L3: Liv 3C 52
Eldon Pl. L3: Liv 3C 52
Eldon Rd. CH42: Rock F 1H 87
CH44: Wall 3D 50
Eldon St. L3: Liv 3C 52
WA10: St H 3C 42
Eldred Rd. L16: Child 3G 73
Eleanor Pk. CH43: Bid 1G 67
Eleanor Rd. CH43: Bid 6H 49
CH46: More 6A 48
L20: Boot 5D 20
Eleanor St. L20: Kirkd 4B 34
WA8: Wid 4E 97
Electric Av. L10: Faz 6F 23
L11: Crox 6F 23
Elephant La. WA9: St H 6B 42
Elfet St. CH41: Birke 1B 68
Elgar Av. CH62: East 2E 121
Elgar Rd. L14: Knott A 2B 56
Elgin Ct. L35: Rainh 5B 60
Elgin Dr. CH45: Wall 1E 51
Elgin Way CH41: Birke 2G 69
Eliot Cl. CH62: New F 4A 88
Eliot St. L20: Boot 6B 20
Elizabeth Ct. WA8: Wid 4F 97
Elizabeth Rd. L10: Faz 4F 23
L20: Boot 5D 20
L36: Huy 1H 75
WA11: Hay 4G 31
Elizabeth St. L3: Liv 5F 53
WA9: Clock F 4A 62
WA9: St H 5A 44
Elizabeth Ter. WA8: Wid 2B 96
Eliza St. WA9: St H 6B 44
Elkan Cl. WA8: Wid 6A 80
Elkan Rd. WA8: Wid 6H 79
Elkstone Rd. L11: Norr G 4F 37
Ellaby Rd. L35: Rainh 3A 60
Ellamsbridge Rd.
WA9: St H 5A 44
Ellel Gro. L6: Liv 2A 54
Ellencliffe Dr. L6: Liv 2A 54
Ellen Gdns. WA9: St H 5A 44
Ellens Cl. L6: Liv 5G 53
Ellen's La. CH63: Beb 6B 88
Ellen St. WA9: St H 6A 44
Elleray Dr. L8: Liv 5F 71
Elleray Pk. Rd. CH45: Wall 6C 32
Ellerby Cl. WA7: Murd 6G 115
Ellergreen Rd. L11: Norr G 3D 36
Ellerman Rd. L3: Liv 6E 71
(not continuous)
Ellerslie Av. L35: Rainh 2H 59
Ellerslie Rd. L13: Liv 1B 54
Ellerton Cl. WA8: Wid 6B 78
Ellerton Way L12: Crox 2A 38
Ellesmere Dr. L10: Ain 1A 22
Ellesmere Gro.
CH45: Wall 1D 50
Ellesmere St. WA7: Run 3F 113
Elliot Dr. L32: Kirkb 3H 23
Elliot St. L1: Liv 4F 5 (6D 52)
WA8: Wid 3F 97
WA10: St H 2C 42
Ellis Ashton St. L36: Huy 5A 58
Ellis La. WA6: Frod 6H 123
Ellison Dr. WA10: St H 1A 42
Ellison Gro. L36: Huy 5F 57
Ellison St. L13: Liv 3D 54
Ellis Pl. L8: Liv 4F 71
Ellis St. WA8: Wid 4E 97
Ellon Av. L35: Rainh 5B 60
Elloway Rd. L24: Speke 2A 110
Ellwood Cl. L24: Hale 3E 111
Elmar Rd. L17: Aig 1C 90
(not continuous)
Elm Av. CH49: Upton 3B 66
L23: Crosb 4H 9
WA8: Wid 1F 97
Elm Bank *L4: Walt 6F 35*
(off Walton Breck Rd.)
Elmbank Rd. CH62: New F 5B 88
L18: Moss H 4C 72
Elmbank St. CH44: Wall 4E 51
Elm Cl. CH61: Pens 1E 101
L12: Crox 2B 38
Elm Ct. CH63: Hghr B 5F 87
L23: Blun 5E 9
Elmcroft Cl. L9: Ain 5B 22
Elmdale Rd. L9: Walt 1G 35
Elmdene Ct. CH49: Grea 1A 84
Elm Dr. CH49: Grea 6A 66
L21: Sea 5H 19
Elmfield Cl. WA9: St H 5C 42
Elmfield Rd. L9: Walt 6G 21
Elm Gdns. *L21: Sea 5A 20*
(off Elm Rd.)
WA11: Rainf 3F 17
Elm Grn. CH64: Will 6H 119
Elm Gro. CH42: Tran 5F 69
CH47: Hoy 2C 64
L7: Liv 6G 53
L34: Eccl P 6F 41
WA8: Wid 2F 97
Elm Hall Dr. L18: Moss H 4E 73
Elmham Cres. L10: Faz 4D 22

Elm Ho. *L22:* Water 2G **19**
    (off Lorne Rd.)
  L34: Presc .1C **58**
Elm Ho. M. *L25:* Gate 5D **74**
Elmhurst Rd. *L25:* Gate 2C **74**
Elmore Cl. *L5:* Liv 2F **53**
  WA7: Wind H 4F **115**
ELM PARK 4A **54**
Elm Pk. Rd. *CH45:* Wall 6C **32**
Elm Rd. *CH42:* Tran 1D **86**
    (Elm Rd. Nth.)
  CH42: Tran 6F **69**
    (Walker M.)
  CH61: Irby 5D **84**
  CH63: Hghr B 4H **87**
  CH64: Will 6H **119**
  L4: Walt .3G **35**
  L21: Sea 5H **19**
  L32: Kirkb 6H **13**
  WA5: Penk 5H **81**
  WA7: Run 5G **113**
  WA9: St H 5B **42**
  WA10: St H 5B **42**
  WA11: Hay 4G **31**
Elm Rd. Nth. *CH42:* Tran 1D **86**
Elms, The *L8:* Liv 5G **71**
  L31: Lyd 4C **6**
  WA7: Run 4D **112**
Elmsdale Rd. *L18:* Moss H 4E **73**
Elmsett Cl. *WA5:* Gt San 4G **81**
Elmsfield Cl. *L25:* Gate 4C **74**
Elmsfield Pk. *L39:* Augh 1F **7**
Elmsfield Rd. *L23:* Thorn 3B **10**
Elms Ho. Rd. *L13:* Liv 4D **54**
Elmsley Cl. *L18:* Moss H 6E **73**
Elmsley Rd. *L18:* Moss H 5D **72**
Elms Pk. *CH61:* Thing 6E **85**
Elms Rd. *L31:* Mag 3B **12**
Elm St. *CH41:* Birke 3F **69**
  L36: Huy 5A **58**
Elmswood Av. *L35:* Rainh 6B **60**
Elmswood Ct. *L18:* Moss H 6D **72**
Elmswood Gro. *L36:* Huy 4E **57**
Elmswood Rd. *CH42:* Tran 5E **69**
  CH44: Wall 3F **51**
  L17: Aig 1B **90**
  L18: Moss H 1C **90**
Elm Ter. *CH47:* Hoy 2C **64**
  L7: Liv 5A **54**
Elmtree Cl. *L12:* W Der 6G **37**
Elm Tree Ct. *CH47:* Hoy 1C **64**
Elmtree Gro. *CH43:* Bid 1A **68**
Elmure Av. *CH63:* Hghr B 6F **87**
Elm Va. *L6:* Liv 3B **54**
Elmway Cl. *L13:* Liv 5D **54**
Elmwood *WA7:* Nort 4E **115**
Elmwood Av. *L23:* Crosb 4A **10**
Elmwood Dr. *CH61:* Hesw 3D **100**
Elphin Gro. *L4:* Walt 4G **35**
Elric Wlk. *L33:* Kirkb 6B **14**
Elsbeck Gro. *WA9:* St H 1H **61**
Elsie Rd. *L4:* Walt 1H **53**
Elsmere Av. *L17:* Aig 6A **72**
Elstead Rd. *L9:* Faz 1C **36**
  L32: Kirkb 2G **23**
Elstow St. *L5:* Kirkd 6D **34**
Elstree Cl. *WA8:* Wid 5H **79**
Elstree Rd. *L6:* Liv 4B **54**
Elswick St. *L8:* Liv 6F **71**
Eltham Av. *L21:* Lith 2B **20**
Eltham Cl. *CH49:* Woodc 1F **85**
  WA8: Wid 6A **80**
Eltham Grn. *CH49:* Woodc 1F **85**
Eltham St. *L7:* Liv 5B **54**
Eltham Wlk. *WA8:* Wid 6A **80**
Elton Av. *L23:* Blun 5E **9**
  L30: N'ton 6E **11**
Elton Cl. *CH62:* East 4E **121**
Elton Dr. *CH63:* Spit 3A **104**
Elton Head Rd. *WA9:* St H 2A **60**
Elton St. *L4:* Walt 3F **35**
Elvington Cl. *WA7:* Sut W 4B **124**
Elwick Dr. *L11:* Crox 3G **37**

Elwood Cl. *L33:* Kirkb 3A **14**
Elworth Av. *WA8:* Wid 4E **79**
Elworthy Av. *L26:* Halew 2H **93**
Elwyn Dr. *L26:* Halew 3H **93**
Elwyn Rd. *CH47:* Meols 6E **47**
Elwy St. *L8:* Liv 4G **71**
Ely Av. *CH46:* More 1A **66**
Ely Cl. *L30:* N'ton 2F **21**
Ely Pk. *WA7:* Nort 3G **115**
Ember Cres. *L6:* Liv 3F **53**
Embledon St. *L8:* Liv 2H **71**
Embleton Gro. *WA7:* Beech 2H **123**
Emerald St. *L30:* N'ton 6H **11**
Emerald St. *L8:* Liv 6G **71**
Emerson St. *L8:* Liv 2F **71**
Emery St. *L4:* Walt 4F **35**
Emily St. *WA8:* Wid 4E **97**
  WA9: St H 6A **42**
Emlyn St. *WA9:* St H 4H **43**
Emmett St. *WA9:* St H 4G **43**
Empire Rd. *L21:* Lith 5B **20**
Empress Cl. *L31:* Mag 6A **6**
Empress Rd. *CH44:* Wall 3E **51**
  L6: Liv 1A **54**
    (not continuous)
Emstrey Wlk. *L32:* Kirkb 1G **23**
Endborne Rd. *L9:* Walt 5G **21**
Endbutt La. *L23:* Crosb 5G **9**
Enderby Av. *WA11:* St H 5H **29**
Endfield Pk. *L19:* Gras 3F **91**
Endmoor Rd. *L36:* Huy 2F **57**
Endsleigh Rd. *L13:* Liv 4C **54**
  L22: Water 1D **18**
Enerby Cl. *CH43:* Bid 2G **67**
Enfield Av. *L23:* Crosb 5G **9**
Enfield Rd. *L13:* Liv 5F **55**
Enfield St. *WA10:* St H 3C **42**
Enfield Ter. *CH43:* O'ton 4D **68**
Enford Dr. *WA9:* St H 6H **43**
Enid St. *L8:* Liv 3F **71**
Ennerdale Av. *CH62:* East 3F **121**
  L31: Mag 5D **6**
  WA11: St H 3F **29**
Ennerdale Cl. *L33:* Kirkb 4H **13**
Ennerdale Dr. *L21:* Lith 3D **20**
  WA6: Frod 6G **123**
Ennerdale Rd. *CH43:* Pren 2A **86**
  CH45: Wall 5B **32**
  L9: Ain .5B **22**
Ennerdale St. *L3:* Liv 3D **52**
Ennis Cl. *L24:* Hale 3D **110**
Ennis Ct. *L11:* Norr G 2F **37**
Ennisdale Dr. *CH48:* W Kir 6C **64**
Ennismore Rd. *L13:* Liv 4D **54**
  L23: Crosb 4E **9**
Ennis Rd. *L12:* W Der 1A **56**
Ensor St. *L20:* Boot 4B **34**
Enstone Av. *L21:* Lith 2A **20**
Enstone Rd. *L25:* Hunts X 5D **92**
Ensworth Rd. *L18:* Moss H 4F **73**
Enterprise Pk. *WA11:* Rainf 5H **17**
Enterprise Way *L13:* Wav 6C **54**
Epping Av. *WA9:* Sut M 4F **61**
Epping Cl. *L35:* Rainh 5B **60**
Epping Ct. *CH60:* Hesw 4E **101**
Epping Gro. *L15:* Wav 3F **73**
Epsom Cl. *L10:* Ain 2C **22**
Epsom Gro. *L33:* Kirkb 3C **14**
Epsom Rd. *CH46:* Leas 4D **48**
Epsom St. *WA9:* St H 1B **44**
Epsom Way *L5:* Liv 2D **52**
Epstein Cl. *L6:* Liv 4H **53**
    (off Coleridge St.)
Epworth Cl. *CH43:* Clau 3C **68**
  WA5: Burtw 1H **63**
Epworth Grange *CH43:* Clau 3C **68**
    (off Park Rd. W.)
Epworth St. *L6:* Liv 5F **53**
Eremon Cl. *L9:* Ain 3B **22**
Erfurt Av. *CH63:* Beb 1A **104**
Erica Cl. *CH60:* Hesw 3C **100**
Erica Pk. *L27:* N'ley 4G **75**

Eric Gro. *CH44:* Wall 3C **50**
Eric Rd. *CH44:* Wall 3C **50**
Eric St. *WA8:* Wid 1G **97**
Eridge St. *L8:* Liv 5G **71**
Erin Cl. *L8:* Liv 3E **71**
Erl St. *L9:* Ain 5G **21**
Ermine Cres. *L5:* Liv 2F **53**
Errington Ct. *L17:* Aig 3C **90**
Errington St. *L5:* Kirkd 1C **52**
Errol St. *L17:* Aig 6H **71**
Erskine Cl. *WA11:* St H 5A **30**
Erskine Ind. Est. *L6:* Liv 4G **53**
Erskine Rd. *CH44:* Wall 4E **51**
Erskine St. *L6:* Liv 5F **53**
Erskine St. Ind. Est. *L6:* Liv 5G **53**
    (off Prospect St.)
Erylmore Rd. *L18:* Moss H 2E **91**
Escolme Dr. *CH49:* Grea 6B **66**
Escor Rd. *L25:* Gate 3C **74**
Escort Cl. *L25:* Hunts X 3E **93**
Eshelby Cl. *L22:* Water 2G **19**
Esher Cl. *CH43:* Bid 2G **67**
  CH62: New F 3B **88**
Eshe Rd. *L23:* Blun 5E **9**
Eshe Rd. Nth. *L23:* Blun 4D **8**
Esher Rd. *CH62:* New F 3B **88**
  L6: Liv 4A **54**
Eskburn Rd. *L13:* Liv 1C **54**
Eskdale Av. *CH46:* More 6A **48**
  CH62: East 2E **121**
  WA11: St H 3F **29**
Eskdale Cl. *WA7:* Beech 2H **123**
Eskdale Rd. *L9:* Walt 6G **21**
Esk St. *L20:* Kirkd 5B **34**
Eslington St. *L19:* Gras 4E **91**
Esmond St. *L6:* Liv 2H **53**
Esonwood Rd. *L35:* Whis 4D **58**
Espin St. *L4:* Walt 4F **35**
Esplanade *CH42:* Rock F 1B **88**
Esplanade, The *CH62:* New F 2B **88**
  L20: Boot 2C **34**
    (off Strand Shop. Cen.)
  L22: Water 3F **19**
Esplen Av. *L23:* Crosb 4H **9**
Essex Rd. *CH48:* W Kir 6C **64**
  L36: Huy 3A **58**
Essex Way *L20:* Boot 1D **34**
Esthwaite Av. *WA11:* St H 3G **29**
Estuary Banks *L24:* Speke 1B **108**
Estuary Blvd. *L24:* Speke 2B **108**
Estuary Commerce Pk. *L24:* Speke . .1B **108**
    (not continuous)
Etal Cl. *L11:* Norr G 4F **37**
Ethelbert Rd. *CH47:* Meols 1C **64**
Ethel Rd. *CH44:* Wall 4F **51**
Etna St. *L13:* Liv 4D **54**
Eton Ct. *L18:* Moss H 4H **73**
Eton Dr. *CH63:* Thorn H 1B **118**
  L10: Ain 1A **22**
Eton Hall Dr. *WA9:* St H 6G **43**
Eton St. *L4:* Walt 4F **35**
Etruscan Rd. *L13:* Liv 3E **55**
Ettington Rd. *L4:* Walt 6H **35**
Ettrick Cl. *L33:* Kirkb 3H **13**
Eurolink *WA9:* St H 3D **60**
Eurolink Bus. Pk. *WA9:* St H 4D **60**
Europa Blvd. *CH41:* Birke 3G **69**
Europa Cen., The *CH41:* Birke 3G **69**
Europa Pools .3F **69**
Europa Sq. *CH41:* Birke 3G **69**
Euston Gro. *CH43:* O'ton 4D **68**
Euston St. *L4:* Walt 3F **35**
Evans Cl. *WA11:* Hay 4H **31**
Evans Rd. *CH47:* Hoy 2B **64**
  L24: Speke 6D **92**
Evans St. *L34:* Presc 6D **40**
Evellynne Cl. *L32:* Kirkb 1H **23**
Evelyn Av. *L34:* Presc 1E **59**
  WA9: St H 2A **44**
Evelyn Rd. *CH44:* Wall 4E **51**
Evelyn St. *L5:* Kirkd 1D **52**
  WA9: St H 2A **44**

Evenson Way L13: Liv .3E **55**
Evenwood WA9: St H .1G **61**
Evenwood Cl. WA7: Manor P .1G **115**
Everdon Wood L33: Kirkb .6B **14**
Evered Av. L9: Walt .1G **35**
Everest Rd. CH42: Tran .1F **87**
L23: Crosb .5G **9**
Evergreen Cl. CH49: Upton .3C **66**
L27: N'ley .3G **75**
Evergreen Way WA9: Bold .6C **44**
Everite Rd. WA8: Wid .4H **95**
Everite Rd. Ind. Est. WA8: Wid .4H **95**
Everleigh Cl. CH43: Bid .2F **67**
Eversleigh Dr. CH63: Beb .1A **104**
Eversley WA8: Wid .1H **95**
Eversley Pk. CH43: O'ton .6D **68**
Eversley St. L8: Liv .3G **71**
(not continuous)
EVERTON .2E **53**
Everton Brow L3: Liv .4E **53**
Everton FC .4F **35**
Everton Gro. WA11: St H .6H **29**
Everton Rd. L6: Liv .3F **53**
Everton Valley L4: Walt .6E **35**
Everton Vw. L20: Boot .3B **34**
Everyman Theatre .6F **53**
Every St. L6: Liv .3H **53**
Evesham Cl. L25: Woolt .1B **92**
Evesham Rd. CH45: Wall .1B **50**
L4: Walt .4B **36**
Ewanville L36: Huy .6G **57**
Ewart Rd. L16: Child .1C **74**
L21: Sea .4H **19**
WA11: St H .5F **29**
Ewden Cl. L16: Child .2A **74**
Exchange Flags L2: Liv .3C **4**
Exchange Pas. E. L2: Liv .3C **4** (5C **52**)
Exchange Pas. W. L2: Liv .3C **4** (5C **52**)
Exchange Pl. L35: Rainh .4A **60**
Exchange St. WA10: St H .2E **43**
Exchange St. E. L2: Liv .3C **4** (5C **52**)
Exchange St. W. L2: Liv .4C **4** (6C **52**)
Exeley L35: Whis .5E **59**
Exeter Cl. L10: Ain .2C **22**
Exeter Rd. CH44: Wall .2E **51**
L20: Boot .3C **34**
Exeter St. WA10: St H .2B **42**
Exford Rd. L12: W Der .5H **37**
Exmoor Cl. CH61: Pens .6D **84**
Exmouth Cl. CH41: Birke .3F **69**
Exmouth Cres. WA7: Murd .1G **125**
Exmouth Gdns. CH41: Birke .3F **69**
Exmouth St. CH41: Birke .3F **69**
Exmouth Way CH41: Birke .3F **69**
WA5: Burtw .1H **63**
Express Ind. Est. WA8: Wid .4G **95**
Extension Vw. WA9: St H .5H **43**

F

Fab4D .5B **4** (6B **52**)
FACT .6G **5** (1E **71**)
Factory La. WA8: Wid .6F **79**
Factory Row WA10: St H .4C **42**
Fairacre Rd. L19: Gras .4E **91**
Fairacres Rd. CH63: Beb .1A **104**
Fairbairn Rd. L22: Water .2G **19**
Fairbank St. L15: Wav .2C **72**
Fairbeech M. CH43: Bid .2G **67**
Fairbrook Dr. CH41: Birke .6A **50**
Fairburn Cl. WA8: Wid .6A **80**
Fairburn Rd. L13: Liv .1C **54**
Fairclough Cl. L35: Rainh .4H **59**
Fairclough Cres. WA11: Hay .5C **30**
Fairclough La. CH43: O'ton .5D **68**
Fairclough Rd. L35: Rainh .4H **59**
L36: Huy .1E **57**
WA10: St H .1A **42**
Fairclough St. L1: Liv .5F **5** (6D **52**)
WA5: Burtw .1G **63**
Fairfax Dr. WA7: Run .3H **113**
Fairfax Pl. L11: Norr G .3B **36**
Fairfax Rd. CH41: Tran .5G **69**
L11: Norr G .3C **36**
FAIRFIELD .4B **54**
Fairfield L23: Crosb .5G **9**
(not continuous)
Fairfield Av. L36: Huy .5C **56**
Fairfield Cl. L36: Huy .5C **56**
Fairfield Cres. CH46: More .1B **66**
L6: Liv .4B **54**
L36: Huy .5C **56**
Fairfield Dr. CH48: W Kir .6E **65**
Fairfield Gdns. WA11: Crank .1C **28**
Fairfield Rd. CH42: Tran .1G **87**
WA8: Wid .2F **97**
WA10: St H .6A **28**
Fairfield St. L7: Liv .4C **54**
Fairford Cres. L14: Knott A .3F **55**
Fairford Rd. L14: Knott A .3F **55**
Fairhaven L33: Kirkb .4A **14**
Fairhaven Cl. CH42: Rock F .1H **87**
Fairhaven Dr. CH63: Brom .2C **120**
Fairhaven Ho. *L19: Aig* .*4D* ***90***
(off The Spinnakers)
Fairhaven Rd. WA8: Wid .1G **97**
Fair Havens Ct. WA8: Wid .3F **97**
Fairholme Av. CH64: Nest .6H **117**
L34: Eccl P .1F **59**
Fairholme Cl. L12: W Der .5E **37**
Fairholme M. *L23: Crosb* .*5G* ***9***
(off Fairholme Rd.)
Fairholme Rd. L23: Crosb .5G **9**
Fairhurst Ter. *L34: Presc* .*1E* ***59***
(off Scotchbarn La.)
Fairlawn Cl. CH63: Raby M .1A **120**
Fairlawn Ct. CH43: O'ton .4B **68**
Fairlawne Cl. L33: Kirkb .4A **14**
Fairlie Cres. L20: Boot .4D **20**
Fairlie Dr. L35: Rainh .5B **60**
Fairmead Rd. CH46: More .6C **48**
L11: Norr G .3C **36**
Fair Oak Ct. WA7: Pres B .4H **125**
Fairoak La. WA7: Pres B .4H **125**
Fairthorn Wlk. L33: Kirkb .6C **14**
Fairview CH41: Tran .5G **69**
Fairview Av. CH45: Wall .2C **50**
Fairview Cl. CH43: O'ton .6D **68**
Fairview Pl. L8: Liv .4G **71**
Fairview Rd. CH43: O'ton .1D **86**
Fairview Way CH61: Pens .2D **100**
Fairway L36: Huy .3A **58**
WA10: Windle .6A **28**
Fairway, The L12: Knott A .3H **55**
Fairway Cres. CH62: Brom .1D **104**
Fairway Nth. CH62: Brom .1D **104**
Fairways CH42: Tran .3D **86**
L23: Crosb .4F **9**
Fairways, The CH48: Caldy .5D **82**
L25: Hunts X .3F **93**
WN4: Ash M .1G **31**
Fairways Cl. L25: Woolt .3D **92**
Fairway Sth. CH62: Brom .2D **104**
Fairway Trad. Est. WA8: Wid .4C **96**
Falcon Cres. L27: N'ley .5H **75**
Falconer St. L20: Boot .5A **20**
Falcongate Ind. Est. CH41: Birke .6D **50**
Falconhall Rd. L9: Faz .1D **36**
Falcon Hey L10: Faz .5E **23**
Falcon Rd. CH41: Birke .5E **69**
Falcons Way WA7: Pal F .1A **124**
Falkirk Av. WA8: Wid .6C **78**
Falkland Rd. CH44: Wall .3F **51**
Falklands App. L11: Norr G .3C **36**
Falkland St. CH41: Birke .1C **68**
L3: Liv .5F **53**
(not continuous)
Falkner Sq. L7: Liv .1G **71**
L8: Liv .2F **71**
(not continuous)
Falkner St. L7: Liv .1G **71**
L8: Liv .6H **5** (1F **71**)
(not continuous)
Falkner Ter. *L8: Liv* .*2G* ***71***
(off Up. Parliament St.)
Fallbrook Dr. L12: W Der .5F **37**
Fallow Cl. WA9: Clock F .3G **61**
Fallowfield L33: Kirkb .5A **14**
WA7: Run .4H **113**
Fallowfield Rd. L15: Wav .3D **72**
Fallows Way L35: Whis .6C **58**
Falls La. L26: Halew .2G **93**
Falmouth Dr. WA5: Penk .6G **81**
Falmouth Pl. WA7: Murd .1G **125**
Falmouth Rd. L11: Crox .6H **23**
Falstaff St. L20: Kirkd .5C **34**
Falstone Dr. WA7: Murd .5G **115**
Faraday Rd. L13: Wav .6C **54**
L33: Know I .4D **24**
WA7: Ast .2H **113**
Faraday St. L5: Liv .2G **53**
Fareham Cl. CH49: Upton .3C **66**
Fareham Rd. L7: Liv .5B **54**
Faringdon Cl. L25: Hunts X .5D **92**
Farley Av. CH62: Brom .4C **104**
Farlow Rd. CH42: Rock F .2H **87**
Farmbrook Rd. L25: Gate .2D **74**
Farm Cl. CH49: Grea .5A **66**
WA9: Clock F .4H **61**
Farmdale Cl. L18: Moss H .1F **91**
Farmdale Dr. L31: Mag .6D **6**
Far Mdw. La. CH61: Irby .5A **84**
Farmer Pl. L20: Boot .4E **21**
Farmers La. WA5: Burtw .1H **63**
Farmfield Dr. CH43: Bid .2G **67**
Far Moss Rd. L23: Blun .3D **8**
Farm Rd. WA9: Clock F .4H **61**
Farmside CH46: Leas .4D **48**
Farm Vw. L21: Ford .1B **20**
Farmview Cl. L27: N'ley .2E **75**
Farnborough Gro. L26: Halew .2H **93**
Farndale WA8: Wid .4E **79**
Farndale Cl. WA5: Gt San .2H **81**
Farndon Av. CH45: Wall .1A **50**
WA9: Sut M .3F **61**
Farndon Dr. CH48: W Kir .6E **65**
Farndon Way CH43: O'ton .5B **68**
Farnham Cl. L32: Kirkb .2B **24**
Farnhill Cl. WA7: Nort .5F **115**
Farnley Cl. WA7: Wind H .4F **115**
Farnside Ct. L17: Aig .4C **90**
FARNWORTH .6F **79**
Farnworth Av. CH46: Leas .4C **48**
Farnworth Cl. WA8: Wid .5F **79**
Farnworth Gro. L33: Kirkb .4A **14**
Farnworth M. WA8: Wid .6F **79**
Farnworth Rd. WA5: Penk .5D **80**
Farnworth St. L6: Liv .4H **53**
WA8: Wid .5F **79**
WA9: St H .1G **43**
Farrant St. WA8: Wid .3F **97**
Farrar St. L13: Liv .6C **36**
Farrell Cl. L31: Mell .5F **13**
Farr Hall Dr. CH60: Hesw .6C **100**
Farr Hall Rd. CH60: Hesw .5C **100**
Farrier Rd. L33: Kirkb .1C **24**
Farriers Wlk. WA9: Clock F .3G **61**
Farriers Way CH48: Frank .1H **83**
L30: N'ton .3F **21**
Farringdon Cl. WA9: St H .2D **60**
Farthing Cl. L25: Hunts X .4C **92**
Farthingstone Cl. L35: Whis .1G **59**
Fatherside Dr. L30: N'ton .6C **10**
Faversham Rd. L11: Norr G .2C **36**
Faversham Way CH42: Rock F .1H **87**
Fawcett Rd. L31: Lyd .4C **6**
Fawley Rd. L18: Moss H .1G **91**
L35: Rainh .6C **60**
FAZAKERLEY .4D **22**
Fazakerley Cl. L9: Walt .1G **35**
Fazakerley Rd. L9: Walt .1G **35**
L35: Presc .3E **59**
Fazakerley Sports Cen. .3D **22**
Fazakerley Station (Rail) .4B **22**
Fazakerley St. L3: Liv .3B **4** (5B **52**)
Fearnley Hall CH41: Birke .4F **69**
Fearnley Rd. CH41: Birke .4F **69**
Fearnside St. L7: Liv .1A **72**

Feather La. CH60: Hesw 5D **100**
Feathers, The WA10: St H 2B **42**
Feeny St. WA9: Sut M 5F **61**
Feilden Rd. CH63: Beb 1A **104**
Felcroft Way L33: Kirkb 1B **24**
Felicity Gro. CH46: More 6B **48**
Fell Gro. WA11: St H 3E **29**
Fell St. CH44: Wall 5G **51**
L7: Liv 5H **53**
Felltor Cl. L25: Woolt 6B **74**
Fellwood Gro. L35: Whis 5E **59**
Felmersham Av. L11: Norr G 2D **36**
Felspar Rd. L32: Kirkb 4B **24**
Felsted Av. L25: Woolt 1E **93**
Felsted Dr. L10: Ain 2C **22**
Felthorpe Cl. CH49: Upton 2F **67**
Felton Cl. CH46: More 1A **66**
Felton Ct. *L17: Aig 6A 72*
(off Lark La.)
Felton Gro. L13: Liv 3D **54**
Feltwell Rd. L4: Walt 1H **53**
Feltwood Cl. L12: W Der 6B **38**
Feltwood Mnr. L12: W Der 6B **38**
Feltwood Rd. L12: W Der 5B **38**
Feltwood Wlk. L12: W Der 6B **38**
Fendale Av. CH46: More 6E **49**
Fender Ct. CH49: Woodc 2H **85**
Fender La. CH43: Bid 6E **49**
CH46: More 6E **49**
Fenderside Rd. CH43: Bid 1G **67**
Fender Vw. Rd. CH46: More 1E **67**
Fender Way CH43: Bid 3F **67**
CH61: Pens 1E **101**
Fenham Dr. WA5: Penk 5G **81**
Fenton Cl. L24: Speke 2F **109**
L30: N'ton 3H **21**
WA8: Wid 6A **78**
WA10: St H 1D **42**
Fenton Grn. L24: Speke 3F **109**
Fenwick La. WA7: Run 1H **123**
Fenwick St. L2: Liv 4C **4** (6C **52**)
Ferguson Av. CH49: Grea 6B **66**
Ferguson Rd. L11: Norr G 5C **36**
L21: Lith 2C **20**
Fern Bank L31: Mag 6D **6**
WA11: Rainf 2E **17**
Fernbank Av. L36: Huy 5F **57**
Fernbank Dr. L30: N'ton 5G **11**
Fernbank La. CH49: Upton 2D **66**
Fern Cl. L27: N'ley 5G **75**
L32: Kirkb 5B **14**
Ferndale Av. CH44: Wall 3E **51**
CH48: Frank 2H **83**
Ferndale Cl. L9: Walt 4G **21**
WA8: Bold H 2A **80**
Ferndale Rd. CH47: Hoy 2B **64**
L15: Wav 3C **72**
L22: Water 1F **19**
Fern Gdns. L34: Eccl P 6F **41**
Fern Gro. CH43: Noct 5H **67**
L8: Liv 3A **72**
L20: Boot 1C **34**
Fern Hey L23: Thorn 4B **10**
Fernhill CH45: New B 5D **32**
Fernhill Av. L20: Boot 2E **35**
Fernhill Cl. L20: Boot 2E **35**
(not continuous)
Fernhill Dr. L8: Liv 3G **71**
Fernhill Gdns. L20: Boot 2E **35**
Fernhill M. E. *L20: Boot 2E 35*
(off Fernhill Rd.)
Fernhill M. W. L20: Boot 2E **35**
Fernhill Rd. L20: Boot 5D **20**
Fernhill Wlk. WA9: Clock F 4G **61**
Fernhill Way L20: Boot 2E **35**
Fernhurst WA7: Run 5H **113**
Fernhurst Rd. L32: Kirkb 2G **23**
Fernie Cres. L8: Liv 4F **71**
Fernlea Av. WA9: St H 6B **42**
Fernlea M. CH43: Bid 1G **67**
Fernlea Rd. CH60: Hesw 5E **101**
Fernleigh Rd. L13: Liv 4F **55**
Fern Lodge L8: Liv 3A **72**
Ferns Cl. CH60: Hesw 4A **100**
Ferns Rd. CH63: Hghr B 6F **87**
Fernwood WA7: Nort 4D **114**
Fernwood Dr. L26: Halew 3G **93**
Fernwood Rd. L17: Aig 1C **90**
Ferny Brow Rd. CH49: Woodc 6F **67**
Ferrey Rd. L10: Faz 4E **23**
Ferries Cl. CH42: Rock F 3A **88**
Ferry Rd. CH62: East 2G **121**
Ferryside CH44: Wall 5G **51**
Ferry Vw. Rd. CH44: Wall 5G **51**
Ferryview Wlk. WA7: Cas 3B **114**
Festival Ct. L11: Norr G 2F **37**
Festival Rd. WA11: Rainf 4G **17**
Festival Ter. *WA7: Run 5G 113*
(off Festival Way)
Festival Way WA7: Run 5G **113**
Ffrancon Dr. CH63: Hghr B 4H **87**
FIDDLER'S FERRY 2F **99**
Fiddlers Ferry Rd. WA8: Wid 3G **97**
Fiddler's Ferry Sailing Club 2G **99**
Fidler St. WA10: St H 4B **42**
Field Av. L21: Lith 3A **20**
Field Cl. CH62: New F 3B **88**
WA9: Clock F 4H **61**
Fieldfare Cl. L25: Gate 4C **74**
Fieldgate WA8: Wid 4H **95**
Field Hey La. CH64: Will 6B **120**
(not continuous)
Field Ho. L12: W Der 6E **37**
Fieldhouse Row WA7: Run 6H **113**
Fieldings, The L31: Lyd 3A **6**
Fielding St. L6: Liv 4G **53**
Field La. L10: Faz 5E **23**
L21: Lith 2A **20**
Field Rd. CH45: New B 6D **32**
WA9: Clock F 4H **61**
Field's End L36: Huy 1G **75**
Fieldsend Cl. L27: N'ley 5G **75**
Fieldside Rd. CH42: Rock F 1G **87**
Field St. L3: Liv 4E **53**
(not continuous)
Fieldsway WA7: West 1E **123**
Fieldton Rd. L11: Norr G 3F **37**
Field Vw. L21: Lith 2A **20**
Field Wlk. L23: Thorn 4B **10**
Field Way L35: Rainh 2A **60**
Fieldway CH45: Wall 2C **50**
CH47: Meols 2F **65**
CH60: Hesw 4G **101**
CH63: Hghr B 3F **87**
L15: Wav 1G **73**
L31: Mag 2C **12**
L36: Huy 1H **75**
WA8: Wid 1A **98**
Fieldway Ct. CH41: Birke 1E **69**
Fifth Av. CH43: Bid 2F **67**
L9: Ain 4C **22**
(Broadway)
L9: Ain 4B **22**
(Sixth Av.)
WA7: Pal F 6B **114**
Filbert Cl. L33: Kirkb 3B **14**
Filby Gdns. WA9: St H 1C **60**
Fillmore Gro. WA8: Wid 6D **78**
Filton Rd. L14: Knott A 2D **56**
Finborough Rd. L4: Walt 3A **36**
FINCHAM 2D **56**
Fincham Cl. L14: Knott A 2D **56**
Fincham Grn. L14: Knott A 2D **56**
Fincham Rd. L14: Knott A 2C **56**
Fincham Sq. L14: Knott A 2C **56**
Finch Av. WA11: Rainf 4G **17**
Finch Cl. WA9: Clock F 4H **61**
Finch Ct. CH41: Birke 2F **69**
Finchdean Cl. CH49: Grea 5A **66**
Finch Dene L14: Knott A 1B **56**
Finch La. L14: Knott A 1B **56**
L26: Halew 5B **94**
Finch Lea Dr. L14: Knott A 2C **56**
Finchley Dr. WA11: St H 4G **29**
Finchley Rd. L4: Walt 6H **35**
Finch Mdw. Cl. L9: Faz 1D **36**
Finch Pl. L3: Liv 5F **53**
Finch Rd. L14: Knott A 1C **56**
Finch Way L14: Knott A 2B **56**
Findley Dr. CH46: Leas 4D **48**
Findon Rd. L32: Kirkb 3B **24**
Fingall Rd. L15: Wav 3F **73**
Finger Ho. La. WA8: Bold H 6H **61**
Fingland Rd. L15: Wav 2C **72**
Finlan Rd. WA8: Wid 4D **96**
Finlay Av. WA5: Penk 6G **81**
Finlay Ct. L30: N'ton 5F **11**
Finlay St. L6: Liv 4A **54**
Finney, The CH48: Caldy 5D **82**
Finney Gro. WA11: Hay 5G **31**
Finsbury Pk. WA8: Wid 4G **79**
Finstall Rd. CH63: Spit 3H **103**
Finvoy Rd. L13: Liv 6C **36**
Fiona Wlk. L10: Faz 4F **23**
Fir Av. L26: Halew 3A **94**
Firbank Cl. WA7: Wind H 4F **115**
Firbrook Ct. CH43: Bid 6G **49**
Fir Cl. L26: Halew 3A **94**
Fir Cotes L31: Mag 6D **6**
Firdale Rd. L9: Walt 1G **35**
Firdene Cres. CH43: Noct 5A **68**
Fire Sta. Rd. L35: Whis 2F **59**
Firethorne Rd. L26: Halew 1F **93**
Fir Gro. L9: Ain 3A **22**
Fir La. L15: Wav 2E **73**
Fir Rd. L22: Water 1G **19**
Firs, The CH43: Bid 1A **68**
Firs Av. CH63: Beb 2H **103**
Firscraig L28: Stockb V 6E **39**
Firshaw Rd. CH47: Meols 6C **46**
First Av. CH43: Bid 3G **67**
L9: Ain 4A **22**
(Higher La.)
L9: Ain 5C **22**
(Second Av.)
L23: Crosb 5F **9**
L35: Rainh 3H **59**
Firstone Gro. L32: Kirkb 3A **24**
Fir St. WA8: Wid 1G **97**
WA10: St H 5B **42**
Firthland Way WA9: St H 3B **44**
Fir Tree Dr. Nth. L12: Crox 2H **37**
Fir Tree Dr. Sth. L12: Crox 2H **37**
Fir Tree La. WA5: Burtw 6H **45**
Fir Way CH60: Hesw 2F **117**
Firwood Gro. WN4: Ash M 1H **31**
Fisher Av. L35: Whis 5D **58**
Fisher Pl. L35: Whis 5D **58**
Fishers La. CH61: Pens 1C **100**
Fisher St. L8: Liv 3D **70**
WA7: Run 2F **113**
WA9: St H 5A **44**
Fishguard Cl. L6: Liv 3F **53**
Fishwicks Ind. Est. WA9: St H 5H **43**
WA11: Hay 3H **31**
Fistral Cl. L10: Faz 5F **23**
Fistral Dr. WA10: Windle 5H **27**
Fitness First
Bromborough 2E **105**
Halton Lea 6A **114**
Liverpool 2H **21**
Fitzclarence Wlk. *L6: Liv 3F 53*
(off Plumpton St.)
Fitzclarence Way L6: Liv 3F **53**
Fitzgerald Rd. L13: Liv 4E **55**
Fitzpatrick Ct. L3: Liv 3C **52**
Fitzroy Way L6: Liv 4G **53**
Fitzwilliam Wlk. WA7: Cas 3C **114**
Fiveways WA10: Eccl 1G **41**
Fiveways Pk. CH64: Nest 4B **118**
Flail Cl. CH49: Grea 5A **66**
Flambards CH49: Woodc 6F **67**
Flander Cl. WA8: Wid 1A **96**
Flatfield Way L31: Mag 6D **6**
Flatt La. CH43: O'ton 6B **68**
Flavian Ct. WA7: Cas 4A **114**
Flawn Rd. L11: Norr G 5C **36**
Flaxhill CH46: More 6B **48**
Flaxman St. L7: Liv 5A **54**

Flaybrick Cl. CH43: Bid 1A 68
Fleck La. L48: Caldy, W Kir 2D 82
Fleetcroft Rd. CH49: Woodc 1E 85
Fleet La. WA9: St H 2A 44
Fleet La. Ind. Est. WA9: St H 3A 44
Fleet St. L1: Liv 5F 5 (6D 52)
Fleetwood Gdns. L33: Kirkb 4B 14
(not continuous)
Fleetwood Pl. L25: Woolt 1B 92
(off Castle St.)
Fleetwoods La. L30: N'ton 5D 10
Fleetwood Wlk. WA7: Murd 6E 115
Fleming Ct. L3: Liv 3C 52
Fleming Rd. L24: Speke 5E 93
Flemington Av. L4: Walt 4B 36
Fleming Way CH46: Leas 5E 49
Fletcher Av. CH42: Rock F 1G 87
L34: Presc 6E 41
Fletcher Cl. CH49: Woodc 6E 67
Fletcher Dr. L19: Gras 4E 91
Fletchers Row WA7: Halt 4B 114
(off Spark La.)
Flint Dr. L12: Crox 4H 37
Flintshire Gdns. WA10: St H 3D 42
Flint St. L1: Liv 2D 70
Flixton Gdns. WA9: St H 1C 60
Floral Pavilion Theatre 4E 33
Floral Wood L17: Aig 1F 89
Florence Av. CH60: Hesw 4D 100
Florence Cl. L9: Walt 2F 35
Florence Ct. L9: Walt 2F 35
(off Buchanan Rd.)
Florence Nightingale Cl.
L30: N'ton 5F 11
Florence Rd. CH44: Wall 4G 51
Florence St. CH41: Birke 3F 69
L4: Walt .5F 35
WA9: St H 6A 42
Florentine Rd. L13: Liv 3E 55
Florida Ct. L19: Gras 3F 91
Florida Way L35: Presc 3D 58
Flowermead Cl. CH47: Meols 6F 47
Fluin La. WA6: Frod 6G 123
Fluker's Brook La. L34: Know 4D 38
(not continuous)
Focus Bldg., The L3: Liv 2E 5
(off Crosshall St.)
Foinavon Cl. L9: Walt 4F 21
Folds, The CH63: Thorn H 1C 118
Folds La. WA11: St H 4E 29
Folds Rd. WA11: Hay 6B 30
Foley Cl. L4: Kirkd 6E 35
Foley St. L4: Kirkd 6E 35
Folkestone Way WA7: Murd 6E 115
Folly La. CH44: Wall 2A 50
(not continuous)
WA7: Run 4B 112
Fontenoy St. L3: Liv 1E 5 (5D 52)
Fonthill Cl. L4: Kirkd 6D 34
Fonthill Rd. L4: Kirkd 5D 34
FORD
CH43 . . . . .3G 67
L21 . . . . .1B 20
Ford Av. L33: Kirkb 3A 14
Ford Cl. CH49: Upton 5F 67
L20: Boot 4E 21
L21: Ford 1B 20
Fordcombe Rd. L25: Gate 5E 75
Ford Dr. CH49: Upton 4F 67
Fordham St. L4: Kirkd 5E 35
Fordhill Vw. CH46: More 1E 67
Ford La. CH49: Upton 4F 67
L21: Ford 1B 20
Fordlea Rd. L12: W Der 5E 37
Fordlea Way L12: W Der 5E 37
Ford Rd. CH49: Upton 4E 67
L35: Presc 1F 59
Ford St. L3: Liv 4C 52
Ford Vw. L21: Ford 6B 10
Ford Way CH49: Upton 5E 67
Ford Way M. CH49: Upton 5E 67
Forefield La. L23: Crosb 4H 9
Foreland Cl. WA5: Gt San 2E 81

Forest Cl. CH47: Meols 6D 46
L34: Eccl P 6F 41
Forest Ct. CH43: Clau 3B 68
Forest Dr. L36: Huy 4E 57
Forest Grn. L12: W Der 5F 37
Forest Gro. L34: Eccl P 6F 41
Forest Lawn L12: W Der 5F 37
Forest Mead WA10: Eccl 2G 41
Forest Rd. CH43: Clau 2C 68
CH47: Meols 6D 46
CH60: Hesw 4E 101
WA9: Sut M 4E 61
Forest Wlk. WA7: Pal F 6B 114
(off Halton Lea Shop. Cen.)
Forfar Rd. L13: Liv 1B 54
Forge Cl. WA8: Cron 4A 78
Forge Cotts. L17: Aig 5A 72
Forge Rd. WA5: Gt San 4H 81
Forge Row L31: Mag 4B 6
Forge St. L20: Kirkd 5C 34
Formby Av. WA10: St H 4B 42
Formby Cl. WA5: Penk 5H 81
Formosa Dr. L10: Faz 4D 22
Formosa Rd. L10: Faz 4D 22
Formosa Way L10: Faz 4D 22
Fornalls Grn. La. CH47: Meols 2E 65
Forrester Av. WA9: St H 6A 42
Forrest St. L1: Liv 6E 5 (1D 70)
Forshaw Av. WA10: St H 5A 42
Forshaw's La. WA5: Coll G 5G 45
Forsythia Cl. L9: Walt 2A 36
Forthlin Rd. L18: Aller 2G 91
(not continuous)
Forth St. L20: Kirkd 4C 34
Forton Lodge Flats L23: Blun 5E 9
(off Blundellsands Rd. E.)
Fort Perch Rock 4D 32
Fort St. CH45: New B 4D 32
Forwood Rd. CH62: Brom 5D 104
Foscote Rd. L33: Kirkb 5C 14
Foster Cl. L35: Whis 2G 59
Fosters Gro. WA11: Hay 5B 30
Fosters Rd. WA11: Hay 5B 30
Foster St. L20: Kirkd 6C 34
WA8: Wid 2F 97
Foundation, The L3: Liv 6F 53
Foundry, The L1: Liv 6F 5
Foundry La. WA8: Hale B 6H 95
Foundry St. WA10: St H 2E 43
(not continuous)
Fountain Ct. L23: Blun 4C 8
Fountain Rd. CH45: New B 6D 32
L34: Know 2F 39
Fountains Av. WA11: Hay 4H 31
Fountains Cl. L4: Walt 6F 35
WA7: Brook 2E 125
Fountains Ct. L5: Kirkd 6D 34
(off Stanley Cl.)
Fountains Rd. L4: Kirkd 6D 34
(not continuous)
Fountain St. CH42: Tran 6E 69
WA9: St H 1A 60
Four Acre Dr. L21: Ford 6B 10
Four Acre La. WA9: Clock F 3F 61
Four Acre Pct. WA9: Clock F 3F 61
Fouracres L31: Mag 2H 11
Four Bridges CH41: Birke 6G 51
Fourth Av. CH43: Bid 3F 67
L9: Ain 4H 21
(Broadway)
L9: Ain 4B 22
(Fifth Av.)
WA7: Pal F 6B 114
Fowell Rd. CH45: New B 5D 32
Fowler Cl. L7: Liv 6A 54
Fox Bank Cl. WA8: Wid 5D 78
Foxcote WA8: Wid 1H 95
Foxcover Rd. CH60: Hesw 6G 101
Foxcovers Rd. CH63: Beb 2A 104
Fox Covert WA7: Nort 6E 115
Foxdale Cl. CH43: O'ton 4C 68
Foxdale Rd. L15: Wav 3D 72
Foxdell Cl. L13: Liv 5E 55

Foxes, The CH61: Thing 5E 85
Foxes Ct. CH43: O'ton 4D 68
Foxfield Rd. CH47: Meols 1D 64
Foxglove L26: Halew 2G 93
Foxglove Cl. L9: Faz 1D 36
Foxglove Rd. CH41: Birke 2B 68
Fox Hey Rd. CH44: Wall 4B 50
Foxhill Cl. L8: Liv 3G 71
Foxhill La. L26: Halew 1G 93
Foxhouse La. L31: Mag 1C 12
Foxhunter Dr. L9: Ain 3A 22
Foxleigh L26: Halew 2F 93
Foxleigh Grange CH41: Birke 6B 50
Foxley Heath WA8: Wid 3C 96
Fox Pl. WA10: St H 1E 43
Fox's Bank La. L35: Whis 3F 77
(not continuous)
Foxshaw Cl. L35: Whis 6D 58
Fox St. CH41: Birke 3E 69
L3: Liv 3E 53
WA7: Run 4E 113
Foxton Cl. CH46: More 6H 47
WA11: St H 4H 29
Foxwood L12: W Der 5A 38
WA9: St H 6A 42
Foxwood Cl. CH48: W Kir 6E 65
Framlington Ct. WA7: Cas 3A 114
Frampton Rd. L4: Walt 3B 36
Francine Cl. L3: Liv 2C 52
Francis Av. CH43: Clau 3D 68
CH46: More 1B 66
Francis Cl. L35: Rainh 3A 60
WA8: Wid 3A 96
Francis Rd. WA6: Frod 6G 123
Francis St. WA9: St H 6B 44
Francis Way L16: Child 1H 73
FRANKBY 1H 83
Frankby Av. CH44: Wall 3C 50
Frankby Cl. CH49: Grea 6H 65
Frankby Grn. CH48: Frank 1G 83
Frankby Gro. CH49: Upton 4D 66
Frankby Rd. CH47: Meols 1D 64
CH48: Frank, W Kir 6D 64
CH49: Grea 6D 64
L4: Walt .5H 35
Frankby Stiles CH48: Frank 6F 65
Franklin Gro. L33: Kirkb 3A 14
Franklin Pl. L6: Liv 2H 53
Franklin Rd. CH46: Leas 3E 49
Frank St. WA8: Wid 2G 97
Franton Wlk. L32: Kirkb 1G 23
Fraser Rd. WA5: Gt San 2E 81
Fraser St. L3: Liv 2G 5 (5E 53)
Freckleton Dr. L33: Kirkb 4C 14
Freckleton Rd. WA10: St H 4H 41
Freda Av. WA9: St H 1G 61
Frederick Banting Cl. L30: N'ton 5F 11
Frederick Gro. L15: Wav 1E 73
Frederick Lunt Av. L34: Know 2E 39
Frederick St. WA8: Wid 2F 97
(not continuous)
WA9: St H 5B 44
Frederick Ter. WA8: Hale B 1G 111
Fredric Pl. WA7: Run 2F 113
Freedom Cl. L7: Liv 1G 71
Freehold St. L7: Liv 4B 54
Freeland St. L4: Kirkd 6E 35
Freeman St. CH41: Birke 2G 69
L7: Liv 1A 72
Freemantle Av. WA9: St H 6C 42
Freemason's Row L3: Liv 1D 4 (4C 52)
Freemont Rd. L12: W Der 6E 37
Freeport Gro. L9: Ain 4H 21
Freesia Av. L9: Walt 1H 35
Freme Cl. L11: Norr G 2F 37
Frenchfield St. WA9: Clock F 4H 61
French St. WA8: Wid 2H 97
WA10: St H 4B 42
Frensham Cl. CH63: Spit 3H 103
Freshfield Cl. L36: Huy 4E 57
Freshfield Gr. L15: Wav 3D 72
Freshford WA9: St H 1H 61
Freshwater Cl. WA5: Gt San 2F 81

Friars Av. WA5: Gt San 4G **81**
Friars Cl. CH63: Beb 6H **87**
Friarsgate Cl. L18: Moss H 4G **73**
Friar St. L5: Liv 2F **53**
WA10: St H 5D **28**
Friends La. WA5: Gt San 3F **81**
Frinsted Rd. L11: Norr G 4E **37**
Frobisher Rd. CH46: Leas 3E **49**
CH64: Nest 6A **118**
FRODSHAM 6G **123**
Frodsham Bus. Cen. WA6: Frod 6G **123**
Frodsham Dr. WA11: St H 6H **29**
Frodsham Pk. Homes WA6: Frod 6E **123**
Frodsham Station (Rail) 6F **123**
Frodsham St. CH41: Tran 5G **69**
(not continuous)
L4: Walt 4F **35**
Frogmore Rd. L13: Liv 4C **54**
Frome Cl. CH61: Irby 4B **84**
Frome Way L25: Hunts X 3F **93**
Frontfield Ct. *WA9: St H 3G 43*
(off Appleton Rd.)
Frost Dr. CH61: Irby 5A **84**
Frost St. L7: Liv 5A **54**
Fryer St. WA7: Run 2E **113**
Fry St. WA9: St H 2A **44**
(not continuous)
Fuchsia Wlk. CH49: Grea 1A **84**
Fulbeck WA8: Wid 1A **96**
Fulbrook Cl. CH63: Spit 3H **103**
Fulbrook Rd. CH63: Spit 3H **103**
Fulford Cl. L12: W Der 1B **56**
Fulford Pk. CH46: More 1C **66**
Fullerton Gro. L36: Huy 3G **57**
Fulmar Cl. L27: N'ley 4G **75**
WA11: St H 5F **29**
Fulmar Gro. L12: Crox 2A **38**
Fulshaw Cl. L27: N'ley 3F **75**
Fulton Av. CH48: W Kir 6D **64**
Fulton St. L5: Liv 2B **52**
Fulwood Cl. L17: Aig 1B **90**
Fulwood Dr. L17: Aig 1A **90**
Fulwood Pk. L17: Aig 2A **90**
Fulwood Rd. L17: Aig 1A **90**
Fulwood Way L21: Ford 5B **10**
Furlong Cl. L9: Ain 3B **22**
Furness Av. L12: W Der 4G **37**
WA10: St H 4C **28**
Furness Cl. CH49: Upton 3C **66**
Furness Ct. WA7: Nort 1H **115**
Furness St. L4: Walt 6E **35**
Furze Way CH46: More 6C **48**

G

Gable Ct. L11: Norr G 2C **36**
Gables, The L31: Mag 2C **12**
L34: Eccl P 1F **59**
Gable Vw. L11: Norr G 2C **36**
Gabriel Cl. CH46: More 1D **66**
Gainford Cl. WA8: Wid 6A **78**
Gainford Rd. L14: Knott A 1C **56**
Gainsborough Av. L31: Mag 1H **11**
Gainsborough Cl. L12: W Der 2A **56**
Gainsborough Ct. WA8: Wid 2H **95**
Gainsborough Rd. CH45: Wall 3A **50**
CH49: Upton 3C **66**
L15: Wav 3C **72**
Gaisgill Ct. WA8: Wid 2A **96**
Gala Bingo
Bromborough 2E 105
Kirkby 1A 24
Liverpool, E. Lancashire Rd. 1E 37
Liverpool, Wavertree Rd. 6A 54
Widnes 3F 97
Gala Cl. L14: Knott A 3A **56**
Gala Leo Casino 2D 70
Galbraith Cl. L17: Aig 1A **90**
Galemeade L11: Norr G 2F **37**
Gale Rd. L21: Lith 2C **20**
L33: Know I 3E **25**
Galion Way WA8: Wid 5D **78**
Gallagher Ind. Est. CH44: Wall 5D **50**
Gallopers La. CH61: Thing 5F **85**
Galloway Rd. L22: Water 1G **19**
Galloway St. L7: Liv 1B **72**
Galston Av. L35: Rainh 5B **60**
Galston Cl. L33: Kirkb 3H **13**
Galsworthy Av. L30: Boot 3D **20**
Galsworthy Pl. L30: Boot 3E **21**
Galsworthy Wlk. L30: Boot 4E **21**
Galton St. L3: Liv 1A **4** (4B **52**)
Galtres Ct. CH63: Hghr B 3G **87**
Galtres Pk. CH63: Hghr B 3G **87**
Galway Av. WA8: Wid 6C **78**
Galway Cres. WA11: Hay 4F **31**
Gambier Ter. L1: Liv 2F **71**
Gamble Av. WA10: St H 5C **28**
Gamlin St. CH41: Birke 1B **68**
Gamston Wood L32: Kirkb 2G **23**
Ganney's Mdw. Rd. CH49: Woodc 1G **85**
Gannock St. L7: Liv 5A **54**
Ganton Cl. WA8: Wid 5F **79**
Ganworth Cl. L24: Speke 3G **109**
Ganworth Rd. L24: Speke 3G **109**
Garage Rd. L24: Halew 6H **93**
Garden Apartments L18: Moss H 6D **72**
Garden Cotts. L12: W Der 3H **55**
Garden Ct. CH42: Tran 2E **87**
Gardeners Vw. L33: Kirkb 3C **14**
Gardeners Way L35: Rainh 2A **60**
Garden Hey Rd. CH46: More 2H **65**
CH47: Meols 1C **64**
Gardenia Gro. L17: Aig 1G **89**
Garden La. CH46: More 6C **48**
L5: Liv 3F **53**
L9: Ain 3B **22**
Garden Lodge Gro. L27: N'ley 4F **75**
Gardenside CH46: Leas 3F **49**
Gardenside St. L6: Liv 4F **53**
Gardens Rd. CH63: Beb 6B **88**
Garden St. L25: Woolt 1C **92**
Garden Wlk. L34: Presc 2D **58**
Gardiner Av. WA11: Hay 5E **31**
Gardner Av. L20: Boot 4D **20**
Gardner Rd. L13: Liv 2C **54**
Gardner's Dr. L6: Liv 3A **54**
Gardner's Row L3: Liv 1E **5** (4D **52**)
Gareth Av. WA11: St H 5F **29**
Garfield Ter. CH49: Upton 4E **67**
Garfourth Cl. L19: Garst 4H **91**
Garfourth Rd. L19: Garst 4H **91**
Garmoyle Cl. L15: Wav 2C **72**
Garmoyle Rd. L15: Wav 2C **72**
Garnet St. L13: Liv 6D **54**
WA9: St H 6H **43**
Garnett Av. L4: Kirkd 5E **35**
Garnetts La. L35: Tar G 2D **94**
WA8: Hale B 1G **111**
Garrick Av. CH46: More 1A **66**
Garrick Rd. CH43: Pren 3B **86**
Garrick St. L7: Liv 2A **72**
Garrigill Cl. WA8: Wid 4F **79**
Garrison Cl. L8: Liv 3H **71**
Garrowby Dr. L36: Huy 4E **57**
Garsdale Av. L35: Rainh 5B **60**
Garsdale Cl. WA5: Gt San 2H **81**
Garsfield Rd. L4: Walt 4B **36**
GARSTON 5G **91**
Garston Ind. Est. L19: Garst 1G **107**
Garston Old Rd. L19: Gras 4F **91**
Garston Way L19: Garst 5G **91**
Garswood Av. WA11: Rainf 2G **17**
Garswood Cl. CH46: Leas 3C **48**
L31: Mag 4D **6**
Garswood Old Rd. WA11: St H 3G **29**
WN4: Garsw 2B **30**
Garswood Rd. WA11: Hay 2D **30**
WN4: Garsw 1E **31**
Garswood St. L8: Liv 6F **71**
WA10: St H 1E **43**
Garter Cl. L11: Crox 2G **37**
Garth, The CH43: O'ton 4A **68**
L36: Huy 4G **57**
Garth Blvd. CH63: Hghr B 3G **87**
Garth Ct. L22: Water 2G **19**
Garthdale Rd. L18: Moss H 5E **73**
Garth Dr. L18: Moss H 5F **73**
Garthowen Rd. L7: Liv 5B **54**
Garth Rd. L32: Kirkb 3C **24**
Garth Wlk. L32: Kirkb 3C **24**
Gartons La. WA9: Clock F, Sut M 4G **61**
Garway L25: Woolt 6E **75**
Gascoyne St. L3: Liv 1C **4** (4C **52**)
Gaskell Ct. WA9: St H 2B **44**
Gaskell Rake *L30: N'ton 4D 10*
(off Higher End Pk.)
Gaskell St. WA9: St H 4G **43**
Gaskill Rd. L24: Speke 1F **109**
Gatclif Rd. L13: Liv 5C **36**
GATEACRE 4D **74**
Gateacre Brow L25: Gate 5D **74**
Gateacre Ct. *L25: Gate 2B 74*
(off Headbourne Cl.)
Gateacre Pk. Dr. L25: Gate 2B **74**
Gateacre Ri. L25: Gate 5D **74**
Gateacre Va. Rd. L25: Woolt 6D **74**
Gateside Cl. L27: N'ley 4G **75**
Gates La. L29: Thorn 1B **10**
Gateway Pk. CH62: Brom 4E **105**
Gathurst Ct. WA8: Wid 3B **96**
Gatley Dr. L31: Mag 2C **12**
Gatley Wlk. L24: Speke 1H **109**
Gaunts Way WA7: Pal F 1A **124**
Gautby Rd. CH41: Birke 6A **50**
Gavin Rd. WA8: Wid 4H **95**
Gawsworth Cl. CH43: O'ton 6B **68**
WA10: Eccl 2H **41**
Gaybeech Cl. CH43: Bid 1F **67**
Gayhurst Cres. L11: Norr G 3E **37**
Gaynor Av. WA11: Hay 4H **31**
GAYTON 6F **101**
Gayton Av. CH45: New B 5D **32**
CH63: Hghr B 3E **87**
Gayton Farm Rd. CH60: Hesw 2E **117**
Gayton La. CH60: Hesw 1F **117**
Gayton Mill Cl. CH60: Hesw 6F **101**
Gayton Parkway CH60: Hesw 2G **117**
Gayton Rd. CH60: Hesw 1D **116**
Gayton Sands Nature Reserve 5D 116
Gaytree Ct. CH43: Bid 2G **67**
Gaywood Av. L32: Kirkb 3B **24**
Gaywood Cl. CH43: Bid 2G **67**
L32: Kirkb 3B **24**
Gaywood Ct. L23: Blun 6D **8**
Gaywood Grn. L32: Kirkb 3B **24**
Gellings La. L34: Know 6C **24**
Gellings Rd. L34: Know 6C **24**
Gelling St. L8: Liv 4F **71**
Gemini Cl. L20: Boot 1B **34**
Gemini Dr. L14: Knott A 3B **56**
Gem St. L5: Liv 2C **52**
General Dr. L12: W Der 6H **37**
Geneva Cl. *L36: Huy 3G 57*
(off Salerno Dr.)
Geneva Rd. CH44: Wall 5F **51**
L6: Liv 4A **54**
Genoa Cl. L25: Gate 2D **74**
Gentwood Pde. L36: Huy 3F **57**
Gentwood Rd. L36: Huy 3E **57**
George Hale Av. L34: Know P 1G **57**
George Harrison Cl. L6: Liv 4H **53**
George Moore Ct. L23: Thorn 3B **10**
George Rd. CH47: Hoy 3C **64**
George's Dock Gates L3: Liv 4B **4** (6B **52**)
Georges Dockway L3: Liv 5C **4** (6B **52**)
George's Rd. L6: Liv 2H **53**
George St. CH41: Birke 2G **69**
L3: Liv 3C **4** (5C **52**)
WA10: St H 2E **43**
Georgia Av. CH62: Brom 2E **105**
L33: Kirkb 3H **13**
Georgia Cl. L20: Boot 2C **34**
Georgian Cl. L26: Halew 5H **93**
L35: Eccl P 1G **59**
Geraint St. L8: Liv 3F **71**
Gerald Rd. CH43: O'ton 5C **68**
Gerard Av. CH45: Wall 6C **32**

Gerard Rd. CH45: Wall 1B 50
CH48: W Kir 6B 64
GERARD'S BRIDGE 6E 29
Gerards Ct. WA11: St H 3F 29
Gerards La. WA9: St H, Sut L 6H 43
Gerard St. L3: Liv 2F 5 (5E 53)
Gerard Way L33: Kirkb 1B 24
Germander Cl. L26: Halew 2G 93
Gerneth Cl. L24: Speke 1E 109
Gerneth Rd. L24: Speke 2D 108
Gerrard's La. L26: Halew 1G 93
Gerrard St. WA8: Wid 3F 97
Gertrude Rd. L4: Walt 1H 53
Gertrude St. CH41: Birke 3H 69
WA9: St H 6A 42
Geves Gdns. L22: Water 2G 19
Ghyll Gro. WA11: St H 2F 29
Gibbons Av. WA10: St H 2A 42
Gibbon's Rd. WN4: Garsw 1F 31
Gibbs Ct. CH61: Irby 5D 84
Gibfield Rd. WA9: St H 2C 60
Gibraltar Row L3: Liv 2B 4 (5B 52)
Gibson Cl. CH61: Pens 2D 100
L33: Kirkb 4H 13
Gibson Rd. L8: Liv 2F 71
Gibson Ter. *CH44: Wall 2F 51*
(off Royden Av.)
Giddygate La. L31: Mag, Mell 1F 13
Gidlow Rd. L13: Liv 4D 54
Gidlow Rd. Sth. L13: Liv 5D 54
Gilbert Cl. CH63: Spit 3H 103
Gilbert Ho. WA7: Run 2C 112
Gilbert Rd. L35: Whis 2F 59
Gilbert St. L1: Liv 6E 5 (1D 70)
Gildarts Gdns. L3: Liv 3C 52
Gildart St. L3: Liv 2H 5 (5F 53)
Gilead St. L7: Liv 5H 53
Gilescroft Av. L33: Kirkb 5C 14
Gilescroft Wlk. L33: Kirkb 5C 14
Gillan Cl. WA7: Brook 2E 125
GILLAR'S GREEN 3E 41
Gillars Grn. Dr. WA10: Eccl 2F 41
Gillar's La. WA10: Eccl 2E 41
Gillbrook Sq. CH41: Birke 1B 68
Gilleney Gro. L35: Whis 2G 59
GILLMOSS 6H 23
Gillmoss Cl. L11: Crox 1G 37
Gillmoss Ind. Est.
L10: Faz 5F 23
Gillmoss La. L11: Crox 6G 23
Gills La. CH61: Barn, Pens 1E 101
Gill St. L3: Liv 3H 5 (5F 53)
Gilman St. L4: Walt 6G 35
Gilmartin Gro. L6: Liv 4G 53
Gilmour Mt. CH43: O'ton 5D 68
Gilpin Av. L31: Mag 5D 6
Gilroy Nature Pk. 5C 64
Gilroy Rd. CH48: W Kir 6C 64
L6: Liv 4H 53
Giltbrook Cl. WA8: Wid 6D 78
Gilwell Av. CH46: More 2C 66
Gilwell Cl. CH46: More 2C 66
Ginnel, The CH62: Port S 6B 88
Gipsy Gro. L18: Moss H 4A 74
Gipsy La. L18: Moss H 4A 74
Girton Av. L20: Boot 3E 35
Girtrell Cl. CH49: Upton 4B 66
Girtrell Rd. CH49: Upton 4B 66
Givenchy Cl. L16: Child 1A 74
Glacier Bldg. L3: Liv 5E 71
Glade, The CH47: Meols 6D 46
Glade Pk. Cl. L8: Liv 5H 71
Glade Rd. L36: Huy 3G 57
Gladeswood Rd. L33: Know I 2D 24
Gladeville Rd. L17: Aig 1C 90
Gladica Cl. L36: Huy 5B 58
Gladstone Av. L16: Child 1C 74
L21: Sea 4A 20
(off Gladstone Rd.)
Gladstone Cl. CH41: Birke 3F 69
Gladstone Ct. *L8: Liv 2F 71*
(off Up. Parliament St.)
Gladstone Hall Rd. CH62: Port S 1B 104
Gladstone Rd. CH42: Rock F 6H 69
CH44: Wall 4F 51
L7: Liv 6H 53
L9: Walt 2G 35
L19: Garst 5G 91
L21: Sea 4H 19
Gladstone St. L3: Liv 1D 4 (4C 52)
L25: Woolt 1B 92
WA8: Wid 3F 97
WA10: St H 2B 42
Gladstone Theatre 1B 104
Gladsville Rd. L27: N'ley 5H 75
Glaisher St. L5: Liv 1G 53
Glamis Cl. CH43: Noct 6H 67
Glamis Gro. WA9: St H 6G 43
Glamis Rd. L13: Liv 1B 54
Glamorgan Cl. WA10: St H 3D 42
Glan Aber Pk. L12: W Der 5A 38
Glasier Rd. CH46: More 6A 48
Glaslyn Way L9: Walt 2G 35
Glassonby Cres. L11: Norr G 4E 37
Glassonby Way L11: Norr G 4E 37
Glastonbury Cl. L6: Liv 6B 36
WA7: Nort 2H 115
Glasven Rd. L33: Kirkb 6B 14
Gleadmere WA8: Wid 1A 96
Gleaner Cl. WA7: Run 2D 112
Gleaston Cl. CH62: Brom 4D 104
Gleave Cl. WA5: Burtw 1H 63
Gleave Cres. L6: Liv 3G 53
Gleave St. WA10: St H 1E 43
Glebe, The WA7: Run 4A 114
Glebe Cl. L31: Mag 6A 6
Glebe End L29: Seft 2F 11
Glebe Hey L27: N'ley 4G 75
Glebe Hey Rd. CH49: Woodc 6E 67
Glebelands Rd. CH46: More 1C 66
Glebe La. WA8: Wid 4E 79
Glebe Rd. CH45: Wall 1C 50
Gleggside CH48: W Kir 1C 82
Glegg St. L3: Liv 3B 52
Glegside Rd. L33: Kirkb 1C 24
Glen, The CH63: Spit 2C 104
L18: Moss H 6G 73
WA7: Pal F 1B 124
Glenacres L25: Woolt 6C 74
Glenalmond Rd. CH44: Wall 3F 51
Glenathol Rd. L18: Moss H 1G 91
Glenavon Rd. CH43: Pren 2C 86
L16: Child 1G 73
Glenbank L22: Water 1E 19
Glenbank Cl. L9: Walt 6G 21
Glenburn Av. CH62: East 3E 121
Glenburn Rd. CH44: Wall 4F 51
Glenby Av. L23: Crosb 1H 19
Glencairn Rd. L13: Liv 4D 54
Glencoe Rd. CH45: Wall 1D 50
Glenconner Rd. L16: Child 6A 56
Glencourse Rd. WA8: Wid 4E 79
Glencroft Cl. L36: Huy 2E 57
Glendale Cl. L8: Liv 6F 71
Glendale Gro. CH63: Spit 3B 104
L33: Kirkb 4C 14
Glendale Rd. WA11: St H 4E 29
Glendevon Rd. L16: Child 6G 55
L36: Huy 6G 57
Glendower Rd. L22: Water 2G 19
Glendower St. L20: Boot 4C 34
Glendyke Rd. L18: Moss H 1G 91
Gleneagles Cl. CH61: Pens 1D 100
L33: Kirkb 3H 13
Gleneagles Dr. WA8: Wid 4E 79
WA11: Hay 6C 30
Gleneagles Rd. L16: Child 6A 56
Glenfield Cl. CH43: Bid 1G 67
CH46: More 6H 47
Glenfield Rd. L15: Wav 3E 73
Glengariff St. L13: Liv 6C 36
Glenham Cl. CH47: Meols 1E 65
Glenhead Rd. L19: Aller 3F 91
Glenholm Rd. L31: Mag 2A 12
Glenista Cl. L9: Walt 2G 35
Glenluce Rd. L19: Aig 3F 91
Glenlyon Rd. L16: Child 1G 73
Glenmarsh Cl. CH63: Hghr B 6F 87
L12: W Der 1G 55
Glenmaye Cl. L12: Crox 3A 38
Glenmore Av. L18: Moss H 6E 73
Glenmore Rd. CH43: O'ton 5C 68
Glenn Pl. WA8: Wid 2C 96
Glen Pk. Rd. CH45: Wall 6C 32
Glen Rd. L13: Liv 5F 55
Glen Ronald Dr. CH49: Grea 4B 66
Glenrose Rd. L25: Woolt 5C 74
Glenside L18: Aller 1G 91
Glentree Cl. CH49: Grea 4B 66
Glentrees Rd. L12: W Der 5F 37
Glentworth Cl. L31: Mag 2B 12
Glenville Cl. L25: Woolt 5D 74
WA7: Run 1F 123
Glenvine Cl. L16: Child 1A 74
Glen Way L33: Kirkb 3B 14
Glenway Cl. L12: Crox 1B 38
Glenwood WA7: Nort 4E 115
Glenwood Cl. L35: Whis 5F 59
Glenwood Dr. CH61: Irby 4C 84
Glenwyllin Rd. L22: Water 1G 19
Globe Rd. L20: Boot 1B 34
Globe St. L4: Walt 6E 35
Gloucester Ct. L6: Liv 4G 53
Gloucester Pl. *L6: Liv 4G 53*
(off Gilmartin Gro.)
Gloucester Rd. CH45: Wall 1A 50
L6: Liv 2B 54
L20: Boot 1D 34
L36: Huy 4A 58
WA8: Wid 6F 79
Gloucester Rd. Nth. L6: Liv 1B 54
Gloucester St. WA9: St H 3H 43
Glover Pl. L20: Boot 1B 34
Glover's Brow L32: Kirkb 5G 13
Glovers Ct. L32: Kirkb 6G 13
Glover's La. L30: N'ton 5E 11
Glover St. CH42: Tran 5E 69
WA10: St H 3D 42
Glyn Av. CH62: Brom 6E 105
Glynne Gro. L16: Child 1C 74
Glynne St. L20: Boot 5D 20
Glynn St. L15: Wav 2D 72
Glyn Rd. CH44: Wall 2D 50
Goddard Rd. WA7: Ast 2A 114
Godetia Cl. L9: Faz 1D 36
Godfrey Pilkington Art Gallery, The 2E 43
(off Victoria Sq.)
Godshill Cl. WA5: Gt San 2F 81
Godstow WA7: Nort 1G 115
Goldcrest Cl. L12: Crox 1B 38
WA7: Beech 2B 124
Goldcrest M. L26: Halew 2G 93
Golden Gro. L4: Walt 4G 35
Golden Triangle Ind. Est.
WA8: Hale B 6H 95
Goldfinch Cl. L26: Halew 2G 93
Goldfinch Farm Rd. L24: Speke 2E 109
Goldie St. L4: Walt 6F 35
Goldsmith Rd. CH43: Pren 2B 86
Goldsmith St. L6: Liv 4H 53
L20: Boot 1A 34
Goldsmith Way CH43: Pren 2B 86
Goldsworth Fold L35: Rainh 4G 59
Golf Links Rd. CH42: Tran 2D 86
Gondover Av. L9: Walt 5F 21
Gonville Rd. L20: Boot 3D 34
Goodacre Rd. L9: Ain 4H 21
Goodakers Ct. *CH49: Woodc 1E 85*
(off Childwall Grn.)
Goodakers Mdw. CH49: Woodc 1E 85
Goodall Pl. L4: Kirkd 5E 35
Goodall St. L4: Kirkd 4E 35
Goodban St. WA9: St H 5A 44
Goodier Ct. WA7: Run 5G 113
Goodison Av. L4: Walt 5F 35
Goodison Pk. 5F 35
Goodison Pl. L4: Walt 4F 35
Goodison Rd. L4: Walt 4F 35
Goodlass Rd. L24: Speke 5C 92

Goodleigh Pl. WA9: Sut L 2G **61**
Good Shepherd Cl. L11: Norr G 3F **37**
Goodwood Cl. L36: Roby 6F **57**
Goodwood Ct. WA9: St H 1B **60**
Goodwood Dr. CH46: Leas 4D **48**
Goodwood St. L5: Liv 2D **52**
Gooseberry Hollow WA7: Wind H 4F **115**
Gooseberry La. WA7: Nort 4F **115**
Goose Grn., The CH47: Meols 6D **46**
Goostrey Cl. CH63: Spit 4B **104**
Gordale Cl. L8: Liv 5G **71**
WA5: Gt San 2H **81**
Gordon Av. CH49: Grea 6C **66**
CH62: Brom 6E **105**
L22: Water 1E **19**
L31: Mag .4B **6**
WA11: Hay 4H **31**
Gordon Ct. CH49: Grea 6C **66**
Gordon Dr. L14: Broad G 4A **56**
L19: Gras 4E **91**
Gordon Pl. L18: Moss H 6E **73**
Gordon Rd. CH45: New B 6E **33**
L21: Sea .4H **19**
Gordon St. CH41: Birke 3E **69**
L15: Wav .2C **72**
Goree L2: Liv 4B **4** (6C **52**)
Goree Piazza *L2: Liv* *4C* ***4***
(off The Strand)
Gores Rd. L33: Know I 2D **24**
Gore St. L8: Liv 3E **71**
Gorleston M. L32: Kirkb 3B **24**
Gorleston Way L32: Kirkb 2B **24**
Gorran Haven WA7: Brook 1E **125**
Gorse Av. L12: W Der 4F **37**
Gorsebank Rd. L18: Moss H 4C **72**
Gorsebank St. CH44: Wall 4E **51**
Gorseburn Rd. L13: Liv 1C **54**
Gorse Cres. CH44: Wall 5E **51**
Gorsedale Pk. CH44: Wall 5F **51**
Gorsedale Rd. CH44: Wall 5D **50**
L18: Moss H 5E **73**
Gorsefield WA9: St H 6B **42**
Gorsefield Av. CH62: Brom 2D **120**
L23: Thorn 4A **10**
Gorsefield Cl. CH62: Brom 2D **120**
Gorsefield Rd. CH42: Tran 6E **69**
Gorse Hey Ct. L13: W Der 2E **55**
Gorsehill Rd. CH45: New B 6C **32**
CH60: Hesw 4E **101**
Gorselands Ct. L17: Aig 1B **90**
Gorse La. CH48: W Kir 2E **83**
Gorse Rd. CH47: Meols 1D **64**
Gorsewood Cl. *L25: Gate* *4E* ***75***
(off Gorsewood Rd.)
Gorsewood Gro. L25: Gate 4D **74**
Gorsewood Rd. L25: Gate 4D **74**
WA7: Murd 1F **125**
Gorsey Av. L30: N'ton 6C **10**
Gorsey Cop Rd. L25: Gate 3C **74**
Gorsey Cop Way L25: Gate 3C **74**
Gorsey Cft. L34: Eccl P 6F **41**
Gorsey La. CH44: Wall 5D **50**
L21: Ford 2B **20**
L30: N'ton 2B **20**
WA5: Burtw 2D **62**
WA8: Wid 3A **98**
WA9: Bold, Clock F 4A **62**
Gorseyville Cres. CH63: Hghr B 6G **87**
Gorseyville Rd. CH63: Hghr B 6G **87**
Gorseywell La. WA7: Pres B 1H **125**
Gorst St. L4: Walt 6F **35**
Gorton Rd. L13: Liv 5F **55**
Gort Rd. L36: Huy 4G **57**
Goschen St. L5: Liv 6F **35**
L13: Liv 4D **54**
Gosford St. L8: Liv 5F **71**
Gosforth Ct. WA7: Pal F 6A **114**
Goswell St. L15: Wav 1C **72**
Gotham Rd. CH63: Spit 3A **104**
Gothic St. CH42: Rock F 1H **87**
Gough Rd. L13: Liv 6C **36**
Goulders Ct. WA7: Brook 2D **124**
Gourley Rd. L13: Liv 6F **55**
Gourleys La. CH48: W Kir 2D **82**
Government Rd. CH47: Hoy 2B **64**
Govett Rd. WA9: St H 6A **42**
Gower St. L3: Liv 1C **70**
L20: Boot 6B **20**
WA9: St H 4H **43**
Gowrie Gro. L21: Lith 4B **20**
GPW Recruitment Stadium, The **2A 42**
Grace Av. L10: Faz 4E **23**
Grace Cl. CH45: Wall 2D **50**
Grace Ho. *WA8: Wid* *2F* ***97***
(off Frederick St.)
Grace Rd. L9: Walt 5G **21**
Grace St. L8: Liv 5F **71**
WA9: St H 5G **43**
Gradwell St. L1: Liv 5E **5** (6D **52**)
Graeme Bryson Ct. L11: Norr G 4D **36**
Grafton Cres. L8: Liv 3E **71**
Grafton Dr. CH49: Upton 5E **67**
Grafton Gro. L8: Liv 5E **71**
Grafton Rd. CH45: New B 6D **32**
Grafton St. CH43: O'ton 4D **68**
L8: Liv 6F **71**
(Beresford Rd.)
L8: Liv 3D **70**
(Stanhope St., not continuous)
WA10: St H 2B **42**
Grafton Wlk. CH48: W Kir 1C **82**
Graham Cl. WA8: Wid 2A **96**
Graham Dr. L26: Halew 3A **94**
Graham Rd. CH48: W Kir 6A **64**
WA8: Wid 3A **96**
Graham's Rd. L36: Huy 5H **57**
Graham St. WA9: St H 1G **43**
Grainger Av. CH43: Pren 1B **86**
CH48: W Kir 5B **64**
L20: Boot 6E **21**
Grain Ind. Est. L8: Liv 5E **71**
Graley Cl. L26: Halew 5H **93**
Grammar School La.
CH48: W Kir 2D **82**
Grampian Av. CH46: More 1D **66**
Grampian Rd. L7: Liv 5C **54**
Grampian Way CH46: More 1C **66**
CH62: East 2E **121**
Granams Cft. L30: N'ton 5D **10**
Granard Rd. L15: Wav 3E **73**
Granary Mill WA4: Pres H 1H **125**
Granary Way L3: Liv 3D **70**
Granborne Chase L32: Kirkb 6F **13**
GRANBY 2G **71**
Granby Cl. WA7: Brook 2E **125**
Granby Cres. CH63: Spit 3A **104**
Granby St. L8: Liv 2G **71**
Grand Central L3: Liv 4G **5**
Grandison Rd. L4: Walt 4A **36**
Grand National Av. L9: Ain 2H **21**
GRANGE 1C **82**
Grange, The CH42: Rock F 2H **87**
CH44: Wall 3E **51**
L20: Boot 5C **20**
Grange Av. CH45: Wall 1D **50**
L12: W Der 2A **56**
L25: Hunts X 4F **93**
Grange Av. Nth. L12: W Der 2A **56**
Grange Ct. CH43: O'ton 6C **68**
L15: Wav *2D* ***72***
(off Grange Ter.)
L23: Blun 6E **9**
Grange Cres. CH66: Hoot 6G **121**
Grange Cross Cl. CH48: W Kir 2E **83**
Grange Cross Hey CH48: W Kir 2E **83**
Grange Cross La. CH48: W Kir 2E **83**
Grange Dr. CH60: Hesw 3D **100**
CH63: Thorn H 6C **102**
WA5: Penk 5H **81**
WA8: Wid 2B **96**
WA10: St H 5H **41**
Grange Farm Cres. CH48: W Kir 6E **65**
Grangehurst Ct. L25: Gate 5D **74**
Grange La. L25: Gate 4C **74**
Grangemeadow Rd. L25: Gate 4C **74**
Grangemoor WA7: Run 6H **113**
Grange Mt. CH43: O'ton 4E **69**
CH48: W Kir 1D **82**
CH60: Hesw 4D **100**
Grange Old Rd. CH48: W Kir 1C **82**
GRANGE PARK 5H **41**
Grange Pk. L31: Mag 2C **12**
Grange Pk. Av. WA7: Run 3G **113**
Grange Pk. Rd. WA10: St H 4A **42**
Grange Pl. CH41: Birke 3E **69**
Grange Pct. CH41: Birke 3G **69**
Grange Rd. CH41: Birke 3F **69**
(not continuous)
CH48: W Kir 1A **82**
CH60: Hesw 3D **100**
L30: N'ton 1H **21**
WA7: Run 3G **113**
WA11: Hay, Newt W 6F **31**
Grange Rd. E. CH41: Birke 3G **69**
Grange Rd. Nth. WA7: Run 3G **113**
Grange Road Sports Cen. **4D 68**
Grange Rd. W. CH41: Birke 3D **68**
CH43: O'ton 3D **68**
Grangeside L25: Gate 4C **74**
Grange St. L6: Liv 2B **54**
Grange Ter. L15: Wav 2D **72**
Grange Valley WA11: Hay 5F **31**
Grange Vw. CH43: O'ton 4E **69**
Grange Wlk. CH48: W Kir 2D **82**
Grange Way L25: Gate 4C **74**
Grangeway WA7: Run 5G **113**
Grangeway Ct. WA7: Run 5G **113**
Grange Weint L25: Gate 5C **74**
Grange Wood CH48: W Kir 2D **82**
Grangewood L16: Child 6B **56**
Granite Ter. L36: Huy 5A **58**
Grant Av. L15: Wav 3D **72**
Grant Cl. L14: Knott A 4C **56**
WA10: St H 1C **42**
Grant Ct. *L20: Boot* *2C* ***34***
(off Clairville Cl.)
Grantham Cl. CH61: Pens 1C **100**
Grantham Cres. WA11: St H 6G **29**
Grantham Rd. L33: Kirkb 4A **14**
Grantham St. L6: Liv 4H **53**
Grantham Way L30: N'ton 5H **11**
Grantley Rd. L15: Wav 3F **73**
Granton Rd. L5: Liv 1F **53**
Grant Rd. CH46: Leas 4F **49**
L14: Knott A 4B **56**
Granville Av. L31: Mag 5B **6**
Granville Cl. CH45: Wall 1A **50**
Granville Ct. CH45: Wall 1A **50**
Granville Rd. L15: Wav 2B **72**
L19: Garst 5G **91**
Granville St. WA7: Run 2E **113**
WA9: St H 2H **43**
Grappenhall Way CH43: Bid 2G **67**
Grasmere Av. CH43: Noct 4G **67**
L34: Presc 1F **59**
WA11: St H 4F **29**
Grasmere Cl. L33: Kirkb 5H **13**
WA11: St H 4F **29**
Grasmere Ct. *CH41: Birke* *4E* ***69***
(off Penrith St.)
WA11: St H 4F **29**
Grasmere Dr. CH45: Wall 1D **50**
L21: Lith 2E **21**
WA7: Beech 2A **124**
Grasmere Fold WA11: St H 4F **29**
Grasmere Gdns. L23: Crosb 6H **9**
Grasmere Ho. *L17: Aig* *1B* ***90***
(off Mossley Hill Dr.)
Grasmere Rd. L31: Mag 5C **6**
WA6: Frod 6G **123**
Grasmere St. L5: Liv 2H **53**
GRASSENDALE 3E **91**
Grassendale Ct. *L19: Gras* *4E* ***91***
(off Grassendale Rd.)
Grassendale Esplanade L19: Gras 5D **90**
Grassendale La. L19: Gras 4E **91**
Grassendale Rd. L19: Gras 4E **91**
Grassington Cres. L25: Woolt 1E **93**
Grassmoor Cl. CH62: Brom 5E **105**

Grasswood Rd. CH49: Woodc 1F **85**
Grasville Rd. CH42: Tran 6G **69**
Gratrix Rd. CH62: Brom 5D **104**
Gray Av. WA11: Hay 5F **31**
Gray Gro. L36: Huy 1H **75**
Graylag Cl. WA7: Beech 2B **124**
Graylands Pl. L4: Walt 4A **36**
Graylands Rd. CH62: Port S 5C **88**
L4: Walt .4A **36**
Graylaw Ind. Est. L9: Ain 5A **22**
Grayling Dr. L12: Crox 2H **37**
Gray's Av. L35: Presc 1F **59**
Grayson M. *CH41: Birke* *2H 69*
(off John St.)
Graysons Rd. WA11: Rainf 1F **17**
Grayson St. L1: Liv 1D **70**
Grayston Av. WA9: Sut L 1H **61**
Gray St. L20: Boot 6A **20**
GREASBY .6B **66**
Greasby Hill Rd.
CH48: W Kir 2C **82**
Greasby Rd. CH44: Wall 3C **50**
CH49: Grea 6A **66**
Great Ashfield WA8: Wid 6B **78**
Gt. Charlotte St. L1: Liv 4F **5** (6D **52**)
(Elliot St.)
L1: Liv 3F **5** (6D **52**)
(Roe St.)
GREAT CROSBY 4G **9**
Gt. Crosshall St. L3: Liv 2D **4** (5C **52**)
Great Delph WA11: Hay 4F **31**
Gt. George Pl. L1: Liv 2E **71**
Gt. George Sq. L1: Liv 1E **71**
Gt. George's Rd. L22: Water 3F **19**
Gt. George's Sq. *L1: Liv* *1E 71*
(off Grenville St. Sth.)
Gt. George St. L1: Liv 1E **71**
Great Hey L30: N'ton 4D **10**
Gt. Homer St. L5: Liv 1E **53**
Gt. Homer St. Shop. Cen.
L5: Liv 2E **53**
Gt. Howard St. L3: Liv 1B **4** (4B **52**)
L5: Liv 1B **52**
GREAT MEOLS 6E **47**
Gt. Mersey St. L5: Kirkd 1D **52**
(not continuous)
Gt. Nelson St. L3: Liv 3D **52**
Gt. Newton St. L3: Liv 3H **5** (5F **53**)
Gt. Orford St. L3: Liv 5H **5** (6F **53**)
Gt. Richmond St. L3: Liv 4E **53**
Great Riding WA7: Nort 6E **115**
GREAT SANKEY 3H **81**
Great Sankey Leisure Cen. 1F **81**
Gt. Western Ho. CH41: Birke 2H **69**
Greaves St. L8: Liv 4F **71**
Grebe Av. WA10: St H 5G **41**
Grecian St. L21: Sea 3H **19**
Grecian Ter. L5: Liv 2F **53**
Gredington St. L8: Liv 5G **71**
Greek St. L3: Liv 3H **5** (5E **53**)
WA7: Run 2D **112**
Green, The CH48: Caldy 4D **82**
CH62: Brom 6D **88**
CH63: Raby 3E **119**
L13: Liv 5G **55**
L23: Crosb .5F **9**
L34: Eccl P 6F **41**
WA7: Halt 4B **114**
Greenacre Cl. L25: Hunts X 3E **93**
Greenacre Dr. CH63: Brom 6C **104**
Greenacre Rd. L25: Hunts X 3E **93**
Greenacres Cl. CH43: Bid 1G **67**
Greenacres Ct. CH43: Bid 1G **67**
Greenall Av. WA5: Penk 5F **81**
Greenall Ct. L34: Presc 1C **58**
Greenall St. WA10: St H 1C **42**
GREEN BANK 3C **42**
Green Bank CH63: Brim 3C **102**
Greenbank L22: Water 3G **19**
Greenbank Av. CH45: New B 6D **32**
L31: Mag .4B **6**
Greenbank Ct. L17: Aig 4C **72**
Greenbank Cres. WA10: St H 2D **42**
Greenbank Dr. CH61: Pens 2D **100**
L10: Faz .4F **23**
L17: Aig .5C **72**
Greenbank La. L17: Aig 5C **72**
Greenbank Rd. CH42: Tran 6E **69**
CH48: W Kir 5B **64**
L18: Moss H 4C **72**
Greenbank Sports Academy 5C **72**
Greenbridge Cl. WA7: Cas 3C **114**
Greenbridge Rd. WA7: Wind H 3D **114**
Greenburn Av. WA11: St H 2G **29**
Green Coppice WA7: Nort 5E **115**
Greencroft Rd. CH44: Wall 4E **51**
Greendale Rd. CH62: Port S 5A **88**
L25: Woolt 5B **74**
Green End La. WA9: St H 5G **43**
Green End Pk. L12: W Der 6E **37**
Greenes Rd. L35: Whis 5D **58**
Greenfield Ct. L18: Aller 2G **91**
Greenfield Dr. L36: Huy 1H **75**
Greenfield Gro. L36: Huy 6H **57**
Greenfield La. CH60: Hesw 3A **100**
L21: Lith .2A **20**
WA6: Frod 6F **123**
Greenfield Rd. L13: Liv 4E **55**
WA10: St H 6B **28**
GREENFIELDS 1G **67**
Greenfields Av. CH62: Brom 6C **104**
Greenfields Cres. CH62: Brom 6C **104**
Greenfield Wlk. L36: Huy 6H **57**
Greenfield Way CH44: Wall 3D **50**
L18: Aller 2F **91**
Greenfinch Cl. L12: Crox 2B **38**
Greenfinch Gro. L26: Halew 2G **93**
Greengables Cl. L8: Liv 4G **71**
Green Gates L36: Huy 1G **57**
Greenham Av. L33: Kirkb 3B **14**
Green Haven CH43: Noct 4H **67**
Greenhaven Cl. L10: Faz 4E **23**
Greenheath Way CH46: Leas 4D **48**
Greenhey Dr. L30: N'ton 1C **20**
Green Heys Dr. L31: Mag 6E **7**
Greenheys Gdns. L8: Liv 3A **72**
Greenheys Rd. CH44: Wall 4D **50**
CH61: Irby 6A **84**
L8: Liv 3H **71**
Greenhill Av. L18: Moss H 4G **73**
Greenhill Cl. L18: Moss H 1F **91**
Greenhill Pl. L36: Huy 6G **57**
Greenhill Rd. L18: Aller, Moss H 6F **73**
L19: Aller 3G **91**
Greenholme Cl. L11: Norr G 2E **37**
Greenhouse Farm Rd. WA7: Pal F . . .1D **124**
Greenhow Av. CH48: W Kir 6B **64**
Green Jones Brow WA5: Burtw 1H **63**
Greenlake Rd. L18: Moss H 1F **91**
Greenlands L36: Huy 6G **57**
Greenland St. L1: Liv 2D **70**
Green La. CH41: Tran 5G **69**
CH45: Wall 2F **49**
(not continuous)
CH62: East 5F **105**
CH63: Beb 6H **87**
L3: Liv 5H **5** (6E **53**)
L13: Liv 2C **54**
L18: Moss H 5F **73**
(not continuous)
L21: Ford .1B **20**
L21: Sea .4A **20**
(not continuous)
L22: Water 1D **18**
L23: Thorn 3B **10**
L31: Mag 5A **6**
WA5: Burtw 6G **45**
WA8: Wid 2C **96**
WA10: Eccl 5E **27**
WA11: Rainf 4G **17**
Green La. Nth. L16: Child 3G **73**
Green Lane Station (Rail) 5H **69**
Green Lawn CH42: Rock F 2H **87**
L36: Huy .3A **58**
Green Lawn Gro. CH42: Rock F 2H **87**
GREEN LEACH 4E **29**
Green Leach Av. WA11: St H 4F **29**
Green Leach Ct. WA11: St H 4F **29**
Green Leach La. WA11: St H 4F **29**
Greenlea Cl. CH63: Beb 5H **87**
Greenleaf St. L8: Liv 2A **72**
Greenleas Cl. CH45: Wall 1H **49**
Greenleas Rd. CH45: Wall 1H **49**
Greenleigh Rd. L18: Moss H 1F **91**
Green Link L31: Mag 5A **6**
Green Mt. CH49: Upton 4E **67**
Greenoaks Farm Ind. Est.
WA8: Wid 2G **97**
Green Oaks Path WA8: Wid 3H **97**
Green Oaks Shop. Cen. WA8: Wid 2F **97**
(Deacon Rd.)
WA8: Wid 3F **97**
(Green Oaks Way)
Green Oaks Way WA8: Wid 3F **97**
Greenock M. WA8: Wid 6C **78**
Greenock St. L3: Liv 1A **4** (4B **52**)
Greenodd Av. L12: W Der 4G **37**
Greenore Dr. L24: Hale 3D **110**
Greenough Av. L35: Rainh 2A **60**
Greenough St. L25: Woolt 1B **92**
Green Pk. L30: N'ton 4F **11**
Green Pk. Dr. L31: Mag 6A **6**
Green Rd. L34: Presc 1C **58**
Greensbridge La. L26: Halew, Tar G . . .2A **94**
L35: Tar G 2B **94**
Greens Health & Fitness
Liverpool 6F **71**
Greenside L6: Liv 4F **53**
Greenside Av. L10: Ain 1C **22**
L15: Wav .1E **73**
Greenside Cl. L33: Kirkb 3C **14**
Green St. L5: Liv 3C **52**
Greens Wlk. *L17: Aig* *6C 72*
(off Aigburth Va.)
Greenville Cl. CH63: Beb 6H **87**
Greenville Dr. L31: Mag 6B **6**
Greenville Rd. CH63: Beb 6H **87**
Greenway CH49: Grea 5C **66**
CH61: Pens 1C **100**
CH62: Brom 2D **104**
CH64: Park 5F **117**
L23: Crosb 4A **10**
L36: Huy .3D **56**
WA5: Gt San 2G **81**
Greenway, The L12: Knott A 3A **56**
Greenway Cl. L36: Huy 3D **56**
Greenway Rd. CH42: Tran 6F **69**
L24: Speke 2A **110**
WA7: Run 4D **112**
WA8: Wid .1F **97**
Greenways Ct. CH62: Brom 1C **120**
Greenwell Rd. WA11: Hay 5E **31**
Greenwich Av. WA8: Wid 5H **79**
Greenwich Ct. L9: Ain 3H **21**
Greenwich Rd. L9: Ain 3H **21**
Greenwood Cl. L34: Presc 1E **59**
Greenwood Ct. WA9: Clock F 3G **61**
Green Wood Dr. WA7: Manor P 1H **115**
Greenwood La. CH44: Wall 2E **51**
Greenwood Rd. CH47: Meols 1E **65**
CH49: Woodc 6E **67**
L18: Aller 2F **91**
Greetham St. L1: Liv 6E **5** (1D **70**)
Gregory Cl. L16: Child 1A **74**
Gregory Way L16: Child 1A **74**
Gregson Ct. CH45: New B 5E **33**
Gregson Rd. L35: Presc 2D **58**
WA8: Wid 2G **97**
Gregson St. L6: Liv 4F **53**
Grenadier Dr. L12: W Der 6A **38**
Grenfell Cl. CH64: Park 6G **117**
Grenfell Ct. CH64: Park 6G **117**
Grenfell Pk. CH64: Park 6G **117**
Grenfell Rd. L13: Liv 5C **36**
Grenfell St. WA8: Wid 3F **97**
Grennan, The CH45: New B 5D **32**
Grennan Ct. *CH45: New B* *5D 32*
(off The Grennan)
Grenville Cres. CH63: Brom 6C **104**

Grenville Dr.—Hall La.

Grenville Dr. CH61: Pens 2C **100**
Grenville Rd. CH42: Tran 6H **69**
CH64: Nest 6A **118**
Grenville St. Sth. L1: Liv 1D **70**
Grenville Way CH42: Tran 6H **69**
Gresford Av. CH43: Pren 1C **86**
CH48: W Kir 6C **64**
L17: Liv 3C **72**
Gresford Cl. L35: Whis 4F **59**
Gresham St. L7: Liv 5C **54**
Gresley Cl. L7: Liv 6A **54**
Gressingham Rd. L18: Moss H 6G **73**
Gretton Rd. L14: Knott A 2D **56**
Greyhound Farm Rd. L24: Speke 2E **109**
Grey Rd. L9: Walt 1F **35**
Greystoke Cl. CH49: Upton 5D **66**
Greystone Cres. L14: Broad G 4A **56**
Greystone Pl. L10: Faz 4D **22**
Greystone Rd. L10: Faz 4C **22**
L14: Broad G 5A **56**
WA5: Penk 5H **81**
Grey St. L8: Liv 3F **71**
Gribble Rd. L10: Faz 4E **23**
Grierson St. L8: Liv 2H **71**
Grieve Rd. L10: Faz 4E **23**
Griffin Av. CH46: More 1C **66**
Griffin Cl. L11: Crox 1G **37**
WA10: Eccl 1F **41**
Griffin M. WA8: Wid 6F **79**
Griffin St. WA9: St H 6A **44**
Griffiths Cl. CH49: Grea 6A **66**
Griffiths Rd. L36: Huy 5G **57**
Griffiths St. L1: Liv 1E **71**
Grimsby Ct. L19: Garst 5F **91**
Grimshaw St. L20: Boot 3B **34**
WA9: Sut L 1G **61**
Grinfield St. L7: Liv 6G **53**
Grinshill Cl. L8: Liv 3G **71**
Grinton Cres. L36: Roby 5F **57**
Grisedale Cl. WA7: Beech 2A **124**
Grisedale Rd. CH62: Brom 5F **105**
Grizedale WA8: Wid 1H **95**
Grizedale Av. WA11: St H 3F **29**
Groarke Dr. WA5: Penk 4F **81**
Groes Rd. L19: Gras 4F **91**
Grogan Sq. L20: Boot 5D **20**
Gronow Pl. *L20: Boot 5E **21***
(off Hughes Dr.)
Grosmont Rd. L32: Kirkb 3B **24**
Grosvenor Av. CH48: W Kir 1B **82**
L23: Crosb 1G **19**
Grosvenor Cl. L30: N'ton 6F **11**
Grosvenor Ct. CH43: O'ton 4D **68**
CH47: Hoy 3B **64**
L15: Wav 2G **73**
L18: Moss H 6C **72**
*L34: Presc 1D **58***
(off Grosvenor Rd.)
Grosvenor Dr. CH45: New B 5D **32**
Grosvenor Pl. CH43: O'ton 4C **68**
Grosvenor Rd. CH43: O'ton 3C **68**
CH45: New B 5D **32**
CH47: Hoy 3B **64**
L4: Walt 3F **35**
L15: Wav 1B **72**
L19: Gras 5E **91**
L31: Mag 3A **12**
L34: Presc 1D **58**
WA8: Wid 5F **79**
WA10: St H 3B **42**
WA11: Hay 4D **30**
Grosvenor St. CH44: Wall 2D **50**
L3: Liv 4D **52**
WA7: Run 2F **113**
Grosvenor Ter. *L8: Liv 5H **71***
(off Wellesley Rd.)
Grove, The CH43: O'ton 6D **68**
CH44: Wall 4E **51**
CH63: Beb 6A **88**
L13: Liv 1D **54**
L28: Stockb V 6E **39**
WA5: Penk 5H **81**
WA10: Windle 6A **28**
Grove Av. CH60: Hesw 4D **100**
Grovedale Dr. CH46: More 6E **49**
Grovedale Rd. L18: Moss H 4D **72**
Grovehurst Av. L14: Knott A 3B **56**
Groveland Av. CH45: Wall 1H **49**
CH47: Hoy 2B **64**
Groveland Rd. CH45: Wall 1H **49**
Grovelands *L7: Liv 1G **71***
(off Falkner St.)
Grove Mead L31: Mag 6E **7**
Grove Pk. L8: Liv 3A **72**
Grove Pk. Av. L12: W Der 5F **37**
Grove Pl. CH47: Hoy 2B **64**
L4: Kirkd 6E **35**
Grove Rd. CH42: Rock F 1H **87**
CH45: Wall 1A **50**
CH47: Hoy 2B **64**
L6: Liv 4B **54**
Groves, The CH43: O'ton 4D **68**
*L7: Liv 1G **71***
(off Grove St.)
L32: Kirkb 4A **24**
Groveside CH48: W Kir 1A **82**
L7: Liv 1G **71**
Grove Sq. CH62: New F 4A **88**
Grove St. CH62: New F 4B **88**
L7: Liv 1G **71**
L15: Wav 1D **72**
L20: Boot 1A **34**
WA7: Run 2D **112**
WA10: St H 2D **42**
Grove Ter. CH47: Hoy 2B **64**
Grove Way L7: Liv 1G **71**
Grovewood Ct. CH43: O'ton 6D **68**
Grovewood Gdns. L35: Whis 4E **59**
Grundy Cl. WA8: Wid 6D **78**
Grundy St. L5: Kirkd 1B **52**
Guardian Ct. CH48: W Kir 2B **82**
Guelph Pl. *L7: Liv 5G **53***
(off Guelph St.)
Guelph St. L7: Liv 5G **53**
Guernsey Rd. L13: Liv 3D **54**
WA8: Wid 6A **80**
Guest St. WA8: Wid 4E **97**
Guffitts Cl. CH47: Meols 6E **47**
Guffitt's Rake CH47: Meols 6E **47**
Guildford Av. L30: N'ton 2F **21**
Guildford St. CH44: Wall 3F **51**
Guildhall Rd. L9: Ain 5G **21**
Guild Hey L34: Know 1F **39**
Guillemot Way L26: Halew 2G **93**
Guilsted Rd. L11: Norr G 3E **37**
Guinea Gap CH44: Wall 4G **51**
Guinea Gap Baths & Recreation Cen. 4G **51**
Guion Rd. L21: Lith 4B **20**
Guion St. L6: Liv 3H **53**
Gulls Way CH60: Hesw 5B **100**
Gunning Av. WA10: Eccl 6H **27**
Gunning Cl. WA10: Eccl 6H **27**
Gurnall St. L4: Walt 6F **35**
Gutticar Rd. WA8: Wid 2H **95**
Guy Cl. CH41: Tran 5G **69**
Gwendoline Cl. CH61: Thing 6E **85**
Gwendoline St. L8: Liv 3F **71**
Gwenfron Rd. L6: Liv 4H **53**
Gwent Cl. L6: Liv 2H **53**
Gwent St. L8: Liv 3G **71**
Gwladys St. L4: Walt 4F **35**
Gwydir St. L8: Liv 4G **71**
Gwydrin Rd. L18: Moss H 4G **73**
Gym, The 5D **4**

H

Hackett Av. L20: Boot 5D **20**
Hackett Pl. L20: Boot 5D **20**
Hackins Hey L2: Liv 3C **4** (5C **52**)
Hackthorpe St. L5: Liv 6E **35**
Hadassah Gro. L17: Aig 5A **72**
Hadden Cl. L35: Rainh 3G **59**
Haddock St. L20: Kirkd 4B **34**
Haddon Av. L9: Walt 5F **21**
Haddon Dr. CH61: Pens 1D **100**
WA8: Wid 5H **77**
Haddon Rd. CH42: Rock F 1A **88**
Haddon Wlk. L12: Crox 2A **38**
Hadfield Av. CH47: Hoy 2C **64**
Hadfield Cl. WA8: Wid 2A **98**
Hadfield Gro. L25: Woolt 6E **75**
Hadleigh Cl. WA5: Gt San 4F **81**
Hadleigh Gro. WA7: Cas 3B **114**
Hadleigh Rd. L32: Kirkb 2B **24**
Hadley Av. CH62: Brom 4C **104**
Haggerston Rd. L4: Walt 3G **35**
Hahnemann Rd. L4: Walt 3E **35**
Haig Av. CH46: More 1D **66**
Haigh Cres. L31: Lyd 3B **6**
Haigh Rd. L22: Water 2G **19**
Haigh St. L3: Liv 3F **53**
(not continuous)
Haig Rd. WA8: Wid 2E **97**
Haileybury Av. L10: Ain 1B **22**
Haileybury Rd. L25: Woolt 3D **92**
Hailsham Rd. L19: Aig 3D **90**
Halby Rd. L9: Ain 5H **21**
Halcombe Rd. L12: W Der 5H **37**
Halcyon Rd. CH41: Birke 5E **69**
Haldane Av. CH41: Birke 2B **68**
Haldane Rd. L4: Walt 3G **35**
HALE 4D **110**
HALE BANK 6H **95**
Halebank Rd. WA8: Hale B 6E **95**
Hale Bank Ter. WA8: Hale B 1G **111**
Hale Ct. WA8: Hale B 1G **111**
Hale Dr. L24: Speke 3F **109**
Halefield St. WA10: St H 1D **42**
(not continuous)
Hale Ga. Rd. WA8: Hale B 3F **111**
Hale Gro. WA5: Gt San 3H **81**
HALE HEATH 3A **110**
Hale M. WA8: Wid 4A **96**
Hale Rd. CH45: Wall 1E **51**
L4: Walt 4E **35**
L24: Speke 2D **108**
WA8: Hale B, Wid 1H **111**
WA8: Wid 4A **96**
Hale Rd. Ind. Est. WA8: Hale B 6H **95**
Hale St. L2: Liv 3D **4** (5C **52**)
Hale Vw. WA7: Run 5C **112**
Hale Vw. Rd. L36: Huy 5A **58**
HALEWOOD 4H **93**
Halewood Caravan Pk. L26: Halew 3C **94**
Halewood Cl. L25: Gate 5D **74**
Halewood Dr. L25: Woolt 1D **92**
(Kings Dr.)
L25: Woolt 1E **93**
(Layton Rd.)
HALEWOOD GREEN 1G **93**
Halewood Leisure Cen. 4A **94**
Halewood Pl. L25: Woolt 6E **75**
Halewood Rd. L25: Gate, Woolt 5D **74**
Halewood Station (Rail) 3H **93**
Halewood Triangle Country Pk. 3F **93**
Halewood Triangle Vis. Cen. 3F **93**
Halewood Way L25: Woolt 1E **93**
Haley Rd. Nth. WA5: Burtw 1G **63**
Haley Rd. Sth. WA5: Burtw 2G **63**
Half Crown St. L5: Kirkd 1C **52**
Halfpenny Cl. L19: Gras 4F **91**
Half-Tide Wharf L3: Liv 2C **70**
Halidon Ct. L20: Boot 1A **34**
Halifax Cres. L23: Thorn 3B **10**
Halkirk Rd. L18: Aller 2G **91**
Halkyn Av. L17: Liv 3B **72**
Halkyn Dr. L5: Liv 2G **53**
Hallam Wlk. *L7: Liv 6A **54***
(off Crosfield Rd.)
Hall Av. WA8: Wid 2G **95**
Hall Dr. CH49: Grea 6A **66**
L32: Kirkb 6A **14**
Hall La. L7: Liv 5G **53**
L9: Ain 4H **21**
L31: Mag 1A **12**
L32: Kirkb 1H **23**

Hall La.—Harrismith Rd.

Hall La. L33: Sim .2B **14**
L34: Presc .2D **58**
L35: Cron, Rainh .1A **78**
L36: Huy .5H **57**
WA5: Burtw .6H **45**
WA8: Cron .2A **78**
WA9: Bold .4B **62**
Hall Nook WA5: Penk .5H **81**
Hall Rd. WA11: Hay .4G **31**
Hall Rd. E. L23: Blun .3D **8**
Hall Road Station (Rail) .3C **8**
Hall Rd. W. L23: Blun .3C **8**
Hallsands Rd. L32: Kirkb .3A **24**
Hallside Cl. L19: Aig .3E **91**
Hall St. WA9: Clock F .4H **61**
WA10: St H .2E **43**
Hall Ter. WA5: Gt San .2G **81**
Halltine Cl. L23: Blun .4C **8**
Hallville Rd. CH44: Wall .4E **51**
L18: Moss H .4E **73**
Hall Wood Av. WA11: Hay .3H **31**
Hallwood Cl. WA7: Run .1F **123**
Hallwood Link Rd. WA7: Pal F .1B **124**
HALLWOOD PARK .1A **124**
Hallwood Pk. Av. WA7: Pal F .1A **124**
Halsall Cl. L23: Crosb .4G **9**
WA7: Brook .2E **125**
Halsall Grn. CH63: Spit .4B **104**
Halsall Rd. L20: Boot .5C **20**
Halsall St. L34: Presc .6D **40**
Halsbury Rd. CH45: Wall .1D **50**
L6: Liv .4A **54**
Halsey Av. L12: W Der .6D **36**
Halsey Cres. L12: W Der .6D **36**
Halsnead Av. L35: Whis .6C **58**
Halsnead Cvn. Est. L35: Whis .6E **59**
Halsnead Cl. L15: Wav .6E **55**
Halstead Rd. CH44: Wall .4E **51**
L9: Walt .5F **21**
Halstead Wlk. *L32: Kirkb .2G 23*
(off Downgreen Cl.)
HALTON .5B **114**
HALTON BROOK .5A **114**
Halton Brook Av. WA7: Run .5H **113**
Halton Brow WA7: Halt .4A **114**
Halton Castle .4B **114**
Halton Ct. WA7: Run .3H **113**
Halton Cres. CH49: Grea .6H **65**
Halton Hey L35: Whis .6D **58**
HALTON LEA .6B **114**
Halton Link Rd. WA7: Pal F .5A **114**
HALTON LODGE .5G **113**
Halton Lodge Av. WA7: Run .6H **113**
Halton Miniature Railway .6D **114**
Halton Rd. CH45: Wall .1C **50**
L31: Lyd .4C **6**
WA5: Gt San .3H **81**
WA7: Run .3F **113**
Halton Stadium .3D **96**
Halton Sta. Rd.
WA7: Sut W .4B **124**
Halton St. WA11: Hay .5G **31**
HALTON VIEW .2G **97**
Halton Vw. Rd. WA8: Wid .2G **97**
HALTON VILLAGE .5B **114**
Halton Wlk. *L25: Gate .3C 74*
(off Hartsbourne Av.)
Halton Wood L32: Kirkb .6F **13**
Hambledon Dr. CH49: Grea .5A **66**
Hamble Dr. WA5: Penk .6H **81**
Hambleton Cl. L11: Crox .1F **37**
WA8: Wid .6A **78**
Hamblett Cres. WA11: St H .5F **29**
Hamer St. WA10: St H .1D **42**
Hamer St. Sth. *WA10: St H .2D 42*
(off Nth. John St.)
Hamil Cl. CH47: Meols .6E **47**
Hamilton Cl. CH64: Park .5F **117**
Hamilton Ct. L23: Blun .5D **8**
Hamilton Ho. L3: Liv .2D **4**
Hamilton La. CH41: Birke .2G **69**
Hamilton Plaza *CH41: Birke .3H 69*
(off Duncan St.)
Hamilton Rd. CH45: New B .5C **32**
L5: Liv .2F **53**
WA10: Windle .5A **28**
Hamilton Sq. CH41: Birke .2H **69**
Hamilton Square Station (Rail) .2H **69**
Hamilton St. CH41: Birke .3G **69**
(not continuous)
Hamlet Ct. L17: Aig .6A **72**
Hamlet Rd. CH45: Wall .1B **50**
Hamlin Cl. WA7: West .1E **123**
Hamlin Rd. L19: Garst .5H **91**
Hammersley Av. WA9: Clock F .4G **61**
Hammersley St. WA9: Clock F .4G **61**
Hammersmith Way WA8: Wid .5H **79**
Hammill Av. WA10: St H .5C **28**
Hammill St. WA10: St H .6B **28**
Hammond Rd. L33: Know I .6E **15**
Hammond St. WA9: St H .3H **43**
Hamnett Rd. L34: Presc .6E **41**
Hampden Gro. CH42: Tran .5G **69**
Hampden Rd. CH42: Tran .5F **69**
Hampden St. L4: Walt .3F **35**
Hampshire Av. L30: N'ton .6C **10**
Hampshire Gdns. WA10: St H .3D **42**
Hampson St. L6: Liv .2A **54**
Hampstead Rd. CH44: Wall .4E **51**
L6: Liv .4A **54**
Hampton Chase CH43: Noct .6H **67**
Hampton Cl. WA8: Wid .6A **80**
Hampton Ct. WA7: Manor P .1E **115**
Hampton Ct. Rd. L12: W Der .2H **55**
Hampton Ct. Way WA8: Wid .5H **79**
Hampton Dr. WA8: Cron .4A **78**
Hampton Pl. WA11: St H .5F **29**
Hampton St. L8: Liv .2F **71**
Hanbury Rd. L4: Walt .5B **36**
Handel Ct. L8: Liv .3H **71**
Handel Rd. L27: N'ley .3E **75**
Handfield Pl. L5: Liv .2G **53**
Handfield Rd. L22: Water .2F **19**
Handfield St. L5: Liv .2G **53**
Handford Av. CH62: East .2F **121**
Handforth La. WA7: Run .1H **123**
Handley Ct. L19: Aig .3D **90**
Handley St. WA7: Run .2D **112**
Hands St. L21: Lith .5B **20**
Hanford Av. L9: Walt .5F **21**
Hankey Dr. L20: Boot .6E **21**
Hankey St. WA7: Run .3D **112**
Hankinson St. L13: Liv .6E **55**
Hankin St. L5: Liv .2D **52**
Hanley Cl. WA8: Wid .2A **96**
Hanley Rd. WA8: Wid .2A **96**
Hanlon Av. *L20: Boot .5D 20*
(off Ainsdale Rd.)
Hanmer Rd. L32: Kirkb .1F **23**
Hannah Cl. CH61: Pens .2C **100**
Hannan Rd. L6: Liv .4A **54**
Hanns Hall Rd. CH64: Nest, Will .6F **119**
Hanover Cl. CH43: Clau .3B **68**
Hanover Ct. WA7: Brook .1D **124**
Hanover St. L1: Liv .6E **5** (6D **52**)
Hansard Ct. WA9: St H .6B **42**
Hansby Dr. L24: Speke .6D **92**
Hanson Pk. CH43: O'ton .4A **68**
Hanson Rd. L9: Ain .6A **22**
Hanson Rd. Bus. Pk. L9: Ain .6A **22**
Hans Rd. L4: Walt .4G **35**
Hanwell St. L6: Liv .1H **53**
Hanworth Cl. L12: Crox .2A **38**
Hapsford Rd. L21: Lith .5B **20**
Hapton St. L5: Liv .1E **53**
Harbern Cl. L12: W Der .1H **55**
Harbord Rd. L22: Water .2E **19**
Harbord St. L7: Liv .6H **53**
Harbord Ter. L22: Water .2E **19**
Harborne Dr. CH63: Spit .3H **103**
Harbour Cl. WA7: Murd .1F **125**
Harbour Dr. L19: Garst .1G **107**
Harbreck Gro. L9: Ain .2B **36**
Harcourt Av. CH44: Wall .4G **51**
Harcourt St. CH41: Birke .2E **69**
L4: Kirkd .6D **34**
Hardie Av. CH46: More .6A **48**
Hardie Cl. WA9: Sut M .4E **61**
Hardie Rd. L36: Huy .4A **58**
Harding Av. CH63: Beb .1H **103**
Harding Cl. L5: Liv .2G **53**
Hardinge Rd. L19: Aller .3G **91**
Hardknott Rd. CH62: Brom .4E **105**
Hard La. WA10: St H .5B **28**
Hardman St. L1: Liv .6H **5** (1E **71**)
Hardshaw Cen.
WA10: St H .2E **43**
Hardshaw St. WA10: St H .2E **43**
Hardwick Rd. WA7: Ast .2H **113**
Hardy St. L1: Liv .2E **71**
(not continuous)
L19: Garst .1H **107**
Harebell Cl. WA8: Wid .5C **78**
Harebell St. L5: Kirkd .6D **34**
Hare Cft. L28: Stockb V .5B **38**
Harefield Grn. L24: Speke .2F **109**
Harefield Rd. L24: Speke .3F **109**
HARESFINCH .4F **29**
Haresfinch Cl. L26: Halew .2A **94**
Haresfinch Rd. WA11: St H .5F **29**
Haresfinch Vw. WA11: St H .5F **29**
Harewell Rd. L11: Norr G .4E **37**
Harewood Cl. L36: Huy .4G **57**
Harewood Rd. CH45: New B .6C **32**
Harewood St. L6: Liv .3G **53**
Harford Cl. WA5: Penk .5H **81**
Hargate Rd. L33: Kirkb .1B **24**
Hargate Wlk. L33: Kirkb .1B **24**
Hargrave Av. CH43: O'ton .6A **68**
Hargrave Cl. CH43: O'ton .6A **68**
Hargrave La. CH64: Will .2H **119**
Hargreaves Ct. WA8: Wid .2H **97**
Hargreaves Ho. *WA8: Wid .2H 97*
(off Hargreaves Ct.)
Hargreaves Rd. L17: Aig .6A **72**
Hargreaves St. WA9: St H .1A **44**
Harkbridge Dr. L7: Liv .1H **71**
Harker St. L3: Liv .1G **5** (4E **53**)
Harland Grn. L24: Speke .2H **109**
Harland Rd. CH42: Tran .5F **69**
Harlech Ct. CH63: Beb .1H **103**
Harlech Gro. WA7: Cas .3B **114**
Harlech Rd. L23: Blun .6E **9**
Harlech St. CH44: Wall .5G **51**
L4: Kirkd, Walt .4E **35**
Harleston Rd. L33: Kirkb .6C **14**
Harleston Wlk. L33: Kirkb .6C **14**
Harley Av. CH63: Hghr B .3E **87**
Harley St. L9: Walt .5G **21**
Harlian Av. CH46: More .2B **66**
Harlow Cl. WA9: St H .6D **42**
Harlow St. L8: Liv .5E **71**
Harlyn Cl. L26: Halew .5G **93**
Harlyn Gdns. WA5: Penk .6F **81**
Harmony Way L13: Liv .6E **55**
Haroldene Gro. L34: Presc .2H **57**
Harold Rd. WA11: Hay .4H **31**
Harper Rd. L9: Walt .1G **35**
Harpers Pond La. L15: Wav .1E **73**
Harper St. L6: Liv .5G **53**
Harps Cft. L30: N'ton .6C **10**
Harptree Cl. L35: Whis .4E **59**
Harradon Rd. L9: Ain .4H **21**
Harrier Dr. L26: Halew .2G **93**
Harringay Av. L18: Moss H .4D **72**
Harrington Av. CH47: Hoy .2C **64**
Harrington Rd. L3: Liv .5E **71**
L21: Lith .2D **20**
L23: Crosb .5F **9**
L36: Huy .3D **56**
Harrington St. L2: Liv .4D **4** (6C **52**)
(not continuous)
Harrington Vw. *CH44: Wall .2F 51*
(off Greenwood La.)
Harris Cl. CH63: Spit .3A **104**
Harris Dr. L20: Boot .5C **20**
L30: Boot .4D **20**
Harris Gdns. WA9: St H .4F **43**
Harrismith Rd. L10: Faz .4D **22**

Harrison Dr. CH45: Wall 6A 32
  L20: Boot 2E 35
  WA11: Hay 5C 30
  WA11: Rainf 1F 17
Harrison Hey L36: Huy 6G 57
Harrison St. WA8: Hale B 5H 95
Harrison's Yd. CH62: East 1F 121
Harrison Way L3: Liv 5E 71
  WA10: St H 1C 42
Harrocks Cl. L30: N'ton 4D 10
Harrock Wood Cl. CH61: Irby 5C 84
Harrogate Cl. CH62: East 3D 120
Harrogate Dr. L5: Liv 2F 53
Harrogate Rd. CH42: Rock F 3A 88
  CH62: East 3D 120
Harrogate Wlk. CH42: Rock F 3A 88
Harron Cl. L32: Kirkb 1G 23
Harrop Rd. WA7: Run 4F 113
Harrops Cft. L30: N'ton 5E 11
Harrowby Cl. L8: Liv 2G 71
Harrowby Rd. CH42: Tran 5E 69
  CH44: Wall 3G 51
  L21: Sea 4H 19
Harrowby Rd. Sth. CH42: Tran 5E 69
Harrowby St. L8: Liv 2G 71
                      (Granby St.)
  L8: Liv 2G 71
                      (Park Way)
Harrow Cl. CH44: Wall 2B 50
  L30: N'ton 6F 11
Harrow Dr. L10: Ain 1B 22
  WA7: Run 3A 114
Harrow Gro. CH62: Brom 5E 105
Harrow Rd. CH44: Wall 2B 50
  L4: Walt 1H 53
Hartdale Rd. L18: Moss H 5E 73
  L23: Thorn 3A 10
Hartford Cl. CH43: O'ton 6B 68
Harthill Av. L18: Moss H 5F 73
Harthill M. CH43: Bid 6G 49
Harthill Rd. L18: Moss H 4G 73
Hartington Av. CH41: Birke 2D 68
Hartington Rd. CH44: Wall 3D 50
  L8: Liv 3A 72
  L12: W Der 1G 55
  L19: Garst 5G 91
  WA10: St H 6A 28
Hartington Ter. L19: Garst 5F 91
              (off St Mary's Rd.)
Hartismere Rd. CH44: Wall 4F 51
Hartland Cl. WA8: Wid 4E 79
Hartland Gdns. WA9: St H 1B 60
Hartland Rd. L11: Norr G 3C 36
Hartley Av. L9: Ain 6H 21
Hartley Cl. L4: Walt 6F 35
Hartley Gro. L33: Kirkb 4B 14
  WA10: St H 5A 42
Hartley Quay L3: Liv 6C 4 (1C 70)
HARTLEY'S VILLAGE 6H 21
Hartley's Village L9: Ain 6H 21
Hartnup St. L5: Liv 1F 53
             (not continuous)
Hartnup Way CH43: Bid 2G 67
Harton Cl. WA8: Wid 6C 78
Hartopp Rd. L25: Gate 3C 74
Hartopp Wlk. L25: Gate 2C 74
             (off Hartopp Rd.)
Hartsbourne Av. L25: Gate 1B 74
             (not continuous)
Hartsbourne Cl. L25: Gate 2B 74
Hartsbourne Wlk. L25: Gate 2C 74
Hart St. L3: Liv 3H 5 (5E 53)
Hartwell St. L21: Lith 5B 20
Hartwood Cl. L32: Kirkb 4B 24
Hartwood Rd. L32: Kirkb 4B 24
Hartwood Sq. L32: Kirkb 4B 24
Harty Rd. WA11: Hay 6C 30
Harvard Cl. WA7: Wind H 3F 115
Harvard Gro. L34: Presc 6E 41
Harvest Cl. CH46: More 6C 48
Harvester Way CH49: Grea 5A 66
  L30: N'ton 5G 11

Harvest La. CH46: More 6B 48
Harvest Way WA9: Clock F 3G 61
Harvey Av. CH49: Grea 6B 66
  WA12: Newt W 2H 45
Harvey Rd. CH45: Wall 1C 50
  CH46: Leas 5E 49
Harwich Gro. L16: Child 1B 74
Harwood Rd. L19: Garst 5H 91
Harworth Rd. WA9: St H 2C 60
Haselbeech Cl. L11: Norr G 2D 36
Haselbeech Cres. L11: Norr G 2D 36
Hasfield Rd. L11: Norr G 3F 37
Haslemere L35: Whis 4F 59
Haslemere Dr. WA5: Penk 5F 81
Haslemere Rd. L25: Gate 3D 74
Haslemere Way L25: Gate 3C 74
Haslingden Cl. L13: Liv 5F 55
Haslington Gro. L26: Halew 5A 94
Hassal Rd. CH42: Rock F 3A 88
Hastie Cl. L27: N'ley 4G 75
Hastings Dr. L36: Huy 1A 76
Hastings Rd. L22: Water 1D 18
Haswell Dr. L28: Stockb V 5C 38
Hatchmere Cl. CH43: O'ton 6B 68
Hatfield Cl. L12: Crox 2B 38
  WA9: St H 6D 42
Hatfield Gdns. L36: Huy 6H 57
Hatfield Rd. L20: Boot 2E 35
Hathaway L31: Mag 2H 11
Hathaway Cl. L25: Gate 3C 74
Hathaway Rd. L25: Gate 3C 74
Hatherley Av. L23: Crosb 1G 19
Hatherley Cl. L8: Liv 2G 71
             (not continuous)
Hatherley St. CH44: Wall 5G 51
  L8: Liv 2G 71
Hathersage Rd. L36: Huy 2G 57
Hatherton Gro. L26: Halew 5A 94
Hatton Av. CH62: East 4E 121
Hatton Cl. CH60: Hesw 4B 100
Hatton Gdn. L3: Liv 2D 4 (5C 52)
Hatton Gdn. Ind. Est. L3: Liv 2E 5
Hatton Hill Rd. L21: Lith 2A 20
Hattons La. L16: Child 3G 73
Hauxwell Gro. WA11: St H 5G 29
Havannah La. WA9: St H 2D 44
Havelock Cl. WA10: St H 2D 42
Havelock Rd. L20: Boot 5C 20
Haven Rd. L10: Faz 3D 22
Haven Wlk. L31: Lyd 3B 6
Havergal St. WA7: Run 4D 112
Haverstock Rd. L6: Liv 4B 54
Haverton Wlk. L12: Crox 2A 38
             (not continuous)
Hawarden Av. CH43: O'ton 3E 69
  CH44: Wall 3E 51
  L17: Liv 3C 72
Hawarden Ct. CH63: Beb 1H 103
Hawarden Gro. L21: Sea 5A 20
Hawdon Ct. L7: Liv 1A 72
Hawes Av. WA11: St H 3G 29
Haweswater Av. WA11: Hay 5C 30
Haweswater Cl. L33: Kirkb 4H 13
  WA7: Beech 2C 124
Haweswater Gro. L31: Mag 5E 7
Hawgreen Rd. L32: Kirkb 1F 23
Hawick Cl. L33: Kirkb 3H 13
Hawke Grn. L35: Tar G 2A 76
Hawke St. L3: Liv 4G 5 (6E 53)
Hawkesworth St. L4: Walt 1G 53
Hawkhurst Cl. L8: Liv 5F 71
Hawkhurst Dr. CH42: Rock F 2A 88
Hawkins Rd. CH64: Nest 6A 118
Hawkins La. L6: Liv 4H 53
Hawks Ct. WA7: Pal F 1A 124
Hawkshead Av. L12: W Der 4G 37
Hawkshead Cl. L31: Mag 5D 6
  WA7: Beech 2C 124
Hawkshead Dr. L21: Lith 3D 20
Hawkshead Rd. CH62: Brom 4E 105
  WA5: Burtw 1G 63
Hawksmoor Cl. L10: Faz 4E 23
Hawksmoor Rd. L10: Faz 5E 23

Hawksmore Cl. CH49: Upton 3B 66
Hawkstone St. L8: Liv 4G 71
             (not continuous)
Hawkstone Wlk. L8: Liv 5G 71
           (off Hawkstone St.)
Hawks Way CH60: Hesw 5C 100
Haworth Dr. L20: Boot 4D 20
Hawthorn Av. WA7: Run 4E 113
  WA8: Wid 1F 97
Hawthorn Cl. WA11: Hay 6C 30
Hawthorn Dr. CH48: W Kir 1E 83
  CH61: Hesw 2D 100
  WA10: Eccl 1H 41
Hawthorne Av. L26: Halew 5G 93
  WA5: Gt San 3H 81
Hawthorne Ct. L21: Lith 3B 20
             (off Sefton Rd.)
Hawthorne Dr. CH64: Will 6B 120
  L33: Kirkb 6B 14
Hawthorne Gro. CH44: Wall 5G 51
Hawthorne Rd. CH42: Tran 6F 69
  L20: Boot 6D 20
  L21: Lith 6D 20
  WA6: Frod 6F 123
  WA9: Sut L 1H 61
Hawthornes, The CH42: Rock F 2A 88
Hawthorn Gro. L7: Liv 6H 53
  L12: W Der 1F 55
Hawthorn La. CH62: Brom 5D 104
Hawthorn Rd. CH64: Park 5F 117
  L34: Presc 1E 59
  L36: Roby 5E 57
Haxted Gdns. L19: Garst 5H 91
Haydn Rd. L14: Knott A 1B 56
HAYDOCK .5E 31
Haydock Cross WA11: Hay 2H 31
Haydock Ind. Est. WA11: Hay 3G 31
Haydock La. WA11: Hay 5E 31
             (not continuous)
Haydock Leisure Cen. 5D 30
Haydock Pk. Rd. L10: Ain 6C 12
Haydock Rd. CH45: Wall 6E 33
Haydock St. WA10: St H 2E 43
  WA12: Newt W 1H 45
Hayes Av. L35: Presc 2D 58
Hayes Cres. WA6: Frod 6G 123
Hayes Dr. L31: Mell 6F 13
Hayes St. WA10: St H 5A 42
Hayfield Cl. L26: Halew 2A 94
Hayfield Pl. CH46: More 1E 67
Hayfield St. L4: Walt 6F 35
Hayfield Way WA9: Clock F 3G 61
Hayles Cl. L25: Gate 3C 74
Hayles Grn. L25: Gate 3C 74
Hayles Gro. L25: Gate 3C 74
Hayling Ho. L19: Aig 4D 90
Haylock Cl. L8: Liv 5F 71
Haymans Cl. L12: W Der 6E 37
Haymans Grn. L12: W Der 6E 37
  L31: Mag 6D 6
Haymans Gro. L12: W Der 6E 37
Haywood Cres. WA7: Wind H 3F 115
Haywood Gdns. WA10: St H 3B 42
Haywood Rd. L28: Stockb V 5D 38
Hazel Av. L32: Kirkb 6G 13
  L35: Whis 4E 59
  WA7: Run 5C 112
Hazel Bus. Pk. WA11: Rainf 5H 17
Hazel Ct. L8: Liv 5G 71
             (off Byles St.)
  L20: Boot 3C 34
Hazeldale Rd. L9: Walt 1G 35
Hazeldene Av. CH45: Wall 2C 50
  CH61: Thing 5F 85
Hazeldene Way CH61: Thing 5F 85
Hazelfield Ct. WA9: Clock F 3G 61
Hazel Gro. CH61: Irby 4B 84
  CH63: Hghr B 1G 103
  L9: Ain 5H 21
  L23: Crosb 6H 9
  WA10: St H 2A 42
Hazelmere Ho. L17: Aig 1B 90
          (off Mossley Hill Dr.)

Hazel M. L31: Mell 6F **13**
Hazel Rd. CH41: Birke 4F **69**
CH47: Hoy 2C **64**
L36: Huy 2H **57**
Hazelslack Rd. L11: Norr G 3E **37**
Hazelwood CH49: Grea 4B **66**
Hazelwood Cl. WA8: Wid 3G **95**
WA9: Sut M 4F **61**
Hazelwood Gro. L26: Halew 1F **93**
Hazlehurst Rd. L4: Walt 6H **35**
Hazleton Rd. L14: Knott A 4G **55**
Headbolt La. L33: Kirkb 5A **14**
Headbourne Cl. L25: Gate 2B **74**
Headbourne Ct. *L25: Gate* *2B* ***74***
(off Headbourne Cl.)
Head Farm Ct. WA12: Newt W 2H **45**
Headingley Cl. L36: Roby 1E **75**
WA9: St H 1G **61**
Headington Rd. CH49: Upton 4B **66**
Headland Cl. CH48: W Kir 3B **82**
Headley Cl. WA10: St H 2D **42**
Head St. L8: Liv 3E **71**
Heald St. L19: Garst 5G **91**
WA12: Newt W 2H **45**
Healy Cl. L27: N'ley 5A **76**
Hearne Rd. WA10: St H 1B **42**
Hearts Health Club
Great Crosby **4F 9**
Wallasey ***3C 50***
(off Wallasey Rd.)
Heartwood Cl. L9: Walt 4G **21**
Heath, The WA7: West 6E **113**
Heathbank Av. CH44: Wall 4C **50**
CH61: Irby 4A **84**
Heathbank Rd. CH42: Tran 6F **69**
Heath Cl. CH48: W Kir 3B **82**
L25: Woolt 4B **74**
L34: Eccl P 6F **41**
Heathcote Cl. L7: Liv 1A **72**
Heathcote Gdns. CH63: Beb 6H **87**
Heathcote Rd. L4: Walt 3F **35**
Heathdale CH63: Beb 2H **103**
Heath Dr. CH49: Upton 4E **67**
CH60: Hesw 4D **100**
WA7: West 6E **113**
Heather Bank CH63: Hghr B 5F **87**
Heather Brae L34: Presc 2A **58**
WA12: Newt W 1H **45**
Heather Brow CH43: Clau 2B **68**
Heather Cl. L4: Walt 5F **35**
L33: Kirkb *5A* ***14***
(off Heathfield Dr.)
WA7: Beech 3A **124**
Heather Ct. *L4: Walt* *5F* ***35***
(off Tetlow St.)
Heatherdale Cl. CH42: Tran 5E **69**
Heatherdale Rd. L18: Moss H 5E **73**
Heather Dene CH62: Brom 2D **104**
Heatherdene Rd. CH48: W Kir 6B **64**
Heatherfield Ct. *CH42: Tran* *5E* ***69***
(off Victoria Flds.)
Heathergreen Ct. L4: Walt 4H **35**
Heatherleigh CH48: Caldy 5D **82**
WA9: St H 1A **60**
Heatherleigh Cl. L9: Walt 4G **21**
Heather Rd. CH60: Hesw 4E **101**
CH63: Hghr B 1F **103**
Heathers Cft. L30: N'ton 6E **11**
Heather Way L23: Thorn 3B **10**
Heathfield CH62: Brom 3D **104**
Heathfield Av. WA9: St H 5C **42**
Heathfield Cl. L21: Lith 5C **20**
Heathfield Dr. L20: Boot 5C **20**
L33: Kirkb 5A **14**
Heathfield Ho. CH61: Thing 5E **85**
Heathfield Pk. WA8: Wid 6B **78**
Heathfield Rd. CH43: O'ton 5E **69**
CH63: Beb 6H **87**
L15: Wav .3E **73**
L22: Water 1E **19**
L31: Mag 2D **12**
Heathfield St. L1: Liv 5G **5** (6E **53**)
(not continuous)
Heathgate Av. L24: Speke 3H **109**
Heath Hey L25: Woolt 4B **74**
Heathland Rd. WA9: Clock F 3G **61**
Heathlands, The CH46: Leas 3C **48**
Heath La. CH64: Will 6C **120**
Heathmoor Rd. CH46: More 6B **48**
Heath Pk. Gro. WA7: Run 5D **112**
Heath Rd. CH63: Beb, Hghr B 6G **87**
L19: Aller 3G **91**
L36: Huy .2E **57**
WA5: Penk 4H **81**
WA7: Run 5E **113**
WA8: Wid 1B **96**
Heath Rd. Cres. WA7: Run 5F **113**
Heath Rd. Sth.
WA7: Run, West 2D **122**
Heathside CH60: Hesw 4A **100**
Heath St. WA9: St H 6B **42**
Heath Vw. L21: Ford 6B **10**
Heathview Cl. WA8: Hale B 6G **95**
Heathview Rd. WA8: Hale B 1G **111**
Heathwaite Cres. L11: Norr G 4E **37**
Heathway CH60: Hesw 6F **101**
Heathwood L12: W Der 2F **55**
Heatley Cl. CH43: Bid 2G **67**
Heaton Cl. L24: Speke 2H **109**
Heatwaves Leisure Cen. **5C 38**
Hebburn Way L12: Crox 2C **38**
Hebden Pde. L11: Norr G 2G **37**
Hebden Rd. L11: Norr G 2F **37**
Hedgebank Cl. L9: Ain 3B **22**
Hedgecote L32: Kirkb 4A **24**
Hedgecroft L23: Thorn 3C **10**
Hedgefield Rd. L25: Gate 4D **74**
Hedge Hey WA7: Cas 4C **114**
Hedgerows, The WA11: Hay 4H **31**
Hedges Cres. L13: Liv 6C **36**
Hedingham Cl. L26: Halew 2A **94**
Hedworth Gdns. WA9: St H 1B **60**
Heigham Gdns. WA9: St H 1C **60**
Helena Rd. WA9: St H 6B **44**
Helena St. CH41: Birke 4G **69**
L7: Liv 6H **53**
L9: Walt 2F **35**
Helen Bank Dr. WA11: Rainf 1F **17**
Helen Ho. *L8: Liv* *2F* ***71***
(off Birley Ct.)
Helford Cl. L35: Whis 1G **59**
Helford Rd. L11: Crox 6H **23**
Heliers Rd. L13: Liv 5F **55**
Helmdon Cl. L11: Norr G 4E **37**
Helmingham Gro. CH41: Tran 5G **69**
Helmsley Rd. L26: Halew 4H **93**
Helsby Av. CH62: East 4F **121**
Helsby Ct. L34: Presc 2D **58**
Helsby Rd. L9: Ain 4H **21**
Helsby St. L7: Liv 6G **53**
WA9: St H 4A **44**
Helston Av. L26: Halew 2H **93**
WA11: St H 4H **29**
Helston Cl. WA5: Penk 4G **81**
WA7: Brook 2D **124**
Helston Grn. L36: Huy 4B **58**
Helston Rd. L11: Crox 6H **23**
Helton Cl. CH43: Noct 6A **68**
Hemans St. L20: Boot 1A **34**
Hemer Ter. L20: Boot 6A **20**
Hemingford St. CH41: Birke 3F **69**
Hemlock Cl. L12: Crox 2H **37**
Hemmingsway L35: Rainh 4G **59**
Hempstead Cl. WA9: St H 6D **42**
Henbury Pl. WA7: Run 1F **123**
Henderson Cl. CH49: Upton 3B **66**
WA5: Gt San 3F **81**
Henderson Dr. WA11: Rainf 1G **17**
Henderson Rd. L36: Huy 4A **58**
WA8: Wid 3D **96**
Hendon Rd. L6: Liv 3B **54**
Hendon Wlk. CH49: Grea 6A **66**
Hengest Cl. L33: Kirkb 3A **14**
Henglers Cl. L6: Liv 4G **53**
Henley Av. L21: Lith 3A **20**
Henley Cl. CH63: Spit 3A **104**
Henley Ct. WA7: Run 3H **113**
WA10: St H 4B **42**
Henley Ho. L19: Aig 4D **90**
Henley Rd. L18: Moss H 4F **73**
Henllan Gdns. WA9: St H 6B **44**
Henlow Av. L32: Kirkb 3B **24**
Hennawood Cl. L6: Liv 2H **53**
Henrietta Gro. L34: Presc 2H **57**
Henry Edward St. L3: Liv 1E **5** (4D **52**)
Henry Hickman Cl. L30: N'ton 5F **11**
Henry St. CH41: Birke 3G **69**
L1: Liv 6E **5** (1D **70**)
L13: Liv 5D **54**
WA8: Wid 2G **97**
WA10: St H 1D **42**
Henthorne Rd. CH62: New F 3B **88**
Henthorne St. CH43: O'ton 4E **69**
Herald Av. L24: Speke 5B **92**
Herald Cl. L11: Crox 2G **37**
Heralds Cl. WA8: Wid 3H **95**
Herbarth Cl. L9: Walt 2F **35**
Herberts La. CH60: Hesw 5D **100**
Herbert St. WA5: Burtw 1G **63**
WA9: St H 6A **44**
Herbert Taylor Cl. L6: Liv 2A **54**
Herculaneum Ct. L8: Liv 6F **71**
Herculaneum Rd. L8: Liv 5E **71**
Hercules Dr. L24: Speke 2B **108**
Herdman Cl. L25: Gate 4D **74**
Hereford Av. CH49: Upton 3C **66**
Hereford Cl. WA10: St H 3D **42**
Hereford Dr. L30: N'ton 2F **21**
Hereford Rd. L15: Wav 3E **73**
L21: Sea .4G **19**
Heriot St. L5: Kirkd 1D **52**
(not continuous)
Hermes Cl. *L30: Boot* *3E* ***21***
(off Atlantic Way)
Hermes Rd. L11: Crox 5F **23**
Hermitage, The *CH60: Hesw* *6D* ***100***
(off School Hill)
Hermitage Gro. L20: Boot 4D **20**
Herm Rd. L5: Liv 2C **52**
Heron Bus. Pk. WA8: Wid 3H **97**
Heron Cl. WA7: Nort 5F **115**
Heron Ct. L26: Halew 2G **93**
Herondale Rd. L18: Moss H 5E **73**
Heron Gro. WA11: Rainf 4H **17**
Heronhall Rd. L9: Faz 1D **36**
Heronpark Way CH63: Spit 3B **104**
Heron Rd. CH47: Meols 2F **65**
CH48: W Kir 2F **65**
Herons Ct. L31: Lyd 3A **6**
Herons Way WA7: Nort 1H **115**
Hero St. L20: Boot 3D **34**
Herrick St. L13: Liv 4D **54**
Herschell St. L5: Liv 1F **53**
Hertford Cl. L26: Halew 4H **93**
Hertford Dr. CH45: Wall 1E **51**
Hertford Rd. L20: Boot 3C **34**
Hertford St. WA9: St H 3H **43**
Hesketh Av. CH42: Rock F 2F **87**
Hesketh Cl. WA5: Penk 5H **81**
Hesketh Ct. WA11: Rainf 5G **17**
Hesketh Dr. CH60: Hesw 4E **101**
L31: Mag .6E **7**
Hesketh Rd. L24: Hale 4E **111**
Hesketh St. L17: Aig 5A **72**
Hesketh Wlk. CH62: Brom 2C **104**
Hesketh Way CH62: Brom 2C **104**
Heskin Cl. L31: Lyd 3C **6**
L32: Kirkb 4A **24**
L35: Rainh 4H **59**
Heskin Rd. L32: Kirkb 4A **24**
Heskin Wlk. L32: Kirkb 4A **24**
Hessle Dr. CH60: Hesw 6D **100**
Hesslewell Ct. CH60: Hesw 4E **101**
HESWALL **5E 101**
Heswall Av. CH63: Hghr B 3E **87**
WA9: Clock F 3F **61**
Heswall Dales Local Nature Reserve
. . . .**4C 100**
Heswall Mt. CH61: Thing 6E **85**

Heswall Point CH60: Hesw 5E **101**
Heswall Rd. L9: Ain 4H **21**
Heswall Station (Rail) 5H **101**
Hever Dr. L26: Halew 2H **93**
Heward Av. WA9: St H 1G **61**
Hewitson Av. L13: Liv 1D **54**
Hewitson Rd. L13: Liv 1D **54**
Hewitt Av. WA10: St H 1A **42**
Hewitt's La. L33: Kirkb 5F **25**
    L34: Know 5F **25**
Hewitts Pl. *L2: Liv* *3D 4*
    (off Vernon St.)
Hexagon, The *L20: Boot* *2C 34*
    (off Strand Shop. Cen.)
Hexham Cl. L30: N'ton 2G **21**
    WA9: St H 1B **60**
Heyburn Rd. L13: Liv 1C **54**
Heydale Rd. L18: Moss H 5E **73**
Heydean Rd. L18: Aller 2G **91**
Heydean Wlk. *L18: Aller* *2G 91*
    (off Heydean Rd.)
Heydon Av. L32: Kirkb 1G **23**
Heydon Cl. L26: Halew 4A **94**
Heyes, The L25: Woolt 1D **92**
Heyes Av. WA11: Hay 6F **31**
    WA11: Rainf 3G **17**
Heyes Dr. CH45: Wall 3G **49**
Heyes Gro. WA11: Rainf 3G **17**
Heyesmere Ct. L17: Aig 4D **90**
Heyes Mt. L35: Rainh 5A **60**
Heyes Rd. WA8: Wid 3A **96**
Heyes St. L5: Liv 2G **53**
Heyeswood WA11: Hay 5F **31**
Heygarth Dr. CH49: Grea 5B **66**
Heygarth Rd. CH62: East 2E **121**
Hey Grn. Rd. L15: Wav 1C **72**
Hey Pk. L36: Huy 5H **57**
Hey Rd. L36: Huy 5H **57**
Heys, The CH62: East 2F **121**
    WA7: Run 4A **114**
Heys Av. CH62: Brom 5D **104**
Heyscroft Rd. L25: Woolt 1D **92**
Heysham Cl. WA7: Murd 1F **125**
Heysham Lawn L27: N'ley 6A **76**
Heysham Rd. L30: N'ton 1G **21**
Heysmoor Hgts. L8: Liv 3H **71**
Heythrop Dr. CH60: Hesw 5G **101**
Heyville Rd. CH63: Hghr B 5G **87**
Heywood Blvd.
    CH61: Thing 5E **85**
Heywood Cl. CH61: Thing 5E **85**
Heywood Ct. L15: Wav 6G **55**
Heywood Gdns. L35: Whis 5E **59**
Heywood Rd. L15: Wav 1G **73**
Heyworth St. L5: Liv 2F **53**
Hibbert St. WA8: Wid 3F **97**
Hickling Gdns. WA9: St H 1C **60**
Hickmans Rd. CH41: Birke 6D **50**
Hickory Gro. L31: Mell 1E **23**
Hickson Av. L31: Mag 4B **6**
Hicks Rd. L21: Sea 4A **20**
    L22: Water 1G **19**
Highacre Rd. CH45: New B 6C **32**
Higham Av. WA10: Eccl 2F **41**
Higham Sq. L5: Liv 3E **53**
High Bank Cl. L43: Noct 4H **67**
Highbank Dr. L19: Garst 5H **91**
Highbanks L31: Lyd 4B **6**
High Beeches L16: Child 6B **56**
High Carrs L36: Roby 5D **56**
Highclere Cres. L36: Huy 2G **57**
Highcroft, The CH63: Beb 6A **88**
Highcroft Av. CH63: Beb 6A **88**
Highcroft Grn. CH63: Beb 6A **88**
Higher Ashton WA8: Wid 6D **78**
HIGHER BEBINGTON 4F **87**
Higher Bebington Rd.
    CH63: Hghr B 5F **87**
Higher End Pk. L30: N'ton 4D **10**
Higher La. L9: Ain, Faz 4A **22**
    (not continuous)
    WA11: Crank, Rainf 1G **17**
Higher Parr St. WA9: St H 2G **43**

Higher Rd. L25: Hunts X 4F **93**
    L26: Halew 5B **94**
    WA8: Hale B 5B **94**
HIGHER RUNCORN 4D **112**
Highfield L33: Kirkb 3B **14**
Highfield Av. WA5: Gt San 4H **81**
Highfield Cl. CH44: Wall 4C **50**
Highfield Cres. CH42: Rock F 2H **87**
    WA8: Wid 1E **97**
Highfield Dr. CH49: Grea 5B **66**
Highfield Gdns. CH43: Clau 3B **68**
Highfield Gro. CH42: Rock F 2H **87**
    L23: Crosb 4H **9**
Highfield Pk. L31: Mag 6E **7**
Highfield Rd. CH42: Rock F 1H **87**
    L9: Walt 1F **35**
    L13: Liv 3E **55**
    L21: Lith 3A **20**
    WA8: Wid 2D **96**
Highfields CH60: Hesw 4D **100**
    L34: Presc 1C **58**
Highfield Sth. CH42: Rock F 4H **87**
Highfield Sq. L13: Liv 3E **55**
Highfield St. L3: Liv 1C **4** (4C **52**)
    (not continuous)
    WA9: St H 5H **43**
Highfield Vw. L13: Liv 3E **55**
Highgate CH60: Hesw 3D **100**
    WA7: Nort 4F **115**
Highgate Ct. *L7: Liv* *6H 53*
    (off Grinfield St.)
Highgate Ct. L31: Lyd 4C **6**
Highgate St. L7: Liv 6G **53**
Highgreen Rd. CH42: Tran 6E **69**
Highgrove Pk. L19: Gras 3E **91**
Highlands Rd. WA7: Run 4D **112**
High Mt. CH60: Hesw 5D **100**
Highoaks Rd. L25: Woolt 2D **92**
Highpark Rd. CH42: Tran 6E **69**
High Pk. St. L8: Liv 4F **71**
Highsted Gro. L33: Kirkb 4A **14**
High St. CH62: Brom 4E **105**
    L2: Liv 3C **4** (5C **52**)
    L15: Wav 1D **72**
    L24: Hale 4D **110**
    L25: Woolt 1C **92**
    L34: Presc 1D **58**
    WA6: Frod 6F **123**
    WA7: Run 3D **112**
Hightor Rd. L25: Woolt 6B **74**
Highville Rd. L16: Child 3H **73**
Highwood Ct. L33: Kirkb 5B **14**
Hignett Av. WA9: St H 3C **44**
Higson Ct. L8: Liv 6G **71**
Hilary Av. L14: Broad G 5A **56**
Hilary Cl. L4: Walt 5A **36**
    L34: Eccl P 6E **41**
    WA5: Gt San 3F **81**
    WA8: Wid 6A **80**
Hilary Dr. CH49: Upton 3E **67**
Hilary Mans. *CH44: Wall* *3C 50*
    (off Colville Rd.)
Hilary Rd. L4: Walt 5A **36**
Hilberry Av. L13: Liv 2C **54**
Hilbre Av. CH44: Wall 3C **50**
    CH60: Hesw 1C **116**
Hilbre Ct. CH48: W Kir 2A **82**
Hilbre Rd. CH48: W Kir 2B **82**
Hilbre St. CH41: Birke 1F **69**
    L3: Liv 4G **5** (6E **53**)
Hilbre Vw. CH48: W Kir 1C **82**
Hilda Rd. L12: W Der 4A **56**
Hildebrand Cl. L4: Walt 5A **36**
Hildebrand Rd. L4: Walt 5A **36**
Hillaby Cl. L8: Liv 3G **71**
Hillam Rd. CH45: Wall 1H **49**
Hillary Cres. L31: Mag 6C **6**
Hillary Dr. L23: Crosb 5A **10**
Hillary Rd. CH62: East 2D **120**
Hillary Wlk. L23: Crosb 5A **10**
Hill Bark Rd. CH48: Frank 1G **83**
Hillbrae Av. WA11: St H 3E **29**
Hillbrook Dr. L9: Ain 2B **36**

Hillburn Dr. CH41: Birke 6A **50**
Hill Crest L20: Boot 3E **35**
Hillcrest L31: Mag 6E **7**
    WA7: Run 4H **113**
Hillcrest Av. L36: Huy 5A **58**
Hillcrest Ct. CH44: Wall 4C **50**
Hillcrest Dr. CH49: Grea 6A **66**
Hillcrest Pde. L36: Huy 5A **58**
Hillcrest Rd. L4: Walt 4B **36**
    L23: Crosb 5A **10**
Hillcroft Rd. CH44: Wall 4E **51**
    L25: Woolt 5B **74**
Hillerton Cl. L12: W Der 3F **37**
Hillfield WA7: Nort 5F **115**
Hillfield Dr. CH61: Hesw 3D **100**
Hillfoot Av. L25: Hunts X 5D **92**
Hillfoot Cl. CH43: Bid 1G **67**
Hillfoot Grn. L25: Woolt 4C **92**
Hillfoot Rd. L25: Hunts X, Woolt ..2B **92**
Hill Gro. CH46: More 2C **66**
Hillhead Rd. L20: Boot 3E **35**
Hillingden Av. L26: Halew 4H **93**
Hillingdon Av. CH61: Hesw 3D **100**
Hillingdon Rd. L15: Wav 3F **73**
Hill Ridge CH43: Noct 4H **67**
Hill Rd. CH43: Clau 2A **68**
Hill School Rd. WA10: St H 5G **41**
Hillside Av. L36: Huy 1E **57**
    WA7: Run 5C **112**
    WA10: St H 5C **28**
    WA12: Newt W 3H **45**
Hillside Cl. CH41: Tran 5G **69**
    L20: Boot 3E **35**
Hillside Ct. CH41: Tran 5G **69**
    L25: Woolt 6C **74**
Hillside Cres. L36: Huy 1E **57**
Hillside Dr. L25: Woolt 6D **74**
Hillside Gro. WA5: Penk 5H **81**
Hillside Rd. CH41: Tran 5G **69**
    CH43: Bid 1H **67**
    CH44: Wall 3A **50**
    CH48: W Kir 1D **82**
    CH60: Hesw 6E **101**
    L18: Moss H 4F **73**
    L36: Huy 2G **57**
Hillside St. L6: Liv 4F **53**
Hillside Vw. CH43: O'ton 6C **68**
Hillsmore Way L5: Liv 1F **53**
Hills Pl. L15: Wav 2E **73**
Hill St. L8: Liv 3D **70**
    (not continuous)
    L34: Presc 1D **58**
    WA7: Run 3E **113**
    WA10: St H 6E **29**
Hill St. Bus. Cen. *L8: Liv* *3D 70*
    (off Hill St.)
Hilltop WA7: Nort 6E **115**
Hilltop La. CH60: Hesw 5F **101**
Hill Top Rd. WA4: Pres H 1H **125**
    WA11: Rainf 1H **27**
Hilltop Rd. L16: Child 2H **73**
Hill Vw. WA8: Wid 4D **78**
Hillview L17: Aig 1C **90**
Hillview Av. CH48: W Kir 6B **64**
Hillview Ct. CH43: Bid 6G **49**
Hill Vw. Dr. CH49: Upton 3E **67**
Hillview Gdns. L25: Woolt 6B **74**
Hillview Rd. CH61: Irby 4A **84**
Hillwood Cl. CH63: Spit 4A **104**
Hilton Cl. CH41: Birke 3E **69**
Hilton Ct. L30: N'ton 5D **10**
Hilton Gro. CH48: W Kir 6A **64**
Hinchley Grn. L31: Mag 6A **6**
Hinckley Rd. WA11: St H 6G **29**
Hindburn Av. L31: Mag 5E **7**
HINDERTON 6D **118**
Hinderton Cl. CH41: Birke 5G **69**
Hinderton Dr. CH48: W Kir 2E **83**
    CH60: Hesw 1D **116**
Hinderton La. CH64: Nest 6C **118**
Hinderton Rd. CH41: Birke 4G **69**
    CH64: Nest 6C **118**
Hindley Beech L31: Mag 5B **6**

Hindley Wlk. L24: Speke 3F 109
Hindlip St. L8: Liv 6G 71
Hind St. CH41: Birke 4G 69
Hinson St. CH41: Birke 3G 69
Hinton Rd. WA7: Run 4E 113
Hinton St. L6: Liv 4A 54
   L21: Lith .5B 20
Hitchens Cl. WA7: Murd 6F 115
HMP Altcourse L9: Faz 5B 22
HMP Kennet L31: Mag 5H 7
HMP Liverpool L9: Walt 6F 21
Hobart Dr. L33: Kirkb 3A 14
Hobart St. St H 5C 42
Hobby Cl. WA7: Pal F 1A 124
Hobhouse Ct. CH43: Clau 3D 68
Hoblyn Rd. CH43: Bid 1A 68
Hockenhall All. L2: Liv 3D 4 (5C 52)
Hockenhull Cl. CH63: Spit 3A 104
Hodder Av. L31: Mag 5E 7
Hodder Cl. L5: Liv 1F 53
Hodder Rd. L5: Liv 1F 53
Hodson Pl. L6: Liv 3G 53
Hogarth Dr. CH43: Noct 6H 67
Hogarth St. L21: Sea 5A 20
   (off Seaforth Va. Nth.)
Hogarth Wlk. L4: Kirkd 5D 34
Hoghton Cl. WA9: St H 5B 44
Hoghton La. WA9: St H 5B 44
   (not continuous)
Hoghton Rd. L24: Hale 3E 111
   WA9: St H 5B 44
Holbeck WA7: Nort 6E 115
Holbeck St. L4: Walt 1H 53
Holborn Ct. WA8: Wid 6D 78
Holborn Hill CH41: Tran 5G 69
Holborn Sq. CH41: Tran 5G 69
Holborn Sq. Ind. Est.
   CH41: Tran 5G 69
Holborn St. L6: Liv 5G 53
Holbrook Cl. WA5: Gt San 3G 81
   WA9: St H 1G 61
Holcombe Cl. CH49: Grea 5B 66
Holden Gro. L22: Water 1E 19
Holden Rd. L22: Water 1D 18
   L35: Presc 3C 58
Holden Rd. E. L22: Water 1E 19
Holden St. L8: Liv 1H 71
Holden Ter. L22: Water 1E 19
Holdsworth Dr. L7: Liv 5H 53
Holford Moss WA7: Nort 2F 115
Holgate L23: Thorn 2B 10
Holgate Pk. L23: Thorn 2B 10
HOLIDAY MOSS 3H 17
Holingsworth Ct. WA10: St H 1F 43
Holkham Cl. WA8: Wid 2D 96
Holkham Gdns. WA9: St H 1B 60
Holland Ct. L30: N'ton 5D 10
Holland Gro. CH60: Hesw 4D 100
Holland Pl. L7: Liv 6H 53
Holland Rd. CH45: Wall 6E 33
   L24: Speke 3G 109
   L26: Halew 5G 93
Holland St. L7: Liv 4B 54
Holland Way L26: Halew 5G 93
Holley Cl. L35: Rainh 4A 60
   (off Rainhill Rd.)
Holliers Cl. L31: Mag 6C 6
Hollies, The L25: Woolt 6A 74
   WA7: Run 5H 113
Hollies Rd. L26: Halew 4H 93
Hollingbourne Pl. L11: Norr G 2E 37
Hollingbourne Rd.
   L11: Norr G 2E 37
Hollinghurst Rd. L33: Kirkb 4B 14
Hollingwood Cl. WN4: Ash M 1H 31
Hollingworth Cl. L9: Walt 2G 35
Hollinhey Cl. L30: N'ton 4G 11
Hollins Cl. L15: Wav 1E 73
Hollins Way WA8: Hale B 6H 95
Hollocombe Rd. L12: W Der 3F 37
Holloway WA7: Run 4D 112
Hollow Cft. L28: Stockb V 4C 38

Holly Av. CH63: Beb 2H 103
Hollybank Ct. CH41: Birke 4F 69
   WA8: Wid 2D 96
Hollybank Grange
   L26: Halew 3H 93
Holly Bank Gro. WA9: St H 1G 43
Hollybank Rd. CH41: Birke 4F 69
   L18: Moss H 4C 72
   WA7: Halt 5B 114
Holly Bank St. WA9: St H 1G 43
Holly Cl. L24: Hale 3D 110
   WA10: Eccl 1H 41
Holly Cres. WA11: Rainf 3G 17
Hollydale Rd. L18: Moss H 4E 73
Holly Farm Ct. WA8: Wid 5D 78
Holly Farm Rd. L19: Garst 5H 91
Hollyfield Rd. L9: Walt 6F 21
Holly Gro. CH42: Tran 5G 69
   L21: Sea .5H 19
   L36: Roby 5D 56
Holly Hey L35: Whis 6D 58
Hollyhurst Cl. L8: Liv 4G 71
Hollymead Cl. L25: Gate 5D 74
Holly M. L23: Crosb 4H 9
Holly Mt. L12: W Der 1E 55
   WA10: St H 3B 42
Holly Pl. CH46: More 2D 66
Holly Rd. L7: Liv 5B 54
   WA5: Penk 4G 81
   WA11: Hay 6B 30
Hollyrood L34: Presc 2A 58
Holly St. L20: Boot 1C 34
   WA5: Penk 5H 81
Hollytree Rd. L25: Woolt 6B 74
Hollywood Bowl
   Liverpool .5D 54
Hollywood Rd. L17: Aig 6C 72
Holman Rd. L19: Garst 5H 91
Holm Cotts. CH43: O'ton 1B 86
Holm Cl. L34: Eccl P 6G 41
Holmefield Av. L19: Aig 2E 91
Holmefield Rd. L19: Aig 3D 90
Holme Rd. WA10: St H 3H 41
Holmes Ct. CH42: Tran 6E 69
Holmes La. L21: Lith 4A 20
   (off Seaforth Rd.)
Holmes St. L8: Liv 2A 72
Holme St. L5: Kirkd 1C 52
Holmesway CH61: Pens 1D 100
Holmfield CH43: O'ton 1B 86
Holmfield Av. WA7: Run 3G 113
Holmfield Gro. L31: Mag 6B 6
   L36: Huy .1H 75
Holm Hey Rd. CH43: Pren 1B 86
Holm Hill CH48: W Kir 2C 82
Holmlands Cres. CH43: O'ton 1A 86
Holmlands Dr. CH43: O'ton 1A 86
Holmlands Way CH43: O'ton 1B 86
Holm La. CH43: O'ton 1B 86
Holmleigh Rd. L25: Gate 3C 74
Holmrook Rd. L11: Norr G 3E 37
Holmside Cl. CH46: More 1D 66
Holmside La. CH43: O'ton 1B 86
Holm Vw. Cl. CH43: O'ton 6C 68
Holmville Rd. CH63: Hghr B 6G 87
Holmway CH63: Hghr B 6H 87
Holmwood Av. CH61: Thing 6G 85
Holmwood Dr. CH61: Thing 6G 85
Holmwood Gdns. CH48: W Kir 2E 83
HOLT 3G 59
Holt Av. CH46: More 1C 66
HOLT GREEN .1G 7
Holt Hill CH41: Birke 5G 69
Holt Hill Ter. CH42: Tran 4G 69
Holt La. L27: N'ley 2G 75
   (not continuous)
   L35: Rainh 3G 59
   WA7: Halt 5B 114
Holt Rd. CH41: Tran 5G 69
   L7: Liv 4A 54
Holt Way L32: Kirkb 1H 23
Holy Cross Cl. L3: Liv 1E 5 (4D 52)

Holyrood L23: Blun 5C 8
Holyrood Av. WA8: Wid 5E 79
Holywell Cl. CH64: Park 6F 117
   WA9: St H 1H 61
Homedove Ho. L23: Blun 5E 9
Home Farm 4H 37
Home Farm Cl. CH49: Woodc 1G 85
Home Farm Rd.
   CH49: Woodc 1F 85
   L34: Know 3E 39
Homer Rd. L34: Know 2E 39
Homerton Rd. L6: Liv 4B 54
Homestall Rd. L11: Norr G 3E 37
Homestead Av. L30: N'ton 6H 11
   WA11: Hay 4G 31
Homestead Cl. L36: Huy 4A 58
Homestead M. CH48: W Kir 1B 82
Honeybourne Dr. L35: Whis 1G 59
Honey Hall Rd. L26: Halew 5G 93
Honeys Grn. Cl. L12: W Der 2H 55
Honeys Grn. La. L12: W Der 2H 55
Honeys Grn. Pct. L12: W Der 2H 55
Honeysuckle Cl. L26: Halew 1F 93
   WA8: Wid 5F 79
Honeysuckle Dr. L9: Walt 2H 35
Honister Av. WA11: St H 3G 29
Honister Gro. WA7: Beech 2A 124
Honister Wlk. L27: N'ley 6A 76
Honiston Av. L35: Rainh 3H 59
Honiton Rd. L17: Aig 2C 90
Honiton Way WA5: Penk 5G 81
Hood Rd. WA8: Wid 2D 96
Hood St. CH44: Wall 4F 51
   L1: Liv 3E 5 (5D 52)
   L20: Boot .6A 20
Hoole Rd. CH49: Woodc 6F 67
Hoose Ct. CH47: Hoy 2C 64
HOOTON 6G 121
Hooton Grn. CH66: Hoot 5G 121
Hooton La. CH66: Hoot 6H 121
Hooton Pk. La. CH65: Hoot 5H 121
Hooton Rd. CH64: Will 6A 120
   CH66: Hoot 6A 120
   L9: Ain 4H 21
Hooton Station (Rail) 6D 120
Hooton Way CH66: Hoot 5F 121
Hooton Works Trad. Est.
   CH66: Hoot 5E 121
Hope Cl. WA10: St H 1C 42
Hope Pk. L16: Child 4H 73
Hope Pl. L1: Liv 6H 5 (1E 71)
Hope St. CH41: Birke 2F 69
   CH45: New B 1D 50
   L1: Liv 6H 5 (1F 71)
   L34: Presc 1D 58
Hope Way L8: Liv 1F 71
Hopfield Rd. CH46: More 1D 66
Hopkins Cl. WA10: St H 1B 42
Hopwood Cres. WA11: Raint 4G 17
Horace St. WA10: St H 1B 42
Horatio St. CH41: Birke 3F 69
Hornbeam Cl. CH46: More 1H 65
   WA7: Wind H 4E 115
   WA11: Hay 6B 30
Hornbeam Rd. L9: Walt 2A 36
   L26: Halew 4A 94
Hornby Av. CH62: Brom 4C 104
   L20: Boot .6B 20
Hornby Blvd. L20: Boot 5B 20
   L21: Lith .5B 20
Hornby Chase L31: Mag 2B 12
Hornby Cl. L9: Walt 1F 35
Hornby Ct. CH62: Brom 4D 104
   L9: Walt 6G 21
Hornby Cres. WA9: Clock F 3H 61
Hornby Flats L21: Lith 5B 20
   (off Linacre Rd.)
Hornby La. L18: Moss H 4H 73
Hornby Pk. L18: Moss H 4H 73
Hornby Pl. L9: Walt 6G 21
Hornby Rd. CH62: Brom 4C 104
   L9: Walt 1F 35

Hornby Rd. L20: Boot 6B 20
  (Knowsley Rd.)
  L20: Boot 1C 34
  (Roby St.)
Hornby St. CH41: Birke 3H 69
  L21: Sea 5A 20
  L23: Crosb 5G 9
Hornby Wlk. L5: Liv 3C 52
Horne St. L6: Liv 3H 53
Hornet Cl. L6: Liv 2G 53
Hornhouse La. L33: Know I 3D 24
Hornsey Rd. L4: Walt 1H 53
Hornspit La. L12: W Der 5E 37
Horringford Rd. L19: Aig 3D 90
Horrocks Av. L19: Garst 5H 91
Horrocks Cl. L36: Huy 3F 57
Horrocks Rd. L36: Huy 4F 57
Horseman Pl. CH44: Wall 5G 51
Horseshoe Dr. L10: Faz 4F 23
Horsey Mere Gdns. WA9: St H 1C 60
Horsfall Gro. L8: Liv 5E 71
Horsfall St. L8: Liv 5E 71
Horton Cl. L33: Kirkb 3A 14
Horwood Av. L35: Rainh 3H 59
Horwood Cl. L12: W Der 3G 37
Hoscar Ct. WA8: Wid 4B 96
Hoscote Pk. CH48: W Kir 1A 82
Hose Side Rd. CH45: Wall 6C 32
Hospital St. WA10: St H 1F 43
Hospital Way WA7: Pal F 6B 114
Hosta Cl. L33: Kirkb 4H 13
Hostock Cl. L35: Whis 5D 58
Hotham St. L3: Liv 3G 5 (5E 53)
Hothfield Rd. CH44: Wall 4F 51
Hotspur St. L20: Boot 5C 34
HOUGH GREEN 2G 95
Hough Grn. Rd. WA8: Wid 1G 95
Hough Green Station (Rail) 2H 95
Houghton Cl. WA8: Wid 1G 97
Houghton Cft. WA8: Cron 4A 78
Houghton La. L1: Liv 4F 5 (6D 52)
Houghton Rd. CH49: Woodc 5F 67
  L24: Hale 3E 111
Houghton's La. WA10: Eccl 5F 27
Houghton St. L1: Liv 4F 5 (6D 52)
  L35: Presc 1D 58
  L35: Rainh 4A 60
  WA8: Wid 1H 97
Houghton Way L1: Liv 4F 5
Hougoumont Av. L22: Water 2G 19
Hougoumont Gro. L22: Water 2G 19
Houlding St. L4: Walt 1G 53
Houlgrave Rd. L5: Liv 2C 52
Houlston Rd. L32: Kirkb 1F 23
Houlston Wlk. L32: Kirkb 1F 23
House La. WA8: Wid 4D 96
Hove, The WA7: Murd 1F 125
  (not continuous)
Hoveton Gdns. WA9: St H 1B 60
Howard Av. CH62: Brom 5E 105
Howard Cl. L21: Ford 1C 20
  (not continuous)
  L31: Mag 6E 7
Howard Ct. CH64: Nest 6B 118
  WA7: Manor P 1E 115
Howard Dr. L19: Gras 4E 91
Howard Florey Av.
  L30: N'ton 5F 11
Howard's La. WA10: Eccl 1E 41
Howards Rd. CH61: Thing 5F 85
Howard St. WA10: St H 5B 42
Howarth Ct. WA7: Run 3F 113
Howbeck Cl. CH43: Clau 3B 68
Howbeck Cl. CH43: O'ton 4B 68
Howbeck Dr. CH43: Clau 3B 68
Howbeck Rd. CH43: O'ton 4B 68
Howden Dr. L36: Huy 4C 56
Howell Dr. CH49: Grea 1B 84
Howell Rd. CH62: New F 4A 88
Howells Cl. L31: Mag 5C 6
Howe St. L20: Boot 4B 34
Howson St. CH42: Rock F 1H 87
HOYLAKE 2B 64

Hoylake Cl. WA7: Murd 1E 125
  (not continuous)
Hoylake Gro. WA9: Clock F 3G 61
Hoylake Rd. CH41: Birke 5H 49
  CH46: More 2H 65
Hoylake Station (Rail) 3B 64
Hoyle Ct. Rd. CH47: Hoy 1B 64
Hoyle Rd. CH47: Hoy 1B 64
Huddleston Cl. CH49: Woodc 6F 67
Hudleston Rd. L15: Wav 6F 55
Hudson Rd. CH46: Leas 3E 49
  L31: Mag 2B 12
Hudswell Cl. L30: N'ton 2H 21
Hughenden Rd. L13: Liv 2D 54
Hughes Av. L35: Presc 3D 58
Hughes Cl. L7: Liv 6A 54
Hughes Dr. L20: Boot 5E 21
Hughes La. CH43: O'ton 6D 68
Hughes St. L6: Liv 3G 53
  (not continuous)
  L19: Garst 6G 91
  WA9: St H 5H 43
Hughestead Gro. L19: Garst 5F 91
Hughson St. L8: Liv 4E 71
Hull Cl. L19: Garst 5F 91
Hulme Cl. CH62: Brom 1C 104
Hulme Wlk. CH62: Brom 1C 104
Hulmewood CH63: Beb 4A 88
Hulton Av. L35: Whis 3F 59
Humber Cl. L4: Kirkd 5E 35
  WA8: Wid 6B 80
Humber Cres. WA9: Sut L 1G 61
Humber St. CH41: Birke 6B 50
Hume Ct. CH47: Meols 1C 64
Humphrey's Cl. WA7: Murd 6F 115
Humphreys Hey L23: Thorn 4B 10
Humphrey St. L20: Boot 5D 20
Huncote Av. WA11: St H 5H 29
Hunslet Rd. L9: Ain 5H 21
Hunstanton Cl. CH49: Upton 2E 67
Hunter Cl. L34: Presc 1E 59
Hunters Ct. WA7: Pal F 1A 124
Hunters La. L15: Wav 2E 73
Hunter St. L3: Liv 2F 5 (5D 52)
  WA9: St H 3G 43
Huntingdon Cl. CH46: More 1H 65
Huntingdon Gro. L31: Lyd 3B 6
Huntley Av. WA9: St H 6G 43
Huntly Rd. WA9: St H 6G 43
Huntly Rd. L6: Liv 4A 54
Hunt Rd. L31: Mag 6C 6
  WA11: Hay 5G 31
Hunts Cross Av. L25: Woolt 6D 74
  (not continuous)
Hunts Cross Shop. Pk.
  L24: Hunts X 5C 92
Hunt's Cross Station (Rail) 4E 93
Huntsman Cl. L25: Hunts X 2F 93
Huntsman Wood L12: W Der 5A 38
Hurlingham Rd. L4: Walt 3A 36
Hurrell Rd. CH41: Birke 6H 49
Hurricane Dr. L24: Speke 2B 108
  (not continuous)
Hursley Rd. L9: Faz 1C 36
Hurst Bank CH42: Rock F 3H 87
Hurstlyn Rd. L18: Aller 2G 91
Hurst Pk. Cl. L36: Huy 3A 58
Hurst Pk. Dr. L36: Huy 3A 58
Hurst Rd. L31: Mag 2C 12
Hurst St. L1: Liv 1D 70
  WA8: Wid 1E 113
Huskisson St. L8: Liv 2F 71
Hutchinson Cl. CH43: Bid 3F 67
Hutchinson St. L6: Liv 4G 53
  WA8: Wid 5D 96
Hutchinson Wlk. L6: Liv 4G 53
Hutfield Rd. L24: Speke 1A 110
Huxley Cl. CH46: More 1H 65
Huxley St. L13: Liv 6B 36
HUYTON 5G 57
Huyton Av. WA10: St H 5C 28

Huyton Brook L36: Huy 1H 75
Huyton Bus. Pk. L36: Huy 6H 57
  (not continuous)
Huyton Chu. Rd. L36: Huy 5G 57
Huyton Gallery 5G 57
Huyton Hall Cres. L36: Huy 5G 57
Huyton Hey Rd. L36: Huy 5G 57
Huyton Ho. Cl. L36: Huy 3D 56
Huyton Ho. Rd. L36: Huy 3D 56
Huyton La. L34: Presc 4G 57
  L36: Huy 4G 57
Huyton Leisure Cen. 6E 57
Huyton Station (Rail) 5G 57
HUYTON-WITH-ROBY 4E 57
Hyacinth Av. L33: Kirkb 4H 13
Hyacinth Cl. WA11: Hay 5H 31
Hyacinth Gro. CH46: More 5E 49
Hyde Cl. WA7: Beech 1H 123
Hyde Rd. L22: Water 2F 19
Hyde's Brow WA11: Rainf 1G 17
Hydrangea Way WA9: Bold 6C 44
Hydro Av. CH48: W Kir 2B 82
Hygeia St. L6: Liv 3G 53
Hylton Av. CH44: Wall 3C 50
Hylton Rd. L19: Aller 3H 91
Hyslop St. L8: Liv 3E 71
Hythe Av. L21: Lith 3C 20
Hythedale Cl. L17: Aig 1A 90

I

Ibbotson's La. L17: Aig 5C 72
Iberis Gdns. WA9: Bold 6C 44
Ibstock Rd. L20: Boot 6B 20
Iffley Cl. CH49: Upton 4B 66
Ikin Cl. CH43: Bid 6G 49
Ilchester Rd. CH41: Birke 6B 50
  CH44: Wall 4F 51
  L16: Child 6A 56
Ilford Av. CH44: Wall 5D 50
  L23: Crosb 4F 9
Ilford St. L3: Liv 2H 5 (5F 53)
Ilfracombe Av. WA9: Sut L 2G 61
Iliad St. L5: Liv 3E 53
Ilkley Wlk. L24: Speke 1F 109
Ilsley Cl. CH49: Upton 5D 66
Imber Rd. L32: Kirkb 3B 24
Imison St. L9: Walt 2F 35
Imison Way L9: Walt 2E 35
Immingham Dr. L19: Garst 5F 91
Imperial Av. CH45: Wall 1E 51
Imperial Chambers L1: Liv 3D 4
Imperial Ct. L2: Liv 3C 4
Imrie St. L4: Walt 3F 35
Ince Av. CH62: East 4E 121
  L4: Walt 5H 35
  L21: Lith 4B 20
  L23: Crosb 4E 9
Ince Cl. CH43: O'ton 5B 68
Ince Gro. CH43: O'ton 5B 68
Ince La. L23: Thorn 1A 10
Incemore Rd. L18: Moss H 2F 91
Ince Rd. L23: Thorn 2A 10
Inchcape Rd. CH45: Wall 2H 49
  L16: Child 6A 56
Index St. L4: Walt 4F 35
Ingestre Cl. CH43: O'ton 6C 68
Ingestre Rd. CH43: O'ton 6C 68
Ingham Rd. WA8: Wid 5D 78
Ingleborough Rd. CH42: Tran 1F 87
Ingleby Rd. CH44: Wall 4C 50
  CH62: New F 3B 88
Ingledene Rd. L18: Moss H 4H 73
Inglefield Ct. CH42: Rock F 2A 88
  (off The Hawthornes)
Ingle Grn. L23: Blun 4C 8
Inglegreen CH60: Hesw 5F 101
Ingleholme Gdns. L34: Eccl P 6G 41
Ingleholme Rd. L19: Aig 2E 91
Inglemere Rd. CH42: Rock F 1G 87
Inglemoss Dr. WA11: Rainf 2H 27
Inglenook Rd. WA5: Penk 5H 81

Ingleside Ct. L23: Blun 6E 9
Ingleton Cl. CH49: Grea 5B 66
Ingleton Dr. WA11: St H 2F 29
Ingleton Grn. L32: Kirkb 3B 24
Ingleton Gro. WA7: Beech 2H 123
Ingleton Rd. L18: Moss H 4D 72
   L32: Kirkb 3B 24
Inglewood L12: Crox 3C 38
Inglewood Av. CH46: More 2B 66
Inglewood Rd. WA11: Rainf 2A 28
Inglis Rd. L9: Ain 4H 21
Ingoe Cl. L32: Kirkb 2F 23
Ingoe La. L32: Kirkb 3F 23
   (not continuous)
Ingrave Rd. L4: Walt 3A 36
Ingrow Rd. L6: Liv 4H 53
Inigo Rd. L13: Liv 3F 55
Inley Cl. CH63: Spit 3A 104
Inley Rd. CH63: Spit 3H 103
Inman Av. WA9: St H 3D 44
Inman Rd. CH49: Upton 3C 66
   L21: Lith 4B 20
Inner Central Rd. L24: Halew 6H 93
Inner Forum L11: Norr G 2C 36
Inner Sth. Rd. L24: Halew 1G 109
Inner W. Rd. L24: Halew 6G 93
Innovation Blvd. L7: Liv 6B 54
Insall Rd. L13: Liv 6F 55
Interchange Motorway Ind. Est.
   L36: Huy 6A 58
International Slavery Mus. 6C 4 (1C 70)
Inveresk Ct. CH43: Noct 3A 68
Invergarry Rd. L11: Crox 1F 37
Invincible Cl. L30: Boot 3E 21
Invincible Way L11: Crox 5G 23
Inwood Rd. L19: Garst 4H 91
Iona Cl. L12: Crox 2C 38
Iona Cres. WA8: Wid 3D 78
Iona Gdns. WA9: St H 6H 43
Ionic Rd. L13: Liv 3E 55
Ionic St. CH42: Rock F 1H 87
   L21: Sea 4H 19
Ipswich Cl. L19: Garst 5F 91
IRBY 5B 84
Irby Av. CH44: Wall 3C 50
IRBY HEATH 5A 84
IRBY HILL .3A 84
Irby Rd. CH61: Hesw, Irby, Pens . . .6B 84
   L4: Walt 5H 35
Irbyside Rd. CH48: Frank 2H 83
Ireland Rd. L24: Hale 4E 111
   WA11: Hay 5E 31
Ireland St. WA8: Wid 2H 97
Irene Av. WA11: St H 4G 29
Irene Rd. L16: Child 3G 73
Ireton St. L4: Walt 3F 35
Iris Av. CH41: Birke 1B 68
Iris Cl. WA8: Wid 1A 96
Iris Gro. L33: Kirkb 4H 13
Iris Pk. Wlk. L31: Mell 6E 13
Irlam Dr. L32: Kirkb 1A 24
Irlam Ho. L20: Boot 2B 34
Irlam Pl. L20: Boot 1B 34
Irlam Rd. L20: Boot 1B 34
Ironbridge Vw. L8: Liv 5F 71
Ironside Rd. L36: Huy 3F 57
Irvine Rd. CH42: Tran 1F 87
Irvine St. L7: Liv 6G 53
Irvine Ter. CH62: New F 3C 88
Irving Cl. L9: Ain 3A 22
Irwell Chambers L3: Liv 3C 4
Irwell Cl. L17: Aig 6C 72
Irwell Ho. L17: Aig 6C 72
Irwell La. L17: Aig 6C 72
   WA7: Run 2F 113
Irwell St. L3: Liv 5C 4 (6C 52)
   WA8: Wid 1E 113
Irwin Rd. WA9: St H 6G 43
Isaac St. L8: Liv 5F 71
Isabel Gro. L13: Liv 6C 36
Island Pl. L19: Garst 5G 91
Island Rd. L19: Garst 5G 91
   L21: Lith 4A 20

Island Rd. Sth. L19: Garst 5H 91
Islands Brow WA11: St H 5F 29
Isleham Cl. L19: Aller 3G 91
Islington L3: Liv 2G 5 (5E 53)
   L23: Crosb 5F 9
Islington Grn. WA8: Wid 5H 79
Islington Sq. L3: Liv 4F 53
Islip Cl. CH61: Irby 4B 84
Ismay Dr. CH44: Wall 2F 51
Ismay Rd. L21: Lith 4B 20
Ismay St. L4: Walt 4F 35
Ivanhoe Rd. L17: Aig 5A 72
   L23: Blun 5E 9
Ivatt Way L7: Liv 6A 54
Iveagh Cl. WA7: Pal F 6C 114
Iver Cl. WA8: Cron 3A 78
Ivernia Rd. L4: Walt 3H 35
Ivor Rd. CH44: Wall 2E 51
Ivory Dr. L33: Kirkb 4A 14
Ivy Av. CH63: Hghr B 6G 87
   L19: Gras 4F 91
   L35: Whis 3G 59
Ivychurch M. WA7: Run 3H 113
Ivy Ct. WA9: St H 1G 43
Ivydale Rd. CH42: Tran 6G 69
   L9: Walt 1H 35
   L18: Moss H 4D 73
Ivy Farm Ct. L24: Hale 4D 110
Ivy Farm Rd. L35: Rainh 3H 59
Ivyhurst Cl. L19: Aig 3D 90
Ivy La. CH46: More 5C 48
Ivy Leigh L13: Liv 2C 54
Ivy St. CH41: Birke 3H 69
   WA7: Run 4E 113

J

Jack McBain Ct. L3: Liv 3C 52
Jack's Brow L34: Know P 2G 39
Jacksfield Way L19: Gras 4D 90
Jackson Cl. CH63: Hghr B 3H 87
   L35: Rainh 6B 60
Jacksons Pond Dr. L25: Gate 2B 74
Jackson St. CH41: Birke 4G 69
   L19: Garst 5G 91
   WA5: Burtw 1G 63
   WA9: St H 2G 43
   WA11: Hay 4C 30
Jackson St. Ind. Est. WA9: St H 3G 43
Jacob Cl. L21: Lith 5B 20
Jacob St. L8: Liv 5F 71
Jacqueline Cl. L36: Roby 5E 57
Jacqueline Dr. L36: Huy 3A 58
Jade Cl. L33: Kirkb 6C 14
Jade Rd. L6: Liv 3H 53
Jamaica St. L1: Liv 2D 70
Jamesbrook Cl. CH41: Birke 1C 68
James Clarke St. L5: Liv 3C 52
James Cl. WA8: Wid 1E 113
James Ct. L25: Woolt 1D 92
James Ct. Apartments L25: Woolt . . .1C 92
James Dixon Ct. L30: N'ton 4D 10
James Dunne Av. L5: Liv 2C 52
James Gro. WA10: St H 3C 42
James Holt Av. L32: Kirkb 2G 23
James Hopkins Way L4: Kirkd 6D 34
James Horrigan Ct. L30: N'ton 6C 10
James Larkin Way L4: Kirkd 6D 34
James Rd. L25: Woolt 1D 92
   WA11: Hay 4H 31
James Simpson Way L30: N'ton 5F 11
   (off Alexander Fleming Av.)
James St. CH43: O'ton 5E 69
   CH44: Wall 5G 51
   L2: Liv 5C 4 (6C 52)
   L19: Garst 5G 91
   WA9: Clock F 4H 61
James Street Station (Rail) . . .5C 4 (6C 52)
Jamieson Av. L23: Crosb 5A 10
Jamieson Rd. L15: Wav 2C 72
Jane St. WA9: St H 6B 44
Janet St. L7: Liv 6H 53

Japonica Gdns. WA9: Bold 6C 44
Jardin M. L17: Aig 5H 71
   (off Parkfield M.)
Jarrett Rd. L33: Kirkb 5C 14
Jarrett Wlk. L33: Kirkb 5C 14
Jarrow Cl. CH43: O'ton 5D 68
Jasmine Cl. CH49: Upton 2B 66
   L5: Liv 3F 53
Jasmine Ct. L36: Huy 2H 57
Jasmine Gdns. WA9: Bold 6C 44
Jasmine Gro. WA8: Wid 3B 96
Jasmine M. L17: Aig 6G 71
Jason St. L5: Liv 1E 53
Jason Wlk. L5: Liv 1E 53
Java Rd. L4: Walt 3B 36
Jay's Cl. WA7: Murd 6G 115
Jean Wlk. L10: Faz 5F 23
Jedburgh Dr. L33: Kirkb 3H 13
Jeffereys Cres. L36: Huy 5D 56
Jefferson Gdns. WA8: Wid 6D 78
Jeffreys Dr. CH49: Grea 4B 66
   L36: Huy 4C 56
Jellicoe Cl. CH48: Caldy 5D 82
Jenkinson St. L3: Liv 4E 53
Jenner Dr. CH46: Leas 5E 49
Jensen Ct. WA7: Ast 2G 113
Jericho Cl. L17: Aig 1B 90
Jericho Ct. L17: Aig 1B 90
Jericho Farm Cl. L17: Aig 2B 90
Jericho Farm Wlk. L17: Aig 2B 90
Jericho La. L17: Aig 2B 90
Jermyn St. L8: Liv 3G 71
Jerningham Rd. L11: Norr G 2B 36
Jersey Av. L21: Lith 2B 20
Jersey Cl. L20: Boot 2C 34
Jersey St. L20: Boot 2C 34
   WA9: Clock F 4G 61
Jesmond St. L15: Wav 1B 72
Jessamine Rd. CH42: Tran 6G 69
Jessop Ho. WA7: Run 2C 112
Jet Cl. L6: Liv 3H 53
Jeudwine Cl. L25: Woolt 2D 92
JJB Fitness Club
   St Helens 4E 43
   Widnes 2G 97
Joan Av. CH46: More 1B 66
   CH49: Grea 5C 66
Jocelyn Cl. CH63: Spit 2A 104
Jockey's Brow La. WA9: St H 5D 42
John Bagot Cl. L5: Liv 2E 53
John Hunter Way L30: N'ton 6F 11
John Lennon Dr. L6: Liv 4H 53
John Lennon Statue 4D 4
   (off Mathew St.)
John Middleton Cl. L24: Hale 3D 110
John Moores Cl. L7: Liv 1G 71
John Moores University
   Aquinas Building 5H 5 (6E 53)
   Blackburne Pl. 1F 71
   (off Blackburne Pl.)
   Brownlow Hill 4H 5 (6E 53)
   Dean Walters Building 1E 71
   Design Academy 4H 5 (6F 53)
   Haigh Building 6H 5
   (off Maryland St.)
   Hope St. 1E 71
   Joe H Makin Drama Cen. 6H 5
   Josephine Butler House 1F 71
   Mount Pleasant Campus 5H 5
   (off Mt. Pleasant)
   Mount St. 6H 5
   Myrtle St. 1F 71
   Rice St. 6H 5 (1F 71)
   Rodney St. 5H 5
   (off Rodney St.)
Johns Av. WA7: Run 5D 112
   WA11: Hay 4G 31
Johnson Av. L35: Presc 3D 58
Johnson Gro. L12: W Der 2A 56
Johnson Rd. CH43: Pren 2B 86
Johnson's La. WA8: Wid 2A 98
Johnson St. L3: Liv 2E 5 (5D 52)
   WA9: St H 1G 43

Johnson Wlk.—Kestrel Gro.

Johnson Wlk. *L7: Liv* *6A* **54**
(off Claughton Cl.)
Johnston Av. L20: Boot 5E **21**
John St. CH41: Birke 2H **69**
L3: Liv 1H **5** (4E **53**)
John Willis Ho. CH42: Rock F 1A **88**
Jones Farm Rd. L25: Gate 4E **75**
Jonson Rd. CH64: Nest 6A **118**
Jonville Rd. L9: Ain 4A **22**
Jordan St. L1: Liv 2D **70**
Joseph Gardner Way L20: Boot 6B **20**
Josephine Butler Sq. *L6: Liv* *4F* **53**
(off Shaw St.)
Joseph Lister Cl. L30: N'ton 6F **11**
Joseph St. WA8: Wid 1G **97**
WA9: St H 6A **44**
Joshua Cl. L5: Liv 1E **53**
Joyce Wlk. L10: Faz 4G **23**
Joy La. WA5: Burtw 3F **63**
WA8: Clock F 5A **62**
WA9: Clock F 5A **62**
Joy Wlk. WA9: Clock F 4A **62**
Jubilee Av. L14: Broad G 6H **55**
WA5: Penk 5G **81**
Jubilee Ct. WA11: Hay 4D **30**
Jubilee Cres. CH62: Port S 6B **88**
WA11: Hay 4H **31**
Jubilee Dr. CH48: W Kir 5A **64**
L7: Liv 5H **53**
L30: N'ton 2G **21**
L35: Whis 5D **58**
Jubilee Rd. L21: Lith 4B **20**
L23: Crosb .6E **9**
Jubilee Way WA8: Wid 2C **96**
Jubits La. WA8: Bold H 1E **79**
WA9: Sut M 1E **79**
Juddfield St. WA11: Hay 5C **30**
Judges Dr. L6: Liv 3A **54**
Judges Way L6: Liv 3A **54**
Jugglers Yd. *L3: Liv* *1D* **4**
(off Marlborough St.)
Julian Way WA8: Wid 5D **78**
Julie Gro. L12: W Der 2B **56**
Juliet Av. CH63: Hghr B 4G **87**
July Rd. L6: Liv 2B **54**
July St. L20: Boot 6C **20**
Junction La. WA9: St H 6A **44**
WA12: Newt W 3H **45**
Junction One Retail Pk.
CH44: Wall 4H **49**
Junction Rd. WA11: Rainf 1E **17**
June Av. CH62: Brom 5E **105**
June Rd. L6: Liv 2B **54**
June St. L20: Boot 1C **34**
Juniper Cl. CH49: Grea 1A **84**
L28: Stockb V 6D **38**
WA10: St H 1B **42**
Juniper Gdns. L23: Thorn 3B **10**
Juniper Gro. WA7: Murd 6F **115**
Juniper St. L20: Kirkd 5C **34**
Justan Rd. L35: Rainh 2H **59**
Juvenal Pl. L3: Liv 3E **53**
Juvenal St. L3: Liv 4D **52**

K

Kaber Ct. L8: Liv 5E **71**
Kaigh Av. L23: Crosb 4F **9**
Kale Cl. CH48: W Kir 2B **82**
Kale Gro. L33: Kirkb 4C **14**
Kara Cl. L20: Boot 2C **34**
Karan Way L31: Mell 6F **13**
Karen Cl. WA5: Burtw 1H **63**
Karonga Rd. L10: Faz 4C **22**
Karonga Way L10: Faz 4D **22**
Karslake Rd. CH44: Wall 4F **51**
L18: Moss H 4D **72**
Katherine Wlk. L10: Faz 4G **23**
Kearsley Cl. L4: Walt 6E **35**
Kearsley St. L4: Walt 6E **35**
Keats Av. L35: Whis 4F **59**
Keats Cl. WA8: Wid 3D **96**
Keats Gro. L36: Huy 6H **57**
Keats St. L20: Boot 6B **20**
Keble Dr. CH45: Wall 1H **49**
L10: Ain 6A **12**
Keble Rd. L20: Boot 4C **34**
Keble St. L6: Liv 4G **53**
WA8: Wid .4F **97**
KECKWICK .1H **115**
Keckwick La. WA4: Dares 1H **115**
Kedleston St. L8: Liv 5G **71**
Keegan Dr. CH44: Wall 5G **51**
Keele Cl. CH43: Bid 5G **49**
Keel Hey CH64: Will 6B **120**
Keel Wharf L3: Liv 2C **70**
Keenan Dr. L20: Boot 6E **21**
Keene Ct. L30: N'ton 5D **10**
Keepers La. CH63: Store 6D **86**
Keepers Wlk. WA7: Cas 3B **114**
Keighley Av. CH45: Wall 2A **50**
Keightley St. CH41: Birke 2F **69**
Keir Hardie Av. L20: Boot 6E **21**
Keith Av. L4: Walt 4F **35**
WA5: Gt San 3F **81**
Keith Dr. CH63: East 2C **120**
Keithley Wlk. L24: Speke 1G **109**
Kelbrook Cl. WA9: St H 1H **61**
Kelburn Gro. L12: W Der 5H **37**
Kelby Cl. L8: Liv 5G **71**
Kelda Ct. L25: Gate 3C **74**
Kelday Cl. L33: Kirkb 1A **24**
Kelk Beck Cl. L31: Mag 5E **7**
Kellet's Pl. CH42: Rock F 6H **69**
Kellett Rd. CH46: Leas 4F **49**
Kellitt Rd. L15: Wav 2C **72**
Kelly Dr. L20: Boot 6E **21**
Kelly St. L34: Presc 1E **59**
Kelmscott Dr. CH44: Wall 3A **50**
Kelsall Av. CH62: East 4E **121**
WA9: Sut M 3F **61**
Kelsall Cl. CH43: O'ton 6B **68**
CH62: East 4E **121**
WA8: Wid .2B **96**
Kelsey Cl. WA10: St H 1B **42**
Kelso Cl. L33: Kirkb 3H **13**
Kelso Rd. L6: Liv 4A **54**
Kelton Gro. L17: Aig 1C **90**
Kelvin Ct. CH44: Wall 6G **51**
Kelvin Gro. L8: Liv 3G **71**
Kelvington Cl. L10: Faz 4D **22**
Kelvin Pk. CH41: Birke 6G **51**
Kelvin Rd. CH41: Tran 5G **69**
CH44: Wall 6G **51**
Kelvinside CH44: Wall 6F **51**
L23: Crosb 1H **19**
Kemberton Dr. WA8: Wid 4E **79**
Kemble St. L6: Liv 4H **53**
L34: Presc 1D **58**
Kemlyn Rd. L4: Walt 6G **35**
Kempsell Wlk. L26: Halew 4A **94**
Kempsell Way L26: Halew 4A **94**
Kempsey Gro. WA9: St H 6C **42**
Kempson Ter. CH63: Beb 1H **103**
Kempston St. L3: Liv 2H **5** (5E **53**)
Kempton Cl. L36: Roby 6E **57**
WA7: Run 1G **123**
Kempton Pk. Rd. L10: Ain 6C **12**
Kempton Rd. CH62: New F 3B **88**
L15: Wav .1B **72**
Kemsley Rd. L14: Knott A 4B **56**
Kenbury Cl. L33: Kirkb 5C **14**
Kenbury Rd. L33: Kirkb 5C **14**
Kendal Cl. CH63: Beb 5H **87**
Kendal Dr. L31: Mag 5C **6**
L35: Rainh 4G **59**
WA11: St H 3F **29**
Kendal Pk. L12: W Der 1H **55**
Kendal Ri. WA7: Beech 2H **123**
Kendal Rd. CH44: Wall 5C **50**
L16: Child 2A **74**
L33: Kirkb 5H **13**
WA8: Wid .2A **96**
Kendal St. CH41: Birke 3G **69**
Kendricks Fold L35: Rainh 4H **59**
Kenilworth Av. WA7: Run 5F **113**
Kenilworth Cl. L25: Woolt 6A **74**
Kenilworth Dr. CH61: Pens 6C **84**
Kenilworth Gdns. CH49: Upton 3C **66**
Kenilworth Rd. CH44: Wall 4F **51**
L16: Child 2H **73**
L23: Blun 5E **9**
Kenilworth St. L20: Boot 2B **34**
Kenilworth Way L25: Woolt 6A **74**
Kenley Av. WA8: Cron 4B **78**
Kenmare Rd. L15: Wav 3C **72**
Kenmay Wlk. L33: Kirkb 6C **14**
Ken M. L20: Boot 5C **20**
Kenmore Rd. CH43: Pren 2A **86**
Kennelwood Av. L33: Kirkb 6B **14**
Kennessee Cl. L31: Mag 1C **12**
KENNESSE GREEN 1B **12**
Kenneth Cl. L30: N'ton 6E **11**
Kenneth Rd. WA8: Wid 4A **96**
Kennet Rd. CH63: Hghr B 6F **87**
WA11: Hay 5E **31**
Kennford Rd. L11: Crox 6G **23**
Kennington Pk. WA8: Wid 6C **78**
KENSINGTON 5H **53**
Kensington L7: Liv 5G **53**
Kensington Av. WA9: St H 6G **43**
Kensington Cl. WA8: Wid 5H **79**
Kensington Dr. L34: Presc 2A **58**
Kensington Gdns. CH46: More 1C **66**
Kensington St. L6: Liv 5G **53**
Kent Av. L21: Lith 3C **20**
Kent Cl. CH63: Brom 5B **104**
L20: Boot *1D* **34**
(off Brookhill Rd.)
Kent Gro. WA7: Run 4F **113**
Kentmere Av. WA11: St H 3G **29**
Kentmere Dr. CH61: Pens 2D **100**
Kent M. *CH43: O'ton* *5D* **68**
(off Kent St.)
Kenton Cl. L25: Gate 2D **74**
Kenton Rd. L26: Halew 4H **93**
Kent Rd. CH44: Wall 4C **50**
WA9: St H 5G **43**
Kents Bank L12: W Der 4G **37**
Kent St. CH43: O'ton 5D **68**
L1: Liv 6F **5** (1D **70**)
WA8: Wid .2F **97**
Kentwell Gro. L12: W Der 6H **37**
Kenview Cl. WA8: Hale B 1G **111**
Kenway WA11: Rainf 3G **17**
Kenwood Cl. L27: N'ley 4H **75**
Kenwright Cres. WA9: St H 5G **43**
Kenwyn Rd. CH45: Wall 2D **50**
Kenyon Av. WA5: Penk 4G **81**
Kenyon Cl. L33: Kirkb 3B **14**
Kenyon Ct. *L8: Liv* *3F* **71**
(off Park Rd.)
Kenyon Rd. L15: Wav 4E **73**
Kenyons La. L31: Lyd, Mag 3C **6**
Kenyons La. Nth. WA11: Hay 3H **31**
Kenyons La. Sth. WA11: Hay 4H **31**
Kenyons Lodge L31: Mag 4D **6**
Kenyons Pl. L31: Lyd 4C **6**
Kenyon Ter. CH43: O'ton 4D **68**
Kepler St. L21: Sea 5A **20**
Keppel St. L20: Boot 4B **34**
Kerman Cl. L12: W Der 4F **37**
Kerr Cl. L33: Kirkb 3A **14**
Kerr Gro. WA9: St H 2A **44**
Kerris Cl. L17: Aig 1A **90**
Kerrysdale Cl. WA9: St H 6H **43**
Kersey Rd. L32: Kirkb 3B **24**
Kersey Wlk. L32: Kirkb 3B **24**
Kershaw Av. L23: Crosb 6H **9**
Kershaw St. WA8: Wid 2B **96**
Kerswell Cl. WA9: St H 1H **61**
Keston Wlk. L26: Halew 5H **93**
Kestrel Av. CH49: Upton 3B **66**
Kestrel Cl. CH49: Upton 3B **66**
WA11: St H 5F **29**
Kestrel Ct. L23: Blun 6C **8**
Kestrel Dene L10: Faz 5E **23**
Kestrel Gro. L26: Halew 2F **93**

Kestrel Rd. CH46: More 6A **48**
CH60: Hesw 6G **101**
Kestrels Way WA7: Pal F 1B **124**
Keswick Av. CH63: East 2C **120**
Keswick Cl. L31: Mag 5D **6**
WA8: Wid 2A **96**
Keswick Dr. L21: Lith 3D **20**
Keswick Gdns. CH63: Brom 2C **120**
Keswick Pl. CH43: Bid 6H **49**
Keswick Rd. CH45: Wall 6A **32**
L18: Aller .1G **91**
WA10: St H 6C **28**
Keswick Vs. *L16: Child* *1C 74*
(off Buttermere Rd.)
Keswick Way L16: Child 1C **74**
Ketterer Ct. WA9: St H 3G **43**
Kevelioc Cl. CH63: Spit 2H **103**
Kew Gdns. Cl. WA8: Wid 5H **79**
Kew St. L5: Liv 2D **52**
Keybank Rd. L12: W Der 5E **37**
Keys Ct. L1: Liv 5E **5** (6D **52**)
Kiddman St. L9: Walt 2F **35**
Kidstone Cl. WA9: St H 6H **43**
Kilbuck La. WA11: Hay 3H **31**
Kilburn Av. CH62: East 1E **121**
Kilburn Gro. WA9: St H 6C **42**
Kilburn St. L21: Lith 5B **20**
Kildale Cl. L31: Mag 5B **6**
Kildare Cl. L24: Hale 3D **110**
Kildonan Rd. L17: Aig 1B **90**
Kilgraston Gdns. L17: Aig 2D **90**
Killarney Gro. CH44: Wall 4C **50**
Killarney Rd. L13: Liv 4F **55**
Killester Rd. L25: Gate 5D **74**
Killington Way L4: Kirkd 5E **35**
Kilmalcolm Cl. CH43: O'ton 5B **68**
Kilmore Cl. L9: Ain 3A **22**
Kilmory Av. L25: Woolt 1E **93**
Kiln Cl. WA10: Eccl 6A **28**
Kilncroft WA7: Brook 2D **124**
(not continuous)
Kiln Hey L12: W Der 2G **55**
Kiln La. WA10: Eccl, Windle 6H **27**
Kiln Rd. CH49: Woodc 6E **67**
Kilnyard Rd. L23: Crosb 5F **9**
Kilrea Cl. L11: Norr G 5D **36**
Kilrea Lodge L11: Norr G 5D **36**
Kilrea Rd. L11: Norr G 5C **36**
Kilsail Rd. L32: Kirkb 4C **24**
Kilsby Dr. WA8: Wid 1A **98**
Kilshaw Rd. WA5: Burtw 1H **63**
Kilshaw St. L6: Liv 3G **53**
(not continuous)
Kimberley Av. L23: Crosb 6F **9**
WA9: St H 6C **42**
Kimberley Cl. L8: Liv 2G **71**
Kimberley Dr. L23: Crosb 6F **9**
Kimberley Rd. CH45: Wall 1D **50**
Kindale Rd. CH43: Pren 2A **86**
Kinder St. L6: Liv 4F **53**
King Arthurs Wlk. WA7: Cas 5C **114**
King Av. L20: Boot 5E **21**
King Edward Cl. L35: Rainh 3H **59**
King Edward Dr. CH62: Port S 5B **88**
King Edward Ind. Est. L3: Liv 2A **4**
King Edward Pde. L3: Liv 2B **4**
King Edward Rd. L35: Rainh 3H **59**
WA10: St H 5B **28**
King Edward St. L3: Liv 2B **4** (5B **52**)
Kingfield Rd. L9: Walt 6F **21**
Kingfisher Bus. Pk. L20: Boot 4C **20**
WA8: Wid 3H **97**
Kingfisher Cl. L27: N'ley 4H **75**
L33: Kirkb 3A **14**
WA7: Beech 2B **124**
Kingfisher Ct. L31: Lyd 3A **6**
Kingfisher Dr. WA11: St H 5F **29**
Kingfisher Gro. L12: W Der 4B **38**
Kingfisher Ho. CH41: Birke 3A **70**
L13: Liv 6E **55**
Kingfisher Way CH49: Upton 3B **66**
King George V Sports Complex **3H 57**
King George Dr. CH44: Wall 1F **51**
King George Rd. WA11: Hay 4H **31**
King George's Dr. CH62: Port S 5B **88**
King George's Way CH43: Bid 2A **68**
Kingham Cl. CH46: Leas 4F **49**
L25: Woolt 1E **93**
WA8: Wid 2H **97**
Kingham M. L25: Woolt 1E **93**
King James Ct. WA7: Pal F 1A **124**
Kinglake Rd. CH44: Wall 3F **51**
Kinglake St. L7: Liv 6H **53**
Kinglass Rd. CH63: Spit 2B **104**
King's Av. CH47: Meols 1D **64**
Kingsbrook Way CH63: Hghr B 3F **87**
King's Brow CH63: Hghr B 5F **87**
Kingsbury CH48: W Kir 6D **64**
Kingsbury Rd. WA8: Wid 5H **79**
King's Bus. Pk. L34: Presc 2A **58**
Kings Cl. CH63: Hghr B 4F **87**
L17: Aig 1A **90**
Kings Ct. CH43: O'ton 5D **68**
CH47: Hoy 2A **64**
CH63: Hghr B 4F **87**
L21: Sea 4H **19**
WA7: Manor P 1F **115**
Kingscourt Rd. L12: W Der 2G **55**
Kingsdale Av. CH42: Tran 1F **87**
L35: Rainh 4B **60**
Kingsdale Rd. L18: Moss H 4E **73**
WA5: Gt San 1H **81**
Kings Dock St. L1: Liv 2D **70**
Kingsdown Rd. L11: Norr G 4E **37**
Kingsdown St. CH41: Tran 5G **69**
Kings Dr. CH48: Caldy 4C **82**
CH61: Pens 6D **84**
L25: Gate .5E **75**
L25: Woolt 1D **92**
L34: Presc 2A **58**
King's Dr. Nth. CH48: W Kir 2D **82**
Kingsfield Rd. L31: Mag 2A **12**
King's Gap, The CH47: Hoy 2A **64**
Kingshead Cl. WA7: Cas 3C **114**
Kingsheath Av. L14: Knott A 3A **56**
Kingsland Cres. L11: Norr G 2C **36**
Kingsland Rd. CH42: Tran 5E **69**
L11: Norr G 2C **36**
King's La. CH63: Hghr B 4F **87**
Kingsley Av. CH62: East 4E **121**
Kingsley Cl. CH61: Pens 2E **101**
L31: Lyd 2B **6**
Kingsley Cres. WA7: Run 4E **113**
Kingsley Rd. CH44: Wall 4D **50**
L8: Liv 2H **71**
WA7: Run 4E **113**
WA10: St H 5B **28**
Kingsley St. CH41: Birke 1C **68**
Kings Lynn Dr. L19: Garst 5F **91**
Kingsmead Dr. L25: Hunts X 4D **92**
Kingsmead Gro. CH43: O'ton 4B **68**
Kings Mdw. WA7: Nort 5E **115**
Kingsmead Rd. CH43: O'ton 4B **68**
CH46: More 5D **48**
Kingsmead Rd. Nth. CH43: O'ton 4B **68**
Kingsmead Rd. Sth. CH43: O'ton 4B **68**
Kings Mt. CH43: O'ton 5D **68**
Kingsnorth L35: Whis 5F **59**
Kings Pde. CH45: Wall, New B 5A **32**
L3: Liv 2C **70**
Kings Pk. L21: Sea 4H **19**
Kings Rd. CH63: Hghr B 3F **87**
L20: Boot .3C **34**
L23: Crosb .5F **9**
WA10: St H 3A **42**
Kings Sq. CH41: Birke 3H **69**
Kings Ter. L20: Boot 4C **34**
Kingsthorne Pk. L25: Hunts X 5E **93**
Kingsthorne Rd. L25: Hunts X 5E **93**
Kingston Av. WA5: Gt San 3G **81**
Kingston Cl. CH46: More 1C **66**
L12: W Der 2A **56**
WA7: Run 3A **114**
King St. CH42: Rock F 2A **88**
CH44: Wall 2F **51**
L19: Garst 1G **107**
King St. L22: Water 2F **19**
WA7: Run 2E **113**
WA10: St H 2D **42**
Kingsville Rd. CH63: Hghr B 6G **87**
Kings Wlk. CH42: Rock F 2A **88**
CH48: W Kir 1C **82**
KINGSWAY **3E 97**
Kingsway CH45: Wall 1C **50**
CH60: Hesw 1G **117**
CH63: Hghr B 4F **87**
L3: Liv 4C **52**
L22: Water 1G **19**
L35: Presc 2D **58**
L36: Huy, Roby 3F **57**
WA8: Wid 4E **97**
WA11: St H 3E **29**
Kingsway Ct. L3: Liv 3D **52**
Kingsway Ho. WA8: Wid 4E **97**
Kingsway Leisure Cen. **4E 97**
Kingsway Pde. L36: Huy 3E **57**
Kingsway Pk. L3: Liv 3D **52**
Kingsway Tunnel App. CH44: Wall 4A **50**
Kingswell Cl. L7: Liv 1H **71**
Kings Wharf CH41: Birke 6H **51**
Kingswood L36: Huy 4F **57**
Kingswood Av. L9: Ain 4H **21**
L22: Water 1H **19**
Kingswood Blvd. CH63: Hghr B 3G **87**
Kingswood Ct. L33: Kirkb 5B **14**
Kingswood Dr. L23: Crosb 6F **9**
Kingswood Rd. CH44: Wall 2E **51**
Kington Rd. CH48: W Kir 6A **64**
Kinley Gdns. *L20: Boot* *6E 21*
(off Wheatley Av.)
Kinloch Cl. L26: Halew 4A **94**
Kinloss Rd. CH49: Grea 6A **66**
Kinmel Cl. CH41: Birke 2F **69**
L4: Walt 5B **36**
Kinmel St. L8: Liv 4G **71**
WA9: St H 5G **43**
Kinnaird Rd. CH45: Wall 1C **50**
Kinnaird St. L8: Liv 6G **71**
Kinnerton Cl. CH46: More 1H **65**
Kinnock Pk. WA5: Burtw 1G **63**
Kinross Rd. CH45: Wall 1H **49**
L10: Faz 4D **22**
L22: Water 3G **19**
Kinsale Dr. L19: Aller 4H **91**
Kinsman Ho. L19: Gras 4D **90**
Kintore Cl. CH63: East 3C **120**
Kintore Dr. WA5: Gt San 3F **81**
Kintore Rd. L19: Gras 4F **91**
Kipling Av. CH42: Rock F 2H **87**
L36: Huy 6A **58**
Kipling Cres. WA8: Wid 3D **96**
Kipling Gro. WA9: Sut M 4E **61**
Kipling St. L20: Boot 6A **20**
Kirby Cl. CH48: W Kir 2C **82**
Kirby Mt. CH48: W Kir 3C **82**
Kirby Pk. CH48: W Kir 2C **82**
Kirby Pk. Mans. CH48: W Kir 2B **82**
Kirby Rd. L20: Boot 5D **20**
Kirkbride Cl. L27: N'ley 5A **76**
Kirkbride Lawn *L27: N'ley* *5A 76*
(off Kirkbride Cl.)
Kirkbride Wlk. *L27: N'ley* *5A 76*
(off Kirkbride Cl.)
Kirkburn Cl. L8: Liv 5F **71**
KIRKBY **1A 24**
Kirkby Bank Rd. L33: Know I 1D **24**
Kirkby Gallery **1A 24**
Kirkby Leisure Cen. **2A 24**
KIRKBY PARK **6G 13**
Kirkby Row L32: Kirkb 6G **13**
Kirkby Station (Rail) **6G 13**
Kirkcaldy Av. WA5: Gt San 3F **81**
Kirk Cotts. CH45: Wall 6D **32**
KIRKDALE **5E 35**
Kirkdale Rd. L5: Kirkd 1D **52**
Kirkdale Station (Rail) **4D 34**
Kirkdale Va. L4: Walt 6E **35**
Kirket Cl. CH63: Beb 1A **104**
Kirket La. CH63: Beb 1H **103**

Kirkfield Gro. CH42: Rock F 2A **88**
Kirkham Rd. WA8: Wid 1G **97**
Kirkland Av. CH42: Tran 1F **87**
Kirkland Cl. L9: Walt 4F **21**
Kirkland Rd. CH45: New B 5E **33**
Kirklands, The CH48: W Kir 2C **82**
Kirkland St. WA10: St H 1D **42**
Kirkmaiden Rd. L19: Aller 3F **91**
Kirkman Fold L35: Rainh 4H **59**
Kirkmore Rd. L18: Moss H 1E **91**
Kirkmount CH49: Upton 4E **67**
Kirk Rd. L21: Lith 5C **20**
Kirkside Cl. L12: Crox 2H **37**
Kirkstead Wlk. L31: Mell 6F **13**
Kirkstone Av. WA11: St H 3G **29**
Kirkstone Cres. WA7: Beech 3C **124**
Kirkstone Rd. Nth. L21: Lith 2C **20**
Kirkstone Rd. Sth. L21: Lith 3D **20**
Kirkstone Rd. W. L21: Ford, Lith 1B **20**
Kirk St. L5: Liv 1E **53**
Kirkwall Dr. WA5: Penk 6H **81**
Kirkway CH45: Wall 6D **32**
CH49: Grea 5C **66**
CH49: Upton 4D **66**
CH63: Hghr B 4F **87**
Kitchener Dr. L9: Walt 5F **21**
Kitchener St. WA10: St H 1B **42**
Kitchen St. L1: Liv 2D **70**
Kitling Rd. L34: Know 6D **24**
Kiverley Cl. L18: Aller 6A **74**
Knap, The CH60: Hesw 1E **117**
Knaresborough Rd. CH44: Wall 3B **50**
Knebworth Cl. L12: W Der 6H **37**
Knighton Rd. L4: Walt 4B **36**
Knight Rd. WA5: Burtw 1H **63**
Knightsbridge Cl. WA8: Wid 5H **79**
Knightsbridge Ct. CH43: Noct 6H **67**
Knightsbridge Wlk. L33: Kirkb 3H **13**
Knights Grange WA9: St H 1G **43**
Knight St. L1: Liv 6G **5** (1E **71**)
Knightsway L22: Water 1H **19**
Knightswood Ct. L18: Aller 3G **91**
Knoclaid Rd. L13: Liv 6C **36**
Knoll, The CH43: O'ton 6C **68**
WA7: Pal F 6B **114**
KNOTTY ASH .4G **55**
Knotty M. L25: Woolt 6E **75**
Knowe, The CH64: Will 6A **120**
Knowle Cl. L12: W Der 3G **37**
Knowles, The L23: Blun 6D **8**
Knowles Ho. Av. WA10: Eccl 2F **41**
Knowles St. CH41: Birke 2E **69**
WA8: Wid 1G **97**
Knowl Hey Rd. L26: Halew 5A **94**
KNOWSLEY 2F **39**
Knowsley Bus. Pk. L34: Know 5C **24**
(not continuous)
Knowsley Cl. CH42: Rock F 2A **88**
Knowsley Ct. CH42: Rock F 2A **88**
Knowsley Ent. Workshops
L33: Know I 2D **24**
Knowsley Expressway L35: Tar G 3D **76**
WA8: Wid 3D **76**
Knowsley Hgts. L36: Huy 2G **57**
Knowsley Ind. Pk. L33: Know I 4D **24**
(Faraday Rd.)
L33: Know I 1E **25**
(Manor Complex)
Knowsley La. L34: Know P 5E **39**
L34: Know, Know P 4E **39**
L36: Huy 5E **39**
Knowsley Outdoor Educational Cen.
. . . . .3H **39**
KNOWSLEY PARK 6H **25**
Knowsley Pk. La. L34: Presc 6C **40**
Knowsley Rd. CH42: Rock F 2A **88**
CH45: Wall 1C **50**
L19: Gras 5E **91**
L20: Boot 6A **20**
L35: Rainh 5B **60**
WA10: St H 2A **42**
Knowsley Safari Pk. 3D **40**
Knowsley St. L4: Walt 3F **35**
Knowsley Vw. WA11: Rainf 1E **17**
Knox Cl. CH62: Port S 5B **88**
Knox St. CH41: Birke 3H **69**
Knutsford Cl. WA10: Eccl 3H **41**
Knutsford Grn. CH46: More 6D **48**
Knutsford Rd. CH46: More 6C **48**
Knutsford Wlk. L31: Lyd 3C **6**
Kramar Wlk. L33: Kirkb 1B **24**
Kremlin Dr. L13: Liv 2D **54**
Kylemore Av. L18: Moss H 6D **72**
Kylemore Cl. CH61: Pens 2C **100**
Kylemore Ct. L26: Halew 4G **93**
Kylemore Dr. CH61: Pens 2C **100**
Kylemore Rd. CH43: O'ton 5C **68**
Kylemore Way CH61: Pens 2C **100**
L26: Halew 4F **93**
Kynance Rd. L11: Crox 6H **23**

L

Laburnham Ter. *L19: Garst* *5G* ***91***
(off Chapel Rd.)
Laburnum Av. L36: Huy 1G **75**
WA11: St H 4H **29**
Laburnum Ct. *L8: Liv* *5G* ***71***
(off Weller Way)
Laburnum Cres. L32: Kirkb 6H **13**
Laburnum Gro. CH61: Irby 5B **84**
L15: Wav *1E* ***73***
(off Chestnut Gro.)
L31: Mag .6E **7**
WA7: Run 5F **113**
Laburnum La. WA5: Gt San 3E **81**
Laburnum Pl. L20: Boot 2D **34**
Laburnum Rd. CH43: O'ton 5E **69**
CH45: New B 6D **32**
L7: Liv 4B **54**
Lace St. L3: Liv 2E **5** (5D **52**)
Lacey Ct. WA8: Wid 4F **97**
Lacey Rd. L34: Presc 2E **59**
Lacey St. WA8: Wid 4E **97**
WA10: St H 5B **42**
Laddock Cl. L4: Walt 6A **36**
Ladies' Wlk. WA9: Bold 4C **62**
Ladybower Cl. CH49: Upton 3C **66**
L7: Liv 1H **71**
Lady Chapel Cl. L1: Liv 2E **71**
Lady Chapel Sq. *L1: Liv* *2E* ***71***
(off Lady Chapel Cl.)
Ladyewood Rd. CH44: Wall 4E **51**
Ladyfield CH43: Bid 2G **67**
Ladyfields L12: W Der 2F **55**
Lady Lever Art Gallery 5B **88**
Lady Mountford Ho. L18: Moss H 6D **72**
Ladypool L24: Hale 4C **110**
Lady Richeld Cl. WA7: Nort 2F **115**
Ladysmith Rd. L10: Faz 4D **22**
LAFFAK 4H **29**
Laffak Rd. WA11: St H 4G **29**
LA Fitness
Mossley Hill 6E **73**
Lagan Ho. CH46: Leas 3C **48**
Laggan St. L7: Liv 5H **53**
Lagrange Arc. WA10: St H 2E **43**
Laird Cl. CH41: Birke 1B **68**
Lairdside Technical Pk. CH41: Tran . . .5H **69**
Lairds Pl. L3: Liv 3D **52**
Laird St. CH41: Birke 1B **68**
Laithwaite Cl. WA9: Sut M 4F **61**
Lake Ent. Pk. CH62: Brom 3E **105**
Lakeland Cl. L1: Liv 6E **5** (1D **70**)
Lakemoor Cl. WA9: St H 6H **43**
Lakenheath Rd. L26: Halew 5G **93**
Lake Pl. CH47: Hoy 2B **64**
Lake Rd. CH47: Hoy 2B **64**
L15: Wav 2E **73**
Lakeside Cl. WA8: Wid 4G **95**
Lakeside Ct. CH45: New B 5E **33**
WA11: Rainf 3G **17**
Lakeside Gdns. WA11: Rainf 3G **17**
Lakeside Lawn L27: N'ley 5A **76**
Lakeside Vw. L22: Water 3F **19**
Lakes Rd. L9: Ain 4B **22**
Lake St. L4: Walt 6G **35**
Lake Vw. L35: Whis 1E **77**
Lake Vw. Ct. L4: Walt 3G **35**
Laleston Cl. WA8: Wid 3C **96**
Lambert St. L3: Liv 2H **5** (5E **53**)
(Kempston St.)
L3: Liv 2H **5**
(Lambert Way)
Lambert Way L3: Liv 2H **5** (5E **53**)
Lambeth Rd. L4: Kirkd 6D **34**
L5: Kirkd .6D **34**
Lambeth Wlk. L4: Kirkd 6D **34**
(not continuous)
Lambourn Av. WA8: Cron 4A **78**
Lambourne Gro. WA9: St H 2C **44**
Lambourne Rd. L4: Walt 4B **36**
Lambrigg Row L5: Liv 6F **35**
Lambshear La. L31: Lyd 3B **6**
Lambsickle Cl. WA7: West 1D **122**
Lambsickle La. WA7: Run, West 1D **122**
Lambton Rd. L17: Aig 6H **71**
Lamerton Cl. WA5: Penk 5F **81**
Lammermoor Rd. L18: Moss H 1E **91**
Lampeter Rd. L6: Liv 1A **54**
Lamport Cl. WA8: Wid 6A **80**
Lamport St. L8: Liv 3E **71**
Lanark Cl. WA10: St H 3D **42**
Lanark Gdns. WA8: Wid 6C **78**
Lancashire Gdns. WA10: St H 3D **42**
Lancaster Av. CH45: Wall 2D **50**
L17: Liv 3B **72**
L23: Crosb 6F **9**
L35: Whis 4D **58**
WA7: Run 5C **112**
WA8: Wid 1G **95**
Lancaster Cl. CH62: Port S 5B **88**
L5: Kirkd .1D **52**
L31: Mag .6E **7**
WA12: Newt W 1H **45**
Lancaster Rd. L36: Huy 3A **58**
WA8: Wid 6E **79**
Lancaster St. L5: Kirkd 1D **52**
L9: Walt .2F **35**
Lancaster Wlk. *L36: Huy* *3A* ***58***
(off Lincoln Cl.)
Lance Cl. L5: Liv 2F **53**
Lancefield Rd. L9: Walt 6F **21**
Lance Gro. L15: Wav 2E **73**
Lance La. L15: Wav 2E **73**
Lancelots Hey L3: Liv 3B **4**
Lancelyn Ct. CH63: Spit 2A **104**
Lancelyn Pct. *CH63: Spit* *2A* ***104***
(off Spital Rd.)
Lancelyn Ter. CH63: Beb 1H **103**
Lancer Ct. WA7: Ast 2A **114**
Lancer Way L12: W Der 6A **38**
Lancing Cl. L25: Hunts X, Woolt 2F **93**
(not continuous)
Lancing Dr. L10: Ain 1B **22**
Lancing Rd. L25: Hunts X 2F **93**
Lancing Way L25: Hunts X 2F **93**
Lancots La. WA9: St H 5H **43**
Land End L31: Mag 6H **7**
Lander Rd. L21: Lith 5B **20**
Landford Av. L9: Faz 1C **36**
Landford Pl. L9: Faz 1C **36**
LANDICAN 3G **85**
Landican Cemetery & Crematorium
CH49: Woodc 2F **85**
Landican La. CH49: Woodc 3G **85**
CH63: Store 5A **86**
Landican Rd. CH49: Woodc 4F **85**
Landor Cl. L5: Liv 2C **52**
Landsdowne Ho. CH41: Birke 3H **69**
Landseer Rd. L5: Liv 2F **53**
LANE ENDS 5E **95**
Lanfranc Cl. L16: Child 1A **74**
Lanfranc Way L16: Child 1A **74**
Langbar L35: Whis 5E **59**
Langdale Av. CH61: Pens 1D **100**
Langdale Cl. L32: Kirkb 2B **24**
WA8: Wid 3A **96**

Langdale Dr. L31: Mag .5D **6**
Langdale Gro. WA11: St H .4F **29**
Langdale Rd. CH45: Wall .6B **32**
CH63: Beb .1G **103**
L15: Wav .3C **72**
WA7: Run .4F **113**
Langdale St. L20: Boot .2D **34**
Langdale Way WA6: Frod .6G **123**
Langfield Gro. CH62: Brom .2D **120**
Langford L24: Hale .3C **110**
Langford Rd. L19: Aig .3D **90**
Langham Av. L17: Aig .6A **72**
Langham Ct. L4: Walt .5F **35**
Langham St. L4: Walt .5F **35**
Langham St. Ind. Est. *L4: Walt .5F **35***
(off Langham St.)
Langholme Hgts. L11: Norr G .1D **36**
Langland Cl. L4: Walt .5B **36**
Lang La. CH48: W Kir .6B **64**
Lang La. Sth. CH48: W Kir .6C **64**
Langley Beck WA8: Wid .5G **79**
Langley Cl. CH63: Spit .3A **104**
L12: Crox .2B **38**
Langley Cl. Shop. Cen. L12: Crox .2B **38**
Langley Rd. CH63: Spit .3A **104**
Langley St. L8: Liv .3E **71**
Langrove St. L5: Liv .2E **53**
Langsdale St. L3: Liv .1H **5** (4E **53**)
(not continuous)
Langshaw Lea L27: N'ley .5H **75**
Langstone Av. CH49: Grea .6A **66**
Langton Cl. WA8: Wid .6H **77**
Langton Rd. L15: Wav .2B **72**
L33: Kirkb .4B **14**
Langtree St. WA9: St H .2G **43**
Langtry Cl. L4: Kirkd .5D **34**
Langtry Rd. L4: Kirkd .5D **34**
Lansbury Av. WA9: St H .3A **44**
Lansbury Rd. L36: Huy .5A **58**
Lansdown L12: W Der .1E **55**
Lansdowne Cl. CH41: Birke .1C **68**
Lansdowne Ct. CH43: Bid .1B **68**
WA9: St H .6H **43**
Lansdowne Pl. CH43: Bid .1B **68**
L5: Liv .1F **53**
Lansdowne Rd. CH41: Birke .1B **68**
CH43: Bid .1B **68**
CH45: Wall .5B **32**
Lansdowne Way L36: Huy .5G **57**
Lanville Rd. L19: Aig .2F **91**
Lanyork Rd. L3: Liv .1B **4** (4B **52**)
Lapford Cres. L33: Kirkb .5C **14**
Lapford Wlk. L33: Kirkb .5C **14**
Lapwing Cl. L12: W Der .4A **38**
Lapwing Ct. L26: Halew .2G **93**
Lapwing Gro. WA7: Pal F .1C **124**
Lapwing La. WA4: Moore .4H **99**
Lapwing Ri. CH60: Hesw .1D **116**
Lapworth Cl. CH46: More .1H **65**
Lapworth St. L5: Kirkd .1D **52**
Larch Av. WA5: Penk .4G **81**
WA8: Wid .1F **97**
Larch Cl. L19: Gras .4D **90**
WA7: Run .6G **113**
Larch Ct. *L8: Liv .5G **71***
(off Weller Way)
Larchdale Gro. L9: Walt .1H **35**
Larchfield Rd. L23: Thorn .4A **10**
Larch Gro. CH43: Bid .1A **68**
L15: Wav .6E **55**
Larch Lea L6: Liv .2H **53**
(not continuous)
Larch Rd. CH42: Tran .4E **69**
L36: Roby .5E **57**
WA7: Run .6G **113**
WA11: Hay .4G **31**
Larchtree M. L12: W Der .5A **38**
Larchwood Av. L31: Mag .2A **12**
Larchwood Cl. CH61: Pens .2D **100**
L25: Gate .4D **74**
Larchwood Dr. CH63: Hghr B .4H **87**
Larcombe Av. CH49: Upton .4D **66**
Larkfield Cl. L17: Aig .1A **90**
Larkfield Ct. WA11: St H .3D **28**
Larkfield Gro. L17: Aig .1A **90**
Larkfield Rd. L17: Aig .1A **90**
Larkfield Vw. L15: Wav .1C **72**
Larkhill Av. CH49: Upton .2E **67**
Larkhill Cl. L13: Liv .6C **36**
Larkhill La. L13: Liv .6C **36**
Larkhill Pl. L13: Liv .6D **36**
Larkhill Vw. L13: Liv .6D **36**
Larkhill Way CH49: Upton .2E **67**
Larkin Cl. CH62: New F .4A **88**
Lark La. L17: Aig .6A **72**
Larkspur Cl. WA7: Beech .3B **124**
Larkspur Ct. L31: Mell .6E **13**
Larksway CH60: Hesw .5F **101**
Lark Way L17: Aig .6A **72**
Larne Ct. WA8: Wid .1C **96**
Larton Farm Cl. CH48: W Kir .1E **83**
Larton Rd. CH48: W Kir .6E **65**
Lartonwood CH48: W Kir .6E **65**
Lascelles Rd. L19: Aller .4H **91**
Lascelles St. WA9: St H .2G **43**
Latchford Rd. CH60: Hesw .1F **117**
Late Moffatt Rd. W. *L9: Ain .4H **21***
(off Moffatt Rd.)
Latham Av. WA7: Run .4F **113**
Latham St. L5: Kirkd .1D **52**
(not continuous)
Latham Way CH63: Spit .3B **104**
Lathbury La. L17: Aig .4C **72**
Lathom Av. CH44: Wall .3D **50**
*L21: Sea .5H **19***
(off Chatham Cl.)
Lathom Cl. *L21: Sea .5H **19***
(off Lathom Av.)
L36: Huy .1A **58**
Lathom Ct. L36: Huy .1A **58**
Lathom Dr. L31: Mag .4D **6**
WA11: Rainf .2F **17**
Lathom Rd. L20: Boot .6C **20**
L36: Huy .4G **57**
Lathum Cl. L35: Presc .2E **59**
Latimer Cl. WA8: Wid .5G **79**
Latimer St. L5: Liv .1D **52**
Latrigg Rd. L17: Aig .1C **90**
Lauder Cl. L33: Kirkb .3H **13**
Launceston Cl. WA7: Brook .1E **125**
Launceston Dr. WA5: Penk .6G **81**
Laund, The CH45: Wall .2B **50**
Laurel Av. CH60: Hesw .4D **100**
CH63: Hghr B .1G **103**
Laurel Bank WA8: Wid .6E **79**
Laurelbanks CH60: Hesw .4C **100**
Laurel Ct. *L7: Liv .4B **54***
(off Laurel Rd.)
WA11: St H .4F **29**
Laurel Dr. CH64: Will .6B **120**
WA10: Eccl .1F **41**
Laurel Gro. L8: Liv .3A **72**
L22: Water .1F **19**
L36: Huy .1G **75**
Laurelhurst Av. CH61: Pens .1E **101**
Laurel Rd. CH42: Tran .5F **69**
L7: Liv .4B **54**
L34: Presc .1E **59**
WA10: St H .3B **42**
WA11: Hay .6B **30**
Laurels, The CH46: Leas .4C **48**
Laurel Way WA10: St H .3B **42**
Laurence Deacon Ct. CH41: Birke .2F **69**
Lauren Cl. L36: Huy .5B **58**
Lauriston Rd. L4: Walt .4A **36**
Laurus Cl. L27: N'ley .4H **75**
Lavan Cl. L6: Liv .4G **53**
Lavan St. L6: Liv .4G **53**
Lavender Cl. WA7: Run .4G **113**
Lavender Cres. L34: Presc .1E **59**
Lavender Gdns. L23: Thorn .4B **10**
WA9: Bold .6C **44**
Lavender Way L9: Walt .1H **35**
Lavrock Bank L8: Liv .5E **71**
Lawford Dr. CH60: Hesw .5G **101**
Lawler Gro. L34: Presc .6E **41**
Lawler St. L21: Lith .5B **20**
Lawnhurst Gro. L17: Aig .3C **90**
Lawns, The CH43: Bid .2H **67**
Lawns Av. CH63: Raby M .1B **120**
Lawnside Cl. CH42: Rock F .2H **87**
Lawrence Cl. L19: Gras .4E **91**
Lawrence Ct. CH42: Rock F .3A **88**
Lawrence Gro. L15: Wav .2C **72**
Lawrence Rd. L15: Wav .2B **72**
WA10: Windle .5A **28**
Lawrenson St. WA10: St H .2C **42**
Lawson Ho. WA7: Run .5E **113**
Lawson Rd. WA7: Run .5E **113**
Lawson Wlk. L12: Crox .2H **37**
Lawton Av. L20: Boot .6E **21**
Lawton Rd. L22: Water .1F **19**
L35: Rainh .5B **60**
L36: Roby .6E **57**
Lawton St. L1: Liv .5G **5** (6E **53**)
Laxey St. L8: Liv .3E **71**
Laxton Rd. L25: Hunts X .4E **93**
Layford Rd. L36: Huy .2F **57**
Layton Av. CH43: Pren .1B **86**
Layton Cl. L25: Woolt .1E **93**
Layton Rd. L25: Woolt .1E **93**
Lazonby Cl. CH43: Bid .1G **67**
Leach Cft. L28: Stockb V .6C **38**
Leach La. WA9: Sut L .3H **61**
Leach St. WA10: St H .1D **42**
Leach Vw. WA11: St H .4F **29**
Leach Way CH61: Irby .5A **84**
Lea Cl. CH43: Noct .5A **68**
Lea Cross Gro. WA8: Wid .6A **78**
Leadenhall Cl. L5: Liv .1F **53**
Leafield Cl. CH61: Irby .5D **84**
Leafield Rd. L25: Hunts X .5D **92**
Leagate L10: Faz .3D **22**
LEA GREEN .2D **60**
Lea Grn. Bus. Pk. WA9: St H .3D **60**
Lea Grn. Ind. Est. WA9: St H .4E **61**
Lea Grn. Rd. WA9: St H .4D **60**
Lea Green Station (Rail) .2F **61**
Leamington Cl. WA5: Gt San .1H **81**
Leamington Rd. L11: Norr G .3B **36**
Leamoore Cl. L12: Knott A .1B **56**
Leander Rd. CH45: Wall .2C **50**
Lea Rd. CH44: Wall .2E **51**
Leas, The CH45: Wall .6A **32**
CH61: Thing .5F **85**
Leaside WA7: Run .4H **113**
WA9: St H .2D **60**
LEASOWE .3F **49**
Leasowe (Park & Ride) .5E **49**
Leasowe Av. CH45: Wall .1A **50**
Leasowe Gdns. CH46: Leas .4C **48**
Leasowe Lighthouse .4A **48**
Leasowe Recreation Cen. .4E **49**
Leasowe Rd. CH44: Wall .3D **48**
CH45: Wall .3D **48**
CH46: Leas .4B **48**
L9: Ain .4H **21**
Leasoweside CH46: Leas .3E **49**
Leasowe Station (Rail) .5D **48**
Leas Pk. CH47: Hoy .5A **64**
Leatherbarrows La. L31: Mag, Mell .2D **12**
Leather La. L2: Liv .3D **4**
Leather's La. L26: Halew .5H **93**
Leathwood L31: Mag .1C **12**
Leaway CH49: Grea .5B **66**
Leawood Gro. CH46: More .1D **66**
L E C Complex L15: Wav .1B **72**
Leckwith Rd. L30: N'ton .1H **21**
Leda Gro. *L17: Aig .5A **72***
(off Hesketh St.)
Ledbury Cl. CH43: O'ton .1A **86**
L12: Crox .1B **38**
WA10: Eccl .2H **41**
Ledger Rd. WA11: Hay .6C **30**
Ledsham Cl. CH43: Noct .5A **68**
Ledsham Rd. L32: Kirkb .1G **23**
Ledsham Wlk. L32: Kirkb .1G **23**
Ledson Pk. L33: Kirkb .3B **14**
Ledsons Gro. L31: Mell .6E **13**

Ledston Cl. WA7: Wind H 4F **115**
Leece St. L1: Liv 6H **5** (1E **71**)
Lee Cl. L35: Rainh 6B **60**
Leecourt Cl. L12: W Der 2H **55**
Leeds St. L3: Liv 1B **4** (4B **52**)
Lee Hall Rd. L25: Gate 4E **75**
Lee Manor Sports Cen. 4F **75**
Leeming Cl. L19: Garst 6G **91**
Lee Pk. Av. L25: Gate 4E **75**
Lee Rd. CH47: Hoy 2C **64**
Lees Av. CH42: Rock F 1H **87**
Leeside Av. L32: Kirkb 3A **24**
Leeside Cl. L32: Kirkb 2B **24**
Lees La. L12: W Der 6H **37**
Lees Rd. L33: Know I 2D **24**
Lee St. WA9: St H 5A **44**
Leeswood L22: Water 2G **19**
Leeswood Rd. CH49: Woodc 6E **67**
Lee Va. Rd. L25: Gate 5E **75**
Leeward Dr. L24: Speke 1C **108**
Legh Rd. CH62: New F 4B **88**
  WA11: Hay 5C **30**
Legh St. WA12: Newt W 2H **45**
  (not continuous)
Legion La. CH62: Brom 4D **104**
Legion Rd. WA10: St H 5B **42**
Leicester Av. L22: Water 6F **9**
Leicester Rd. L20: Boot 1D **34**
Leicester St. WA9: St H 5B **42**
Leigh Av. WA8: Wid 2D **96**
Leigh Bri. Way L5: Liv 2C **52**
  (off New Hedley Gro.)
Leigh Grn. Cl. WA8: Wid 3A **96**
Leigh Pl. L1: Liv 4F **5**
Leigh Rd. CH48: W Kir 6B **64**
Leighs Hey Cres. L32: Kirkb 1B **24**
Leigh St. L1: Liv 4E **5** (6D **52**)
  (not continuous)
Leighton Av. CH47: Meols 1E **65**
  L31: Mag 5C **6**
Leighton Chase CH64: Nest 6H **117**
Leighton Rd. CH41: Tran 5G **69**
  CH64: Nest 4G **117**
Leighton St. L4: Kirkd 4E **35**
Leinster Gdns. WA7: Run 2D **112**
Leinster Rd. L13: Liv 4F **55**
Leinster St. WA7: Run 2D **112**
Leiria Way WA7: Run 3E **113**
Leison St. L4: Kirkd 6D **34**
  L5: Kirkd 1D **52**
Leiston Cl. CH61: Irby 4C **84**
Lemon Cl. L7: Liv 6A **54**
Lemon Gro. L8: Liv 3A **72**
Lemon St. L5: Kirkd 1D **52**
Lemon Tree Wlk. WA10: St H 4B **42**
Lenfield Dr. WA11: Hay 5B **30**
Lenham Way L24: Speke 1D **108**
Lennox Av. CH45: New B 6D **32**
Lennox La. CH43: Bid 6G **49**
Lennox Way L7: Liv 5H **53**
Lenthall St. L4: Walt 3F **35**
Lenton Rd. L25: Gate 4E **75**
Lentworth Ct. L17: Aig 4D **90**
Leo Cl. L14: Knott A 3B **56**
Leominster Rd. CH44: Wall 3D **50**
Leonard Cheshire Dr.
  L30: N'ton 6F **11**
Leonard Ho. CH41: Birke 5H **51**
Leonards Cl. L36: Huy 1F **57**
Leonard St. WA7: West P 6B **112**
  WA9: St H 6B **44**
Leon Cl. WA5: Gt San 2F **81**
Leonora St. L8: Liv 5G **71**
Leopold Gro. WA9: Sut L 2G **61**
Leopold Rd. L7: Liv 5H **53**
  (not continuous)
  L22: Water 1E **19**
Leopold St. CH44: Wall 4G **51**
Leslie Av. CH49: Grea 6B **66**
Leslie Rd. WA10: St H 5A **42**
Lesseps Rd. L8: Liv 2A **72**
Lessingham Rd. WA8: Wid 6D **78**
Lester Cl. L4: Kirkd 6E **35**

Lester Dr. CH61: Irby 4A **84**
  WA10: Eccl 6G **27**
Lester Gro. L36: Huy 3H **57**
Lestock St. L8: Liv 2E **71**
Leta St. L4: Walt 4F **35**
  (not continuous)
Letchworth St. L6: Liv 2A **54**
Lethbridge Cl. L5: Kirkd 1C **52**
Letitia St. L8: Liv 4F **71**
Levens Hey CH46: More 1B **66**
Leven St. L4: Kirkd 5E **35**
Levens Way WA8: Wid 3A **96**
Lever Av. CH44: Wall 5G **51**
Lever C'way. CH63: Hghr B, Store . . .6C **86**
Lever Ct. L1: Liv 6E **5** (1D **70**)
Leveret Rd. L24: Speke 2A **110**
Leverhulme Ct. CH63: Beb 1A **104**
Levers St. WA9: Clock F 4H **61**
Lever Ter. CH42: Tran 6G **69**
  (off Summerford Cl.)
Leveson Rd. L13: Liv 6F **55**
Lewis Cres. WA8: Wid 4E **97**
Lewis Gro. WA8: Wid 2B **96**
Lewisham Rd. CH62: Port S 5C **88**
  L11: Norr G 3D **36**
Lewis St. WA10: St H 2C **42**
Lewis Wlk. L33: Kirkb 3A **14**
Lexham Rd. L14: Knott A 4G **55**
Lexington Way L33: Kirkb 3A **14**
Leybourne Cl. L25: Gate 3C **74**
Leybourne Grn. L25: Gate 4C **74**
Leybourne Gro. L25: Gate 4C **74**
Leybourne Rd. L25: Gate 3C **74**
Leyburn Cl. L32: Kirkb 4A **24**
  (not continuous)
Leyburn Rd. CH45: Wall 1B **50**
Ley Cl. WA9: Clock F 3G **61**
Leyfield Cl. L12: W Der 1H **55**
Leyfield Ct. L12: W Der 1H **55**
Leyfield Rd. L12: W Der 1G **55**
Leyfield Wlk. L12: W Der 1H **55**
Leyland Gro. WA11: Hay 5D **30**
Leyland Rd. WA11: Rainf 3F **17**
Leyland St. L34: Presc 1D **58**
Leyton Cl. WA7: Run 1F **123**
Liberton Ct. L5: Liv 1G **53**
  (off St Domingo Va.)
Liberty Pl. WA10: St H 2B **42**
Liberty St. L15: Wav 2C **72**
Libra Cl. L14: Knott A 2C **56**
Library St. WA10: St H 2E **43**
Librex Cl. L21: Lith 5C **20**
Lichfield Av. L22: Water 6F **9**
Lichfield Cl. L30: N'ton 2G **21**
Lichfield Rd. L15: Wav 3E **73**
  L26: Halew 5G **93**
Lichfield St. CH45: New B 6E **33**
Lickers La. L35: Whis 5D **58**
Liddell Av. L31: Mell 5E **13**
Liddell Rd. L12: W Der 6D **36**
Lidderdale Ct. L15: Wav 3C **72**
  (off Lidderdale Rd.)
Lidderdale Rd. L15: Wav 3C **72**
Lidgate Cl. L33: Kirkb 4A **14**
Liebig St. WA8: Wid 3F **97**
Liege Ho. CH49: Upton 3D **66**
  (off Manorside Cl.)
Lifestyles
  Alsop 3F **35**
  Austin Rawlinson 2G **109**
  Cardinal Heenan 2H **55**
  Croxteth 1G **37**
  Ellergreen 3E **37**
  Everton .1E **53**
  Garston 4G **91**
  Millennium 3E **5**
  Park Road 4F **71**
  Peter Lloyd 2D **54**
  Tennis Cen. 2D **72**
  Toxteth Sports Cen. 3F **71**
  Walton .3H **35**
  Woolton Swimming Pool 1C **92**

Liffey Ct. L3: Liv 5F **53**
  (off London Rd.)
Liffey St. L8: Liv 2H **71**
Lifton Rd. L33: Kirkb 1C **24**
Lightbody St. L5: Liv 2B **52**
Lightburn St. WA7: Run 4D **112**
Lightfoot Cl. CH60: Hesw 6F **101**
Lightfoot La. CH60: Hesw 6F **101**
Lighthouse Rd. CH47: Hoy 3B **64**
  L24: Hale 6E **111**
Lightoaks Dr. L26: Halew 2B **94**
Lightstream Dr. L24: Speke 5D **92**
Lightwood Dr. L7: Liv 1A **72**
Lightwood St. L7: Liv 1A **72**
Lilac Av. WA8: Wid 1F **97**
Lilac Cres. WA7: Run 5G **113**
Lilac Gro. L36: Huy 1F **75**
  WA11: Hay 6B **30**
Lilford Av. L9: Walt 5F **21**
Lilford Dr. WA5: Gt San 3H **81**
Lilley Rd. L7: Liv 4B **54**
Lillian Rd. L4: Walt 1H **53**
Lillie Cl. CH43: Bid 1G **67**
Lillyfield CH60: Hesw 1D **116**
Lilly Grn. L4: Walt 4H **35**
  (off Lilly Gro.)
Lilly Gro. L4: Walt 4H **35**
  (not continuous)
Lilly Va. L7: Liv 4B **54**
Lily Gro L7: Liv 6H **53**
  (off Dorothy St.)
Lily Rd. L21: Lith 5B **20**
Limbo La. CH61: Irby 3B **84**
Lime Av. CH63: Hghr B 1F **103**
  WA8: Wid 1F **97**
  L13: Liv 3E **55**
Limedale Rd. L18: Moss H 4E **73**
Lime Gro. L8: Liv 3A **72**
  L21: Sea 5A **20**
  WA7: Run 5G **113**
  WA11: Rainf 3F **17**
Limehurst Gro. CH62: Brom 1D **120**
Limekiln La. CH44: Wall 5C **50**
  L3: Liv .3D **52**
  (not continuous)
  L5: Liv .2D **52**
  WA5: Burtw 4G **63**
Limekiln Row WA7: Cas 5C **114**
Limerick Cl. WA8: Wid 6C **78**
Limes, The CH49: Upton 4D **66**
Lime St. L1: Liv 3F **5** (5D **52**)
Lime St. Chambers L1: Liv 3G **5**
Lime Street Station (Rail) 3G **5** (6E **53**)
Lime Tree Cl. L9: Walt 1H **35**
Lime Tree Gro. CH60: Hesw 5G **101**
Lime Va. Rd. WN5: Bil 1G **29**
Linacre Ho. L20: Boot 3C **34**
Linacre La. L20: Boot 6C **20**
  WA8: Wid 4C **78**
Linacre Rd. L21: Lith 4B **20**
Lincoln Cl. L6: Liv 3H **53**
  L36: Huy 4B **58**
  WA7: Run 1G **123**
Lincoln Cres. WA11: St H 5F **29**
Lincoln Dr. CH45: Wall 1E **51**
  L10: Ain 6B **12**
Lincoln Grn. L31: Mag 1H **11**
Lincoln Rd. WA10: St H 3B **42**
Lincoln Sq. WA8: Wid 1F **97**
Lincoln St. CH41: Birke 6C **50**
  L19: Garst 1G **107**
Lincoln Way L35: Rainh 6B **60**
  L36: Huy 4B **58**
  (off Lincoln Cl.)
Lincombe Rd. L36: Huy 3D **56**
Lindale Cl. CH46: More 6E **49**
Lindale Dr. WA9: Clock F 3G **61**
Lindale Rd. L7: Liv 4C **54**
Lindby Cl. L32: Kirkb 3C **24**
Lindby Rd. L32: Kirkb 3C **24**
Linden Av. L23: Blun 5E **9**
  L30: N'ton 1F **21**
Linden Ct. WA8: Wid 5D **78**

Linden Dr. CH43: Pren .2A **86**
L36: Huy .1G **75**
Linden Gro. CH45: Wall .6D **32**
Linden Rd. L27: N'ley .4G **75**
Lindens, The CH43: O'ton .4E **69**
L31: Mag .2A **12**
Linden Way WA8: Wid .5D **78**
WA10: Eccl .1H **41**
Lindenwood L32: Kirkb .3B **24**
Lindeth Av. CH44: Wall .5D **50**
Lindfield Cl. L8: Liv .5F **71**
Lindisfarne Ct. WA8: Wid .3D **78**
Lindisfarne Dr. L12: Crox .2B **38**
Lindley Cl. L7: Liv .1A **72**
Lindley St. L7: Liv .1A **72**
Lindrick Cl. L35: Rainh .3G **59**
Lindsay Rd. L4: Walt .5B **36**
Lindsay St. WA9: Clock F .4H **61**
Lind St. L4: Walt .4F **35**
Lindwall Cl. CH43: Bid .6G **49**
Linear Pk. CH46: More .6A **48**
Lineside Cl. L25: Gate .4D **74**
Linford Gro. WA11: St H .6G **29**
Lingdale Av. CH43: Clau .3B **68**
Lingdale Ct. CH43: Clau .2B **68**
CH48: W Kir .1A **82**
Lingdale Rd. CH43: Clau .2B **68**
CH48: W Kir .6A **64**
Lingdale Rd. Nth. CH41: Birke .2B **68**
Lingfield Cl. L30: N'ton .2G **21**
L36: Roby .6E **57**
Lingfield Gro. L14: Broad G .5H **55**
Lingfield Rd. L14: Broad G .5G **55**
WA7: Run .5C **112**
Lingford Cl. L27: N'ley .5H **75**
Lingham Cl. CH46: More .6B **48**
Lingham La. CH46: More .4A **48**
(not continuous)
Lingholme Rd. WA10: St H .1C **42**
LINGLEY GREEN .2F **81**
Lingley Grn. Av. WA5: Gt San .3E **81**
LINGLEY MERE .6F **63**
Lingley Mere Bus. Pk. WA5: Gt San .1F **81**
Lingley Rd. WA5: Gt San .3F **81**
Lingmell Av. WA11: St H .2F **29**
Lingmell Rd. L12: W Der .5F **37**
Ling St. L7: Liv .5H **53**
Lingtree Rd. L32: Kirkb .1F **23**
Lingwell Av. WA8: Wid .1B **96**
Lingwell Pk. WA8: Wid .1B **96**
Lingwood Rd. WA5: Gt San .3H **81**
Linhope Way L17: Aig .6A **72**
Link Av. L23: Thorn .4A **10**
WA11: St H .5A **30**
Linkfield Cl. L27: N'ley .3F **75**
Link Rd. L36: Huy .6B **58**
Links, The CH43: O'ton .4B **68**
Links Cl. CH45: Wall .6B **32**
CH48: W Kir .2D **82**
CH63: Raby M .1B **120**
Links Hey Rd. CH48: Caldy .5E **83**
Linkside CH63: Hghr B .4F **87**
Linkside Ct. L23: Blun .4C **8**
Linkside Rd. L25: Woolt .2E **93**
Links Rd. L32: Kirkb .2C **24**
Linkstor Rd. L25: Woolt .1B **92**
Links Vw. CH43: O'ton .4A **68**
CH45: Wall .5B **32**
Linksview L25: Woolt .1B **92**
Linksway CH45: Wall .6B **32**
Linkway WA7: Run .5G **113**
WA10: Windle .5H **27**
Linkway E. WA9: St H .3F **43**
Linkway W. WA9: St H .2D **42**
WA10: St H .2D **42**
Linner Rd. L24: Speke .3E **109**
Linnet Cl. L17: Aig .4A **72**
Linnet Ct. L17: Aig .5A **72**
Linnet Ho. L17: Aig .4A **72**
Linnet La. L17: Aig .4H **71**
Linnets Pk. WA7: Run .2F **113**
Linnets Way CH60: Hesw .5C **100**
Linnet Way L33: Kirkb .2A **14**
Linslade Cl. L33: Kirkb .5B **14**
Linslade Cres. L33: Kirkb .5B **14**
Linton Pl. L32: Kirkb .6G **13**
Linton St. L4: Walt .4F **35**
Linum Gdns. WA9: Bold .6D **44**
Linville Av. L23: Blun .5D **8**
Linwood Cl. WA7: Brook .2E **125**
Linwood Gro. L35: Whis .5E **59**
Linwood Rd. CH42: Tran .6G **69**
Lionel St. WA9: St H .6B **44**
Lions Cl. CH43: Clau .3B **68**
Lipton Cl. L20: Boot .3C **34**
Lisburn La. L13: Liv .6C **36**
Lisburn Rd. L17: Aig .1C **90**
LISCARD .2D **50**
Liscard Cres. CH44: Wall .3D **50**
Liscard Gro. CH44: Wall .3C **50**
Liscard Ho. CH44: Wall .3D **50**
Liscard Rd. CH44: Wall .3D **50**
L15: Wav .2B **72**
Liscard Village CH45: Wall .2D **50**
Liscard Way CH44: Wall .3D **50**
Liskeard Cl. WA7: Brook .1D **124**
Lisleholme Cl. L12: W Der .1G **55**
Lisleholme Cres. L12: W Der .1G **55**
Lisleholme Rd. L12: W Der .1G **55**
Lismore Ct. L23: Blun .5E **9**
Lismore Rd. L18: Moss H .1E **91**
Lister Av. CH46: Leas .5E **49**
Lister Cres. L7: Liv .5A **54**
Lister Dr. L6: Liv .3C **54**
L13: Liv .3C **54**
Lister Rd. L7: Liv .4A **54**
WA7: Ast .2G **113**
Liston St. L4: Walt .3F **35**
Litcham Cl. CH49: Upton .2E **67**
Litchborough Gro. L35: Whis .1G **59**
LITHERLAND .3B **20**
Litherland Av. CH46: More .6B **48**
Litherland Cres. WA11: St H .4G **29**
Litherland Ho. L20: Boot .1D **34**
Litherland Pk. L21: Lith .3B **20**
Litherland Rd. L20: Boot .5C **20**
Litherland Sports Pk. .2D **20**
Lithou Cl. L5: Liv .2D **52**
Little Acre L31: Mag .1C **12**
Lit. Barn Hey L30: N'ton .5D **10**
LITTLE BONGS .3H **55**
Littlebourne WA7: Murd .6G **115**
Lit. Brook La. L32: Kirkb .3H **23**
Lit. Canning St. L8: Liv .2F **71**
Lit. Catharine St. L8: Liv .2F **71**
Littlecote Cl. WA9: Clock F .3G **61**
Little Ct. L3: Liv .3C **52**
Little Cft. L35: Whis .4D **58**
LITTLE CROSBY .1F **9**
Lit. Crosby Rd. L23: Crosb, Lit C .1F **9**
Littledale L14: Knott A .4H **55**
Littledale Rd. CH44: Wall .4F **51**
WA5: Gt San .2H **81**
Little Delph WA11: Hay .4E **31**
Littlegate WA7: Run .5A **114**
Lit. Hardman St. L1: Liv .6H **5** (1E **71**)
Lit. Heath Rd. L24: Speke .3G **109**
Lit. Heyes St. L5: Liv .1G **53**
Lit. Howard St. L3: Liv .3B **52**
Lit. Huskisson St. L8: Liv .2F **71**
Little La. CH64: Park .6G **117**
Littlemore Cl. CH49: Upton .4B **66**
Lit. Moss Hey L28: Stockb V .6D **38**
Lit. Parkfield Rd. L17: Aig .5H **71**
Littler Rd. WA11: Hay .6C **30**
Little St Bride St. L8: Liv .1F **71**
Littlestone Cl. WA8: Wid .5E **79**
Lit. Storeton La. CH63: Store .5C **86**
Little St. WA9: St H .4A **44**
Littleton Cl. CH43: Noct .5A **68**
Littlewood Cl. L35: Whis .4E **59**
Lit. Woolton St. L7: Liv .6G **53**
Littondale Av. L35: Rainh .5B **60**
Liver Ind. Est. L9: Ain .1A **36**
Livermore Ct. L8: Liv .3A **72**
LIVERPOOL .4F **5** (6D **52**)
Liverpool Aquatics Cen. .2D **72**
Liverpool Arts Village L1: Liv .6E **5**
Liverpool Cathedral Church of Christ .2E **71**
Liverpool College Sports Cen. .*5D 72*
(off Queens Dr.)
Liverpool Empire Theatre .3G **5** (5E **53**)
Liverpool FC .6G **35**
Liverpool Intermodal Freeport Terminal
L20: Boot .1A **34**
Liverpool International Bus. Pk.
L24: Speke .2B **108**
LIVERPOOL JOHN LENNON AIRPORT .4E **109**
Liverpool John Moores University
Avril Robarts Cen. .2D **4** (5C **52**)
Byrom St. .1F **5** (4D **52**)
IM Marsh Campus .2D **90**
The Henry Cotton Campus .2E **5**
William Brown St. .2F **5** (5D **52**)
Liverpool Metropolitan Cathedral of Christ the King (RC) .6F **53**
Liverpool One L1: Liv .5D **4** (6C **52**)
Liverpool Parish Church .4B **4**
Liverpool Pl. WA8: Wid .2A **96**
Liverpool Playhouse .4F **5** (6D **52**)
Liverpool Rd. CH64: Nest .6A **118**
(not continuous)
L23: Crosb .4G **9**
L31: Lyd .4B **6**
L34: Presc .1B **58**
L36: Huy .3D **56**
(not continuous)
WA5: Gt San .3E **81**
WA8: Wid .2H **95**
WA10: St H .2D **42**
WA11: Hay .4C **30**
(not continuous)
WN4: Ash M, Garsw .3C **30**
Liverpool Rd. Nth. L31: Mag .4B **6**
Liverpool Rd. Sth. L31: Mag .6B **6**
Liverpool Sailing Club .3A **108**
Liverpool St. WA10: St H .2D **42**
Liverpool Way, The L33: Kirkb .2C **24**
Liversidge Rd. CH42: Tran .5F **69**
Liver St. L1: Liv .6D **4** (1C **70**)
Livingston Av. L17: Aig .5A **72**
Livingston Ct. L17: Aig .5A **72**
(not continuous)
Livingston Dr. L17: Aig .6A **72**
Livingston Dr. Nth. L17: Aig .6A **72**
Livingston Dr. Sth. L17: Aig .6A **72**
Livingstone Gdns. CH41: Birke .2E **69**
Livingstone Rd. CH46: Leas .3E **49**
Livingstone St. CH41: Birke .2E **69**
Llanrwst Cl. L8: Liv .4E **71**
Lloyd Av. CH41: Birke .2D **68**
Lloyd Cl. L6: Liv .3F **53**
Lloyd Cres. WA12: Newt W .2H **45**
Lloyd Dr. CH49: Grea .6A **66**
Lloyd Rd. L34: Presc .6E **41**
Lloyd St. WA11: Hay .5B **30**
Lobelia Av. L9: Walt .1H **35**
Lobelia Gro. WA7: Beech .2B **124**
Lochinvar St. L9: Walt .2F **35**
Lochmore Rd. L18: Moss H .2F **91**
Lochryan Rd. L19: Aller .3F **91**
Loch St. WA7: Run .3E **113**
(not continuous)
Lockerby Rd. L7: Liv .4B **54**
Locker Pk. CH49: Grea .5A **66**
Locke St. L19: Garst .1G **107**
Lockett Rd. WA8: Wid .1E **97**
Lockfield WA7: Run .3C **112**
Lockfields Vw. L3: Liv .2C **52**
Lockgate E. WA7: Wind H .3E **115**
Lockgate W. WA7: Wind H .3D **114**
Lockington Cl. L8: Liv .5G **71**
Lock Rd. CH62: East .5G **105**
Lock St. WA9: St H .6G **29**
Lockton Rd. L34: Know .6D **24**
Lockwood Vw. WA7: Pres B .2H **125**
Loddon Cl. CH49: Upton .2F **67**

Lodge, The CH43: Noct 3H 67
Lodge La. CH62: Port S 5B 88
    L8: Liv 2H 71
    WA7: Halt 5A 114
    WA8: Cron 5G 77
Lodge Rd. WA8: Wid 3H 95
Lodge Works L33: Know I 6E 15
Lodwick St. L20: Kirkd 4B 34
Lofthouse Ga. WA8: Wid 6D 78
Logan Rd. CH41: Birke 6D 50
Logfield Dr. L19: Garst 6H 91
Lognor Rd. L32: Kirkb 1G 23
Lognor Wlk. L32: Kirkb 1G 23
Logwood Rd. L36: Huy 1A 76
Lois Ct. CH45: Wall 1E 51
Lombard Rd. CH46: More 5D 48
Lombardy Av. CH49: Grea 1H 83
Lomond Gro. CH46: More 1D 66
Lomond Rd. L7: Liv 4C 54
Londonderry Rd. L13: Liv 6B 36
London Rd. L3: Liv 3G 5 (5E 53)
    (not continuous)
Longacre Cl. CH45: Wall 2H 49
Longacre Rd. CH64: Nest 5A 118
Long Acres CH49: Grea 4B 66
Long Av. L9: Ain 5H 21
Longbenton Way WA7: Manor P 1D 114
Longborough Rd.
    L34: Know 2E 39
Longcroft Av. L19: Aller 4H 91
Longcroft Sq. L19: Aller 4H 91
Longdale La. L29: Seft 2D 10
Longdown Rd. L10: Faz 5F 23
Longfellow Cl. L32: Kirkb 3H 23
Longfellow Dr. CH62: New F 4A 88
Longfellow St. L8: Liv 2A 72
    (not continuous)
    L20: Boot .6A 20
Longfield Av. L23: Crosb 3G 9
Longfield Cl. CH49: Grea 5B 66
Longfield Pk. WA9: Clock F 3H 61
Longfield Rd. L21: Lith 5B 20
Longfield Wlk. L23: Crosb 3G 9
Longfold L31: Mag 6D 6
Longford Dr. WA8: Wid 1C 96
Longford St. L8: Liv 6G 71
Long Hey L35: Whis 5D 58
Long Hey Rd. L48: Caldy 4E 83
Longland Rd. CH45: Wall 1D 50
Long La. L9: Ain, Faz 5H 21
    L15: Wav .1D 72
    L19: Garst 4G 91
    L29: Thorn 1A 10
Long Meadow CH60: Hesw 1D 116
    WA10: Eccl 1H 41
Longmeadow Rd. L34: Know 1F 39
Longmoor Cl. L10: Faz 4C 22
Longmoor Gro. L9: Ain 5H 21
Longmoor La. L9: Ain 5H 21
    L10: Faz 5H 21
Long Moss L30: N'ton 6C 10
Longreach Rd. L14: Knott A 3B 56
Longridge Av. CH49: Upton 3C 66
    WA11: St H 6H 29
Longridge Wlk. L4: Kirkd 5E 35
Long Spinney WA7: Nort 5E 115
Longstone Wlk. L7: Liv 1H 71
Longton La. L35: Rainh 2H 59
LONGVIEW .2H 57
Longview Av. CH45: Wall 2C 50
    L35: Rainh 3G 59
Longview Cres. L36: Huy 4H 57
Longview Dr. L36: Huy 3H 57
Longview La. L36: Huy 2H 57
Longview Rd. L35: Rainh 3G 59
    L36: Huy 4H 57
Longville St. L8: Liv 4E 71
Longwood Cl. WA11: Rainf 2A 28
Longworth Way L25: Woolt 6C 74
Lonie Gro. WA10: St H 5A 42
Lonsboro Rd. CH44: Wall 4E 51
Lonsdale Av. CH45: Wall 1C 50
    WA10: St H 6H 41

Lonsdale Cl. L21: Ford 1B 20
    WA5: Gt San 1G 81
    WA8: Wid .3A 96
Lonsdale M. L21: Ford 1B 20
Lonsdale Rd. L21: Ford 1B 20
    L26: Halew 5G 93
Lonsdale Vs. CH45: Wall 1C 50
    (off Seaview Rd.)
Looe Cl. WA8: Wid 1C 96
Looe Rd. L11: Crox 6H 23
Looms, The CH64: Park 5F 117
Loomsway CH61: Irby 5A 84
Loraine St. L5: Liv 2F 53
Lordens Cl. L14: Knott A 2C 56
Lordens Rd. L14: Knott A 2C 56
Lord Nelson St. L1: Liv 3G 5 (5E 53)
    L3: Liv 3G 5 (5E 53)
Lords Av. CH43: Bid 1G 67
Lords Fold WA11: Rainf 2E 17
Lord St. CH41: Birke 2G 69
    L2: Liv 4D 4 (6C 52)
    L19: Garst 1H 107
    WA7: Run .2D 112
    WA10: St H 6D 28
    (not continuous)
Loreburn Rd. L15: Wav 3E 73
Lorenzo Dr. L11: Norr G 4C 36
Loretto Dr. CH49: Upton 3E 67
Loretto Rd. CH44: Wall 2B 50
Lorn Ct. CH41: Birke 3G 69
Lorne Ct. CH43: O'ton 5D 68
Lorne Rd. CH43: O'ton 5C 68
    L22: Water 2F 19
Lorne St. L7: Liv 4C 54
Lorn St. CH41: Birke 3G 69
Lorton Av. WA11: St H 3E 29
Lorton St. L8: Liv 2H 71
Lothair Rd. L4: Walt 6G 35
Lothian St. L8: Liv 3G 71
Lotus Gdns. WA9: Bold 6C 44
Loudon Gro. L8: Liv 3G 71
Lough Grn. CH63: Spit 3A 104
Loughlin Dr. L33: Kirkb 4B 14
Loughrigg Av. WA11: St H 2F 29
Louis Braille Cl. L30: N'ton 5F 11
Louis Pasteur Av. L30: N'ton 5F 11
Lovelace Rd. L19: Gras 3A 92
Love La. CH44: Wall 4C 50
    L3: Liv 3C 52
Lovel Rd. L24: Speke 3F 109
Lovel Ter. WA8: Hale B 6H 95
Lovel Way L24: Speke 2F 109
Lovett Dr. L35: Presc 2E 59
Lowbridge Ct. L19: Garst 5H 91
Lowden Av. L21: Lith 1B 20
Lowell St. L4: Walt 4F 35
Lwr. Appleton Rd.
    WA8: Wid .2F 97
Lwr. Bank Vw. L20: Kirkd 4B 34
LOWER BEBINGTON 6A 88
Lwr. Breck Rd. L6: Liv 1H 53
Lwr. Castle St. L2: Liv 4C 4 (6C 52)
Lwr. Church St. WA8: Wid 6E 97
Lower Cl. L26: Halew 3A 94
Lwr. Farm Rd. L25: Gate 2C 74
Lwr. Flaybrick Rd. CH43: Bid 1A 68
Lwr. Gill St. L3: Liv 5F 53
Lower Grn. CH49: Woodc 6E 67
Lwr. Hall St. WA10: St H 1F 43
Lower Hey L23: Thorn 4B 10
LOWER HOUSE 3C 96
Lower Ho. La. L11: Norr G 1E 37
    WA8: Wid .4D 96
Lower La. L9: Faz 4C 22
Lwr. Mersey Vw. L20: Kirkd 4B 34
Lwr. New Hall Pl. L3: Liv 3B 4
Lower Rd. CH62: Port S 5B 88
    L26: Halew 3B 94
    WA8: Hale B 3B 94
Lower Sandfield L25: Gate 5D 74
Lowerson Cres. L11: Norr G 5C 36
Lowerson Rd. L11: Norr G 5C 36
Lwr. Thingwall La. CH61: Thing 5G 85

Lowestoft Dr. L19: Garst 5F 91
Lowe St. WA10: St H 1D 42
Lowe St. Sth. WA10: St H 2D 42
Loweswater Cres. WA11: Hay 5C 30
Loweswater Way L33: Kirkb 4H 13
Lowfield Ind. Est. WA9: St H 3D 60
Lowfield La. WA9: St H 1D 60
Lowfield Rd. L14: Knott A 4G 55
Lowfields Av. CH62: East 4D 120
Lowfields Cl. CH62: East 4E 121
Low Hill L6: Liv 4G 53
Lowlands Rd. WA7: Run 3D 112
Lowndes Rd. L6: Liv 1B 54
Lowood Gro. CH41: Birke 4F 69
Lowood Rd. CH41: Birke 4F 69
Lowry Bank CH44: Wall 4G 51
Lowry Cl. L33: Kirkb 3A 14
Lowther Av. L10: Ain 1B 22
    L31: Mag 5D 6
Lowther Cres. WA10: St H 5H 41
Lowther Dr. L35: Rainh 4H 59
Lowther St. L8: Liv 2G 71
Low Wood Gro. CH61: Barn 1G 101
Low Wood St. L6: Liv 4G 53
Loxdale Cl. L8: Liv 5G 71
Loxwood Cl. L25: Gate 2D 74
Loyola Hey L35: Rainh 1C 78
Lucan Rd. L17: Aig 1C 90
Lucerne Rd. CH44: Wall 5F 51
Lucerne St. L17: Aig 6A 72
Lucius Cl. L9: Walt 4F 21
Lucknow St. L17: Aig 5A 72
Ludlow Cl. CH48: W Kir 2B 82
Ludlow Cres. WA7: Run 5F 113
Ludlow Dr. CH48: W Kir 2B 82
Ludlow Gro. CH62: Brom 4D 104
Ludlow St. L4: Kirkd 4F 35
Ludwig Rd. L4: Walt 1H 53
Lugard Rd. L17: Aig 1C 90
LUGSDALE .4G 97
Lugsdale Rd. WA8: Wid 4E 97
Lugsmore La. WA10: St H 4B 42
Luke St. CH44: Wall 5G 51
    L8: Liv 3F 71
Lulworth Av. L22: Water 1E 19
Lulworth Rd. L25: Gate 4E 75
Lumber La. WA5: Burtw 5G 45
Lumina CH62: Brom 3E 105
Lumley Rd. CH44: Wall 4F 51
Lumley St. L19: Garst 4F 91
Lumley Wlk. L24: Hale 4E 111
Lunar Dr. L30: N'ton 4F 11
Lunar Rd. L9: Ain 5H 21
Lune Av. L31: Mag 5D 6
Lunesdale Av. L9: Ain 4H 21
Lune St. L23: Crosb 5G 9
Lune Way WA8: Wid 2A 96
Lunsford Rd. L14: Knott A 3B 56
LUNT 1D 10
Lunt Av. L30: N'ton 1G 21
    L35: Whis .4E 59
Lunt La. L29: Seft 1D 10
Lunt Rd. L20: Boot 5C 20
    L29: Seft, Thorn 1C 10
LUNTS HEATH 5F 79
Lunts Heath Rd. WA8: Wid 4E 79
Lupin Dr. WA11: Hay 5H 31
Lupton Dr. L23: Crosb 5A 10
Luscombe Cl. L26: Halew 3A 94
Lusitania Rd. L4: Walt 3G 35
Luther Gro. WA9: St H 3D 44
Luton Gro. L4: Walt 5F 35
Luton St. L5: Kirkd 1B 52
    WA8: Wid .4E 97
Lutyens Cl. L4: Walt 5F 35
Luxmore Rd. L4: Walt 4G 35
Lycett Rd. CH44: Wall 2A 50
    L4: Walt 6A 36
Lyceum Pl. L1: Liv 5F 5
Lycroft Cl. WA7: Run 1F 123
Lydbrook Cl. CH42: Rock F 6H 69
Lydbury Cres. L32: Kirkb 3B 24
Lydford Rd. L12: W Der 5F 37

Lydia Ann St.—Malvern Cl.

Lydia Ann St. L1: Liv 6E **5** (1D **70**)
LYDIATE 2A **6**
Lydiate, The CH60: Hesw 6D **100**
Lydiate La. CH64: Will 6G **119**
L23: Seft, Thorn 3B **10**
L25: Woolt 1E **93**
L26: Halew 1F **93**
L29: Thorn 3B **10**
WA7: West P 6B **112**
Lydiate Pk. L23: Thorn 3B **10**
Lydiate Rd. L20: Boot 6C **20**
Lydia Wlk. L10: Faz 4F **23**
Lydieth Lea L27: N'ley 3G **75**
Lydney Rd. L36: Huy 3D **56**
Lyelake Cl. L32: Kirkb 2B **24**
Lyelake Gdns. *L32: Kirkb* *2B* ***24***
(off Lyelake Rd.)
Lyelake Rd. L32: Kirkb 2B **24**
Lyle St. L5: Liv 2D **52**
Lyme Cl. L36: Huy 2A **58**
Lymecroft L25: Woolt 1B **92**
Lyme Cross Rd. L36: Huy 1G **57**
Lyme Gro. L36: Huy 2H **57**
Lyme St. WA11: Hay 5G **31**
WA12: Newt W 1G **45**
Lyme Tree Ct. WA8: Cron 3A **78**
Lymewood Ct. WA11: Hay 4G **31**
Lymington Gro. L30: N'ton 6F **11**
Lymington Rd. CH44: Wall 3B **50**
Lymm Rd. CH43: Bid 2H **67**
Lynas Gdns. L19: Gras 3F **91**
Lynas St. CH41: Birke 1F **69**
Lyncot Rd. L9: Ain 3H **21**
Lyncroft Rd. CH44: Wall 5E **51**
Lyndale WA7: Run 5G **113**
Lyndale Av. CH62: East 3E **121**
Lyndene Rd. L25: Gate 3C **74**
Lyndhurst L31: Mag 6C **6**
Lyndhurst Av. CH61: Pens 2E **101**
L18: Moss H 6D **72**
Lyndhurst Cl. CH61: Thing 6E **85**
Lyndhurst Rd. CH45: Wall 1B **50**
CH47: Meols 6E **47**
CH61: Irby 6A **84**
L18: Moss H 5D **72**
L23: Crosb 5A **10**
Lyndhurst Way L36: Huy 5G **57**
Lyndon Dr. L18: Moss H 5F **73**
Lyndon Gro. WA7: Run 5F **113**
Lyndor Cl. L25: Woolt 2D **92**
Lyndor Rd. L25: Woolt 2D **92**
Lyneham L35: Whis 5F **59**
Lynholme Rd. L4: Walt 6H **35**
Lynmouth Rd. L17: Aig 3C **90**
Lynnbank CH43: O'ton 5D **68**
Lynnbank Rd. L18: Moss H 4H **73**
Lynn Cl. WA7: Run 6G **113**
WA10: St H 1A **42**
Lynscot Pl. L16: Child 1H **73**
Lynsted Rd. L14: Knott A 3B **56**
Lynton Cl. CH60: Hesw 1F **117**
L19: Aller 3F **91**
WA5: Penk 5G **81**
Lynton Ct. L23: Blun 5D **8**
Lynton Cres. WA8: Wid 1C **96**
Lynton Dr. CH63: Beb 2A **104**
Lynton Grn. L25: Woolt 5B **74**
Lynton Gro. WA9: Sut L 2G **61**
Lynton Rd. CH45: Wall 1A **50**
L36: Huy 4B **58**
Lynton Way WA10: Windle 5H **27**
Lynwood Av. CH44: Wall 4C **50**
Lynwood Dr. CH61: Irby 5C **84**
Lynwood Gdns. L9: Walt 6F **21**
Lynwood Rd. L9: Walt 6F **21**
Lynxway, The L12: Knott A 3H **55**
Lyon Cl. WA10: St H 2D **42**
Lyon Ind. Est. WA9: St H 1A **62**
Lyon Rd. L4: Walt 1H **53**
Lyons Cl. CH46: More 6C **48**
Lyons Pl. L25: Hunts X 3F **93**
Lyons Rd. CH46: More 6C **48**
WA5: Penk 5H **81**
Lyon St. L19: Garst 1G **107**
WA10: St H 2C **42**
Lyra Rd. L22: Water 2F **19**
Lysander Cl. L6: Liv 3G **53**
Lyster Rd. L20: Boot 2A **34**
Lytham Cl. L10: Faz 2D **22**
Lytham Ct. L32: Kirkb 5G **13**
Lytham Rd. WA8: Wid 1F **97**
Lytham Way L12: W Der 1B **56**
Lyttelton Rd. L17: Aig 1C **90**
Lytton Av. CH42: Rock F 2H **87**
Lytton Gro. *L21: Sea* *5A* ***20***
(off Ash Gro.)
Lytton St. L6: Liv 4F **53**

M

Maberley Vw. L15: Wav 6E **55**
Mab La. L12: W Der 5B **38**
McAllester Lodge *CH43: O'ton* *5B* ***68***
(off Bidston Rd.)
Macalpine Cl. CH49: Upton 3E **67**
Macbeth St. L20: Kirkd 4C **34**
McBride St. L19: Garst 5G **91**
McClellan Pl. WA8: Wid 2F **97**
McCormack Av. WA9: St H 1A **44**
McCulloch St. WA9: St H 2G **43**
Macdermott Rd. WA8: Wid 6D **96**
Macdona Dr. CH48: W Kir 3B **82**
Macdonald Av. WA11: St H 6A **30**
Macdonald Dr. CH49: Grea 6B **66**
Macdonald Rd. CH46: More 1A **66**
Macdonald St. L15: Wav 1C **72**
Mace Rd. L11: Crox 2G **37**
McFarlane Av. WA10: St H 1A **42**
Macfarren St. L13: Liv 4E **55**
McGill Ct. *CH41: Birke* *2F* ***69***
(off Cathcart St.)
McGough Cl. WA9: Sut M 4E **61**
McKeagney Gdns. WA8: Wid 4B **96**
Mackenzie Rd. CH46: Leas 4F **49**
McKeown Cl. L5: Liv 2D **52**
Mackets Cl. L25: Woolt 2E **93**
Macket's La. L25: Woolt 1E **93**
Mack Gro. L30: N'ton 1D **20**
McKinley Way WA8: Wid 6D **78**
McMinnis Av. WA9: St H 3C **44**
McNair Hall L18: Moss H 6D **72**
Macqueen St. L13: Liv 5E **55**
McVinnie Rd. L35: Presc 1F **59**
Maddock Rd. CH44: Wall 2F **51**
Maddocks St. L13: Liv 5E **55**
Maddock St. CH41: Birke 1E **69**
Maddrell St. L3: Liv 3B **52**
Madeira Dr. L25: Gate 3D **74**
Madelaine St. L8: Liv 3G **71**
Madeleine McKenna Ct. WA8: Wid . . .6H **77**
Madeley Cl. CH48: W Kir 2B **82**
Madeley Dr. CH48: W Kir 2B **82**
Madeley St. L6: Liv 4A **54**
Madison Sq. L1: Liv 6G **5** (1E **71**)
Madryn Av. L33: Kirkb 1C **24**
Madryn St. L8: Liv 4G **71**
Maelor Cl. CH63: Brom 1C **120**
Mafeking Cl. L15: Wav 6D **54**
Magazine Av. CH45: New B 6D **32**
Magazine Brow CH45: New B 6E **33**
Magazine La. CH45: New B 6D **32**
Magazine Rd. CH62: Brom 2D **104**
Magazines Prom. CH45: New B 5E **33**
Magazine Wlk. CH62: Brom 2D **104**
Magdala St. L8: Liv 2A **72**
Magdalen Ho. L20: Boot 3C **34**
Magdalen Sq. L30: N'ton 5F **11**
Maggots Nook Rd. WA11: Rainf 1G **17**
MAGHULL 5C **6**
Maghull La. L31: Mag 6G **7**
Maghull Smallholdings Est.
L31: Mag .4F **7**
Maghull Station (Rail) 2C **12**
Magnolia Cl. L26: Halew 1F **93**
WA11: Hay 6B **30**
Magnolia Dr. WA7: Beech 3B **124**
Magnolia Wlk. CH49: Grea 1A **84**
Magnus Cl. L13: Liv 2D **54**
Maguire Av. L20: Boot 1E **35**
Mahon Av. L20: Boot 5D **20**
Mahon Ct. *L8: Liv* *2F* ***71***
(off Morpeth St.)
Maiden La. L13: Liv 6B **36**
Maidford Rd. L14: Knott A 2B **56**
Maidstone Cl. L25: Hunts X 3E **93**
Maidstone Dr. L12: W Der 2B **56**
Main Av. WA10: St H 5A **42**
Main Cl. WA11: Hay 5C **30**
Main Dr. L35: Whis 6D **58**
Main Front L35: Whis 1E **77**
Main Rd. CH62: Port S 1B **104**
Mainside Rd. L32: Kirkb 2B **24**
Main St. WA6: Frod 6F **123**
WA7: Halt 4B **114**
Maintree Cres. L24: Speke 1A **110**
Mainwaring Rd. CH44: Wall 4F **51**
CH62: Brom 5D **104**
Maisemore Flds. WA8: Wid 6C **78**
Maitland Cl. L8: Liv 2H **71**
Maitland Rd. CH45: New B 5E **33**
Maitland St. L8: Liv 2H **71**
Majestic Cl. L11: Crox 2G **37**
Major Cross St. WA8: Wid 4E **97**
Major St. L5: Kirkd 1D **52**
Makepeace Wlk. *L8: Liv* *3F* ***71***
(off Thackeray Cl.)
Makin St. L4: Walt 3F **35**
Malahide Ct. WA8: Wid 1C **96**
Malcolm Cres. CH63: Brom 1C **120**
Malcolm Gro. L20: Kirkd 4D **34**
Malcolm Pl. L15: Wav 6D **54**
Malcolm St. WA7: Run 3F **113**
Malden Rd. L6: Liv 4A **54**
Maldon Cl. L26: Halew 5H **93**
Maldwyn Rd. CH44: Wall 2D **50**
Maley Cl. L8: Liv 5G **71**
Malham Cl. WA5: Gt San 1G **81**
Malhamdale Av. L35: Rainh 5B **60**
Malin Cl. L24: Hale 3D **110**
Mall, The L5: Liv 2G **53**
Mallaby Ct. *CH41: Birke* *1C* ***68***
(off Mallaby St.)
Mallaby St. CH41: Birke 1C **68**
Mallard Cl. L12: Crox 2B **38**
L26: Halew 2G **93**
WA7: Beech 2B **124**
Mallard Gdns. WA9: St H 1C **60**
Mallard Ho. L31: Lyd 3A **6**
Mallard Way CH46: More 6A **48**
WA11: St H 5F **29**
Malleson Rd. L13: Liv 6C **36**
Mallins Cl. L8: Liv 5G **71**
Mallory Av. L31: Lyd 3A **6**
Mallory Gro. WA11: St H 5H **29**
Mallory Rd. CH42: Tran 1F **87**
Mallowdale Cl. CH62: East 2F **121**
Mallow Rd. L6: Liv 4A **54**
Mallow Way L36: Huy 1H **75**
Malmesbury Cl. CH49: Grea 5A **66**
Malmesbury Pk. WA7: Nort 2F **115**
Malmesbury Rd. L11: Norr G 3C **36**
Malpas Av. CH43: Pren 1C **86**
Malpas Dr. CH63: Hghr B 4G **87**
Malpas Gro. CH45: Wall 1C **50**
Malpas Rd. CH45: Wall 1B **50**
L11: Crox 6H **23**
WA7: Run 6F **113**
Malta Cl. L36: Huy 4F **57**
Malta St. L8: Liv 4F **71**
Malta Wlk. L8: Liv 4F **71**
Maltby Cl. WA9: St H 2C **60**
Malt Ho. Ct. WA10: Windle 5A **28**
Malton Cl. WA8: Cron 4A **78**
Malton Rd. L25: Woolt 2D **92**
Malt St. L7: Liv 1H **71**
Malvern Av. L14: Broad G 5B **56**
Malvern Cl. L32: Kirkb 5G **13**
WA5: Gt San 1H **81**

Malvern Cres. L14: Broad G 5B **56**
Malvern Gro. CH42: Tran 1F **87**
   L10: Ain 1A **22**
Malvern Rd. CH45: Wall 2H **49**
   L6: Liv 4A **54**
   L20: Boot .6C **20**
   WA9: Sut H 2B **44**
Malwood St. L8: Liv 5F **71**
Manchester Rd. L34: Presc 1B **58**
Mandela Ct. L8: Liv 4H **71**
Manderston Dr. L12: W Der 6H **37**
Mandeville St. L4: Walt 3F **35**
Manesty's La. L1: Liv 5E **5** (6D **52**)
Manfred St. L6: Liv 5G **53**
Manica Cres. L10: Faz 4D **22**
Manion Av. L31: Lyd 2A **6**
Manion Cl. L31: Lyd 2A **6**
Manley Cl. CH43: O'ton 6B **68**
Manley Pl. WA9: St H 6C **42**
Manley Rd. L22: Water 1E **19**
   L36: Huy .1A **76**
Mannering Ct. L17: Aig 5A **72**
           (off Mannering Rd.)
Mannering Rd. L17: Aig 5H **71**
Manners La. CH60: Hesw 1C **116**
Manningham Rd. L4: Walt 1H **53**
Manning St. WA10: St H 2D **42**
Mannington Cl. CH47: Meols 1E **65**
Mann Island L3: Liv 5B **4** (6B **52**)
Mann St. L8: Liv 3E **71**
Manor Av. L23: Crosb 4F **9**
   L35: Rainh 5A **60**
   WA12: Newt W 1H **45**
Manorbier Cres. L9: Walt 2G **35**
Manor Cl. L20: Boot 3E **35**
Manor Complex L33: Know I 1E **25**
Manor Ct. CH48: W Kir 6A **64**
            (off Bridge Rd.)
   CH49: Grea 6A **66**
   CH61: Irby 5B **84**
   WA9: Sut L 3H **61**
Manor Cres. L25: Woolt 2D **92**
Manor Dr. CH49: Upton 2D **66**
   L23: Crosb 4F **9**
   L30: N'ton 6H **11**
Mnr. Farm Ct. WA6: Frod 6G **123**
Mnr. Farm M. WA7: Manor P 1F **115**
Mnr. Farm Rd. L36: Huy 6H **57**
   WA7: Manor P 1E **115**
Manor Fell WA7: Pal F 6D **114**
MANOR GREEN 2G **67**
Manor Gro. L32: Kirkb 1F **23**
Manor Hill CH43: Clau, O'ton 3C **68**
Manor Ho. CH62: Brom 5D **104**
   L17: Aig 6H **71**
Manor Ho., The CH49: Upton 2D **66**
Manor Ho. Cl. L31: Mag 6B **6**
   WA11: St H 2E **29**
Manor La. CH42: Rock F 1A **88**
   CH45: Wall 2E **51**
Manor M. CH45: Wall 2E **51**
MANOR PARK 1E **115**
Manor Pk. Av. WA7: Manor P 1E **115**
Manor Pk. Bus. Pk.
   WA7: Manor P 1D **114**
Manor Pk. Cl. CH61: Thing 5E **85**
Manor Pk. Ct. WA7: Manor P 1E **115**
Manor Pl. CH62: Brom 6D **88**
   WA8: Wid .2H **95**
Manor Rd. CH44: Wall 2D **50**
   CH45: Wall 2D **50**
   CH47: Hoy 1C **64**
   CH61: Irby 5B **84**
   CH62: East 1D **120**
   CH63: Thorn H 4B **102**
   L23: Blun, Crosb 3E **9**
   L25: Woolt 2D **92**
   WA6: Frod 6G **123**
   WA7: Run 3H **113**
   WA8: Wid .2H **95**
   WA11: Hay 4G **31**
Manor Road Station (Rail) 2C **64**
Manorside Cl. CH49: Upton 3D **66**

Manor St. WA9: St H 3G **43**
Manor Vw. L12: W Der 4B **38**
Manor Way CH43: Bid 2G **67**
   L25: Woolt 2D **92**
            (not continuous)
Manorwood Dr. L35: Whis 5E **59**
Mansell Cl. WA8: Wid 4G **79**
Mansell Dr. L26: Halew 5G **93**
Mansell Rd. L6: Liv 4A **54**
Mansfield St. L3: Liv 1G **5** (4E **53**)
Mansion Dr. L11: Crox 1F **37**
Manston Rd. WA5: Penk 6H **81**
Manton Rd. L6: Liv 4A **54**
Manvers Rd. L16: Child 1A **74**
Manville Rd. CH45: New B 6D **32**
Manville St. WA9: St H 4G **43**
Maple Av. WA7: Run 5G **113**
   WA7: Sut W 3C **124**
   WA8: Wid .4F **97**
   WA11: Hay 4D **30**
Maple Cl. L12: Crox 2H **37**
   L21: Sea .5A **20**
   L35: Whis 4E **59**
Maple Ct. L21: Lith 3B **20**
   L34: Know 1E **39**
Maple Cres. L36: Roby 5F **57**
   WA5: Penk 5H **81**
Mapledale Rd. L18: Moss H 4F **73**
Maple Gro. CH62: Brom 5C **104**
   L8: Liv 3A **72**
   L35: Presc 2E **59**
   WA10: St H 2A **42**
Maple Leaf Dr. L36: Huy 1F **57**
Maples Ct. CH43: O'ton 6C **68**
Maple St. CH41: Birke 4F **69**
Mapleton Cl. CH43: Pren 2A **86**
Mapleton Dr. WA7: Sut W 4B **124**
Maple Tree Gro.
   CH60: Hesw 5G **101**
Maplewood L32: Kirkb 3B **24**
Maplewood Cl. L27: N'ley 4G **75**
   WA8: Wid .4G **95**
Maplewood Gro. CH43: Bid 1A **68**
Marathon Cl. L6: Liv 3F **53**
Marble Cl. L20: Boot 3C **34**
Marbury Rd. L32: Kirkb 1G **23**
Marc Av. L31: Mell 5F **13**
Marcham Way L11: Norr G 4F **37**
Marchfield Rd. L9: Walt 6F **21**
March Rd. L6: Liv 2B **54**
Marchwood Way L25: Gate 2C **74**
Marcien Way WA8: Wid 6D **78**
Marcot Rd. L6: Liv 3B **54**
Marcus Ct. L36: Huy 3A **58**
           (off Mosscroft Cl.)
Marcus St. CH41: Birke 2G **69**
Mardale Av. WA11: St H 3F **29**
Mardale Cl. L27: N'ley 6A **76**
Mardale Lawn L27: N'ley 6A **76**
Mardale Rd. L36: Huy 2E **57**
Mardale Wlk. L27: N'ley 6A **76**
           (off Mardale Cl.)
   L36: Huy .2E **57**
Mareth Cl. L18: Moss H 1E **91**
Marford Rd. L12: W Der 6F **37**
Marfords Av. CH63: Brom 6C **104**
Margaret Av. L20: Boot 5C **20**
   WA9: St H 5G **43**
Margaret Ct. WA8: Wid 4F **97**
   WA10: St H 4B **42**
Margaret Rd. L4: Walt 3E **35**
   L23: Blun .4C **8**
Margaret St. L6: Liv 3G **53**
   WA9: Clock F 4A **62**
Margery Rd. WA10: St H 4A **42**
Marian Av. WA12: Newt W 2H **45**
Marian Cl. L35: Rainh 5A **60**
Marian Cl., The L30: N'ton 5E **11**
Marian Dr. CH46: More 1C **66**
   L35: Rainh 5H **59**
Marian Rd. WA11: Hay 4G **31**
Marian Sq. L30: N'ton 6F **11**
Marian Way, The L30: N'ton 5E **11**

Maria Rd. L9: Walt 2F **35**
Marie Curie Av. L30: N'ton 5F **11**
            (not continuous)
Marigold Way WA9: Bold 6C **44**
Marina Av. L21: Lith 4B **20**
   WA9: St H 6G **43**
Marina Cres. L30: N'ton 2G **21**
   L36: Huy .6F **57**
Marina Gro. WA7: Run 3F **113**
Marina La. WA7: Murd 6G **115**
Marina Village WA7: Pres B 6G **115**
Marine AFC 6E **9**
Marine Cres. L22: Water 2F **19**
Marine Dr. CH60: Hesw 6B **100**
Marine Pk. CH48: W Kir 5B **64**
Marine Pk. Mans.
   CH45: New B 4D **32**
Marine Prom. CH45: New B 4D **32**
Mariner Cl. WA7: Murd 1F **125**
Marine Rd. CH47: Hoy 2A **64**
Mariners Pk. CH44: Wall 1F **51**
Mariners Rd. CH45: New B 6E **33**
   L23: Blun .1D **18**
Mariners Way L20: Boot 2C **34**
       (off Strand Shop. Cen.)
Mariners Wharf L3: Liv 3C **70**
Marine Ter. CH45: Wall 6E **33**
   L22: Water 3F **19**
Marion Dr. WA7: West 1D **122**
Marion Gro. L18: Moss H 1G **91**
Marion Rd. L20: Boot 5D **20**
Marion St. CH41: Birke 3G **69**
Maritime Cen. L21: Sea 4G **19**
Maritime Ct. CH49: Woodc 2F **85**
           (off Childwall Grn.)
   L12: W Der 5E **37**
   L30: N'ton 4F **11**
Maritime Ent. Pk. L20: Boot 2B **34**
Maritime Grange CH44: Wall 5G **51**
Maritime Gro. CH43: O'ton 4D **68**
Maritime Lodge L5: Liv 1F **53**
            (off Towson St.)
Maritime Pk. CH43: O'ton 4E **69**
Maritime Pl. L3: Liv 1H **5** (4E **53**)
Maritime Vw. CH47: Tran 6F **69**
Maritime Way L1: Liv 6E **5** (1D **70**)
Marius Cl. L4: Walt 5F **35**
Markden M. L8: Liv 2F **71**
Market Pl. L34: Presc 1D **58**
   WA8: Wid .4E **97**
Market Pl. Sth. CH41: Birke 3H **69**
Market Sq. L1: Liv 4F **5**
   L32: Kirkb 1A **24**
Market St. CH41: Birke 3G **69**
   CH47: Hoy 3B **64**
   WA8: Wid .4E **97**
   WA10: St H 2E **43**
   WA12: Newt W 1H **45**
Market Way L1: Liv 4F **5**
Markfield Cres. L25: Woolt 2E **93**
   WA11: St H 6G **29**
Markfield Rd. L20: Boot 6B **20**
Markham Gro. CH43: Bid 1B **68**
Mark Rake CH62: Brom 4D **104**
Mark St. CH44: Wall 5G **51**
   L5: Liv 6E **35**
Marksway CH61: Pens 1E **101**
Marlborough Av. L30: N'ton 1G **21**
   L31: Lyd 4C **6**
Marlborough Ct. L17: Aig 1C **90**
           (off Aigburth Va.)
Marlborough Cres. WA8: Wid 4E **79**
Marlborough Gro. CH43: O'ton 5E **69**
Marlborough Pl. L3: Liv 1D **4** (4C **52**)
Marlborough Rd. CH45: New B 6E **33**
   L13: Liv 1B **54**
   L22: Water 3G **19**
   L23: Crosb 6F **9**
   L34: Presc 6E **41**
Marlborough St. L3: Liv 1D **4** (4C **52**)
Marlborough Way WA11: Hay 3G **31**
Marlbrook Rd. L25: Gate 3D **74**
Marlcroft Dr. L17: Aig 3C **90**

Marldon Av. L23: Crosb 1G **19**
Marldon Rd. L12: W Der 5E **37**
Marled Hey L28: Stockb V 5C **38**
Marley Cl. L35: Rainh 6C **60**
Marlfield La. CH61: Pens 1E **101**
Marlfield Rd. L12: W Der 1F **55**
Marline Av. CH63: Brom 1C **120**
Marling Pk. WA8: Wid 2H **95**
Marlowe Cl. WA8: Wid 2D **96**
Marlowe Dr. L12: W Der 1E **55**
Marlowe Rd. CH44: Wall 3C **50**
CH64: Nest 6A **118**
Marl Rd. L30: N'ton 6H **11**
L33: Know I 6E **15**
Marlsford St. L6: Liv 4A **54**
Marlston Av. CH61: Irby 5D **84**
Marlston Pl. WA7: Run 1F **123**
Marlwood Av. CH45: Wall 2A **50**
Marmaduke St. L7: Liv 6H **53**
Marmion Av. L20: Boot 4E **21**
Marmion Rd. CH47: Hoy 2B **64**
L17: Aig 5A **72**
Marmonde St. L4: Walt 5E **35**
Marnell Cl. L5: Liv 2C **52**
Marnwood Rd. L32: Kirkb 2H **23**
Marnwood Wlk. L32: Kirkb 2G **23**
Marple Cl. CH43: O'ton 6A **68**
Marquis St. CH41: Tran 5G **69**
CH62: New F 4B **88**
L3: Liv 3H **5** (5E **53**)
Marram Cl. CH46: More 5E **49**
Marsden Av. WA10: St H 1B **42**
Marsden Cl. CH44: Wall 2F **51**
Marsden Ct. CH45: New B 6D **32**
WA8: Wid 5C **78**
Marsden Rd. L26: Halew 5H **93**
Marsden St. L6: Liv 4G **53**
Marsden Way L6: Liv 4G **53**
MARSH, THE 6C **96**
Marshall Av. WA9: St H 5G **43**
Marshall Cl. L33: Kirkb 4B **14**
Marshall Pl. L3: Liv 3C **52**
Marshall's Cl. L31: Lyd 3B **6**
MARSHALL'S CROSS 2F **61**
Marshalls Cross (Park & Ride) 1F **61**
Marshalls Cross Rd. WA9: St H 1F **61**
Marshall St. CH41: Birke 1E **69**
Marsham Cl. CH49: Upton 2E **67**
Marsham Rd. L25: Gate 4E **75**
Marsh Av. L20: Boot 5E **21**
Marshfield Cl. L36: Huy 4H **57**
Marshfield Ct. CH46: Leas 4C **48**
Marshfield Rd. L11: Norr G 4F **37**
(not continuous)
Marshgate WA8: Wid 4H **95**
Marshgate Pl. WA6: Frod 5H **123**
Marshgate Rd. L12: W Der 3F **37**
Marsh Hall Pad WA8: Wid 5F **79**
Marsh Hall Rd. WA8: Wid 5F **79**
Marshlands Rd. CH45: Wall 1A **50**
Marsh La. CH63: Hghr B 4E **87**
L20: Boot 1A **34**
WA5: Cuerd 1E **99**
WA7: Ast 2B **114**
Marshside Cl. L8: Liv 4F **71**
Marsh St. L20: Kirkd 4D **34**
WA8: Wid 5E **97**
WA9: St H 2G **43**
Marsland Gro. WA9: St H 5A **44**
Marston Cl. CH43: O'ton 6B **68**
CH62: East 4E **121**
Marsworth Dr. L6: Liv 3F **53**
Marten Av. CH63: Brom 6C **104**
Martensen St. L7: Liv 6H **53**
Martham Gdns. WA9: St H 1C **60**
Martial Arts Studio, The *1E* ***43***
(off Tolver St.)
Martin Av. WA10: St H 5D **28**
Martin Cl. CH61: Irby 5A **84**
L18: Moss H 2E **91**
L35: Rainh 3G **59**
WA7: Pal F 6C **114**
Martindale Gro. WA7: Beech 2H **123**
Martindale Rd. CH62: Brom 4E **105**
L18: Moss H 4H **73**
WA11: St H 1F **29**
Martine Cl. L31: Mell 5F **13**
Martin Gro. L35: Presc 2E **59**
Martinhall Rd. L9: Faz 1D **36**
Martin Rd. L18: Moss H 2E **91**
Martin's La. CH44: Wall 3E **51**
Martland Av. L10: Ain 6C **12**
Martland Rd. L25: Gate 5E **75**
Martlesham Cres. CH49: Grea 6H **65**
Martlett Rd. L12: W Der 2H **55**
Martock L35: Whis 5F **59**
Marton Cl. L24: Speke 3F **109**
Marton Grn. L24: Speke 3F **109**
Marton Rd. L36: Huy 1G **57**
Marvin St. L6: Liv 4G **53**
Marwood Towers *L5: Liv 1E* ***53***
(off Boundary St.)
Marybone L3: Liv 2D **4** (5D **52**)
Marybone Apartments *L3: Liv 1E* ***5***
(off Marybone)
Marybone Student Village *L3: Liv 2E* ***5***
(off Marybone)
Maryhill Rd. WA7: Run 5E **113**
Maryland Ho. *L20: Boot 2C* ***34***
(off Georgia Cl.)
Maryland La. CH46: More 6B **48**
Maryland St. L1: Liv 6H **5** (1E **71**)
Marylebone Av. WA9: St H 1D **60**
Marymount Cl. CH44: Wall 4D **50**
Maryport Cl. L5: Liv 1F **53**
Mary Rd. L20: Boot 5D **20**
Mary Stockton Ct. *L21: Sea 5A* ***20***
(off Seaforth Va. W.)
Mary St. WA8: Wid 4H **97**
WA9: Clock F 4A **62**
Maryton Grange L18: Aller 1H **91**
Maryville Rd. L34: Presc 1E **59**
Marywell Cl. WA9: St H 6H **43**
Marzhan Way WA8: Wid 2G **97**
Masefield Av. WA8: Wid 3D **96**
Masefield Cl. CH62: New F 4A **88**
Masefield Cres. L30: Boot 3D **20**
Masefield Gro. L16: Child 1B **74**
WA10: St H 6B **28**
Masefield Pl. L30: Boot 3E **21**
Masefield Rd. L23: Thorn 3C **10**
Maskell Rd. L13: Liv 4D **54**
Mason Av. WA8: Wid 5E **79**
Mason St. CH45: New B 5D **32**
L7: Liv 6G **53**
L22: Water 2F **19**
L25: Woolt 1C **92**
WA7: Run 2G **113**
Massam Cl. WA11: Rainf 3G **17**
Masseyfield Rd. WA7: Brook 2C **124**
Massey Pk. CH45: Wall 2C **50**
Massey St. CH41: Birke 1F **69**
WA9: St H 5G **43**
Master's Way L19: Garst 1H **107**
Matchwood Cl. L19: Garst 6H **91**
Matchworks, The
L19: Garst 6A **92**
Mater Cl. L9: Ain 2B **36**
Mather Av. L18: Aller, Moss H 5F **73**
L19: Aller 1G **91**
WA7: West P 6B **112**
WA9: St H 2A **44**
Mather Ct. CH43: O'ton 4D **68**
Mather Rd. CH43: O'ton 4D **68**
Mathew St. L2: Liv 4D **4** (6C **52**)
Mathieson Rd. WA8: Wid 6C **96**
Matlock Av. L9: Walt 5G **21**
Matlock Cl. WA5: Gt San 6H **63**
Matthew Cl. CH44: Wall 5G **51**
Matthew St. CH44: Wall 5G **51**
Maud Roberts Ct. L21: Lith 3A **20**
Maud St. L8: Liv 3G **71**
Maunders Ct. L23: Crosb 4H **9**
Maureen Wlk. L10: Faz 4F **23**
Mauretania Rd. L4: Walt 3G **35**
Maurice Jones Ct. CH46: More 6C **48**
Mavis Dr. CH49: Woodc 6E **67**
Max Rd. L14: Knott A 2B **56**
Maxton Rd. L6: Liv 4A **54**
Maxwell Cl. CH49: Upton 3E **67**
Maxwell Ct. CH42: Tran 6E **69**
Maxwell Pl. L13: Liv 1D **54**
Maxwell Rd. L13: Liv 1D **54**
Maxwell St. WA10: St H 2C **42**
May Av. CH44: Wall 5F **51**
Maybank Gro. L17: Aig 2D **90**
Maybank Rd. CH42: Tran 5F **69**
Maybury Way L17: Aig 1A **90**
May Cl. L21: Lith 5B **20**
Mayer Av. CH63: Beb 1H **103**
Mayew Rd. CH61: Irby 5D **84**
Mayfair Av. L14: Broad G 5B **56**
L23: Crosb 4G **9**
Mayfair Cl. L6: Liv 3H **53**
WA5: Gt San 2F **81**
Mayfair Ct. *CH43: O'ton 6D* ***68***
(off The Grove)
Mayfair Gro. WA8: Wid 2B **96**
Mayfayre Av. L31: Lyd 2A **6**
Mayfield L4: Kirkd 5E **35**
Mayfield Av. WA8: Wid 2H **95**
WA9: St H 5C **42**
Mayfield Cl. L12: W Der 1G **55**
Mayfield Ct. WA8: Wid 1E **97**
Mayfield Dr. CH62: East 1H **121**
Mayfield Gdns. CH64: Nest 6A **118**
L19: Gras 4E **91**
Mayfield Rd. CH45: Wall 2B **50**
CH63: Beb 2A **104**
L19: Gras 4E **91**
Mayfields Ho. *CH62: New F 4B* ***88***
(off Mayfields Nth.)
Mayfields Nth. CH62: New F 4B **88**
Mayfields Sth. CH62: New F 4B **88**
Mayflower Av. L24: Speke 5C **92**
Mayford Cl. L25: Gate 3E **75**
Mayhall Ct. L31: Mag 5C **6**
May Pl. L13: Liv 5E **55**
Maypole Ct. L30: N'ton 4D **10**
L34: Know 6E **25**
May Rd. CH60: Hesw 5E **101**
May St. L3: Liv 5H **5** (6E **53**)
L20: Boot 6C **20**
Maytree Cl. L27: N'ley 3E **75**
Mayville Rd. L18: Moss H 4F **73**
Mazenod Ct. L3: Liv 1E **5**
Mazzini Cl. L5: Liv 2E **53**
Mead Av. L21: Lith 3C **20**
Meade Cl. L35: Rainh 6B **60**
Meade Rd. L13: Liv 1C **54**
Meadfoot Rd. CH46: More 6B **48**
Meadow, The CH49: Woodc 6F **67**
(not continuous)
Meadow Av. WA9: Clock F 4H **61**
Meadow Bank L31: Mag 5A **6**
L32: Kirkb 5G **13**
Meadowbank Cl. L12: W Der 2A **56**
Meadowbarn Cl. L32: Kirkb 2A **24**
Meadow Brook Cl. L10: Faz 4F **23**
Meadowbrook Rd. CH46: More 2B **66**
Meadow Cl. CH64: Will 6H **119**
WA8: Wid 6B **78**
WA12: Newt W 2H **45**
Meadow Ct. L11: Norr G 2F **37**
L25: Woolt 6D **74**
Meadow Cres. CH49: Woodc 1E **85**
Meadow Cft. CH64: Will 6G **119**
Meadowcroft CH60: Hesw 4G **101**
WA9: St H 1G **61**
Meadowcroft Ct. WA7: Cas 5C **114**
Meadowcroft Pk. L12: W Der 3H **55**
Meadowcroft Rd. CH45: Wall 1B **50**
CH47: Meols 6E **47**
Meadow Dr. L36: Huy 1H **75**
Meadowfield Cl. CH42: Rock F 1H **87**
L9: Walt 4G **21**
Meadowgate CH48: Caldy 6D **82**
Meadow Hey L20: Boot 6A **20**
Meadow Hey Cl. L25: Woolt 6D **74**

Meadow La. CH42: Rock F 1H **87**
CH64: Will 6G **119**
L12: W Der 4F **37**
L31: Mag 6D **6**
WA9: St H 3B **44**
Meadow Oak Dr. L25: Gate 5C **74**
Meadow Pk. CH42: Rock F 1H **87**
Meadow Rd. CH48: W Kir 6F **65**
Meadow Row WA7: Cas 4C **114**
Meadows, The *CH41: Birke 2F 69*
(off Conway St.)
CH62: Brom 6D **104**
L31: Mag 6C **6**
L35: Rainh 4A **60**
Meadowside CH46: Leas 3F **49**
Meadowside Dr. L33: Kirkb 3B **14**
Meadowside Rd. CH62: Brom 6D **104**
Meadow St. CH45: New B 5C **32**
Meadowsweet Rd. L33: Kirkb 5B **14**
Meadow Vw. L21: Ford 6B **10**
Meadow Wlk. CH61: Pens 2C **100**
WA7: Pal F 6B 114
(off Halton Lea Shop. Cen.)
Meadow Way L12: W Der 4F **37**
Meads, The L34: Eccl P 6G **41**
Meadway CH45: Wall 2C **50**
CH49: Upton 3F **67**
CH60: Hesw 1D **116**
CH62: Spit 3C **104**
L15: Wav 1G **73**
L30: N'ton 1G **21**
L31: Mag 2H **11**
L35: Whis 3F **59**
WA7: Run 4A **114**
WA8: Wid 2G **95**
Mealor's Weint CH64: Park 6F **117**
Meander, The L12: W Der 4A **38**
Measham Cl. WA11: St H 6G **29**
Measham Way L12: Crox 2A **38**
Mecca Bingo
Birkenhead 3F 69
Liverpool 3A 56
St Helens 1D 42
Medbourne Cres. L32: Kirkb 3B **24**
Medea Cl. L5: Liv 1E **53**
Medlock Ct. CH43: O'ton 4C **68**
Medlock St. L4: Kirkd 5E **35**
Medway *L20: Boot 2C 34*
(off Strand Shop. Cen.)
Medway Ct. WA9: St H 2B **44**
Medway Rd. CH42: Rock F 1A **88**
Meerbrook Gro. *L33: Kirkb 4B 14*
(off Langton Rd.)
Meeting La. WA5: Penk 4F **81**
Mega Centre, The 3C 52
Melbourne Cl. L24: Speke 1D **108**
Melbourne St. CH45: New B 5C **32**
WA9: St H 6C **42**
Melbreck Rd. L18: Aller 2F **91**
Melbury Rd. L14: Knott A 1D **56**
Melda Cl. L6: Liv 4F **53**
Meldon Cl. L12: W Der 3G **37**
Meldrum Rd. L15: Wav 3F **73**
Melford Dr. CH43: Pren 2A **86**
WA7: Run 4G **113**
Melford Gro. L6: Liv 1B **54**
Meliden Gdns. WA9: St H 6B **44**
Melksham Dr. CH61: Irby 4B **84**
MELLING 4D 12
Melling Av. L9: Ain 4H **21**
Melling Ct. CH45: New B 6E **33**
Melling Dr. L32: Kirkb 6A **14**
Melling La. L31: Mag 2C **12**
MELLING MOUNT 2G 13
Melling Rd. CH45: New B 6E **33**
L9: Ain 3H **21**
L20: Boot 6C **20**
Melling Way L32: Kirkb 6A **14**
Melloncroft Dr. CH48: Caldy 3B **82**
Melloncroft Dr. W. CH48: Caldy 4C **82**
Mellor Cl. L35: Tar G 2A **76**
WA7: Wind H 5F **115**
Mellor Rd. CH42: Tran 1E **87**
Melly Rd. L17: Aig 6H **71**
Melrose CH46: More 6E **49**
Melrose Av. CH47: Hoy 2B **64**
L23: Crosb 6G **9**
WA5: Burtw 6H **45**
WA10: Eccl 6H **27**
Melrose Gdns. CH43: Pren 3B **86**
Melrose Pk. *L22: Water 3G 19*
(off Melrose Rd.)
Melrose Rd. L4: Kirkd 5D **34**
L22: Water 3G **19**
L33: Kirkb 3H **13**
Melton Cl. CH49: Upton 4C **66**
Melton Rd. WA7: Run 1G **123**
Melverley Rd. L32: Kirkb 1F **23**
Melville CH62: New F 2B **88**
Melville Av. CH42: Rock F 2A **88**
Melville Cl. WA8: Wid 2H **97**
WA10: St H 1B **42**
Melville Pl. L7: Liv 1G **71**
Melville Rd. CH63: Hghr B 6G **87**
L20: Boot 4C **20**
Melville St. L8: Liv 4G **71**
Melwood Dr. L12: W Der 6G **37**
Melwood (Liverpool FC Training Ground)
6G 37
Menai M. *L34: Presc 1E 59*
(off St James' Rd.)
Menai Rd. L20: Boot 5D **20**
Menai St. CH41: Birke 3E **69**
Mendell Cl. CH62: Brom 5E **105**
Mendip Cl. CH42: Tran 2E **87**
L26: Halew 4G **93**
Mendip Gro. WA9: St H 2B **44**
Mendip Rd. CH42: Tran 2E **87**
L15: Wav 3E **73**
Mendips (Childhood Home of John Lennon)
6A 74
Menlo Av. CH61: Irby 5D **84**
Menlo Cl. CH43: O'ton 5A **68**
Menlove Av. L18: Moss H 4F **73**
L25: Woolt 5H **73**
Menlove Ct. L18: Moss H 4G **73**
Menlove Gdns. Nth. L18: Moss H 4F **73**
Menlove Gdns. Sth. L18: Moss H 4F **73**
Menlove Gdns. W. L18: Moss H 4F **73**
Menlove Mans. L18: Moss H 3G **73**
Menstone Rd. L13: Liv 3D **54**
Mentmore Cres. L11: Norr G 4F **37**
Mentmore Rd. L18: Moss H 1E **91**
MEOLS 1E 65
Meol's Cl. L24: Hale 3E **111**
Meols Ct. CH47: Hoy 3A **64**
Meols Dr. CH47: Hoy 6A **64**
CH48: W Kir 6A **64**
Meols Pde. CH47: Meols 1B **64**
Meols Station (Rail) 1E 65
Mercer Av. L32: Kirkb 1G **23**
Mercer Ct. L12: W Der 1A **56**
L20: Boot 2C 34
(off Clairville Cl.)
Mercer Dr. L4: Kirkd 6E **35**
Mercer Rd. CH43: Bid 1A **68**
WA11: Hay 5F **31**
Mercer St. L19: Garst 6G **91**
WA5: Burtw 1G **63**
Merchant Cl. L30: N'ton 3H **21**
Merchants Ct. L1: Liv 5D **4**
Mercury Ct. L3: Liv 2C **4** (5C **52**)
Mere Av. CH63: Raby M 1B **120**
Mere Bank L17: Aig 5C **72**
Merebank CH43: O'ton 5A **68**
Merecliff L28: Stockb V 5E **39**
Merecroft Av. CH44: Wall 5E **51**
Meredale Rd. L18: Moss H 5E **73**
Meredith St. L19: Garst 6A **92**
Mere Farm Gro. CH43: O'ton 5B **68**
Mere Farm Rd. CH43: O'ton 5A **68**
Mere Grn. L4: Walt 4G **35**
Mere Gro. WA11: St H 2F **29**
Mereheath CH46: Leas 4C **48**
Mereheath Gdns. *CH46: Leas 4C 48*
(off Mereheath)
Mere Hey WA10: Eccl 2G **41**
Mereland Way WA9: St H 3B **44**
Mere La. CH45: Wall 6A **32**
CH60: Hesw 3C **100**
L5: Liv 2F **53**
Mere Pk. L23: Blun 5E **9**
Mere Pk. Rd. CH49: Grea 6A **66**
Meres Rd. L9: Ain 4C **22**
Merevale Cl. WA7: Beech 1A **124**
Mereview Cres. L12: Crox 2H **37**
Merewood L32: Kirkb 3B **24**
Mereworth CH48: Caldy 5D **82**
Meribel Cl. L23: Crosb 4A **10**
Meribel Sq. L34: Presc 1D **58**
Meriden Av. CH63: Spit 4A **104**
Meriden Cl. WA11: St H 5H **29**
Meriden Rd. L25: Gate 3D **74**
Meridian Bus. Village L24: Speke 5E **93**
Merlin Av. CH49: Upton 3B **66**
Merlin Cl. CH49: Upton 3B **66**
WA7: Cas 4C **114**
WA11: St H 5F **29**
Merlin Ct. L26: Halew 2F **93**
Merlin Rd. CH42: Tran 6E **69**
Merlin St. L8: Liv 3F **71**
Merrills La. CH49: Upton 4E **67**
Merrilocks Grn. L23: Blun 4C **8**
Merrilocks Rd. L23: Blun 4C **8**
Merrilox Av. L31: Lyd 4C **6**
Merrion Cl. L25: Woolt 6B **74**
Merritt Av. CH41: Birke 1D **68**
Merrivale Rd. L25: Woolt 1E **93**
Merrydale Dr. L11: Crox 2G **37**
Mersey Av. L19: Aig 3D **90**
L31: Mag 5E **7**
Merseybank Ho. *CH62: New F 3B 88*
(off New Ferry Rd.)
Merseybank Rd. CH62: New F 3B **88**
Mersey Cotts. L19: Garst 6H **91**
Mersey Ct. *CH44: Wall 5G 51*
(off Borough Rd. E.)
L23: Crosb 6E **9**
Mersey Ho. L20: Boot 1B **34**
Mersey Indoor Karting Cen. 1C 72
Mersey La. Sth. CH42: Rock F 1A **88**
Mersey Rd. CH42: Rock F 1A **88**
L17: Aig 4C **90**
L23: Blun, Crosb 6E **9**
WA7: Run 2E **113**
WA8: Wid 1E **113**
Merseyside Maritime Mus. 6C 4 (1C 70)
Merseyside Youth Challenge Trust 2B 92
Merseysport 3D 70
Mersey St. CH44: Wall 5G **51**
WA9: St H 2C **44**
Mersey Tunnel - Toll L3: Liv 4H **51**
(not continuous)
Mersey Vw. *CH41: Tran 5G 69*
(off Marquis St.)
CH63: Hghr B 5F **87**
L22: Water 1E **19**
WA7: West P 6B **112**
Mersey Vw. Cotts. WA7: West 1D **122**
Mersey Vw. Rd. WA8: Hale B 1H **111**
Mersey Wlk. CH42: Tran 6G **69**
Mersham Ct. WA8: Wid 5D **78**
Merstone Cl. L26: Halew 4H **93**
Merthyr Gro. L16: Child 6A **56**
Merton Bank Rd. WA9: St H 6G **29**
Merton Cl. L36: Huy 5D **56**
Merton Cres. L36: Huy 5D **56**
Merton Dr. CH49: Woodc 6E **67**
L36: Huy 5C **56**
Merton Gro. L20: Boot 2C **34**
L23: Blun 6E **9**
Merton Ho. L20: Boot 2C **34**
Merton Pl. CH43: O'ton 3E **69**
Merton Rd. CH45: Wall 2C **50**
CH65: Hoot 4H **121**
L20: Boot 2C **34**
Merton St. WA9: St H 6G **29**
Merton Towers L20: Boot 2D **34**
Mesham Cl. CH49: Upton 4C **66**

Metcalf Cl.—Mithril Cl.

Metcalf Cl. L33: Kirkb .3H **13**
Methuen St. CH41: Birke .1C **68**
L15: Wav .1C **72**
Metquarter L1: Liv .4E **5** (6D **52**)
Mevagissey Rd. WA7: Brook .2E **125**
Mews, The L17: Aig .2D **90**
L23: Crosb .6G **9**
L28: Stockb V .6E **39**
WA5: Burtw .1G **63**
Meyrick Ct. WA12: Newt W .2H **45**
Meyrick Rd. L11: Norr G .3C **36**
Micawber Cl. L8: Liv .4F **71**
Michael Dragonette Ct. L3: Liv .3C **52**
Michigan Cl. L27: N'ley .4G **75**
Mickering La. L39: Augh .1G **7**
Micklefield Rd. L15: Wav .3D **72**
Micklegate WA7: Murd .6F **115**
Micklehead Bus. Village WA9: St H .4E **61**
MICKLEHEAD GREEN .4E **61**
Micklehead Grn. WA9: St H .4D **60**
Middlefield Rd. L18: Aller .6A **74**
Middleham Cl. L32: Kirkb .2G **23**
Middlehey Av. L34: Know .1F **39**
Middlehurst Av. WA10: St H .1D **42**
Middlehurst Cl. L34: Eccl P .6G **41**
Middlemass Hey L27: N'ley .4G **75**
Middle Rd. L24: Halew .6H **93**
(not continuous)
Middlesex Rd. L20: Boot .1D **34**
Middleton Ct. L24: Speke .3G **109**
Middleton Rd. L7: Liv .5C **54**
L22: Water .1H **19**
Middle Way L11: Crox .1H **37**
Middlewood L32: Kirkb .3B **24**
Midghall St. L3: Liv .1D **4** (4C **52**)
Midhurst Rd. L12: Crox .2B **38**
Midland St. CH43: O'ton .4E **69**
WA8: Wid .2F **97**
Midland Ter. L22: Water .2F **19**
Midlothian Dr. L23: Blun .6E **9**
Midway Rd. L36: Huy .3G **57**
Midwood St. WA8: Wid .3F **97**
Milbrook Cres. L32: Kirkb .6A **14**
Milbrook Dr. L32: Kirkb .6A **14**
Milbrook Wlk. L32: Kirkb .6A **14**
Mildenhall Rd. L25: Gate .3C **74**
Mildenhall Way *L25: Gate .3D 74*
(off Mildenhall Rd.)
Mildmay Rd. L11: Norr G .3C **36**
L20: Boot .6B **20**
Mile End L5: Liv .3D **52**
Miles Cl. CH49: Grea .6A **66**
Miles La. CH49: Grea .1A **84**
Miles St. L8: Liv .5G **71**
Milestone Hey L28: Stockb V .5D **38**
Milford Dr. L12: Crox .2A **38**
Milford St. L5: Kirkd .1C **52**
Milk St. WA10: St H .2E **43**
Millachip Ct. *L6: Liv .3H 53*
(off White Rock St.)
Milland Cl. L11: Crox .2G **37**
Millar Cres. WA8: Wid .4E **97**
Mill Av. WA5: Gt San .2G **81**
Mill Bank L13: Liv .1D **54**
Millbank Cotts. L31: Mag .4D **6**
Millbank Ct. L9: Ain .3B **22**
Millbank La. L31: Augh, Mag .4E **7**
L39: Augh .4F **7**
Mill Bank Rd. CH44: Wall .4C **50**
Millbeck Cl. L32: Kirkb .5A **14**
Millbeck Gro. WA11: St H .1F **29**
Mill Brook Bus. Pk. WA11: Rainf .6H **17**
Millbrook Ct. L34: Know .6E **25**
Millbrook La. WA10: Eccl .1H **41**
Millbrook Rd. CH41: Birke .5D **50**
Mill Brow CH63: Hghr B .5F **87**
WA8: Wid .1G **97**
WA9: Sut L .2H **61**
WA10: Eccl .1H **41**
Mill Brow Cl. WA9: Sut L .2H **61**
Millbutt Cl. CH63: Hghr B .5F **87**
Mill Cl. CH42: Tran .5F **69**
L23: Crosb .3G **9**
Mill Ct. L30: N'ton .4D **10**
Mill Cft. CH64: Nest .6A **118**
Millcroft L23: Crosb .4A **10**
Millcroft Pk. CH49: Grea .6H **65**
Millcroft Rd. L25: Woolt .2E **93**
Millennium Ct. CH64: Nest .6A **118**
Millennium Rd. L8: Liv .3G **71**
Miller Av. L23: Crosb .4F **9**
Millers Bri. L20: Boot .3B **34**
Millers Bri. Ind. Est. L20: Boot .3B **34**
Millers Cl. CH46: More .2H **65**
Millerscroft L32: Kirkb .6G **13**
Millersdale WA9: Clock F .3G **61**
Millersdale Av. L9: Ain .4H **21**
Millersdale Cl. CH62: East .2F **121**
Millersdale Gro. WA7: Beech .1H **123**
Millersdale Rd. L18: Moss H .5E **73**
Millers Fold WA10: Eccl .1H **41**
Millers Way CH46: More .1A **66**
Millfield CH64: Nest .6A **118**
Millfield Bus. Pk. WA11: Hay .3G **31**
Millfield Cl. CH63: Hghr B .6F **87**
L13: W Der .1E **55**
Millfield La. WA11: Hay .1G **31**
WN4: Ash M .1G **31**
Millfield Rd. WA8: Wid .1G **97**
Millfields WA10: Eccl .2G **41**
Mill Grn. CH64: Will .6H **119**
Millgreen Cl. L12: Crox .2A **38**
Mill Grn. La. WA8: Wid .4H **79**
Mill Gro. L21: Lith .3B **20**
Mill Hey L35: Rainh .6C **60**
Mill Hey Rd. CH48: Caldy .5D **82**
Mill Hill CH43: O'ton .6C **68**
Mill Hill Rd. CH61: Irby .3A **84**
Millhouse Cl. CH46: More .6H **47**
Millhouse Ct. L12: W Der .1E **55**
Millhouse La. CH46: More .6H **47**
Millington Cl. CH43: Pren .2A **86**
WA7: Sut W .3B **124**
WA8: Wid .3D **96**
Mill La. CH44: Wall .4C **50**
CH49: Grea .6A **66**
CH60: Hesw .5F **101**
CH64: Will .6G **119**
L3: Liv .2F **5** (5D **52**)
L12: W Der .1E **55**
L13: Liv .5E **55**
L15: Wav .5E **55**
L20: Boot .2D **34**
L32: Kirkb .5G **13**
L34: Know .6F **25**
L35: Rainh .5A **60**
WA6: Frod .5A **124**
WA8: Cron .4B **78**
WA8: Wid, Bold H .4H **79**
WA9: Sut L .2G **61**
WA11: Rainf .6H **17**
Millom Av. L35: Rainh .3H **59**
Millom Gro. L12: W Der .4G **37**
WA10: St H .5A **42**
Mill Pk. Dr. CH62: East .4E **121**
Mill Rd. CH61: Thing .5E **85**
CH62: Brom .2D **104**
CH63: Hghr B .4F **87**
L6: Liv .3F **53**
(not continuous)
Mill Spring Ct. L20: Boot .2D **34**
Mill Sq. L10: Ain .1C **22**
Millstead Rd. L15: Wav .1E **73**
Millstead Wlk. *L15: Wav .1E 73*
(off Millstead Rd.)
Mill Stile L25: Woolt .1C **92**
Mill Stream Cl. L29: Seft .2F **11**
Mill St. CH42: Tran .5F **69**
L8: Liv .3E **71**
L25: Woolt .1C **92**
L34: Presc .1D **58**
WA10: St H .1D **42**
Mill Ter. CH63: Hghr B .6F **87**
Millthwaite Ct. CH44: Wall .3B **50**
Millthwaite Rd. CH44: Wall .3B **50**
Millvale St. L6: Liv .4A **54**
Mill Vw. L8: Liv .4E **71**
Millview L32: Kirkb .5G **13**
Mill Vw. Dr. CH63: Hghr B .5E **87**
Millway Rd. L24: Speke .1A **110**
Mill Weir Gdns. L29: Seft .2F **11**
Millwood CH63: Hghr B .5F **87**
WA7: Nort .4E **115**
Millwood Av. WA10: Eccl .2F **41**
Millwood Ct. L24: Speke .1A **110**
Millwood Gdns. L35: Whis .5F **59**
Millwood Rd. L24: Speke .2G **109**
MILL YARD .3H **55**
Mill Yd. CH61: Thing .5F **85**
Milman Ct. L25: Woolt .6A **74**
Milman Rd. L4: Walt .4F **35**
Milman Way CH49: Upton .5D **66**
Milner Cop CH60: Hesw .5E **101**
Milne Rd. L13: Liv .5C **36**
Milner Rd. CH60: Hesw .5E **101**
L17: Aig .2C **90**
Milner St. CH41: Birke .1C **68**
Milnthorpe Cl. L4: Kirkd .5E **35**
Milnthorpe Rd. WA5: Burtw .1G **63**
Milnthorpe St. L19: Garst .5G **91**
Milroy St. L7: Liv .6H **53**
Milton Av. L14: Broad G .5A **56**
L35: Whis .4E **59**
WA8: Wid .3D **96**
Milton Cl. L35: Whis .4E **59**
Milton Cres. CH60: Hesw .4E **101**
Milton Grn. CH61: Thing .5F **85**
Milton Pavement CH41: Birke .3F **69**
Milton Rd. CH42: Tran .5E **69**
CH44: Wall .5F **51**
CH48: W Kir .6A **64**
L4: Walt .3E **35**
L7: Liv .5C **54**
L22: Water .1G **19**
WA8: Wid .3D **96**
Milton Rd. E. CH42: Tran .5F **69**
Milton St. L20: Boot .1B **34**
WA8: Wid .6E **97**
WA9: Sut M .5E **61**
Milton Way L31: Mag .6A **6**
Milverny Way WA9: St H .4E **43**
Milverton St. L6: Liv .3A **54**
Mimosa Rd. L15: Wav .2F **73**
Mindale Rd. L15: Wav .1D **72**
Minehead Gro. WA9: Sut L .2H **61**
Minehead Rd. L17: Aig .2C **90**
Miners Way L24: Speke .2A **110**
WA8: Wid .4E **97**
Mines Av. L17: Aig .4D **90**
L34: Presc .1E **59**
Mine Way WA11: Hay .4H **31**
Minstead Av. L33: Kirkb .1B **24**
Minster Ct. L7: Liv .1G **71**
WA7: Run .5C **112**
Minto Cl. L7: Liv .5A **54**
Minton Cl. L12: Crox .2B **38**
Minton Way WA8: Wid .4F **79**
Mintor Rd. L33: Kirkb .1C **24**
Minver Rd. L12: W Der .6H **37**
Miranda Av. CH63: Hghr B .4G **87**
Miranda Pl. L20: Kirkd .4D **34**
Miranda Rd. L20: Boot .4D **34**
Miranda Rd. Sth. L20: Kirkd .4D **34**
Mirfield Cl. L26: Halew .5H **93**
Mirfield St. L6: Liv .4H **53**
Miriam Pl. CH41: Birke .1B **68**
Miriam Rd. L4: Walt .1G **53**
Miskelly St. L20: Kirkd .5C **34**
Missouri Dr. WA5: Gt San .2H **81**
Missouri Rd. L13: Liv .6B **36**
Mistle Thrush Way L12: Crox .2B **38**
Miston St. L20: Kirkd .5C **34**
Misty Cl. WA8: Wid .1A **96**
Mitchell Av. WA5: Burtw .2G **63**
Mitchell Cres. L21: Lith .3B **20**
Mitchell Pl. L1: Liv .4G **5** (6D **52**)
Mitchell Rd. L34: Presc .1C **58**
WA10: St H .4A **42**
Mithril Cl. WA8: Wid .6A **80**

Mitre Cl. L35: Whis . . . 6D **58**
Mitylene St. L5: Liv . . . 1E **53**
Mobberley Ct. CH63: Spit . . . 2A **104**
Mobberley Way CH63: Spit . . . 2A **104**
Mockbeggar Dr. CH45: Wall . . . 6A **32**
Mockbeggar Wharf CH45: Wall . . . 6A **32**
Modred St. L8: Liv . . . 4F **71**
Moel Famau Vw. L17: Aig . . . 1H **89**
Moffatdale Rd. L4: Walt . . . 5A **36**
Moffatt Rd. L9: Ain . . . 4A **22**
Moira Sephton Ct. *CH43: Noct . . . 5H 67*
(off Sandalwood Dr.)
Molesworth Gro. L16: Child . . . 6B **56**
Molineux Av. L14: Broad G . . . 6H **55**
Molland Cl. L12: W Der . . . 5H **37**
Mollington Av. L11: Norr G . . . 3D **36**
Mollington Link CH41: Birke . . . 4G **69**
Mollington Rd. CH44: Wall . . . 4E **51**
L32: Kirkb . . . 1G **23**
Mollington St. CH41: Birke . . . 4G **69**
Molly's La. L33: Kirkb . . . 4F **25**
Molton Rd. L16: Child . . . 1G **73**
Molyneux Cl. CH49: Upton . . . 4D **66**
L35: Presc . . . 3D **58**
L36: Huy . . . 5H **57**
Molyneux Ct. L11: Norr G . . . 2F **37**
L14: Broad G . . . 6H 55
(off Molyneux Av.)
Molyneux Dr. CH45: New B . . . 5D **32**
L35: Presc . . . 3D **58**
Molyneux Rd. L6: Liv . . . 4H **53**
L18: Moss H . . . 5D **72**
L22: Water . . . 1G **19**
L31: Mag . . . 2D **12**
Molyneux Way L10: Ain . . . 6A **12**
Monaghan Cl. L9: Walt . . . 4G **21**
Monarchs Quay L3: Liv . . . 2C **70**
Monash Cl. L33: Kirkb . . . 3A **14**
Monash Rd. L11: Norr G . . . 5D **36**
Monastery La. WA9: St H . . . 6H **43**
Monastery Rd. L6: Liv . . . 1A **54**
WA9: St H . . . 6A **44**
Mona St. CH41: Birke . . . 2B **68**
L20: Boot . . . 5D **20**
WA10: St H . . . 3B **42**
Mond Rd. L10: Faz . . . 4E **23**
WA8: Wid . . . 3E **97**
Monfa Rd. L20: Boot . . . 5C **20**
Monica Dr. WA8: Wid . . . 4E **79**
Monica Rd. L25: Woolt . . . 2D **92**
Monkfield Way L19: Garst . . . 1H **107**
Monk Rd. CH44: Wall . . . 3D **50**
Monksdown Rd. L11: Norr G . . . 4E **37**
Monks Ferry CH41: Birke . . . 3H **69**
Monksferry Wlk. L19: Gras . . . 4D **90**
Monk St. *CH41: Birke . . . 3H 69*
(off Cross St.)
L5: Liv . . . 1F **53**
Monks Way CH48: W Kir . . . 1B **82**
CH63: Beb . . . 1H **103**
L25: Woolt . . . 1D **92**
WA7: Pres B . . . 2G **125**
(not continuous)
Monkswell Dr. L15: Wav . . . 1E **73**
Monkswell St. L8: Liv . . . 6G **71**
Monmouth Dr. L10: Ain . . . 2D **22**
Monmouth Gro. WA9: St H . . . 3H **43**
Monmouth Rd. CH44: Wall . . . 3B **50**
Monro Cl. L8: Liv . . . 5F **71**
Monro St. L8: Liv . . . 5F **71**
Mons Sq. *L20: Boot . . . 2C 34*
(off Strand Shop. Cen.)
Montague Rd. L13: Liv . . . 5E **55**
WA8: Wid . . . 5G **95**
Montclair Dr. L18: Moss H . . . 3F **73**
Monterey Rd. L13: Liv . . . 5F **55**
Montfort Dr. L19: Gras . . . 4E **91**
Montgomery Cl. L35: Whis . . . 5D **58**
WA5: Gt San . . . 1H **81**
Montgomery Hill CH48: Caldy, Frank . . . 3F **83**
Montgomery Rd. L9: Walt . . . 5G **21**
L36: Huy . . . 3F **57**
WA8: Wid . . . 3B **96**
Montgomery Way L6: Liv . . . 3H **53**
Montpelier Av. WA7: West . . . 1D **122**
Montpelier Dr. L8: Liv . . . 5F **71**
Montpellier Ct. *CH45: New B . . . 5C 32*
(off Montpellier Cres.)
Montpellier Cres. CH45: New B . . . 5C **32**
Montpellier Ho. CH45: New B . . . 5C **32**
Montreal Rd. L27: N'ley . . . 4G **75**
Montrose Av. CH44: Wall . . . 6G **51**
Montrose Bus. Pk. *L7: Liv . . . 5C 54*
(off Tattersall Way)
Montrose Ct. CH47: Hoy . . . 3B **64**
L12: W Der . . . 6B **38**
Montrose Pl. L26: Halew . . . 5H **93**
Montrose Rd. L13: Liv . . . 1B **54**
Montrose Way L13: Liv . . . 5D **54**
Montrovia Cres. L10: Faz . . . 4D **22**
Monument Pl. L3: Liv . . . 3H **5** (5F **53**)
Monville Rd. L9: Ain . . . 4A **22**
Moorbridge Cl. L30: N'ton . . . 5G **11**
Moor Cl. L23: Crosb . . . 4H **9**
Moor Coppice L23: Crosb . . . 4H **9**
Moor Ct. L10: Faz . . . 4E **23**
Moorcroft Rd. CH45: Wall . . . 2H **49**
L18: Aller . . . 2G **91**
L36: Huy . . . 2G **57**
Moorditch La. WA6: Frod . . . 6D **122**
Moor Dr. L23: Crosb . . . 4G **9**
Moore Av. CH42: Rock F . . . 1G **87**
WA9: St H . . . 2D **44**
Moore Cl. WA8: Wid . . . 1H **97**
Moore Dr. WA11: Hay . . . 4H **31**
Moore's Ho. L4: Walt . . . 3F **35**
Moore St. L20: Boot . . . 6B **20**
Mooreway L35: Rainh . . . 6C **60**
Moorfield L33: Kirkb . . . 4B **14**
Moorfield Cen. L33: Kirkb . . . 3B **14**
Moorfield Dr. CH64: Park . . . 5G **117**
Moorfield Rd. L23: Crosb . . . 4A **10**
WA8: Wid . . . 5H **79**
WA10: St H . . . 6A **28**
Moorfields L2: Liv . . . 3D **4** (5C **52**)
Moorfields Av. CH43: Noct . . . 5H **67**
Moorfields Station (Rail) . . . 3D **4** (5C **52**)
Moorfoot Rd. WA9: St H . . . 2B **44**
Moorfoot Rd. Ind. Est. WA9: St H . . . 1B **44**
Moorfoot Way L33: Kirkb . . . 3H **13**
Moorgate Av. L23: Crosb . . . 6H **9**
Moorgate La. L32: Kirkb . . . 3C **24**
Moorgate Point L33: Know I . . . 4C **24**
Moorgate Rd. L33: Kirkb . . . 5B **24**
Moorgate Rd. Sth. L34: Know . . . 5B **24**
Moorgate St. L7: Liv . . . 6H **53**
Moorhead Cl. L21: Lith . . . 4A **20**
Moorhey Rd. L31: Mag . . . 3A **12**
Moor Ho. L23: Crosb . . . 4G **9**
Mooring Cl. WA7: Murd . . . 1F **125**
Moorings, The CH41: Birke . . . 4F **69**
CH60: Hesw . . . 5A **100**
L31: Lyd . . . 3A **6**
Moorings Cl. CH64: Park . . . 6F **117**
Moorland Av. L23: Crosb . . . 4G **9**
Moorland Cl. CH60: Hesw . . . 6E **101**
Moorland Dr. WA7: Murd . . . 6G **115**
Moorland Pk. CH60: Hesw . . . 6E **101**
Moorland Rd. CH42: Tran . . . 6G **69**
L31: Mag . . . 3A **12**
Moorlands Rd. L23: Thorn . . . 3B **10**
Moor La. CH60: Hesw . . . 5D **100**
L4: Walt . . . 2G **35**
L10: Faz . . . 4E **23**
L23: Crosb . . . 4G **9**
L23: Crosb, Thorn . . . 4G **9**
L29: Seft . . . 1D **10**
L32: Kirkb . . . 3F **23**
WA6: Frod . . . 6F **123**
WA8: Wid . . . 4D **96**
(not continuous)
Moor La. Bus. Cen. WA8: Wid . . . 4E **97**
Moor La. Sth. WA8: Wid . . . 4D **96**
MOOR PARK . . . 3G **9**
Moor Pl. L3: Liv . . . 3H **5** (5E **53**)
Moorside Cl. L23: Crosb . . . 5H **9**
Moorside Ct. WA8: Wid . . . 4D **96**
Moorside Rd. L23: Crosb . . . 5H **9**
Moor St. L2: Liv . . . 4C **4** (6C **52**)
Moorway CH60: Hesw . . . 5F **101**
Moorwood Cres. WA9: Clock F . . . 3G **61**
Moray Cl. WA10: St H . . . 6C **28**
Morcott La. L24: Hale . . . 3D **110**
Morden St. L6: Liv . . . 4A **54**
Morecambe St. L6: Liv . . . 2A **54**
Morecroft Rd. CH42: Rock F . . . 2A **88**
Morella Rd. L4: Walt . . . 5A **36**
Morello Cl. WA10: St H . . . 6D **28**
Morello Dr. CH63: Spit . . . 3B **104**
Moresby Cl. WA7: Murd . . . 6G **115**
Moret Cl. L23: Crosb . . . 4A **10**
MORETON . . . 1C **66**
Moreton Av. WA9: Clock F . . . 3G **61**
MORETON COMMON . . . 3B **48**
Moreton Gro. CH45: Wall . . . 1A **50**
Moreton Hills Golf Cen. . . . 5B **48**
Moreton Rd. CH49: Upton . . . 2D **66**
Moreton Station (Rail) . . . 5C **48**
Morgan M. L30: N'ton . . . 6D **10**
Morgan St. WA9: St H . . . 3H **43**
Morland Av. CH62: Brom . . . 1D **120**
Morley Av. CH41: Birke . . . 1D **68**
Morley Ct. L14: Knott A . . . 3A **56**
Morley Rd. CH44: Wall . . . 4C **50**
WA7: Run . . . 4E **113**
Morley St. L4: Walt . . . 6E **35**
WA10: St H . . . 6D **28**
(not continuous)
Morley Way WA10: St H . . . 1D **42**
Morningside L23: Crosb . . . 6H **9**
Morningside Pl. L11: Norr G . . . 4D **36**
Morningside Rd. L11: Norr G . . . 4D **36**
Morningside Vw. L11: Norr G . . . 5D **36**
Morningside Way L11: Norr G . . . 5D **36**
Mornington Av. L23: Crosb . . . 1G **19**
Mornington Rd. CH45: New B . . . 1D **50**
Mornington St. L8: Liv . . . 4E **71**
Morpeth Cl. CH46: More . . . 1H **65**
Morpeth Rd. CH47: Hoy . . . 4A **64**
Morpeth St. L8: Liv . . . 2F **71**
Morpeth Wharf CH41: Birke . . . 1G **69**
Morris Cl. WA11: Hay . . . 6C **30**
Morris Ct. CH43: O'ton . . . 4B **68**
Morrison Cl. WA5: Gt San . . . 4H **81**
Morrison M. WA8: Wid . . . 1B **96**
Morrissey Cl. WA10: St H . . . 1B **42**
Morris St. WA9: St H . . . 4A **44**
Morston Av. L32: Kirkb . . . 3A **24**
Morston Cres. L32: Kirkb . . . 3A **24**
Morston Wlk. L32: Kirkb . . . 3A **24**
Mortar Mill Quay CH41: Birke . . . 6F **51**
Mortimer St. CH41: Birke . . . 3H **69**
Mortlake Cl. WA8: Wid . . . 6A **78**
Morton Ho. L18: Moss H . . . 6D **72**
Morton Rd. WA7: Nort . . . 5F **115**
Morton St. L8: Liv . . . 4F **71**
(not continuous)
Mortuary Rd. CH45: Wall . . . 1D **50**
Morvah Cl. L12: W Der . . . 3G **37**
Morval Cres. L4: Walt . . . 3E **35**
WA7: Run . . . 4H **113**
Moscow Dr. L13: Liv . . . 2D **54**
Mosedale Av. WA11: St H . . . 2F **29**
Mosedale Gro. WA7: Beech . . . 2A **124**
Mosedale Rd. CH62: Brom . . . 3E **105**
L9: Walt . . . 6G **21**
Moseley Av. CH45: Wall . . . 3C **50**
Moseley Rd. CH63: Spit . . . 4A **104**
Moses St. L8: Liv . . . 5F **71**
MOSS BANK
WA8 . . . 4H **97**
WA11 . . . 3E **29**
Moss Bank Pk. L21: Lith . . . 3A **20**
Moss Bank Rd. WA8: Wid . . . 4H **97**
WA11: St H . . . 3D **28**
Mossborough Hall La. WA11: Rainf . . . 6B **16**
Mossborough Rd. WA11: Rainf . . . 1D **26**
Moss Brow WA11: Rainf . . . 2F **17**
Mossbrow Rd. L36: Huy . . . 3G **57**

Mosscraig L28: Stockb V 6E **39**
Mosscroft Cl. L36: Huy 3A **58**
Mossdale Cl. WA5: Gt San 2H **81**
Mossdale Dr. L35: Rainh 4B **60**
Mossdale Rd. L33: Kirkb 4B **14**
Mossdene Rd. CH44: Wall 3B **50**
Moss End Way L33: Know I 6F **15**
Mossfield Rd. L9: Walt 5F **21**
Moss Ga. Gro. L14: Knott A 4C **56**
Moss Ga. Rd. L14: Knott A 4C **56**
Moss Grn. Way WA9: St H 4C **44**
Moss Gro. CH42: Tran 1D **86**
L8: Liv 3A **72**
Mosshey Ct. CH63: Spit 2A **104**
Mosshill Cl. L31: Mag 4B **6**
Mosslands WA10: Eccl 1G **41**
Mosslands Dr. CH44: Wall 2A **50**
CH45: Wall 2A **50**
Moss La. CH42: Tran 1D **86**
L9: Walt 5F **21**
L20: Boot 5E **21**
L21: Lith 3B **20**
L23: Lit C 1F **9**
L31: Lyd 2A **6**
L31: Mag 5D **6**
L33: Kirkb 6D **14**
L33: Sim 1B **14**
WA9: St H 3C **44**
WA11: Windle 4F **27**
Mosslawn Rd. L32: Kirkb 2C **24**
Mosslea Pk. L18: Moss H 5D **72**
Mossley Av. CH62: Brom 5D **104**
L18: Moss H 4D **72**
Mossley Ct. L18: Moss H 6E **73**
MOSSLEY HILL 6D **72**
Mossley Hill Dr. L17: Aig 4B **72**
(not continuous)
Mossley Hill Rd. L18: Moss H 1D **90**
L19: Aig 1D **90**
Mossley Hill Station (Rail) 6E **73**
Mossley Rd. CH42: Tran 6G **69**
MOSS NOOK 4B **44**
Moss Nook La. L31: Mag, Mell 1E **13**
WA11: Rainf 3E **17**
Moss Pits Cl. L10: Faz 4D **22**
Moss Pits La. L10: Faz 4C **22**
L15: Wav 3F **73**
MOSS SIDE
L31 . . . . . 5D **6**
WA4 . . . . . 4H **99**
Moss Side L14: Knott A 4C **56**
Moss Side La. WA4: Moore 4G **99**
Moss St. L6: Liv 5F **53**
L19: Garst 5G **91**
L34: Presc 6D **40**
WA8: Wid 4H **97**
Moss Vw. L21: Lith 3C **20**
L31: Mag 6E **7**
Mossville Cl. L18: Moss H 1E **91**
Mossville Rd. L18: Moss H 1F **91**
Moss Way L11: Crox 6G **23**
Mossy Bank Rd. CH44: Wall 3F **51**
Mostyn Av. CH48: W Kir 2B **82**
CH60: Hesw 5A **100**
L10: Ain 6A **12**
L19: Aller 3H **91**
Mostyn Cl. L4: Kirkd 6E **35**
Mostyn Gdns. CH64: Park 6F **117**
Mostyn Sq. CH64: Park 6F **117**
Mostyn St. CH44: Wall 4D **50**
Motherwell Cl. WA8: Wid 6C **78**
Mottershead Cl. WA8: Wid 3E **97**
Mottershead Rd. WA8: Wid 3E **97**
Mottram Cl. L33: Kirkb 1B **24**
Moughland La. WA7: Run 4D **112**
Mould St. L5: Liv 1D **52**
Moulton Cl. WA7: Sut W 3B **124**
Mounsey Rd. CH42: Tran 4F **69**
Mount, The CH44: Wall 3E **51**
CH60: Hesw 5D **100**
Mount Av. CH60: Hesw 5D **100**
CH63: Hghr B 4F **87**
L20: Boot 4D **20**
Mount Cl. L32: Kirkb 5G **13**
Mount Ct. CH45: Wall 5C **32**
CH60: Hesw 5D **100**
Mount Cres. L32: Kirkb 5G **13**
Mount Dr. CH63: Hghr B 4F **87**
Mount Gro. CH41: Birke 4E **69**
Mount Gro. Pl. *CH41: Birke 4E* ***69***
(off Mount Gro.)
Mt. Haven Cl. CH49: Upton 4E **67**
Mount Olive CH43: O'ton 6C **68**
Mount Pk. CH63: Hghr B 4F **87**
L25: Woolt 6C **74**
Mount Pk. Ct. L25: Woolt 6C **74**
Mt. Pleasant CH43: O'ton 6D **68**
L3: Liv 5G **5** (6E **53**)
L22: Water 2F **19**
WA8: Wid 1F **97**
Mt. Pleasant Av. WA9: St H 2C **44**
Mt. Pleasant Cl. CH45: New B 6D **32**
Mt. Pleasant Rd. CH45: New B, Wall . . . 1C **50**
Mount Rd. CH42: Tran 2E **87**
CH45: Wall 5C **32**
CH48: W Kir 2C **82**
CH49: Upton 4E **67**
CH63: Hghr B, Spit 3E **87**
L32: Kirkb 6F **13**
(not continuous)
WA7: Halt 5B **114**
Mount St. L1: Liv 6H **5** (1E **71**)
L22: Water 2F **19**
L25: Woolt 1C **92**
WA8: Wid 1F **97**
Mount Vernon L7: Liv 6G **53**
Mt. Vernon Grn. L7: Liv 5G **53**
Mt. Vernon Rd. L7: Liv 5G **53**
Mt. Vernon St. L7: Liv 5G **53**
Mountview Cl. L8: Liv 4G **71**
Mount Way CH63: Hghr B 4F **87**
Mountwood Rd. CH42: Tran 3E **87**
Mowbray Av. WA11: St H 6G **29**
Mowbray Ct. L20: Kirkd 4C **34**
Mowbray Gro. L13: Liv 6E **55**
Mowcroft La. WA5: Cuerd 6C **80**
Moxon St. WA10: St H 3A **42**
Moyles Ct. WA8: Wid 1B **96**
Mozart Cl. L8: Liv 3H **71**
Mr Hardman's Photographic Studio . . . 1E **71**
Muirfield Cl. L12: W Der 1A **56**
Muirfield Rd. L36: Roby 6E **57**
Muirhead Av. L6: Liv 3A **54**
L13: Liv, W Der 1C **54**
L13: W Der 6D **36**
Muirhead Av. E. L11: Norr G 5E **37**
Muir Rd. L9: Ain 5B **22**
Mulberry Av. WA8: Wid 4G **97**
WA10: St H 2A **42**
Mulberry Cl. L33: Kirkb 3B **14**
Mulberry Ct. *L7: Liv 1F* ***71***
(off Mulberry St.)
Mulberry Gro. CH44: Wall 4F **51**
Mulberry Pl. L7: Liv 1F **71**
Mulberry Rd. CH42: Rock F 1H **87**
Mulberry St. L7: Liv 1F **71**
Mulcrow Cl. WA9: St H 1H **43**
Mulgrave St. L8: Liv 2G **71**
Mulliner St. L7: Liv 2A **72**
Mullion Cl. L26: Halew 3G **93**
WA7: Brook 1D **124**
Mullion Rd. L11: Crox 6G **23**
Mullion Wlk. L11: Crox 6G **23**
Mullrea Cl. L27: N'ley 3E **75**
Mullwood Cl. L12: Crox 2B **38**
Mulrankin Ct. L13: Liv 5F **55**
Mulveton Rd. CH63: Spit 2H **103**
Mumfords Gro. CH47: Meols 6E **47**
Mumfords La. CH47: Meols 6D **46**
(not continuous)
Muncaster Cl. CH62: Brom 4D **104**
Muncaster Ct. WA7: Cas 3B **114**
Muncaster Dr. WA11: Rainf 2G **17**
Munster Rd. L13: Liv 4F **55**
Murat Gro. L22: Water 2E **19**
Murat St. L22: Water 2E **19**
Murcote Rd. L14: Knott A 2B **56**
MURDISHAW 1F **125**
Murdishaw Av. WA7: Brook, Murd . . . 2E **125**
Murdock Way L10: Faz 5F **23**
Muriel Cl. WA5: Gt San 3F **81**
Muriel St. L4: Walt 5G **35**
Murphy Gro. WA9: St H 1A **44**
Murrayfield Dr. CH46: Leas 3D **48**
Murrayfield Rd. L25: Gate 3D **74**
Murrayfield Wlk. *L25: Gate 2D* ***74***
(off Murrayfield Rd.)
Murray Gro. CH48: W Kir 6A **64**
Museum of Liverpool
(Due open 2011) . . . . . **6B 4 (1B 70)**
Musker Dr. L30: N'ton 6C **10**
Musker Gdns. L23: Crosb 6H **9**
Musker St. L23: Crosb 6H **9**
Muspratt Rd. L21: Sea 6A **20**
Muttocks Rake *L30: N'ton 4D* ***10***
(off Great Hey)
Mycroft Cl. L5: Liv 1F **53**
Myers Av. L35: Whis 2G **59**
Myerscough Av. L20: Boot 6E **21**
Myers Ct. L23: Crosb 1H **19**
Myers Rd. E. L23: Crosb 6G **9**
Myers Rd. W. L23: Crosb 6F **9**
Mylia Cl. L14: Knott A 4C **56**
Mynsule Rd. CH63: Spit 2H **103**
Myrtle Av. WA11: Hay 4D **30**
Myrtle Ct. L7: Liv 1G **71**
L8: Liv 1G **71**
Myrtle Gro. CH44: Wall 4G **51**
L22: Water 1F **19**
WA8: Wid 3B **96**
Myrtle Pde. L7: Liv 1F **71**
Myrtle Rd. CH49: Woodc 5F **67**
Myrtle St. L7: Liv 1F **71**
Mystery Cl. L15: Wav 2C **72**

N

Naburn Gro. CH46: More 2C **66**
Nairn Cl. CH63: East 3D **120**
Nansen Gro. L4: Walt 4G **35**
Nant Pk. Ct. CH45: New B 5E **33**
Nantwich Cl. CH49: Woodc 1E **85**
Napier Cl. WA10: St H 2C **42**
Napier Dr. CH46: More 1D **66**
Napier Rd. CH62: New F 3B **88**
Napier St. L20: Boot 4B **34**
WA10: St H 2C **42**
Naples Rd. CH44: Wall 4F **51**
Napps Cl. L25: Gate 2B **74**
Napps Wlk. *L25: Gate 2B* ***74***
(off Napps Cl.)
Napps Way CH61: Hesw 3E **101**
L25: Gate 1B **74**
Naseby Cl. CH43: Noct 5G **67**
Naseby St. L4: Walt 3F **35**
Natal Rd. L9: Ain 5H **21**
Nathan Dr. WA11: Hay 5G **31**
Nathan Gro. L33: Kirkb 5B **14**
National Conservation Cen. . . . **3E 5 (5D 52)**
National Wildflower Cen. **6B 56**
Naughton Lea WA8: Wid 6B **78**
Naughton Rd. WA8: Wid 3E **97**
Navigation Cl. L30: N'ton 5G **11**
WA7: Murd 1F **125**
Navigation Rd. WA9: St H 1G **43**
Navigation Wharf L3: Liv 3D **70**
Naylor Rd. CH43: Bid 1A **68**
WA8: Wid 2H **97**
Naylorsfield Dr. L27: N'ley 3E **75**
Naylor's Rd. L25: Gate 4F **75**
L27: N'ley 3F **75**
Naylor St. L3: Liv 1D **4** (4C **52**)
Nazareth Ho. La. WA8: Wid 4A **96**
Nazeby Av. L23: Crosb 6A **10**
Neale Dr. CH49: Grea 6C **66**
Neasham Cl. L26: Halew 3H **93**
Nedens Gro. L31: Lyd 4B **6**
Nedens La. L31: Lyd 4B **6**

Needham Cl. WA7: Run 3H **113**
Needham Cres. CH43: Noct 5H **67**
Needham Rd. L7: Liv 5A **54**
Needwood Dr. CH63: Beb 2H **103**
Neills Rd. WA9: Bold 2D **62**
Neilson Rd. L17: Aig 6H **71**
Neilson St. L17: Aig 6H **71**
Neil St. WA8: Wid 1F **97**
Nell's La. L39: Augh 2E **7**
Nelson Av. L35: Whis 5E **59**
Nelson Ct. CH42: Rock F 2A **88**
CH45: New B 4D **32**
Nelson Dr. CH61: Pens 1C **100**
WA7: West 1D **122**
Nelson Ho. CH42: Rock F 2A **88**
Nelson Memorial ***3C 4***
(off Exchange Pas. E.)
Nelson Pl. L35: Whis 5E **59**
Nelson Rd. CH42: Rock F 2A **88**
L7: Liv 6H **53**
L21: Lith .4B ***20***
(off Bridge Rd.)
Nelson's Cft. CH63: Beb 2A **104**
Nelson St. CH45: New B 6E **33**
L1: Liv 2D **70**
(not continuous)
L15: Wav .1C **72**
L20: Boot .3B **34**
WA7: Run 3E **113**
WA8: Wid .5E **97**
WA12: Newt W 2H **45**
(not continuous)
Nelville Rd. L9: Ain 4A **22**
Neptune Cl. WA7: Murd 6F **115**
Neptune St. CH41: Birke 1F **69**
Neptune Theatre . . . . **5F 5 (6D 52)**
Ness Gro. L32: Kirkb 1G **23**
NESTON **6A 118**
Neston Av. WA9: Clock F 3F **61**
Neston Gdns. *CH41: Birke 1D* ***68***
(off Churchview Rd.)
Neston Recreation Cen. **6B 118**
Neston Rd. CH63: Thorn H 3B **118**
CH64: Nest 3B **118**
Neston St. L4: Walt 4F **35**
Netherby St. L8: Liv 6F **71**
Netherfield WA8: Wid 3B **96**
Netherfield Cl. CH43: Noct 5G **67**
Netherfield Rd. Nth. L5: Liv 1E **53**
Netherfield Rd. Sth. L5: Liv 3E **53**
NETHERLEY **4G 75**
Netherley Rd. L35: Tar G 4H **75**
WA8: Wid .6C **76**
NETHERTON **6F 11**
Netherton Activity Cen. **5E 11**
Netherton Grange L30: N'ton 6H **11**
Netherton Grn. L30: N'ton 4F **11**
Netherton Ind. Est. L30: N'ton 3F **21**
Netherton La. L30: N'ton 4E **11**
(not continuous)
Netherton Pk. Rd. L21: Lith 3D **20**
Netherton Rd. CH46: More 1C **66**
L18: Moss H 2E **91**
L20: Boot .5D **20**
Netherton Way *L30: Boot 3E* ***21***
(off Captain's La.)
L30: Boot, N'ton 2E **21**
(not continuous)
Netherwood Rd. L11: Norr G 3C **36**
Netley St. L4: Kirkd 5E **35**
Nettle Hill CH48: W Kir 6A **64**
Nettlestead Rd. L11: Norr G 5E **37**
Neva Av. CH46: More 1B **66**
Neville Av. WA9: St H 3D **44**
Neville Cl. CH43: Noct 5G **67**
Neville Cres. WA5: Penk 6H **81**
Neville Rd. CH44: Wall 3C **50**
CH62: Brom 6E **105**
L22: Water 2G **19**
Neville St. WA12: Newt W 1H **45**
Nevin St. L6: Liv 4G **53**
Nevison St. L7: Liv 6H **53**
Nevitte Cl. L28: Stockb V 5C **38**
New Acres Cl. CH43: Bid 1G **67**
New Albert Ter. *WA7: Run 2F* ***113***
(off Fredric Pl.)
Newark Cl. CH43: Noct 5G **67**
L30: N'ton 4H **11**
L36: Huy .1F **57**
Newark St. L4: Walt 4F **35**
New Bank Pl. WA8: Wid 2H **95**
New Bank Rd. WA8: Wid 2H **95**
New Barnet WA8: Wid 6D **78**
New Bird St. L1: Liv 2D **70**
New Bold Ct. WA9: Bold 6C **44**
Newbold Cres. CH48: W Kir 6E **65**
Newbold Gro. L12: Crox 3B **38**
Newborough Av. L18: Moss H 4D **72**
L23: Crosb 5A **10**
NEW BOSTON **5G 31**
Newbridge Cl. CH49: Woodc 5F **67**
WA7: Brook 1E **125**
Newbridge Farm Cvn. Pk. L33: Sim . . .2G **15**
NEW BRIGHTON **4D 32**
New Brighton Station (Rail) **5C 32**
Newburgh Cl. WA7: Wind H 4F **115**
Newburn CH43: O'ton 4D **68**
Newburns La. CH43: O'ton 6D **68**
Newburn St. L4: Walt 3F **35**
Newbury Cl. L36: Roby 6F **57**
WA8: Wid .6E **79**
Newbury Way CH46: Leas 4D **48**
L12: W Der 2A **56**
Newby Av. L35: Rainh 3G **59**
Newby Dr. L36: Huy 4E **57**
Newby Gro. L12: W Der 3G **37**
Newby Pl. WA11: St H 3E **29**
Newby St. L4: Walt 5F **35**
Newcastle Rd. L15: Wav 3E **73**
New Chester Rd. CH41: Birke, Tran . . .4H **69**
CH42: Rock F, Tran 5H **69**
CH62: Brom, East, New F, Port S
. . . . .1A **88**
CH66: Hoot 5G **121**
Newchurch Cl. L27: N'ley 5H **75**
Newcombe St. L6: Liv 2H **53**
Newcroft Rd. L25: Woolt 5B **74**
New Cross St. L34: Presc 6D **40**
WA10: St H 1D **42**
(Henry St.)
WA10: St H 2D **42**
(Westfield St.)
New Cross St. Sth. *WA10: St H 2D* ***42***
(off Nth. John St.)
New Cut La. L33: Kirkb, Rainf 4A **26**
Newdales Cl. CH43: Bid 1G **67**
Newdown Rd. L11: Crox 6H **23**
Newdown Wlk. L11: Crox 6H **23**
Newell Rd. CH44: Wall 2D **50**
Newenham Cres. L14: Knott A 3A **56**
NEW FERRY **4B 88**
New Ferry By-Pass
CH62: New F, Port S 3B **88**
New Ferry Rd. CH62: New F 4B **88**
Newfield Cl. L23: Thorn 3C **10**
Newfields WA10: St H 1A **42**
New Fort Way L20: Boot 5A **20**
New Glade Hill WA11: St H 5H **29**
New Grey Rock Cl. L6: Liv 3H **53**
New Hall L10: Faz 3D **22**
New Hall La. CH47: Hoy 3B **64**
L11: Norr G 5C **36**
New Hall Mnr. CH64: Nest 1A **118**
New Hall Pl. L3: Liv 3B **4** (5B **52**)
Newhall St. L1: Liv 2D **70**
Newhall Swimming Pool **3D 22**
Newhaven Rd. CH45: New B 6E **33**
New Hawthorne Gdns. L18: Moss H . . .6D **72**
New Hedley Gro. L5: Liv 2C **52**
New Henderson St. L8: Liv 3E **71**
New Hey L12: W Der 2E **55**
New Heyes CH64: Nest 6A **118**
New Hey Rd. CH49: Woodc 5F **67**
New Heys Dr. L18: Aller 2H **91**
Newholme Cl. L12: Crox 2A **38**
Newhope Rd. CH41: Birke 2E **69**
Newhouse Rd. L15: Wav 2B **72**
New Hutte La. L26: Halew 5G **93**
Newick Pk. L32: Kirkb 2G **23**
Newick Rd. L32: Kirkb 2G **23**
Newington L1: Liv 5G **5** (6E **53**)
Newington Way WA8: Wid 6D **78**
New Islington L3: Liv 2H **5** (5E **53**)
Newland Cl. WA8: Wid 6A **78**
Newland Ct. L17: Aig 6A **72**
Newland Dr. CH44: Wall 3C **50**
Newlands Rd. CH63: Beb 1B **104**
WA11: St H 4G **29**
Newling St. CH41: Birke 2E **69**
Newlyn Av. L21: Lith 2A **20**
L31: Mag 6D **6**
Newlyn Cl. CH47: Meols 6E **47**
WA7: Brook 1D **124**
Newlyn Gdns. WA5: Penk 6F **81**
Newlyn Gro. WA11: St H 4H **29**
Newlyn Rd. CH47: Meols 6E **47**
L11: Crox .6H **23**
Newlyn Wlk. L11: Crox 6H **23**
Newman St. L4: Kirkd 6D **34**
New Mkt. Cl. L21: Lith 4B **20**
Newmarket Gdns. WA9: St H 1A **60**
New Mkt. Hall *WA7: Run 2E* ***113***
(off Granville St.)
New Mersey Retail Pk. L24: Speke 6B **92**
New Mersey Shop. Pk. L24: Speke 6B **92**
New Mill Stile L25: Woolt 6C **74**
Newmoore La. WA7: Nort 2G **115**
Newmorn Ct. L17: Aig 1A **90**
New Palace Amusement Pk. **4D 32**
Newport Av. CH45: Wall 6A **32**
Newport Cl. CH43: Noct 5G **67**
Newport Ct. L5: Liv 2C **52**
New Quay L3: Liv 3B **4** (5B **52**)
Newquay Cl. WA7: Brook 1D **124**
New Quay Ter. L3: Liv 3B **4**
New Red Rock Vw. L6: Liv 3H **53**
New Rd. L13: Liv 2C **54**
L34: Eccl P 6E **41**
New Rd. Ct. *L13: Liv 2C* ***54***
(off Oak Leigh)
New School La. CH66: Chil T 6H **121**
Newsham Cl. WA8: Wid 5H **77**
Newsham Dr. L6: Liv 3A **54**
(not continuous)
Newsham Rd. L36: Huy 1A **76**
Newsham St. L5: Liv 2D **52**
News La. WA11: Rainf 1G **17**
Newstead Av. L23: Blun 6D **8**
Newstead Rd. L8: Liv 2A **72**
WA8: Wid .5F **95**
Newstet Rd. L33: Know I 1D **24**
New St. CH44: Wall 5G **51**
WA7: Run 3E **113**
WA8: Wid .3F **97**
WA9: St H, Sut L 2G **61**
NEWTON **1E 83**
Newton Cl. L12: W Der 5F **37**
NEWTON COMMON **2G 45**
Newton Ct. *CH42: Rock F 2A* ***88***
(off New Chester Rd.)
L13: Wav .6C **54**
Newton Cross La. CH48: W Kir 1E **83**
Newton Dr. CH48: W Kir 1E **83**
Newton Pk. Rd. CH48: W Kir 1E **83**
Newton Rd. CH44: Wall 3C **50**
CH47: Hoy 2C **64**
L13: Liv 3C **54**
WA9: St H 2C **44**
Newton St. CH41: Birke 2F **69**
Newton Wlk. *L20: Boot 1B* ***34***
(off Capricorn Way)
Newton Way CH49: Upton 4D **66**
L3: Liv 4H **5** (6F **53**)
New Tower Ct. CH45: New B 5E **33**
NEWTOWN **6H 123**
Newtown Gdns. L32: Kirkb 1A **24**
New Way L14: Knott A 2C **56**
New Way Bus. Cen. CH44: Wall 5F **51**
Nicander Rd. L18: Moss H 4D **72**

Nicholas Ho. L23: Blun 5D 8
Nicholas Rd. L23: Blun 5D 8
  WA8: Wid 3A 96
Nicholas St. L3: Liv 4D 52
Nicholl Rd. WA10: Eccl 5G 27
Nicholls Dr. CH61: Pens 1D 100
Nichols Grn. L8: Aller 2G 91
Nicholson St. WA9: St H 1A 44
Nickleby Cl. L8: Liv 4F 71
Nickleford Hall Dr. WA8: Wid 3D 78
Nicola Ct. CH45: Wall 1E 51
Nidderdale Av. L35: Rainh 4B 60
Nigel Rd. CH60: Hesw 5G 101
Nigel Wlk. WA7: Cas 3C 114
Nightingale Cl. L27: N'ley 4H 75
  L32: Kirkb 6F 13
  WA7: Beech 2B 124
Nightingale Rd. L12: Crox 2B 38
Nimrod St. L4: Walt 4F 35
Ninth Av. L9: Ain 4B 22
Nithsdale Rd. L15: Wav 3C 72
Nixon St. L4: Walt 3F 35
NOCTORUM 5H 67
Noctorum Av. CH43: Noct 4G 67
Noctorum Dell CH43: Noct 5H 67
Noctorum La. CH43: Noct, O'ton 3H 67
Noctorum Rd. CH43: Noct 4H 67
Noctorum Way CH43: Noct 5H 67
Noel St. L8: Liv 2A 72
Nook, The CH43: O'ton 3D 68
  CH48: Frank 1H 83
  L25: Gate 6D 74
  WA10: Windle 5H 27
Nook La. WA9: St H 4B 44
Nook Ri. L15: Wav 1F 73
Noonan Cl. L9: Walt 1F 35
Norbreck Av. L14: Broad G 5A 56
Norbury Av. CH63: Hghr B 6G 87
  L18: Moss H 4D 72
Norbury Cl. CH63: Hghr B 6H 87
  L32: Kirkb 1H 23
  WA8: Wid 2H 97
Norbury Fold L35: Rainh 6C 60
Norbury Rd. L32: Kirkb 1H 23
Norbury Wlk. L32: Kirkb 1H 23
Norcliffe Rd. L35: Rainh 3H 59
Norcott Dr. WA5: Burtw 1H 63
Norfolk Cl. CH43: Noct 5G 67
  L20: Boot 1D 34
  (off Brookhill Rd.)
Norfolk Dr. CH48: W Kir 2C 82
  WA5: Gt San 3G 81
Norfolk Pl. L21: Sea 4A 20
  WA8: Wid 3A 96
Norfolk Rd. L31: Mag 2A 12
  WA10: St H 4B 42
Norfolk St. L1: Liv 2D 70
  WA7: Run 2F 113
Norgate St. L4: Walt 6F 35
Norgrove Cl. WA7: Murd 5F 115
Norlands Ct. CH42: Rock F 2G 87
Norland's La. L35: Rainh 1C 78
  WA8: Cron, Wid 1C 78
Norlands Pk. WA8: Wid 3D 78
Norland St. WA8: Wid 2H 97
Norleane Cres. WA7: Run 5F 113
Norley Av. CH62: East 4E 121
Norley Dr. WA10: Eccl 2G 41
Norley Pl. L26: Halew 5G 93
Norman Av. WA11: Hay 4H 31
Normandale Rd. L4: Walt 4B 36
Normandy Rd. L36: Huy 4F 57
Norman Rd. CH44: Wall 5G 51
  L20: Boot 4C 20
  L23: Crosb 6F 9
  WA7: Run 4E 113
Norman Salisbury Ct. WA10: St H 6E 29
Normans Rd. WA9: St H 6B 44
Normanston Cl. CH43: O'ton 5D 68
Normanston Rd. CH43: O'ton 5D 68
Norman St. CH41: Birke 1B 68
  L3: Liv 5F 53
  (off London Rd.)

Normanton Av. L17: Aig 6A 72
Norma Rd. L22: Water 2G 19
Normington Cl. L31: Lyd 3B 6
Norris Cl. CH43: Noct 5G 67
NORRIS GREEN 3D 36
Norris Grn. Cres. L11: Norr G 4D 36
Norris Grn. Rd. L12: W Der 1F 55
Norris Grn. Way L11: Norr G 4E 37
Norris Gro. WA8: Hale B 6A 96
Norris Rd. L34: Presc 1C 58
Norseman Cl. L12: W Der 5F 37
Nth. Atlantic Cl. L36: Huy 3G 57
North Av. L10: Ain 1C 22
  L24: Speke 5C 92
Nth. Barcombe Rd.
  L16: Child 2H 73
Northbrook Cl. L8: Liv 2G 71
Nth. Brooke Way CH49: Woodc 6E 67
Northbrook Rd. CH44: Wall 4F 51
Northbrook St. L8: Liv 2G 71
  (Granby St.)
  L8: Liv 2G 71
  (Rosebery St.)
Nth. Cantril Av. L12: W Der 5A 38
Nth. Cheshire Trad. Est.
  CH43: Pren 3A 86
North Cl. CH62: Brom 3C 104
Northcote Cl. L5: Liv 3F 53
Northcote Rd. CH45: Wall 1H 49
  L9: Walt 2F 35
Northdale Rd. L15: Wav 1D 72
North Dingle L4: Kirkd 5D 34
  (not continuous)
North Dr. CH45: Wall 5B 32
  CH60: Hesw 6E 101
  L12: W Der 2E 55
  L15: Wav 1D 72
NORTH END 6G 75
North End La. L26: Halew 6G 75
Northern La. WA8: Wid 6G 77
Northern Perimeter Rd.
  L30: N'ton 4E 11
Northfield Cl. L33: Kirkb 5C 14
  WA9: Clock F 4H 61
Northfield Rd. L20: Boot 5E 21
NORTH FLORIDA 3F 31
Nth. Florida Rd. WA11: Hay 3F 31
North Front L35: Whis 6E 59
Northgate Rd. L13: Liv 2E 55
North Gro. L18: Aller 2G 91
Nth. Hill St. L8: Liv 4F 71
Nth. John St. L2: Liv 3D 4 (6C 52)
  WA10: St H 2D 42
  (not continuous)
Nth. Linkside Rd. L25: Woolt 2E 93
Nth. Manor Way L25: Woolt 2E 93
North Meade L31: Mag 5A 6
Northmead Rd. L19: Aller 4A 92
Nth. Mersey Bus. Cen.
  L33: Know I 5E 15
Nth. Mossley Hill Rd.
  L18: Moss H 5D 72
Nth. Mount Rd. L32: Kirkb 5F 13
Northop Rd. CH45: Wall 1B 50
North Pde. CH47: Hoy 2A 64
  CH64: Park 5F 117
  L24: Speke 2G 109
  L32: Kirkb 1A 24
North Pk. Ct. *CH44: Wall* 4G 51
  (off Demesne St.)
North Pk. Rd. L32: Kirkb 5F 13
Nth. Parkside Wlk. *L12: W Der* 5E 37
  (off Parkside Dr.)
Nth. Perimeter Rd. L33: Know I 5E 15
Northridge Rd. CH61: Pens 6E 85
North Rd. CH42: Tran 6E 69
  CH48: W Kir 1A 82
  CH65: Ell P 3H 121
  L14: Broad G 5G 55
  L19: Gras 5D 90
  L24: Halew 6G 93
  WA10: St H 6D 28

North St. L3: Liv 2E 5 (5D 52)
  WA11: Hay 5G 31
  WA12: Newt W 1H 45
Nth. Sudley Rd. L17: Aig 1C 90
North Ter. CH47: Meols 6D 46
Northumberland Gro. L8: Liv 4D 70
Northumberland St. L8: Liv 4E 71
Northumberland Ter. L5: Liv 1E 53
Northumberland Way L30: N'ton 6C 10
North Vw. L7: Liv 6G 53
  L36: Huy 5A 58
  WA5: Gt San 2G 81
Nth. Wallasey App. CH45: Wall 1G 49
Northway CH60: Hesw 4H 101
  L15: Wav 6F 55
  L31: Augh, Lyd, Mag 2A 12
  (not continuous)
  L39: Augh 2E 7
  WA7: Pal F 5B 114
  WA8: Wid 2B 96
Northways CH62: Brom 2D 104
North West Mus. of Road Transport 1E 43
Northwich Cl. L23: Thorn 3B 10
Northwich Rd. WA4: Dutt, Lwr W 3F 125
  WA7: Brook 2D 124
  WA7: Dutt, Pres B 3F 125
Nth. William St. CH44: Wall 5G 51
North Wirral Coastal Pk. 5F 47
NORTHWOOD 1B 24
Northwood Rd. CH43: Pren 1B 86
  L36: Huy 3H 57
  WA7: Run 3A 114
NORTON 5F 115
Norton Av. WA5: Penk 4G 81
Norton Dr. CH61: Irby 4A 84
Norton Ga. WA7: Nort 5E 115
Norton Gro. L31: Mag 3B 12
  WA9: St H 6B 42
Norton Hill WA7: Wind H 4E 115
Norton La. WA7: Halt, Nort 5C 114
  (not continuous)
  WA7: Nort 4F 115
Norton Priory Gdns. 2D 114
Norton Priory Mus. 2D 114
Norton Rd. CH48: W Kir 6A 64
Norton Sta. Rd. WA7: Murd, Nort 5F 115
Norton St. L3: Liv 2G 5 (5E 53)
  L20: Boot 6B 20
Norton Vw. WA7: Nort 5C 114
Norton Village WA7: Nort 5F 115
Norton Village Gdns. WA7: Nort 5F 115
Nortonwood La. WA7: Wind H 5E 115
Norville Rd. L14: Broad G 5G 55
Norwich Dr. CH49: Upton 2E 67
Norwich Rd. L15: Wav 3E 73
Norwich Way L32: Kirkb 1A 24
Norwood Av. L21: Lith 2B 20
Norwood Cl. CH49: Grea 6B 66
Norwood Ct. CH49: Grea 6B 66
Norwood Gro. L6: Liv 3H 53
  WA11: Rainf 3G 17
Norwood Rd. CH44: Wall 5D 50
  CH49: Grea 5B 66
Norwyn Rd. L11: Norr G 3C 36
Nottingham Cl. L35: Rainh 2A 60
Nottingham Rd. L36: Roby 6E 57
Nowshera Av. CH61: Pens 6D 84
Nuffield Cl. CH49: Upton 5D 66
Nun Cl. CH43: O'ton 6D 68
Nunn St. WA9: St H 2H 43
Nunsford Cl. L21: Lith 1D 20
Nunthorpe Av. L34: Know 6D 24
Nurse Rd. CH61: Thing 5F 85
Nursery Cl. CH43: O'ton 6D 68
  L25: Hunts X 3E 93
  WA8: Wid 6H 79
Nursery La. L19: Garst 4G 91
Nursery Rd. L31: Lyd 3B 6
  WA9: St H 6B 42
NUT GROVE 1A 60
Nutgrove Av. WA9: St H 6B 42
Nutgrove Hall Dr. WA9: St H 6B 42
Nutgrove Rd. WA9: St H 1A 60
Nut St. WA9: St H 6B 42

Nuttall St. L7: Liv 6H 53
Nyland Rd. L36: Huy 2F 57

O

Oak Av. CH49: Upton 3B 66
   L9: Ain 5H 21
   WA11: Hay 4G 31
Oak Bank CH41: Birke 4E 69
Oakbank Rd. L18: Moss H 4C 72
Oakbank St. CH44: Wall 4E 51
Oakbourne Cl. L17: Aig 1A 90
Oak Cl. CH46: More 2B 66
   L12: W Der 4B 38
   L35: Whis 4E 59
Oak Ct. L8: Liv 5G 71
   (off Weller Way)
   WA7: Cas 3C 114
Oakcross Gdns. L25: Woolt 1E 93
Oakdale Av. CH44: Wall 5F 51
Oakdale Cl. L32: Kirkb 2G 23
Oakdale Dr. CH49: Grea 1A 84
Oakdale Rd. CH44: Wall 5F 51
   L18: Moss H 4E 73
   L22: Water 1F 19
Oakdale Row L32: Kirkb 3B 24
Oakdene Cl. CH62: Brom 2D 120
Oakdene Ct. L35: Rainh 5B 60
Oakdene Rd. CH42: Tran 6E 69
   L4: Walt 6H 35
Oak Dr. M24: Speke 6G 113
Oakenholt Rd. CH46: More 6C 48
Oakes St. L3: Liv 5F 53
Oakfield L4: Walt 1H 53
Oakfield Av. L25: Gate 5C 74
Oakfield Cl. WA9: St H 6B 42
Oakfield Dr. L36: Huy 1H 75
   WA8: Wid 3G 95
Oakfield Gro. L36: Huy 1H 75
Oakfield Rd. CH62: Brom 5C 104
   L4: Walt 1G 53
Oak Gdns. WA5: Penk 5F 81
Oakgate Cl. L11: Norr G 2F 37
Oak Grange L26: Halew 3H 93
Oakham Dr. CH46: More 6H 47
   L10: Ain 2D 22
Oakham St. L8: Liv 3D 70
Oakhill Cl. L12: Crox 2H 37
   L31: Mag 5C 6
Oakhill Cott. La. L31: Lyd 3C 6
Oakhill Dr. L31: Lyd 3C 6
OAK HILL PARK 5F 55
Oakhill Pk. L13: Liv 5F 55
Oakhill Rd. L13: Liv 5F 55
   L31: Mag 5C 6
Oakhouse Pk. L9: Walt 2F 35
Oakhurst Cl. L25: Gate 4D 74
Oakland Cl. L21: Lith 5C 20
Oakland Dr. CH49: Upton 3E 67
Oakland Rd. L19: Aig 3D 90
Oaklands CH62: Brom 1D 120
   L35: Rainh 4A 60
Oaklands Av. L23: Crosb 4G 9
Oaklands Bus. Cen.
   CH66: Hoot 5E 121
Oaklands Ct. WA9: Clock F 3G 61
Oaklands Dr. CH61: Hesw 4E 101
   CH63: Beb 5A 88
Oaklands Ter. CH61: Hesw 3E 101
Oakland St. WA8: Wid 1E 113
Oakland Va. CH45: New B 5E 33
Oak La. L12: W Der 4G 37
Oak La. Nth. L12: Crox 3G 37
Oakleaf M. CH43: Noct 4H 67
Oaklea Rd. CH61: Irby 5D 84
Oaklee Gro. L33: Kirkb 5C 14
Oak Leigh L13: Liv 2C 54
Oakleigh Gro. CH63: Beb 5H 87
Oakley Cl. L12: Crox 2A 38
Oak Mdws. L35: Rainh 6C 60
Oakmere Cl. CH46: Leas 3C 48
   L9: Walt 4G 21

Oakmere Dr. CH49: Grea 5A 66
   WA5: Penk 6H 81
Oakmere St. WA7: Run 3E 113
Oakmoore WA7: Nort 1H 115
Oakridge Cl. CH62: Spit 3C 104
Oakridge Rd. CH62: Spit 3C 104
Oak Rd. CH63: Hghr B 4H 87
   CH66: Hoot 6E 121
   L35: Whis 4E 59
   L36: Huy 1F 75
   WA5: Penk 6H 81
Oaks, The CH62: Brom 5C 104
   L12: Crox 2B 38
   WA8: Wid 5H 79
   (off Hampton Ct. Way)
   WA9: Sut L 3H 61
Oaks Cl. WA9: Clock F 4H 61
Oaks La. CH61: Pens 1E 101
Oaksmeade Cl. L12: Crox 3B 38
Oaks Pl. WA8: Wid 4E 97
Oakston Av. L35: Rainh 5B 60
Oak St. L20: Boot 1C 34
   (off Holly St.)
   WA9: St H 5A 44
Oaksway CH60: Hesw 1F 117
Oak Ter. L7: Liv 5A 54
Oakthorn Gro. WA11: Hay 5E 31
Oaktree Pl. CH42: Rock F 6H 69
Oak Tree Rd. WA10: Eccl 6G 27
Oak Va. L13: Liv 5F 55
OAK VALE PARK 5F 55
Oak Vw. L24: Speke 2A 110
Oakwood Cl. L25: Gate 4D 74
Oakwood Dr. CH43: Bid 1A 68
   L36: Huy 6H 57
Oakwood Pk. CH43: Bid 1A 68
   CH62: Brom 2D 120
Oakwood Rd. L26: Halew 4G 93
Oakworth Cl. L33: Kirkb 5A 14
Oakworth Dr. CH62: New F 4C 88
   L35: Tar G 2A 76
Oarside Dr. CH45: Wall 1C 50
Oatfield La. L21: Ford 1B 20
Oatlands, The CH48: W Kir 2C 82
Oatlands Rd. L32: Kirkb 1G 23
Oban Dr. CH60: Hesw 5E 101
Oban Rd. L4: Walt 1H 53
Oberon St. L20: Boot 4C 34
O'Brien Gro. WA9: St H 1A 44
Observatory Rd. CH43: Bid 1A 68
Oceanic Rd. L13: Liv 5D 54
Ocean Pk. CH44: Wall 6F 51
Ocean Rd. L21: Lith 4B 20
O'Connell Cl. WA11: Hay 5E 31
O'Connell Rd. L3: Liv 3D 52
O'Connor Gro. L33: Kirkb 3A 14
Octavia Ct. L36: Huy 6H 57
Octavia Hill Rd. L21: Ford 2C 20
October Dr. L6: Liv 1B 54
Oddfellows Arms Yd.
   L25: Woolt 1C 92
   (off Allerton Rd.)
Odeon Cinema
   Bootle 6G 11
   Bromborough 2E 105
   Liverpool 5D 4 (6C 52)
   Mossley Hill 5F 73
Odsey St. L7: Liv 5A 54
Odyssey Cen. CH41: Birke 1E 69
Office Quarter, The L24: Speke . . .1B 108
Ogden Cl. L13: W Der 5E 37
Ogle Cl. L35: Presc 2E 59
OGLET .5G 109
Oglet La. L24: Hale 5F 109
   L24: Speke 3E 109
Ogle Way L36: Huy 2G 57
Oil St. L3: Liv 3B 52
O'Keeffe Rd. WA9: St H 1G 43
Okehampton Rd. L16: Child 1H 73
Okell Dr. L26: Halew 1F 93
Okell St. WA7: Run 3E 113
Old Albert Ter. WA7: Run 2F 113
   (off Thomas St.)

Old Barn Rd. CH44: Wall 4C 50
   L4: Walt 1H 53
Old Bidston Rd. CH41: Birke 1D 68
OLD BOSTON 4H 31
Oldbridge Rd. L24: Speke 3H 109
Old Chester Rd. CH41: Tran 5G 69
   CH42: Rock F, Tran 5G 69
   CH63: Beb, Hghr B 2H 87
Old Church Cl. L9: Ain 4H 21
Old Church Yd. L2: Liv 4C 4 (6B 52)
Old Clatterbridge Rd.
   CH63: Spit 3G 103
Old Coach Rd. WA7: Run 2D 112
Old College Pl. L7: Liv 6A 54
Old Colliery Rd. L35: Whis 4D 58
Old Court Ho. Rd. CH62: Brom 6D 88
Old Distillery Rd. L24: Speke 6E 93
Old Dover Rd. L36: Roby 6E 57
Old Eccleston La. WA10: St H 2A 42
Old Farm Rd. L23: Crosb 5H 9
   L32: Kirkb 5B 24
Oldfield L35: Whis 3F 59
Oldfield Cl. CH60: Hesw 3C 100
Oldfield Dr. CH60: Hesw 3B 100
Oldfield Gdns. CH60: Hesw 4B 100
Oldfield La. CH48: W Kir 5G 65
Oldfield Rd. CH45: Wall 1B 50
   CH60: Hesw 3B 100
   L19: Aig 3E 91
Oldfield Wlk. WA10: St H 6D 28
Oldfield Way CH60: Hesw 3B 100
Oldgate WA8: Wid 4A 96
Old Gorsey La. CH44: Wall 5D 50
Old Greasby Rd. CH49: Upton 4D 66
Old Hall L35: Whis 1E 77
Old Hall Cl. L31: Mag 2B 12
Old Hall Dr. WN4: Ash M 1H 31
Old Hall Gdns. WA11: Rainf 2G 17
Old Hall La. L32: Kirkb 1H 23
Old Hall Rd. CH62: Brom 4E 105
   L31: Mag 1B 12
Old Hall St. L3: Liv 2B 4 (5B 52)
Oldham Pl. L1: Liv 5H 5 (6E 53)
Oldham St. L1: Liv 6G 5 (1E 71)
Old Haymarket L1: Liv 3E 5 (5D 52)
   (not continuous)
Old Higher Rd. WA8: Hale B 6D 94
Old Hutte La. L24: Halew 6A 94
   L26: Halew 5A 94
Old Kennel Cl. L12: W Der 5B 38
Old La. CH60: Hesw 5H 101
   L31: Lyd 3D 6
   L34: Eccl P 6F 41
   L35: Eccl P 6F 41
   L35: Rainh 4H 59
   WA8: Wid 4B 96
   WA11: Rainf 2F 17
Old Leeds St. L3: Liv 2B 4 (5B 52)
Old Lodge Cl. L12: W Der 5F 37
Old Maryland La. CH46: More 6C 48
Old Meadow L34: Know 1F 39
Old Meadow Rd. CH61: Pens 1C 100
Old Mill Av. WA9: Sut L 2H 61
Old Mill Cl. CH60: Hesw 6F 101
   L15: Wav 1E 73
Old Mill La. L15: Wav 1E 73
   L34: Know 1G 39
Old Nook La. WA11: St H 5A 30
Old Orchard L35: Whis 6E 59
Old Post Office Pl. L1: Liv 5E 5
Old Prescot Cl. L31: Mag 5H 7
Old Pump La. CH49: Grea 6A 66
Old Quarry, The L25: Woolt 1C 92
Old Quay St. WA7: Run 2F 113
Old Racecourse Rd. L31: Mag 1H 11
Old Rectory Grn. L29: Seft 2E 11
Old Riding L14: Knott A 2B 56
Old Roan Station (Rail) 6H 11
Old Ropery L2: Liv 4C 4
Old Rough La. L33: Kirkb 6A 14
Old School Ho., The CH43: O'ton . . .4C 68
   (off Beresford Rd.)
Old School Way CH41: Birke 2A 68

Old Stable Yd., The L7: Liv 6G **53**
OLD SWAN .4E **55**
Old Thomas La. L14: Broad G 6H **55**
Old Upton La. WA8: Wid 5C **78**
Old Whint Rd. WA11: Hay 5C **30**
(not continuous)
Old Wood La. L27: N'ley 5H **75**
Old Wood Rd. CH61: Pens 1D **100**
Oleander Dr. WA10: St H 1A **42**
Olga Rd. WA9: St H 6G **43**
Olinda St. CH62: New F 4B **88**
Olive Cl. L31: Mell 1E **23**
Olive Cres. CH41: Tran 5G **69**
Olivedale Rd. L18: Moss H 4D **72**
Olive Gro. L15: Wav 6E **55**
L30: N'ton 2G **21**
L36: Roby 5F **57**
Olive La. L15: Wav 6E **55**
Olive Mt. CH41: Tran 5G **69**
Olive Mt. Hgts. L15: Wav 1F **73**
Olive Mt. Rd. L15: Wav 1E **73**
Olive Mt. Vs. L15: Wav 6E **55**
Olive Mt. Wlk. *L15: Wav* *1F 73*
(off Olive Mt. Rd.)
Oliver La. CH41: Birke 3G **69**
Oliver Lyme Ho. L34: Presc 1E **59**
Oliver Lyme Rd. L34: Presc 1E **59**
Olive Rd. L22: Water 3G **19**
Oliver Rd. WA10: St H 4A **42**
Oliver St. CH41: Birke 3F **69**
Oliver St. E. CH41: Birke 3G **69**
Olivetree Rd. L15: Wav 1F **73**
Olive Va. L15: Wav 1D **72**
Olivia Cl. CH43: Noct 5G **67**
Olivia M. CH43: Noct 5G **67**
Olivia St. L20: Boot 4D **34**
Olivia Way L36: Huy 5B **58**
Ollerton Cl. CH43: Noct 5G **67**
Ollerton Pk. WA5: Burtw 6G **45**
Ollery Grn. L30: N'ton 5H **11**
Ollier St. WA8: Wid 4E **97**
Olney St. L4: Walt 3F **35**
Olton St. L15: Wav 1C **72**
Olympia St. L6: Liv 4G **53**
Olympic Way L30: N'ton 3H **21**
Omega Blvd. WA5: Gt San 6F **63**
O'Neill St. L20: Boot 1B **34**
One Park W. L1: Liv 5D **4** (6C **52**)
Onslow Rd. CH45: New B 5D **32**
CH62: New F 3B **88**
L6: Liv 4A **54**
Ontario Cl. L27: N'ley 4G **75**
Ontario Way L36: Huy 1F **57**
Opal Cl. L6: Liv 3H **53**
L21: Lith .3C **20**
Opal Ct. *L3: Liv* *5F 53*
(off London Rd.)
Opco Complex L24: Speke 6D **92**
Open Air Theatre
Liverpool **5H 73**
Open Eye Gallery **5F 5**
Openfields Cl. L26: Halew 1G **93**
Oppenheim Av. WA10: St H 5A **42**
Orange Gro. L8: Liv 3A **72**
Orange Tree Cl. L28: Stockb V 5D **38**
Oran Way L36: Huy 4F **57**
Orb Cl. L11: Crox 2G **37**
Orb Wlk. *L11: Crox* *2G 37*
(off Sceptre Rd.)
Orchard, The CH45: Wall 6C **32**
L17: Aig .2D **90**
L35: Rainh 2A **60**
L36: Huy .5G **57**
Orchard Av. L14: Broad G 6H **55**
Orchard Cl. L34: Eccl P 6G **41**
L35: Whis 6E **59**
WA11: St H 4H **29**
Orchard Ct. CH41: Tran 6H **69**
L31: Mag .6E **7**
Orchard Dale L23: Crosb 5H **9**
Orchard Dene L35: Rainh 4A **60**
Orchard Gdns. L35: Whis 1E **77**
Orchard Grange CH46: More 2A **66**
Orchard Hey L30: N'ton 5H **11**
L31: Mag .1C **12**
WA10: Eccl 2G **41**
Orchard Pl. CH62: Spit 3B **104**
Orchard Rd. CH46: More 6C **48**
Orchard Wlk. *WA7: Pal F* *6B 114*
(off Halton Lea Shop. Cen.)
Orchard Way CH63: Hghr B 5F **87**
WA8: Wid 6G **77**
Orchid Gro. L17: Aig 6F **71**
Orchid Way WA9: Bold 6D **44**
O'Reilly Ct. L3: Liv 3C **52**
Orford Cl. L24: Hale 3E **111**
Orford St. L15: Wav 1D **72**
Oriel Cl. L2: Liv 4C **4**
L10: Ain 6B **12**
Oriel Ct. CH42: Tran 2D **86**
Oriel Cres. L20: Kirkd 4C **34**
Oriel Dr. L10: Ain 6A **12**
Oriel Lodge L20: Boot 3C **34**
Oriel Rd. CH42: Tran 6G **69**
L20: Boot 2B **34**
L20: Kirkd 4C **34**
Oriel St. L3: Liv 1D **4** (4C **52**)
Orient Dr. L25: Woolt 6D **74**
Origen Rd. L16: Child 6H **55**
Oriole Cl. WA10: St H 6H **41**
Orion Blvd. WA5: Gt San 6G **63**
Orith Av. WA10: Eccl 2F **41**
Orkney Cl. WA8: Wid 6A **80**
WA11: St H 4H **29**
Orlando Cl. CH43: Noct 5G **67**
Orlando St. L20: Boot 4C **34**
Orleans Rd. L13: Liv 4E **55**
Ormande St. WA9: St H 4F **43**
Ormerod Ct. CH63: Beb 6A **88**
Ormesby Gdns. WA9: St H 1C **60**
Ormesby Gro. CH63: Raby M 1B **120**
Ormiston Rd. CH45: New B 6D **32**
Ormond Cl. WA8: Wid 1A **96**
Ormonde Av. L31: Mag 2A **12**
Ormonde Cres. L33: Kirkb 1C **24**
Ormonde Dr. L31: Mag 1A **12**
Ormond M. CH43: Noct 5G **67**
Ormond St. CH45: Wall 2D **50**
L3: Liv 3C **4** (5C **52**)
Ormond Way CH43: Noct 5G **67**
Ormsby St. L15: Wav 2C **72**
Ormside Gro. WA9: St H 6H **43**
Ormskirk Rd. L9: Ain 3H **21**
L10: Ain, N'ton 5H **11**
L34: Know 5F **25**
WA11: Rainf 1D **16**
Ormskirk St. WA10: St H 1E **43**
Orphan Dr. L6: Liv 2B **54**
Orphan St. L7: Liv 1G **71**
ORRELL 4D **20**
Orrell Cl. WA5: Gt San 3H **81**
Orrell Hey L20: Boot 4D **20**
Orrell La. L9: Walt 4E **21**
L20: Boot 4E **21**
Orrell Lodge L20: Boot 5E **21**
Orrell Mt. L20: Boot 4C **20**
Orrell Mt. Ind. Est.
L20: Boot 4C **20**
ORRELL PARK 5F **21**
Orrell Park Station (Rail) 5G **21**
Orrell Rd. CH45: New B 6E **33**
L20: Boot 3C **20**
L21: Lith .3C **20**
Orrell St. WA9: St H 2G **43**
Orret's Mdw. Rd. CH49: Woodc 6F **67**
Orrysdale Rd. CH48: W Kir 6A **64**
Orry St. L5: Liv 2D **52**
Orsett Rd. L32: Kirkb 3B **24**
Orston Cres. CH63: Spit 3A **104**
Ortega Cl. CH62: New F 4C **88**
Orthes St. L3: Liv 6F **53**
Orton Rd. L16: Child 1G **73**
Orville St. WA9: St H 6B **44**
Orwell Cl. WA9: Sut M 4E **61**
Orwell Rd. L4: Kirkd 5D **34**
Osbert Rd. L23: Blun 5D **8**
Osborne Av. CH45: New B 6D **32**
Osborne Ct. *CH43: O'ton* *3D 68*
(off Osborne Rd.)
CH62: Port S 5B **88**
WA10: St H 5A **42**
Osborne Gro. CH45: New B 1D **50**
L34: Presc 2A **58**
Osborne Rd. CH43: O'ton 4D **68**
CH45: New B 6E **33**
L13: Liv 1C **54**
L21: Lith .2C **20**
(not continuous)
WA10: Eccl 6G **27**
Osborne Va. CH45: New B 6D **32**
Osborne Wood L17: Aig 2B **90**
Osbourne Cl. CH62: Brom 6E **105**
Osmaston Rd. CH42: Tran 1C **86**
Osprey Cl. L27: N'ley 4G **75**
WA7: Beech 2B **124**
Ossett Cl. CH43: Noct 5G **67**
WA7: Nort 5F **115**
Osterley Gdns. L9: Walt 5F **21**
O'Sullivan Cres. WA11: St H 6A **30**
Oswald Cl. L33: Kirkb 3A **14**
Oteley Av. CH62: Brom 5D **104**
Othello Cl. L20: Kirkd 4C **34**
Otterburn Cl. CH46: More 1H **65**
Otterburn St. WA7: Nort 2G **115**
OTTERSPOOL 2A **90**
Otterspool Dr. L17: Aig 3B **90**
Otterspool Rd. L17: Aig 2B **90**
Otterton Rd. L11: Crox 6G **23**
Ottley St. L6: Liv 4A **54**
Otway St. L19: Garst 6G **91**
Oulton Cl. CH43: O'ton 6A **68**
L31: Lyd 3A **6**
Oulton Gdns. WA9: St H 1C **60**
Oulton La. L36: Roby 1F **75**
Oulton Rd. L16: Child 3H **73**
Oulton Way CH43: O'ton 1A **86**
Oundle Dr. L10: Ain 6A **12**
Oundle Pl. L25: Hunts X 4D **92**
Oundle Rd. CH46: More 6C **48**
Outer Central Rd. L24: Halew 6G **93**
Outer Forum L11: Norr G 2C **36**
Out La. L25: Woolt 1C **92**
Outlet La. L31: Bic, Mell 1A **14**
Oval, The **4H 87**
Oval, The CH45: Wall 1B **50**
Overbrook Ho. L34: Know 6E **25**
Overbrook La. L34: Know 6D **24**
Overbury St. L7: Liv 6H **53**
Overchurch Rd. CH49: Upton 3C **66**
Overdale Av. CH61: Barn 6H **85**
Overdale Rd. CH64: Will 6A **120**
Overdene Wlk. L32: Kirkb 2B **24**
Overgreen Gro. CH46: More 6B **48**
Overstrand CH48: W Kir 1A **82**
Overton Av. L21: Lith 2B **20**
Overton Cl. CH43: O'ton 6B **68**
L32: Kirkb 2H **23**
Overton Rd. CH44: Wall 3D **50**
Overton St. L7: Liv 6H **53**
Overton Way CH43: O'ton 6B **68**
Ovington Cl. WA7: Sut W 4B **124**
Ovolo Rd. L13: Liv 3E **55**
Owen Cl. WA10: St H 4B **42**
Owen Dr. L24: Speke 2D **108**
Owen Rd. L4: Kirkd 5D **34**
L33: Know I 4E **25**
L35: Rainh 5A **60**
Owen St. WA10: St H 4B **42**
Oxborough Cl. WA8: Wid 5D **78**
Oxbow Rd. L12: W Der 5A **38**
Oxendale Cl. L8: Liv 2H **71**
Oxenholme Cres. L11: Norr G 4E **37**
Oxford Av. L20: Boot 2E **35**
L21: Lith .3B **20**
Oxford Cl. L17: Aig 1A **90**
Oxford Ct. L22: Water 1E **19**
Oxford Dr. CH63: Thorn H 1B **118**
L22: Water 1E **19**
L26: Halew 3H **93**

Oxford Ho.—Park Rd. W.

Oxford Ho. *L20: Boot* *2E 35*
(off Fernhill Rd.)
Oxford Rd. CH44: Wall 3E **51**
L9: Ain 3H **21**
L20: Boot 2D **34**
L22: Water 1E **19**
L36: Huy 3A **58**
WA7: Run 4E **113**
Oxford St. L7: Liv 6F **53**
WA8: Wid 3F **97**
WA10: St H 1D **42**
(Cooper St.)
WA10: St H 6D **28**
(Rutland St.)
Oxford St. E. L7: Liv 6G **53**
Oxheys WA7: Nort 5E **115**
Ox La. L35: Tar G 5B **76**
Oxley Av. CH46: Leas 4F **49**
Oxley St. WA9: St H 6H **43**
Oxmoor Cl. WA7: Brook 2C **124**
Oxmoor Local Nature Reserve **6F 99**
OXTON **5B 68**
Oxton Cl. L17: Aig 1A **90**
L32: Kirkb 3F **23**
WA8: Wid 5A **78**
Oxton Ct. CH43: O'ton 5D **68**
Oxton Rd. CH41: Birke 4E **69**
CH44: Wall 4D **50**
Oxton St. L4: Walt 5F **35**

P

Pacific Rd. CH41: Birke 2H **69**
L20: Boot 2B **34**
(Atlantic Rd.)
L20: Boot 1B **34**
(Globe Rd.)
Packenham Rd. L13: Liv 1D **54**
Padbury St. L8: Liv 4G **71**
Paddington L7: Liv 6G **53**
Paddock, The CH46: More 2A **66**
CH49: Upton 4F **67**
CH60: Hesw 5G **101**
L25: Gate 5D **74**
L32: Kirkb 4H **23**
L34: Eccl P 6G **41**
Paddock Cl. L23: Blun 3D **8**
Paddock Dr. CH64: Park 5H **117**
Paddock Gro. WA9: Clock F 4H **61**
Paddock Ri. WA7: Beech 3A **124**
Paddock Rd. L34: Presc 1A **58**
Padeswood Cl. WA9: St H 1G **61**
Padstow Cl. L26: Halew 2G **93**
WA5: Penk 6G **81**
Padstow Dr. WA10: Windle 5H **27**
Padstow Rd. CH49: Grea 6A **66**
L16: Child 1H **73**
Padstow Sq. WA7: Brook 2D **124**
Pagebank Rd. L14: Knott A 4C **56**
Pagefield Rd. L15: Wav 3E **73**
Page Grn. L36: Huy 4E **57**
Page La. WA8: Wid 2G **97**
PAGE MOSS **5D 56**
Page Moss Av. L36: Huy 3D **56**
Page Moss La. L14: Knott A 4C **56**
Page Moss Pde. L36: Huy 3D **56**
Page Wlk. L3: Liv 1H **5** (4E **53**)
(not continuous)
Pagewood Cl. CH43: Noct 5G **67**
Paignton Cl. L36: Huy 4B **58**
WA5: Penk 5G **81**
Paignton Rd. CH45: Wall 1B **50**
L16: Child 1H **73**
Paisley Av. CH62: East 3E **121**
WA11: St H 4H **29**
Paisley Ct. L14: Knott A 3B **56**
Paisley St. L3: Liv 1A **4** (4B **52**)
PALACE FIELDS **1C 124**
Palacefields Av. WA7: Pal F 1B **124**
Palacefields Local Cen.
WA7: Pal F 1C **124**
Palace Rd. L9: Ain 5G **21**
Palatine, The L20: Boot 2C **34**
Palatine Arc. WA10: St H 2E **43**
Palatine Rd. CH44: Wall 5F **51**
CH62: Brom 4C **104**
Palermo Cl. CH44: Wall 5F **51**
Paley Cl. L4: Walt 6F **35**
Palin Dr. WA5: Gt San 3H **81**
Palladio Rd. L13: Liv 3F **55**
Pall Mall L3: Liv 1C **4** (4C **52**)
Palmarsh Rd. WA8: Hale B 6H **95**
Palm Cl. L9: Walt 2A **36**
Palm Ct. *L8: Liv* *5G 71*
(off Weller Way)
Palmer Cl. CH43: Noct 6H **67**
WA10: St H 1D **42**
Palmerston Av. L21: Lith 4A **20**
Palmerston Cl. L18: Moss H 6D **72**
Palmerston Ct. L18: Moss H 6E **73**
Palmerston Cres.
L19: Garst 5G **91**
Palmerston Dr. L21: Lith 4B **20**
L25: Hunts X 4F **93**
Palmerston Rd. CH44: Wall 3B **50**
L18: Moss H 6D **72**
L19: Garst 5G **91**
Palmerston St. CH42: Rock F 1H **87**
Palmer Vs. CH42: Rock F 2G **87**
Palm Gro. CH43: O'ton 3D **68**
L25: Woolt 2D **92**
Palm Hill CH43: O'ton 5D **68**
Palmwood Av. L35: Rainh 5B **60**
Palmwood Cl. CH43: Pren 2A **86**
Paltridge Way CH61: Pens 1D **100**
Pamela Cl. L10: Faz 5F **23**
Pampas Gro. L9: Walt 1H **35**
Pankhurst Rd. L21: Ford 1C **20**
Pansy St. L5: Kirkd 6D **34**
Panton Way L10: Faz 5F **23**
Papillon Dr. L9: Ain 3B **22**
Parade, The CH64: Park 5F **117**
L15: Wav 6F **55**
L26: Halew 4G **93**
Parade Cres. L24: Speke 3G **109**
Parade St. WA10: St H 1E **43**
Paradise Gdns. L15: Wav 2D **72**
Paradise Island Bingo **4E 35**
Paradise La. L35: Whis 5D **58**
Paradise Pl. L1: Liv 5E **5**
Paradise St. L1: Liv 6E **5** (1D **70**)
Paragon Cl. WA8: Wid 4F **79**
Parbold Av. WA11: St H 6H **29**
Parbold Ct. WA8: Wid 3B **96**
Parbrook Cl. L36: Huy 1F **57**
Parbrook Rd. L36: Huy 1F **57**
Parc Play & Resource Cen. **2C 24**
Parish M. L14: Knott A 3A **56**
Park, The L36: Huy 6G **57**
WA5: Penk 6F **81**
Park & Ride
Leasowe **5E 49**
Marshalls Cross **1F 61**
Park Av. CH44: Wall 4F **51**
L9: Ain 4B **22**
L18: Moss H 6C **72**
L23: Crosb 4G **9**
L31: Lyd 4C **6**
L34: Eccl P 6F **41**
L35: Rainh 3A **60**
WA8: Wid 1F **97**
WA11: Hay 5C **30**
Parkbourn L31: Mag 5F **7**
Parkbourn Dr. L31: Mag 5F **7**
Parkbourn Nth. L31: Mag 5F **7**
Parkbourn Sq. L31: Mag 5F **7**
Parkbridge Rd. CH42: Tran 6E **69**
Park Brow Dr. L32: Kirkb 3B **24**
Parkbury Ct. CH43: O'ton 6C **68**
Park Cl. CH41: Birke 3E **69**
L32: Kirkb 5F **13**
(not continuous)
Park Ct. CH48: W Kir 1A **82**
L22: Water 3G **19**
L32: Kirkb 6G **13**
Park Ct. WA7: Run 5E **113**
WA9: St H 5F **43**
Parkdale CH48: Caldy 5D **82**
Parkdale Av. L9: Walt 4G **21**
Park Dr. CH41: Birke 2C **68**
(not continuous)
CH43: Clau 2C **68**
L23: Blun 4C **8**
L23: Thorn 2A **10**
Parkend Rd. CH42: Tran 6E **69**
Parker Av. L21: Sea 4H **19**
Parker Cl. L30: N'ton 2H **21**
Parkers Ct. WA7: Pal F 1A **124**
Parker St. L1: Liv 4F **5** (6D **52**)
WA7: Run 2F **113**
Parkfield Av. CH41: Birke 3F **69**
L30: N'ton 3G **21**
Parkfield Dr. CH44: Wall 3D **50**
Parkfield Gro. L31: Mag 6B **6**
Parkfield M. L17: Aig 5H **71**
Parkfield Pl. CH41: Birke 3F **69**
Parkfield Rd. CH63: Beb 2A **104**
L17: Aig 5H **71**
L22: Water 1G **19**
PARKGATE **6G 117**
Parkgate Cl. L17: Aig 2C **90**
Parkgate Ho. *CH64: Park* *5F 117*
(off Greenway)
Parkgate Ho. Ct. CH64: Park 6F **117**
Parkgate La. CH64: Nest 2A **118**
Parkgate Way WA7: Murd 6E **115**
Park Gro. CH41: Birke 4F **69**
Parkhill Ct. *L8: Liv* *5F 71*
(off Park Hill Rd.)
Park Hill Rd. L8: Liv 5F **71**
Parkhill Rd. CH42: Tran 6E **69**
Parkholme L22: Water 2G **19**
Parkhurst Rd. CH42: Tran 1E **87**
L11: Norr G 4D **36**
Park Ind. Est. WN4: Ash M 1G **31**
Parkinson Rd. L9: Walt 1G **35**
Parkland Cl. L8: Liv 4G **71**
Parkland Ct. CH43: Bid 1G **67**
CH49: Woodc *1E 85*
(off Childwall Grn.)
Parklands L34: Know 2F **39**
WA8: Wid 6A **78**
WA11: Rainf 2F **17**
Parklands Dr. CH60: Hesw 1F **117**
Parklands Way L22: Water 2G **19**
Park La. CH47: Meols 6F **47**
L1: Liv 6E **5** (1D **70**)
L20: Boot 4D **20**
L30: N'ton 1F **21**
L31: Mag 4E **7**
Park La. Cvn. Site
CH47: Meols 5G **47**
Park La. Dr. L31: Mag 5F **7**
Park La. W. L30: N'ton 6F **11**
Park Pl. L8: Liv 3E **71**
L20: Boot 2C **34**
Park Rd. CH42: Tran 6G **69**
CH44: Wall 4E **51**
CH47: Meols 6E **47**
CH48: W Kir 1A **82**
CH60: Hesw 4F **101**
CH62: East 1F **121**
CH62: Port S 6B **88**
CH64: Will 6B **120**
L8: Liv 3F **71**
L22: Water 2G **19**
L32: Kirkb 6F **13**
(not continuous)
L34: Presc 6C **40**
WA5: Gt San 2E **81**
WA7: Run 5D **112**
WA8: Wid 2F **97**
WA9: St H 2G **43**
WA11: St H 2G **43**
Park Rd. E. CH41: Birke 3E **69**
Park Rd. Nth. CH41: Birke 2C **68**
Park Rd. Sth. CH43: Clau 3D **68**
Park Rd. W. CH43: Clau 2C **68**

Parkside CH44: Wall 4E **51**
  L20: Boot 1C **34**
    (off Strand Shop. Cen.)
Parkside Av. WA9: Sut M 4F **61**
Parkside Cl. CH63: Beb 5A **88**
  L27: N'ley .5G **75**
Parkside Ct. WA8: Wid 1E **97**
Parkside Dr. L12: W Der 5E **37**
Parkside Mans. L36: Huy 5B **58**
Parkside Rd. CH42: Tran 6G **69**
  CH63: Beb 5A **88**
Parkside St. L6: Liv 4F **53**
Parkstile La. L11: Crox 1G **37**
Parkstone Rd. CH42: Tran 6E **69**
Park St. CH41: Birke 3F **69**
  (not continuous)
  CH44: Wall 3E **51**
  L8: Liv 4E **71**
  (not continuous)
  L20: Boot .2C **34**
  (not continuous)
  WA9: St H 1G **43**
  WA11: Hay 5B **30**
Park Ter. L22: Water 3G **19**
Parkvale Av. CH43: Pren 3A **86**
Park Va. Rd. L9: Walt 5G **21**
Park Vw. CH62: Brom 5C **104**
  L6: Liv 2B **54**
  L9: Walt 1G **35**
  (off Brook Rd.)
  L17: Aig 4C **72**
  L22: Water 1F **19**
  L23: Thorn 2B **10**
  L36: Huy .3E **57**
Parkview CH49: Woodc 2E **85**
Parkview Cl. CH41: Birke 2E **69**
Parkview Ct. CH60: Hesw 5D **100**
Parkview Dr. L27: N'ley 5G **75**
Park Vw. Flats L21: Lith 3A **20**
Parkview Rd. L11: Crox 5H **23**
Park Wall Rd. L29: Ince B, Thorn 1A **10**
Park Way L8: Liv 2F **71**
  (not continuous)
  L36: Huy .6F **39**
Parkway CH45: Wall 6A **32**
  CH47: Meols 1E **65**
  CH61: Irby 4D **84**
  L23: Crosb 1H **19**
  L30: N'ton 4F **11**
Parkway Cl. CH61: Irby 4D **84**
Parkway E. L32: Kirkb 6F **13**
Parkway W. L32: Kirkb 6F **13**
Park W. CH60: Hesw 6B **100**
Parkwood Cl. CH62: Brom 4E **105**
Parkwood Rd. L25: Woolt 5C **74**
  L35: Whis 5E **59**
Parlane St. WA9: St H 1G **43**
  (not continuous)
Parle Ct. L6: Liv 2H **53**
Parliament Bus. Pk. L8: Liv 2H **71**
  (off Commerce Way)
Parliament Cl. L1: Liv 2E **71**
Parliament Pl. L8: Liv 2F **71**
Parliament St. L8: Liv 2D **70**
  WA9: St H 6B **42**
Parlington Cl. WA8: Wid 4A **96**
Parlow Rd. L11: Norr G 5C **36**
Parnell Rd. CH63: Spit 3A **104**
PARR 2A **44**
Parren Av. L35: Whis 6C **58**
Parr Gro. CH49: Grea 5A **66**
  WA11: Hay 5C **30**
Parr Ind. Est. WA9: St H 3A **44**
Parr Mt. Ct. WA9: St H 2G **43**
Parr Mt. St. WA9: St H 2G **43**
Parrs Cnr. Trad. Est. L20: Boot 1C **34**
  (off Stanley Rd.)
Parr's Brk. CH43: O'ton 6D **68**
PARR STOCKS 3H **43**
Parr Stocks Rd. WA9: St H 3H **43**
Parr St. L1: Liv 6F **5** (1D **70**)
  WA8: Wid .2G **97**
  WA9: St H 2F **43**

Parr Swimming & Fitness Cen. 1H **43**
Parry's La. WA7: Run 4E **113**
Parry St. CH44: Wall 5F **51**
Parsonage Rd. WA8: Wid 1D **112**
Parsonage Way WA5: Gt San 4H **81**
Parson's Brow WA11: Rainf 3E **17**
Parthenon Dr. L11: Norr G 2B **36**
Partington Av. L20: Boot 1E **35**
Partington Sq. WA7: Nort 1H **115**
Parton St. L6: Liv 4A **54**
Partridge Cl. L12: Crox 2B **38**
Partridge Rd. L23: Blun 5D **8**
  L32: Kirkb 6F **13**
Pass Way WA11: St H 3G **29**
  (off Honister Av.)
Pasture Av. CH46: More 5C **48**
Pasture Cl. L25: Woolt 2D **92**
  WA9: Clock F 3G **61**
Pasture Cres. CH46: More 6C **48**
Pasture La. WA11: Rainf 5G **17**
Pasture La. Bus. Cen. WA11: Rainf . .5G **17**
Pasture Rd. CH46: More 4B **48**
Pastures, The CH48: W Kir 1F **83**
  WA9: Bold 6C **44**
Pateley Cl. L32: Kirkb 2G **23**
Pateley Wlk. L24: Speke 1H **109**
Paterson St. L4: Birke 3E **69**
Patmos Cl. L5: Liv 1E **53**
Paton Cl. CH48: W Kir 6D **64**
Patricia Av. CH41: Birke 6B **50**
Patricia Ct. WA10: St H 1D **42**
  (off Albion St.)
Patricia Gro. L20: Boot 5D **20**
Patrick Av. L20: Boot 4D **20**
Pattens Cl. L30: N'ton 5D **10**
Patten St. CH41: Birke 1D **68**
Patten's Wlk. L34: Know P 6F **25**
Patterdale Cres. L31: Mag 5D **6**
Patterdale Dr. WA10: St H 5H **41**
Patterdale Rd. CH63: Beb 2H **103**
  L15: Wav 3D **72**
Paul Cl. WA5: Gt San 3F **81**
Pauldings La. L21: Lith 3A **20**
Pauline Wlk. L10: Faz 4F **23**
Paul McCartney Way L6: Liv 4H **53**
Paul Orr Ct. L3: Liv 3C **52**
Paulsfield Dr. CH46: More 2C **66**
Paul St. L3: Liv 1D **4** (4C **52**)
Paulton Cl. L8: Liv 5F **71**
Paverley Bank L27: N'ley 3F **75**
Pavilion Bingo Club 2H **71**
  (off Lodge La.)
Pavilion Cl. L8: Liv 2H **71**
Pavilion Ct. WA12: Newt W 2H **45**
Pavilions, The CH43: O'ton 5C **68**
Pavilion Sports Cen. 1E **55**
Paxton Rd. L36: Huy 3G **57**
Peacehaven Cl. L16: Child 1B **74**
Peach Gro. L31: Mell 5F **13**
  WA11: Hay 4G **31**
Peach St. L7: Liv 6F **53**
Peach Tree Cl. L24: Hale 3E **111**
Pearce Cl. L25: Woolt 3B **74**
Pear Gro. L6: Liv 4H **53**
Pearl Way L6: Liv 3H **53**
Pearson Ct. L15: Wav 3E **73**
Pearson Dr. L20: Boot 4E **21**
Pearson Rd. CH42: Tran 4G **69**
Pearson St. L15: Wav 2D **72**
Pear Tree Av. WA7: Run 6G **113**
Peartree Av. L12: W Der 4B **38**
Pear Tree Cl. CH60: Hesw 4G **101**
  L24: Hale 4E **111**
  WA6: Frod 6H **123**
Pear Tree Rd. L36: Huy 1G **75**
Peasefield Rd. L14: Knott A 3C **56**
PEASLEY CROSS 4G **43**
Peasley Cross La. WA9: St H 2F **43**
Peatwood Av. L32: Kirkb 4B **24**
Peckers Hill Rd. WA9: St H 6A **44**
Peckfield Cl. WA7: Brook 2C **124**
Peckforton Cl. L13: Liv 1C **54**
Peckforton Dr. WA7: Sut W 3B **124**

Peckmill Grn. L27: N'ley 5H **75**
Pecksniff Cl. L8: Liv 4F **71**
Peebles Av. WA11: St H 4H **29**
Peebles Cl. L33: Kirkb 3H **13**
Peel Av. CH42: Tran 6H **69**
Peel Cl. L35: Whis 4E **59**
Peel Ho. L21: Sea 5A **20**
Peel Ho. La. WA8: Wid 6F **79**
Peel Pl. L8: Liv 2F **71**
  WA10: St H 6E **29**
Peel Rd. L20: Boot 6A **20**
Peel St. L8: Liv 5G **71**
  WA7: Run 2D **112**
Peet Wlk. L31: Mag 5A **6**
Peet St. L7: Liv 6H **53**
Pelham Gro. L17: Aig 5A **72**
Pelham Rd. CH44: Wall 4C **50**
Pelwood Cl. CH49: Woodc 6F **67**
Pemberton Rd. CH49: Woodc 6F **67**
  L13: Liv 4E **55**
Pembertons Ct. L34: Presc 1E **59**
  (off Scotchbarn La.)
Pemberton St. WA10: St H 2C **42**
Pembrey Way L25: Hunts X 3F **93**
Pembroke Av. CH46: More 2C **66**
Pembroke Cl. WA10: St H 3C **42**
Pembroke Ct. CH41: Tran 5H **69**
  WA7: Manor P 6E **99**
Pembroke Gdns. L3: Liv 5F **53**
Pembroke Ho. L6: Liv 3A **54**
Pembroke Pl. L3: Liv 3H **5** (5E **53**)
Pembroke Rd. L20: Boot 2C **34**
Pembroke St. L3: Liv 5F **53**
Pembury Cl. L12: Crox 2A **38**
Penare WA7: Brook 2E **125**
Penarth Cl. L7: Liv 1H **71**
Pencombe Rd. L36: Huy 3D **56**
Penda Dr. L33: Kirkb 3A **14**
Pendennis Ct. WA7: Cas 3B **114**
Pendennis Rd. CH44: Wall 4E **51**
Pendennis St. L6: Liv 2H **53**
Pendine Cl. L6: Liv 3A **54**
Pendle Av. WA11: St H 6H **29**
Pendlebury St. WA9: Clock F 4G **61**
Pendle Cl. CH49: Upton 3C **66**
Pendle Dr. L21: Ford 5C **10**
Pendleton Grn. L26: Halew 4G **93**
  (not continuous)
Pendleton Rd. L4: Walt 3G **35**
Pendle Vw. L21: Ford 5C **10**
Pendle Vs. L21: Ford 6C **10**
Penfold L31: Mag 6D **6**
Penfold Cl. L18: Moss H 4H **73**
Penfolds WA7: Run 4H **113**
Pengwern Gro. L15: Wav 1B **72**
Pengwern St. L8: Liv 4G **71**
Pengwern Ter. CH45: Wall 6E **33**
  (off Holland Rd.)
Penhale Cl. L17: Aig 1H **89**
Peninsula Cl. CH45: Wall 5A **32**
PENKETH 5G **81**
Penketh Cl. WA5: Penk 5F **81**
  WA7: Run 3F **113**
Penketh Grn. L24: Speke 1G **109**
Penketh Parish Swimming Pool 5G **81**
Penketh Rd. L24: Speke 2G **109**
Penketh's La. WA7: Run 2E **113**
Penkett Ct. CH45: Wall 1E **51**
Penkett Gdns. CH45: Wall 1E **51**
Penkett Gro. CH45: Wall 1E **51**
Penkett Rd. CH45: Wall 1D **50**
Penkford La. WA5: Coll G 4F **45**
Penkford St. WA12: Newt W 2G **45**
Penlake Ind. Est. WA9: St H 1A **62**
Penlake La. WA9: St H 6B **44**
Penley Cres. L32: Kirkb 1F **23**
Penlinken Dr. L6: Liv 3H **53**
Penmann Cl. L26: Halew 3H **93**
Penmann Cres. L26: Halew 3H **93**
Penmon Dr. CH61: Pens 2D **100**
Pennant Av. L12: W Der 4G **37**
Pennard Av. L36: Huy 2F **57**

Pennine Cl. WA9: St H 2A 44
Pennine Dr. WA9: St H 2B 44
Pennine Rd. CH42: Tran 2E 87
CH44: Wall 3B 50
Pennine Way L32: Kirkb 5G 13
Pennington Av. L20: Boot 4E 21
Pennington Cl. WA6: Frod 5H 123
Pennington Gdns. *L34: Presc 1D 58*
(off Houghton St.)
Pennington La. WA9: Coll G, St H 2E 45
Pennington Rd. L21: Lith 5C 20
Pennington St. L4: Walt 3F 35
Penn La. WA7: Run 3D 112
Pennsylvania Rd. L13: Liv 6B 36
Pennycress Dr. L11: Norr G 3D 36
Pennyford Dr. L18: Moss H 6C 72
Penny La. L18: Moss H 5D 72
WA5: Coll G 5F 45
WA8: Cron 2F 77
WA11: Hay 4H 31
Penny La. Neighbourhood Cen.
L15: Wav 3E 73
Pennystone Cl. CH49: Upton 3B 66
Pennywood Dr. L35: Whis 5E 59
Penpoll Cl. L20: Boot 5C 20
Penpoll Trad. Est. L20: Boot 5C 20
Penrhos Rd. CH47: Hoy 3A 64
Penrhyd Rd. CH61: Irby 6B 84
Penrhyn Av. CH61: Thing 5E 85
L21: Lith 4B 20
Penrhyn Cres. WA7: Run 6F 113
Penrhyn Rd. L34: Know 6D 24
Penrhyn St. L5: Liv 2D 52
Penrith Cl. WA6: Frod 6H 123
Penrith Cres. L31: Mag 5D 6
Penrith Rd. WA10: St H 5H 41
Penrith St. CH41: Birke 4E 69
Penrose Av. E. L14: Broad G 5B 56
Penrose Av. W. L14: Broad G 5A 56
Penrose Gdns. WA5: Penk 6F 81
Penrose St. L5: Liv 1F 53
Penryn Av. WA11: St H 4H 29
Penryn Cl. WA5: Penk 6G 81
Pensall Dr. CH61: Hesw 3D 100
Pensarn Rd. L13: Liv 5D 54
PENSBY 1E 101
Pensby Cl. CH61: Thing 6E 85
Pensby Hall La. CH61: Hesw 3D 100
Pensby Rd. CH60: Hesw 4E 101
CH61: Hesw, Irby, Pens 4E 101
Pensby St. CH41: Birke 1E 69
Penshaw Cl. L14: Knott A 1C 56
Penshaw Ct. WA7: Pal F 6A 114
Pentire Av. WA10: Windle 5H 27
Pentire Cl. L10: Faz 5F 23
Pentland Av. L4: Walt 4G 35
WA9: St H 2B 44
Pentland Rd. L33: Kirkb 5C 14
Penuel Rd. L4: Walt 3F 35
Penvalley Cres. L6: Liv 3A 54
Peony Gdns. WA9: Bold 6D 44
Peover St. L3: Liv 1F 5 (4D 52)
Peploe Rd. L4: Walt 3B 36
Peplow Rd. L32: Kirkb 1F 23
Pepper St. L24: Hale 4D 110
Pera Cl. L6: Liv 4G 53
Percival Ct. WA7: Run 4B 112
Percival La. WA7: Run 4B 112
Percival Way WA10: St H 6A 28
Percy Rd. CH44: Wall 5G 51
Percy St. L8: Liv 2F 71
L20: Boot 6B 20
WA9: St H 5B 44
Percy Vs. *L9: Walt 1G 35*
(off Cedardale Rd.)
Perimeter Rd. L33: Know I 3F 25
Perriam Rd. L19: Aller 3H 91
Perrin Av. WA7: Run 5C 112
Perrin Rd. CH45: Wall 2A 50
Perrins Rd. WA5: Burtw 1H 63
Perrygate Cl. L7: Liv 1H 71
Perry St. L8: Liv 3D 70
WA7: Run 3F 113
Pershore Ho. CH42: Tran 2D 86
Pershore Rd. L32: Kirkb 3A 24
Perth Av. WA9: St H 6C 42
Perth Cl. L33: Kirkb 3H 13
Perth St. L6: Liv 4G 53
Peterborough Dr. L30: N'ton 5E 11
Peterborough Rd. L15: Wav 3E 73
Peter Ho. L3: Liv 2D 4
Peterhouse M. L20: Boot 2D 34
Peterlee Cl. WA9: St H 6D 42
Peterlee Way L30: N'ton 2G 21
Peter Mahon Way L20: Boot 1B 34
Peter Price's La. CH63: Hghr B 1G 103
Peter Rd. L4: Walt 3E 35
(not continuous)
Peters Arc. L1: Liv 5E 5
Petersfield Cl. L30: N'ton 2F 21
Petersgate WA7: Murd 6F 115
Peter's La. L1: Liv 5E 5 (6D 52)
Peter St. CH44: Wall 5G 51
L1: Liv 3E 5 (5D 52)
WA10: St H 1C 42
Peterwood CH42: Rock F 2A 88
Petham Ct. WA8: Wid 5C 78
Petherick Rd. L11: Crox 6G 23
Petra Ct. L4: Walt 6A 36
Petunia Cl. L14: Knott A 3C 56
WA9: Bold 6C 44
Petworth Cl. L24: Speke 1D 108
Peveril St. L9: Walt 2F 35
PEWFALL 2E 31
PEX HILL 3C 78
Pex Hill Ct. WA8: Wid 4C 78
Pharmacy Rd. L24: Speke 1E 109
Pheasant Fld. L24: Hale 3C 110
Pheasant Gro. L26: Halew 2G 93
Philbeach Rd. L4: Walt 3B 36
L11: Norr G 3B 36
Philharmonic Ct. *L8: Liv 1F 71*
(off Catharine St.)
Philharmonic Hall 1F 71
Philip Gro. WA9: St H 6G 43
Philip Leverhume Lodge
CH62: Port S 5B 88
Philip Rd. WA8: Wid 3H 95
Phillimore Rd. L6: Liv 4A 54
Phillip Gro. L12: W Der 2B 56
Phillips Cl. L23: Thorn 3B 10
Phillips Dr. WA5: Gt San 3G 81
Phillips St. L3: Liv 1D 4 (4C 52)
Phillips Way CH60: Hesw 5C 100
Phipps' La. WA5: Burtw 5G 45
Phoenix Brow WA9: St H 2F 43
Phoenix Dr. L14: Knott A 3C 56
Phoenix Pk. L24: Speke 6C 92
Physics Rd. L24: Speke 6E 93
Phythian Cl. L6: Liv 4H 53
Phythian Cres. WA5: Penk 5H 81
Phythian St. L6: Liv 4G 53
WA11: Hay 5B 30
Pickerill Rd. CH49: Grea 6B 66
Pickering Rake *L30: N'ton 4D 10*
(off Red Lomes)
Pickering Rd. CH45: New B 5D 32
Pickerings Cl. WA7: Run 1G 123
Pickerings Pasture Local Nature Reserve
2H 111
Pickerings Pasture Vis. Cen. 1H 111
Pickerings Rd. WA8: Hale B 6H 95
Pickering St. L6: Liv 2G 53
Pickmere Dr. CH62: East 4F 121
(not continuous)
WA7: Brook 2E 125
Pickop St. L3: Liv 1D 4 (5C 52)
Pickwick St. L8: Liv 3F 71
Pickworth Way L31: Mell 1F 23
Picow Farm Rd.
WA7: Run, West P 4C 112
Picow St. WA7: Run 4D 112
Picton Av. WA7: Run 4F 113
Picton Cl. CH43: O'ton 5B 68
CH62: East 4D 120
Picton Cres. L15: Wav 1C 72
Picton Gro. L15: Wav 1B 72
Picton Hall *5D 52*
(off Cuerden St.)
Picton Rd. L15: Wav 1B 72
L22: Water 2F 19
Picton Sports Cen. 1D 72
Piele Rd. WA11: Hay 4F 31
Pier Head L3: Liv 5B 4 (6B 52)
Pighue La. L7: Liv 6C 54
L13: Liv 6E 55
Pigot St. WA10: St H 2C 42
Pigott's Rake *L30: N'ton 4D 10*
(off Higher End Pk.)
Pike Ho. Rd. WA10: Eccl 6G 27
Pike Pl. WA10: Eccl 1H 41
Pikes Bri. Fold WA10: Eccl 1G 41
Pikes Hey Rd. CH48: Caldy 4F 83
Pilch Bank Rd. L14: Knott A 3A 56
Pilch La. L14: Knott A 3A 56
Pilch La. E. L36: Huy 5C 56
Pilgrim St. CH41: Birke 3H 69
L1: Liv 6H 5 (1E 71)
Pilgrims Way WA7: Nort 2F 115
Pilkington Sailing Club 2G 41
Pilkington Ct. L34: Presc 2D 58
Pilkington St. WA11: Rainf 3F 17
Pilling La. L31: Lyd 2A 6
Pilot Gro. L15: Wav 1B 72
Pimblett Rd. WA11: Hay 4G 31
Pimbley Gro. E. L31: Mag 3A 12
Pimbley Gro. W. L31: Mag 3A 12
Pimhill Cl. L8: Liv 3G 71
Pimlico Rd. WA7: Run 3C 112
Pincroft Way *L4: Kirkd 6D 34*
(off Fountains Rd.)
Pine Av. CH63: Beb 2H 103
WA8: Wid 1F 97
WA10: St H 5D 28
Pine Cl. L32: Kirkb 6G 13
L35: Whis 4E 59
L36: Huy 3F 57
WA11: Hay 5E 31
Pine Ct. CH41: Birke 3F 69
L8: Liv 5G 71
(off Byles St.)
Pine Dale WA11: Rainf 2E 17
Pinedale Cl. CH43: Noct 5H 67
Pinefield Cl. L5: Liv 1F 53
Pine Gro. L20: Boot 1D 34
L22: Water 1F 19
Pine Hey CH64: Nest 6H 117
Pinehurst Av. L4: Walt 6H 35
L22: Water 6E 9
Pinehurst Rd. L4: Walt 6H 35
Pinellas WA7: Run 2F 113
Pine Lodge L4: Walt 5A 36
Pine M. L1: Liv 2E 71
Pinemore Rd. L18: Moss H 1E 91
Pineridge Cl. CH62: Spit 2C 104
Pine Rd. CH60: Hesw 4G 101
WA7: Run 6G 113
Pines, The CH63: Spit 2B 104
L12: Crox 1B 38
WA8: Wid 5H 79
(off Hampton Ct. Way)
Pinetop Cl. L6: Liv 3A 54
Pine Tree Av. CH43: Noct 5G 67
Pinetree Cl. CH46: More 1D 66
L30: N'ton 6F 11
Pinetree Ct. CH44: Wall 2B 50
Pinetree Dr. CH48: W Kir 2D 82
Pinetree Gro. CH46: More 1D 66
Pinetree Rd. L36: Huy 1F 75
Pine Vw. Dr. CH61: Hesw 3D 100
Pine Walks CH42: Tran 2D 86
CH48: W Kir 2D 82
Pinewalks Ridge CH42: Tran 3E 87
Pine Way CH60: Hesw 3C 100
Pinewood WN4: Ash M 1H 31
Pinewood Av. L12: Crox 2H 37
Pinewood Cl. L27: N'ley 3G 75
Pinewood Dr. CH60: Hesw 5F 101
Pinewood Gdns. L33: Kirkb 4A 14

Pinewood Rd. WA5: Burtw 6H **45**
Pinfold Cl. L30: N'ton 4D **10**
Pinfold Cottage Woodland Pk. 4E **11**
Pinfold Ct. CH48: W Kir 5A **64**
  L23: Crosb 4F **9**
Pinfold Cres. L32: Kirkb 3C **24**
Pinfold Dr. WA10: Eccl 2G **41**
Pinfold La. CH48: W Kir 5A **64**
  L34: Know .2D **38**
Pinfold Rd. L25: Hunts X 4E **93**
Pingwood La. L33: Kirkb 3C **14**
Pinners Fold WA7: Nort 4D **114**
Pinnington Pl. L36: Huy 5F **57**
Pinnington Rd. L35: Whis 4E **59**
Pintail Cl. WA11: St H 5F **29**
Pipers, The CH60: Hesw 4B **100**
Piper's Cl. CH60: Hesw 5B **100**
Piper's End CH60: Hesw 5B **100**
Pipers La. CH60: Hesw 3A **100**
                                        (not continuous)
Pipistrelle Ri. CH43: Noct 5H **67**
Pipit Cl. L26: Halew 1G **93**
Pippits Row WA7: Beech 3A **124**
Pirrie Rd. L9: Ain 2B **36**
Pitch Cl. CH49: Grea 5B **66**
Pit La. WA8: Wid 5E **79**
Pit Pl. L25: Woolt 1C **92**
Pitsmead Rd. L32: Kirkb 2A **24**
Pitts Heath La. WA7: Nort 2F **115**
Pitt St. L1: Liv 1D **70**
  WA8: Wid 6E **97**
  WA9: St H 2G **43**
Pitville Av. L18: Moss H 6E **73**
Pitville Cl. L18: Moss H 1E **91**
Pitville Gro. L18: Moss H 6F **73**
Pitville Rd. L18: Moss H 6E **73**
Pitville Ter. WA8: Wid 4A **96**
Plaistow Ct. WA7: Pal F 6A **114**
Plane Cl. L9: Walt 2A **36**
Plane Tree Gro. WA11: Hay 4H **31**
Plane Tree Rd. CH63: Hghr B 1G **103**
Planetree Rd. L12: W Der 6B **38**
Plantation Bus. Pk. CH62: Brom . . .3F **105**
Plantation Cl. WA7: Cas 4C **114**
Plantation Ct. CH62: Brom 3F **105**
Plantation Rd. CH62: Brom 4F **105**
Planters, The CH49: Grea 5A **66**
  L30: N'ton 5G **11**
                                  (off Harvester Way)
Platinum Ct. L33: Know I 4D **24**
Platt Gro. CH64: Rock F 3A **88**
Platts St. WA11: Hay 5C **30**
Plattsville Rd. L18: Moss H 4E **73**
Playfield Rd. L12: W Der 6B **38**
Playfield Wlk. L12: W Der 6B **38**
Plaza Blvd. L8: Liv 3D **70**
Plaza Cinema
  Waterloo 2G **19**
Pleasant Hill St. L8: Liv 3D **70**
Pleasant St. CH45: New B 6D **32**
  L3: Liv 5H **5** (6E **53**)
  L20: Boot 3B **34**
Pleasant Vw. L20: Boot 3B **34**
Pleasington Cl. CH43: Noct 5A **68**
Pleasington Dr. CH43: Noct 5A **68**
Plemont Rd. L13: Liv 2E **55**
Plimsoll St. L7: Liv 6H **53**
Plover Dr. WA7: Nort 5F **115**
Pluckington Rd. L36: Huy 4B **58**
Plumbers Way L36: Huy 5H **57**
Plumer St. CH41: Birke 1C **68**
  L15: Wav 2C **72**
Plumley Gdns. WA8: Wid 1G **95**
Plumpstons La. WA6: Frod 6F **123**
Plumpton M. WA8: Wid 2G **97**
Plumpton St. L6: Liv 3F **53**
Plum Tree Cl. L28: Stockb V 5D **38**
  L35: Presc .1G **59**
Plymouth Cl. L19: Garst 6F **91**
  WA7: Murd 1G **125**
Plymyard Av. CH62: Brom, East . . .1D **120**
Plymyard Cl. CH62: Brom 2D **120**
Plymyard Copse CH62: Brom 2D **120**

Plymyard Ct. CH62: Brom 1C **120**
                                    (off Plymyard Av.)
Pochard Ri. WA7: Nort 5F **115**
POCKET NOOK 2G **43**
Pocket Nook St. WA9: St H 1G **43**
Podium Rd. L13: Liv 3E **55**
Poets Cnr. CH62: Port S 6B **88**
Poets Grn. L35: Whis 4F **59**
                                    (not continuous)
Poleacre Dr. WA8: Wid 1B **96**
Polinda Gdns. WA10: St H 5A **42**
Pollard Rd. L15: Wav 6E **55**
POLL HILL 3D **100**
Poll Hill Rd. CH60: Hesw 4D **100**
Pollitt Cres. WA9: Clock F 4G **61**
Pollitt Sq. CH62: New F 3C **88**
Pollitt St. WA9: Clock F 4G **61**
Polperro Cl. L11: Crox 6H **23**
Pomfret St. L8: Liv 3F **71**
Pomona St. L3: Liv 5H **5** (6E **53**)
Pond Cl. L6: Liv 3A **54**
Pond Grn. Way WA9: St H 4B **44**
Pond Vw. Cl. CH60: Hesw 5G **101**
Pond Wlk. WA9: St H 4C **44**
Pondwater Cl. L32: Kirkb 2A **24**
Ponsonby Rd. CH45: Wall 2A **50**
Ponsonby St. L8: Liv 3G **71**
Pool Bank CH62: Port S 4B **88**
Poolbank Rd. CH62: New F 4B **88**
Pool End WA9: St H 3B **44**
Poole Rd. CH44: Wall 2F **51**
Pool Hey L28: Stockb V 5D **38**
                                    (not continuous)
Pool Hollow WA7: Run 4F **113**
Pool La. CH49: Woodc 1E **85**
  CH62: Brom 6C **88**
  WA7: Run 2F **113**
Poolside Rd. WA7: Run 4F **113**
Pool St. CH41: Birke 2F **69**
  WA8: Wid 4F **97**
Poolwood Rd. CH49: Woodc 5F **67**
Pope St. L20: Boot 6B **20**
Poplar Av. CH49: Upton 4D **66**
  L23: Crosb .4H **9**
  WA5: Penk .5G **81**
  WA7: Run .6G **113**
  WA10: Eccl 1G **41**
Poplar Bank L36: Huy 5G **57**
Poplar Cl. L26: Halew 2A **94**
  WA7: Run .6G **113**
Poplar Ct. L8: Liv 5G **71**
                                      (off Byles St.)
Poplar Dr. CH63: Beb 1B **104**
  L5: Liv 2G **53**
  L32: Kirkb 6H **13**
Poplar Farm Cl. CH46: More 3A **66**
Poplar Gro. CH42: Tran 5F **69**
                                      (off Ash Rd.)
  L21: Sea 5H **19**
  L35: Presc .2E **59**
  WA10: St H 2A **42**
  WA11: Hay .5E **31**
Poplar Rd. CH43: O'ton 5D **68**
  L25: Woolt .6C **74**
  WA11: Hay .5E **31**
Poplar St. CH45: New B 6D **32**
Poplar Way L4: Kirkd 5D **34**
Poppleford Cl. L25: Gate 5F **75**
Poppy Cl. CH46: More 5E **49**
Poppy Rd. L23: Thorn 4B **10**
Porchester Rd. L11: Norr G 4D **36**
Porchfield Cl. L11: Norr G 2F **37**
Porlock Av. L16: Child 4A **74**
  WA9: Sut L .2G **61**
Porlock Cl. CH60: Hesw 1F **117**
  WA5: Penk .5G **81**
Portalbot Cl. L19: Garst 5G **91**
Portal M. CH61: Pens 2D **100**
Portal Rd. CH61: Pens 2D **100**
Portal Way L11: Crox 4G **23**
Portbury Cl. CH62: Port S 5C **88**
Portbury Wlk. CH62: Port S 5B **88**

Portbury Way CH62: Port S 5C **88**
Port C'way. CH62: Brom 1C **104**
Portelet Rd. L13: Liv 3D **54**
Porter Cl. L35: Rainh 6B **60**
Porter St. L3: Liv 3B **52**
  WA7: Run .3G **113**
Portgate Cl. L12: W Der 3G **37**
Porthcawl Cl. WA8: Wid 6A **78**
Porthleven Rd. WA7: Brook 2D **124**
Portia Av. CH63: Hghr B 4G **87**
Portia St. L20: Kirkd 4C **34**
                                                6H **41**
Portico Av. L35: Eccl P 1G **59**
Portico Ct. L35: Eccl P 1G **59**
                                      (off Portico La.)
Portico La. L34: Eccl P 6G **41**
  L35: Eccl P .1G **59**
  L35: Presc, Eccl P 1F **59**
Portland Av. L22: Water 1E **19**
Portland Ct. CH45: New B 4C **32**
Portland Gdns. L5: Liv 3C **52**
                                      (off Green St.)
Portland Ga. CH62: Port S 5C **88**
                                    (off Portbury Cl.)
Portland Pl. L5: Liv 3E **53**
Portland Rd. WA5: Gt San 1H **81**
  CH41: Birke 1C **68**
  CH45: New B 4C **32**
  L5: Liv 3C **52**
  WA7: Run .2D **112**
  WA12: Newt W 1H **45**
Portland Way WA9: St H 4B **44**
Portlemouth Rd. L11: Crox 6G **23**
Portloe Av. L26: Halew 2H **93**
Portman Rd. L15: Wav 2B **72**
Porto Hey Rd. CH61: Irby 6B **84**
Porton Rd. L32: Kirkb 2G **23**
Portreath Way
  WA10: Windle 5H **27**
Portree Av. CH63: East 2D **120**
Portree Cl. L9: Walt 1F **35**
Portrush Cl. WA8: Wid 6C **78**
Portrush St. L13: Liv 1C **54**
Portside WA7: Pres B 6G **115**
Portsmouth Pl. WA7: Murd 1G **125**
PORT SUNLIGHT 6B **88**
Port Sunlight Driving Range 6C **88**
Port Sunlight Station (Rail) 6B **88**
Portway L25: Hunts X 4E **93**
Portwood Cl. L7: Liv 1H **71**
Post Office La. WA7: West P 6B **112**
Potters La. L18: Moss H 4G **73**
  WA8: Hale B 1F **111**
Pottery, The L31: Mell 1E **23**
Pottery Cl. L35: Whis 4C **58**
Pottery Flds. L34: Presc 1D **58**
Pottery La. L35: Whis 4C **58**
  L36: Huy 4B **58**
Poulevara Ho. L13: Liv 5F **55**
                                  (off W. Oakhill Pk.)
Poulsom Dr. L30: N'ton 1C **20**
Poulter Rd. L9: Ain 4H **21**
POULTON
  CH44 . . . . .4D **50**
  CH63 . . . . .3A **104**
Poulton Bri. Rd. CH41: Birke 5B **50**
  CH44: Wall .4C **50**
Poulton Cl. L26: Halew 5F **93**
Poulton Dr. WA8: Wid 4B **96**
Poulton Grn. Cl. CH63: Spit 4H **103**
  CH63: Raby M 6A **104**
Poulton Rd. CH44: Wall 4C **50**
  CH63: Spit .2A **104**
Poulton Royd Dr. CH63: Spit 3H **103**
Poulton Va. CH44: Wall 5C **50**
Poverty La. L31: Mag 1C **12**
Powder Works La. L31: Mag 4H **7**
Powell St. WA9: St H 6A **44**
Powerhouse L8: Liv 2H **71**
                                (off Commerce Way)
Powerleague Soccer Cen.
  Liverpool 6E **35**

Power Rd. CH42: Rock F 3A **88**
   CH62: Brom 4F **105**
Powis St. L8: Liv 4G **71**
Pownall Sq. L3: Liv 2D **4** (5C **52**)
Pownall St. L1: Liv 6D **4** (1C **70**)
Poynter St. WA9: St H 6C **42**
Pratt Rd. L34: Presc 1C **58**
Precinct, The CH62: Brom 4D **104**
Precincts, The L23: Crosb 5G **9**
Preece Cl. WA8: Wid 6B **78**
Preesall Way L11: Crox 6G **23**
   (not continuous)
Premier St. L5: Liv 2F **53**
   (not continuous)
Prentice Rd. CH42: Rock F 2G **87**
PRENTON .3B **86**
Prenton Av. WA9: Clock F 3G **61**
Prenton Dell Av. CH43: Pren 3C **86**
Prenton Dell Rd. CH43: Pren 2A **86**
Prenton Farm Rd. CH43: Pren 3C **86**
Prenton Grn. L24: Speke 2G **109**
Prenton Hall Rd. CH43: Pren 2B **86**
Prenton La. CH42: Tran 2D **86**
Prenton Pk. 1E **87**
Prenton Pk. Rd. CH42: Tran 6E **69**
Prenton Rd. E. CH42: Tran 1E **87**
Prenton Rd. W. CH42: Tran 1E **87**
Prenton Village Rd. CH43: Pren 2B **86**
Prenton Way CH43: Pren 2H **85**
Prenton Way Bus. Units
   CH43: Pren 2H **85**
Prentonwood Ct. CH42: Tran 2E **87**
PRESCOT .1D **58**
Prescot Bus. Pk. L34: Presc 2C **58**
Prescot By-Pass L34: Presc 1B **58**
Prescot Cables FC 6D **40**
Prescot Cen. L34: Presc 1D **58**
Prescot Dr. L6: Liv 4B **54**
Prescot Leisure Cen. 2E **59**
Prescot Mus. 1D **58**
   (off Church St.)
Prescot Rd. L7: Liv 4B **54**
   L13: Liv 4B **54**
   L31: Mag, Mell 5G **13**
   L39: Augh, Mag, Mell, Orm 4H **7**
   WA8: Cron 5F **77**
   WA8: Wid 6B **78**
   WA10: St H 5G **41**
Prescot School Sports Cen. 6C **40**
Prescot Station (Rail) 2E **59**
Prescot St. CH45: New B 5C **32**
   L7: Liv 5F **53**
Prescot Trade Cen. L34: Presc 1E **59**
Preseland Rd. L23: Crosb 6G **9**
Prestbury Av. CH43: O'ton 1A **86**
Prestbury Cl. CH43: O'ton 1A **86**
   WA8: Wid 3C **96**
Prestbury Dr. WA10: Eccl 3H **41**
Prestbury Rd. L11: Norr G 1D **36**
Preston Av. L34: Presc 2C **58**
PRESTON BROOK 1H **125**
Preston Gro. L6: Liv 2A **54**
PRESTON ON THE HILL 1H **125**
Preston St. L1: Liv 3E **5** (5D **52**)
   WA9: Sut M 5E **61**
Preston Way L23: Crosb 5A **10**
Prestwick Cl. WA8: Wid 6D **78**
Prestwick Dr. L23: Blun 3E **9**
Prestwood Cres. L14: Knott A 3B **56**
Prestwood Rd. L14: Knott A 3B **56**
Pretoria Rd. L9: Ain 5H **21**
Price Gro. WA9: St H 3C **44**
Price's La. CH43: O'ton 5D **68**
Price St. CH41: Birke 1D **68**
   L1: Liv 6E **5** (1C **70**)
Price St. Bus. Cen. CH41: Birke 1E **69**
Primary Av. L30: N'ton 5H **11**
Primrose Cl. WA7: Cas 5C **114**
   WA8: Wid 2C **96**
Primrose Ct. CH45: New B 5D **32**
   (off Egerton St.)
   L36: Huy 1G **57**
Primrose Dr. L36: Huy 2G **57**

Primrose Gro. CH44: Wall 5G **51**
   WA11: Hay 4G **31**
Primrose Hill CH62: Port S 5A **88**
   L3: Liv 2E **5** (5D **52**)
Primrose Rd. CH41: Birke 2B **68**
   L18: Moss H 4G **73**
Primrose St. L4: Kirkd 6D **34**
Primula Cl. WA9: Bold 6C **44**
Primula Dr. L9: Walt 1H **35**
Prince Albert St. WA9: St H 4B **44**
Prince Albert M. L1: Liv 2E **71**
   (off Up. Frederick St.)
Prince Alfred Rd. L15: Wav 2E **73**
Prince Andrew's Gro. WA10: Windle . . .5A **28**
Prince Edward St. CH41: Birke 2E **69**
Prince Edwin St. L5: Liv 3E **53**
Prince Rupert's Tower 3F **53**
Princes Av. CH48: W Kir 1B **82**
   CH62: East 1E **121**
   L8: Liv 2F **71**
   L23: Crosb 5F **9**
Princes Blvd. CH63: Hghr B 3F **87**
Prince's Cl. WA7: Cas 4B **114**
Princes Ct. L8: Liv 3H **71**
Princes Ga. E. L8: Liv 3H **71**
Princes Ga. Ho. L8: Liv 3H **71**
   (off Kingsley Rd.)
Princes Ga. W. L8: Liv 3H **71**
Princes Pde. L3: Liv 2A **4** (5B **52**)
PRINCES PARK 3H **71**
Princes Pk. Mans. L8: Liv 4H **71**
Princes Pavement CH41: Birke 3G **69**
Princes Pl. WA8: Wid 2C **96**
Princes Rd. L8: Liv 2F **71**
   WA10: St H 4A **42**
Princess Av. WA5: Gt San 2G **81**
   WA10: St H 6C **28**
   WA11: Hay 4H **31**
Princess Dr. L12: W Der 5A **38**
   L14: Knott A 5A **38**
Princess Gdns. L3: Liv 1C **4** (4C **52**)
Princess Rd. CH45: New B 6D **32**
Princess St. WA7: Run 2E **113**
Princess Ter. CH43: O'ton 4E **69**
Princes St. L2: Liv 3D **4** (5C **52**)
   L20: Boot 4B **34**
   WA8: Wid 3E **97**
Princess Way L21: Sea 5H **19**
Prince St. L22: Water 3G **19**
Princes Way WA11: St H 3E **29**
Princesway CH45: Wall 1C **50**
Prince William St. L8: Liv 3E **71**
Priors Cl. L25: Woolt 1D **92**
Priorsfield CH46: More 1C **66**
Priorsfield Rd. L25: Woolt 1D **92**
Prior St. L20: Boot 5A **20**
Priory, The CH64: Nest 6H **117**
   L15: Wav 6D **54**
   L35: Rainh 4A **60**
Priory Cl. CH63: Beb 2A **104**
   L17: Aig 1H **89**
   L35: Whis 6C **58**
   WA7: Halt 4C **114**
Priory Ct. L36: Huy 5F **57**
   WA7: Pres B 2G **125**
Priory Farm Cl. L19: Gras 4E **91**
Priory Gdns. WA10: St H 4D **28**
Priory M. CH41: Birke 3H **69**
Priory Rd. CH44: Wall 4G **51**
   CH48: W Kir 1C **82**
   L4: Walt 5G **35**
   WA7: Wind H 3E **115**
Priory St. CH41: Birke 3H **69**
   L19: Garst 1H **107**
Priory Way L25: Woolt 1D **92**
Priory Wharf CH41: Birke 3H **69**
Pritchard Av. L21: Sea 4H **19**
Pritt St. L3: Liv 1G **5** (4E **53**)
Private Dr. CH61: Barn 6H **85**
Prizett Rd. L19: Gras 4F **91**
Probyn Rd. CH45: Wall 2A **50**
Procter Rd. CH42: Rock F 2A **88**
Proctor Ct. L30: N'ton 5D **10**

Proctor Rd. CH47: Hoy 3C **64**
Proctors Cl. WA8: Wid 1G **97**
Progress Pl. L1: Liv 3D **4**
Promenade, The L17: Aig 2H **89**
   L19: Aig 4B **90**
Promenade Gdns. L17: Aig 6F **71**
Prophet Wlk. L8: Liv 4F **71**
Prospect Cl. L6: Liv 4B **54**
   (off Prospect Va.)
Prospect Point L6: Liv 5F **53**
Prospect Rd. CH42: Tran 2D **86**
   WA9: St H 1H **43**
Prospect Row WA7: West 6D **112**
Prospect St. L6: Liv 5G **53**
Prospect Va. CH45: Wall 2B **50**
   L6: Liv 3B **54**
Prospect Way L30: N'ton 6H **11**
Proudman Dr. CH43: Bid 2G **67**
Providence Cl. WA10: St H 1E **43**
Providence Cres. L8: Liv 3E **71**
Provident St. WA9: St H 2C **44**
Province Pl. L20: Boot 5D **20**
Province Rd. L20: Boot 5D **20**
Prussia St. L3: Liv 2C **4** (5C **52**)
   (not continuous)
Public Hall St. WA7: Run 2E **113**
Pudsey St. L1: Liv 3G **5** (5E **53**)
Pugin St. L4: Walt 6E **35**
Pulford Av. CH43: Pren 1C **86**
Pulford Cl. WA7: Beech 1A **124**
Pulford Rd. CH63: Beb 6H **87**
Pulford St. L4: Walt 6F **35**
Pullman Cl. CH60: Hesw 5H **101**
Puma Cl. L36: Huy 2C **58**
Pumpfields Rd. L3: Liv 1C **4** (4C **52**)
Pump La. CH61: Grea 4H **65**
   WA7: Halt 5B **114**
Purbeck Dr. CH61: Irby 4B **84**
Purley Gro. L18: Moss H 1E **91**
Purley Rd. L22: Water 1E **19**
Purser Gro. L15: Wav 1B **72**
Putney Ct. WA7: Pal F 6A **114**
Pyecroft Cl. WA5: Gt San 3F **81**
Pyecroft Rd. WA5: Gt San 3F **81**
Pye Rd. CH60: Hesw 5D **100**
Pyes Gdns. WA11: St H 4F **29**
Pyes La. L36: Huy 6E **39**
Pye St. L15: Wav 2E **73**
PYGON'S HILL 1C **6**
Pygon's Hill La. L31: Lyd 1C **6**
Pym St. L4: Walt 3F **35**
Pyramids Shop. Cen., The
   CH41: Birke 3F **69**

Q

Quadrangle, The L18: Moss H 5F **73**
Quadrant, The CH47: Hoy 3B **64**
Quadrant Cl. WA7: Murd 1F **125**
Quaker La. CH60: Hesw 4C **100**
Quaker St. L2: Liv 3D **4**
Quakers Mdw. L34: Know 1F **39**
Quarry Av. CH63: Beb 1H **103**
Quarry Bank CH41: Birke 4F **69**
   L33: Kirkb 6B **14**
Quarry Bank Flats CH41: Birke 4F **69**
   (off Quarry Bank)
Quarrybank St. CH41: Birke 4E **69**
Quarrybank Workshops CH41: Birke . . .4E **69**
   (off Quarrybank St.)
Quarry Cl. CH61: Hesw 3D **100**
   L13: Liv 2E **55**
   L33: Kirkb 6B **14**
   WA7: Run 4H **113**
Quarry Ct. WA8: Wid 2A **96**
Quarry Dale L33: Kirkb 6B **14**
Quarry Grn. L33: Kirkb 6B **14**
Quarry Grn. Flats L33: Kirkb 6B **14**
Quarry Hey L33: Kirkb 6B **14**
Quarry La. CH61: Thing 5E **85**
Quarry Pk. L35: Rainh 6B **60**
   (off Lincoln Way)

Quarry Pl. *L25: Woolt* . . . *1B 92*
(off Quarry St.)
Quarry Rd. CH64: Nest . . . 6D **118**
L13: Liv . . . 2D **54**
L20: Boot . . . 3D **34**
L23: Thorn . . . 3A **10**
Quarry Rd. E. CH60: Hesw . . . 4C **100**
CH61: Hesw . . . 4C **100**
CH63: Beb . . . 1A **104**
Quarry Rd. W. CH60: Hesw . . . 4C **100**
Quarryside Dr. L33: Kirkb . . . 6C **14**
Quarry St. L25: Woolt . . . 6B **74**
Quarry St. Sth. L25: Woolt . . . 1C **92**
Quarry Way L36: Huy . . . 5A **58**
Quartz Way L21: Lith . . . 3C **20**
Quay, The WA6: Frod . . . 5H **123**
Quayle Cl. WA11: Hay . . . 5E **31**
Quay Pl. WA7: Pres B . . . 6G **115**
Quay Side WA6: Frod . . . 5H **123**
Quebec Quay L3: Liv . . . 3C **70**
Queen Anne Pde. L3: Liv . . . 3B **4**
Queen Anne St. L3: Liv . . . 1G **5** (4E **53**)
Queen Av. L2: Liv . . . 4D **4**
Queen Elizabeth Ct. L21: Lith . . . 3A **20**
Queen Mary's Dr. CH62: Port S . . . 5B **88**
Queen's Av. CH47: Meols . . . 1D **64**
WA8: Wid . . . 3H **95**
Queensberry St. L8: Liv . . . 4F **71**
Queensbury CH48: W Kir . . . 6D **64**
Queensbury Av. CH62: Brom . . . 4E **105**
Queensbury Way WA8: Wid . . . 6B **78**
Queens Cl. L19: Garst . . . 5G **91**
WA7: Run . . . 4D **112**
Queens Ct. CH47: Hoy . . . 2B **64**
L6: Liv . . . 2G **53**
L15: Wav . . . 6G **55**
Queenscourt Rd. L12: W Der . . . 2G **55**
Queensdale Rd. L18: Moss H . . . 4E **73**
Queens Dock Commercial Cen.
L1: Liv . . . 2D **70**
Queens Dr. CH43: Pren . . . 2C **86**
CH60: Hesw . . . 5C **100**
L12: W Der . . . 3F **55**
WA10: Windle . . . 5A **28**
Queens Dr. Mossley Hill
L18: Moss H . . . 5C **72**
Queens Dr. Stoneycroft L13: Liv . . . 2E **55**
Queens Dr. Walton L4: Walt . . . 3G **35**
Queens Dr. Wavertree L15: Wav . . . 6G **55**
Queens Dr. W. Derby L13: W Der . . . 5C **36**
Queensland Av. WA9: St H . . . 6C **42**
Queensland Pl. WA9: St H . . . 6C **42**
Queensland St. L7: Liv . . . 6H **53**
Queens M. L6: Liv . . . 3G **53**
Queens Pk. Leisure Cen. . . . **1C 42**
Queen Sq. L1: Liv . . . 3F **5** (5D **52**)
Queens Rd. CH42: Rock F . . . 2A **88**
CH44: Wall . . . 3G **51**
CH47: Hoy . . . 2A **64**
L6: Liv . . . 2G **53**
L20: Boot . . . 3C **34**
L23: Crosb . . . 5G **9**
L34: Presc . . . 1E **59**
WA7: Run . . . 4D **112**
WA10: St H . . . 4A **42**
WA11: Hay . . . 4H **31**
Queen St. CH41: Tran . . . 5G **69**
CH45: Wall . . . 2D **50**
L19: Garst . . . 6G **91**
L22: Water . . . 3F **19**
WA7: Run . . . 2E **113**
WA10: St H . . . 6D **28**
Queen's Wlk. *L1: Liv* . . . *2E 71*
(off Lady Chapel Cl.)
Queensway CH41: Birke . . . 5A **4** (1A **70**)
CH45: Wall . . . 1C **50**
CH60: Hesw . . . 1G **117**
L22: Water . . . 1H **19**
WA7: Run . . . 2D **112**
WA8: Wid . . . 5D **96**
WA11: Rainf . . . 4G **17**
WA11: St H . . . 3E **29**
Queensway Trad. Est. WA8: Wid . . . 6E **97**
Queens Wharf L3: Liv . . . 2C **70**
Queenswood Av. CH63: Hghr B . . . 3G **87**
Quernmore Rd. L33: Kirkb . . . 6C **14**
Quernmore Wlk. L33: Kirkb . . . 6C **14**
Quickswood Cl. L25: Woolt . . . 4B **74**
Quickswood Dr. L25: Woolt . . . 4B **74**
Quickswood Grn. L25: Woolt . . . 4B **74**
Quickthorn Cres. L28: Stockb V . . . 6D **38**
Quigley Av. L30: N'ton . . . 2G **21**
Quigley St. CH41: Tran . . . 5H **69**
Quinesway CH49: Upton . . . 4D **66**
Quinn St. WA8: Wid . . . 4F **97**
Quintbridge Cl. L26: Halew . . . 4G **93**
Quorn St. L7: Liv . . . 5H **53**

R

RABY . . . **3E 119**
Raby Av. CH63: Raby M . . . 1B **120**
Raby Cl. CH60: Hesw . . . 6D **100**
CH63: Raby M . . . 6A **104**
WA8: Wid . . . 1A **98**
Raby Dell CH63: Raby M . . . 1B **120**
Raby Dr. CH46: More . . . 2B **66**
CH63: Raby M . . . 6A **104**
Raby Gro. CH63: Hghr B . . . 3F **87**
Raby Hall Rd.
CH63: Brom, Raby M . . . 2G **119**
RABY MERE . . . **6A 104**
Raby Mere Rd.
CH63: Raby, Raby M . . . 3E **119**
(not continuous)
Raby Pk. Rd. CH64: Nest . . . 6A **118**
Raby Rd. CH63: Raby, Thorn H . . . 1D **118**
Racecourse Retail Pk. L9: Ain . . . 1H **21**
Rachel St. L5: Liv . . . 3D **52**
Radburn Cl. L23: Thorn . . . 4B **10**
Radburn Rd. L23: Thorn . . . 4B **10**
Radford Av. CH63: Spit . . . 3B **104**
Radford Cl. WA8: Wid . . . 4A **96**
Radlett Cl. WA5: Penk . . . 6G **81**
Radley Dr. CH63: Thorn H . . . 1B **118**
L10: Ain . . . 6A **12**
Radley Rd. CH44: Wall . . . 2B **50**
Radleys Ct. *L8: Liv* . . . *3F 71*
(off Up. Warwick St.)
Radley St. WA9: St H . . . 6C **42**
Radmore Rd. L14: Knott A . . . 4H **55**
Radnor Av. CH60: Hesw . . . 4D **100**
Radnor Cl. L26: Halew . . . 5G **93**
Radnor Dr. CH45: Wall . . . 1E **51**
L20: Boot . . . 2E **35**
WA8: Wid . . . 1B **96**
Radnor Pl. CH43: O'ton . . . 3E **69**
L6: Liv . . . 2B **54**
Radshaw Nook L32: Kirkb . . . 5A **24**
Radstock Gro. WA9: Sut L . . . 2H **61**
Radstock Rd. CH44: Wall . . . 2A **50**
L6: Liv . . . 4A **54**
Radstock Wlk. L26: Halew . . . 5H **93**
Radway Rd. L36: Huy . . . 2H **57**
Raeburn Av. CH48: W Kir . . . 6C **64**
CH62: East . . . 1D **120**
Raffles Rd. CH42: Tran . . . 4E **69**
Raffles St. L1: Liv . . . 2E **71**
Rafter Av. L20: Boot . . . 5E **21**
Raglan St. L19: Garst . . . 6G **91**
Railbrook Hey L13: Liv . . . 6E **55**
Railside Ct. L5: Liv . . . 2C **52**
Railton Av. L35: Rainh . . . 5B **60**
Railton Cl. L35: Rainh . . . 6B **60**
Railton Rd. L11: Norr G . . . 3C **36**
Railway Cotts. CH66: Hoot . . . 6D **120**
L25: Hunts X . . . 4E **93**
Railway St. L19: Garst . . . 6G **91**
WA10: St H . . . 1F **43**
Railway Vw. L32: Kirkb . . . 6G **13**
Railyard, The L7: Liv . . . 1G **71**
Rainbow Cl. WA8: Wid . . . 6A **78**
Rainbow Dr. L26: Halew . . . 3G **93**
L31: Mell . . . 5F **13**
Raines Cl. CH49: Grea . . . 5C **66**
RAINFORD . . . **2G 17**
Rainford Av. L20: Boot . . . 6E **21**
Rainford By-Pass WA11: Rainf . . . 1D **16**
Rainford Gdns. L2: Liv . . . 4E **5**
Rainford Hall Cotts. WA11: Crank . . . 1D **28**
Rainford Ind. Est. WA11: Rainf . . . 5H **17**
(not continuous)
Rainford Rd. WA10: St H, Windle . . . 4A **28**
WA11: Windle . . . 4A **28**
(not continuous)
Rainford Sq. L2: Liv . . . 4D **4** (6C **52**)
Rainham Cl. L19: Aller . . . 3G **91**
RAINHILL . . . **4A 60**
Rainhill Rd. L35: Rainh . . . 3A **60**
WA9: St H . . . 3A **60**
Rainhill Station (Rail) . . . **4A 60**
RAINHILL STOOPS . . . **6C 60**
Rainhill Trials Exhibition . . . **4A 60**
Rake, The CH62: Brom . . . 5C **104**
Rake Cl. CH49: Upton . . . 5E **67**
Rake Hey CH46: More . . . 1H **65**
Rake Hey Cl. CH46: More . . . 1A **66**
Rake La. CH45: New B, Wall . . . 6D **32**
CH49: Upton . . . 5E **67**
Rake M. CH49: Upton . . . 5E **67**
Rakersfield Ct. CH45: New B . . . 5E **33**
Rakersfield Rd. CH45: New B . . . 5E **33**
Rakes La. L29: Seft . . . 2C **10**
Raleigh Av. L35: Whis . . . 5D **58**
Raleigh Rd. CH46: Leas . . . 3E **49**
CH64: Nest . . . 6B **118**
Raleigh St. L20: Boot . . . 4B **34**
Rambaldi Sq. *WA8: Wid* . . . *2F 97*
(off Cross St.)
Rame Cl. L10: Faz . . . 5F **23**
Ramford St. WA9: St H . . . 3H **43**
Ramilies Rd. L18: Moss H . . . 4D **72**
Ramleh Pk. L23: Blun . . . 6C **8**
Rampit Cl. WA11: Hay . . . 4H **31**
Ramsbrook Cl. L24: Speke . . . 1E **109**
Ramsbrook La. L24: Hale . . . 6C **94**
WA8: Hale B . . . 6C **94**
Ramsbrook Rd. L24: Speke . . . 1E **109**
Ramsey Cl. L19: Aller . . . 3H **91**
L35: Whis . . . 4E **59**
WA8: Wid . . . 6A **80**
Ramsey Ct. CH48: W Kir . . . 3B **82**
Ramsey Rd. L19: Aller . . . 3H **91**
Ramsfield Rd. L24: Speke . . . 1A **110**
Ramsons Cl. L26: Halew . . . 2G **93**
Randall Dr. L30: N'ton . . . 1C **20**
Randle Av. WA11: Rainf . . . 1E **17**
Randle Brook Ct. WA11: Rainf . . . 1E **17**
Randle Cl. CH63: Spit . . . 3A **104**
Randle Hgts. L11: Crox . . . 6A **24**
L34: Know . . . 6A **24**
Randle M. WA8: Wid . . . 2F **97**
Randles Rd. L34: Know . . . 6C **24**
Randolph St. L4: Walt . . . 6F **35**
Randon Gro. WA10: St H . . . 1D **42**
Ranelagh Av. L21: Lith . . . 3A **20**
Ranelagh Dr. Nth. L19: Gras . . . 3E **91**
Ranelagh Dr. Sth. L19: Gras . . . 3E **91**
Ranelagh Pl. L3: Liv . . . 4G **5** (6E **53**)
Ranelagh St. L1: Liv . . . 5F **5** (6D **52**)
Ranfurly Rd. L19: Gras . . . 4F **91**
Rangemore Rd. L18: Moss H . . . 2E **91**
Rankin Hall L18: Moss H . . . 1C **90**
Rankin St. CH44: Wall . . . 5C **50**
Rankin Way CH62: Brom . . . 4E **105**
Ranworth Cl. L11: Norr G . . . 2C **36**
Ranworth Gdns. WA9: St H . . . 1B **60**
Ranworth Pl. L11: Norr G . . . 2C **36**
Ranworth Rd. WA5: Gt San . . . 3G **81**
Ranworth Sq. L11: Norr G . . . 2D **36**
Ranworth Way L11: Norr G . . . 2D **36**
Rappart Rd. CH44: Wall . . . 4F **51**
Rashid Mufti Ct. L8: Liv . . . 3G **71**
Ratcliffe Pl. L35: Rainh . . . 3H **59**
Rathbone Hall L17: Aig . . . 5C **72**
Rathbone Rd. L13: Wav . . . 1D **72**
L15: Wav . . . 1D **72**
Rathlin Cl. WA8: Wid . . . 6A **80**

Rathmore Av.—Richard Gro.

Rathmore Av. L18: Moss H 6E **73**
Rathmore Cl. CH43: O'ton 6C **68**
Rathmore Dr. CH43: O'ton 5C **68**
Rathmore Rd. CH43: O'ton 5C **68**
Raven Cl. L6: Liv 4G **53**
Ravendale Cl. CH43: Noct 5H **67**
Ravenfield Cl. L26: Halew 3G **93**
Ravenfield Dr. WA8: Wid 6A **78**
Ravenglass Av. L31: Mag 5C **6**
RAVENHEAD 3C 42
Ravenhead Av. L32: Kirkb 4A **24**
Ravenhead Pk. WA9: St H 4E **43**
Ravenhead Rd. WA10: St H 4C **42**
Ravenhead Row WA10: St H 4C **42**
Ravenhill Cres. CH46: Leas 3D **48**
Ravenhurst Way L35: Whis 6D **58**
Ravenna Rd. L19: Aller 3H **91**
Ravens Ct. L26: Halew 4H **93**
Ravenscroft Rd. CH43: O'ton 4E **69**
Ravensthorpe Grn. L11: Norr G 2D **36**
Ravenstone Cl. CH49: Upton 2D **66**
Ravenstone Dr. WA9: St H 6H **43**
Ravenstone Rd. L19: Aller 3F **91**
Ravenswood Av. CH42: Rock F 3H **87**
Ravenswood Rd. CH61: Hesw 3E **101**
L13: Liv 4E **55**
Raven Way *L20: Boot 2C 34*
(off Strand Shop. Cen.)
Rawcliffe Cl. WA8: Wid 5D **78**
Rawcliffe Rd. CH42: Tran 4F **69**
L9: Walt 1F **35**
Rawdon Cl. WA7: Pal F 6C **114**
Rawlinson Cres. L26: Halew 3B **94**
Rawlinson Rd. L13: Liv 4D **54**
Rawlins St. L7: Liv 4B **54**
Rawson Cl. L21: Sea 4H **19**
Rawson Rd. L21: Sea 3H **19**
(not continuous)
Raydale Cl. L9: Walt 2G **35**
Raymond Av. L30: N'ton 2G **21**
Raymond Pl. L5: Liv 3D **52**
Raymond Rd. CH44: Wall 4E **51**
Raynham Rd. L13: Liv 5D **54**
Rayrig Fold WA11: Rainf 3F **17**
Reach, The L3: Liv 1E **5** (4D **52**)
Reade Cl. CH63: Spit 4A **104**
Reading Cl. L5: Kirkd 6D **34**
Reading St. L5: Kirkd 6D **34**
Reads Ct. L9: Walt 5F **21**
Reapers Way L30: N'ton 5G **11**
Rear Comn. Pas. L6: Liv 4B **54**
Reay Ct. CH44: Wall 4G **51**
Reay St. WA8: Wid 1G **97**
Rebecca Gdns. WA9: St H 6G **43**
Recreation St. WA9: St H 1G **43**
Rector Rd. L6: Liv 6A **36**
Rectory Cl. CH42: Tran 5F **69**
CH60: Hesw 6D **100**
Rectory Dr. L26: Halew 2H **93**
Rectory Gdns. WA9: St H 1G **61**
Rectory La. CH60: Hesw 6C **100**
Rectory Rd. CH48: W Kir 2B **82**
Redacre Cl. WA4: Dutt 4H **125**
Redbourne Av. L26: Halew 5H **93**
Redbourne Dr. WA8: Wid 5H **77**
Redbourn St. L6: Liv 1A **54**
Redbrook Cl. CH62: Brom 1D **120**
Redbrook St. L6: Liv 1A **54**
Red Brow La. WA4: Dares 5G **115**
WA7: Murd 5G **115**
Redbrow Way L33: Kirkb 5A **14**
Redburn Cl. L8: Liv 5G **71**
Redcap Cl. CH45: Wall 5A **32**
Redcar Dr. CH62: East 2D **120**
Redcar M. L6: Liv 1H **53**
Redcar Rd. CH45: Wall 1H **49**
Redcar St. L6: Liv 1A **54**
Redcote Ct. CH48: W Kir 2A **82**
Redcroft CH49: Grea 6A **66**
Red Cross St. L1: Liv 5C **4** (6C **52**)
Red Cut La. L33: Kirkb 3G **25**
Redditch Cl. CH49: Grea 5A **66**
Redfern St. L20: Kirkd 5C **34**
Redfield Cl. CH44: Wall 3F **51**
Redford Cl. CH49: Grea 5A **66**
Redford St. L6: Liv 1A **54**
Redgate Av. L23: Crosb 5A **10**
Redgate Dr. WA9: St H 2H **43**
Redgrave Ct. L20: Boot 3C **34**
Redgrave St. L7: Liv 5A **54**
Redhill Av. L32: Kirkb 3B **24**
Red Hill Rd. CH63: Store 6D **86**
Redhouse Bank CH48: W Kir 6A **64**
Redhouse La. CH48: W Kir 6A **64**
Redington Rd. L19: Aller 3H **91**
Redland Rd. *L9: Ain 3H 21*
(off Lyncot Rd.)
Red Lion Cl. L31: Mag 6B **6**
Red Lion Shop. Cen. L31: Mag 6B **6**
Red Lomes L30: N'ton 4D **10**
Redmain Way L12: Crox 3B **38**
Redmere Dr. CH60: Hesw 5H **101**
Redmires Cl. L7: Liv 1H **71**
Redmont St. CH41: Tran 5G **69**
Redmoor Cres. L33: Kirkb 4A **14**
Redoaks Way L26: Halew 2B **94**
Redpoll Gro. L26: Halew 1G **93**
Red Rocks Marsh Nature Reserve 5A 64
Red Rock St. L6: Liv 3H **53**
Red Rum Cl. L9: Ain 3B **22**
Redruth Av. WA11: St H 4H **29**
Redruth Cl. WA7: Brook 1E **125**
Redruth Rd. L11: Crox 6H **23**
Redstone Cl. CH47: Meols 1D **64**
Redstone Dr. CH60: Hesw 4A **100**
Redstone Pk. CH45: Wall 5B **32**
Redstone Ri. CH43: Noct 3H **67**
Redstone Way L35: Whis 2G **59**
Redtail Cl. WA7: Run 2D **112**
Redvers Av. CH66: Hoot 5G **121**
Redvers Dr. L9: Walt 5F **21**
Redwald Cl. L33: Kirkb 3B **14**
Redwing La. L25: Gate 5C **74**
Redwing Way L26: Halew 1F **93**
Redwood Av. L31: Lyd 4B **6**
Redwood Cl. CH43: O'ton 1B **86**
L25: Gate 4E **75**
Redwood Ct. *L8: Liv 5G 71*
(off Byles St.)
Redwood Dr. WA11: Hay 6B **30**
Redwood Gro. *L20: Boot 1C 34*
(off Strand Rd.)
Redwood Rd. L25: Gate 4D **74**
Redwood Way L33: Kirkb 3A **14**
Reedale Cl. L18: Moss H 5E **73**
Reedale Rd. L18: Moss H 5E **73**
Reeds Av. E. CH46: Leas 4D **48**
Reeds Av. W. CH46: Leas 4D **48**
Reeds Brow WA11: Rainf 1H **17**
Reeds La. CH46: Leas, More 3D **48**
WA11: Rainf 5E **17**
Reeds Rd. L36: Huy 3G **57**
Reedville CH43: O'ton 4D **68**
Reedville Gro. CH46: Leas 5D **48**
Reedville Rd. CH63: Beb 6H **87**
Reeve Ct. Village WA9: St H 1A **60**
Reeves Av. L20: Boot 6E **21**
Reeves St. WA9: St H 2A **44**
Reflection Ct. WA10: St H 2D **42**
Regal Cres. WA8: Wid 3H **95**
Regal Dr. WA10: Windle 6A **28**
Regal Rd. L11: Crox 2G **37**
Regal Wlk. L4: Walt 6F **35**
Regency Ct. *CH42: Rock F 2A 88*
(off Rock La. W.)
Regency Pk. WA8: Wid 6C **78**
Regent Av. L14: Broad G 5A **56**
L30: N'ton 6F **11**
WA11: Hay 4D **30**
Regent Pk. L36: Huy 2G **57**
Regent Rd. CH45: Wall 1H **49**
L3: Liv 1B **52**
L5: Kirkd, Liv 3B **34**
L20: Boot, Kirkd 6H **19**
L23: Crosb 5F **9**
WA8: Wid 2F **97**
Regents Cl. CH61: Thing 5F **85**
Regents Rd. WA10: St H 3A **42**
Regent St. L3: Liv 3B **52**
WA7: Run 2E **113**
WA12: Newt W 2H **45**
Regents Way CH63: Hghr B 3F **87**
Regiment Way L12: W Der 6H **37**
Regina Av. L22: Water 1E **19**
Reginald Rd. WA9: St H 1A **62**
Regina Rd. L9: Walt 5G **21**
Reigate Cl. L25: Woolt 6E **75**
Reins Cft. CH64: Nest 6A **118**
Rembury Pl. WA4: Dutt 4H **125**
Renaissance Way L24: Halew 6F **93**
Rendal Cl. L5: Liv 2G **53**
Rendcombe Grn. L11: Norr G 2D **36**
Rendelsham Cl. CH49: Upton 4C **66**
Rendel St. CH41: Birke 2F **69**
Renfrew Av. CH62: East 2E **121**
WA11: St H 4H **29**
Renfrew St. L7: Liv 5G **53**
Renlake Ind. Est. WA9: St H 1B **62**
Rennell Rd. L14: Knott A 4G **55**
Rennie Av. WA10: St H 1A **42**
Renown Way L24: Speke 5C **92**
Renshaw St. L1: Liv 5G **5** (6E **53**)
Renton Av. WA7: Run 3H **113**
Renville Rd. L14: Broad G 5G **55**
Renwick Av. L35: Rainh 3G **59**
Renwick Rd. L9: Walt 6G **21**
Repton Gro. L10: Ain 1A **22**
Repton Rd. L16: Child 1H **73**
Reservoir Rd. CH42: Tran 2D **86**
L25: Woolt 6B **74**
Reservoir Rd. Nth. CH42: Tran 1D **86**
Reservoir St. L6: Liv 3G **53**
WA9: St H 6A **42**
Rest Hill Rd. CH63: Store 6D **86**
Retford Rd. L33: Kirkb 1B **24**
Retford Wlk. L33: Kirkb 1B **24**
Reva Rd. L14: Broad G 4B **56**
Revesby Cl. WA8: Wid 1B **96**
Rex Cohen Ct. L17: Aig 4C **72**
Rexmore Rd. L18: Moss H 1E **91**
Rexmore Way L15: Wav 2C **72**
Reynolds Av. WA9: St H 3D **44**
Reynolds Cl. L6: Liv 3G **53**
Reynolds Way L25: Woolt 1C **92**
Rhiwlas St. L8: Liv 4G **71**
Rhodesia Rd. L9: Ain 5H **21**
Rhodesway CH60: Hesw 6F **101**
Rhona Cl. CH63: East 3C **120**
Rhona Dr. WA5: Gt San 3G **81**
Rhosesmor Cl. L32: Kirkb 4B **24**
Rhosesmor Rd. L32: Kirkb 5B **24**
Rhuddlan Cl. L13: Liv 5D **54**
Rhyl St. L8: Liv 4F **71**
WA8: Wid 4D **96**
Rialto Cl. L8: Liv 2F **71**
Ribble Av. L31: Mag 5D **6**
L35: Rainh 4A **60**
Ribble Cl. WA8: Wid 6B **80**
Ribbledale Rd. L18: Moss H 5E **73**
Ribble Ho. L25: Gate 5E **75**
Ribble Rd. L25: Gate 6E **75**
Ribbler's La. L32: Kirkb 4H **23**
L34: Know 5B **24**
Ribblesdale Av. L9: Ain 4H **21**
Ribblesdale Rd. CH62: East 2F **121**
Ribble St. CH41: Birke 6B **50**
Ribchester Way L35: Tar G 2A **76**
Rice Hey Rd. CH44: Wall 2E **51**
Rice La. CH44: Wall 2E **51**
(not continuous)
L9: Walt 2F **35**
Rice Lane City Farm 1F 35
Rice Lane Station (Rail) 6G 21
Rice St. L1: Liv 6H **5** (1E **71**)
Richard Allen Way *L5: Liv 3F 53*
(off Netherfield Rd. Sth.)
Richard Chubb Dr. CH44: Wall 1F **51**
Richard Cl. WA7: Cas 4C **114**
Richard Gro. L12: W Der 2A **56**

Richard Hesketh Dr. L32: Kirkb 1G 23
Richard Kelly Cl. L4: Walt 5B 36
Richard Kelly Dr. L4: Walt 3B 36
Richard Kelly Pl. L4: Walt 5B 36
Richard Martin Rd. L21: Ford 2C 20
Richard Rd. L23: Blun 4C 8
Richards Gro. WA9: St H 1A 44
Richardson Rd. CH42: Rock F 2G 87
Richardson St. L7: Liv 2A 72
Richland Rd. L13: Liv 2D 54
Richmond Av. L21: Lith 3A 20
  WA7: Run .3A 114
  WA11: Hay 4D 30
Richmond Cl. CH63: Beb 5A 88
  WA10: Eccl 1G 41
Richmond Ct. L6: Liv 2G 53
                          (off Richmond Ter.)
  L21: Lith 4B 20
                             (off Delta Rd.)
  WA8: Wid 5H 79
Richmond Cres. L30: N'ton 6F 11
Richmond Gro. L31: Lyd 4D 6
Richmond Pk. L6: Liv 1H 53
Richmond Rd. CH63: Beb 5H 87
  L23: Crosb .4G 9
Richmond Row L3: Liv 1G 5 (4E 53)
Richmond St. CH45: New B 4D 32
  L1: Liv 4E 5 (6D 52)
  WA8: Wid .2G 97
Richmond Ter. L6: Liv 2H 53
Richmond Way CH61: Hesw 3D 100
  CH61: Thing 4E 85
  L35: Tar G .2A 76
Rich Vw. CH43: O'ton 6D 68
Rickaby Cl. CH63: Brom 5C 104
Rickman St. L4: Kirkd 6D 34
Rickman Way L36: Huy 1H 75
Ridding La. WA7: Brook 2D 124
Riddock Rd. L21: Lith 6B 20
Rides, The WA11: Hay 5F 31
Ridge, The CH60: Hesw 3B 100
Ridgefield Rd. CH61: Pens 6D 84
Ridgemere Rd. CH61: Pens 6D 84
Ridgetor Rd. L25: Woolt 6B 74
Ridgeview Rd. CH43: Noct 4H 67
Ridgeway, The CH47: Meols 2E 65
  CH60: Hesw 6F 101
  CH63: Hghr B 3F 87
  L25: Woolt 6C 74
  WA7: Murd 1F 125
  WA8: Cron 3A 78
Ridgeway Dr. L31: Lyd 3C 6
Ridgewell Cl. L21: Lith 4A 20
Ridgewood Dr. CH61: Pens 1C 100
  WA9: St H 1G 61
Ridgewood Way L18: Wor 4G 21
Ridgmont Av. L11: Norr G 3D 36
Riding Cl. WA9: Clock F 3G 61
Ridingfold L26: Halew 1F 93
Riding Hill Rd. L34: Know 3F 39
Riding Hill Wlk. L34: Know 3F 39
Ridings, The CH43: Noct 4H 67
Ridings Hey CH43: Noct 5H 67
Riding St. L3: Liv 3H 5 (5F 53)
Ridley Gro. CH48: W Kir 6A 64
Ridley La. L31: Mag 6C 6
Ridley Rd. L6: Liv 4A 54
Ridley St. CH43: O'ton 4E 69
Ridsdale WA8: Wid 3A 96
Ridsdale Lawn L27: N'ley 6A 76
Riesling Dr. L33: Kirkb 4H 13
Rigby Dr. CH49: Grea 1B 84
Rigby Rd. L31: Mag 4A 6
Rigby St. L3: Liv 2B 4 (5B 52)
  WA10: St H 2D 42
                            (Clock Twr. St.)
  WA10: St H 1D 42
                              (Henry St.)
Rigby St. Sth. WA10: St H 2D 42
                           (off Nth. John St.)
Riley Av. L20: Boot 6D 20
Riley Dr. WA7: Run 5E 113
Rimmer Av. L16: Child 6C 56

Rimmerbrook Rd. L25: Gate 2D 74
Rimmer Cl. L21: Lith 4B 20
Rimmer Gro. WA9: St H 2A 44
Rimmer St. L3: Liv 2H 5 (5E 53)
Rimmington Rd. L17: Aig 1C 90
Rimrose Bus. Pk. L20: Boot 1A 34
Rimrose Rd. L20: Boot 6A 20
Rimrose Valley Country Pk. 5B 10
Rimrose Valley Rd. L23: Crosb 6A 10
Rimsdale Cl. L17: Aig 4C 90
Rindlebrook La. L34: Presc 2C 58
Ringcroft Rd. L13: Liv 4F 55
Ringo Starr Dr. L6: Liv 4H 53
Ringsfield Rd. L24: Speke 3A 110
Ringway CH64: Nest 6B 118
Ringway Rd. L25: Gate 5E 75
  WA7: Run .3H 113
Ringways CH62: Brom 2D 104
Ringwood Av. L14: Broad G 5B 56
Ringwood Rd. CH43: O'ton 6C 68
Rio Ct. L34: Presc 6D 40
Ripley Av. L21: Lith 2B 20
Ripley Cl. L31: Mag 6D 6
Ripon Cl. L30: N'ton 2F 21
  L36: Huy 4A 58
Ripon Rd. CH45: Wall 1A 50
Ripon Row WA7: Run 1H 123
Ripon St. CH41: Tran 5G 69
  L4: Walt 4F 35
Risbury Rd. L11: Norr G 3D 36
Rishton Cl. L5: Liv 2G 53
Rishton St. L5: Liv 2G 53
                         (off Tynemouth Cl.)
Ritchie Av. L9: Ain 5A 22
Ritherup La. L35: Rainh 3A 60
Ritson St. L8: Liv 3H 71
Rivacre Rd. CH62: East 2G 121
  CH66: Ell P, Hoot 5H 121
Riva La. CH60: Hesw 3C 100
Riveacre Rd. CH65: Hoot 2G 121
Rivenmill Cl. WA8: Wid 4G 79
River Avon St. L8: Liv 2A 72
                            (not continuous)
Riverbank Cl. CH60: Hesw 1D 116
Riverbank Rd. CH60: Hesw 1C 116
  CH62: Brom 1E 105
  L19: Gras 4E 91
River Gro. CH62: New F 3B 88
Riverpark Gdns. L8: Liv 3E 71
                            (off Hyslop St.)
Riversdale WA6: Frod 6G 123
Riversdale Cl. L33: Kirkb 5B 14
Riversdale Ct. L19: Aig 3D 90
Riversdale M. L19: Aig 3D 90
Riversdale Rd. CH44: Wall 3F 51
  CH48: W Kir 1A 82
  L19: Aig 4D 90
  L21: Sea 4B 20
  WA7: Halt .4A 114
Riverside CH48: W Kir 3B 82
  CH62: Port S 6B 88
  L12: W Der 4A 38
Riverside Bowl 4D 32
Riverside Cl. L20: Boot 6A 20
Riverside Ct. CH62: New F 2B 88
Riverside Dr. L3: Liv 6E 71
  L17: Aig 1G 89
Riverside Gro. WA9: St H 6H 43
Riverside Ho. CH41: Birke 6H 51
Riverside Trad. Est. WA5: Penk 2F 99
Riverside Vw. L17: Aig 2A 90
Riverside Wlk. L3: Liv 4D 70
                            (Atlantic Way)
  L3: Liv 6B 4 (1B 70)
                           (The Colonnades)
Riverslea Rd. L23: Blun 1D 18
River Vw. CH41: Tran 5G 69
                            (off Marquis St.)
  CH62: New F 3C 88
  L22: Water .1E 19
Riverview CH49: Woodc 2E 85
Riverview Gdns. CH42: Rock F 1H 87
River Vw. Res. Cvn. Pk. WA8: Wid . . .3G 97

Riverview Rd. CH44: Wall 4G 51
  CH62: Brom 2F 105
Riverview Wlk. L8: Liv 5F 71
                           (off Cockburn St.)
River Wlk. WA7: Pal F 6B 114
                       (off Halton Lea Shop. Cen.)
River Way L25: Gate 6E 75
Riverwood Rd. CH62: Brom 4F 105
Riviera Dr. CH42: Rock F 2F 87
  L11: Crox 1G 37
Rivington Av. CH43: Noct 5A 68
  WA9: St H .5C 28
Rivington Rd. CH44: Wall 4F 51
  WA7: Pres B 4H 125
  WA10: St H 2B 42
Rivington St. WA10: St H 3B 42
Roadwater Cl. L25: Gate 2D 74
Robarts Rd. L4: Walt 1H 53
ROBBINS BRIDGE 2D 6
Robbins Bri. L31: Lyd 2D 6
Robeck Rd. L13: Liv 6F 55
Robert Dr. CH49: Grea 6C 66
Robert Gro. L12: W Der 2A 56
Roberts Av. WA11: Hay 6C 30
Roberts Ct. WA7: Pal F 1B 124
Robertson St. L8: Liv 4E 71
Roberts St. L3: Liv 1A 4 (4B 52)
Robert St. CH41: Birke 2F 69
  WA7: Run .3G 113
  WA8: Wid .2F 97
Robina Rd. WA9: St H 5H 43
Robin Cl. WA7: Murd 6F 115
Robins La. WA9: St H 5G 43
Robinson Pl. WA9: St H 2H 43
Robinson Rd. L21: Lith 2C 20
Robin Way CH49: Woodc 1F 85
Robsart St. L5: Liv 2C 52
Robson St. L4: Walt 6F 35
  L13: Liv 6E 55
ROBY 5E 57
Roby Cl. L35: Rainh 3A 60
Roby Ct. L36: Roby 6F 57
Roby Gro. WA5: Gt San 3H 81
Roby Mt. Av. L36: Roby 5F 57
Roby Rd. L14: Broad G 6B 56
  L36: Roby .5C 56
                            (not continuous)
Roby Station (Rail) 5E 57
Roby St. L15: Wav 2C 72
  L20: Boot 1C 34
  WA10: St H 4B 42
Rocastle Cl. L6: Liv 4G 53
Rochester Av. L30: N'ton 2F 21
Rochester Gdns. WA10: St H 4B 42
Rochester Rd. CH42: Rock F 1A 88
Rock Av. CH60: Hesw 4D 100
Rock Bank CH49: Upton 4E 67
Rockbank Rd. L13: Liv 2D 54
Rockbourne Av. L25: Woolt 4B 74
Rockbourne Grn. L25: Woolt 4B 74
Rockbourne Way L25: Woolt 4B 74
Rock Cl. CH42: Rock F 1H 87
Rocket Trad. Cen. L14: Broad G 6G 55
ROCK FERRY 1H 87
Rock Ferry By-Pass CH42: Rock F . . .6A 70
Rock Ferry Station (Rail) 1H 87
Rockfield Cl. WA8: Wid 5B 96
Rockfield Gdns. L31: Mag 6E 6
                            (off East Meade)
Rockfield Rd. L4: Walt 6F 35
Rockford Av. L32: Kirkb 4A 24
Rockford Cl. L32: Kirkb 4A 24
Rockford Gdns. WA5: Gt San 1H 81
Rockford Wlk. L32: Kirkb 4A 24
Rock Gro. L13: Liv 4E 55
Rockhill Rd. L25: Woolt 1D 92
Rockhouse St. L6: Liv 2A 54
Rockingham Ct. L33: Kirkb 6B 14
Rockland Rd. CH45: Wall 6B 32
  L22: Water .1G 19
Rocklands, The CH43: Noct 3H 67

Rocklands Av. CH63: Beb 4A **88**
Rocklands La. CH63: Thorn H 5E **103**
Rock La. L31: Mell 3D **12**
WA8: Wid 5D **78**
Rock La. E. CH42: Rock F 2A **88**
(not continuous)
Rock La. W. CH42: Rock F 2H **87**
Rockley St. L4: Kirkd 5E **35**
(not continuous)
Rockmount Cl. L25: Woolt 6B **74**
Rockmount Pk. L25: Woolt 6B **74**
Rockmount Rd. L17: Aig 2D **90**
Rock Pk. CH42: Rock F 1A **88**
(not continuous)
Rock Pk. Rd. CH42: Rock F 2B **88**
Rockpoint Av. CH45: New B 6E **33**
Rock Retail Pk. CH41: Birke 4G **69**
ROCKSAVAGE 2G **123**
Rocksavage Expressway
WA7: Clftn 2H **123**
Rocksavage Way WA7: Run 2E **123**
Rockside Rd. L18: Moss H 2E **91**
Rock St. L13: Liv 4E **55**
WA10: St H 5A **42**
Rock Vw. L31: Mell 5E **13**
Rockville Rd. L14: Broad G 6G **55**
Rockville St. CH42: Rock F 1H **87**
Rockwell Cl. L12: W Der 5H **37**
Rockwell Rd. L12: W Der 5H **37**
Rocky Bank Rd. CH42: Tran 6F **69**
Rocky La. CH60: Hesw 5D **100**
L6: Liv 2A **54**
L16: Child 1G **73**
Rocky La. Sth. CH60: Hesw 5E **101**
Rococo Sq. CH45: New B 4E **33**
Roderick Rd. L4: Walt 3G **35**
Roderick St. L3: Liv 1H **5** (4E **53**)
Rodgers Cl. WA6: Frod 6F **123**
Rodick St. L25: Woolt 1B **92**
Rodmell Rd. L9: Ain 5H **21**
Rodney St. CH41: Birke 4F **69**
L1: Liv 6H **5** (1E **71**)
WA10: St H 2C **42**
Roe All. L1: Liv 5F **5**
Roeburn Way WA5: Penk 6F **81**
Roedean Cl. L25: Woolt 2D **92**
L31: Mag 5C **6**
Roehampton Dr. L23: Blun 3E **9**
WA7: Pal F 6A **114**
Roemarsh Cl. L12: W Der 3F **37**
Roemarsh Ct. WA7: Pal F 1A **124**
Roe St. L1: Liv 4F **5** (6D **52**)
Roften Works Ind. Est.
CH66: Hoot 6D **120**
Roger Arden Ct. L20: Boot 1D **34**
Rogers Av. L20: Boot 6E **21**
Rogersons Grn. L26: Halew 1G **93**
Rokeby Cl. L3: Liv 4E **53**
L20: Boot 4E **21**
Rokeby Ct. WA7: Manor P 6F **99**
Rokeby St. L3: Liv 4E **53**
Roker Av. CH44: Wall 4C **50**
Rokesmith Av. L7: Liv 1A **72**
Roklis Bldg. *CH44: Wall* *3F* ***51***
(off Liscard Rd.)
Roklis Ct. *CH49: Upton* *5E* ***67***
(off Rake La.)
Roland Av. CH63: Hghr B 5F **87**
WA7: Run 4D **112**
WA11: St H 4G **29**
Rolands Wlk. WA7: Cas 4B **114**
Roleton Cl. L30: N'ton 5H **11**
Rollesby Gdns. WA9: St H 1C **60**
Rolleston Dr. CH45: Wall 6B **32**
CH63: Beb 1A **104**
Rolling Mill La. WA9: St H 5B **44**
Rollo St. L4: Kirkd 6D **34**
Roman Cl. WA7: Cas 3A **114**
Roman Rd. CH43: Pren 3C **86**
CH47: Meols 6D **46**
CH63: Store 3C **86**
Roman Way L33: Kirkb 6C **14**
Rome Cl. L36: Huy 4F **57**
Romer Rd. L6: Liv 4A **54**
Romford Way L26: Halew 5H **93**
(not continuous)
Romilly St. L6: Liv 4H **53**
Romley St. L4: Walt 4F **35**
Romney Cl. WA8: Wid 1A **98**
Romulus St. L7: Liv 5B **54**
Ronald Cl. L22: Water 2H **19**
Ronald Rd. L22: Water 2H **19**
Ronald Ross Av. L30: N'ton 6F **11**
Ronaldshay WA8: Wid 1A **98**
Ronald St. L13: Liv 4D **54**
Ronaldsway CH49: Upton 3D **66**
CH60: Hesw 1D **116**
L10: Faz 4E **23**
L23: Thorn 3A **10**
L26: Halew 3A **94**
Ronan Cl. L20: Boot 1A **34**
Ronan Rd. WA8: Wid 6C **96**
Rone Cl. CH46: More 1B **66**
Rookery Dr. L19: Aig 3D **90**
WA11: Rainf 3G **17**
Rookery La. WA11: Rainf 4G **17**
Rookley Cl. L27: N'ley 5H **75**
Rooks Way CH60: Hesw 5C **100**
Rooley, The L36: Huy 6F **57**
Roosevelt Dr. L9: Ain 3H **21**
Roper's Bri. Cl. L35: Whis 5D **58**
Ropers Ct. L34: Presc 2D **58**
Roper St. L8: Liv 4F **71**
WA9: St H 1G **43**
Ropewalk, The CH64: Park 6G **117**
Ropewalks Sq. L1: Liv 6G **5**
Ropeworks Cl. L20: Boot 6D **20**
Rosalind Av. CH63: Hghr B 4G **87**
Rosalind Way L20: Kirkd 4D **34**
Rosam Ct. WA7: Pal F 1A **124**
Rosclare Dr. CH45: Wall 1B **50**
Roscoe & Gladstone Hall L17: Aig 5C **72**
Roscoe Cl. L35: Tar G 2A **76**
Roscoe Cres. WA7: West P 6C **112**
Roscoe La. L1: Liv 6G **5**
Roscoe Pl. L1: Liv 6G **5** (1E **71**)
Roscoe St. L1: Liv 6H **5** (1E **71**)
WA10: St H 2B **42**
Roscommon St. L5: Liv 3E **53**
Roscommon Way WA8: Wid 6C **78**
Roscote, The CH60: Hesw 6D **100**
Roscote Cl. CH60: Hesw 6D **100**
Roseacre CH48: W Kir 6A **64**
Roseate Ct. CH45: Wall 5A **32**
Rose Av. L20: Boot 4C **20**
WA9: St H 6G **43**
WA11: Hay 5G **31**
Rose Bank Rd. L16: Child 2H **73**
Rosebank Rd. L36: Huy 2E **57**
Rosebank Way L36: Huy 2E **57**
Rosebery Av. CH44: Wall 3E **51**
L22: Water 1E **19**
Rosebery Gro. CH42: Tran 1D **86**
Rosebery Rd. WA10: St H 6B **28**
Rosebery St. L8: Liv 2G **71**
Rosebourne Cl. L17: Aig 1A **90**
Rose Brae L18: Moss H 5F **73**
Rosebrae Ct. CH41: Birke 2A **70**
CH60: Hesw 4E **101**
Rose Brow L25: Woolt 5C **74**
Rose Cl. L26: Halew 4A **94**
WA7: Murd 2F **125**
Rose Ct. CH41: Birke 3F **69**
L15: Wav 2C **72**
Rose Cres. WA8: Wid 4D **96**
Rosecroft CH62: Brom 1C **120**
Rosecroft Ct. CH47: Hoy 3A **64**
Rosedale Av. L23: Crosb 5G **9**
Rosedale Cl. L9: Walt 1H **35**
Rosedale Rd. CH42: Tran 6G **69**
L18: Moss H 5F **73**
Rose Dr. WA11: Rainf 4G **17**
Rosefield Av. CH63: Hghr B 4G **87**
Rosefield Rd. L25: Woolt 2E **93**
Rosegarth Grn. *L13: Liv* *3F* ***55***
(off Black Horse La.)
Roseheath Dr. L26: Halew 4H **93**
Rose Hill L3: Liv 4D **52**
Rosehill Av. WA9: Bold 2D **62**
Rosehill Ct. L25: Woolt 5C **74**
Roseland Cl. L31: Lyd 3A **6**
Roselands Ct. CH42: Rock F 2G **87**
Rose La. L18: Moss H 6D **72**
Rose Lea Cl. WA8: Wid 5E **79**
Roselee Ct. CH42: Rock F 2A **88**
Rosemary Av. WA7: Beech 3B **124**
Rosemary Cl. CH43: Bid 1A **68**
L7: Liv 1G **71**
Rosemead Av. CH61: Pens 1D **100**
Rosemont Rd. L17: Aig 1D **90**
Rosemoor Dr. L23: Crosb 4A **10**
Rosemoor Gdns. L11: Norr G 3E **37**
Rose Mt. CH43: O'ton 6D **68**
Rosemount Cl. CH43: O'ton 6C **68**
Rose Mt. Dr. CH45: Wall 1C **50**
Rosemount Pk. CH43: O'ton 5C **68**
Rose Pl. CH42: Tran 5F **69**
L3: Liv 4D **52**
(not continuous)
WA11: Rainf 4G **17**
Roseside Dr. L27: N'ley 3H **75**
Rose St. L1: Liv 3F **5** (6D **52**)
L25: Woolt 1B **92**
WA8: Wid 4D **96**
Rose Ter. L18: Moss H 5E **73**
Rose Va. L5: Liv 3E **53**
(not continuous)
Rose Vw. Av. WA8: Wid 1E **97**
Rose Vs. L15: Wav 2D **72**
Rosewarne Cl. L17: Aig 1H **89**
Rosewood Cl. L27: N'ley 4G **75**
L28: Stockb V 6D **38**
WA8: Wid 3H **95**
Rosewood Dr. CH46: More 1H **65**
Rosewood Farm Ct. WA8: Wid 4C **78**
Rosewood Gdns. L11: Norr G 4F **37**
Roseworth Av. L9: Walt 4G **21**
Roskell Rd. L25: Hunts X 4E **93**
Roslin Ct. CH43: O'ton 5D **68**
Roslin Rd. CH43: O'ton 5D **68**
CH61: Irby 5B **84**
Roslyn St. CH42: Tran 6H **69**
Rossall Av. L10: Ain 6B **12**
Rossall Cl. L24: Hale 3E **111**
Rossall Ct. CH46: Leas 5D **48**
Rossall Rd. CH46: More 6D **48**
L13: Liv 5F **55**
WA8: Wid 1H **97**
Ross Av. CH46: Leas 3G **49**
Ross Cl. L34: Know 2F **39**
Rosscourt Vw. CH42: Rock F 1B **88**
Rossendale Cl. CH43: Noct 5H **67**
Rossett Av. L17: Liv 3C **72**
Rossett Rd. L23: Crosb 6E **9**
Rossett St. L6: Liv 2A **54**
Rossington Gdns. WA9: St H 2D **60**
Rossini St. L21: Sea 5A **20**
Rossiter Dr. CH43: Bid 3G **67**
Rosslyn Av. L31: Mag 1H **11**
Rosslyn Cres. CH46: More 1C **66**
Rosslyn Dr. CH46: More 1C **66**
Rosslyn Pk. CH46: More 2C **66**
Rosslyn St. L17: Aig 6H **71**
Rossmore Gdns. L4: Walt 5A **36**
Ross St. WA8: Wid 2F **97**
Ross Twr. Ct. CH45: New B 5E **33**
Rostherne Av. CH44: Wall 4C **50**
Rostherne Cres. WA8: Wid 1B **96**
Rosthwaite Gro. WA11: St H 2F **29**
Rosthwaite Rd. L12: W Der 1G **55**
Roswell Ct. L28: Stockb V 1D **56**
Rothay Dr. WA5: Penk 6F **81**
Rothbury Cl. CH46: More 1A **66**
WA7: Beech 1A **124**
Rothbury Ct. WA9: Sut M 5F **61**
Rothbury Rd. L14: Knott A 1B **56**
Rotherham Cl. L36: Huy 3G **57**
Rotherwood CH43: Noct 4H **67**
Rotherwood Cl. CH63: Hghr B 5F **87**

Rothesay Cl. WA7: Cas 3B 114
  WA11: St H 4A 30
Rothesay Ct. CH63: Beb 1H 103
Rothesay Dr. CH62: East 3E 121
  L23: Crosb 6G 9
Rothesay Gdns. CH43: Pren 2B 86
Rothsay Cl. L5: Liv 3F 53
Rothwells La. L23: Thorn 3B 10
Rothwell St. L6: Liv 3G 53
Rotunda St. L5: Liv 2D 52
Roughdale Av. L32: Kirkb 4B 24
  WA9: Sut M 3F 61
Roughdale Cl. L32: Kirkb 4B 24
Roughley Ho. CH41: Birke 2H 69
          (off Bridge St.)
Roughsedge Ho. L28: Stockb V . . .5D 38
Roughwood Dr. L33: Kirkb 6B 14
Roundabout, The WA8: Cron 3B 78
Round Hey L28: Stockb V 5C 38
Round Meade, The L31: Mag 5A 6
Roundwood Dr. WA9: St H 4F 43
Routledge St. WA8: Wid 2F 97
Row, The CH47: Hoy 2B 64
Rowan Av. L12: W Der 4B 38
Rowan Cl. WA5: Gt San 3H 81
  WA7: Run 6G 113
  WA11: Hay 6B 30
  WA11: St H 4H 29
Rowan Ct. CH49: Grea 1H 83
  CH63: Hghr B 5F 87
  L17: Aig 1C 90
Rowan Dr. L32: Kirkb 6G 13
Rowan Gro. CH63: Hghr B 1G 103
  L36: Huy 1F 75
Rowans, The L39: Augh 1F 7
  WA8: Wid 5H 79
     (off Hampton Ct. Way)
Rowan Tree Cl. CH49: Grea 6H 65
Rowena Cl. L23: Crosb 5H 9
Rowlings Way L32: Kirkb 3B 24
Rowsley Gro. L9: Ain 4H 21
Rowson Ct. CH45: New B 5D 32
     (off Pickering Rd.)
Rowson St. CH45: New B 4D 32
  L34: Presc 6D 40
Rowthorn Cl. WA8: Wid 3C 96
Rowton Cl. CH43: O'ton 6B 68
Roxborough Cl. WA5: Burtw 1H 63
Roxborough Wlk. L25: Woolt 6E 75
Roxburgh Av. CH42: Tran 1F 87
  L17: Aig 6A 72
Roxburgh St. L4: Kirkd 3E 35
  L20: Boot 3E 35
Royal, The CH47: Hoy 3A 64
Royal Av. WA8: Wid 3H 95
Royal Ct. CH42: Rock F 2A 88
     (off Rock La. W.)
Royal Court Theatre 3F 5 (6D 52)
Royal Cft. L12: W Der 3F 55
Royal Gro. WA10: St H 4B 42
Royal Liverpool Golf Course 4A 64
Royal Mail St. L3: Liv 4G 5 (6E 53)
Royal Pl. WA8: Wid 3H 95
Royal Quay L3: Liv 1C 70
Royal Standard Way CH42: Tran . . .6H 69
Royal St. L4: Walt 6E 35
Royden Av. CH44: Wall 2F 51
  WA7: Run 5D 112
Royden Rd. CH49: Upton 3C 66
      (not continuous)
Royden Way L3: Liv 6E 71
Roysten Gdns. WA9: St H 3H 43
Royston Av. CH44: Wall 3F 51
Royston St. L7: Liv 6H 53
Royton Cl. L26: Halew 5H 93
Royton Rd. L22: Water 1H 19
Rubbing Stone CH48: Caldy 5D 82
Ruby Cl. L21: Lith 3C 20
Ruby St. L8: Liv 6F 71
      (not continuous)
Rudd Av. WA9: St H 3D 44
Rudd St. CH47: Hoy 2B 64

Rudgate L35: Whis 5E 59
Rudgrave Av. CH44: Wall 2F 51
Rudgrave Pl. CH44: Wall 2F 51
Rudgrave Sq. CH44: Wall 2F 51
Rudheath La. WA7: Nort 2F 115
Rudley Wlk. L24: Speke 3H 109
Rudston Rd. L16: Child 1G 73
Rudyard Cl. L14: Knott A 4G 55
Rudyard Rd. L14: Knott A 4G 55
Rufford Av. L31: Mag 4D 6
Rufford Cl. L10: Faz 2D 22
  L35: Presc 2F 59
  WA11: Rainf 1A 96
Rufford Rd. CH44: Wall 4E 51
  L6: Liv .4A 54
  L20: Boot 6C 20
  WA11: Rainf 2F 17
Rufford Wlk. WA11: St H 5A 30
Rugby Dr. L10: Ain 2C 22
Rugby Rd. CH44: Wall 2B 50
  L9: Ain .3H 21
Ruislip Cl. L25: Woolt 1E 93
Rullerton Rd. CH44: Wall 3G 50
Rumford Pl. L3: Liv 3B 4 (5C 52)
Rumford St. L2: Liv 3C 4 (5E 52)
Rumney Pl. L4: Kirkd 5E 35
      (not continuous)
Rumney Rd. L4: Kirkd 5E 35
Rumney Rd. W. L4: Kirkd 5D 34
Runcorn WA7: Run 3C 112
Runcorn East Station (Rail) 6F 115
Runcorn FC Halton 3D 96
     (off Lower Ho. La.)
Runcorn Hill Local Nature Reserve
  . . . . .5D 112
Runcorn Hill Vis. Cen. 5D 112
Runcorn Rd.
  WA4: Dares, Hghr Wal, Moore . . .1H 115
Runcorn Ski & Snowboard Cen. . . .6D 114
Runcorn Spur Rd. WA7: Run 3F 113
Runcorn Station (Rail) 3D 112
Runcorn Swimming Pool 2F 113
Rundle Rd. L17: Aig 1C 90
Rundle St. CH41: Birke 1C 68
Runic St. L13: Liv 5D 54
Runnell, The CH64: Nest 4H 117
Runnell's La. L23: Thorn 4C 10
Runnymead Wlk. WA8: Wid 1G 97
     (off William St.)
Runnymede L36: Huy 3F 57
Runnymede Cl. L25: Woolt 5C 74
Runnymede Ct. WA8: Wid 2G 97
     (off William St.)
Runnymede Dr. WA11: Hay 5C 30
Runnymede Gdns. WA8: Wid 2G 97
     (off Cliffe St.)
Runton Rd. L25: Gate 4E 75
Rupert Dr. L6: Liv 3G 53
Rupert Rd. L36: Huy 4E 57
Rupert Row WA7: Cas 5C 114
Ruscar Cl. L26: Halew 1G 93
Ruscolm Cl. WA5: Gt San 2F 81
Ruscombe Rd. L14: Knott A 2B 56
Rushbury Ct. L15: Wav 1D 72
Rushden Rd. L32: Kirkb 2C 24
Rushey Hey Rd. L32: Kirkb 1A 24
Rushfield Cres. WA7: Brook 2D 126
Rushgreen Cl. CH43: Bid 2G 67
Rushlake Dr. L27: N'ley 4F 75
Rushmere Rd. L11: Norr G 4E 37
Rushmore Dr. WA8: Wid 6D 78
Rusholme Cl. L26: Halew 5A 94
Rushton Cl. WA5: Burtw 6H 45
  WA8: Wid 6D 78
Rushton Pl. L25: Woolt 1C 92
Rushton's Wlk. L30: N'ton 4D 10
Rushy Vw. WA12: Newt W 1H 45
Ruskin Av. CH42: Rock F 2F 87
  CH44: Wall 4C 50
Ruskin Cl. L20: Boot 2C 34
Ruskin Dr. WA10: St H 1B 42

Ruskin Leisure 6B 28
Ruskin St. L4: Kirkd 4E 35
Ruskin Way CH43: Noct 6H 67
  L36: Huy 6F 57
Rusland Av. CH61: Pens 1D 100
Rusland Rd. L32: Kirkb 3B 24
Russell Cl. WA8: Wid 5F 79
Russell Pl. L19: Garst 5G 91
Russell Rd. CH42: Rock F 6H 69
     (not continuous)
  CH44: Wall 2A 50
  L18: Moss H 4D 72
  L19: Garst 5G 91
  L36: Huy 5B 58
  WA7: Run 4C 112
Russell St. CH41: Birke 2G 69
  L3: Liv 3H 5 (6E 53)
Russet Cl. L27: N'ley 4G 75
  WA10: St H 6D 28
Russian Av. L13: Liv 2D 54
Russian Dr. L13: Liv 2D 54
Rutherford Cl. L13: Wav 6C 54
Rutherford Rd. L18: Moss H 3F 73
  L31: Mag 2C 12
  WA10: Windle 5A 28
Rutherglen Av. L23: Crosb 1H 19
Ruth Evans Ct. L35: Rainh 3G 59
Ruthven Ct. L21: Lith 4A 20
Ruthven Rd. L13: Liv 6F 55
  L21: Lith 4A 20
Rutland Av. L17: Liv 3B 72
  L26: Halew 3H 93
Rutland Cl. L5: Liv 2G 53
Rutland Ho. L17: Aig 4B 72
  L23: Blun 6D 8
Rutland St. L20: Boot 1D 34
  WA7: Run 3D 112
  WA10: St H 6D 28
Rutland Way L36: Huy 4B 58
Rutter St. L8: Liv 4E 71
Rycot Rd. L24: Speke 1D 108
Rycroft Rd. CH44: Wall 4E 51
  CH47: Meols 1E 65
  L10: Faz 3C 22
Rydal Av. CH43: Noct 4G 67
  L23: Crosb 1H 19
  L34: Presc 1F 59
Rydal Bank CH44: Wall 3E 51
  CH63: Beb 4A 88
Rydal Cl. CH61: Pens 1D 100
  L10: Ain 1D 22
  L33: Kirkb 5H 13
  WA11: St H 4E 29
Rydal Rd. L36: Huy 6G 57
Rydal St. L5: Liv 1G 53
Rydal Way WA8: Wid 2A 96
Rydecroft L25: Woolt 1B 92
Ryder Cl. L35: Rainh 3G 59
Ryder Ct. L35: Rainh 1H 59
Rye Cl. WA9: Clock F 3G 61
Ryecote L32: Kirkb 4A 24
Ryecroft L21: Ford 6B 10
Ryecroft Rd. CH60: Hesw 6G 101
Ryedale Cl. L8: Liv 2H 71
Ryefield La. L21: Ford 6B 10
Ryegate Rd. L19: Gras 3F 91
Rye Gro. L12: W Der 1A 56
Rye Hey Rd. L32: Kirkb 1A 24
Ryland Pk. CH61: Thing 6E 85
Rylands Hey CH49: Grea 5B 66
Rylands St. WA8: Wid 3F 97
Ryleys Gdns. L2: Liv 3D 4
Rymer Gro. L4: Walt 4G 35

S

Sabre Cl. WA7: Murd 6F 115
Sackville Rd. WA10: Windle 5A 28
Saddle Cl. L9: Ain 3B 22

Saddlers Ri.—St Marks Ct.

Saddlers Ri. WA7: Nort 5E **115**
Saddlestone Gro. L8: Liv 4E **71**
Sadler's La. WA11: Windle 4E **27**
Sadler St. WA8: Wid 2G **97**
Saffron Gdns. WA9: St H 3H **43**
Saffron M. L23: Thorn 3B **10**
St Agnes Rd. L4: Kirkd 5D **34**
L36: Huy 5G **57**
St Aidans Ct. CH43: Clau 3B **68**
WA9: Clock F 4A **62**
St Aidans Dr. WA8: Wid 3D **78**
St Aidan's Gro. L36: Huy 6E **39**
St Aidan's Ter. CH43: Clau 3B **68**
St Aidan's Way L30: N'ton 6D **10**
St Alban Rd. WA5: Penk 4G **81**
St Albans L6: Liv 2H **53**
St Albans Cl. WA11: Hay 4H **31**
St Albans Ct. L5: Liv 2C **52**
St Albans Rd. CH43: Clau 2C **68**
CH44: Wall 3D **50**
L20: Boot 2C **34**
St Alban's Sq. L20: Boot 3C **34**
St Alexander Cl. L20: Kirkd 4D **34**
St Ambrose Cft. L30: N'ton 5E **11**
St Ambrose Gro. L4: Walt 1H **53**
St Ambrose Rd. WA8: Wid 2G **97**
St Ambrose Way *L5: Liv 3E **53***
(off Everton Brow)
St Andrew Rd. L4: Walt 1H **53**
St Andrews Av. L12: W Der 1A **56**
St Andrews Ct. CH43: Noct 3H **67**
L22: Water 3G **19**
St Andrews Dr. L23: Blun 3E **9**
L36: Huy 6E **39**
St Andrews Gdns. L3: Liv 3H **5**
St Andrews Gro. L30: N'ton 6C **10**
WA11: St H 5F **29**
St Andrews Pl. *L17: Aig 6A **72***
(off Normanton Av.)
St Andrews Rd. CH43: O'ton 3D **68**
CH63: Beb 1A **104**
L20: Boot 5C **20**
L23: Blun 3D **8**
St Andrew St. L3: Liv 4H **5** (6F **53**)
St Andrews Vw. L33: Kirkb 3A **14**
St Annes Cl. CH41: Birke 2F **69**
St Anne's Cotts.
*L14: Knott A 4G **55***
(off Rudyard Cl.)
St Annes Ct. *L3: Liv 4E **53***
(off St Anne St.)
L13: Liv 4D **54**
L17: Aig 2C **90**
St Annes Gdns. L17: Aig 2D **90**
St Annes Gro. CH41: Birke 1E **69**
L17: Aig 2C **90**
St Anne's Ho. *L20: Boot 3D **34***
(off University Rd.)
St Annes Pl. CH41: Birke 1E **69**
St Annes Rd. L17: Aig 2D **90**
L36: Huy 6G **57**
WA8: Wid 1F **97**
St Annes Ter. CH41: Birke 1E **69**
St Anne St. CH41: Birke 2E **69**
(Livingstone Gdns.)
CH41: Birke 2F **69**
(Robert St.)
CH41: Birke 1E **69**
(St Anne's Pl.)
L3: Liv 1G **5** (3E **53**)
St Annes Way CH41: Birke 2F **69**
St Ann Pl. L35: Rainh 3A **60**
ST ANNS 3B **42**
St Ann's Rd. WA10: St H 2A **42**
St Anthony's Cl. L36: Huy 6E **39**
St Anthony's Gro. L30: N'ton 6D **10**
St Anthony's Rd. L23: Blun 4D **8**
St Anthony's Shop. Cen.
L5: Liv 2E **53**
St Asaph Gro. L30: N'ton 2F **21**
St Augustine St. L5: Liv 2D **52**
St Augustine's Way L30: N'ton 5D **10**
St Austell Cl. CH46: More 6H **47**
WA5: Penk 6G **81**
WA7: Brook 1D **124**
St Austells Rd. L4: Walt 3E **35**
St Bartholomew Rd. L3: Liv 1E **5** (4D **52**)
St Bartholomews Ct. L36: Huy 5E **57**
St Bedes Vw. WA8: Wid 2E **97**
St Benedict's Gro. L36: Huy 6E **39**
St Benet's Way L30: N'ton 6E **11**
St Bernards Cl. L8: Liv 2H **71**
L30: N'ton 6D **10**
St Bernard's Dr. L30: N'ton 6D **10**
St Brendan's Cl. L36: Huy 6E **39**
St Brides Cl. WA5: Penk 6G **81**
St Bride's Rd. CH44: Wall 2F **51**
St Bride St. L8: Liv 1F **71**
St Bridgets Cl. WA8: Wid 6E **97**
St Bridget's Gro. L30: N'ton 6D **10**
St Bridget's La. CH48: W Kir 2B **82**
St Brigid's Cres. *L5: Liv 2C **52***
(off Silvester St.)
St Catherine's Cl. L36: Huy 6G **57**
St Catherines Gdns. CH42: Tran 5F **69**
St Catherine's Rd. L20: Boot 2C **34**
St Chad's Dr. L32: Kirkb 1A **24**
St Chads Pde. L32: Kirkb 1A **24**
St Christoper's Dr. L36: Huy 6E **39**
St Christopher's Av. L30: N'ton 5D **10**
St Columba's Cl. CH44: Wall 2F **51**
St Cuthberts Cl. L12: Crox 2A **38**
St Cyrils Cl. L27: N'ley 3E **75**
St Cyril's Ct. L27: N'ley 3E **75**
St Damian's Cft. L30: N'ton 6E **11**
St David Rd. CH43: Clau 3C **68**
CH62: East 1G **121**
St David's Cl. L35: Rainh 3A **60**
St David's Gro. L30: N'ton 1D **20**
St Davids La. CH43: Noct 4H **67**
St Davids Rd. L4: Walt 1H **53**
L14: Knott A 2D **56**
St Domingo Gro. L5: Liv 1G **53**
St Domingo Rd. L5: Liv 6E **35**
St Domingo Va. L5: Liv 1F **53**
St Dunstan's Gro. L30: N'ton 6D **10**
St Edmond's Rd. L20: Boot 3C **34**
St Edmund's Rd. CH63: Beb 6H **87**
St Edwards Cl. CH41: Birke 1D **68**
St Edwards M. *CH41: Birke 1D **68***
(off Old Bidston Rd.)
St Elmo Rd. CH44: Wall 2F **51**
St Gabriel's Av. L36: Huy 5A **58**
St George's Av. CH42: Tran 1F **87**
WA10: Windle 6A **28**
St Georges Ct. L31: Mag 1B **12**
WA8: Wid 3B **96**
St George's Gro. CH46: More 1B **66**
L30: N'ton 1D **20**
St George's Hall 3F 5 (5D 52)
St George's Hill L5: Liv 2F **53**
St George's Mt. CH45: New B 5D **32**
St George's Pk. CH45: New B 5D **32**
St George's Pl. L1: Liv 3F **5** (5D **52**)
St Georges Rd. CH45: Wall 1A **50**
L36: Huy 2G **57**
WA10: St H 3B **42**
St George's Way CH63: Thorn H 1C **118**
L1: Liv 4F **5**
St Gerard Cl. L5: Liv 1D **52**
St Gregory's Cft. L30: N'ton 5E **11**
ST HELENS 2E **43**
St Helens Central Station (Rail) 2F **43**
St Helens Cl. CH43: Clau 3D **68**
St Helens Crematorium
WA10: Windle 4A **28**
St Helens Junction Station (Rail) 6B **44**
St Helens Linkway L35: Rainh 6D **60**
WA9: St H 3E **43**
St Helens Retail Pk. WA9: St H 2F **43**
St Helens RLFC 2A 42
St Helens Rd. L34: Presc, Eccl P 6D **40**
WA11: Rainf 1H **27**
St Helens Theatre Royal 2E 43
St Hilary Brow CH44: Wall 3B **50**
St Hilary Dr. CH45: Wall 2B **50**
St Hilda's Dr. WA6: Frod 6G **123**
St Hilda St. L4: Walt 5E **35**
St Hugh's Cl. CH43: Clau 3D **68**
St Hugh's Ho. L20: Boot 3C **34**
St Ives Ct. CH43: Clau 2C **68**
St Ives Gro. L13: Liv 4D **54**
St Ives Rd. CH43: Clau 3C **68**
St Ives Way L26: Halew 3H **93**
St James Cl. CH49: Grea 5B **66**
L12: W Der 1E **55**
WA6: Frod 6F **123**
St James Ct. *CH45: New B 5D **32***
(off Victoria Rd.)
St James Dr. L20: Boot 1B **34**
St James M. L20: Boot 1B **34**
St James Mt. L35: Rainh 5A **60**
St James Pl. L8: Liv 2E **71**
St James Rd. CH41: Birke 1B **68**
CH45: New B 5D **32**
L1: Liv 2E **71**
L34: Eccl P 6E **41**
L34: Presc 1E **59**
L35: Rainh 5A **60**
L36: Huy 6G **57**
St James St. L1: Liv 2D **70**
St James Way *L30: N'ton 5D **10***
(off St Nicholas' Dr.)
St Jerome's Way L30: N'ton 5E **11**
St Johns Av. L9: Walt 6G **21**
St Johns Brow WA7: Run 2F **113**
St John's Cen. L1: Liv 4F **5** (6D **52**)
St John's Cl. CH47: Meols 1D **64**
St John's Ct. L22: Water 2F **19**
St John's Ho. L20: Boot 2D **34**
St John's La. L1: Liv 3F **5** (5D **52**)
St John's Pavement CH41: Birke 3F **69**
St John's Pl. L22: Water 2F **19**
St John's Rd. CH45: Wall 2A **50**
CH62: East 2G **121**
L20: Boot 3B **34**
L22: Water 2F **19**
L36: Huy 6H **57**
St John's Sq. CH41: Birke 3F **69**
L1: Liv 4F **5**
St John's Ter. *L20: Boot 4B **34***
(off St John's Rd.)
St John St. CH41: Birke 3F **69**
WA7: Run 2F **113**
WA10: St H 5B **42**
WA12: Newt W 2H **45**
St Johns Vs. WA8: Wid 1B **96**
St John's Way L1: Liv 4F **5**
St Josephs Cl. L36: Huy 6E **39**
WA5: Penk 4G **81**
*WA9: St H 4G **43***
(off Cleveland St.)
St Josephs Cres. L3: Liv 1G **5** (4E **53**)
St Jude's Cl. L36: Huy 6E **39**
St Kevin's Dr. L32: Kirkb 5A **14**
L33: Kirkb 5A **14**
St Kilda's Rd. CH46: More 2C **66**
St Laurence Cl. CH41: Birke 2F **69**
St Laurence Dr. CH41: Birke 2F **69**
St Laurence Gro. L32: Kirkb 3B **24**
St Lawrence Cl. L8: Liv 5G **71**
St Leonard's Cl. L30: N'ton 5D **10**
St Lucia Rd. CH44: Wall 2F **51**
St Lukes Cl. L14: Knott A 1B **56**
St Luke's Ct. L4: Walt 3G **35**
St Luke's Cres. WA8: Wid 5F **79**
St Luke's Gro. *L30: N'ton 5D **10***
(off Dartmouth Dr.)
St Lukes Pl. L1: Liv 6G **5** (1E **71**)
St Luke's Rd. L23: Crosb 5F **9**
WA10: St H 2B **42**
St Luke's Way L36: Huy 6E **39**
WA6: Frod 6F **123**
St Margaret's Gro. L30: N'ton 1C **20**
St Margaret's Rd. CH47: Hoy 3A **64**
St Marks Ct. CH43: O'ton 4D **68**

St Mark's Gro. L30: N'ton 5C 10
St Mark's Rd. L36: Huy 6H 57
St Mark's St. WA11: Hay 5C 30
St Martins Gro. L32: Kirkb 4B 24
St Martin's Ho. L20: Boot 2C 34
St Martin's La. WA7: Murd 6F 115
St Martins M. L5: Liv 3E 53
St Mary's Arc. WA10: St H 2E 43
   (within St Mary's Mkt.)
St Mary's Av. CH44: Wall 3D 50
   L4: Walt 3G 35
St Mary's Cl. L13: Liv 6D 54
   L20: Boot 2B 34
   L24: Hale 3D 110
St Marys Ct. CH49: Upton 5E 67
   L25: Woolt 1C 92
St Mary's Ga. CH41: Birke 3H 69
St Mary's Gro. L4: Walt 3G 35
   L30: N'ton 6C 10
St Mary's La. L4: Walt 3G 35
St Mary's Mkt. WA10: St H 2E 43
St Mary's Pl. L4: Walt 3G 35
St Marys Rd. L19: Garst, Gras 4F 91
   L22: Water 2H 19
   L36: Huy 5G 57
   WA5: Gt San, Penk 4H 81
   WA7: Halt 4B 114
   WA8: Wid 1E 113
St Mary's St. CH44: Wall 3D 50
   L25: Woolt 1C 92
St Mary's Tower 3H 69
St Mathews Cl. L4: Walt 3B 36
   L36: Huy 4H 57
St Matthew's Av. L21: Lith 3C 20
St Matthews Gro. WA10: St H 5A 42
St Mawes Cl. Wid 1C 96
St Mawes Way WA10: Windle 5H 27
St Michael Rd. L39: Augh 1E 7
St Michael's Chu. Rd. L17: Aig 6H 71
St Michaels Cl. L17: Aig 1A 90
   WA8: Wid 4A 96
St Michaels Cl. L36: Huy 4G 57
St Michaels Gro. CH46: More 1B 66
   L6: Liv .3H 53
   L30: N'ton 6C 10
St Michael's Hall L17: Aig 1H 89
ST MICHAEL'S HAMLET 1H 89
St Michael's Ind. Est. WA8: Wid 4A 96
St Michaels Pk. CH62: Port S 5B 88
St Michaels Rd. L17: Aig 1H 89
   L23: Blun, Crosb 4D 8
   WA8: Wid 4A 96
   WA9: St H 4E 61
St Michael's Station (Rail) 1H 89
St Michael's Vw. WA8: Wid 4B 96
St Monica's Dr. L30: N'ton 5D 10
St Nicholas' Dr. L30: N'ton 5D 10
St Nicholas Gro. WA9: St H 6H 43
St Nicholas Pl. L3: Liv 4A 4 (6B 52)
   (not continuous)
St Nicholas Rd. CH45: Wall 2H 49
   L35: Whis 6D 58
St Oswald's Av. CH43: Bid 6G 49
St Oswald's Cl. L30: N'ton 6F 11
St Oswald's La. L30: N'ton 6F 11
St Oswald's M. CH43: Bid 6G 49
St Oswald's St. L13: Liv 5E 55
St Paschal Baylon Blvd.
   L16: Child 1B 74
St Patricks Cl. L33: Kirkb 4A 14
   WA8: Wid 6E 97
St Patrick's Dr. L30: N'ton 5D 10
St Paul's Av. CH44: Wall 5G 51
St Pauls Cl. CH42: Rock F 1G 87
   L33: Kirkb 4H 13
St Pauls Pl. L20: Boot 3D 34
St Paul's Rd. CH42: Rock F 1H 87
   CH44: Wall 5F 51
   WA8: Wid 3F 97
St Paul's Sq. L3: Liv 2B 4 (5B 52)
St Paul St. WA10: St H 2C 42
St Paul's Vs. CH42: Rock F 1H 87

St Peters Cl. CH60: Hesw 6D 100
   L33: Kirkb 4H 13
St Peter's Ct. CH42: Rock F 2A 88
   L17: Aig 5H 71
St Peter's Ho. L20: Boot 3D 34
St Peter's M. CH42: Rock F 2B 88
St Peter's Rd. CH42: Rock F 2A 88
   L9: Ain .4A 22
St Peters Row L31: Mag 3B 12
St Peter's Sq. L1: Liv 6G 5
St Peter's Way CH43: Noct 5G 67
St Philip's Av. L21: Lith 3C 20
St Richards Cl. L20: Kirkd 4D 34
St Seiriol Gro. CH43: Clau 3C 68
St Stephen Rd. WA5: Gt San, Penk 4H 81
St Stephens Cl. CH60: Hesw 1G 117
   L25: Gate 4E 75
St Stephen's Ct. CH42: Tran 2B 88
St Stephen's Gro. L30: N'ton 6D 10
St Stephen's Pl. L3: Liv 1E 5 (4D 52)
St Stephen's Rd. CH42: Tran 1D 86
St Teresa's Cl. L11: Norr G 3D 36
St Teresa's Rd. WA10: St H 1B 42
St Thomas Cl. WA10: St H 5B 28
St Thomas Ct. WA8: Wid 2B 96
St Thomas's Dr. L30: N'ton 6D 10
St Vincent Rd. CH43: Clau 3C 68
   CH44: Wall 2F 51
   WA5: Penk 4H 81
St Vincents Cl. L12: W Der 1A 56
St Vincent St. L3: Liv 3H 5 (5E 53)
St Vincent Way L3: Liv 3H 5
St Werburgh's Sq. CH41: Birke 3G 69
St William Rd. L23: Thorn 4B 10
St William Way L23: Thorn 3B 10
St Winifred Rd. CH45: New B 6D 32
   L35: Rainh 2H 59
Saker St. L4: Walt 6F 35
Salacre Cl. CH49: Upton 5F 67
Salacre Cres. CH49: Upton 5E 67
Salacre La. CH49: Upton 4E 67
Salacre Ter. CH49: Upton 4E 67
   (off Salacre La.)
Salcombe Dr. L25: Hunts X 4D 92
Salem Vw. CH43: O'ton 6D 68
Salerno Dr. L36: Huy 3F 57
Saleswood Av. WA10: Eccl 2G 41
Salhouse Gdns. WA9: St H 1B 60
Saline Cl. L14: Knott A 1C 56
Salisbury Av. CH48: W Kir 1A 82
   L30: N'ton 2G 21
Salisbury Dr. CH63: Raby M 5H 89
Salisbury Hall L18: Moss H 1D 90
Salisbury Ho. L20: Boot 1B 34
Salisbury Pk. L16: Child 4H 73
Salisbury Rd. CH45: New B 5C 32
   L5: Liv 1F 53
   L15: Wav 2B 72
   L19: Gras 4E 91
   L20: Boot 1B 34
   WA11: Hay 3G 31
Salisbury St. CH41: Birke 4F 69
   L3: Liv 1H 5 (3F 53)
   L34: Presc 1D 58
   WA7: Run 4E 113
   WA8: Wid 3F 97
Salisbury Ter. L15: Wav 1D 72
Salop St. L4: Walt 5F 35
Saltash Cl. L26: Halew 3G 93
   WA7: Brook 1D 124
Saltburn Rd. CH45: Wall 2H 49
Saltergate Rd. L8: Liv 5G 71
Salthouse Quay L3: Liv 6C 4 (1C 70)
Saltney St. L3: Liv 3B 52
Saltpit La. L31: Mag 6D 6
Saltwood Dr. WA7: Brook 2E 125
Saltworks Cl. WA6: Frod 5H 123
Salvia Way L33: Kirkb 4H 13
Samaria Av. CH62: New F 4C 88
Samphire Gdns. WA9: Bold 6D 44
Samuel St. WA9: St H 6B 42
Sanbec Gdns. WA8: Cron 4B 78

Sandalwood L23: Crosb 5F 9
   (off Coronation Rd.)
   WA7: Nort 4D 114
Sandalwood Cl. L6: Liv 2H 53
Sandalwood Dr. CH43: Noct 5H 67
Sandalwood Gdns. WA9: St H 6G 43
Sandbanks CH47: Hoy 2A 64
Sandbeck St. L8: Liv 6F 71
Sandbourne CH46: More 1E 67
Sandbrook Ct. CH46: More 1C 66
Sandbrook La. CH46: More 1C 66
Sandbrook Rd. L25: Gate 1C 74
Sandcliffe Rd. CH45: Wall 5A 32
Sandeman Rd. L4: Walt 5B 36
Sanderling Rd. L33: Kirkb 6C 14
Sanders Hey Cl. WA7: Brook 2C 124
Sanderson Cl. WA5: Gt San 3F 81
Sandfield L36: Huy 5F 57
Sandfield Av. CH47: Meols 6D 46
Sandfield Cl. CH63: Hghr B 5F 87
   L12: W Der 2G 55
Sandfield Ct. WA6: Frod 6F 123
Sandfield Cres. WA10: St H 2D 42
   (off Liverpool Rd.)
Sandfield Hey L12: W Der 1G 55
   (off Sandfield Pk. E.)
SANDFIELD PARK 2F 55
Sandfield Pk. CH60: Hesw 5B 100
Sandfield Pk. E. L12: W Der 1G 55
Sandfield Pl. L20: Boot 1B 34
Sandfield Rd. CH45: New B 6D 32
   CH49: Woodc 1F 85
   CH63: Hghr B 5F 87
   L20: Boot 3D 34
   L25: Gate 5D 74
   WA10: Eccl 6G 27
Sandfield Ter. CH45: New B 6D 32
Sandfield Wlk. L12: W Der 3F 55
Sandford Dr. L31: Mag 5C 6
Sandford St. CH41: Birke 2G 69
Sandforth Cl. L12: W Der 1E 55
Sandforth Ct. L13: W Der 2E 55
Sandforth Rd. L12: W Der 2E 55
Sandgate Cl. L24: Speke 1D 108
Sandham Gro. CH60: Hesw 5G 101
Sandham Rd. L24: Speke 1A 110
Sandhead St. L7: Liv 1B 72
Sandhey Rd. CH47: Meols 1C 64
Sandheys Av. L22: Water 2E 19
Sandheys Cl. L4: Walt 6E 35
Sandheys Gro. L22: Water 1E 19
Sandheys Rd. CH45: New B 6D 32
Sandheys Ter. L22: Water 2E 19
Sandhills, The CH46: Leas 4C 48
Sandhills Bus. Est. L5: Kirkd 1C 52
Sandhills Bus. Pk. L5: Kirkd 6C 34
Sandhills La. L5: Kirkd 6B 34
Sandhills Station (Rail) 1C 52
Sandhills Vw. CH45: Wall 2H 49
Sandhurst L23: Blun 5E 9
Sandhurst Cl. L21: Sea 4H 19
Sandhurst Dr. L10: Ain 1C 22
Sandhurst Rd. L26: Halew 5A 94
   L35: Rainh 2G 59
Sandhurst St. L17: Aig 6H 71
Sandhurst Way L31: Lyd 2A 6
Sandicroft Rd. L12: Crox 3B 38
Sandino St. L8: Liv 3F 71
Sandiway CH47: Meols 6D 46
   CH63: Brom 1C 120
   L35: Whis 5D 58
   L36: Huy 6H 57
Sandiway Av. WA8: Wid 2G 95
Sandiways L31: Mag 6D 6
Sandiways Av. L30: N'ton 1G 21
Sandiways Rd. CH45: Wall 1A 50
Sandlea Pk. CH48: W Kir 1A 82
Sandlewood Gro. L33: Kirkb 5B 14
Sandon Cl. L35: Rainh 3H 59
Sandon Ct. L22: Water 2F 19
   (off Sandon St.)

Sandon Gro.—Seaforth

Sandon Gro. WA11: Rainf 3G **17**
Sandon Ind. Est. L5: Kirkd 1B **52**
Sandon Lodge *L21: Sea* *5A 20*
(off Seaforth Rd.)
Sandon Pl. WA8: Wid 2H **97**
Sandon Prom. CH44: Wall 3G **51**
Sandon Rd. CH44: Wall 3G **51**
Sandon St. L8: Liv 1F **71**
L22: Water 2F **19**
Sandon Way L5: Kirkd 1B **52**
Sandown Cl. WA7: Run 1G **123**
Sandown Ct. L15: Wav 1D **72**
Sandown La. L15: Wav 1D **72**
SANDOWN PARK . . . . **.6D 54**
Sandown Pk. Rd. L10: Ain 6C **12**
Sandown Rd. L15: Wav 6D **54**
L21: Sea .4H **19**
Sandpiper Cl. CH49: Upton 3B **66**
Sandpiper Gro. L26: Halew 2G **93**
Sandpipers Ct. CH47: Hoy 2B **64**
L22: Water . . . . *.1E 19*
(off Bridge Rd.)
Sandridge Rd. CH45: New B 6D **32**
CH61: Pens 6D **84**
Sandringham Av. CH47: Meols 1C **64**
L22: Water 3G **19**
Sandringham Cl. CH47: Meols 2C **64**
CH62: New F 4A **88**
L33: Kirkb 4A **14**
Sandringham Dr. CH45: New B 5C **32**
L17: Aig .5H **71**
WA9: St H 1G **61**
Sandringham M. CH47: Meols 2C **64**
Sandringham Rd. L13: Liv 1C **54**
L22: Water 3G **19**
L31: Mag .1A **12**
WA8: Wid .5E **79**
Sandrock Cl. CH45: New B 6D **32**
Sandrock Rd. CH45: New B 6D **32**
Sands Rd. L18: Moss H 5D **72**
Sandstone CH45: Wall 2E **51**
Sandstone Cl. L35: Rainh 6A **60**
Sandstone Dr. CH48: W Kir 1E **83**
L35: Whis 2G **59**
Sandstone M. WA8: Wid 5C **78**
Sandstone Rd. E. L13: Liv 3E **55**
Sandstone Rd. W. L13: Liv 3D **54**
Sandstone Wlk. CH60: Hesw 6E **101**
Sandwash Cl. WA11: Rainf 5H **17**
Sandway Cres. L11: Norr G 3E **37**
Sandy Brow La. L33: Kirkb 4G **25**
Sandy Grn. L9: Ain 5A **22**
Sandy Gro. L13: Liv 1D **54**
Sandy Ho. L21: Sea 4H **19**
Sandy Knowle L15: Wav 6E **55**
Sandy La. CH45: Wall 1A **50**
CH48: W Kir 3B **82**
CH60: Hesw 4E **101**
CH61: Irby 4A **84**
L9: Ain 5H **21**
L13: Liv .1D **54**
L21: Sea .4A **20**
(not continuous)
L31: Lyd .1A **6**
L31: Mell 4E **13**
L39: Augh 1G **7**
WA5: Penk 5H **81**
WA7: Pres B 1G **125**
WA7: West P 6B **112**
WA8: Cron 4B **78**
WA8: Wid .3C **80**
WA11: St H 2C **28**
Sandy La. Nth. CH61: Irby 4A **84**
SANDYMOOR . . . . **.2F 115**
Sandymoor La. WA7: Nort 2F **115**
(not continuous)
Sandymount Dr. CH45: Wall 6C **32**
CH63: Beb 1H **103**
Sandy Rd. L21: Sea 3H **19**
(not continuous)
Sandyville Gro. L4: Walt 5C **36**
Sandyville Rd. L4: Walt 5B **36**
Sandy Way CH43: O'ton 4C **68**
Sankey (for Penketh) Station (Rail) . . **.3H 81**
Sankey Mnr. WA5: Gt San 3H **81**
Sankey Rd. L31: Mag 2B **12**
WA11: Hay 6B **30**
Sankey St. L1: Liv 1E **71**
WA8: Wid .5E **97**
WA9: St H 3H **43**
Sankey Valley Country Pk. . . . . **.1C 44**
Sankey Valley Country Pk. Vis. Cen.
. . . . **.5A 30**
Santon Av. L13: Liv 2C **54**
Sapphire Dr. L33: Kirkb 4A **14**
Sapphire St. L13: Liv 6D **54**
Sarah's Cft. L30: N'ton 6E **11**
Sark Rd. L13: Liv 3D **54**
Sartfield Cl. L16: Child 1A **74**
Sarum Rd. L25: Gate 2C **74**
Sarus Ct. WA7: Manor P 1D **114**
Satinwood Cl. WN4: Ash M 1H **31**
Satinwood Cres. L31: Mell 6E **13**
SAUGHALL MASSIE . . . . **.3A 66**
Saughall Massie La.
CH49: Upton 4C **66**
Saughall Massie Rd.
CH48: W Kir 6D **64**
CH49: Grea, Upton 6D **64**
Saughall Rd. CH46: More 2A **66**
CH49: Upton 2A **66**
Saunby Cl. L19: Garst 6G **91**
Saunders Av. L35: Presc 3D **58**
Saunderton Cl. WA11: Hay 4E **31**
Saville Rd. L13: Liv 5F **55**
L31: Lyd .4B **6**
Savoylands Cl. L17: Aig 1A **90**
Sawley Cl. WA7: Murd 6G **115**
Sawpit La. L36: Huy 5H **57**
Saxby Rd. L14: Knott A 2C **56**
Saxon Cl. L6: Liv 3H **53**
Saxon Ct. WA10: St H 6C **28**
Saxonia Rd. L4: Walt 3H **35**
Saxon Rd. CH46: More 6D **48**
CH47: Meols 1C **64**
L23: Crosb 6F **9**
WA7: Run 3G **113**
Saxon Ter. WA8: Wid 2F **97**
Saxon Way L33: Kirkb 3A **14**
Saxony Rd. L7: Liv 5G **53**
(not continuous)
Sayce St. WA8: Wid 2F **97**
Scafell Cl. CH62: East 4D **120**
Scafell Lawn L27: N'ley 6A **76**
Scafell Rd. WA11: St H 3D **28**
Scafell Wlk. L27: N'ley 5A **76**
(not continuous)
Scape La. L23: Crosb 4G **9**
Scargreen Av. L11: Norr G 2D **36**
Scarisbrick Av. L21: Lith 4B **20**
Scarisbrick Cl. L31: Mag 4D **6**
Scarisbrick Cres.
L11: Norr G 2B **36**
Scarisbrick Dr. L11: Norr G 2B **36**
Scarisbrick Pl. L11: Norr G 3B **36**
Scarisbrick Rd. L11: Norr G 3B **36**
WA11: Rainf 2F **17**
Scarsdale Rd. L11: Norr G 4D **36**
Sceptre Cl. WA12: Newt W 2H **45**
Sceptre Rd. L11: Crox 1G **37**
Sceptre Wlk. L11: Crox 2G **37**
Scholar St. L7: Liv 2A **72**
Scholes, The WA10: St H 6H **41**
Scholes La. WA9: St H 6H **41**
WA10: St H 6H **41**
Scholes Pk. WA10: St H 6H **41**
Schomberg St. L6: Liv 4G **53**
School Cl. CH46: More 6D **48**
L27: N'ley 2E **75**
Schoolfield Cl. CH49: Woodc 1F **85**
Schoolfield Rd. CH49: Woodc 1F **85**
School Hill CH60: Hesw 6D **100**
School La. CH43: Bid 6G **49**
CH44: Wall 2A **50**
School La. CH45: Wall 3A **50**
CH47: Hoy 2B **64**
(not continuous)
CH47: Meols 6D **46**
CH61: Thurs 5H **83**
CH62: New F 4B **88**
CH63: Hghr B 5F **87**
CH64: Nest 5D **118**
CH64: Park 6F **117**
CH66: Chil T 6F **121**
L1: Liv 5E **5** (6D **52**)
L10: Ain .2B **22**
L21: Lith .3B **20**
L21: Sea .4A **20**
L25: Woolt 4C **92**
L31: Mag .5F **7**
L31: Mell 4E **13**
L34: Know 5C **24**
L35: Rainh 6C **60**
(not continuous)
L36: Huy 5A **58**
WA7: Halt 5B **114**
WA8: Bold H 2A **80**
School St. WA11: Hay 5B **30**
School Way L24: Speke 2D **108**
WA8: Wid .6H **79**
Schooner Cl. WA7: Murd 1F **125**
Science Rd. L24: Speke 1E **109**
Scone Cl. L11: Crox 2G **37**
Score, The WA9: St H 1E **61**
(not continuous)
Scorecross WA9: St H 5F **43**
Score La. L16: Child 6G **55**
Scoresby Rd. CH46: Leas 4F **49**
Scorpio Cl. L14: Knott A 2C **56**
Scorton St. L6: Liv 2A **54**
Scotchbarn La. L34: Presc 1E **59**
L35: Presc 1E **59**
Scotchbarn Sports Cen. . . . . **.2E 59**
Scoter Rd. L33: Kirkb 1B **24**
Scotia Av. CH62: New F 4C **88**
Scotia Rd. L13: Liv 3E **55**
Scotland Rd. L3: Liv 1F **5** (4D **52**)
L5: Liv 4D **52**
Scott Av. L35: Whis 4F **59**
L36: Huy 6A **58**
WA8: Wid 3D **96**
WA9: Sut M 4E **61**
Scott Cl. L4: Walt 6F **35**
L31: Mag .6C **6**
Scotts Pl. CH41: Birke 2B **68**
Scotts Quays CH41: Birke 6G **51**
Scott St. CH45: Wall 2D **50**
L20: Boot 6B **20**
Scythes, The CH49: Grea 5A **66**
L30: N'ton 5H **11**
Scythia Cl. CH62: New F 3C **88**
Seabank Av. CH44: Wall 2E **51**
Seabank Ct. CH48: W Kir 2A **82**
Seabank Rd. CH44: Wall 5D **32**
CH45: New B, Wall 5D **32**
CH60: Hesw 1C **116**
Seacole Cl. L8: Liv 3H **71**
SEACOMBE . . . . **.6F 51**
Seacombe Prom.
CH44: Wall 3G **51**
(not continuous)
Seacombe Vw. CH44: Wall 5G **51**
Sea Ct. CH45: Wall 6B **32**
Seacroft Cl. L14: Knott A 1C **56**
Seacroft Rd. L14: Knott A 1C **56**
Seafarers Dr. L25: Gate 5C **74**
Seafield Av. CH60: Hesw 1C **116**
L23: Crosb 6G **9**
Seafield Dr. CH45: Wall 6C **32**
Seafield Rd. CH62: New F 3B **88**
L9: Walt .6F **21**
L20: Boot . . . . *.1B 34*
(off Cleary St.)
Seaford Cl. WA7: Wind H 4F **115**
Seafore Cl. L31: Lyd 3A **6**
SEAFORTH . . . . **.4H 19**

Seaforth Dr. CH46: More 2C **66**
Seaforth & Litherland Station (Rail)
. . . . .4A **20**
Seaforth Nature Reserve 4E **19**
Seaforth Rd. L21: Sea 6A **20**
Seaforth Va. Nth. L21: Sea 5A **20**
Seaforth Va. W. L21: Sea 5A **20**
Seagram Cl. L9: Ain 3A **22**
Sea La. WA7: Run 3H **113**
Sealy Cl. CH63: Spit 4A **104**
Seaman Rd. L15: Wav 2C **72**
Seaport St. L8: Liv 3H **71**
Sea Rd. CH45: Wall 5B **32**
Seascale Av. WA10: St H 5H **41**
Seath Av. WA9: St H 1A **44**
Seathwaite Cl. L23: Blun 6D **8**
WA7: Beech 2A **124**
Seathwaite Cres. L33: Kirkb 5H **13**
Seaton Cl. L12: Crox 2C **38**
Seaton Gro. WA9: St H 1B **60**
Seaton Pk. WA7: Nort 2G **115**
Seaton Rd. CH42: Tran 5E **69**
CH45: Wall 1C **50**
Seaview CH47: Hoy 2B **64**
Seaview Av. CH45: Wall 2C **50**
CH61: Irby 5B **84**
CH62: East 1H **121**
Seaview La. CH61: Irby 5B **84**
Sea Vw. Rd. L20: Boot 1A **34**
Seaview Rd. CH45: Wall 1C **50**
Seaview Ter. L22: Water 2E **19**
Seawood Gro. CH46: More 2B **66**
Second Av. CH43: Bid 3F **67**
L9: Ain 5C **22**
(First Av.)
L9: Ain 4B **22**
(Third Av.)
L23: Crosb 5F **9**
L35: Rainh 3H **59**
WA7: Pal F 5B **114**
Sedbergh Av. L10: Ain 6A **12**
Sedbergh Gro. WA7: Beech 2A **124**
Sedbergh Rd. CH44: Wall 2B **50**
Sedburgh Gro. L36: Huy 4D **56**
Sedburn Rd. L32: Kirkb 4C **24**
Seddon Cl. WA10: Eccl 2F **41**
Seddon Ct. L34: Presc 1D **58**
Seddon Rd. L19: Garst 5G **91**
WA10: St H 5H **41**
Seddon St. L1: Liv 6E **5** (1D **70**)
WA10: St H 4D **28**
Sedgefield Cl. CH46: More 1E **67**
Sedgefield Rd. CH46: More 1E **67**
Sedgeley Wlk. L36: Huy 2H **57**
Sedgemoor Rd. L11: Norr G 2C **36**
Sedgewick Cres. WA5: Burtw 1G **63**
Sedley St. L6: Liv 1H **53**
Sedum Gro. L33: Kirkb 4H **13**
Seeds La. L9: Ain 3A **22**
Seeley Av. CH41: Birke 2C **68**
Seel Rd. L36: Huy 5H **57**
Seel St. L1: Liv 5F **5** (6D **52**)
SEFTON 2F **11**
Sefton Av. L21: Lith 4B **20**
WA8: Wid 6E **79**
Sefton Bus. Pk. L30: N'ton 3G **21**
(not continuous)
Sefton Cl. L32: Kirkb 6G **13**
Sefton Dr. L8: Liv 4A **72**
L10: Ain .1C **22**
L23: Thorn 2A **10**
L31: Mag 1H **11**
L32: Kirkb 6G **13**
Sefton Gro. L17: Aig 5A **72**
Sefton Ho. L9: Ain 4H **21**
Sefton La. L31: Mag 1G **11**
Sefton La. Ind. Est. L31: Mag 1G **11**
Sefton Mill La. L29: Seft 2F **11**
Sefton Mills L29: Seft 2F **11**
Sefton Moss La. L30: N'ton 6D **10**
Sefton Moss Vs. L21: Lith 3B **20**
SEFTON PARK 5C **72**
Sefton Pk. Ct. *L17: Aig* *1C* ***90***
(off Aigburth Va.)
Sefton Pk. Palm House 5B **72**
Sefton Pk. Rd. L8: Liv 3H **71**
Sefton Rd. CH42: Rock F 2A **88**
CH45: New B 6D **32**
CH62: New F 3A **88**
L9: Ain 4B **22**
L9: Walt .1G **35**
L20: Boot 6D **20**
L21: Lith 3B **20**
Sefton St. L8: Liv 3D **70**
L21: Lith 3B **20**
(not continuous)
WA12: Newt W 2H **45**
SEFTON TOWN 5D **10**
Sefton Vw. L21: Lith 3B **20**
L23: Crosb 5A **10**
Seiont Ho. L8: Liv 4F **71**
Selborne L35: Whis 5F **59**
Selborne Cl. L8: Liv 2G **71**
Selborne St. L8: Liv 2F **71**
Selbourne Cl. CH49: Woodc 6G **67**
Selby Cl. WA7: Nort 1G **115**
WA10: St H 3B **42**
Selby Gro. L36: Huy 4B **58**
Selby Rd. L9: Walt 5G **21**
Selby St. CH45: Wall 2D **50**
Seldon St. L6: Liv 4H **53**
Selina Rd. L4: Walt 3E **35**
Selkirk Av. CH62: East 3E **121**
Selkirk Dr. WA10: Eccl 6H **27**
Selkirk Rd. L13: Liv 4D **54**
Sellar St. L4: Kirkd 6E **35**
Selsdon Rd. L22: Water 1E **19**
Selsey Cl. L7: Liv 1H **71**
Selside Lawn *L27: N'ley* *5A* ***76***
(off Selside Wlk.)
Selside Wlk. L27: N'ley 6A **76**
Selston Cl. CH63: Spit 3A **104**
Selworthy Grn. L16: Child 3H **73**
Selwyn Cl. WA8: Wid 6A **80**
Selwyn St. L4: Kirkd 4E **35**
Senator Point L33: Know I 3E **25**
Senator Rd. WA9: St H 6B **42**
Seneschal Ct. WA7: Pal F 1A **124**
Sennen Cl. WA7: Brook 2D **124**
Sennen Rd. L32: Kirkb 3B **24**
Sentinel Way L30: N'ton 3G **21**
September Rd. L6: Liv 2A **54**
Serenade Rd. L33: Kirkb 3B **14**
Sergeant Rd. L12: W Der 6A **38**
Sergrim Rd. L36: Huy 4E **57**
Serpentine, The L19: Gras 3E **91**
L23: Blun 5C **8**
Serpentine Nth., The
L23: Blun 4C **8**
Serpentine Rd. CH44: Wall 2E **51**
Serpentine Sth., The L23: Blun 5D **8**
Servia Rd. L21: Lith 4B **20**
Servite Cl. L22: Water 1E **19**
Servite Ct. L25: Woolt 3E **93**
Servite Ho. L17: Aig 5H **71**
Sessions Rd. L4: Kirkd 5E **35**
Seth Powell Way L36: Huy 1E **57**
Settrington Rd. L11: Norr G 4D **36**
Seven Acre Rd. L23: Thorn 4B **10**
Seven Acres La.
CH61: Thing 5E **85**
Sevenoak Gro. L35: Tar G 2B **76**
Sevenoaks Cl. L5: Liv 2E **53**
Seventh Av. L9: Ain 4B **22**
(Lakes Rd.)
L9: Ain 4B **22**
(Sixth Av.)
Severn Cl. WA8: Wid 6B **80**
WA9: Sut L 2G **61**
Severn Rd. L33: Kirkb 3B **14**
L35: Rainh 4H **59**
Severn St. CH41: Birke 6C **50**
L5: Liv 1F **53**
Severs St. L6: Liv 3H **53**
Sewell St. L34: Presc 1D **58**
WA7: Run 3F **113**
(not continuous)
Sextant Cl. WA7: Murd 2F **125**
Sexton Av. WA9: St H 3D **44**
Sexton Way L14: Broad G 5B **56**
Seymour Ct. CH42: Tran 5G **69**
L14: Broad G 6H **55**
WA7: Manor P 2E **115**
Seymour Dr. L31: Mag 4D **6**
Seymour Pl. E. CH45: New B 5E **33**
Seymour Pl. W.
CH45: New B 5D **32**
Seymour Rd. L14: Broad G 5H **55**
L21: Lith *4B* ***20***
(off Bridge Rd.)
Seymour St. CH42: Tran 5G **69**
CH45: New B 5D **32**
L3: Liv 3H **5** (5E **53**)
L20: Boot 3B **34**
Seymour Ter. L3: Liv 3H **5**
Shacklady Rd. L33: Kirkb 5C **14**
Shackleton Rd. CH46: Leas 3F **49**
Shadowbrook Dr. L24: Speke 5E **93**
Shadwell St. L5: Liv 2B **52**
Shaftesbury Av. L33: Kirkb 4A **14**
WA5: Penk 1G **99**
Shaftesbury Rd. L23: Crosb 5F **9**
Shaftesbury St. L8: Liv 3E **71**
Shaftesbury Ter. L13: Liv 4E **55**
Shaftesbury Way WA5: Burtw 6H **45**
Shaftway Cl. WA11: Hay 4H **31**
Shakespeare Av. CH42: Rock F 2H **87**
L32: Kirkb 3H **23**
Shakespeare Cl. L6: Liv 3G **53**
Shakespeare Rd. CH44: Wall 5F **51**
CH64: Nest 6A **118**
WA8: Wid 2E **97**
WA9: Sut M 4E **61**
Shakespeare St. L20: Boot 6A **20**
Shalcombe Cl. L26: Halew 4A **94**
Shaldon Cl. L32: Kirkb 3C **24**
Shaldon Gro. L32: Kirkb 3C **24**
Shaldon Rd. L32: Kirkb 4C **24**
Shaldon Wlk. L32: Kirkb 3C **24**
Shalem Ct. CH63: Hghr B 5F **87**
Shalford Gro. CH48: W Kir 1D **82**
Shallcross Ct. *L6: Liv* *3G* ***53***
(off Shallcross Pl.)
Shallcross Pl. L6: Liv 3G **53**
Shallmarsh Cl. CH63: Hghr B 6F **87**
Shallmarsh Rd. CH63: Hghr B 6F **87**
Shalom Ct. L17: Aig 3C **72**
Shamrock Rd. CH41: Birke 2B **68**
Shand St. L19: Garst 1G **107**
Shanklin Cl. WA5: Gt San 3E **81**
Shanklin Rd. L15: Wav 6D **54**
Shannon Gro. WA8: Wid 1C **96**
Shannon Ho. CH46: Leas 3C **48**
Shannons La. L34: Know 4E **39**
Shannon St. CH41: Birke 6B **50**
Shard Cl. L11: Crox 6F **23**
Shard St. WA9: St H 6A **44**
Sharpeville Cl. L4: Kirkd 6D **34**
Sharples Cres. L23: Crosb 5H **9**
Sharp St. WA8: Wid 3E **97**
Sharwood Rd. L27: N'ley 5H **75**
Shavington Av. CH43: O'ton 6B **68**
Shawbury Av. CH63: Hghr B 4F **87**
Shawell Ct. WA8: Wid 1A **98**
Shaw Entry L35: Whis 1F **77**
Shaw Hill St. L1: Liv 3E **5** (5D **52**)
Shaw La. CH49: Grea 1A **84**
L35: Presc, Whis 3D **58**
Shaw Rd. L24: Speke 6E **93**
Shaws All. L1: Liv 1D **70**
Shaws Dr. CH47: Meols 1D **64**
Shaw St. CH41: Birke 4F **69**
CH47: Hoy 2B **64**
L6: Liv 3F **53**
WA7: Run 3D **112**
(not continuous)

Shaw St. WA10: St H 2F **43**
WA11: Hay 5G **31**
Shawton Rd. L16: Child 1H **73**
Shearman Cl. CH61: Pens 1E **101**
Shearman Rd. CH61: Pens 1E **101**
Shearwater Cl. L27: N'ley 5H **75**
Sheen Rd. CH45: New B 6E **33**
Sheila Wlk. L10: Faz 5F **23**
Sheil Pl. L6: Liv 4A **54**
Sheil Rd. L6: Liv 3A **54**
Shelagh Av. WA8: Wid 2E **97**
Sheldon Cl. CH63: Spit 4A **104**
Sheldon Rd. L12: W Der 5H **37**
Shelley Cl. L36: Huy 6H **57**
Shelley Ct. L32: Kirkb 3H **23**
Shelley Pl. L35: Whis 4F **59**
Shelley Rd. WA8: Wid 2E **97**
Shelley St. L20: Boot 1B **34**
(not continuous)
WA9: Sut M 5F **61**
Shelley Way CH48: W Kir 3B **82**
SHELL GREEN 2A **98**
Shell Grn. Est., The WA8: Wid 3A **98**
Shell Grn. Ho. WA8: Wid 3A **98**
Shellingford Rd. L14: Knott A 3C **56**
Shelmore Dr. L8: Liv 5F **71**
Shelton Cl. L13: Liv 5E **55**
WA8: Wid 6B **80**
Shelton Rd. CH45: Wall 1C **50**
Shenley Cl. CH63: Beb 5H **87**
Shenley Rd. L15: Wav 1G **73**
Shenstone St. L7: Liv 6H **53**
Shenton Av. WA11: St H 5H **29**
Shepherd Cl. CH49: Grea 5A **66**
Shepherds Fold Cl. L8: Liv 3G **71**
Shepherds Row WA7: Cas 3B **114**
Shepherd St. L6: Liv 5F **53**
Sheppard Av. L16: Child 1C **74**
Shepston Av. L4: Walt 4G **35**
Shepton Rd. L36: Huy 1F **57**
Sherborne Av. L25: Hunts X 3F **93**
L30: N'ton 5E **11**
Sherborne Cl. WA7: Nort 2G **115**
Sherborne Rd. CH44: Wall 2B **50**
Sherborne Sq. L36: Huy 5G **57**
Sherbourne Way WA5: Burtw 1H **63**
Sherbrooke Cl. L14: Knott A 3A **56**
Sherburn Cl. L9: Ain 3B **22**
Sherdley Bus. Pk. WA9: St H 4F **43**
Sherdley Ct. L35: Rainh 3A **60**
Sherdley Pk. 6F **43**
Sherdley Pk. Dr. WA9: St H 6G **43**
Sherdley Pk. Golf Driving Range 6F **43**
Sherdley Rd. WA9: St H 1D **60**
(not continuous)
Sherdley Rd. Cvn. Site WA9: St H 5E **43**
Sherdley Rd. Ind. Est. WA9: St H 4F **43**
Sherford Cl. L27: N'ley 5H **75**
Sheridan Way WA7: Nort 3F **115**
Sheriff Cl. L5: Liv 3E **53**
Sheringham Cl. CH49: Upton 2E **67**
WA9: St H 2H **43**
Sheringham Rd. WA5: Gt San 3G **81**
Sherlock Av. WA11: Hay 4G **31**
Sherlock La. CH44: Wall 5C **50**
Sherman Dr. L35: Rainh 6B **60**
Sherry Ct. L17: Aig 4C **72**
Sherry La. CH49: Woodc 1E **85**
Sherwell Cl. L15: Wav 6E **55**
Sherwood Av. CH61: Irby 4A **84**
L23: Crosb 4F **9**
Sherwood Cl. L35: Rainh 2H **59**
WA8: Wid 2A **96**
Sherwood Ct. L12: Crox 2B **38**
L36: Huy 5H **57**
Sherwood Cres. WA5: Burtw 1G **63**
Sherwood Dr. CH63: Hghr B 4G **87**
L35: Whis 5F **59**
Sherwood Gro. CH47: Meols 1F **65**
Sherwood Rd. CH44: Wall 4E **51**
CH47: Meols 1F **65**
L23: Crosb 4E **9**
Sherwood Row L26: Halew 5G **93**
Sherwood's La. L10: Faz 3D **22**
Sherwood St. L3: Liv 3B **52**
Sherwyn Rd. L4: Walt 5A **36**
Shetland Cl. WA8: Wid 6A **80**
Shetland Dr. CH62: Brom 5E **105**
Shevington Cl. WA8: Wid 6A **80**
WA9: St H 6G **43**
Shevington's La. L33: Kirkb 4H **13**
Shevington Wlk. WA8: Wid 6A **80**
Shewell Cl. CH42: Tran 5F **69**
Shiel Rd. CH45: New B 6D **32**
Shimmin St. L7: Liv 6G **53**
Shipley Wlk. L24: Speke 1F **109**
Ship St. WA6: Frod 6F **123**
Shipton Cl. CH43: Pren 2A **86**
L19: Aller 3F **91**
WA8: Wid 6B **78**
Shirdley Av. L32: Kirkb 4B **24**
Shirdley Wlk. L32: Kirkb 4B **24**
Shirebourne Av. WA11: St H 4F **29**
Shiregreen WA9: St H 1G **61**
Shires, The WA10: St H 3C **42**
Shirley Rd. L19: Aller 3G **91**
Shirley St. CH44: Wall 4G **51**
Shirwell Gro. WA9: Sut L 3G **61**
Shobdon Cl. L12: Crox 1B **38**
Shop La. L31: Mag 6B **6**
Shop Rd. L34: Know 1E **39**
Shore Bank CH62: New F 3C **88**
Shore Dr. CH62: Port S 5C **88**
Shorefields CH62: New F 3C **88**
Shorefields Ho. CH62: New F 4C **88**
Shorefields Village L8: Liv 6F **71**
Shoreham Dr. WA5: Penk 6H **81**
Shore La. CH48: Caldy 4C **82**
Shore Rd. CH41: Birke 2H **69**
CH48: Caldy 4C **82**
L20: Boot 6H **19**
Shore Road Pumping Station 2H **69**
Shorewell Cl. WA5: Gt San 2E **81**
Short Cl. WA12: Newt W 2G **45**
Shortfield Rd. CH49: Upton 5E **67**
Shortfield Way CH49: Upton 5E **67**
Short St. WA8: Wid 6E **97**
WA11: Hay 5G **31**
WA12: Newt W 2G **45**
Shortwood Rd. L14: Knott A 4B **56**
Shottesbrook Grn. L11: Norr G 2D **36**
Showcase Cinema
Liverpool 1E **37**
Shrewsbury Av. L10: Ain 6A **12**
L22: Water 6F **9**
Shrewsbury Cl. CH43: Clau 3B **68**
Shrewsbury Dr. CH49: Upton 3E **67**
Shrewsbury Pl. *L19: Garst* *5G* ***91***
(off Shrewsbury Rd.)
Shrewsbury Rd. CH43: Clau 2B **68**
CH44: Wall 2B **50**
CH48: W Kir 2A **82**
CH60: Hesw 4E **101**
L19: Garst 5G **91**
Shrewton Rd. L25: Gate 2C **74**
Shropshire Cl. L30: N'ton 5G **11**
Shropshire Gdns.
WA10: St H 3D **42**
Sibford Rd. L12: W Der 2H **55**
Siddall St. WA10: St H 4D **28**
Siddeley Dr. WA12: Newt W 2H **45**
Siddeley St. L17: Aig 6A **72**
Sidgreave St. WA10: St H 2C **42**
Siding Ct. WA8: Wid 4E **97**
Siding La. L33: Sim 3E **15**
WA11: Rainf 1C **16**
Sidings, The *L7: Liv* *1G* ***71***
(off Crown St.)
Sidlaw Av. WA9: St H 2B **44**
Sidmouth Cl. WA5: Penk 5G **81**
WA10: Windle 5A **28**
Sidney Av. CH45: New B 5C **32**
Sidney Cl. CH64: Nest 6B **118**
Sidney Ct. CH42: Tran 6G **69**
Sidney Pl. L7: Liv 6G **53**
Sidney Powell Av. L32: Kirkb 1G **23**
Sidney Rd. CH42: Tran 5G **69**
CH64: Nest 6B **118**
L20: Boot 3D **34**
Sidney St. CH41: Birke 2G **69**
WA10: St H 1B **42**
Sidney Ter. CH42: Tran 6G **69**
Sidwell St. L19: Garst 5G **91**
Sienna Cl. L27: N'ley 3E **75**
Signal Works Rd.
L9: Ain, Faz 3C **22**
Silcroft Rd. L32: Kirkb 3A **24**
Silkhouse Ct. L2: Liv 3C **4**
Silkhouse La. L3: Liv 3C **4**
Silkstone Cl. L7: Liv 1H **71**
WA10: St H 2B **42**
Silkstone Cres. WA7: Pal F 6D **114**
Silkstone St. WA10: St H 2B **42**
(not continuous)
Silloth Cl. L19: Garst 5F **91**
Silver Av. WA11: Hay 6C **30**
Silverbeech Av. L18: Moss H 5F **73**
Silverbeech Rd. CH44: Wall 4E **51**
Silverbirch Gdns. CH44: Wall 2A **50**
Silver Birch Way L31: Lyd 2A **6**
Silverbrook Rd. L27: N'ley 2F **75**
Silverburn Av. CH46: More 6C **48**
Silverdale Av. L13: Liv 2C **54**
Silverdale Cl. L36: Huy 1G **75**
Silverdale Dr. L21: Lith 3D **20**
Silverdale Gro. WA11: St H 3E **29**
Silverdale Rd. CH43: O'ton 5C **68**
CH63: Hghr B 4H **87**
Silverlake Cl. L4: Walt 2G **35**
Silverlea Av. CH45: Wall 2D **50**
Silver Leigh L17: Aig 2B **90**
Silverlime Gdns. WA9: St H 6A **42**
Silverstone Dr. L36: Roby 1F **75**
Silverstone Gro. L31: Lyd 2A **6**
Silverton Rd. L17: Aig 3C **90**
Silverwell Rd. L11: Crox 6H **23**
Silverwell Wlk. L11: Crox 6H **23**
Silverwing Ho. L19: Aig 4D **90**
Silvester St. L5: Liv 2C **52**
Simms Av. WA9: St H 2A **44**
SIMM'S CROSS 3F **97**
Simm's Rd. L6: Liv 1B **54**
Simnel Cl. L25: Gate 3D **74**
Simon Ct. CH48: W Kir 1A **82**
Simonsbridge CH48: Caldy 5D **82**
Simons Cl. L35: Whis 1D **76**
Simon's Cft. L30: N'ton 6C **10**
Simonside WA8: Wid 1A **96**
Simonstone Gro. WA9: St H 6H **43**
SIMONSWOOD 3C **14**
Simonswood Ind. Pk.
L33: Sim 3D **14**
Simonswood La. L33: Kirkb 2C **24**
Simonswood Wlk. L33: Kirkb 1C **24**
Simpson St. CH41: Birke 3F **69**
L1: Liv 2D **70**
Sim St. L3: Liv 1H **5** (4E **53**)
Sinclair Av. L35: Presc 2F **59**
WA8: Wid 3D **96**
Sinclair Cl. L35: Presc 1F **59**
Sinclair Dr. L18: Moss H 3F **73**
Sinclair St. L19: Garst 6G **91**
Sinclair Way L34: Presc 2C **58**
Sineacre La. L33: Sim 1G **15**
L39: Bic 1G **15**
Singleton Av. CH42: Tran 6E **69**
WA11: St H 6H **29**
Singleton Dr. L34: Know 2F **39**
Sirdar Cl. L7: Liv 1H **71**
Sir Howard St. L8: Liv 1F **71**
Sir Howard Way *L8: Liv* *1F* ***71***
(off Sir Howard St.)
Sir Thomas St. L1: Liv 3D **4** (5D **52**)
Siskin Grn. L25: Gate 5C **74**
Sisters Way CH41: Birke 3F **69**
Six Acre La. WA4: Moore 6H **99**

Sixth Av. L9: Ain 4C **22**
(Broadway)
L9: Ain 4B **22**
(Seventh Av.)
Skeffington St. L35: Whis 5E **59**
Skelhorne St. L3: Liv 4G **5** (6E **53**)
Skelton Cl. WA11: St H 4F **29**
Skerries Rd. L4: Walt 1G **53**
Skiddaw Cl. WA7: Beech 3C **124**
Skiddaw Rd. CH62: Brom 3E **105**
Skipton Cl. WA7: Cas 4B **114**
Skipton Rd. L4: Walt 6H **35**
L36: Huy 4B **58**
Skirving Pl. L5: Liv 1D **52**
Skirving St. L5: Liv 1E **53**
Skye Cl. WA8: Wid 6A **80**
Skyhawk Av. L19: Speke 1A **108**
Sky Lark Ri. WA9: St H 2C **44**
Sky Pk. Ind. Est. L24: Speke 2D **108**
Slag La. WA11: Hay 3D **30**
(not continuous)
Slater Pl. L1: Liv 6F **5** (1D **70**)
Slater St. L1: Liv 6F **5** (1D **70**)
Slatey Rd. CH43: O'ton 3D **68**
Sleaford Rd. L14: Knott A 2D **56**
Sleepers Hill L4: Walt 6F **35**
Slessor Av. CH48: W Kir 6D **64**
Slim Rd. L36: Huy 4G **57**
Slingsby Dr. CH49: Upton 5E **67**
Smallholdings, The L31: Mag 4E **7**
Smallridge Cl. CH61: Pens 1C **100**
Smallwood M. CH60: Hesw 3C **100**
Smeaton St. L4: Kirkd 4E **35**
(not continuous)
Smethick Wlk. L30: N'ton 5G **11**
Smilie Av. CH46: More 6A **48**
Smith Av. CH41: Birke 1D **68**
Smithdown Gro. L7: Liv 1G **71**
Smithdown La. L7: Liv 6G **53**
(Elm Gro.)
L7: Liv 1H **71**
(Malt St.)
Smithdown Pl. L15: Wav 4E **73**
Smithdown Rd. L7: Liv 2A **72**
L15: Wav 2A **72**
Smith Dr. L20: Boot 6E **21**
Smithfield St. L3: Liv 2D **4** (5C **52**)
WA9: St H 3H **43**
Smithford Wlk. L35: Tar G 2B **76**
Smith Pl. L5: Kirkd 1D **52**
Smith Rd. WA8: Wid 4D **96**
Smith St. L5: Kirkd 6E **35**
L34: Presc 1E **59**
WA9: St H 6A **44**
Smithy Cl. WA8: Cron 4A **78**
Smithy Heritage Cen. 6H **27**
Smithy Hey CH48: W Kir 1C **82**
Smithy Hill CH63: Thorn H 1C **118**
Smithy La. L39: Augh 1E **7**
WA8: Cron 3A **78**
Smithystone Cl. L15: Wav 2E **73**
Smollett St. L6: Liv 4H **53**
L20: Boot 5B **20**
Smugglers Way CH45: Wall 5A **32**
Smyth Rd. WA8: Wid 1H **97**
Snaefell Av. L13: Liv 2C **54**
Snaefell Gro. L13: Liv 2C **54**
Snave Cl. L21: Lith 6B **20**
Snowberry Cl. WA8: Wid 5A **80**
Snowberry Rd. L14: Knott A 1C **56**
Snowden Rd. CH46: More 1A **66**
Snowdon Cl. WA5: Gt San 3G **81**
Snowdon Gro. WA9: St H 6G **43**
Snowdon La. L5: Liv 2C **52**
Snowdon Rd. CH42: Tran 1F **87**
Snowdrop Av. CH41: Birke 1B **68**
Snowdrop Cl. WA7: Beech 3B **124**
Snowdrop M. L21: Lith 5B **20**
Snowdrop St. L5: Kirkd 6D **34**
Soho Pl. L3: Liv 1H **5** (4E **53**)
Soho St. L3: Liv 1H **5** (4E **53**)
(not continuous)

Solar Rd. L9: Ain 5H **21**
Solly Av. CH42: Rock F 1G **87**
Solomon St. L7: Liv 5H **53**
Solway Gro. WA7: Beech 2H **123**
Solway St. CH41: Birke 6C **50**
Solway St. E. L8: Liv 2H **71**
Solway St. W. L8: Liv 2H **71**
Soma Av. L21: Lith 3C **20**
Somerford Ho. L23: Blun 6D **8**
Somerford Rd. L14: Knott A 3C **56**
Somerford Wlk. WA8: Wid 6A **80**
(off Barneston Rd.)
Somerley Cl. L12: W Der 5H **37**
Somerset Pl. L6: Liv 2B **54**
Somerset Rd. CH45: Wall 2A **50**
CH48: W Kir 6C **64**
CH61: Pens 1C **100**
L20: Boot 1D **34**
L22: Water 1E **19**
Somerset St. WA9: St H 3H **43**
Somerton St. L15: Wav 1C **72**
Somerville Cl. CH63: Brom 1B **120**
Somerville Gro. L22: Water 1F **19**
Somerville Rd. L22: Water 1F **19**
WA8: Wid 3B **96**
Sommer Av. L12: W Der 6E **37**
Sonning Av. L21: Lith 2A **20**
Sonning Rd. L4: Walt 3B **36**
Sorany Cl. L23: Thorn 3A **10**
Sorogold St. WA9: St H 2G **43**
Sorrel Cl. CH43: Noct 4H **67**
Sorrell Way WA9: Clock F 4H **61**
Sth. Albert Rd. L17: Aig 5H **71**
Southampton Dr. L19: Garst 5F **91**
Southampton Way WA7: Murd 1G **125**
South Av. L34: Presc 1B **58**
South Bank CH43: O'ton 6D **68**
Sth. Bank Rd. L7: Liv 5B **54**
L19: Gras 5E **91**
Sth. Bank Ter. WA7: Run 2D **112**
Sth. Barcombe Rd.
L16: Child 2A **74**
Sth. Boundary Rd. L33: Know I 3D **24**
Southbourne Rd. CH45: Wall 2H **49**
Southbrook Rd. L27: N'ley 3E **75**
Southbrook Way L27: N'ley 3E **75**
Sth. Cantril Av. L12: W Der 6B **38**
Sth. Chester St. L8: Liv 3F **71**
Southcroft L33: Kirkb 5A **14**
Southcroft Rd. CH45: Wall 2H **49**
South Dale WA5: Penk 4H **81**
Southdale Rd. CH42: Rock F 1G **87**
L15: Wav 1D **72**
Southdean Rd. L14: Knott A 1D **56**
SOUTHDENE 3B **24**
South Dr. CH49: Upton 4E **67**
CH60: Hesw 6E **101**
CH61: Irby 6A **84**
L12: W Der 2F **55**
L15: Wav 1D **72**
Southern Cres. L8: Liv 4E **71**
Southern Rd. L24: Speke 3G **109**
Southern's La. WA11: Rainf 3G **17**
Southey Cl. WA8: Wid 3D **96**
Southey Gro. L31: Mag 3B **12**
Southey Rd. WA10: St H 5A **42**
Southey St. L15: Wav 2C **72**
L20: Boot 1B **34**
(not continuous)
Sth. Ferry Quay L3: Liv 3D **70**
Southfield Rd. L9: Walt 5F **21**
Southfields Av. WA5: Gt San 4H **81**
South Front L35: Whis 6E **59**
(not continuous)
Southgate Cl. L12: Crox 2A **38**
Southgate Rd. L13: Liv 4F **55**
South Gro. L8: Liv 5G **71**
L18: Aller 2G **91**
South Hey Rd. CH61: Irby 6B **84**
Sth. Highville Rd. L16: Child 3H **73**
South Hill Gro. CH43: O'ton 6D **68**
L8: Liv 5G **71**

South Hill Rd. CH43: O'ton 5E **69**
L8: Liv 6F **71**
Sth. Hunter St. L1: Liv 6H **5** (1F **71**)
Sth. John St. L1: Liv 5D **4** (6C **52**)
Southlands Av. WA5: Penk 6H **81**
Southlands Ct. WA7: Run 5D **112**
(off Southlands M.)
Southlands M. WA7: Run 5D **112**
South La. WA8: Wid 5A **80**
South La. Entry WA8: Wid 5B **80**
South Mnr. Way L25: Woolt 2E **93**
South Meade L31: Mag 6A **6**
Southmead Gdns. L19: Aller 4A **92**
Southmead Rd. L19: Aller 4A **92**
Sth. Mossley Hill Rd.
L19: Aig, Gras 2E **91**
Southney Cl. L31: Mell 6F **13**
Sth. Pde. CH48: W Kir 1A **82**
L23: Crosb 6H **9**
L24: Speke 2G **109**
L32: Kirkb 1A **24**
WA7: West P 6B **112**
South Pk. Ct. CH44: Wall 4G **51**
(off Demesne St.)
L32: Kirkb 6G **13**
South Pk. Rd. L32: Kirkb 6F **13**
Sth. Parkside Dr. L12: W Der 6G **37**
Sth. Parkside Wlk. L12: W Der 5F **37**
(off Parkside Dr.)
South Pk. Way L20: Boot 3D **34**
Southport Rd. L20: Boot 5E **21**
L23: Thorn 2A **10**
L31: Lyd 1A **6**
Southport St. WA9: St H 2C **44**
South Quay L3: Liv 2C **70**
Southridge Rd. CH61: Pens 6E **85**
South Rd. CH42: Tran 6E **69**
CH48: W Kir 2A **82**
CH65: Hoot 4H **121**
L9: Ain 5B **22**
L14: Broad G 4H **55**
L19: Gras 5E **91**
L22: Water 3F **19**
L24: Halew 1G **109**
WA7: West P 6B **112**
Sth. Sefton Bus. Cen. L20: Boot 2B **34**
South Sta. Rd. L25: Gate 4D **74**
South St. L8: Liv 4G **71**
WA8: Wid 3F **97**
WA9: St H 6B **42**
Sth. Sudley Rd. L19: Aig 2E **91**
South Vw. CH62: Brom 6D **88**
L8: Liv 5G **71**
(off Dentwood St.)
L22: Water 3G **19**
L36: Huy 5B **58**
South Vw. Ct. L22: Water 3G **19**
South Vw. Ter. WA5: Cuerd 6C **80**
South Vs. CH45: New B 6D **32**
Southwark Gro. L30: N'ton 2F **21**
South Way L15: Wav 1F **73**
Southway WA7: Pal F 6B **114**
(not continuous)
WA8: Wid 3B **96**
Southwell Pl. L8: Liv 4E **71**
Southwell St. L8: Liv 4E **71**
Southwick Rd. CH42: Tran 6G **69**
Sth. Wirral Retail Pk. CH62: Brom . . .2D **104**
Southwold Cres. WA5: Gt San 3F **81**
Southwood Av. WA7: Wind H 3E **115**
Southwood Cl. L32: Kirkb 3C **24**
Southwood Rd. CH62: Brom 4F **105**
L17: Aig 1H **89**
Sovereign Cl. WA7: Murd 6F **115**
Sovereign Hey L11: Crox 2G **37**
Sovereign Rd. L11: Crox 2G **37**
Sovereign Way CH41: Birke 6F **51**
L11: Crox 2G **37**
Spaceport 5H **51**
Spark La. WA7: Halt 4B **114**
Sparks La. CH61: Thing 5E **85**

Sparling St. L1: Liv 2D 70
  (not continuous)
SPARROW HALL 1D 36
Sparrow Hall Cl. L9: Faz 1C 36
Sparrow Hall Rd. L9: Faz 1D 36
Sparrowhawk Cl. L26: Halew 2G 93
  WA7: Pal F 6C 114
Speakman Rd. WA10: St H 5B 28
Speakman St. WA7: Run 2D 112
Speedwell Cl. CH60: Hesw 5G 101
Speedwell Dr. CH60: Hesw 5G 101
Speedwell Rd. CH41: Birke 2B 68
SPEKE 3G 109
Speke Blvd. L24: Speke 1D 108
Speke Chu. Rd. L24: Speke 2D 108
Speke Hall .3B 108
Speke Hall Av. L24: Speke 2C 108
Speke Hall Ind. Est.
  L24: Speke 2C 108
Speke Hall La. L25: Hunts X 6C 92
Speke Hall Rd. L24: Speke 6C 92
Speke Ho. L24: Speke 3A 110
Spekeland Rd. L7: Liv 1A 72
Speke Rd. L19: Garst 6G 91
  L24: Speke 6H 91
  L25: Hunts X, Woolt 1D 92
  L26: Halew 5C 94
  WA8: Wid 5C 94
Speke Town La. L24: Speke 1D 108
Spellow La. L4: Walt 5F 35
Spellow Pl. L3: Liv 3B 4
Spence Av. L20: Boot 6D 20
Spencer Av. CH46: More 6E 49
Spencer Cl. L36: Huy 1H 75
Spencer Gdns. WA9: St H 5H 43
Spencer Pl. L20: Boot 4D 20
Spencer's La. L31: Mell 1C 22
Spencer St. L6: Liv 3F 53
Spenders La. WA7: Aston 6F 125
Spennymoor Ct. WA7: Pal F 6A 114
Spenser Av. CH42: Rock F 2H 87
Spenser Cl. WA8: Wid 2D 96
Spenser Rd. CH64: Nest 6A 118
Spenser St. L20: Boot 1B 34
Spicer Gro. L32: Kirkb 1A 24
Spice St. L9: Ain 5H 21
Spike Island Vis. Cen. 6E 97
Spindle Cl. L6: Liv 3F 53
Spindrift Ct. CH48: W Kir 2A 82
Spindus Rd. L24: Speke 2C 108
Spinnaker Cl. WA7: Murd 1F 125
Spinnakers, The L19: Aig 4D 90
Spinners Dr. WA9: St H 5B 44
Spinney, The CH48: W Kir 1E 83
  CH49: Upton 3E 67
  CH60: Hesw 2G 117
  CH63: Spit 2B 104
  CH64: Park 6H 117
  L28: Stockb V 6D 38
  L34: Presc 6C 40
  WA11: Rainf 2F 17
Spinney Av. WA8: Wid 2G 95
Spinney Cl. L33: Know I 3E 25
  WA9: Clock F 3G 61
Spinney Cres. L23: Blun 3D 8
Spinney Grn. WA10: Eccl 2G 41
Spinney Rd. L33: Know I 3F 25
Spinney Vw. L33: Know I 3F 25
Spinney Wlk. WA7: Cas 4C 114
Spinney Way L36: Huy 4E 57
Spire Grn. L9: Walt 5G 21
Spires, The WA10: Eccl 1G 41
SPITAL 2B 104
Spital Heyes CH63: Spit 2B 104
Spital Rd. CH62: Brom, Spit 2A 104
  CH63: Spit 2A 104
Spital Station (Rail) 2B 104
Spitfire Rd. L24: Speke 5B 92
Spofforth Rd. L7: Liv 1B 72
Spooner Av. L21: Lith 4C 20
Sprainger St. L3: Liv 3B 52
Sprakeling Pl. L20: Boot 4E 21

Spray St. WA10: St H 1C 42
Spreyton Cl. L12: W Der 3G 37
Sprig Cl. L9: Ain 3B 22
Springbank Cl. WA7: Run 1F 123
Spring Bank Rd. L4: Walt 2H 53
Springbourne Rd.
  L17: Aig .1H 89
Springbrook Cl. WA10: Eccl 1G 41
Spring Cl. L33: Kirkb 4C 14
Spring Ct. WA7: Run 3F 113
Springcroft CH64: Park 6G 117
Springdale Cl. CH46: More 6E 49
  L12: W Der 6G 37
Springfield L3: Liv 1G 5 (4E 53)
  (not continuous)
Springfield Av. CH48: W Kir 6E 65
  L21: Lith .3C 20
Springfield Cl. CH49: Woodc 1G 85
  WA10: St H 5A 42
Springfield La. WA10: Eccl 6G 27
Springfield Pk. WA11: Hay 4E 31
Springfield Rd. L39: Augh 2E 7
  WA8: Wid 3G 95
  WA10: St H 5A 42
Springfield Sq. L4: Walt 5F 35
Springfield Way L12: W Der 5A 38
Spring Gdns. L31: Mag 1C 12
Spring Gro. L12: W Der 1G 55
Springhill Av. CH62: Brom 1D 120
Springhill Cl. L15: Wav 3E 73
Springmeadow Rd. L25: Gate 4C 74
Springpool WA9: St H 6H 43
Springs Cl. L20: Boot 1D 34
  (off Davies St.)
Springside Cl. L36: Huy 1E 57
Spring St. CH42: Tran 5H 69
  WA8: Wid 5E 97
SPRINGVALE 1G 17
Spring Va. CH45: Wall 6A 32
Springvale Cl. L32: Kirkb 2H 23
Springville Rd. L9: Ain 4A 22
Springwell Rd. L20: Boot 4C 20
Springwood Av. L19: Aller 3H 91
  L25: Woolt 3H 91
Springwood Ct. L19: Aller 4H 91
  (off Brocklebank La.)
Springwood Crematorium
  L25: Aller 4H 91
Springwood Gro. L32: Kirkb 4B 24
Springwood Way CH62: New F 3A 88
Spruce Cl. CH42: Tran 5F 69
Spruce Gro. L28: Stockb V 6D 38
Sprucewood Cl. L6: Liv 2H 53
Spur, The L12: Crosb 6F 9
Spur Cl. L11: Crox 2G 37
Spurgeon Cl. L5: Liv 2F 53
Spurling Rd. WA5: Burtw 1H 63
Spurriers La. L31: Mell 1G 13
Spurstow Cl. CH43: O'ton 5B 68
Squibb Dr. CH46: Leas 5E 49
Squires Av. WA8: Wid 2D 96
Squires Cl. WA11: Hay 5D 30
Squires St. L7: Liv 6G 53
Stable Cl. CH49: Grea 5B 66
Stables, The L23: Crosb 4A 10
Stables Bus. Cen., The L13: Liv 6C 36
  (off Larkhill La.)
Stables Ct. WA9: St H 3G 43
  (off Appleton Rd.)
Stableyard Cotts. WA11: Crank 1C 28
Stackfield, The CH48: W Kir 6F 65
Stadium Rd. CH62: Brom 2E 105
Stadt Moers Pk. 5B 58
Stadt Moers Vis. Cen. 5C 58
Stafford Cl. L36: Huy 3A 58
Stafford Moreton Way L31: Mag 6B 6
Stafford Rd. WA10: St H 4B 42
Staffordshire Cl. L5: Liv 1E 53
Stafford St. L3: Liv 2H 5 (5E 53)
Stag Rd. L24: Speke 5A 92
Stainburn Av. L11: Norr G 2D 36

Stainer Cl. L14: Knott A 2B 56
Stainton Cl. L26: Halew 3G 93
  WA11: St H 3F 29
Stairhaven Rd. L19: Aller 2F 91
Stakes, The CH46: Leas 4C 48
Stalbridge Av. L18: Moss H 4D 72
Stalbridge Dr. WA7: Nort 1H 115
Staley Av. L23: Crosb 6H 9
Staley St. L20: Boot 5C 20
Stalisfield Av. L11: Norr G 3E 37
Stalisfield Gro. L11: Norr G 3E 37
Stalisfield Pl. L11: Norr G 3E 37
Stalmine Rd. L9: Walt 1G 35
Stamford Ct. L20: Boot 2D 34
Stamfordham Dr. L19: Aller 3G 91
Stamfordham Gro. L19: Aller 4H 91
Stamfordham Pl. L19: Aller 4H 91
Stamford St. L7: Liv 5A 54
Stanbury Av. CH63: Beb 5A 88
Standale Rd. L15: Wav 1D 72
Standard Rd. L11: Crox 1G 37
Standedge Way L14: Knott A 1C 56
Standen Cl. WA10: St H 1C 42
Stand Farm Rd. L12: Crox 2B 38
Standish Cl. WA8: Wid 3B 96
Standish Dr. WA11: Rainf 2G 17
Standish St. L3: Liv 1E 5 (5D 52)
  WA10: St H 1E 43
Stand Pk. Av. L30: N'ton 1F 21
Stand Pk. Cl. L30: N'ton 1F 21
Stand Pk. Rd. L16: Child 3H 73
Stand Pk. Way L30: N'ton 6E 11
Standring Gdns. WA10: St H 5H 41
Stanfield Av. L5: Liv 2F 53
Stanfield Dr. CH63: Beb 2H 103
Stanford Av. CH45: New B 6D 32
Stanford Cres. L25: Hunts X 2F 93
Stangate L31: Mag 5A 6
Stanhope Dr. CH62: Brom 4D 104
  L36: Huy .4E 57
Stanhope St. L8: Liv 3D 70
  (not continuous)
  WA10: St H 6D 28
Stanier Way L7: Liv 6A 54
Staniforth Pl. L16: Child 6H 55
STANLEY 5C 54
Stanley Av. CH45: Wall 1H 49
  CH63: Hghr B 3D 86
  WA5: Gt San 2F 81
  WA11: Rainf 2E 17
Stanley Bank Rd. WA11: Hay 4C 30
Stanley Bank Way WA11: Hay 5B 30
Stanley Bungalows L34: Know 2E 39
Stanley Cl. CH44: Wall 5G 51
  L4: Kirkd .6D 34
  WA8: Wid 1G 97
Stanley Ct. CH42: Tran 6H 69
Stanley Cres. L34: Presc 1C 58
Stanley Gdns. L9: Walt 6F 21
Stanley Ho. L20: Boot 1B 34
Stanley La. CH62: East 3F 121
STANLEY PARK 3D 2
Stanley Pk. .5G 35
Stanley Pk. L21: Lith 2A 20
Stanley Pk. Av. Nth. L4: Walt 4H 35
  (not continuous)
Stanley Pk. Av. Sth. L4: Walt 5H 35
Stanley Pct. L20: Boot 2C 34
Stanley Rd. CH41: Birke 6B 50
  CH47: Hoy 3A 64
  CH62: New F 3A 88
  L5: Kirkd .5D 34
  L20: Boot, Kirkd 5C 20
  L20: Kirkd 4D 34
  L22: Water 3G 19
  L31: Mag .3A 12
  L36: Huy .5G 57
Stanley St. CH44: Wall 5G 51
  L1: Liv 3D 4 (5C 52)
  L7: Liv 6C 54
  L19: Garst 1H 107
  WA7: Run 2F 113

Stanley Ter. CH45: New B 6D **32**
L8: Liv 2F 71
(off Up. Parliament St.)
L18: Moss H 6E **73**
Stanley Theatre 6F 53
Stanley Vs. WA7: Run 4D **112**
Stanlowe Vw. L19: Gras 5D **90**
Stanmore Pk. CH49: Grea 6H **65**
Stanmore Rd. L15: Wav 3F **73**
WA7: Run 3H **113**
Stanney Cl. CH62: East 4E **121**
Stannyfield Cl. L23: Thorn 3B **10**
Stannyfield Dr. L23: Thorn 3B **10**
Stansfield Av. L31: Mag 6E **7**
Stanstead Av. WA5: Penk 6H **81**
Stanton Av. L21: Lith 2A **20**
Stanton Cl. L30: N'ton 4D **10**
WA11: Hay 5E **31**
Stanton Cres. L32: Kirkb 1G **23**
Stanton Rd. CH63: Beb 2G **103**
L18: Moss H 4D **72**
Stanwood Cl. WA10: Eccl 2F **41**
Stanwood Gdns. L35: Whis 4E **59**
Stanza Ct. L5: Liv 2E **53**
Stapehill Cl. L13: Liv 5F **55**
Stapeley Gdns. L26: Halew 5A **94**
Staplands Rd. L14: Broad G 5H **55**
Stapleford Rd. L25: Gate 3E **75**
Staplehurst Cl. L12: Crox 2A **38**
Staplehurst Dr. CH42: Rock F 2H **87**
Stapleton Av. CH49: Grea 5B **66**
L24: Speke 2F **109**
L35: Rainh 3A **60**
Stapleton Cl. L25: Gate 2D **74**
L35: Rainh 3A **60**
Stapleton Rd. L35: Rainh 2H **59**
Stapleton Way WA8: Hale B 6H **95**
Stapley Cl. WA7: Run 4D **112**
Stargazer, The 5A 50
Starling Cl. WA7: Murd 6F **115**
Starling Gro. L12: W Der 4B **38**
Star St. L8: Liv 3E **71**
Starworth Dr. CH62: New F 4C **88**
Statham Rd. CH43: Bid 1G **67**
Station App. CH46: More 5C **48**
CH47: Meols 1E **65**
Station Cl. L25: Hunts X 4E **93**
Station M. L32: Kirkb 6G **13**
Station Pas. *L9: Walt 1G 35*
(off Walton Pk.)
Station Rd. CH41: Birke 6B **50**
CH44: Wall 3C **50**
CH47: Hoy 3B **64**
CH60: Hesw 1D **116**
CH61: Barn 6H **85**
CH61: Thurs 6G **83**
CH63: Store 6H **85**
CH64: Park 6G **117**
L25: Gate 4C **74**
L31: Lyd 1A **6**
L31: Mag 1C **12**
L31: Mell 6E **13**
L34: Presc 1D **58**
(not continuous)
L35: Rainh 4A **60**
L36: Roby 5E **57**
WA5: Gt San 4H **81**
WA5: Penk 6F **81**
WA7: Run 3D **112**
WA7: Sut W 3D **124**
WA8: Wid 5G **79**
WA9: St H 6A **44**
WA11: Hay 5E **31**
Station St. L35: Rainh 4A **60**
Statton Rd. L13: Liv 6F **55**
Staveley Rd. L19: Gras 3F **91**
Stavert Cl. L11: Norr G 2F **37**
Staverton Pk. L32: Kirkb 2G **23**
Stavordale Rd. CH46: More 6D **48**
Steble St. L8: Liv 4F **71**
Steel Av. CH45: Wall 1E **51**
Steel Ct. L5: Liv 2C **52**
Steeple, The CH48: Caldy 5D **82**
Steeplechase Cl. L9: Ain 3A **22**
Steeple Vw. L33: Kirkb 4A **14**
Steers Cft. L28: Stockb V 5B **38**
Steinberg Ct. L3: Liv 3C **52**
Steley Way L34: Presc 2D **58**
Stella Pct. L21: Sea 5A **20**
Stenhills Cres. WA7: Run 3G **113**
Stephens La. L2: Liv 3D **4**
Stephenson Ct. *L7: Liv 6A 54*
(off Crosfield Rd.)
Stephenson Ho. L7: Liv 1G **71**
Stephenson Rd. L13: Liv 5E **55**
Stephenson Way L13: Wav 6C **54**
Stephen Way L35: Rainh 2H **59**
Stepney Gro. L4: Walt 4G **35**
Sterling Way L5: Kirkd 1D **52**
Sterndale Cl. L7: Liv 1H **71**
Sterrix Av. L30: N'ton 1C **20**
Sterrix Grn. L21: Lith 1C **20**
Sterrix La. L21: Lith 1C **20**
L30: N'ton 1C **20**
Steve Biko Cl. L8: Liv 2H **71**
Stevenage Cl. WA9: St H 6D **42**
Stevenson Cres. WA10: St H 1B **42**
Stevenson Dr. CH63: Spit 2H **103**
Stevenson St. L15: Wav 1D **72**
Stevens Rd. CH60: Hesw 6G **101**
Stevens St. WA9: St H 5B **42**
Steventon WA7: Nort 1G **115**
Steward Ct. L35: Presc 2F **59**
Stewards Av. WA8: Wid 3D **96**
Stewart Av. L20: Boot 1E **35**
Stewart Cl. CH61: Pens 2D **100**
Stile Hey L23: Thorn 4B **10**
Stiles Rd. L33: Kirkb 3B **14**
Stillington Rd. L8: Liv 5G **71**
Stirling Av. L23: Crosb 6G **9**
Stirling Cres. WA9: St H 1F **61**
Stirling La. L25: Hunts X 4F **93**
Stirling Rd. L24: Speke 2D **108**
Stirling St. CH44: Wall 5D **50**
Stockbridge La. L36: Huy 2D **56**
(not continuous)
Stockbridge Pl. L5: Liv 2G **53**
Stockbridge St. L5: Liv 2G **53**
STOCKBRIDGE VILLAGE 5C 38
Stockdale Cl. L3: Liv 1D **4** (4C **52**)
Stockdale Ct. WA5: Gt San 2G **81**
Stockdale Dr. WA5: Gt San 2G **81**
Stockham Cl. WA7: Halt 5C **114**
Stockham La.
WA7: Brook, Halt, Pal F 5C **114**
WA7: Brook, Pal F 5C **114**
WA7: Murd 2E **125**
Stockham Lodge Racquet & Health Club
. . . . . .6D 114
Stockmoor Rd. L11: Norr G 2D **36**
Stockpit Rd. L33: Know I 1E **25**
Stocks Av. WA9: St H 2A **44**
Stocks La. WA5: Gt San, Penk 4F **81**
Stockswell Farm Ct.
WA8: Wid 5C **78**
Stockswell Rd. WA8: Wid 5F **77**
Stockton Cres. L33: Kirkb 3H **13**
Stockton Gro. WA9: St H 1B **60**
Stockton Wood Rd. L24: Speke 2E **109**
Stockville Rd. L18: Moss H 5A **74**
Stoddart Rd. L4: Walt 3G **35**
Stoke Cl. CH62: East 4E **121**
Stoker Way L9: Walt 6G **21**
Stokesay CH43: Noct 3H **67**
Stokes Cl. L26: Halew 2A **94**
Stokesley Av. L32: Kirkb 1G **23**
Stoke St. CH41: Birke 1D **68**
Stonebarn Dr. L31: Mag 4B **6**
Stone Barn La. WA7: Pal F 1C **124**
Stonebridge La. L10: Faz 5E **23**
L11: Crox 6F **23**
Stoneby Dr. CH45: Wall 6C **32**
Stonechat Cl. L27: N'ley 5G **75**
WA7: Beech 2A **124**
Stone Ct. WA11: Hay 5D **30**
Stonecrop L18: Moss H 4A **74**
Stonecrop Cl. WA7: Beech 3B **124**
Stone Cross Dr. WA8: Wid 4C **78**
Stonecross Dr. L35: Rainh 6B **60**
Stonedale Cres. L11: Crox 1F **37**
Stonedale Pk. L11: Crox 1E **37**
Stonefield Rd. L14: Knott A 3B **56**
Stonefont Cl. L9: Walt 2G **35**
Stonegate Dr. L8: Liv 5F **71**
Stonehaven Cl. L16: Child 1B **74**
Stone Hey L35: Whis 6D **58**
Stonehey Dr. CH48: W Kir 2C **82**
Stonehey Rd. L32: Kirkb 3A **24**
Stone Hey Wlk. L32: Kirkb 3A **24**
Stonehill Av. CH63: Beb 5A **88**
L4: Walt .1H 53
(off Stonehill St.)
Stonehills Ct. WA7: Run 3G **113**
Stonehills La. WA7: Run 3G **113**
Stonehill St. L4: Walt 1H **53**
Stonehouse M. L18: Aller 6H **73**
Stonehouse Rd. CH44: Wall 2A **50**
Stonelea WA7: Wind H 4D **114**
Stoneleigh Gro. CH42: Rock F 3H **87**
Stonemasons Ct. *L25: Woolt 6C 74*
(off Clay Cross Rd.)
Stoneridge Ct. CH43: Bid 1G **67**
Stone Sq. L20: Boot 6E **21**
Stone St. L3: Liv 3B **52**
L34: Presc 1D **58**
Stoneville Rd. L13: Liv 3E **55**
STONEYCROFT 3E 55
Stoneycroft L12: W Der 3F **55**
Stoneycroft Cl. L13: Liv 2E **55**
Stoneycroft Cres. L13: Liv 2E **55**
Stoney Hey Rd. CH45: New B 6C **32**
Stoneyhurst Av. L10: Ain 6A **12**
Stoney La. L35: Rainh, Whis 3F **59**
Stoney La. Ind. Est.
L35: Rainh 4G **59**
Stoney Vw. L35: Rainh 4H **59**
Stonham Cl. CH49: Upton 4C **66**
Stonyfield L30: N'ton 4E **11**
Stony Holt WA7: Nort 5E **115**
Stonyhurst Cl. WA11: St H 4F **29**
Stonyhurst Rd. L25: Woolt 2D **92**
Stopford St. L8: Liv 5F **71**
Stopgate La. L9: Ain, Faz 1B **36**
L33: Sim 3C **14**
Store St. L20: Kirkd 4D **34**
STORETON .6C 86
STORETON BRICKFIELDS 6A 86
Storeton Cl. CH43: O'ton 6D **68**
Storeton La. CH61: Barn 2G **101**
Storeton Rd. CH42: Tran 6D **68**
CH43: O'ton 6D **68**
Stormont Rd. L19: Garst 4F **91**
Storrington Av. L11: Norr G 2F **37**
Storrington Heys L11: Norr G 1F **37**
Storrsdale Rd. L18: Moss H 6F **73**
Stour Av. L35: Rainh 4A **60**
Stourcliffe Rd. CH44: Wall 3C **50**
Stourport Cl. CH49: Grea 5A **66**
Stourton Rd. L32: Kirkb 3A **24**
Stourton St. CH44: Wall 5E **51**
Stourvale Rd. L26: Halew 4H **93**
Stowe Av. L10: Ain 1C **22**
Stowe Cl. L25: Hunts X 4C **92**
Stowell St. L7: Liv 1F **71**
Stowford Cl. L12: W Der 3G **37**
Strada Way L3: Liv 1H **5** (4F **53**)
Strafford Dr. L20: Boot 1E **35**
Strand, The L2: Liv 4C **4** (6C **52**)
Strand Rd. CH47: Hoy 2B **64**
L20: Boot 2A **34**
Strand Shop. Cen.
L20: Boot 2C **34**
Strand St. L1: Liv 5C **4** (6C **52**)
Strand Vw. L20: Boot 2A **34**
Stratford Rd. L19: Aig 3D **90**
Strathallan Cl. CH60: Hesw 3C **100**

Strathcona Rd. CH45: Wall 1D 50
   L15: Wav 2C 72
Strathearn Rd. CH60: Hesw 1D 116
Strathlorne Cl. CH42: Tran 6H 69
Strathmore Dr. L23: Crosb 6G 9
Strathmore Gro. WA9: St H 1G 61
Strathmore Rd. L6: Liv 3A 54
Stratton Cl. CH45: Wall 1E 51
   L18: Aller 1A 92
   WA7: Brook 1D 124
Stratton Dr. WA9: St H 1B 60
Stratton Pk. WA8: Wid 4D 78
Stratton Rd. L32: Kirkb 2G 23
Stratton Wlk. L32: Kirkb 2G 23
Strauss Cl. L8: Liv 3H 71
Strawberry Field 6A 74
Strawberry Rd. L11: Norr G 3C 36
Streatham Av. L18: Moss H 4D 72
Street Hey La. CH64: Will 5B 120
Stretford Cl. L33: Kirkb 4A 14
Stretton Av. CH44: Wall 3C 50
   WA9: St H 2B 44
Stretton Cl. L13: O'ton 6A 68
   CH62: East 4E 121
   L12: Crox 2C 38
Stretton Way L36: Huy 1B 76
Strickland St. WA10: St H 6F 29
Stringhey Rd. CH44: Wall 2E 51
Stroma Rd. L18: Aller 2F 91
Stroud Cl. CH37: Grea 6A 66
Stuart Av. CH46: More 6D 48
   L25: Hunts X 4E 93
Stuart Cl. CH46: More 1E 67
Stuart Dr. L14: Broad G 4A 56
Stuart Gro. L20: Kirkd 4D 34
Stuart Rd. CH42: Tran 6F 69
   L4: Walt 3E 35
   L22: Water 1G 19
   L23: Crosb 1G 19
   L31: Mell 6F 13
   WA7: Manor P 1D 114
   WA10: Windle 5A 28
Stuart Rd. Nth. L20: Boot 2E 35
Stubbs La. CH43: Noct 6A 68
Studholme St. L20: Kirkd 6C 34
Studland Rd. L9: Faz 1C 36
Studley Rd. CH45: Wall 1A 50
Sturdee Rd. L13: Liv 6F 55
Sturgess St. WA12: Newt W 2H 45
Suburban Rd. L6: Liv 1A 54
Sudbury Cl. L25: Woolt 1F 93
Sudbury Gdns. WA9: St H 1A 60
Sudbury Rd. L22: Water 1D 18
Sudell Av. L31: Mag 5E 7
Sudell La. L31: Lyd 1C 6
   L39: Augh 1C 6
Sudley Grange L17: Aig 2C 90
Sudley House 1D 90
Sudworth Rd. CH45: New B 6C 32
Suffield Rd. L4: Kirkd 5D 34
Suffolk Pl. WA8: Wid 4A 96
Suffolk St. L1: Liv 6F 5 (1D 70)
   L20: Boot 1D 34
   WA7: Run 2D 112
Suffton Pk. L32: Kirkb 2G 23
Sugarbrook La. L10: Faz 6D 22
Sugar La. L34: Know 2E 39
Sugar St. L9: Ain 6H 21
Sugnall St. L7: Liv 1F 71
     (not continuous)
Sulby Av. L13: Liv 2C 54
Sulgrave Cl. L16: Child 6G 55
Sullington Dr. L27: N'ley 3G 75
     (not continuous)
Sullivan Av. CH49: Upton 5D 66
Sullivan Rd. WA8: Wid 4H 97
Sullivans Way L17: Liv 5F 43
Sumley Cl. WA11: St H 6H 29
Summer Cl. WA7: Halt 4B 114
Summerfield CH62: Brom 3D 104
Summerfield Av. WA10: Eccl 2F 41
Summerford Cl. CH42: Tran 6G 69

Summerhill Dr. L31: Mag 2D 12
Summer La.
   WA4: Dares, Hatt, Pres H 1H 125
   WA7: Halt 4B 114
Summer Rd. L20: Boot 6C 20
Summers Av. L20: Boot 1E 35
Summer Seat L3: Liv 3D 52
   L20: Boot 2A 34
Summers Rd. L3: Liv 4D 70
Summertrees Av. CH49: Grea 5B 66
Summertrees Cl. CH49: Grea 5B 66
Summerwood CH61: Irby 4B 84
Summit, The CH44: Wall 2E 51
Summit Way L25: Woolt 4D 94
Sumner Cl. L5: Liv 2C 52
   L35: Rainh 6B 60
Sumner Gro. L33: Kirkb 4B 14
     (off Mossdale Rd.)
Sumner Rd. CH43: Bid 1B 68
Sumners Farm Ct. WA4: Pres H 1H 125
Sumner St. WA11: Hay 5C 30
Sunbeam Cl. WA7: Run 2D 112
Sunbourne Rd. L17: Aig 1H 89
Sunbury Rd. CH44: Wall 4E 51
   L4: Walt 6H 35
Sunbury St. WA10: St H 5A 42
Suncroft Rd. CH60: Hesw 6G 101
Sundale Av. L35: Presc 1F 59
Sundene Lodge L22: Water 4G 19
Sundew Cl. L9: Walt 4F 21
Sundridge St. L8: Liv 5G 71
Sunfield Rd. CH46: More 5D 48
Sunflower Cl. WA9: Bold 1G 63
Sunlight Lodge CH62: Port S 5B 88
Sunlight St. L6: Liv 2A 54
Sunlight Vision Mus. 5B 88
Sunloch Cl. L9: Ain 3B 22
Sunningdale CH46: More 1E 67
Sunningdale Av. WA8: Wid 2H 95
Sunningdale Cl. L36: Roby 6E 57
   WA5: Burtw 6H 45
Sunningdale Dr. CH61: Thing 6E 85
   CH63: Brom 1B 120
   L23: Blun 3E 9
Sunningdale Rd. CH45: Wall 5B 32
   L15: Wav 1D 72
Sunniside La. WA7: Nort 1G 115
Sunny Bank CH63: Hghr B 5F 87
Sunnybank Av. CH43: Noct 5H 67
Sunny Bank Rd. L16: Child 2H 73
Sunnydale L35: Rainh 4B 60
Sunnygate Rd. L19: Gras 3E 91
Sunnymede Dr. L31: Lyd 4C 6
Sunnyside CH46: More 5B 48
   L8: Liv .4H 71
   WA5: Gt San 3G 81
Sunrise Cl. L19: Gras 4F 91
Sunsdale Rd. L18: Moss H 4E 73
Sunset Cl. L33: Kirkb 4C 14
     (off Freckleton Dr.)
Superior Cl. L27: N'ley 4G 75
Surby Cl. L16: Child 1A 74
Surlingham Gdns. WA9: St H 1C 60
Surrey Av. CH49: Upton 4C 66
Surrey Dr. CH48: W Kir 3C 82
Surrey St. CH44: Wall 4C 50
   L1: Liv 6E 5 (1D 70)
   L20: Boot 1D 34
   WA7: Run 3E 113
   WA9: St H 3H 43
Susan Dr. WA5: Penk 4F 81
Susan Gro. CH46: More 1B 66
Susan St. WA8: Wid 1G 97
Susan Wlk. L35: Whis 2F 61
Sussex Cl. CH61: Pens 1C 100
   L20: Boot 1D 34
Sussex Gro. WA9: St H 3G 43
Sussex Rd. CH48: W Kir 6C 64
   L31: Mag 2B 12

Sussex St. L20: Boot 1D 34
   L22: Water 1E 19
   WA8: Wid 2H 97
Sutcliffe St. L6: Liv 4H 53
Sutherland Ct. WA7: Run 3F 113
Sutherland Dr. CH62: East 3D 120
Sutherland Rd. L34: Presc 1E 59
SUTTON 5B 44
Sutton C'way. WA6: Frod 5A 124
Sutton Cl. CH62: East 4E 121
Sutton Fields Golf Driving Range . . .4E 125
Sutton Fold WA9: St H 5H 43
Sutton Fold Ind. Pk. WA9: St H 5A 44
SUTTON HEATH 6D 42
Sutton Heath Rd. WA9: St H 1C 60
SUTTON LEACH 2H 61
Sutton Leisure Cen. 1F 61
SUTTON MANOR 5F 61
Sutton Moss Rd. WA9: St H 5B 44
Sutton Oak Dr. WA9: St H 4H 43
Sutton Pk. Dr. WA9: St H 6G 43
Sutton Quays Bus. Pk.
   WA7: Sut W 4A 124
Sutton Rd. CH45: New B 6D 32
   WA9: St H 4G 43
Suttons La. WA8: Wid 4F 97
Sutton St. L13: Liv 2C 54
   WA7: Run 3F 113
Suttons Way L26: Halew 2G 93
     (off Betony Cl.)
SUTTON WEAVER 4C 124
Sutton Wood Rd. L24: Speke 2E 109
Suzanne Boardman Ho. L6: Liv 2A 54
Swainson Rd. L10: Faz 4D 22
Swale Av. L35: Rainh 4A 60
Swaledale Av. L35: Rainh 4B 60
Swaledale Cl. CH62: East 2E 121
   WA5: Gt San 2H 81
Swalegate L31: Mag 5B 6
Swallow Cl. L12: Crox 2B 38
   L27: N'ley 4H 75
   L33: Kirkb 2A 14
Swallow Ct. WA10: St H 2B 42
Swallow Flds. L9: Faz 1D 36
Swallowhurst Cres. L11: Norr G 3E 37
Swan Av. WA9: St H 3C 44
Swan Ct. CH43: Pren 1B 86
Swan Cres. L15: Wav 1F 73
Swan Gdns. WA9: St H 1C 60
Swan Hey L31: Mag 2C 12
Swan La. L39: Augh 1D 6
Swan Rd. WA12: Newt W 1F 45
Swansea Cl. L19: Garst 5F 91
SWANSIDE 5B 56
Swanside Av. L14: Broad G 4A 56
Swanside Pde. L14: Knott A 4A 56
Swanside Rd. L14: Broad G 4A 56
Swanston Av. L4: Walt 4G 35
Swan St. L13: Liv 4D 54
Swan Wlk. L31: Mag 2C 12
Sweden Gro. L22: Water 2F 19
Sweet Briar Ct. WA9: Clock F 5H 61
Sweeting St. L2: Liv 4D 4 (6C 52)
Swift Gro. L12: Crox 1B 38
Swift's Cl. L30: N'ton 5D 10
Swift's La. L30: N'ton 5D 10
Swift St. WA10: St H 6E 29
Swift's Weint CH64: Park 6F 117
     (off Coastguard La.)
Swinbrook Grn. L11: Norr G 2D 36
Swinburne Cl. L16: Child 1B 74
Swinburne Rd. WA10: St H 6B 28
Swindale Cl. L8: Liv 2H 71
Swinden Cl. WA7: Wind H 3F 115
Swinderby Dr. L31: Mell 6F 13
Swindon Cl. CH49: Grea 5A 66
   L5: Kirkd 6D 34
Swindon St. L5: Kirkd 6D 34
Swinford Av. WA8: Wid 1A 98
Swisspine Gdns. WA9: St H 6A 42
Swiss Rd. L6: Liv 4A 54
SWITCH ISLAND 4H 11

Switch Island Leisure Pk.
L30: N'ton 6G 11
Sword Cl. L11: Crox 2G 37
Sword Wlk. L11: Crox 2G 37
Swynnerton Way WA8: Wid 4F 79
Sybil Rd. L4: Walt 6G 35
Sycamore Av. CH49: Upton 2B 66
L23: Crosb 3H 9
L26: Halew 5H 93
WA8: Wid 1F 97
WA11: Hay 6C 30
Sycamore Cl. CH49: Upton 2B 66
L9: Walt 2A 36
WA10: Eccl 1H 41
Sycamore Ct. *L8: Liv* *5G 71*
(off Weller Way)
WA7: Manor P 1F 115
Sycamore Dr. L33: Kirkb 6B 14
WA7: Sut W 3C 112
Sycamore Gdns. WA10: St H 5C 28
Sycamore Pk. L18: Aller 1H 91
Sycamore Ri. CH49: Grea 1A 84
Sycamore Rd. CH42: Tran 5F 69
L22: Water 1G 19
L36: Huy 1G 75
WA7: Run 5G 113
Sydenham Av. L17: Liv 4A 72
Sydenham Ho. L17: Aig 4B 72
Syder's Gro. L34: Know 2E 39
Sydney St. L9: Ain 5G 21
WA7: West P 6B 112
Sylvan Ct. L25: Woolt 2D 92
Sylvandale Gro. CH62: Brom 3D 104
Sylvania Rd. L4: Walt 3G 35
Sylvia Cl. L10: Faz 5F 23
Syren St. L20: Kirkd 5C 34
Syston Av. WA11: St H 5G 29

T

Tabley Av. WA8: Wid 1A 96
Tabley Cl. CH43: O'ton 1B 86
Tabley Gdns. WA9: St H 1B 60
Tabley Rd. L15: Wav 2B 72
Tabley St. L1: Liv 1D 70
Tace Cl. L8: Liv 2F 71
Taggart Av. L16: Child 3H 73
Tagus Cl. L8: Liv 3H 71
Tagus St. L8: Liv 3H 71
Tailor's La. L31: Mag 1C 12
Talbot Av. CH63: Brim 4C 102
Talbot Cl. WA10: St H 1D 42
Talbot Ct. CH43: O'ton 5C 68
L36: Huy 6G 57
Talbot Rd. CH43: O'ton 5C 68
Talbotville Rd. L13: Liv 6G 55
Talgarth Way L25: Gate 2C 74
Taliesin St. L5: Liv 2D 52
Talisman Cl. WA7: Murd 6G 115
Talisman Way L20: Boot 1A 34
Talland Cl. L26: Halew 2G 93
Tallarn Rd. L32: Kirkb 1F 23
Tall Trees WA9: St H 5F 43
Talton Rd. L15: Wav 2B 72
Tamar Cl. L6: Liv 3G 53
Tamar Gro. CH46: More 1B 66
Tamarisk Gdns. WA9: St H 6A 42
Tamar Rd. WA11: Hay 5E 31
Tamerton Cl. L18: Aller 1A 92
Tam O'Shanter Urban Farm 2A 68
Tamworth St. L8: Liv 4E 71
WA10: St H 1C 42
Tanar Cl. CH63: Spit 2B 104
Tanat Dr. L18: Moss H 5F 73
Tancred Rd. CH45: Wall 2C 50
L4: Walt 6G 35
Tanhouse WA7: Halt 4A 114
Tan Ho. La. WA5: Burtw 3H 63
Tanhouse La. WA8: Wid 3G 97
Tanhouse Rd. L23: Thorn 4B 10
Tannery La. WA5: Penk 6E 81

Tansley Cl. CH48: W Kir 1E 83
Tanworth Dr. CH46: More 6H 47
Tapestry Gdns. CH41: Birke 6B 50
Tapley Pl. L13: Liv 5D 54
Taplow St. L6: Liv 1H 53
Tapton Way L13: Wav 6D 54
Tara Pk. Cvn. Site L3: Liv 4B 52
Tarbock Pk. Cvn. Site L3: Liv 5C 76
TARBOCK GREEN 2C 76
TARBOCK INTERCHANGE 2C 76
Tarbock Hey CH46: More 1A 66
Tarbot Hey CH46: More 1A 66
Tarbrock Ct. *L30: N'ton* *4D 10*
(off Great Hey)
Target Rd. CH60: Hesw 5A 100
Tariff St. L5: Liv 2D 52
Tarleton Cl. L26: Halew 4G 93
Tarleton St. L1: Liv 4E 5 (6D 52)
Tarlton Cl. L35: Rainh 2G 59
Tarnbeck WA7: Nort 6E 115
Tarncliff L28: Stockb V 5E 39
Tarn Gro. WA11: St H 3F 29
Tarnmere Cl. L4: Walt 2G 35
Tarporley Cl. CH43: O'ton 6B 68
Tarragon Cl. L23: Thorn 4B 10
Tarran Dr. CH46: More 5B 48
Tarran Rd. CH46: More 5B 48
Tarran Way E. CH46: More 5B 48
Tarran Way Nth. CH46: More 5B 48
Tarran Way Sth. CH46: More 5B 48
Tarran Way W. CH46: More 4B 48
Tarves Wlk. L33: Kirkb 1B 24
Tarvin Cl. WA7: Run 1G 123
WA9: Sut M 3F 61
Tarvin Rd. CH62: East 3F 121
Tasker Ter. L35: Rainh 3A 60
Tasman Gro. WA9: St H 6C 42
Tate Cl. WA8: Wid 1B 96
Tate Liverpool 6B 4 (1B 70)
Tate St. L4: Walt 5F 35
Tatlock St. L5: Liv 3C 52
Tattersall Pl. L20: Boot 3B 34
Tattersall Rd. L21: Lith 4A 20
Tattersall Way L7: Liv 5C 54
Tatton Rd. CH42: Tran 4F 69
L9: Walt 5G 21
Taunton Av. WA9: Sut L 2H 61
Taunton Dr. L10: Ain 1C 22
Taunton Rd. CH45: Wall 1A 50
L36: Huy 5B 58
Taunton St. L15: Wav 1C 72
Taurus Rd. L14: Knott A 3C 56
Tavener Cl. CH63: Brom 2C 120
Tavington Rd. L26: Halew 2A 94
Tavistock Rd. CH45: Wall 1A 50
WA5: Penk 5G 81
Tavy Rd. L6: Liv 3G 53
Tawd St. L4: Kirkd 5E 35
Tawny Ct. WA7: Pal F 6A 114
Taylforth Cl. L9: Walt 6G 21
Taylor Cl. WA9: St H 5A 44
Taylor Rd. WA11: Hay 5G 31
Taylors Cl. L9: Walt 2E 35
Taylors La. L9: Walt 2E 35
WA5: Cuerd 1C 98
Taylors Row WA7: Run 3G 113
Taylor St. CH41: Birke 2G 69
L5: Liv 2D 52
WA8: Wid 2G 97
WA9: St H 5A 44
Taylor St. Ind. Est. L5: Liv 2E 53
Teakwood Cl. L6: Liv 2H 53
Teal Av. WA11: St H 5F 29
Teal Gro. L26: Halew 2G 93
Teals Way CH60: Hesw 5B 100
Teasville Rd. L18: Moss H 5A 74
Tebay Cl. L31: Mag 6F 7
Tebay Rd. CH62: East 5E 105
Teck St. L7: Liv 5G 53
Tedburn Cl. L25: Gate 5E 75
Tedbury Cl. L32: Kirkb 3A 24
Tedbury Wlk. L32: Kirkb 3A 24

Tedder Sq. WA8: Wid 3B 96
Teehey Cl. CH63: Hghr B 5F 87
Teehey Gdns. CH63: Hghr B 5F 87
Teehey La. CH63: Hghr B 5F 87
Tees Cl. L4: Kirkd 4E 35
Teesdale Cl. WA5: Gt San 2H 81
Teesdale Rd. CH63: Beb 1G 103
WA11: Hay 4E 31
Teesdale Way L35: Rainh 2A 60
Tees Pl. L4: Kirkd 4E 35
Tees St. CH41: Birke 6B 50
L4: Kirkd 4D 34
Teign Cl. L6: Liv 3G 53
Teignmouth Cl. L19: Garst 5F 91
Teilo St. L8: Liv 4G 71
Telary Cl. L5: Liv 2C 52
Telegraph Ho. L23: Crosb 4G 9
Telegraph La. CH45: Wall 2G 49
Telegraph Rd. CH48: Caldy 4F 83
CH60: Hesw 1A 100
CH61: Thurs 4F 83
Telegraph Way L32: Kirkb 1A 24
Telford Cl. CH43: O'ton 5D 68
WA8: Wid 5B 78
Telford Ct. L7: Liv 6H 53
Telford Dr. WA9: St H 6B 44
Tempest Hey L2: Liv 3C 4 (6C 52)
Temple Cl. L2: Liv 4D 4 (6C 52)
Temple La. L2: Liv 3D 4 (5C 52)
Templemore Av. L18: Moss H 6E 73
Templemore Rd. CH43: O'ton 5C 68
Temple Rd. CH42: Tran 1E 87
Temple St. L2: Liv 3D 4 (5C 52)
Templeton Cres. L12: W Der 4F 37
Tenbury Cl. WA5: Gt San 1H 81
Tenby Av. L21: Lith 2A 20
Tenby Dr. CH46: More 1D 66
WA7: Run 3H 113
Tenby St. L5: Liv 1G 53
Tennis St. WA10: St H 6C 28
Tennis St. Nth. WA10: St H 6C 28
Tennyson Av. CH42: Rock F 2H 87
Tennyson Rd. L36: Huy 1A 76
WA8: Wid 2E 97
Tennyson St. L20: Boot 6B 20
WA9: Sut M 5E 61
Tennyson Way L32: Kirkb 2H 23
Tenpin
Bootle 6G 11
Tensing Rd. L31: Mag 6C 6
Tenterden St. L5: Liv 3D 52
Tenth Av. L9: Ain 4B 22
Terence Rd. L16: Child 3H 73
Terminus Rd. CH62: Brom 2D 104
L36: Huy 2D 56
Tern Cl. L33: Kirkb 2A 14
WA8: Wid 5F 79
Ternhall Rd. L9: Faz 1D 36
Tern Way CH46: More 6H 47
WA10: St H 6G 41
Terrace Rd. WA8: Wid 6E 97
Terret Cft. L28: Stockb V 6D 38
Tetbury St. CH41: Birke 4E 69
Tetchill Cl. WA7: Nort 5F 115
Tetlow St. L4: Walt 5F 35
Tetlow Way L4: Walt 5F 35
Teulon Cl. L4: Walt 5F 35
Tewit Hall Cl. L24: Speke 2E 109
Tewit Hall Rd. L24: Speke 2E 109
Tewkesbury Cl. L12: Crox 1B 38
L25: Woolt 1F 93
Teynham Av. L34: Know 1F 39
Teynham Cres. L11: Norr G 3D 36
Thackeray Cl. L8: Liv 3F 71
Thackeray St. *L8: Liv* *3F 71*
(off Pomfret St.)
Thackeray Gdns. L30: Boot 3D 20
Thackray Rd. WA10: St H 5B 42
Thames Rd. WA9: Sut L 1G 61
Thames St. L8: Liv 3H 71
Thatchers Mt. WA5: Coll G 4F 45
THATTO HEATH 5C 42

Thatto Heath Rd. WA9: St H 5B **42**
   WA10: St H 5B **42**
Thatto Heath Station (Rail) 5B **42**
The . . . .
   Names prefixed with 'The' for
   example 'The Aerodrome' are
   indexed under the main name
   such as 'Aerodrome, The'
Thermal Rd. CH62: Brom 1D **104**
Thermopylae Pas. CH43: Noct 3H **67**
Thetford Rd. WA5: Gt San 3G **81**
Thickwood Moss La. WA11: Rainf 4F **17**
THINGWALL 6F **85**
Thingwall Av. L14: Knott A 5H **55**
Thingwall Dr. CH61: Irby 5E **85**
Thingwall Grange CH61: Thing 5F **85**
Thingwall Hall Dr. L14: Broad G 5H **55**
Thingwall La. L14: Knott A 4H **55**
Thingwall Recreation Cen. 5F **85**
Thingwall Rd. CH61: Irby 5B **84**
   L15: Wav 2F **73**
Thingwall Rd. E. CH61: Thing 5E **85**
Third Av. CH43: Bid 3F **67**
   L9: Ain .4B **22**
               (Fourth Av.)
   L9: Ain .4C **22**
              (Lower La.)
   L23: Crosb 5F **9**
   WA7: Pal F 5B **114**
Thirlmere Av. CH43: Noct 3G **67**
   L21: Lith 3D **20**
   WA11: St H 3E **29**
Thirlmere Cl. L31: Mag 5D **6**
   WA6: Frod 6H **123**
Thirlmere Ct. L5: Liv *2G* **53**
             (off Harding Cl.)
Thirlmere Dr. CH45: Wall 2D **50**
   L21: Lith 3D **20**
Thirlmere Grn. L5: Liv 2G **53**
Thirlmere Rd. L5: Liv 2G **53**
Thirlmere Wlk. L33: Kirkb 5H **13**
Thirlmere Way WA8: Wid 3A **96**
Thirlstane St. L17: Aig 6H **71**
Thirsk Cl. WA7: Run 1G **123**
Thistledown Cl. L17: Aig 6G **71**
Thistleton Av. CH41: Birke 1B **68**
Thistleton Cl. WA9: St H 1A **44**
Thistlewood Rd. L7: Liv 5C **54**
Thistley Hey Rd. L32: Kirkb 1B **24**
Thomas Cl. L19: Garst 6G **91**
Thomas Ct. CH43: O'ton 4E **69**
   WA7: Pal F 6B **114**
Thomas Dr. L14: Broad G 5G **55**
   L35: Presc 3C **58**
Thomas Jones Way WA7: Run 3E **113**
Thomas La. L14: Knott A 3H **55**
Thomas Steers Way L1: Liv . . .6D **4** (6C **52**)
Thomas St. CH41: Birke 4G **69**
   WA7: Run 2F **113**
   WA8: Wid 4E **97**
Thomaston St. L5: Liv 1E **53**
          (not continuous)
Thomas Winder Ct. L5: Kirkd 1D **52**
          (off Sterling Way)
Thompson St. CH41: Tran 5G **69**
   WA10: St H 4B **42**
Thomson Rd. L21: Sea 4H **19**
          (not continuous)
Thomson St. L6: Liv 3H **53**
Thorburn Cl. CH62: New F 3B **88**
Thorburn Ct. CH62: New F 2B **88**
Thorburn Cres. CH62: New F 3B **88**
Thorburn Lodge CH62: New F 3B **88**
Thorburn Rd. CH62: New F 3B **88**
Thorburn St. L7: Liv 6H **53**
Thorley Cl. L15: Wav 6E **55**
Thornaby Gro. WA9: St H 1B **60**
Thornbeck Cl. L12: Crox 2B **38**
Thornbridge Av. L21: Lith 3D **20**
Thornbrook Cl. L12: W Der 6H **37**
Thornbury Rd. L4: Walt 6A **36**
Thorncliffe Rd. CH44: Wall 4C **50**

Thorn Cl. WA5: Penk 6H **81**
   WA7: Run 6G **113**
Thorncroft Dr. CH61: Barn 1F **101**
Thorndale Rd. L22: Water 1F **19**
Thorndyke Cl. L35: Rainh 6C **60**
Thorne La. CH44: Wall 2B **50**
Thornes Rd. L6: Liv 4H **53**
Thorness Cl. CH49: Grea 1A **84**
Thorneycroft St. CH41: Birke 1C **68**
Thornfield Hey CH63: Spit 3A **104**
Thornfield Rd. L9: Walt 6F **21**
   L23: Thorn 3A **10**
Thornham Av. WA9: St H 5G **43**
Thornham Cl. CH49: Upton 2E **67**
Thornhead La. L12: W Der 1H **55**
Thornhill Rd. L15: Wav 2E **73**
Thornholme Cres. L11: Norr G 4E **37**
Thornhurst L32: Kirkb 4A **24**
Thornleigh Av. CH62: East 4F **121**
Thornley Rd. CH46: More 2A **66**
Thornridge CH46: More 1E **67**
Thorn Rd. WA7: Run 6G **113**
   WA10: St H 2A **42**
Thorns, The L31: Mag 5A **6**
Thorns Dr. CH49: Grea 1A **84**
Thornside Wlk. L25: Gate 5D **74**
THORNTON 3A **10**
Thornton WA8: Wid 3C **96**
Thornton Av. CH63: Hghr B 3F **87**
   L20: Boot 5D **20**
Thornton Comn. Rd.
   CH63: Raby M, Thorn H 6D **102**
Thornton Crematorium
   L23: Thorn 3C **10**
Thornton Cres. CH60: Hesw 1F **117**
Thorntondale Dr. WA5: Gt San 2G **81**
Thornton Gro. CH63: Hghr B 3F **87**
THORNTON HOUGH 1C **118**
Thornton Rd. CH45: Wall 1C **50**
   CH63: Hghr B 3F **87**
   L16: Child 6A **56**
   L20: Boot 6C **20**
          (not continuous)
Thornton St. CH41: Birke 1C **68**
   L21: Lith 5B **20**
Thorn Tree Cl. L24: Hale 4E **111**
Thorntree Cl. L17: Aig 6G **71**
Thornwood Cl. L6: Liv 2H **53**
Thornycroft Rd. L15: Wav 2B **72**
Thorpe Bank CH42: Rock F 3H **87**
Thorstone Dr. CH61: Irby 4A **84**
Thorsway CH42: Rock F 1H **87**
   CH48: Caldy 3D **82**
Threadneedle Ct. WA9: St H 5B **44**
Three Acres Cl. L25: Woolt 6A **74**
Three Butt La. L12: W Der 1D **54**
THREE LANES END 4H **65**
Threlfall St. L8: Liv 5G **71**
Thresher Av. CH49: Grea 5A **66**
Threshers, The L30: N'ton *5H* **11**
          (off Reapers Way)
Throne Rd. L11: Crox 2G **37**
Throne Wlk. L11: Crox *1G* **37**
          (off Throne Rd.)
Thurne Way L25: Gate 3C **74**
Thurnham St. L6: Liv 2A **54**
Thursby Cl. L32: Kirkb 3B **24**
Thursby Cres. L32: Kirkb 2B **24**
Thursby Dr. L32: Kirkb 3B **24**
Thursby Rd. CH62: Brom 3E **105**
Thursby Wlk. L32: Kirkb 3B **24**
THURSTASTON 6H **83**
Thurstaston Common Local Nature Reserve
   . . . . .3G **83**
Thurstaston Rd. CH60: Hesw 4C **100**
   CH61: Irby, Thurs 6H **83**
Thurston Billiard & Snooker Mus.
   . . . . .1G **5** (4E **53**)
Thurston Rd. L4: Walt 1H **53**
Tibb's Cross La. WA8: Bold H 1H **79**
Tiber St. L8: Liv 3H **71**
Tichbourne Way L6: Liv 4F **53**

Tickford Bank WA8: Wid 1C **96**
Tickle Av. WA9: St H 2H **43**
Tideswell Cl. L7: Liv 1H **71**
Tide Way CH45: Wall 5A **32**
Tiger Ct. L34: Presc 2A **58**
Tilbey Dr. WA6: Frod 6E **123**
Tilbrook Dr. WA9: St H 1H **61**
Tilbury Pl. WA7: Murd 1G **125**
Tildsley Cres. WA7: West 1D **125**
Tillotson Cl. L8: Liv 4E **71**
Tilney St. L9: Walt 5G **21**
Tilstock Av. CH62: New F 3B **88**
Tilstock Cl. L26: Halew 1A **94**
Tilstock Cres. CH43: Pren 2B **86**
Tilston Cl. L9: Faz 2B **36**
Tilston Rd. CH45: Wall 1C **50**
   L9: Faz 1B **36**
   L32: Kirkb 1G **23**
Timberland Cl. L25: Gate 2C **74**
Time Pk. L35: Whis 2F **59**
Timmis Cres. WA8: Wid 2E **97**
Timon Av. L20: Boot 1E **35**
Timor Av. WA9: St H 5C **42**
Timperley Ct. WA8: Wid *3F* **97**
          (off Alfred Cl.)
Timpron St. L7: Liv 1A **72**
Timway Dr. L12: W Der 5A **38**
Tinas Way CH49: Upton 4E **67**
Tinling Cl. L34: Presc 1E **59**
Tinsley Cl. L26: Halew 1G **93**
Tinsley St. L4: Walt 6G **35**
Tintagel Cl. WA7: Brook 1E **125**
Tintagel Rd. L11: Crox 6H **23**
Tintern Dr. CH46: More 1C **66**
Tiptree Cl. L12: Crox 1B **38**
Titchfield St. L3: Liv 3C **52**
   L5: Liv 3C **52**
Tithebarn Cl. CH60: Hesw 6D **100**
Tithebarn Dr. CH64: Park 5F **117**
Tithebarn Gro. L15: Wav 2E **73**
Tithe Barn La. L32: Kirkb 2H **23**
Tithebarn La. L31: Mell 4E **13**
Tithebarn Rd. L23: Crosb 5H **9**
   L34: Know 1F **39**
   WN4: Garsw 1E **31**
Tithebarn St. L2: Liv 3C **4** (5D **52**)
Titherington Way L15: Wav 3B **72**
Tithings, The WA7: Run 4A **114**
Tiverton Av. CH44: Wall 3C **50**
Tiverton Cl. L36: Huy 4B **58**
   WA8: Wid 6A **78**
Tiverton Rd. L26: Halew 5G **93**
Tiverton Sq. WA5: Penk 5G **81**
Tiverton St. L15: Wav 1C **72**
Tobermory Cl. WA11: Hay 6C **30**
Tobin Cl. L5: Liv 3C **52**
Tobin St. CH44: Wall 3F **51**
Tobruk Rd. L36: Huy 3F **57**
Todd Rd. WA9: St H 2F **43**
Toft Cl. WA8: Wid 2D **96**
Toft St. L7: Liv 5A **54**
Toftwood Av. L35: Rainh 6B **60**
Toftwood Gdns. L35: Rainh 6B **60**
Tokenspire Pk. L33: Know I 4D **24**
Toleman Av. CH63: Beb 6A **88**
Tollemache Rd. CH41: Birke 2B **68**
   CH43: Bid 2A **68**
   CH43: Clau 2B **68**
Tollemache St. CH45: New B 5E **33**
Tollerton Rd. L12: W Der 1D **54**
Tolpuddle Rd. L25: Woolt 6B **74**
Tolpuddle Way L4: Kirkd 5D **34**
Tolver Ho. WA10: St H 1E **43**
          (off Tolver St.)
Tolver St. WA10: St H 1E **43**
Tom Mann Cl. L3: Liv 2F **5** (5D **52**)
Tommy Gent Way L31: Mag 1B **12**
Tonbridge Cl. L24: Speke 1D **108**
Tonbridge Dr. L10: Ain 6B **12**
Topaz Cl. L4: Walt 3E **35**
Topcliffe Gro. L12: Crox 2C **38**
Topgate Cl. CH60: Hesw 5F **101**

Topham Dr. L9: Ain 1H **21**
Topham Ter. L9: Ain 3H **21**
Topsham Cl. L25: Gate 5E **75**
Torcross Way L25: Gate 5E **75**
L26: Halew 2G **93**
Tordelow Cl. L6: Liv 3G **53**
Toronto Cl. L36: Huy 6F **39**
Toronto St. CH44: Wall 4G **51**
Torpoint Cl. L14: Knott A 1C **56**
Torr Dr. CH62: East 6G **105**
Torrington Dr. CH61: Thing 5F **85**
L26: Halew 4G **93**
Torrington Gdns. CH61: Thing 4F **85**
Torrington Rd. CH44: Wall 3C **50**
L19: Gras 4F **91**
Torrisholme Rd. L9: Ain 2B **36**
Torr St. L5: Liv 1E **53**
(not continuous)
Torus Rd. L13: Liv 3E **55**
Tor Vw. L15: Wav 3E **73**
Torwood CH43: Noct 2H **67**
Total Fitness
Bootle 5H **11**
Liverpool 5D **54**
Prenton 3H **85**
Tothale Turn L27: N'ley 5H **75**
Totland Cl. WA5: Gt San 2E **81**
Totnes Av. L26: Halew 2H **93**
Totnes Rd. L11: Crox 6G **23**
Tourist Info. Cen.
Liverpool John Lennon Airport **3E 109**
Liverpool, Salthouse Quay **1C 70**
Liverpool, Williamson St. . . . . . **4E 5 (6D 52)**
Runcorn **4F 113**
St Helens **2E 43**
Towcester St. L21: Lith 5B **20**
Tower Gdns. L3: Liv 4C **4** (6B **52**)
TOWER HILL **3B 14**
Tower Hill CH42: Tran 6F **69**
Towerlands St. L7: Liv 6H **53**
Tower La. WA7: Nort 6E **115**
Tower Prom. CH45: New B 4E **33**
Tower Quays CH41: Birke 1G **69**
Tower Rd. CH41: Birke 1G **69**
CH42: Tran 2D **86**
(Reservoir Rd.)
CH42: Tran 6F **69**
(Tower Hill)
Tower Rd. Nth. CH60: Hesw 3C **100**
Tower Rd. Sth. CH60: Hesw 4D **100**
Towers, The CH42: Tran 1G **87**
Towers Av. L31: Mag 5B **6**
Towers Rd. L16: Child 3G **73**
Tower St. L3: Liv 4D **70**
Tower Way L25: Woolt 6C **74**
Tower Wharf CH41: Birke 1G **69**
Towneley Ct. WA8: Wid 2E **97**
TOWN END **3A 78**
Townfield Cen. CH43: O'ton 6A **68**
Townfield Cl. CH43: O'ton 6A **68**
Townfield Gdns. CH63: Hghr B 4H **87**
Townfield La. CH43: O'ton 6A **68**
CH63: Beb 4H **87**
CH63: Beb, Hghr B 4H **87**
WA6: Frod 6H **123**
Townfield Rd. CH48: W Kir 1B **82**
WA7: Wind H 3E **115**
Town Flds. CH45: Wall 1A **50**
Townfield Vw. WA7: Wind H 3E **115**
Townfield Way CH44: Wall 3D **50**
Town Hall Dr. WA7: Run 4F **113**
Town La. CH63: Hghr B 5F **87**
L24: Hale 4D **110**
Townley Ct. *CH47: Hoy* *2B* ***64***
(off Seaview)
Town Mdw. La. CH46: More 1H **65**
Town Rd. CH42: Tran 6F **69**
Town Row L12: W Der 6F **37**
Townsend Av. L11: Norr G 5C **36**
L13: Liv 5C **36**
Townsend La. L4: Walt 1H **53**
L6: Liv 1A **54**
L13: Liv 1A **54**
Townsend St. CH41: Birke 6A **50**
L5: Kirkd 1C **52**
Townsend Vw. L11: Norr G 2C **36**
L21: Ford 1B **20**
Townshend Av. CH61: Irby 6B **84**
Town Sq. *WA7: Pal F* *6B* ***114***
(off Halton Lea Shop. Cen.)
Town Vw. CH43: O'ton 4E **69**
Town Vw. M. CH43: O'ton 4E **69**
Town Wlk. *WA7: Pal F* *6B* ***114***
(off Halton Lea Shop. Cen.)
Towson St. L5: Liv 1F **53**
(not continuous)
TOXTETH **3E 71**
Toxteth Gro. L8: Liv 5G **71**
Toxteth St. L8: Liv 4F **71**
(not continuous)
Tradewind Sq. L1: Liv 6F **5**
TRAFALGAR **1A 104**
Trafalgar Av. CH44: Wall 2F **51**
Trafalgar Ct. WA8: Wid 5E **97**
Trafalgar Dr. CH63: Beb 1A **104**
Trafalgar Rd. CH44: Wall 2E **51**
Trafalgar St. WA10: St H 1C **42**
Trafalgar Way L6: Liv 4F **53**
Trafford Cres. WA7: Run 1G **123**
Tragan Dr. WA5: Penk 6F **81**
Tramway Rd. L17: Aig 6A **72**
TRANMERE **6G 69**
Tranmere Recreation Cen. **1E 87**
Tranmere Rovers FC **1E 87**
Trapwood Cl. WA10: Eccl 2H **41**
Travanson Cl. L10: Faz 5F **23**
Travers' Entry WA9: Bold 6C **44**
Traverse St. WA9: St H 2G **43**
Travis Dr. L33: Kirkb 4B **14**
Travis St. WA8: Wid 3F **97**
Trawden Way L21: Ford 5C **10**
Traynor Ct. *CH43: O'ton* *4C* ***68***
(off Beresford Rd.)
Treborth St. L8: Liv 4G **71**
Trecastle Rd. L33: Kirkb 5C **14**
Tree Bank Cl. WA7: Run 5E **113**
Treetop Ct. L6: Liv 3A **54**
Treetops Dr. CH41: Birke 6H **49**
Tree Vw. Ct. L31: Mag 1C **12**
Trefoil Cl. L8: Liv 3F **71**
Treforris Rd. CH45: Wall 6B **32**
Trefula Pk. L12: W Der 1E **55**
Trelawney Cl. L25: Gate 3D **74**
Tremore Cl. L12: W Der 4F **37**
Trenance Cl. WA7: Brook 2E **125**
Trendeal Rd. L11: Crox 6H **23**
Trent Av. L14: Broad G 4B **56**
L31: Mag 5E **7**
Trent Cl. L12: Crox 2H **37**
L35: Rainh 4H **59**
WA8: Wid 5F **79**
WA9: Sut L 2G **61**
Trentham Av. L18: Moss H 4D **72**
Trentham Cl. WA8: Wid 5F **79**
Trentham Rd. CH44: Wall 4E **51**
L32: Kirkb 2G **23**
Trentham St. WA7: Run 2D **112**
Trentham Wlk. L32: Kirkb 2G **23**
Trent Pl. L35: Rainh 4H **59**
Trent Rd. L35: Rainh 4H **59**
Trent St. CH41: Birke 6B **50**
L5: Kirkd 1C **52**
Trent Way CH60: Hesw 1F **117**
L21: Lith 2A **20**
Tressel Dr. WA9: Sut M 4E **61**
Tressell St. L9: Walt 2F **35**
Trevelyan St. L9: Walt 2F **35**
Treviot Cl. L33: Kirkb 3H **13**
Trevor Dr. L23: Crosb 6H **9**
Trevor Rd. L9: Walt 5G **21**
Triad, The L20: Boot 1C **34**
Trident Pk. WA7: Pal F 6A **114**
Trimley Cl. CH49: Upton 4C **66**
Tring Cl. CH49: Upton 2E **67**
Trinity Ct. CH47: Hoy 2B **64**
Trinity Gdns. CH43: O'ton 4B **68**
CH47: Hoy 2B **64**
WA6: Frod 6G **123**
Trinity Gro. L23: Blun 6D **8**
Trinity Ho. WA6: Frod 6G **123**
Trinity La. CH41: Birke 2G **69**
Trinity Pl. L20: Boot 2D **34**
WA8: Wid 4F **97**
Trinity Rd. CH44: Wall 2D **50**
CH47: Hoy 2B **64**
L20: Boot 3C **34**
Trinity St. CH41: Birke 2E **69**
WA7: Run 2F **113**
WA9: St H 1G **43**
Trinity Wlk. L3: Liv 1H **5**
Trispen Cl. L26: Halew 3G **93**
Trispen Rd. L11: Crox 1H **37**
Trispen Wlk. *L11: Crox* *1H* ***37***
(off Trispen Rd.)
Tristram's Cft. L30: N'ton 6D **10**
Triumph Trading Pk., The
L24: Speke 5B **92**
Triumph Way L24: Hunts X, Speke 5B **92**
Troon Cl. CH63: Brom 2C **120**
L12: W Der 1A **56**
WA11: Hay 6C **30**
Trooper Cl. L12: W Der 6A **38**
Trotwood Cl. L9: Ain 3B **22**
Troutbeck Av. L31: Mag 5D **6**
WA12: Newt W 1G **45**
Troutbeck Cl. CH49: Woodc 1E **85**
WA7: Beech 2C **124**
Troutbeck Gro. WA11: St H 1F **29**
Troutbeck Rd. L18: Moss H 4H **73**
Trouville Rd. L4: Walt 6A **36**
Trowbridge St. L3: Liv 4H **5** (6E **53**)
Trueman Cl. CH43: Bid 1G **67**
Trueman St. L3: Liv 2E **5** (5D **52**)
Truman Cl. WA8: Wid 6D **78**
Truro Av. L30: N'ton 5F **11**
Truro Cl. WA7: Brook 1E **125**
WA11: St H 4H **29**
Truro Rd. L15: Wav 3E **73**
Tudor Av. CH44: Wall 5G **51**
CH63: Beb 2A **104**
Tudor Cl. L7: Liv 6F **53**
WA11: Rainf 1E **17**
Tudor Ct. *L19: Gras* *4E* ***91***
(off Dugdale Cl.)
Tudor Grange CH49: Grea 6B **66**
Tudor Rd. CH42: Tran 6G **69**
L23: Crosb 6F **9**
L25: Hunts X 4E **93**
WA7: Manor P 2D **114**
Tudor St. Nth. L6: Liv 4H **53**
Tudor St. Sth. L6: Liv 4H **53**
Tudor Vw. L33: Kirkb 4A **14**
(not continuous)
Tudorville Rd. CH63: Beb 6H **87**
Tudor Way CH60: Hesw 5F **101**
TUE BROOK **1C 54**
Tue La. WA8: Cron 3H **77**
Tuffins Cnr. L27: N'ley 4F **75**
Tulip Av. CH41: Birke 1B **68**
Tulip Rd. L15: Wav 2F **73**
WA11: Hay 5H **31**
Tullimore Rd. L18: Moss H 2E **91**
Tullis St. WA10: St H 3C **42**
Tulloch St. L6: Liv 4H **53**
Tully Av. WA12: Newt W 2G **45**
Tumilty Av. L20: Boot 1E **35**
Tunbridge Cl. WA5: Gt San 1H **81**
Tunnage Sq. L1: Liv 6F **5**
Tunnel Rd. CH41: Birke 4H **69**
L7: Liv 1H **71**
Tunnel Top Nth. WA4: Dutt 1H **125**
WA7: Pres B 1H **125**
Tunstall Cl. CH49: Upton 4C **66**
Tunstall St. L7: Liv 2A **72**

Tunstalls Way. WA9: Clock F 3H **61**
Tupelo Cl. L12: Crox 1B **38**
Tupman St. L8: Liv 4F **71**
Turmar Av. CH61: Thing 5F **85**
Turnacre L14: Broad G 4A **56**
Turnall Rd. WA8: Wid 4H **95**
Turnberry Cl. CH46: More 6H **47**
   L12: W Der 1B **56**
   L36: Roby 6E **57**
Turnbridge Rd. L31: Mag 4B **6**
Turner Av. L20: Boot 4E **21**
Turner Cl. L8: Liv 6G **71**
   WA8: Wid 6B **78**
Turner Gro. L33: Kirkb 3A **14**
Turner Home, The L8: Liv 5H **71**
Turners Ct. L25: Gate 6E **75**
Turner St. CH41: Birke 4E **69**
Turney Rd. CH44: Wall 3C **50**
Turnstone Bus. Pk. WA8: Wid 4G **97**
Turnstone Cl. L12: Crox 2A **38**
Turnstone Dr. L26: Halew 2G **93**
Turret Rd. CH45: Wall 1C **50**
Turriff Dr. CH63: East 3C **120**
Turriff Rd. L14: Knott A 2C **56**
Turton Cl. L24: Hale 4D **110**
Turton St. L5: Kirkd 1D **52**
Tuscan Cl. WA8: Wid 4F **79**
Tuson Dr. WA8: Wid 5D **78**
Tweed Cl. L6: Liv 3A **54**
Tweed St. CH41: Birke 6C **50**
Twickenham Dr. CH46: Leas 4D **48**
   L36: Roby 6E **57**
Twickenham St. L6: Liv 1H **53**
Twigden Cl. L10: Faz 3D **22**
Twig La. L31: Mag 6D **6**
   L36: Huy 4E **57**
Two Butt La. L35: Whis, Rainh 2G **59**
Twomey Cl. L5: Liv 3C **52**
Twyford Cl. L21: Lith 2B **20**
Twyford Cl. L31: Mag 6D **6**
   WA8: Wid 5F **79**
Twyford La. WA8: Wid 2G **79**
Twyford Pl. WA9: St H 2G **43**
Twyford St. L6: Liv 1H **53**
Tyberton Pl. L25: Hunts X 5E **93**
Tyburn Cl. CH63: Spit 3H **103**
Tyburn Rd. CH63: Spit 3H **103**
Tyndall Av. L22: Water 3H **19**
Tyne Cl. L4: Kirkd 5E **35**
   WA9: St H 1B **60**
Tynemouth Cl. L5: Liv 2G **53**
Tynemouth Rd. WA7: Murd 1E **125**
Tyne St. CH41: Birke 6B **50**
Tynron Gro. CH43: Noct 5H **67**
Tynville Rd. L9: Ain 4A **22**
Tynwald Cl. L13: Liv 2D **54**
Tynwald Cres. WA8: Wid 4D **78**
Tynwald Hill L13: Liv 3D **54**
Tynwald Pl. L13: Liv 3D **54**
Tynwald Rd. CH48: W Kir 1A **82**
Tyrer Gro. L34: Presc 6E **41**
Tyrers Av. L31: Lyd 2A **6**
Tyrer St. CH41: Birke 6B **50**
   L1: Liv 4F **5** (6D **52**)

U

U-boat Story 2A **70**
Uldale Cl. L11: Norr G 3E **37**
Uldale Way L11: Norr G 3E **37**
Ullet Rd. L8: Liv 5H **71**
   L17: Aig 5H **71**
Ullet Wlk. L17: Aig 4B **72**
Ullswater Av. CH43: Noct 3H **67**
   WA11: St H 3E **29**
Ullswater Cl. L33: Kirkb 5H **13**
Ullswater Gro. WA7: Beech 2H **123**
Ullswater Ho. L17: Aig 1B **90**
Ullswater St. L5: Liv 1G **53**
Ulster Rd. L13: Liv 4F **55**

Ulverscroft CH43: O'ton 5B **68**
Ulverston Cl. L31: Mag 5D **6**
   WA11: Hay 5C **30**
Ulverston Lawn L27: N'ley 5H **75**
Undercliffe Rd. L13: Liv 3E **55**
Underhill Rd. WA10: St H 3B **42**
Underley St. L7: Liv 2A **72**
Underley Ter. CH62: New F 4B **88**
Underwater Street *4B 4*
   (in Cunard Building, Water St.)
Underway, The WA7: Halt 5B **114**
Unicorn Cl. L11: Crox 1G **37**
Unicorn Way CH41: Tran 4H **69**
Union Bank La. WA8: Bold H 2E **62**
Union Ct. L2: Liv 4D **4** (6C **52**)
Union St. CH42: Tran 6H **69**
   CH44: Wall 3F **51**
   L3: Liv 3B **4** (5B **52**)
   WA7: Run 3F **113**
   WA10: St H 6E **29**
Union Ter. CH45: New B 4D **32**
Unity Bldg. L3: Liv 3B **4**
Unity Gro. L34: Know 6C **24**
Unity Theatre 6H **5**
University of Liverpool
   Biosciences Building 6G **53**
   Cambridge St. 1F **71**
   Central Campus *6F 53*
       (off Mt. Pleasant)
   North Campus 6F **53**
   Peach St. 6G **53**
University of Liverpool Library *1G 71*
       (off Chatham St.)
University of Liverpool Sports Cen. . .6F **53**
University Rd. L20: Boot 3D **34**
Upavon Av. CH49: Grea 2H **65**
Upchurch Cl. L8: Liv 5F **71**
Upland Cl. WA10: St H 5H **41**
Upland Rd. CH49: Upton 3D **66**
   WA10: St H 5H **41**
Uplands, The CH43: O'ton 5A **68**
   WA7: Pal F 6C **114**
Uplands Rd. CH62: Brom 4C **104**
Up. Baker St. L6: Liv 4G **53**
Up. Beau St. L5: Liv 3E **53**
Up. Beckwith St. CH41: Birke 1D **68**
UPPER BIDSTON VILLAGE 6G **49**
Up. Brassey St. CH41: Birke 1B **68**
Up. Bute St. L5: Liv 3E **53**
Up. Duke St. L1: Liv 6G **5** (1E **71**)
Up. Essex St. L8: Liv 4F **71**
Up. Flaybrick Rd. CH41: Birke 2A **68**
Up. Frederick St. L1: Liv 6E **5** (1D **70**)
       (not continuous)
Up. Hampton St. L8: Liv 2F **71**
Up. Harrington St. L8: Liv 3E **71**
Up. Hill St. L8: Liv 3E **71**
       (not continuous)
Up. Hope Pl. L7: Liv 6H **5** (1F **71**)
Up. Huskisson St. L8: Liv 2G **71**
Up. Mann St. L8: Liv 3E **71**
       (not continuous)
Up. Mason St. L7: Liv 6G **53**
Up. Mersey Rd. WA8: Wid 6E **97**
Up. Newington L1: Liv 5G **5** (6E **53**)
Up. Park St. L8: Liv 4F **71**
Up. Parliament St. L8: Liv 2E **71**
Up. Pitt St. L1: Liv 1D **70**
       (not continuous)
Up. Pownall St. L1: Liv 1D **70**
Up. Raby Rd. CH64: Nest 5C **118**
Up. Rice La. CH44: Wall 2E **51**
Up. Stanhope St. L8: Liv 2E **71**
       (not continuous)
Up. Warwick St. L8: Liv 3F **71**
Up. William St. L3: Liv 3B **52**
Uppingham Av. L10: Ain 1C **22**
Uppingham Rd. CH44: Wall 2B **50**
   L13: Liv 2D **54**
UPTON
   CH49 . . . . .4E **67**
   WA8 .6H **77**

Upton Barn L31: Mag 5B **6**
Upton Bridle Path WA8: Wid 5D **78**
       (not continuous)
Upton By-Pass CH49: Upton 3C **66**
Upton Cl. CH49: Upton 4D **66**
   L24: Speke 2G **109**
Upton Ct. CH49: Upton 3E **67**
Upton Dr. WA5: Penk 4H **81**
Upton Grange WA8: Wid 6B **78**
Upton Grn. L24: Speke 2G **109**
Upton La. WA8: Wid 5C **78**
Upton Pk. Dr. CH49: Upton 3E **67**
Upton Rd. CH41: Birke 4G **67**
   CH43: Bid, Noct 4G **67**
   CH46: More 1C **66**
UPTON ROCKS 6D **78**
Upton Rocks Av. WA8: Wid 5C **78**
Upton Rocks M. WA8: Wid 5C **78**
Upton Station (Rail) 4G **67**
Urmson Rd. CH45: Wall 2D **50**
Ursula St. L20: Boot 4D **34**
Utkinton Cl. CH43: O'ton 6B **68**
Utting Av. L4: Walt 4H **35**
Utting Av. E. L11: Norr G 4C **36**
UVECO Bus. Cen. CH41: Birke 6D **50**
Uxbridge St. L7: Liv 6H **53**

V

Vahler Ter. WA7: Run 3G **113**
Vale Ct. *L21: Sea* *5A 20*
       (off Seaforth Va. Nth.)
Vale Dr. CH45: New B 6E **33**
Vale Gro. L32: Kirkb 2C **24**
Vale Lodge L9: Walt 1F **35**
Valencia Gro. L34: Eccl P 6G **41**
Valencia Rd. L15: Wav 1E **73**
Valentia Rd. CH47: Hoy 3A **64**
Valentine Gro. L10: Ain 2C **22**
Valentine Rd. WA12: Newt W 2H **45**
Valentines Bldg. L9: Ain 2A **22**
Valentines Way L9: Ain 1A **22**
Valerian Rd. CH41: Birke 2B **68**
Valerie Cl. L10: Faz 5F **23**
Valerie Pk. 6D **40**
Vale Rd. L23: Crosb 5F **9**
   L25: Woolt 6A **74**
Valescourt Rd. L12: W Der 2G **55**
Valiant Cl. L12: Crox 3C **38**
Valiant Ho. CH41: Birke 3H **69**
Valiant Way CH41: Tran 5H **69**
Valkyrie Rd. CH45: Wall 2C **50**
Vallance Rd. L4: Walt 6A **36**
Valleybrook Gro. CH63: Spit 3B **104**
Valley Cl. L10: Ain 2D **22**
   L23: Crosb 5B **10**
Valley Community Theatre 4F **75**
Valley Rd. CH41: Birke 5H **49**
   CH62: Brom 5D **104**
   L4: Walt 1G **53**
   L32: Faz, Kirkb 4E **23**
Valley Rd. Bus. Pk. CH41: Birke 6A **50**
Vanbrugh Cres. L4: Walt 6A **36**
Vanbrugh Rd. L4: Walt 5A **36**
Vancouver Rd. L27: N'ley 4G **75**
Vanderbilt Av. L9: Ain 3H **21**
Vanderbyl Av. CH62: Spit 3C **104**
Vandries St. L3: Liv 3B **52**
Vandyke St. L8: Liv 2A **72**
Vanguard St. L5: Liv 1F **53**
Vanguard Way CH41: Tran 6H **69**
Vardon St. CH41: Birke 1F **69**
Varley Rd. L19: Aig 2E **91**
   WA9: St H 1G **43**
Varthen St. L5: Liv 1G **53**
Vaughan Rd. CH45: New B 5E **33**
Vaughan St. CH41: Birke 1B **68**
Vaux Cres. L20: Boot 6D **20**
VAUXHALL 3C **52**
Vauxhall Bus. Cen. *L3: Liv* *4C 52*
       (off Eaton St.)

Vauxhall Cl. WA5: Penk 5H 81
Vauxhall Rd. L3: Liv 1D 4 (4C 52)
L5: Liv 4C 52
Vaux Pl. L20: Boot 6D 20
Venables Cl. CH63: Spit 4B 104
Venables Dr. CH63: Spit 3A 104
Venice St. L5: Liv 1F 53
Venmore St. L5: Liv 1F 53
(not continuous)
Ventnor Cl. WA5: Gt San 2E 81
Ventnor Rd. L15: Wav 1D 72
Venture Ct. CH41: Birke 4G 69
Venture Point W. L24: Speke 6D 92
Venture Works L33: Know I 2E 25
Verbena Cl. WA7: Beech 3B 124
Verdala Pk. L18: Moss H 1G 91
Verdi Av. L21: Sea 5A 20
Verdi St. L21: Sea 5H 19
Verdi Ter. L21: Sea 6H 19
Vere St. L8: Liv 4E 71
Vermont Av. L23: Crosb 5F 9
Vermont Cl. L33: Kirkb 2H 13
Vermont Rd. L23: Crosb 5F 9
Vermont Way L20: Boot 1C 34
Verney Cres. L19: Aller 3G 91
Verney Cres. Sth. L19: Aller 3G 91
Vernon Av. CH44: Wall 5F 51
CH66: Hoot 5G 121
Vernon St. L2: Liv 3D 4 (5C 52)
WA9: St H 1G 43
Verona St. L5: Liv 1F 53
Veronica Cl. L12: Crox 2A 38
Veronica M. WA8: Wid 2B 96
Verulam Cl. L3: Liv 2G 71
Verwood Cl. CH61: Irby 4B 84
Verwood Dr. L12: Crox 2C 38
Veryan Cl. L26: Halew 2H 93
Vescock St. L5: Liv 3D 52
Vesta Rd. L19: Garst 1H 107
Vesty Bus. Pk. L30: N'ton 3G 21
Vesty Rd. L30: N'ton 3G 21
Vesuvian Dr. L19: Garst 1H 107
Vesuvius Pl. L5: Kirkd 1D 52
Vesuvius St. L5: Kirkd 1D 52
Viaduct St. WA12: Newt W 2H 45
Vicarage Cl. CH42: Tran 2D 86
L18: Moss H 1F 91
L24: Hale 4E 111
Vicarage Dr. WA11: Hay 4C 30
Vicarage Gro. CH44: Wall 2E 51
Vicarage Lawn L25: Gate 4E 75
Vicarage Pl. L34: Presc 1C 58
Vicarage Rd. WA8: Wid 4E 97
WA11: Hay 4C 30
Vicar Rd. L6: Liv 6A 36
Viceroy St. L5: Liv 1F 53
Vickers Rd. WA8: Wid 6D 96
Victoria Av. CH60: Hesw 1D 116
L14: Broad G 5H 55
L15: Wav 1D 72
L23: Blun 5E 9
WA5: Gt San 3F 81
WA8: Wid 6E 79
WA11: St H 3E 29
Victoria Cl. L17: Aig 6C 72
Victoria Ct. CH42: Rock F 2A 88
L15: Wav 1E 73
L17: Aig 5H 71
(off Lit. Parkfield Rd.)
Victoria Dr. CH42: Rock F 2A 88
CH48: W Kir 1A 82
L9: Walt 5F 21
Victoria Falls Rd. L27: N'ley 5H 75
Victoria Flds. CH42: Tran 5E 69
Victoria Gallery & Mus. 6F 53
Victoria Gdns. CH43: O'ton 5D 68
Victoria Gro. WA8: Wid 6E 79
Victoria Hall L2: Liv 2D 4
Victoria Ho. L34: Presc 1D 58
WA11: Rainf 2F 17
Victoria La. CH43: O'ton 5D 68
Victoria Mt. CH43: O'ton 5D 68

Victoria Pde. CH45: New B 4E 33
VICTORIA PARK
L9 . . . . .4E 21
L15 . . . . .1E 73
Victoria Pk.
City Rd. 5D 28
Victoria Pk. Glasshouses 2E 97
Victoria Pk. Rd. CH42: Tran 1F 87
Victoria Pl. CH44: Wall 5H 51
L35: Rainh 4A 60
Victoria Prom. WA8: Wid 1E 113
Victoria Rd. CH42: Tran 5E 69
CH45: New B 5C 32
CH48: W Kir 2A 82
CH63: Hghr B 5F 87
L13: Liv 1C 54
L17: Aig 1C 90
L22: Water 3G 19
L23: Crosb 5F 9
L36: Huy 5H 57
WA5: Penk 5F 81
WA7: Run 3E 113
(not continuous)
WA8: Wid 4E 97
Victoria Rd. W. L23: Blun 5E 9
Victoria Sq. WA8: Wid 4E 97
WA10: St H 1E 43
Victoria St. CH62: Port S 6B 88
L1: Liv 4D 4 (6C 52)
L2: Liv 4D 4 (6C 52)
L35: Rainh 4A 60
WA8: Wid 4E 97
WA10: St H 6E 29
WA11: Rainf 2F 17
Victoria Ter. L15: Wav 3E 73
(off Prince Alfred Rd.)
L35: Rainh 4A 60
Victoria Trad. Est. L35: Rainh 4A 60
(off Victoria St.)
WA8: Wid 5E 97
Victoria Vs. L35: Rainh 4A 60
Victor St. L15: Wav 1B 72
Victory Cl. L30: Boot 3E 21
Vienna St. L5: Liv 1F 53
Viennese Rd. L25: Gate 3D 74
View 146 L5: Liv 2E 53
Viewpark Cl. L16: Child 2B 74
View Rd. L35: Rainh 5A 60
Viking Cl. L21: Lith 4A 20
Viking Ct. WA8: Wid 4E 97
(off Vine St.)
Village, The CH63: Beb 5A 88
Village Cl. CH45: Wall 1A 50
WA7: Cas 5C 114
Village Ct. CH43: O'ton 5C 68
CH61: Irby 5B 84
L17: Aig 1A 90
Village Courts L30: N'ton 4F 11
Village Grn. Ct. CH43: Bid 1G 67
Village M. CH45: Wall 1A 50
CH63: Hghr B 5F 87
Village Nook L10: Ain 1C 22
Village Rd. CH43: O'ton 5C 68
CH48: W Kir 2B 82
CH60: Hesw 6D 100
CH63: Hghr B 5F 87
Village St. L6: Liv 3F 53
WA7: Nort 3G 115
Village Way CH45: Wall 2A 50
Villa Gloria Cl. L19: Aig 3E 91
Villas Rd. L31: Mag 6G 7
Villiers Ct. L34: Know 6D 24
Villiers Cres. WA10: Eccl 6F 27
Villiers Rd. L34: Know 5D 24
Vincent Cl. L1: Liv 6F 5 (1D 70)
Vincent Naughton Ct.
CH41: Birke 4G 69
Vincent Rd. L21: Lith 2C 20
L35: Rainh 3H 59
Vincent St. CH41: Birke 2F 69
L13: Liv 6E 55
WA10: St H 1E 43

Vine Cres. WA5: Gt San 3H 81
Vine Ho. L21: Sea 5A 20
Vineries, The L25: Woolt 6A 74
Vineside Rd. L12: W Der 2H 55
Vine St. L7: Liv 1G 71
WA7: Run 3E 113
WA8: Wid 4E 97
Vine Ter. WA8: Wid 1G 95
Vineyard St. L19: Garst 6A 92
Vining Ho. L35: Presc 1F 59
Vining St. L8: Liv 3F 71
Viola Cl. L33: Kirkb 4H 13
Viola St. L20: Boot 4C 34
Violet Rd. CH41: Birke 2B 68
L21: Lith 5B 20
Violet St. WA8: Wid 4E 97
Virgil St. L5: Liv 3E 53
WA10: St H 1C 42
Virginia Av. L31: Lyd 4C 6
Virginia Gro. L31: Lyd 4B 6
Virginia Rd. CH45: New B 4D 32
Virgin's La. L23: Thorn 2H 9
Viscount Cen. L24: Speke 6F 93
Viscount Dr. L24: Hale 3G 109
Vista Rd. WA7: Run 5E 113
WA11: Hay 4H 31
WA12: Newt W 1H 45
Vista Way WA12: Newt W 1H 45
Vitesse Rd. L24: Speke 5B 92
Vittoria Cl. CH41: Birke 2F 69
Vittoria Ct. CH41: Birke 2F 69
Vittoria St. CH41: Birke 2E 69
Vivian Av. CH44: Wall 5G 51
Vixen Gro. WA8: Wid 5D 78
Voelas St. L8: Liv 3G 71
Vogan Av. L23: Crosb 6A 10
Volunteer St. WA6: Frod 6H 123
WA10: St H 1D 42
Vronhill Cl. L8: Liv 3G 71
Vue Cinema
Birkenhead 3G 69
Vulcan Cl. CH41: Birke 1B 68
L19: Garst 1G 107
Vulcan St. CH41: Birke 1B 68
L3: Liv 3B 52
L19: Garst 1G 107
L20: Boot 1A 34
Vyner Cl. CH43: Noct 3A 68
Vyner Ct. CH43: Noct 3A 68
Vyner Pk. CH43: Noct 3A 68
Vyner Rd. CH45: Wall 2B 50
Vyner Rd. Nth. CH43: Bid 2H 67
L25: Gate 4C 74
Vyner Rd. Sth. CH43: Bid, Noct 3H 67
L25: Gate 4D 74
Vyrnwy St. L5: Liv 1G 53

W

WADDICAR .5F 13
Waddicar La. L31: Mell 6E 13
Wadebridge Rd. L10: Faz 5F 23
Wadeson Rd. L4: Walt 3B 36
Wadham Pk. L20: Boot 3D 34
Wadham Rd. L20: Boot 4C 34
Wagon La. WA11: Hay 1D 44
Waine Gro. L35: Whis 2G 59
Waine St. WA9: St H 1H 43
WA11: Hay 5B 30
Wainwright Cl. L7: Liv 1A 72
Wainwright Gro.
L19: Garst 5G 91
Wakefield Dr. CH46: Leas 3D 48
Wakefield Rd. L30: N'ton 1G 34
Wakefield St. L3: Liv 1G 5 (4E 53)
Walby Cl. CH49: Woodc 1G 85
Walden Rd. L14: Knott A 4G 55
Waldgrave Pl. L15: Wav 6E 55
Waldgrave Rd. L15: Wav 6E 55
Waldron Cl. L3: Liv 1D 4 (4C 52)
Walford Cl. CH63: Spit 3H 103

Walk, The L24: Speke 3B **108**
*L28: Stockb V 6E **39***
(off Dannette Hey)
Walker Art Gallery 2F 5 (5D 52)
Walker Av. WA9: Sut M 4F **61**
Walker Dr. L20: Boot 4C **20**
Walker Hgts. *CH42: Tran 6F **69***
(off Walker St.)
Walker M. CH42: Tran 6F **69**
Walker Pl. CH42: Tran 6F **69**
Walker Rd. L21: Lith 4A **20**
Walker's Cft. CH45: Wall 2B **50**
Walkers La. WA5: Penk 6G **81**
WA9: Sut M 4E **61**
Walker St. CH42: Tran 6F **69**
CH47: Hoy 2B **64**
CH62: Port S 5B **88**
L6: Liv 4G **53**
Walker Way L9: Walt 5F **21**
Wallace Av. L36: Huy 3A **58**
Wallace Dr. L36: Huy 3H **57**
Wallace St. L9: Ain 5G **21**
WA8: Wid 3E **97**
Wallacre Rd. CH44: Wall 3A **50**
WALLASEY 2A **50**
Wallasey Bri. Rd. CH41: Birke 6B **50**
Wallasey Grove Road Station (Rail) 1A **50**
Wallasey Rd. CH44: Wall 3B **50**
CH45: Wall 3B **50**
Wallasey Village CH44: Wall 1A **50**
CH45: Wall 1A **50**
Wallasey Village Station (Rail) 2A **50**
Waller Cl. L4: Kirkd 6E **35**
Waller St. L20: Boot 5B **20**
Wallgate Rd. L25: Gate 3B **74**
Wallgate Way L25: Gate 3B **74**
Wallingford Rd. CH49: Upton 5D **66**
Wallrake CH60: Hesw 6D **100**
Wallsend Ct. WA8: Wid 6D **78**
Wall St. L1: Liv 5D **4** (6C **52**)
Walmer Rd. L22: Water 3G **19**
Walmersley Dr. WA11: Rainf 4G **17**
Walmesley Rd. WA10: Eccl 6G **27**
Walmsley St. CH44: Wall 2E **51**
L5: Liv 2C **52**
WA8: Wid 3G **97**
Walney Rd. L12: W Der 5E **37**
Walney Ter. L12: W Der 5E **37**
Walnut Av. L9: Walt 2A **36**
Walnut Gro. L31: Mell 6E **13**
WA9: St H 5F **43**
Walnut St. *L7: Liv 6F **53***
(off Mt. Pleasant)
Walpole Av. L35: Whis 4F **59**
Walpole Rd. WA7: Run 1F **123**
Walsham Gdns. WA9: St H 1C **60**
Walsh Cl. L5: Liv 3C **52**
Walsh Rd. L14: Broad G 5G **55**
Walsingham Ct. *CH44: Wall 4F **51***
(off Liscard Rd.)
Walsingham Dr. WA7: Nort 3F **115**
Walsingham Rd. CH44: Wall 4F **51**
L16: Child 6A **56**
WA5: Penk 4H **81**
Walter Beilin Ct. L17: Aig 4C **72**
Walter Gro. WA9: St H 6B **44**
Walter St. L5: Liv 2B **52**
WA8: Wid 2H **97**
Waltham Ct. WA7: Nort 1G **115**
Waltham Rd. L6: Liv 1A **54**
Waltho Av. L31: Mag 6D **6**
WALTON 3H **35**
Walton Av. WA5: Penk 4G **81**
Walton Breck Rd. L4: Walt 6F **35**
Walton Hall Av. L4: Walt 3G **35**
L11: Norr G 2B **36**
Walton Hall Rd. L4: Walt 3H **35**
Walton La. L4: Walt 6F **35**
Walton Pk. L9: Walt 1G **35**
Walton Rd. L4: Walt 6E **35**
WA10: St H 5B **28**
Walton Station (Rail) 1F **35**
Walton St. CH41: Birke 3G **69**
WA7: Run 3E **113**
Walton Va. L9: Walt, Ain 5G **21**
Walton Village L4: Walt 3F **35**
(not continuous)
Wambo La. L25: Gate 4E **75**
Wandsworth Rd. L11: Norr G 4D **36**
Wandsworth Way
WA8: Wid 6D **96**
Wango La. L10: Ain 2C **22**
Wantage Vw. L36: Roby 1E **75**
Wapping L1: Liv 6D **4** (1C **70**)
Wapshare Rd. L11: Norr G 4C **36**
Warbler Cl. L26: Halew 1F **93**
Warbreck Av. L9: Walt, Ain 4G **21**
Warbreck Moor L9: Ain 5H **21**
WARBRECK PARK 4G **21**
Warbreck Rd. L9: Walt 5G **21**
Warburton Hey L35: Rainh 3H **59**
Warden St. L4: Walt 5E **35**
Wardgate Av. L12: Crox 2A **38**
Ward Gro. CH42: Rock F 3H **87**
Ward Rake *L30: N'ton 5D **10***
(off Granams Cft.)
Ward Rd. L23: Blun 4C **8**
Ward St. L3: Liv 3G **5** (5E **53**)
L34: Presc 6D **40**
WA10: St H 1E **43**
Wareham Cl. WA11: Hay 4E **31**
Wareing Rd. L9: Ain 5A **22**
Waresley Cres. L9: Faz 1C **36**
Warham Rd. L4: Walt 6A **36**
Waring Av. CH42: Tran 1F **87**
WA9: St H 3D **44**
Warkworth Cl. L36: Huy 1A **76**
WA8: Wid 6A **78**
Warmington Rd. L14: Knott A 4G **55**
Warner Dr. L4: Walt 5A **36**
Warnerville Rd. L13: Liv 6F **55**
Warnley Cl. WA8: Wid 6B **78**
Warren, The CH49: Upton 4F **67**
WA12: Newt W 2H **45**
Warren Cft. WA7: Nort 6E **115**
Warrender Dr. CH43: Bid 1B **68**
Warren Dr. CH43: Bid 3G **67**
CH45: Wall, New B 5B **32**
Warren Hey CH63: Spit 4A **104**
Warrenhouse Av. L22: Water 1D **18**
Warrenhouse Rd. L33: Kirkb 5C **14**
Warren Hurst CH45: New B 5C **32**
Warren Pk. CH45: Wall 6B **32**
Warren Rd. CH47: Hoy 2A **64**
L23: Blun 4C **8**
Warren St. L3: Liv 4H **5** (6E **53**)
Warren Way CH60: Hesw 4B **100**
Warrington New Rd.
WA9: St H 2F **43**
Warrington Old Rd.
WA9: St H 3F **43**
Warrington Rd. L34: Presc 1D **58**
L35: Presc, Rainh, Whis 1D **58**
L35: Rainh 1D **58**
WA5: Penk 5G **81**
WA7: Cas 3A **114**
WA7: Manor P 1C **114**
(not continuous)
WA8: Bold H 1D **78**
WA8: Wid 3G **97**
Warrington St. CH41: Tran 5G **69**
Warton Cl. L25: Woolt 1E **93**
WA5: Penk 6H **81**
Warton St. L20: Boot 5B **20**
Warton Ter. L20: Boot 5B **20**
Warwick Av. L23: Crosb 6F **9**
WA5: Gt San 2F **81**
Warwick Cl. CH43: O'ton 4E **69**
L36: Huy 4A **58**
Warwick Ct. *L8: Liv 3G **71***
(off Gwent St.)
Warwick Dr. CH45: Wall 1E **51**
CH48: W Kir 3C **82**
Warwick Gro. WA7: Cas 4B **114**
Warwick Rd. CH49: Upton 4C **66**
L20: Boot 1D **34**
L36: Huy 4A **58**
Warwick St. L8: Liv 3E **71**
WA10: St H 2B **42**
Wasdale Av. L31: Mag 5E **7**
WA11: St H 3F **29**
Wasdale Rd. L9: Walt 6G **21**
Washbrook Av. CH43: Bid 1G **67**
Washbrook Cl. WA10: Eccl 1H **41**
Washington Cl. WA8: Wid 6D **78**
Washington Dr. L33: Kirkb 3H **13**
Washington Pde. L20: Boot 1C **34**
Washington Rd. L27: N'ley 5H **75**
Washway La. WA10: St H 4D **28**
WA11: St H 4D **28**
Wastdale Ct. CH46: More 6A **48**
Wastdale Dr. CH46: More 6A **48**
Wastdale M. CH46: More 6A **48**
Wastle Bri. Rd. L36: Huy 2G **57**
Waterdale Cres. WA9: St H 6H **43**
Waterdale Pl. WA9: St H 6H **43**
Waterfall Dr. L4: Walt 2G **35**
Waterfield Cl. CH63: Hghr B 6F **87**
Waterfield Way L21: Lith 2A **20**
Waterford Rd. CH43: O'ton 4B **68**
L27: N'ley 3E **75**
Waterford Way WA7: Murd 1E **125**
(not continuous)
Waterfront WA4: Pres H 1H **125**
Waterfront Bus. Area L8: Liv 2E **71**
Waterfront Bus. Area Parliament St. Nth.
*L1: Liv 2E **71***
(off New Bird St.)
*L1: Liv 2D **70***
(off Simpson St.)
Waterfront Bus. Area Parliament St. Sth.
*L8: Liv 3E **71***
(off Stanhope St.)
Water Gdns. L23: Thorn 3B **10**
Watergate La. L25: Woolt 1D **92**
Watergate Way L25: Woolt 1D **92**
Waterhouse Cl. L6: Liv 1H **53**
Waterland La. WA9: St H 3B **44**
Water La. L35: Tar G 5C **76**
WATERLOO 2G **19**
Waterloo Cen. WA8: Wid 5E **97**
Waterloo Cl. L22: Water 3F **19**
Waterloo Ct. CH63: Beb 5A **88**
Waterloo Dock L3: Liv 4B **52**
WATERLOO PARK 2H **19**
Waterloo Pl. CH41: Birke 4G **69**
Waterloo Quay L3: Liv 1A **4** (4B **52**)
Waterloo Rd. CH45: New B 4D **32**
L3: Liv 1A **4** (3B **52**)
L21: Sea 5G **19**
L22: Water 3G **19**
WA7: Run 3D **112**
WA8: Wid 6E **97**
Waterloo Station (Rail) 2G **19**
Waterloo St. L15: Wav 2E **73**
WA10: St H 2D **42**
Watermead Dr. WA7: Pres B 2H **125**
Waterpark Cl. CH43: Pren 2B **86**
Waterpark Dr. L28: Stockb V 5B **38**
Waterpark Ho. *CH42: Tran 1D **86***
(off Storeton Rd.)
Waterpark Rd. CH42: Tran 2B **86**
CH43: Pren 2B **86**
Watersedge WA6: Frod 5H **123**
Watersedge Apartments
*CH45: New B 4E **33***
(off Tower Prom.)
Waterside L30: N'ton 4E **11**
WA9: St H 1F **43**
Waterside Ct. WA7: Run 2C **112**
WA9: St H 1F **43**
Waterside Dr. WA6: Frod 5G **123**
Waterside La. WA8: Hale B 6A **96**
Waterside Pk. L36: Roby 6F **57**
Waterstone Cl. L11: Norr G 2F **37**

Water St. CH41: Birke 3H **69**
CH44: Wall 3F **51**
CH62: Port S 6C **88**
L2: Liv 4C **4** (6C **52**)
L3: Liv 4B **4** (6B **52**)
*L22: Water 3G **19***
(off Brunswick Pde.)
L23: Thorn 3B **10**
WA7: Run 2E **113**
WA8: Wid .5E **97**
WA10: St H 2D **42**
Water Twr. Rd. CH64: Nest 6A **118**
Waterway Av. L30: N'ton 6H **11**
Waterworks La. CH66: Hoot 6E **121**
Waterworks St. L20: Boot 2D **34**
Watery La. WA9: St H 5A **44**
WA10: Windle 4G **27**
WA11: Windle 4F **27**
Watford Rd. L4: Walt 6H **35**
Watkin Cl. L30: N'ton 2H **21**
Watkins Av. WA12: Newt W 2H **45**
Watkinson St. L1: Liv 2D **70**
Watkinson Way WA8: Wid 1D **78**
Watling Av. L21: Lith 2A **20**
Watling Way L35: Whis 1G **59**
Watmough St. L5: Liv 3E **53**
Watson Ct. *CH41: Birke 2H **69***
(off Argyle St.)
Watson St. CH41: Birke 2F **69**
Watton Beck Cl. L31: Mag 5E **7**
Watton Cl. L12: Crox 3C **38**
Watts Clift Way WA9: St H 2F **43**
Watts Cl. L33: Kirkb 5C **14**
Watts La. L20: Boot 5E **21**
Wauchope St. L15: Wav 1C **72**
Wavell Av. WA8: Wid 3A **96**
Wavell Rd. L36: Huy 3G **57**
Waverley Dr. L34: Presc 2H **57**
Waverley Gro. CH42: Tran 1E **87**
Waverley Ho. L19: Aig 4D **90**
Waverley Rd. CH47: Hoy 2C **64**
L17: Aig 5A **72**
L23: Blun 6E **9**
Waverley St. L20: Boot 2B **34**
Waverly Ct. WA9: St H 4G **43**
Waverton Av. CH43: O'ton 1A **86**
WAVERTREE 1D 72
Wavertree Athletics Cen. **2D 72**
Wavertree Av. L13: Wav 6C **54**
WA8: Wid .3D **96**
Wavertree Blvd. L7: Liv 6B **54**
Wavertree Blvd. Sth. L7: Liv 6C **54**
Wavertree Bus. Pk. L15: Wav 2D **72**
Wavertree Gdns. *L15: Wav 2D **72***
(off Prince Alfred Rd.)
WAVERTREE GREEN 3E 73
Wavertree Grn. L15: Wav 2E **73**
Wavertree Ho. *L13: Liv 6E **55***
(off Binns Rd.)
Wavertree Nook Rd. L15: Wav 6G **55**
Wavertree Retail Pk. L7: Liv 6A **54**
Wavertree Rd. L7: Liv 6H **53**
Wavertree Sports Pk. **2D 72**
Wavertree Technology Pk.
L7: Liv 6B **54**
L13: Wav .6C **54**
Wavertree Technology Park Station (Rail)
. . . .**6D 54**
Wavertree Va. L15: Wav 1B **72**
Wayford Cl. WA6: Frod 6F **123**
Wayford M. WA6: Frod 6F **123**
Waylands Dr. L25: Hunts X 4D **92**
Waymark Gdns. WA9: Sut M 4F **61**
Wayville Cl. L18: Moss H 1F **91**
Weardale Rd. L15: Wav 3C **72**
Weasdale Cl. WA9: St H 6H **43**
Weates Cl. WA8: Wid 6A **80**
Weatherstones Cotts.
CH64: Nest 6F **119**
Weaver Av. L33: Kirkb 3B **14**
L35: Rainh 4H **59**
Weaver Ct. L25: Gate 6E **75**
Weaver Cres. WA6: Frod 6H **123**
Weaver Gro. WA9: St H 2C **44**
Weaver Ho. *L25: Gate 6E **75***
(off Ribble Rd.)
Weaver Ind. Est. L19: Garst 1G **107**
Weaver La. WA6: Frod 5F **123**
Weaver Pk. Ind. Est.
WA6: Frod 5H **123**
Weaver Rd. WA6: Frod 6H **123**
WA7: West 1E **123**
Weaver Sailing Club **5H 123**
Weaverside Av. WA7: Sut W 3B **124**
Weavers La. L31: Mag 3D **12**
Weaver St. L9: Walt 2F **35**
Webb Cl. L7: Liv 6A **54**
Webb Dr. WA5: Burtw 1H **63**
Webber Rd. L33: Know I 2D **24**
Webb St. L7: Liv 2A **72**
WA9: St H 4H **43**
Web Complex, The
L33: Know I 3E **25**
Webster Av. CH44: Wall 2F **51**
L20: Boot .1E **35**
Webster Dr. L32: Kirkb 1A **24**
Webster Rd. L7: Liv 2B **72**
Websters Holt CH49: Upton 3D **66**
Webster St. L3: Liv 2E **5** (5D **52**)
L21: Lith .5B **20**
Wedge Av. WA11: Hay 6C **30**
Wedgewood Gdns. WA9: St H 1H **59**
Wedgewood St. L7: Liv 5H **53**
Wedgwood Dr. WA8: Wid 5F **79**
Wednesbury Dr. WA5: Gt San 3H **81**
Weightman Gro. L9: Ain 5G **21**
Weirside WA9: St H 1H **61**
Welbeck Av. L18: Moss H 4D **72**
Welbeck Ct. *L22: Water 2F **19***
(off Mt. Pleasant)
Welbourne Rd. L16: Child 6G **55**
Weld Blundell Av. L31: Lyd 3A **6**
Weldon St. L4: Walt 3F **35**
Weld Rd. L23: Blun 6E **9**
Welford Av. CH43: Pren 1B **86**
Welland Cl. L26: Halew 5G **93**
Welland Rd. CH63: Hghr B 6F **87**
Wellbank Dr. L26: Halew 2A **94**
Wellbrae Cl. CH49: Upton 4B **66**
Wellbrook Cl. L24: Speke 1F **109**
WA7: Brook 2E **125**
Wellbrook Grn. L24: Speke 2F **109**
Wellbrow Rd. L4: Walt 3G **35**
Wellcroft Rd. L36: Huy 3G **57**
Weller St. L8: Liv 4F **71**
Weller Way L8: Liv 5G **71**
Wellesbourne Pl. L11: Norr G 3E **37**
Wellesbourne Rd. L11: Norr G 2E **37**
Wellesley Gro. CH63: Beb 5A **88**
Wellesley Rd. CH44: Wall 3D **50**
(not continuous)
L8: Liv 5G **71**
Wellesley Ter. L8: Liv 5G **71**
Wellfarm Cl. L9: Ain 2B **36**
Wellfield WA7: Pres B 2G **125**
WA8: Wid .6E **79**
WA11: Rainf 5G **17**
Wellfield Av. L32: Kirkb 2A **24**
Wellfield Pl. L8: Liv 5G **71**
Wellfield Rd. L9: Walt 1G **35**
Wellgreen Rd. L25: Gate 2B **74**
Wellgreen Wlk. *L25: Gate 2C **74***
(off Wellgreen Rd.)
Wellingford Av. WA8: Hale B 6H **95**
Wellington Av. L15: Wav 3B **72**
Wellington Cl. CH63: Beb 5A **88**
L10: Ain 6A **12**
Wellington Employment Pk. Sth.
L5: Kirkd .1C **52**
Wellington Flds. L15: Wav 3B **72**
Wellington Gdns. *L22: Water 2F **19***
(off Wellington St.)
Wellington Ga. L24: Hale 3D **110**
Wellington Gro. L15: Wav 1C **72**
Wellington Mans. *CH45: New B 4C **32***
(off Atherton St.)
Wellington Rd. CH43: O'ton 4C **68**
CH45: New B 4C **32**
CH63: Beb 5A **88**
L8: Liv 5F **71**
L15: Wav .2C **72**
L21: Lith .4A **20**
Wellington St. L3: Liv 4D **52**
L19: Garst 5G **91**
L22: Water 2F **19**
WA7: Run 2E **113**
WA8: Wid .5E **97**
Wellington St. Ind. Est. *WA8: Wid 5E **97***
(off Wellington St.)
Wellington Ter. CH41: Birke 4F **69**
L8: Liv 4G **71**
WA10: St H 6E **29**
Well La. CH42: Rock F, Tran 6F **69**
CH49: Grea 6A **66**
CH60: Hesw 1E **117**
CH63: Hghr B 5F **87**
L16: Child 2B **74**
L20: Boot .2D **34**
L25: Gate .2B **74**
WA5: Penk 6G **81**
(not continuous)
Well La. Gdns. L20: Boot 2D **34**
Wells St. L15: Wav 2D **72**
Wellstead Cl. L15: Wav 1E **73**
Wellstead Rd. L15: Wav 1E **73**
Wellstead Wlk. *L15: Wav 1E **73***
(off Wellstead Rd.)
Welsh Rd.
CH66: Led, Lit Sut, Chil T 6G **121**
Welton Av. CH49: Upton 4D **66**
Welton Cl. L24: Speke 2F **109**
Welton Grn. L24: Speke 2F **109**
Welton Rd. CH62: Brom 3D **104**
Welwyn Cl. WA9: St H 1D **60**
Wembley Gdns. L9: Walt 5F **21**
Wembley Rd. L18: Moss H 5F **73**
L23: Crosb .6H **9**
Wendell St. L8: Liv 2A **72**
Wendover Av. L17: Aig 6A **72**
Wendover Cl. CH43: Noct 5H **67**
WA11: Hay 4F **31**
Wendron Rd. L11: Crox 6H **23**
Wenger Rd. WA8: Wid 4F **79**
Wenlock Ct. L26: Halew 4G **93**
Wenlock Dr. L26: Halew 4G **93**
Wenlock Rd. L4: Walt 6H **35**
WA7: Beech 3C **124**
Wenning Av. L31: Mag 5D **6**
Wensley Av. L26: Halew 4H **93**
Wensley Dale L9: Walt 4G **21**
Wensleydale Av. CH62: East 2E **121**
L35: Rainh 4B **60**
Wensleydale Cl. L31: Mag 5A **6**
WA5: Gt San 1H **81**
Wensley Rd. L9: Walt 4G **21**
Wentworth Av. CH45: New B 6D **32**
Wentworth Cl. CH43: Noct 5H **67**
WA8: Wid .4E **79**
Wentworth Dr. CH63: Brom 2C **120**
L5: Liv 3F **53**
Wentworth Gro. L36: Huy 5D **56**
Wernbrook Cl. CH43: Noct 5H **67**
Wernbrook Rd. L4: Walt 6A **36**
Wervin Cl. CH43: O'ton 1A **86**
Wervin Rd. CH43: O'ton 1A **86**
L32: Kirkb .2H **23**
Wesley Av. CH44: Wall 2E **51**
WA11: Hay 4H **31**
Wesley Gro. CH44: Wall 4G **51**
Wesley Hall Gdns. WA9: St H 1B **60**
Wesley Pl. L15: Wav 1D **72**
Wesley St. L22: Water 3F **19**
W. Albert Rd. L17: Aig 5H **71**
W. Alfred Ct. *CH43: O'ton 4E **69***
(off Alfred Rd.)
West Allerton Station (Rail) **2F 91**

WEST BANK 1E 113
Westbank Av. CH45: New B 6E **33**
W. Bank Dock Est. WA8: Wid 6C **96**
W. Bank Rd. L7: Liv 5C **54**
Westbank Rd. CH42: Tran 6E **69**
W. Bank St. WA8: Wid 6E **97**
Westbourne Av. CH48: W Kir 1B **82**
L23: Thorn 3B **10**
Westbourne Gro. CH48: W Kir 1B **82**
Westbourne Rd. CH43: O'ton 4E **69**
CH44: Wall 3B **50**
CH48: W Kir 1A **82**
Westbrook Av. L34: Presc 1B **58**
Westbrook Rd. CH46: More 2A **66**
L25: Gate 4E **75**
W. Brow Gdns. CH43: Bid 1G **67**
Westbury Cl. L17: Aig 2A **90**
L25: Hunts X 3F **93**
Westbury St. CH41: Tran 5G **69**
Westcliffe Ct. WA8: Wid 5F **79**
Westcliffe Rd. L12: W Der 6E **37**
West Cl. CH43: Noct 4H **67**
L34: Eccl P 6G **41**
Westcombe Rd. L4: Walt 6A **36**
Westcott Rd. L4: Walt 1H **53**
Westcott Way CH43: Noct 5H **67**
Westdale Rd. CH42: Rock F 1G **87**
L15: Wav 1D **72**
Westdale Vw. L15: Wav 1D **72**
WEST DERBY 6F 37
W. Derby Rd. L6: Liv 4G **53**
(Low Hill)
L6: Liv 2B **54**
(Orphan Dr.)
L13: Liv 1D **54**
W. Derby St. L7: Liv 5G **53**
W. Derby Village L12: W Der 6F **37**
West Dr. CH49: Upton 4E **67**
CH60: Hesw 6E **101**
West End Gro. WA11: Hay 5B **30**
West End Rd. WA11: Hay 5B **30**
Westerhope Way WA8: Wid 6D **78**
Western Approaches Mus. (Underground Wartime Mus.) 3C **4** (5C **52**)
Western Av. CH62: Brom 2D **104**
L24: Speke 3E **109**
L36: Huy 4C **56**
Western Dr. L19: Gras 4E **91**
Westerton Rd. L12: W Der 1A **56**
Westfield Av. L14: Broad G 5A **56**
Westfield Cres. WA7: Run 4C **112**
Westfield Dr. L12: Crox 3A **38**
Westfield M. WA7: Run 4D **112**
Westfield Rd. CH44: Wall 6F **51**
L9: Walt 5E **21**
WA7: Run 4C **112**
Westfield St. WA10: St H 2D **42**
(not continuous)
Westfield Wlk. L32: Kirkb 1F **23**
W. Float Ind. Est.
CH41: Birke 5D **50**
Westgate WA8: Wid 4H **95**
Westgate Rd. CH62: Port S 1B **104**
L15: Wav 4E **73**
West Gro. CH60: Hesw 5D **100**
Westhead Av. L33: Kirkb 1B **24**
Westhead Cl. L33: Kirkb 2C **24**
Westhead Wlk. L33: Kirkb 1B **24**
(not continuous)
Westhouse Cl. CH63: Brom 2C **120**
WEST KIRBY 1A 82
West Kirby Concourse (Leisure Cen.) 6A **64**
W. Kirby Rd. CH46: More 3A **66**
West Kirby Station (Rail) 1A 82
West Knowe CH43: O'ton 5B **68**
Westlands Cl. CH64: Nest 6B **118**
West La. WA7: Pal F 6A **114**
Westleigh Pl. WA9: Sut L 2G **61**
W. Lodge Dr. CH48: W Kir 6A **64**
West Mains L24: Speke 2A **110**
West Meade L31: Mag 5A **6**
Westminster Av. L30: N'ton 5E **11**
Westminster Chambers *L1: Liv* *3E 5*
(off Crosshall St.)
Westminster Cl. L4: Kirkd 5E **35**
WA8: Wid 3H **95**
Westminster Ct. CH43: O'ton 4B **68**
Westminster Dr. CH62: Brom 6D **104**
WA11: Hay 4H **31**
Westminster Gro. L34: Presc 2A **58**
Westminster Rd. CH44: Wall 3D **50**
L4: Kirkd 4D **34**
Westmoreland Rd.
CH45: New B 6E **33**
Westmorland Av. L30: N'ton 6C **10**
WA8: Wid 2F **97**
Westmorland Dr. L3: Liv 1D **4** (4C **52**)
Westmorland Pl. L5: Liv 2D **52**
Westmorland Rd. L36: Huy 5G **57**
W. Oakhill Pk. L13: Liv 5E **55**
WESTON 1D 122
Weston Ct. L23: Blun 6D **8**
WA7: West 6D **112**
Weston Cres. WA7: West 1D **122**
Weston Gro. L26: Halew 5A **94**
L31: Mag 3B **12**
WESTON POINT 6B 112
Weston Point Docks WA7: West P . . . 6B **112**
Weston Point Expressway
WA7: Run, West 4C **112**
Weston Rd. WA7: Run, West 5C **112**
Weston Vw. WA7: Clftn 3H **123**
W. Orchard La. L9: Ain 3B **22**
Westover Cl. L31: Mag 6B **6**
Westover Rd. L31: Mag 6B **6**
WEST PARK 3B 42
West Pk. Gdns. CH43: Bid 1G **67**
West Pk. Rd. WA10: St H 3B **42**
Westport Bus. Pk. L20: Kirkd 6C **34**
West Rd. CH43: Noct 4H **67**
CH65: Ell P, Hoot 4H **121**
L14: Broad G 5G **55**
WA7: West P 6B **112**
Westry Cl. CH46: More 1H **65**
West Side WA9: St H 3G **43**
W. Side Av. WA11: Hay 5C **30**
Westside Ind. Est. WA9: St H 3G **43**
West St. CH45: Wall 2D **50**
L34: Presc 1C **58**
WA10: St H 4B **42**
West Twr. L3: Liv 2B **4**
WESTVALE 1G 23
West Vw. CH41: Tran 5H **69**
L36: Huy 5B **58**
West Vw. Av. L36: Huy 5B **58**
West Vw. Cl. L36: Huy 5B **58**
Westview Cl. CH43: Noct 5H **67**
Westward Ho CH48: Caldy 5D **82**
Westward Vw. L17: Aig 6G **71**
L22: Water 1D **18**
Westway CH43: Noct 5H **67**
CH46: More 6C **48**
CH49: Grea 5B **66**
CH60: Hesw 1D **116**
L15: Wav 1F **73**
L31: Mag 5B **6**
WA7: Pal F 6A **114**
Westway Sq. CH46: More 6C **48**
Westwick Pl. L36: Huy 4D **56**
Westwood WA7: Wind H 4E **115**
Westwood Ct. CH43: O'ton 4B **68**
CH64: Nest 5A **118**
Westwood Gro. CH44: Wall 3C **50**
Westwood Rd. CH43: Bid 3G **67**
L18: Aller 3G **91**
Wetherby Av. CH45: Wall 2A **50**
Wetherby Ct. L36: Huy 2E **57**
Wethersfield Rd. CH43: Noct 6A **68**
Wetstone La. CH48: W Kir 2C **82**
Wexford Av. L24: Hale 3D **110**
Wexford Cl. CH43: O'ton 5A **68**
WA11: Hay 4F **31**
Wexford Rd. CH43: O'ton 5B **68**
Wexwood Gro. L35: Whis 5F **59**
Weybourne Cl. CH49: Upton 2E **67**
Weyman Av. L35: Whis 4E **59**
Weymoor Cl. CH63: Spit 3H **103**
Weymouth Av. WA9: St H 4B **44**
Weymouth Cl. L16: Child 1B **74**
WA7: Murd 1G **125**
Weymouth Rd. WA5: Burtw 1H **63**
Whaley La. CH61: Irby 5D **84**
Whalley Av. WA10: St H 4C **28**
WA11: Rainf 3F **17**
Whalley Ct. L30: N'ton 5D **10**
Whalley Gro. WA8: Wid 6H **79**
Whalley Rd. CH42: Tran 4F **69**
Whalley St. L8: Liv 5F **71**
Wharf, The WA7: Pres B 1H **125**
Wharfdale Cl. WA5: Gt San 2H **81**
Wharfedale WA7: Pal F 1D **124**
Wharfedale Av. CH42: Tran 1D **86**
Wharfedale Dr. CH62: East 2F **121**
L35: Rainh 4B **60**
Wharfedale Rd. CH45: Wall 1B **50**
Wharfedale St. L19: Garst 6A **92**
Wharford La. WA7: Nort 2G **115**
Wharf Rd. WA12: Newt W 3G **45**
Wharf St. CH62: Port S 6C **88**
Wharmby Rd. WA11: Hay 5G **31**
Wharncliffe Rd. L13: Liv 4E **55**
Wharton Cl. CH49: Upton 3B **66**
Wharton St. WA9: St H 4F **43**
Whatcroft Cl. WA7: Run 1H **123**
Wheatcroft Rd. L18: Aller 1G **91**
Wheatear Cl. L27: N'ley 5G **75**
Wheatfield Cl. CH46: More 2D **66**
L30: N'ton 6H **11**
Wheatfield Rd. WA8: Cron 4A **78**
Wheatfield Vw. L21: Ford 1B **20**
Wheat Hill Rd. L36: Huy 2G **75**
Wheathills Ind. Est. L27: N'ley 3F **75**
Wheatland Bus. Pk.
CH44: Wall 5F **51**
Wheatland Cl. WA9: Clock F 3G **61**
Wheatland La. CH44: Wall 4F **51**
Wheatland Rd. CH60: Hesw 6G **101**
Wheatlands WA7: Run 4A **114**
Wheatley Av. L20: Boot 6E **21**
Wheatsheaf Av. WA9: Sut L 1H **61**
Wheeler Dr. L31: Mell 6F **13**
Whelan Gdns. WA9: St H 1C **60**
Wheldon Rd. WA8: Wid 4F **95**
Whernside WA8: Wid 6A **78**
Whetstone Ct. *CH41: Birke* *4F 69*
(off Whetstone La.)
Whetstone La. CH41: Birke 4F **69**
Whickham Cl. WA8: Wid 6D **78**
Whimbrel Cl. WA7: Beech 2B **124**
Whimbrel Pk. L26: Halew 2G **93**
Whinberry Dr. L32: Kirkb 2H **23**
Whinbury Ct. WA9: Clock F 3G **61**
Whincraig L28: Stockb V 6D **38**
Whinfell Gro. WA7: Beech 2A **124**
Whinfell Rd. L12: W Der 2G **55**
Whinfield Rd. L9: Walt 5F **21**
L23: Thorn 3A **10**
Whinhowe Rd. L11: Norr G 3F **37**
Whinmoor Cl. CH43: Noct 3H **67**
Whinmoor Rd. L10: Faz 4E **23**
L12: W Der 2G **55**
Whinney Gro. E. L31: Mag 3A **12**
Whinney Gro. W. L31: Mag 3A **12**
WHISTON 4E 59
WHISTON CROSS 4D 58
Whiston La. L36: Huy 3A **58**
WHISTON LANE ENDS 5E 59
Whiston Station (Rail) 4E 59
Whitburn Rd. L33: Kirkb 5C **14**
Whitby Av. CH45: Wall 2A **50**
Whitby Rd. WA7: Run 4E **113**
Whitby St. L6: Liv 1B **54**
Whitchurch Way WA7: Run 1H **123**
Whitcroft Rd. L6: Liv 4B **54**

Whitebeam Cl. L33: Kirkb 3B **14**
WA7: Wind H 4E **115**
Whitebeam Dr. L12: Crox 2H **37**
Whitebeam Gdns. WA9: St H 1A **60**
Whitebeam Wlk. CH49: Grea 1H **83**
Whitechapel L1: Liv 4E **5** (6D **52**)
Whitefield Av. L4: Kirkd 5E **35**
Whitefield Cl. CH49: Woodc 6F **67**
Whitefield Dr. L32: Kirkb 1F **23**
Whitefield La. L35: Tar G 4A **76**
Whitefield Rd. L6: Liv 3H **53**
WA10: St H 6B **28**
WHITEFIELDS CROSS 6B **80**
Whitefield Way L6: Liv 3G **53**
White Friars WA10: Eccl 1G **41**
Whitegate Cl. L34: Know 1F **39**
Whitegates Cl. CH64: Will 6G **119**
Whitegates Cres. CH64: Will 6G **119**
Whitehall Cl. L4: Kirkd 4E **35**
Whitehart Cl. L4: Walt 4H **35**
Whitehaven Rd. L5: Liv 1F **53**
Whiteheath Way CH46: Leas 4D **48**
Whitehedge Rd. L19: Garst 4F **91**
WHITEHOUSE 3H **125**
White Ho. Cl. WA11: Hay 5D **30**
Whitehouse Expressway
WA7: Brook, Pal F 1A **124**
Whitehouse Ind. Est. WA7: Pres B . . .3G **125**
(not continuous)
Whitehouse La. CH60: Hesw 4G **101**
CH63: Brim 4G **101**
Whitehouse Rd. L13: Liv 5F **55**
Whitelands Mdw. CH49: Upton 4C **66**
White Lodge Av. L36: Huy 4F **57**
White Lodge Cl. CH62: Brom 2D **120**
Whitely Gro. L33: Kirkb 3C **14**
White Mdw. Dr. L23: Thorn 4A **10**
White Oak Lodge *L19: Gras 4D* ***90***
(off Beechwood Rd.)
White Rock St. L6: Liv 3H **53**
Whiteside Av. WA11: St H 6A **30**
Whiteside Cl. CH49: Upton 5E **67**
L5: Liv 2D **52**
Whiteside Rd. WA11: Hay 5D **30**
Whitestone Cl. L34: Know 3E **39**
White St. WA8: Wid 6E **97**
Whitethorn Av. WA5: Gt San 4H **81**
Whitethorn Dr. L28: Stockb V 5D **38**
Whitewell Dr. CH49: Upton 3D **66**
Whitewood Pk. L9: Ain 5B **22**
Whitfield Ct. CH42: Tran 5F **69**
Whitfield Gro. WA11: Hay 5C **30**
Whitfield La. CH60: Hesw 3E **101**
Whitfield Rd. L9: Walt 6G **21**
WHITFIELDS CROSS 6A **80**
Whitfield St. CH42: Tran 5F **69**
Whitford Rd. CH42: Tran 5E **69**
Whitham Av. L23: Crosb 6H **9**
Whithorn St. L7: Liv 1B **72**
Whitland Rd. L6: Liv 4B **54**
Whitley Cl. WA7: Run 5D **112**
Whitley Dr. CH44: Wall 2F **51**
Whitley St. L3: Liv 3B **52**
Whitman St. L15: Wav 2C **72**
Whitmoor Cl. L35: Rainh 6C **60**
Whitney Pl. L25: Woolt 1E **93**
Whitney Rd. L25: Woolt 6E **75**
Whitstable Pk. WA8: Wid 5C **78**
Whitstone Cl. L18: Aller 1A **92**
Whittaker Cl. L13: Liv 6D **54**
Whittaker St. WA9: St H 4H **43**
Whittier St. L8: Liv 2A **72**
Whittington Ho. *L21: Lith 4A* ***20***
(off Beach Rd.)
Whittle Av. WA5: Gt San 1H **81**
WA11: Hay 6C **30**
Whittle Cl. L5: Kirkd 1E **53**
Whittle Hall La. WA5: Gt San 3H **81**
Whittle St. L5: Kirkd 1E **53**
WA10: St H 4B **42**
Whittlewood Ct. L33: Kirkb 5B **14**
Whitwell Cl. WA5: Gt San 2F **81**
Whitworth Ct. WA7: Manor P 1F **115**
Wicket Cl. L11: Crox 6H **23**
Wickham Cl. CH44: Wall 5F **51**
Wicksten Dr. WA7: Run 3G **113**
Widdale Av. L35: Rainh 4B **60**
Widdale Cl. WA5: Gt San 2H **81**
Widgeons Covert CH63: Thorn H 2B **118**
Widmore Rd. L25: Gate 5E **75**
WIDNES 3F **97**
Widnes Crematorium
WA8: Wid .6E **79**
Widnes Rd. WA5: Cuerd, Penk 1B **98**
WA8: Wid .4E **97**
(not continuous)
Widnes Station (Rail) 6E **79**
Widnes Trade Pk. WA8: Wid 4G **97**
Widnes Vikings RLFC 3D **96**
Wiend, The CH42: Rock F 2F **87**
CH63: Beb 6A **88**
Wigg Island Community Pk.
Local Nature Reserve 2H **113**
Wightman St. L6: Liv 4H **53**
Wignall Cl. L32: Kirkb 4A **24**
Wilberforce Rd. L4: Walt 4H **35**
Wilbraham Pl. L5: Liv 2D **52**
Wilbraham St. CH41: Birke 3G **69**
L5: Liv 2D **52**
WA9: Clock F 4A **62**
Wilburn St. L4: Walt 4F **35**
Wilbur St. WA9: St H 6A **44**
Wilcock Cl. L5: Liv 2D **52**
Wilcote Cl. WA8: Wid 5G **79**
Wildbrook Dr. CH41: Birke 6H **49**
Wildcherry Gdns. WA9: St H 6H **41**
Wilde St. L3: Liv 2G **5** (5E **53**)
Wilding Av. WA7: Run 3F **113**
Wild Pl. L20: Boot 4E **21**
Wilfer Cl. L7: Liv 1A **72**
Wilfred Owen Dr. CH41: Birke 2A **68**
Wilkes Av. CH46: Leas 4F **49**
Wilkie St. L15: Wav 2C **72**
Wilkinson Cl. WA8: Wid 6E **97**
Wilkinson Ct. *L15: Wav 1B* ***72***
(off Willow Rd.)
Wilkinson St. CH41: Birke 4E **69**
Wilkin St. L4: Kirkd 6E **35**
Willan St. CH43: O'ton 5D **68**
Willard St. L20: Boot 5D **20**
Willaston Dr. L26: Halew 5A **94**
Willaston Rd. CH46: More 6B **48**
CH63: Raby, Thorn H 1F **119**
L4: Walt 4H **35**
Willedstan Av. L23: Crosb 6G **9**
William Brown St. L3: Liv 3F **5** (5D **52**)
(not continuous)
William Ct. CH64: Nest 5B **118**
William Harvey Cl. L30: N'ton 6F **11**
William Henry St. L3: Liv 1H **5** (4E **53**)
L20: Boot 3B **34**
William Jessop Way L3: Liv . . .2A **4** (5B **52**)
William Morris Av. L20: Boot 6E **21**
William Moult St. L5: Liv 2D **52**
William Penn Cl. WA5: Penk 4G **81**
William Rd. WA11: Hay 6B **30**
William Roberts Av. L32: Kirkb 1G **23**
Williams Av. L20: Boot 6E **21**
Williamson Art Gallery & Mus. 4D **68**
Williamson Ct. L25: Woolt 2E **93**
L26: Halew 2A **94**
Williamson Sq. L1: Liv 4E **5** (6D **52**)
Williamson St. L1: Liv 4E **5** (6D **52**)
WA9: St H 1G **43**
Williamson Student Village
L7: Liv 6G ***53***
(off Paddington)
Williamson Tunnels Heritage Cen. . . . *6G* ***53***
(off The Old Stableyard)
Williams St. L34: Presc 1D **58**
William St. CH41: Birke 3G **69**
CH44: Wall 5G **51**
WA8: Wid .1G **97**
WA10: St H 1E **43**
William Wall Rd. L21: Ford 1B **20**
Willingdon Rd. L16: Child 6A **56**
Willington Av. CH62: East 4E **121**
Willink Rd. WA11: St H 4G **29**
Willis Cl. L35: Whis 5D **58**
Willis La. L35: Whis 5D **58**
Williton Rd. L16: Child 4A **74**
Willmer Rd. CH42: Tran 4E **69**
L4: Walt 6H **35**
Willoughby Dr. WA10: St H 5H **41**
Willoughby Rd. CH44: Wall 3B **50**
L14: Broad G 5A **56**
L22: Water 2G **19**
Willow Av. L32: Kirkb 6G **13**
L35: Whis .4E **59**
L36: Huy .1G **75**
WA8: Wid .1F **97**
Willowbank Cl. L36: Huy 2E **57**
Willowbank Rd. CH42: Tran 6F **69**
CH62: New F 5B **88**
Willowbrow Rd. CH63: Raby 3E **119**
Willow Cl. L14: Broad G 5A **56**
WA7: Run 6F **113**
Willow Ct. CH63: Hghr B 5F **87**
WA9: Clock F 3H ***61***
(off Clock Face Rd.)
Willowcroft Rd. CH44: Wall 5E **51**
Willowdale Rd. L9: Walt 1G **35**
L18: Moss H 4D **72**
Willow Grn. L25: Woolt 5B **74**
Willow Gro. CH46: More 2B **66**
L15: Wav .1E **73**
L35: Presc 2E **59**
Willowherb Cl. L26: Halew 1F **93**
Willow Hey L31: Mag 2C **12**
Willow Ho. L21: Sea 5A **20**
Willow La. CH63: Raby 4F **119**
Willow Lea CH43: O'ton 5C **68**
Willowmeade L11: Norr G 2F **37**
Willow Moss Cl.
CH46: More 5E **49**
Willow Pk. CH49: Grea 5A **66**
Willow Ri. L33: Kirkb 6B **14**
Willow Rd. L15: Wav 1C **72**
WA10: St H 2A **42**
WA11: Hay 4G **31**
Willows, The CH45: Wall 6A **32**
WA5: Gt San 4H **81**
WA9: Clock F 3G **61**
Willow Tree Av. WA9: Sut L 3H **61**
Willow Tree Ct. WA8: Wid 1H **97**
Willow Way L11: Crox 6H **23**
L23: Crosb 4G **9**
Wills Av. L31: Mag 5B **6**
Willsford Av. L31: Mell 6F **13**
Wilmere La. WA8: Wid 4E **79**
Wilmot Av. WA5: Gt San 3H **81**
Wilne Rd. CH45: Wall 1C **50**
Wilsden Rd. WA8: Wid 2H **95**
Wilson Av. CH44: Wall 3G **51**
Wilson Bus. Cen.
L36: Huy .6A **58**
Wilson Cl. WA8: Wid 2H **97**
WA10: St H 2C **42**
Wilson Gro. L19: Garst 5G **91**
Wilson Rd. CH44: Wall 3G **51**
L35: Presc 4D **58**
L36: Huy .6H **57**
Wilson's La. L21: Lith 3B **20**
Wilstan Av. CH63: Hghr B 6F **87**
Wilstone Cl. L6: Liv 3F **53**
Wilton Grange CH48: W Kir 5A **64**
Wilton Gro. L13: Liv 5E **55**
Wilton Rd. CH42: Rock F 2A **88**
L36: Huy .6F **57**
Wilton's Dr. L34: Know 2E **39**
Wilton St. CH44: Wall 3D **50**
L3: Liv 1H **5**
Wiltshire Dr. *L30: N'ton 6D* ***10***
(off Simon's Cft.)
Wiltshire Gdns. WA10: St H 3D **42**
Wimbald Cl. L25: Gate 4E **75**

Wimbledon St. CH45: Wall .2D **50**
L15: Wav .2C **72**
Wimborne Av. CH61: Thing .6E **85**
Wimborne Cl. L14: Knott A .1D **56**
Wimborne Pl. L14: Knott A .2D **56**
Wimborne Rd. L14: Knott A .1C **56**
Wimborne Way CH61: Irby .4B **84**
Wimbrick Cl. CH46: More .1D **66**
Wimbrick Ct. CH46: More .1D **66**
Wimbrick Hey CH46: More .1D **66**
Wimpole St. L7: Liv .5H **53**
Winchester Av. L10: Ain .6B **12**
L22: Water .1E **19**
Winchester Cl. L25: Woolt .4D **92**
Winchester Dr. CH44: Wall .3C **50**
Winchester Pl. WA8: Wid .3A **96**
Winchester Rd. L6: Liv .1A **54**
WA11: Hay .2G **31**
Winchfield Rd. L15: Wav .3D **72**
Windbourne Rd. L17: Aig .1H **89**
Windermere Av. WA8: Wid .5F **79**
WA11: St H .3E **29**
Windermere Ct. *CH41: Birke .4E 69*
(off Penrith St.)
Windermere Dr. L12: W Der .4G **37**
L31: Mag .5D **6**
L33: Kirkb .5H **13**
Windermere Ho. L17: Aig .1B **90**
Windermere Pl. WA11: St H .3E **29**
Windermere Rd. CH43: Noct .4G **67**
WA11: Hay .5D **30**
Windermere St. L5: Liv .1G **53**
WA8: Wid .5F **79**
Windermere Ter. L8: Liv .4H **71**
Windfield Cl. L33: Kirkb .3C **14**
Windfield Grn. L19: Garst .2H **107**
Windfield Rd. L19: Garst .1H **107**
WINDLE .5H **27**
Windle Ash L31: Mag .5B **6**
Windle Av. L23: Crosb .5A **10**
Windlebrook Cres. WA10: Windle .5H **27**
Windle City WA10: St H .5D **28**
Windle Ct. CH64: Nest .5A **118**
Windle Gro. WA10: Windle .5A **28**
Windle Hall Dr. WA10: St H .4C **28**
WINDLE HILL .6E **119**
WINDLEHURST .4D **28**
Windlehurst Av. WA10: St H .5C **28**
WINDLES GREEN .4B **10**
Windleshaw Rd. WA10: St H .5B **28**
Windle St. WA10: St H .6D **28**
Windle Va. WA10: St H .6C **28**
Windmill Av. L23: Crosb .4H **9**
Windmill Cl. L33: Kirkb .4A **14**
Windmill Gdns. CH43: Bid .1G **67**
WA9: St H .1H **43**
WINDMILL HILL .3E **115**
Windmill Hill Av. E.
WA7: Nort, Wind H .3F **115**
Windmill Hill Av. Nth.
WA7: Wind H .2F **115**
Windmill Hill Av. Sth.
WA7: Wind H .4F **115**
Windmill Hill Av. W.
WA7: Wind H .3E **115**
Windmill La. WA4: Pres H .6H **115**
WA5: Penk .4G **81**
Windmill Shop. Cen.
WA8: Wid .3F **97**
Windmill St. WA7: Run .3F **113**
Window La. L19: Garst .1G **107**
Windsor Av. L21: Lith .3A **20**
Windsor Cl. CH49: Grea .6B **66**
CH62: New F .4A **88**
L30: N'ton .4F **11**
Windsor Ct. *L8: Liv .3F 71*
(off Northumberland St.)
L20: Boot .6E 21
(off Windsor Rd.)
Windsor Gro. WA7: Run .5F **113**
Windsor M. CH62: New F .4A **88**
Windsor Pk. Rd. L10: Ain .6C **12**
Windsor Rd. L9: Walt .5G **21**
L13: Liv .1B **54**
L20: Boot .6E **21**
L23: Crosb .4F **9**
L31: Mag .1A **12**
L35: Presc .3F **59**
L36: Huy .5C **56**
WA8: Wid .5E **79**
WA10: St H .2B **42**
Windsor St. CH41: Birke .4E **69**
CH45: New B .4D **32**
L8: Liv .2F **71**
Windsor Vw. L8: Liv .2H **71**
Windus St. WA10: St H .2C **42**
Windwood Dr. L24: Speke .1B **108**
WINDY ARBOR .1B **76**
Windy Arbor Brow L35: Whis .1C **76**
Windy Arbor Cl. L35: Whis .1D **76**
Windy Arbor Rd. L35: Whis .5D **58**
Windy Bank CH62: Port S .5B **88**
(not continuous)
Wineva Gdns. L23: Crosb .6H **9**
Winfield Way WA8: Wid .3F **97**
Winford St. CH44: Wall .4F **51**
Winfrith Cl. CH63: Spit .3H **103**
Winfrith Dr. CH63: Spit .3H **103**
Winfrith Rd. L25: Gate .5E **75**
Wingate Av. WA9: St H .1B **60**
Wingate Cl. CH43: Noct .5A **68**
Wingate Rd. CH62: East .2E **121**
L17: Aig .1C **90**
L33: Kirkb .5B **14**
Wingate Towers L36: Huy .3F **57**
Wingate Wlk. L33: Kirkb .6C **14**
Wingfield Cl. L29: Seft .1D **10**
Wingrave Way L11: Norr G .4F **37**
Winhill L25: Woolt .5C **74**
Winifred Rd. L10: Faz .4F **23**
Winifred St. L7: Liv .6H **53**
Winkle St. L8: Liv .4F **71**
Winmoss Dr. L33: Kirkb .4B **14**
Winnbourne Gdns. *WA9: Sut M .5F 61*
(off Chandlers Way)
Winnington Rd. CH47: Hoy .4A **64**
Winnipeg Dr. L27: N'ley .4G **75**
Winnows, The WA7: Run .4H **113**
Winsford Cl. WA11: Hay .4H **31**
Winsford Dr. WA5: Burtw .6G **45**
Winsford Rd. L13: Liv .1D **54**
Winsham Cl. L32: Kirkb .3B **24**
Winsham Rd. L32: Kirkb .3A **24**
Winskill Rd. L11: Norr G .4E **37**
Winslade Ct. L4: Walt .3H **35**
Winslade Rd. L4: Walt .4H **35**
Winslow Cl. WA7: Nort .5F **115**
Winslow St. L4: Walt .4F **35**
Winstanley Ho. *CH62: New F .4B 88*
(off Winstanley Rd.)
Winstanley Rd. CH62: New F .4B **88**
L22: Water .1G **19**
Winster Dr. L27: N'ley .5A **76**
Winster M. WA10: St H .5H **41**
Winston Av. WA9: St H .3D **44**
Winston Dr. CH43: Noct .4G **67**
Winstone Rd. L14: Knott A .3C **56**
Winston Gro. CH46: More .1C **66**
Winterburn Cres. L12: W Der .6H **37**
Winter Gro. WA9: St H .2D **44**
Winterhey Av. CH44: Wall .5D **50**
Winterley Dr. L26: Halew .5A **94**
Winter St. L6: Liv .4G **53**
Winthrop Pk. CH43: O'ton .4A **68**
Winton Cl. CH45: New B .5C **32**
Winton Gro. WA7: Wind H .4F **115**
Winwick Vw. WA5: Coll G .4F **45**
Winwood Hall L25: Woolt .2C **92**
Wirral Beach Cvn. Pk. CH47: Meols .5F **47**
Wirral Bus. Cen. CH41: Birke .5E **51**
Wirral Cl. CH63: Beb .2H **103**
Wirral Gdns. CH63: Beb .2H **103**
Wirral Intl. Bus. Pk. CH62: Brom .4F **105**
Wirral Leisure Pk. CH62: Brom .2E **105**
Wirral Little Theatre .3E **69**
Wirral Mt. CH45: Wall .2B **50**
CH48: W Kir .1D **82**
Wirral Mus. .3H **69**
Wirral Sailing Cen. .1A **82**
Wirral Tennis & Sports Cen. .5H **49**
Wirral Transport Mus. .2G **69**
Wirral Vw. L19: Gras .5D **90**
Wirral Vs. CH45: Wall .1A **50**
Wirral Way CH43: Noct .4G **67**
Wisenholme Cl. WA7: Beech .2A **124**
Wisteria Way WA9: Bold .6C **44**
Witham Cl. L30: N'ton .5G **11**
Withburn Cl. CH49: Upton .3C **66**
Withens, The L28: Stockb V .6D **38**
Withensfield CH45: Wall .1D **50**
Withens La. CH44: Wall .2E **51**
CH45: Wall .1D **50**
Withens Rd. L31: Lyd .4C **6**
Withert Av. CH63: Hghr B .3F **87**
Withington Rd. CH44: Wall .4E **51**
L24: Speke .2H **109**
Withins Rd. WA11: Hay .3G **31**
Within Way L24: Hale .4E **111**
Withnell Cl. L13: Liv .5F **55**
Withnell Rd. L13: Liv .5F **55**
Withycombe Rd. WA5: Penk .5G **81**
Witley Av. CH46: More .6C **48**
Witley Cl. CH46: More .6C **48**
Witney Cl. CH49: Grea .6A **66**
Wittenham Cl. CH49: Upton .5D **66**
Wittering La. CH60: Hesw .5B **100**
Witterings, The CH64: Nest .6A **118**
Witton Rd. L13: Liv .1B **54**
Witton Way WA11: Rainf .2F **17**
Witt Rd. WA8: Wid .4E **97**
Wivenhoe Ho. *L19: Aig .4D 90*
(off The Spinnakers)
Wivern Pl. WA7: Run .2F **113**
Woburn Cl. L13: Liv .3D **54**
WA11: Hay .4H **31**
Woburn Dr. WA8: Cron .3B **78**
Woburn Grn. *L13: Liv .3D 54*
(off Woburn Hill)
Woburn Hill L13: Liv .3D **54**
Woburn Pl. CH42: Rock F .1H **87**
Woburn Rd. CH45: Wall .1D **50**
Wokefield Way WA10: St H .1A **42**
Wokingham Gro. L36: Huy .1G **75**
Wolfenden Av. L20: Boot .6E **21**
Wolfe Rd. WA9: St H .3A **44**
Wolferton Cl. CH49: Upton .2F **67**
Wolfe St. L8: Liv .4E **71**
Wolfrick Dr. CH63: Spit .4B **104**
Wolseley Rd. WA10: St H .6D **28**
Wolsey St. L20: Kirkd .4C **34**
Wolstenholme Sq. L1: Liv .6F **5** (1D **70**)
Wolverton Dr. WA7: Wind H .4F **115**
Wolverton St. L6: Liv .2A **54**
Womack Gdns. WA9: St H .1C **60**
Woodale Cl. WA5: Gt San .2G **81**
Woodall Dr. WA7: Run .4F **113**
Wood Av. L20: Boot .6E **21**
Woodbank Cl. L16: Child .1B **74**
Woodbank Pk. CH43: O'ton .5B **68**
Woodbank Rd. WA5: Penk .5H **81**
Woodberry Cl. CH43: Noct .5H **67**
L33: Kirkb .3B **14**
Woodbine St. L5: Kirkd .6D **34**
Woodbourne Rd. L14: Knott A .3H **55**
Woodbridge Av. L26: Halew .1F **93**
Woodbrook Av. L9: Walt .4F **21**
Woodburn Blvd. CH63: Hghr B .3G **87**
Woodburn Dr. CH60: Hesw .1D **116**
WOODCHURCH .1F **85**
Woodchurch Ct. CH42: Tran .6E **69**
Woodchurch La. CH42: Tran .1D **86**
CH49: Woodc .3G **85**
Woodchurch Leisure Cen. .6G **67**
Woodchurch Rd. CH41: Birke .6E **69**
CH42: Tran .2F **85**
CH43: Pren .2F **85**

Woodchurch Rd. CH49: Woodc 2F **85**
L13: Liv 3E **55**
Wood Cl. CH41: Birke 2F **69**
CH66: Hoot 6G **121**
L32: Kirkb 1H **23**
Woodcote Bank CH42: Rock F 4A **88**
Woodcote Cl. L33: Kirkb 5C **14**
Woodcotes, The CH62: Brom 1D **120**
Woodcot La. CH60: Hesw 4C **100**
Woodcroft Dr. CH61: Hesw 3D **100**
Woodcroft La. CH63: Hghr B 3H **87**
Woodcroft Rd. L15: Wav 2B **72**
Woodcroft Way WA9: Clock F 3G **61**
WOODEND 5F **97**
Woodend CH61: Pens 6D **84**
L35: Whis 1E **77**
WA7: Murd 6G **115**
Woodend Av. L23: Crosb 3G **9**
L24: Speke 5E **93**
L25: Hunts X 5E **93**
L31: Mag 2A **12**
Woodend Ct. WA8: Wid 1H **97**
Woodend Ind. Est. L24: Speke 6F **93**
Woodend La. L24: Speke 1E **109**
WOOD END PARK 4D **90**
Woodene Cl. L32: Kirkb 4C **24**
Woodfarm Hey L28: Stockb V 5C **38**
Woodfield Av. CH63: Hghr B 4G **87**
Woodfield Cres. WN4: Ash M 1H **31**
Woodfield Rd. CH61: Pens 1C **100**
CH63: Beb 2A **104**
L9: Walt 6F **21**
L36: Huy 5E **57**
Woodford Cl. WA7: Run 1F **123**
Woodford Rd. CH62: New F 3B **88**
L14: Knott A 3A **56**
WA10: Windle 5A **28**
Woodgate L27: N'ley 3E **75**
Woodger St. L19: Garst 6G **91**
Wood Grn. CH43: Bid 1G **67**
L34: Presc 1C **58**
Woodgreen Rd. L13: Liv 3E **55**
Wood Gro. L13: Liv 5D **54**
Woodhall Av. CH44: Wall 3F **51**
Woodhall Rd. L13: Liv 4E **55**
Woodhatch Rd. WA7: Brook 2D **124**
Woodhead Rd. CH62: Port S 5C **88**
Woodhead Row CH62: Port S 6C **88**
Woodhead St. CH62: New F 4B **88**
Wood Heath Way CH62: East 6G **105**
WOODHEY 4G **87**
Woodhey Ct. CH63: Hghr B 3H **87**
Woodhey Gro. CH63: Hghr B 4H **87**
Woodhey Rd. CH63: Hghr B 4H **87**
L19: Gras 3E **91**
Woodholme Ct. L25: Gate 5D **74**
Woodhouse Cl. L4: Walt 6E **35**
Woodhurst Cl. L36: Huy 1E **57**
Woodhurst Cres. L14: Knott A 3C **56**
Woodin Rd. CH42: Rock F 3A **88**
Woodkind Hey CH63: Spit 3A **104**
Woodland Av. CH47: Meols 6D **46**
WA8: Wid 2D **96**
Woodland Dr. CH45: New B 6E **33**
CH49: Woodc 6E **67**
Woodland Gro. CH42: Rock F 3H **87**
Woodland Rd. CH42: Rock F 3H **87**
CH48: W Kir 1E **83**
CH49: Woodc 6E **67**
L4: Walt 5B **36**
L21: Sea 4H **19**
L26: Halew 4G **93**
L31: Mell 5E **13**
Woodlands, The CH41: Birke 4F **69**
CH49: Upton 3D **66**
L34: Eccl P 6F **41**
Woodlands Dr. CH61: Barn 1G **101**
Woodlands La. CH48: W Kir 2D **82**
Woodlands Pk. L12: W Der 2E **55**
Woodlands Rd. CH61: Irby 6B **84**
CH64: Park 6H **117**
L9: Ain 5B **22**
Woodlands Rd. L17: Aig 1C **90**
L36: Huy 5D **56**
WA11: St H 5F **29**
Woodlands Sq. *L27: N'ley 5A* ***76***
(off Wood La.)
Woodland Vw. L23: Thorn 2A **10**
Woodland Wlk. CH62: Brom 4C **104**
WA7: Cas 4C **114**
Wood La. CH45: Wall 1A **50**
CH49: Grea 4B **66**
CH64: Park 5G **117**
CH64: Will 6A **120**
L27: N'ley 4H **75**
L34: Presc 2B **58**
L36: Huy 5B **58**
WA7: Beech, Sut W 3B **124**
WA7: Murd 1E **125**
Wood Lea L12: Crox 2A **38**
Woodlea Cl. CH62: Brom 2D **120**
Woodlee Rd. L25: Gate 5E **75**
Woodleigh Cl. L31: Lyd 2A **6**
Woodley Fold WA5: Penk 6H **81**
Woodley Rd. L31: Mag 3A **12**
Woodpecker Cl. CH49: Upton 4B **66**
L12: W Der 4B **38**
Woodpecker Dr. L26: Halew 1G **93**
Woodridge WA7: Wind H 4E **115**
Wood Rd. L26: Halew 4G **93**
Woodrock Rd. L25: Woolt 1D **92**
Woodruff St. L8: Liv 5F **71**
Woodside Av. CH46: More 2B **66**
WA11: St H 3D **28**
Woodside Bus. Pk.
CH41: Birke 2H **69**
Woodside Cl. L12: W Der 5F **37**
Woodside Ferry App.
CH41: Birke 2H **69**
Woodside Rd. CH61: Irby 5C **84**
WA5: Gt San 2H **81**
WA11: Hay 4G **31**
Woodside St. L7: Liv 6H **53**
Woodside Way L33: Kirkb 4B **14**
Woodsome Pk. L25: Gate 6E **75**
Woodsorrel Rd. CH41: Birke 2B **68**
L15: Wav 2F **73**
Woodstock Gro. WA8: Wid 1B **96**
Woodstock Rd. CH44: Wall 4C **50**
Woodstock St. L5: Liv 2D **52**
Wood St. CH41: Birke 2F **69**
CH47: Hoy 2B **64**
CH62: Port S 6B **88**
L1: Liv 5F **5** (6D **52**)
L19: Garst 5G **91**
L21: Lith 4B **20**
L34: Presc 1D **58**
WA8: Wid 2G **97**
WA9: St H 1G **43**
Woodthorn Cl. WA4: Dares 1H **115**
Wood Va. WA9: St H 1C **60**
Woodvale Cl. CH43: Bid 1G **67**
Woodvale Ct. *CH49: Woodc 2E* ***85***
(off Childwall Grn.)
Woodvale Rd. L12: Crox 2B **38**
L25: Woolt 1D **92**
Woodview L34: Know 2F **39**
Woodview Av. CH44: Wall 5G **51**
Woodview Cres. WA8: Wid 3G **95**
Woodview Rd. L25: Woolt 5B **74**
WA8: Wid 3G **95**
Woodville Av. L23: Crosb 6F **9**
Woodville Pl. WA8: Wid 2B **96**
Woodville Rd. CH42: Tran 5E **69**
Woodville St. WA10: St H 1F **43**
(not continuous)
Woodville Ter. L6: Liv 2H **53**
Woodward Rd. CH42: Rock F 3A **88**
L33: Know I 5E **15**
Woodway CH49: Grea 5B **66**
Woodway Ct. CH62: Brom 3E **105**
Woodyear Rd. CH62: Brom 6E **105**
Woolacombe Av. WA9: Sut L 2G **61**
Woolacombe Rd. L16: Child 3A **74**
Wooler Cl. CH46: More 1A **66**
Woolfall Cl. L36: Huy 3D **56**
Woolfall Cres. L36: Huy 3D **56**
WOOLFALL HEATH 2E **57**
Woolfall Heath Av.
L36: Huy 2E **57**
Woolfall Ter. L21: Sea 5A **20**
Woolhope Rd. L4: Walt 3H **35**
Woolley Cl. WA6: Frod 5H **123**
Woolmoore Rd. L24: Speke 5E **93**
Woolston Rd. WA11: Hay 4E **31**
WOOLTON 1C **92**
Woolton Cinema, The 1C **92**
WOOLTON HILL 6A **74**
Woolton Hill Rd. L25: Woolt 5A **74**
Woolton M. *L25: Woolt 1B* ***92***
(off Quarry St.)
Woolton Mt. L25: Woolt 6C **74**
WOOLTON PARK 5C **74**
Woolton Pk. L25: Woolt 5C **74**
Woolton Pk. Cl. L25: Woolt 6C **74**
Woolton Rd. L15: Wav 2E **73**
L16: Child 3G **73**
L19: Aller, Garst 5G **91**
L25: Aller 5H **91**
L25: Woolt 4A **74**
Woolton St. L25: Woolt 1C **92**
(not continuous)
Woolton Views L25: Hunts X 3F **93**
Worcester Av. L13: Liv 6B **36**
L22: Water 1E **19**
Worcester Cl. WA10: St H 3D **42**
Worcester Ct. L20: Boot 2D **34**
Worcester Dr. L13: Liv 6B **36**
Worcester Dr. Nth. L13: Liv 6B **36**
Worcester Rd. CH43: Bid 1H **67**
L20: Boot 1D **34**
Wordsworth Av. CH42: Rock F 2H **87**
WA8: Wid 3D **96**
WA9: Sut M 4E **61**
Wordsworth St. L8: Liv 2A **72**
L20: Boot 6A **20**
Wordsworth Wlk. CH48: W Kir 3B **82**
Wordsworth Way L36: Huy 6H **57**
Wordworth Ct. L32: Kirkb 3G **23**
World Mus. Liverpool 2F **5** (5D **52**)
World of Glass, The 2E **43**
Worrow Cl. L11: Norr G 2F **37**
Worrow Rd. L11: Norr G 2F **37**
WORSLEY BROW 5A **44**
Worsley Brow WA9: St H 5A **44**
Worsley St. WA11: Hay 5B **30**
Worthing St. L22: Water 1E **19**
Worthington Cl. WA7: Pal F 6C **114**
Wortley Rd. L10: Faz 3C **22**
Wray Av. WA9: Clock F 3H **61**
Wrayburn Cl. L7: Liv 1A **72**
Wray Ct. WA9: Clock F 3H **61**
Wrekin Cl. L25: Woolt 2D **92**
Wrekin Dr. L10: Ain 1C **22**
Wrenbury Cl. CH43: O'ton 1B **86**
WA7: Sut W 3B **124**
Wrenbury St. L7: Liv 5A **54**
Wren Cl. WA7: Pal F 1C **124**
Wrenfield Gro. L17: Aig 1A **90**
Wren Gro. L26: Halew 2G **93**
Wright Cres. WA8: Wid 6E **97**
Wrights La. WA5: Burtw 3G **63**
WA5: Cuerd 1B **98**
Wrights Ter. L15: Wav 2E **73**
Wright St. CH44: Wall 3F **51**
L5: Liv 2D **52**
Wrigley Rd. WA11: Hay 5G **31**
Wroxham Cl. CH49: Upton 4E **67**
Wroxham Ct. *CH49: Upton 4E* ***67***
(off Wroxham Cl.)
Wroxham Dr. CH49: Upton 5E **67**
Wroxham Rd. WA5: Gt San 3F **81**
Wroxham Way CH49: Upton 4E **67**
Wryneck Cl. WA10: St H 5H **41**
Wrynose Rd. CH62: Brom 5E **105**
Wulstan St. L4: Kirkd 6D **34**

Wycherley Rd. CH42: Tran 6F **69**
Wycherley St. L34: Presc 1D **58**
Wychwood CH49: Upton 4D **66**
Wycliffe Rd. L4: Walt 6A **36**
 WA11: Hay 4G **31**
Wycliffe St. CH42: Rock F 1H **87**
Wye Cl. CH42: Rock F 6H **69**
Wyedale Rd. WA11: Hay 4E **31**
Wye St. L5: Liv 1F **53**
Wykeham St. L4: Kirkd 6D **34**
Wykeham Way L4: Kirkd 6D **34**
Wyken Gro. WA11: St H 6G **29**
Wyke Rd. L35: Presc 2E **59**
Wyllin Rd. L33: Kirkb 1C **24**
Wylva Av. L23: Crosb 6A **10**
Wylva Rd. L4: Walt 1G **53**
Wyncroft Cl. WA8: Wid 4A **96**
Wyncroft Rd. WA8: Wid 4A **96**
Wyncroft St. L8: Liv 5G **71**
Wyndale Cl. L18: Moss H 6F **73**
Wyndcote Rd. L18: Moss H 4F **73**
Wyndham Av. L14: Broad G 5C **56**
Wyndham Rd. CH45: Wall 2H **49**
Wyndham St. L4: Walt 3F **35**
Wynne Rd. WA10: St H 6C **28**
Wynnstay Av. L31: Lyd 4C **6**
Wynnstay St. L8: Liv 3G **71**
Wynstay Rd. CH47: Meols 1C **64**
Wynwood Pk. L36: Roby 6E **57**
Wyre Rd. L5: Liv 6F **35**
Wyrescourt Rd. L12: W Der 2H **55**
Wyresdale Av. WA10: St H 4C **28**
Wyresdale Rd. L9: Ain 4H **21**
Wysall Cl. WA11: St H 6H **29**
Wyswall Cl. L26: Halew 2G **93**
Wythburn Cres. WA11: St H 3F **29**
Wythburn Gro. WA7: Beech 2A **124**
Wyvern Rd. CH46: More 1C **66**

X

X Building L3: Liv 2C **4** (5C **52**)

Y

Yanwath St. L8: Liv 2H **71**
Yarcombe Cl. L26: Halew 2H **93**
Yardley Cen. L33: Know I 1E **25**
Yardley Dr. CH63: Spit 4A **104**
Yardley Rd. L33: Know I 2E **25**
Yarmouth Rd. WA5: Gt San 3G **81**
Yarn Cl. WA9: St H 5B **44**
Yarrow Av. L31: Mag 5E **7**
Yates Cl. L34: Presc 2D **58**
Yates St. L8: Liv 4E **71**
Yeadon Wlk. L24: Speke 2E **109**
Yellow Submarine 3E **109**
Yelverton Cl. L26: Halew 2H **93**
Yelverton Rd.
 CH42: Tran 6G **69**
 L4: Walt 6A **36**
Yeoman Cotts. CH47: Hoy 3C **64**
Ye Priory Ct. L25: Aller 2A **92**
Yew Bank Rd. L16: Child 2H **73**
Yewdale Av. WA11: St H 2F **29**
Yewdale Pk. CH43: O'ton 5D **68**
Yewdale Rd. L9: Walt 1H **35**
Yew Tree Av. WA9: St H 1G **61**
Yew Tree Cl. CH49: Woodc 1E **85**
 L12: W Der 1B **56**
Yew Tree Grn. L31: Mell 5F **13**
Yew Tree La. CH48: W Kir 1B **82**
 L12: W Der 2A **56**
Yew Tree Rd. CH46: More 5D **48**
 CH63: Hghr B 1G **103**
 L9: Walt 1F **35**
 L18: Aller 6H **73**
 L25: Hunts X 3E **93**
 L36: Huy 1F **75**
Yew Tree Trad. Est.
 WA11: Hay 3H **31**
Yew Way CH46: More 6D **48**
Yorkaster Rd. L18: Aller 2G **91**
York Av. CH44: Wall 4F **51**
 CH48: W Kir 3B **82**

York Av. L17: Liv 3B **72**
 L23: Crosb 5F **9**
 WA5: Gt San 2G **81**
York Cl. L30: N'ton 4F **11**
 WA10: St H 1D **42**
York Cotts. L25: Gate 5D **74**
York Ho. L17: Aig 4B **72**
York Pl. WA7: Run 3F **113**
York Rd. CH44: Wall 5F **51**
 L23: Crosb 5G **9**
 L31: Mag 2B **12**
 L36: Huy 4A **58**
 WA8: Wid 3A **96**
Yorkshire Gdns.
 WA10: St H 3D **42**
York St. CH62: Brom 6D **88**
 L1: Liv 6E **5** (1D **70**)
 L9: Walt 2F **35**
 L19: Garst 1G **107**
 L22: Water 3F **19**
 WA7: Run 3E **113**
York Ter. L5: Liv 1E **53**
York Way L19: Garst 1H **107**
 L36: Huy 4A **58**
Youatt Av. L35: Presc 3E **59**
Youens Way L14: Knott A 3A **56**
Yoxall Dr. L33: Kirkb 4H **13**

Z

Zander Gro. L12: Crox 2C **38**
Zante Cl. L5: Liv 1E **53**
Zara Ct. WA11: Hay 4E **31**
Zenith Wlk. L25: Gate 2C **74**
Zetland Rd. CH45: Wall 6B **32**
 L18: Moss H 4D **72**
Zetland St. CH41: Birke 4F **69**
Zig Zag Rd. CH45: Wall 1D **50**
 L12: W Der 2H **55**
Zircon Cl. L21: Lith 3C **20**

SAFETY CAMERA INFORMATION

Safety camera locations are publicised by the Safer Roads Partnership which operates them in order to encourage drivers to comply with speed limits at these sites. It is the driver's absolute responsibility to be aware of and to adhere to speed limits at all times.

By showing this safety camera information it is the intention of Geographers' A-Z Map Company Ltd., to encourage safe driving and greater awareness of speed limits and vehicle speed. Data accurate at time of printing.

HOSPITALS, TREATMENT CENTRES, WALK-IN CENTRES and HOSPICES covered by this atlas.

N.B. Where it is not possible to name these facilities on the map, the reference given is for the road in which they are situated.

ALDER HEY CHILDREN'S HOSPITAL 3G **55**
Eaton Road
West Derby
LIVERPOOL
L12 2AP
Tel: 0151 2284811

ARROWE PARK HOSPITAL 2E **85**
Arrowe Park Road
WIRRAL
CH49 5PE
Tel: 0151 6785111

ASHTON HOUSE HOSPITAL 5D **68**
26 Village Road
Oxton
PRENTON
CH43 5SR
Tel: 0151 6539660

ASHWORTH HOSPITAL 4G **7**
Parkbourn
LIVERPOOL
L31 1HW
Tel: 0151 473 0303

BROADGREEN HOSPITAL 5G **55**
Thomas Drive
LIVERPOOL
L14 3LB
Tel: 0151 2826000

CHESHIRE & MERSEYSIDE NHS TREATMENT CENTRE
....1B **124**
Earls Way
RUNCORN
WA7 2HH
Tel: 01928 574001

CLAIRE HOUSE CHILDREN'S HOSPICE 4F **103**
Clatterbridge Road
WIRRAL
CH63 4JD
Tel: 0151 3344626

CLATTERBRIDGE CENTRE FOR ONCOLOGY 4F **103**
Clatterbridge Road
WIRRAL
CH63 4JY
Tel: 0151 3341155

CLATTERBRIDGE HOSPITAL 4F **103**
Clatterbridge Road
WIRRAL
CH63 4JY
Tel: 0151 3344000

FAIRFIELD INDEPENDENT HOSPITAL 1C **28**
Crank Road
Crank
ST HELENS
WA11 7RS
Tel: 01744 739311

HALTON GENERAL HOSPITAL 1B **124**
Hospital Way
RUNCORN
WA7 2DA
Tel: 01928 714567

HALTON HAVEN HOSPICE 2E **125**
Barnfield Avenue.
Murdishaw
RUNCORN
WA7 6EP
Tel: 01928 712728

LIVERPOOL HEART & CHEST HOSPITAL 5G **55**
Thomas Drive
LIVERPOOL
L14 3PE
Tel: 0151 2281616

LIVERPOOL SPIRE HOSPITAL 4D **72**
57 Greenbank Road
LIVERPOOL
L18 1HQ
Tel: 0151 5221826

LIVERPOOL UNIVERSITY DENTAL HOSPITAL 5F **53**
Pembroke Place
LIVERPOOL
L3 5PS
Tel: 0151 7062000

LIVERPOOL WOMEN'S HOSPITAL 1G **71**
Crown Street
LIVERPOOL
L8 7SS
Tel: 0151 7089988

MARIE CURIE CENTRE, LIVERPOOL 1D **92**
Speke Road
Woolton
LIVERPOOL
L25 8QA
Tel: 0151 8011400

MOSSLEY HILL HOSPITAL 6C **72**
Park Avenue
Mossley Hill
LIVERPOOL
L18 8BU
Tel: 0151 2503000

MURRAYFIELD SPIRE HOSPITAL 6H **85**
Holmwood Drive
Heswall
WIRRAL
CH61 1AU
Tel: 0845 6002110

NHS CHILDREN'S WALK-IN CENTRE (SMITHDOWN) 3B **72**
Smithdown Road
LIVERPOOL
L15 2LQ
Tel: 0151 2854820

NHS WALK-IN CENTRE (KNOWSLEY - HUYTON) 5G **57**
Nutgrove Villa
Westmorland Road
Huyton
LIVERPOOL
L36 6GA
Tel: 0151 290 3333

NHS WALK-IN CENTRE (KNOWSLEY - KIRKBY) 1A **24**
St Chad's Clinic
St Chad's Drive
LIVERPOOL
L32 8RE
Tel: 0151 244 3180

NHS WALK-IN CENTRE (LITHERLAND TOWN HALL) 3B **20**
Hatton Hill Road
LIVERPOOL
L21 9JN
Tel: 0151 475 4667

NHS WALK-IN CENTRE (LIVERPOOL CITY CENTRE)
. . . . .4F **5** (6D **52**)
Unit 4
Charlotte Row
53 Great Charlotte Street
LIVERPOOL
L1 1HU
Tel: 0151 285 3535

NHS WALK-IN CENTRE (LIVERPOOL - OLD SWAN) 5E **55**
Old Swan Health Centre
St. Oswalds Street
LIVERPOOL
L13 2GA
Tel: 0151 285 3565

NHS WALK-IN CENTRE (ST HELENS) 2F **43**
Millennium Building
Bickerstaffe Street
ST HELENS
WA10 1DH
Tel: SEE NOTES

NHS WALK-IN CENTRE
    (SIR ALFRED JONES MEMORIAL HOSPITAL) 5G **91**
Sir Alfred Jones Memorial Hospital
Church Road
Garston
LIVERPOOL
L19 2LP
Tel: SEE NOTES

NHS WALK-IN CENTRE (WIRRAL) .4D **50**
Victoria Central Hospital
Mill Lane
WALLASEY
CH44 5UF
Tel: 0151 678 5111

NHS WALK-IN CENTRE (WIRRAL ARROWE PARK) 2E **85**
Arrowe Park Hospital
Arrowe Park Road
WIRRAL
CH49 5PE
Tel: 0151 488 3706

PARK LODGE HOSPITAL 2B **54**
Orphan Drive
LIVERPOOL
L6 7UN
Tel: 0151 3308901

PRIMARY CARE TREATMENT CENTRE
(SIR ALFRED JONES MEMORIAL HOSPITAL) 5G **91**
LIVERPOOL
L19 2LP
Tel: 0151 330 8301

RATHBONE HOSPITAL 5E **55**
Mill Lane
Old Swan
LIVERPOOL
L13 4AW
Tel: 0151 2503000

ROYAL LIVERPOOL UNIVERSITY HOSPITAL 5F **53**
Prescot Street
LIVERPOOL
L7 8XP
Tel: 0151 7062000

ST BARTHOLOMEW'S DAY HOSPITAL 5E **57**
Station Road
Huyton
LIVERPOOL
L36 4HU
Tel: 0151 4896241

ST CATHERINE'S HOSPITAL (BIRKENHEAD) 5F **69**
Church Road
BIRKENHEAD
CH42 0LQ
Tel: 0151 6787272

ST HELENS HOSPITAL (MERSEYSIDE) 4G **43**
Marshalls Cross Road
ST HELENS
WA9 3DA
Tel: 0151 4261600

ST JOHN'S HOSPICE IN WIRRAL 4G **103**
Mount Road
Higher Bebington
WIRRAL
CH63 6JE
Tel: 0151 3342778

ST JOSEPH'S HOSPICE 1H **9**
Ince Road
LIVERPOOL
L23 4UE
Tel: 0151 924 3812

SCOTT CLINIC 2A **60**
Rainhill Road
ST HELENS
WA9 5BD
Tel: 0151 4306300

SEFTON ABBEY HOSPITAL 5C **22**
University Hospital Aintree
Lower Lane
LIVERPOOL
L9 7AL
Tel: 0151 2576700

SIR ALFRED JONES MEMORIAL HOSPITAL 5G **91**
Church Road
Garston
LIVERPOOL
L19 2LP
Tel: 0151 2503000

SMITHDOWN HEALTH PARK 3B **72**
Smithdown Road
LIVERPOOL
L15 2HE
Tel: 0151 33080/54/74/10

UNIVERSITY HOSPITAL AINTREE 5C **22**
Longmoor Lane
LIVERPOOL
L9 7AL
Tel: 0151 5255980

VICTORIA CENTRAL HOSPITAL 4D **50**
Mill Lane
WALLASEY
CH44 5UF
Tel: 0151 6785111

WALTON CENTRE FOR NEUROLOGY AND NEUROSURGERY
.... 4C **22**
Lower Lane
LIVERPOOL
L9 7LJ
Tel: 0151 5253611

WALTON HOSPITAL 2F **35**
Rice Lane
LIVERPOOL
L9 1AE
Tel: 0151 5253611

WATERLOO DAY HOSPITAL 2G **19**
Park Road
Waterloo
LIVERPOOL
L22 3XR
Tel: 0151 928 7243

WHISTON HOSPITAL 3F **59**
Warrington Road
PRESCOT
L35 5DR
Tel: 0151 4261600

WILLOWBROOK HOSPICE 6G **41**
Portico Lane
Eccleston Park
PRESCOT
L34 2QT
Tel: 0151 4308736

WILLOW HOUSE RESOURCE CENTRE (DAY HOSPITAL) 4E **59**
168 Dragon Lane
Whiston
PRESCOT
L35 3QY
Tel: 0151 2895827

WOODLANDS HOSPICE 5B **22**
Longmoor Lane
LIVERPOOL
L9 7LA
Tel: 0151 5292299

ZOE'S PLACE - BABY HOSPICE 2A **56**
Yew Tree Lane
LIVERPOOL
L12 9HH
Tel: 0151 2280353